A Distant Mirror

Europe in the 14th Century

A Distant Mirror

The Calamitous 14th Century

Barbara W. Tuchman

BALLANTINE BOOKS • NEW YORK

"For mankind is ever the same and nothing is lost out of nature, though everything is altered."

—JOHN DRYDEN,
"On the Characters in the Canterbury Tales,"
in Preface to *Fables, Ancient and Modern*

Acknowledgments

I would like to express my thanks to all who have helped me in one way or another to write this book: to Maître Henri Crepin, Deputy Mayor of Coucy-le-Château and president of the Association for Restoration of the Castle of Coucy and Its Environs, for his hospitality and guidance; to my editor Robert Gottlieb for enthusiasm and belief in the book as well as judicious improvements; to my daughter Alma Tuchman for substantial research, my friend Katrina Romney for sustained interest and to both for critical reading. For first aid in medieval complexities, I am especially indebted to Professors Elizabeth A. R. Brown and John Henneman; also to Professor Howard Garey for elucidating problems of medieval French, and to Mr. Richard Famiglietti for the benefit of his familiarity with sources in the period. For various advice, guidance, translations and answers to queries, I am grateful to Professors John Benton, Giles Constable, Eugene Cox, J. N. Hillgarth, Harry A. Miskimin, Lynn White, Mrs. Phyllis W. G. Gordan, John Plummer of the Morgan Library, and, in France, Professors Robert Fossier of the Sorbonne, Raymond Cazelles of Chantilly, Philippe Wolff of Toulouse, Mme. Therese d'Alveney of the Bibliothèque Nationale, M. Yves Metman of the Archives Nationales, Bureaux des Sceaux, M. Georges Dumas of the Archives de l'Aisne, and M. Depouilly of the Museum of Soissons; also to Professor Irwin Saunders for introductions to the Institute for Balkan Studies in Sofia, and to Professors Topkova-Zaimova and Elisabeth Todorova of that Institute for assisting my visit to Nicopolis; also to Widener Library at Harvard and Sterling Library at Yale for borrowing privileges, and to the helpful and knowledgeable staff of the New York Public Library for assistance of many kinds. To unnamed others who appeared briefly to lend a hand on my journey of seven years, my gratitude is equal.

Contents

ℭaps and ℑllustrations

Maps

Illustrations

Foreword

The Period, the Protagonist, the Hazards

The genesis of this book was a desire to find out what were the effects on society of the most lethal disaster of recorded history—that is to say, of the Black Death of 1348-50, which killed an estimated one third of the population living between India and Iceland. Given the possibilities of our own time, the reason for my interest is obvious. The answer proved elusive because the 14th century suffered so many "strange and great perils and adversities" (in the words of a contemporary) that its disorders cannot be traced to any one cause; they were the hoofprints of more than the four horsemen of St. John's vision, which had now become seven—plague, war, taxes, brigandage, bad government, insurrection, and schism in the Church. All but plague itself arose from conditions that existed prior to the Black Death and continued after the period of plague was over.

Although my initial question has escaped an answer, the interest of the period itself—a violent, tormented, bewildered, suffering and disintegrating age, a time, as many thought, of Satan triumphant—was compelling and, as it seemed to me, consoling in a period of similar disarray. If our last decade or two of collapsing assumptions has been a period of unusual discomfort, it is reassuring to know that the human species has lived through worse before.

Curiously, the "phenomenal parallels" have been applied by another historian to earlier years of this century. Comparing the aftermaths of the Black Death and of World War I, James Westfall Thompson found all the same complaints: economic chaos, social unrest, high prices, profiteering, depraved morals, lack of production, industrial indolence, frenetic gaiety, wild expenditure, luxury, debauchery, social and religious hysteria, greed, avarice, maladministration, decay of manners. "History never repeats itself," said Voltaire; "man always does." Thucydides, of course, made that principle the justification of his work.

Simply summarized by the Swiss historian, J. C. L. S. de Sismondi, the 14th century was "a bad time for humanity." Until recently, historians tended to dislike and to skirt the century because it could not be made to fit into a pattern of human progress. After the experiences of the terrible 20th century, we have greater fellow-feeling for a distraught age whose rules were breaking down under the pressure of adverse and violent events. We recognize with a painful twinge the marks of "a period of anguish when there is no sense of an assured future."

The interval of 600 years permits what is significant in human character to stand out. People of the Middle Ages existed under mental, moral, and physical circumstances so different from our own as to constitute almost a foreign civilization. As a result, qualities of conduct that we recognize as familiar amid these alien surroundings are revealed as permanent in human nature. If one insists upon a lesson from history, it lies here, as discovered by the French medievalist Edouard Perroy when he was writing a book on the Hundred Years' War while dodging the Gestapo during World War II. "Certain ways of behavior," he wrote, "certain reactions against fate, throw mutual light upon each other."

The fifty years that followed the Black Death of 1348-50 are the core of what seems to me a coherent historical period extending approximately from 1300 to 1450 plus a few years. To narrow the focus to a manageable area, I have chosen a particular person's life as the vehicle of my narrative. Apart from human interest, this has the advantage of enforced obedience to reality. I am required to follow the circumstances and the sequence of an actual medieval life, lead where they will, and they lead, I think, to a truer version of the period than if I had imposed my own plan.

The person in question is not a king or queen, because everything about such persons is *ipso facto* exceptional, and, besides, they are overused; nor a commoner, because commoners' lives in most cases did not take in the wide range that I wanted; nor a cleric or saint, because they are outside the limits of my comprehension; nor a woman, because any medieval woman whose life was adequately documented would be atypical.

The choice is thus narrowed to a male member of the Second Estate—that is, of the nobility—and has fallen upon Enguerrand de

Coucy VII, last of a great dynasty and "the most experienced and skillful of all the knights of France." His life from 1340 to 1397 coincided with the period that concerned me, and, from the death of his mother in the great plague to his own perfectly timed death in the culminating fiasco of the century, seemed designed for my purpose.

Through marriage to the eldest daughter of the King of England, he acquired a double allegiance bridging two countries at war, which enlarged the scope and enriched the interest of his career; he played a role, usually major, in every public drama of his place and time, and he had the good sense to become a patron of the greatest contemporary chronicler, Jean Froissart, with the result that more is known about him than might otherwise have been the case. He has one grievous imperfection—that no authentic portrait of him exists. He has, however, a compensating advantage, for me: that, except for a single brief article published in 1939, nothing has been written about him in English, and no formal, reliable biography in French except for a doctoral thesis of 1890 that exists only in manuscript. I like finding my own way.

I must beg the reader to have patience in making Coucy's acquaintance because he can only be known against the background and events of his time which fill the first half dozen chapters. Enguerrand (pronounced with a hard "g") made his first mark on history at the age of eighteen in 1358, which does not occur until Chapter 7.

I come now to the hazards of the enterprise. First are uncertain and contradictory data with regard to dates, numbers, and hard facts. Dates may seem dull and pedantic to some, but they are fundamental because they establish sequence—what precedes and what follows—thereby leading toward an understanding of cause and effect. Unfortunately, medieval chronology is extremely hard to pin down. The year was considered to begin at Easter and since this could fall any time between March 22 and April 22, a fixed date of March 25 was generally preferred. The change over to New Style took place in the 16th century but was not everywhere accepted until the 18th, which leaves the year to which events of January, February, and March belong in the 14th century a running enigma—further complicated by use of the regnal year (dating from the reigning King's accession) in official English documents of the 14th century and use of the papal year in certain other cases. Moreover, chroniclers did not date an event by the day of the month but by the religious calendar—speaking, for example, of two days before the Nativity of the Virgin, or the Monday after Epiphany, or St. John the Baptist's Day, or the third Sunday in Lent.

The result is to confuse not only the historian but the inhabitants of the 14th century themselves, who rarely if ever agree on the same date for any event.

Numbers are no less basic because they indicate what proportion of the population is involved in a given situation. The chronic exaggeration of medieval numbers—of armies, for example—when accepted as factual, has led in the past to a misunderstanding of medieval war as analogous to modern war, which it was not, in means, method, or purpose. It should be assumed that medieval figures for military forces, battle casualties, plague deaths, revolutionary hordes, processions, or any groups en masse are generally enlarged by several hundred percent. This is because the chroniclers did not use numbers as data but as a device of literary art to amaze or appall the reader. Use of Roman numerals also made for lack of precision and an affinity for round numbers. The figures were uncritically accepted and repeated by generation after generation of historians. Only since the end of the last century have scholars begun to re-examine the documents and find, for instance, the true strength of an expeditionary force from paymasters' records. Yet still they disagree. J. C. Russell puts the pre-plague population of France at 21 million, Ferdinand Lot at 15 or 16 million, and Edouard Perroy at a lowly 10 to 11 million. Size of population affects studies of everything else—taxes, life expectancy, commerce and agriculture, famine or plenty—and here are figures by modern authorities which differ by 100 percent. Chroniclers' figures which seem obviously distorted appear in my text in quotation marks.

Discrepancies of supposed fact were often due to mistakes of oral transmission or later misreading of a manuscript source, as when the Dame de Courcy, subject of an international scandal, was mistaken by an otherwise careful 19th century historian for Coucy's second wife, at a cost, for a while, of devastating confusion to the present author. The Comte d'Auxerre in the Battle of Poitiers was variously rendered by English chroniclers as Aunser, Aussure, Soussiere, Usur, Waucerre, and by the *Grandes Chroniques* of France as Sancerre, a different fellow altogether. Enguerrand was written as Ingelram in England. It is not surprising that I took the name Canolles to be a variant of the notorious brigand captain Arnaut de Cervole, only to find, when the circumstances refused to fit, that it was instead a variant of Knowles or Knollys, an equally notorious English captain. Though minor, this sort of difficulty can be unnerving.

Isabeau of Bavaria, Queen of France, is described by one historian as a tall blonde and by another as a "dark, lively, little woman." The Turkish Sultan Bajazet, reputed by his contemporaries to be bold, enterprising, and avid for war, and surnamed Thunderbolt for the rapidity of his strikes, is described by a modern Hungarian historian as "effeminate, sensual, irresolute and vacillating."

It may be taken as axiomatic that any statement of fact about the Middle Ages may (and probably will) be met by a statement of the opposite or a different version. Women outnumbered men because men were killed off in the wars; men outnumbered women because women died in childbirth. Common people were familiar with the Bible; common people were unfamiliar with the Bible. Nobles were tax exempt; no, they were not tax exempt. French peasants were filthy and foul-smelling and lived on bread and onions; French peasants ate pork, fowl, and game and enjoyed frequent baths in the village bathhouses. The list could be extended indefinitely.

Contradictions, however, are part of life, not merely a matter of conflicting evidence. I would ask the reader to expect contradictions, not uniformity. No aspect of society, no habit, custom, movement, development, is without cross-currents. Starving peasants in hovels live alongside prosperous peasants in featherbeds. Children are neglected and children are loved. Knights talk of honor and turn brigand. Amid depopulation and disaster, extravagance and splendor were never more extreme. No age is tidy or made of whole cloth, and none is a more checkered fabric than the Middle Ages.

One must also remember that the Middle Ages change color depending on who is looking at them. Historians' prejudices and points of view—and thus their selection of material—have changed considerably over a period of 600 years. During the three centuries following the 14th, history was virtually a genealogy of nobility, devoted to tracing dynastic lines and family connections and infused by the idea of the noble as a superior person. These works of enormous antiquarian research teem with information of more than dynastic interest, such as Anselm's item about the Gascon lord who bequeathed a hundred livres for the dowries of poor girls he had deflowered.

The French Revolution marks the great reversal, following which historians saw the common man as hero, the poor as *ipso facto* virtuous, nobles and kings as monsters of iniquity. Simeon Luce, in his history of the Jacquerie, is one of these, slanted in his text, yet unique in his research and invaluable for his documents. The giants of the 19th and early 20th centuries who unearthed and published the sources, annotated and edited the chronicles, collected the literary works, read and excerpted masses of sermons, treatises, letters, and other primary material, provided the ground on which we latecomers walk. Their work is now supplemented and balanced by modern medievalists of the post-Marc Bloch era who have taken a more sociological approach and turned up detailed hard facts about daily life—for example, the number of communion wafers sold in a particular diocese, as an indicator of religious observance.

My book is indebted to all these groups, beginning with the primary chroniclers. I realize it is unfashionable among medievalists today to rely on the chroniclers, but for a sense of the period and its attitudes I find them indispensable. Furthermore, their form is narrative and so is mine.

With all this wealth, empty spaces nevertheless exist where the problem is not contradictory information but no information. To bridge the gap, one must make use of what seems the likely and natural explanation, which accounts for the proliferation of "probably" and "presumably" in my text—annoying but, in the absence of documented certainty, unavoidable.

A greater hazard, built into the very nature of recorded history, is overload of the negative: the disproportionate survival of the bad side—of evil, misery, contention, and harm. In history this is exactly the same as in the daily newspaper. The normal does not make news. History is made by the documents that survive, and these lean heavily on crisis and calamity, crime and misbehavior, because such things are the subject matter of the documentary process—of lawsuits, treaties, moralists' denunciations, literary satire, papal Bulls. No Pope ever issued a Bull to approve of something. Negative overload can be seen at work in the religious reformer Nicolas de Clamanges, who, in denouncing unfit and worldly prelates in 1401, said that in his anxiety for reform he would not discuss the good clerics because "they do not count beside the perverse men."

Disaster is rarely as pervasive as it seems from recorded accounts. The fact of being on the record makes it appear continuous and ubiquitous whereas it is more likely to have been sporadic both in time and place. Besides, persistence of the normal is usually greater than the effect of disturbance, as we know from our own times. After absorbing the news of today, one expects to face a world consisting entirely of strikes, crimes, power failures, broken water mains, stalled trains, school shutdowns, muggers, drug addicts, neo-Nazis, and rapists. The fact is that one can come home in the evening—on a lucky day—without having encountered more than one or two of these phenomena. This has led me to formulate Tuchman's Law, as follows: "The fact of being reported multiplies the apparent extent of any deplorable development by five- to tenfold" (or any figure the reader would care to supply).

Difficulty of empathy, of genuinely entering into the mental and emotional values of the Middle Ages, is the final obstacle. The main barrier is, I believe, the Christian religion as it then was: the matrix and law of medieval life, omnipresent, indeed compulsory. Its insistent principle that the life of the spirit and of the afterworld was superior to the here and now, to material life on earth, is one that the modern world does not share, no matter how devout some present-day Christians may be. The rupture of this principle and its replacement by belief in the worth of the individual and of an active life not necessarily focused on God is, in fact, what created the modern world and ended the Middle Ages.

What compounds the problem is that medieval society, while professing belief in renunciation of the life of the senses, did not renounce it in practice, and no part of it less so than the Church itself. Many tried, a few succeeded, but the generality of mankind is not made for renunciation. There never was a time when more attention was given to money and possessions than in the 14th century, and its concern with the flesh was the same as at any other time. Economic man and sensual man are not suppressible.

The gap between medieval Christianity's ruling principle and everyday life is the great pitfall of the Middle Ages. It is the problem that runs through Gibbon's history, which he dealt with by a delicately malicious levity, pricking at every turn what seemed to him the hypocrisy of the Christian ideal as opposed to natural human functioning. I do not think, however great my appreciation of the master otherwise, that Gibbon's method meets the problem. Man himself was the formulator of the impossible Christian ideal and tried to uphold it, if not live by it, for more than a millennium. Therefore it must represent a need, something more fundamental than Gibbon's 18th century enlightenment allowed for, or his elegant ironies could dispose of. While I recognize its presence, it requires a more religious bent than mine to identify with it.

Chivalry, the dominant political idea of the ruling class, left as great a gap between ideal and practice as religion. The ideal was a vision of order maintained by the warrior class and formulated in the image of the Round Table, nature's perfect shape. King Arthur's knights adventured for the right against dragons, enchanters, and wicked men, establishing order in a wild world. So their living counterparts were supposed, in theory, to serve as defenders of the Faith, upholders of justice, champions of the oppressed. In practice, they were themselves the oppressors, and by the 14th century the violence and lawlessness of men of the sword had become a major agency of disorder. When the gap between ideal and real becomes too wide, the system breaks down. Legend and story have always reflected this; in the Arthurian romances the Round Table is shattered from within. The sword is returned to the lake; the effort begins anew. Violent, destructive, greedy, fallible as he may be, man retains his vision of order and resumes his search.

A Note on Money

Medieval currencies derived originally from the *libra* (livre or pound) of pure silver from which were struck 240 silver pennies, later established as twelve pennies to the shilling or sous and 20 shillings or sous to the pound or livre. The florin, ducat, franc, livre, écu, mark, and English pound were all theoretically more or less equivalent to the original pound, although in the course of things their weight and gold content varied. The nearest to a standard was the coin containing 3.5 grams of gold minted by Florence (the florin) and Venice (the ducat) in the mid-13th century. The word "gold" attached to the name of a coin, as franc d'or, écu d'or, or mouton d'or, signified a real coin. When expressed by the name of the currency alone, or, in France, as a livre in one of its various forms—*parisis, tournois, bordelaise,* each differing slightly in value—the currency in question represented money of account which existed only on paper.

Given this glimpse of the complications of the problem, the non-specialist reader would be well advised not to worry about it, because the names of coins and currency mean nothing anyway except in terms of purchasing power. From time to time, in mention of the pay of men-at-arms, the wages of laborers, the price of a horse or a plow, the living expenses of a bourgeois family, the amounts of hearth taxes and sales taxes, I have tried to relate monetary figures to actual values. I have not attempted to translate various currencies into the equivalent of only one, such as livres or francs, because equivalency kept changing as did the gold or silver content of the coinage; moreover, real coins and money of account under the same name differed in value. I have, therefore, in each case, simply adopted the currency named by the document or chronicler, and would urge the reader simply to think of any given amount as so many pieces of money.

References to Sources

Sources will be found in the Bibliography and, for a particular item, in the Reference Notes at the end of the book, located by page number and an identifying phrase from the text.

Part One

Chapter 1

"I Am the Sire de Coucy":
The Dynasty

Formidable and grand on a hilltop in Picardy, the five-towered castle of Coucy dominated the approach to Paris from the north, but whether as guardian or as challenger of the monarchy in the capital was an open question. Thrusting up from the castle's center, a gigantic cylinder rose to twice the height of the four corner towers. This was the *donjon* or central citadel, the largest in Europe, the mightiest of its kind ever built in the Middle Ages or thereafter. Ninety feet in diameter, 180 feet high, capable of housing a thousand men in a siege, it dwarfed and protected the castle at its base, the clustered roofs of the town, the bell tower of the church, and the thirty turrets of the massive wall enclosing the whole complex on the hill. Travelers coming from any direction could see this colossus of baronial power from miles away and, on approaching it, feel the awe of the traveler in infidel lands at first sight of the pyramids.

Seized by grandeur, the builders had carried out the scale of the *donjon* in interior features of more than mortal size: risers of steps were fifteen to sixteen inches, window seats three and a half feet from the ground, as if for use by a race of titans. Stone lintels measuring two cubic yards were no less heroic. For more than four hundred years the dynasty reflected by these arrangements had exhibited the same quality of excess. Ambitious, dangerous, not infrequently ferocious, the Coucys had planted themselves on a promontory of land which was formed by nature for command. Their hilltop controlled passage through the valley of the Ailette to the greater valley of the Oise. From here they had challenged kings, despoiled the Church, departed for and died on crusades, been condemned and excommunicated for crimes, progressively enlarged their domain, married royalty, and nurtured a pride that took for its battle cry, *"Coucy à la merveille!"* Holding one of the four great baronies of France, they scorned territorial titles and adopted their motto of simple arrogance,

> *Roi ne suis,*
> *Ne prince ne duc ne comte aussi;*
> *Je suis le sire de Coucy.*

> (Not king nor prince,
> Duke nor count am I;
> I am the lord of Coucy.)

Begun in 1223, the castle was a product of the same architectural explosion that raised the great cathedrals whose impulse, too, sprang from northern France. Four of the greatest were under construction, at the same time as the castle—at Laon, Reims, Amiens, and Beauvais, within fifty miles of Coucy. While it took anywhere from 50 to 150 years to finish building a cathedral, the vast works of Coucy with *donjon*, towers, ramparts, and subterranean network were completed, under the single compelling will of Enguerrand de Coucy III, in the astonishing space of seven years.

The castle compound enclosed a space of more than two acres. Its four corner towers, each 90 feet high and 65 in diameter, and its three outer sides were built flush with the edge of the hill, forming the ramparts. The only entrance to the compound was a fortified gate on the inner side next to the *donjon*, protected by guard towers, moat, and portcullis. The gate opened onto the *place d'armes*, a walled space of about six acres, containing stables and other service buildings, tiltyard, and pasture for the knights' horses. Beyond this, where the hill widened out like the tail of a fish, lay the town of perhaps a hundred houses and a square-towered church. Three fortified gates in the outer wall encircling the hilltop commanded access to the outside world. On the south side facing Soissons, the hill fell away in a steep, easily defensible slope; on the north facing Laon, where the hill merged with the plateau, a great moat made an added barrier.

Within walls eighteen to thirty feet thick, a spiral staircase connected the three stories of the *donjon*. An open hole or "eye" in the roof, repeated in the vaulted ceiling of each level, added a little extra light and air to the gloom, and enabled arms and provisions to be hoisted from floor to floor without the necessity of climbing the stairs. By the same means, orders could be given vocally to the entire garrison at one time. As many as 1,200 to 1,500 men-at-arms could assemble to hear what was said from the middle level. The *donjon* had kitchens, said an awed contemporary, "worthy of Nero," and a rainwater fishpond on the roof. It had a well, bread ovens, cellars, storerooms, huge fireplaces with chimneys on each floor, and latrines. Vaulted underground passageways led to every part of the castle, to the open court, and to secret exits outside the ramparts, through which a besieged garrison could be provisioned. From the top of the *donjon* an observer could see the whole region as far as the forest of Compiègne thirty miles away, making Coucy proof against surprise. In design and execution the fortress was the most nearly perfect military structure of medieval Europe, and in size the most audacious.

One governing concept shaped a castle: not residence, but defense. As fortress, it was an emblem of medieval life as dominating as the cross. In the *Romance of the Rose*, that vast compendium of everything but romance, the castle enclosing the Rose is the central structure, which must be besieged and penetrated to reach the goal of sexual desire. In real life, all its arrangements testified to the fact of violence, the expectation of attack, which had carved the history of the Middle Ages. The castle's predecessor, the Roman villa, had been unfortified, depending on Roman law and the Roman legions for its ramparts. After the Empire's collapse, the medieval society that emerged was a set of disjointed and clashing parts subject to no central or effective secular authority. Only the Church offered an organizing principle, which was the reason for its success, for society cannot bear anarchy.

Out of the turbulence, central secular authority began slowly to cohere in the monarchy, but as soon as the new power became effective it came into conflict with the Church on the one hand and the barons on the other. Simultaneously the bourgeois of the towns were developing their own order and selling their support to barons, bishops, or kings in return for charters of liberties as free "communes." By providing the freedom for the development of commerce, the charters marked the rise of the urban Third Estate. Political balance among the competing groups was unstable because the king had no permanent armed force at his command. He had to rely on the feudal obligation of his vassals to perform limited military service, later supplemented by paid service. Rule was still personal, deriving from the fief of land and oath of homage. Not citizen to state but vassal to lord was the bond that underlay political structure. The state was still struggling to be born.

By virtue of its location in the center of Picardy, the domain of Coucy, as the crown acknowledged, was "one of the keys of the kingdom." Reaching almost to Flanders in the north and to the Channel and borders of Normandy on the west, Picardy was the main avenue of northern France. Its rivers led both southward to the Seine and westward to the Channel. Its fertile soil made it the primary agricultural region of France, with pasture and fields of grain, clumps of forest, and a comfortable sprinkling of villages. Clearing, the first act of civilization, had started with the Romans. At the opening of the 14th century Picardy supported about 250,000 households or a population of more than a million, making it the only province of France, other than Toulouse in the south, to have been more populous in medieval times than in modern. Its temper was vigorous and independent, its towns the earliest to win charters as communes.

In the shadowed region between legend and history, the domain of Coucy was originally a fief of the Church supposedly bestowed on St. Remi, first Bishop of Reims, by Clovis, first Christian King of the Franks, in about the year 500. After his conversion to Christianity by St. Remi, King Clovis gave the territory of Coucy to the new bishopric of Reims, grounding the Church in the things of Caesar, as the Emperor Constantine had traditionally grounded the Church of Rome. By Constantine's gift, Christianity was both officially established and fatally compromised. As William Langland wrote,

> When the kindness of Constantine gave Holy Church endowments
> In lands and leases, lordships and servants,
> The Romans heard an angel cry on high above them,
> "This day *dos ecclesiae* has drunk venom
> And all who have Peter's power are poisoned forever."

That conflict between the reach for the divine and the lure of earthly things was to be the central problem of the Middle Ages. The claim of the Church to spiritual leadership could never be made wholly credible to all its communicants when it was founded in material wealth. The more riches the Church amassed, the more visible and disturbing became the flaw; nor could it ever be resolved, but continued to renew doubt and dissent in every century.

In the earliest Latin documents, Coucy was called Codiciacum or

Codiacum, supposedly derived from *Codex, codicis*, meaning a tree trunk stripped of its branches such as those the Gauls used to build their palisades. For four centuries through the Dark Ages the place remained in shadow. In 910–20 Hervé, Archbishop of Reims, built the first primitive castle and chapel on the hill, surrounded by a wall as defense against Norsemen invading the valley of the Oise. Settlers from the village below, taking refuge within the Bishop's walls, founded the upper town, which came to be known as Coucy-le-Château, as distinguished from Coucy-la-Ville below. In those fierce times the territory was a constant bone of conflict among barons, archbishops, and kings, all equally bellicose. Defense against invaders—Moors in the south, Norsemen in the north—had bred a class of hard-bitten warriors who fought among themselves as willingly and savagely as against outsiders. In 975 Oderic, Archbishop of Reims, ceded the fief to a personage called the Comte d'Eudes, who became the first lord of Coucy. Nothing is known of this individual except his name, but once established on the hilltop, he produced in his descendants a strain of extraordinary strength and fury.

The dynasty's first recorded act of significance, religious rather than bellicose, was the founding by Aubry de Coucy in 1059 of the Benedictine Abbey of Nogent at the foot of the hill. Such a gesture, on a larger scale than the usual donation for perpetual prayers, was meant both to display the importance of the donor and to buy merit to assure his salvation. Whether or not the initial endowment was meager, as the monastery's rancorous Abbot Guibert complained in the next century, the abbey flourished and, supported by a flow of funds from successive Coucys, outlived them all.

Aubry's successor, Enguerrand I, was a man of many scandals, obsessed by lust for women, according to Abbot Guibert (himself a victim of repressed sexuality, as revealed in his *Confessions*). Seized by a passion for Sybil, wife of a lord of Lorraine, Enguerrand succeeded, with the aid of a compliant Bishop of Laon who was his first cousin, in divorcing his first wife, Adèle de Marle, on charges of adultery. Afterward he married Sybil with the sanction of the Church while her husband was absent at war and while the lady herself was pregnant as the result of still a third liaison. She was said to be of dissolute morals.

Out of this vicious family situation came that "raging wolf" (in the words of another famous abbot, Suger of St. Denis), the most notorious and savage of the Coucys, Thomas de Marle, son of the repudiated Adèle. Bitterly hating the father who had cast his paternity in doubt, Thomas grew up to take part in the ceaseless war originally launched against Enguerrand I by the discarded husband of Sybil.

These private wars were fought by the knights with furious gusto and a single strategy, which consisted in trying to ruin the enemy by killing or maiming as many of his peasants and destroying as many crops, vineyards, tools, barns, and other possessions as possible, thereby reducing his sources of revenue. As a result, the chief victim of the belligerents was their respective peasantry. Abbot Guibert claimed that in the "mad war" of Enguerrand against the Lorrainer, captured men had their eyes put out and feet cut off with results that could still be seen in the district in his time. The private wars were the curse of Europe which the crusades, it has been thought, were subconsciously invented to relieve by providing a vent for aggression.

When the great summons of 1095 came to take the cross and save the Holy Sepulcher on the First Crusade, both Enguerrand I and his son Thomas joined the march, carrying their feud to Jerusalem and back with mutual hate undiminished. From an exploit during the crusade the Coucy coat-of-arms derived, although whether the protagonist was Enguerrand or Thomas is disputed. One or the other with five companions, on being surprised by a party of Moslems when out of armor, took off his scarlet cloak trimmed with vair (squirrel fur), tore it into six pieces to make banners for recognition, and thus equipped, so the story goes, fell upon the Moslems and annihilated them. In commemoration a shield was adopted bearing the device of six horizontal bands, pointed, of red on white, or in heraldic terms, "Barry of six, vair and gules" (gules meaning red).

As his mother's heir to the territories of Marle and La Fère, Thomas added them to the Coucy domain to which he succeeded in 1116. Untamed, he pursued a career of enmity and brigandage, directed in varying combinations against Church, town, and King, "the Devil aiding him," according to Abbot Suger. He seized manors from convents, tortured prisoners (reportedly hanging men up by their testicles until these tore off from the weight of the body), personally cut the throats of thirty rebellious bourgeois, transformed his castles into "a nest of dragons and a cave of thieves," and was excommunicated by the Church, which ungirdled him—in absentia—of the knightly belt and ordered the anathema to be read against him every Sunday in every parish in Picardy. King Louis VI assembled a force for war upon Thomas and succeeded in divesting him of stolen lands and castles. In the end, Thomas was not proof against that hope of salvation and fear of hell which brought the Church so many rich legacies through the centuries. He left a generous bequest to the Abbey of Nogent, founded another abbey at Prémontré nearby, and died in bed in 1130. He had been married three times. Abbot Guibert thought him "the wickedest man of his generation."

What formed a man like Thomas de Marle was not necessarily aggressive genes or father-hatred, which can occur in any century, but a habit of violence that flourished because of a lack of any organ of effective restraint.

While political power centralized during the 12th and 13th centuries, the energies and talents of Europe were gathering in one of civilization's great bursts of development. Stimulated by commerce, a surge took place in art, technology, building, learning, exploration by land and sea, universities, cities, banking and credit, and every sphere that enriched life and widened horizons. Those 200 years were the High Middle Ages, a period that brought into use the compass and mechanical clock, the spinning wheel and treadle loom, the windmill and watermill; a period when Marco Polo traveled to China and Thomas Aquinas set himself to organize knowledge, when universities were established at Paris, Bologna, Padua, and Naples, Oxford and Cambridge, Salamanca and Valladolid, Montpellier and Toulouse; when Giotto painted human feeling, Roger Bacon delved into experimental science, Dante framed his great design of human fate and wrote it in the vernacular; a period when religion was expressed both in the gentle preaching of St. Francis and in the cruelty of the Inquisition, when the Albigensian Crusade in the name of faith drenched southern France in blood and massacre while the soaring cathedrals rose arch upon arch, triumphs of creativity, technology, and faith.

They were not built by slave labor. Though limited serfdom existed, the rights and duties of serfs were fixed by custom and legal memory, and the work of medieval society, unlike that of the ancient world, was done by its own members.

At Coucy after the death of Thomas, a sixty-year period of more respectable lordship followed under his son and grandson, Enguerrand II and Raoul I, who cooperated with the crown to the benefit of their domain. Each responded to the renewed crusades of the 12th century, and each in turn lost his life in the Holy Land. Perhaps suffering from financial stringency imposed by these expeditions, the widow of Raoul sold to Coucy-le-Château in 1197 its charter of liberties as a free commune for 140 livres.

Such democratization, as far as it went, was not so much a step in a steady march toward liberty—as 19th century historians liked to envision the human record—as it was the inadvertent by-product of the nobles' passionate pursuit of war. Required to equip himself and his retainers with arms, armor, and sound horses, all of them costly, the crusader—if he survived—usually came home poorer than he went, or left his estate poorer, especially since none of the crusades after the First was either victorious or lucrative. The only recourse, since it was unthinkable to sell land, was to sell communal privileges or commute labor services and bonds of serfdom for a money rent. In the expanding economy of the 12th and 13th centuries, the profits of commerce and agricultural surplus brought burghers and peasants the cash to pay for rights and liberties.

In Enguerrand III, called "the Great," builder of the reconstructed castle and *donjon,* the excess of the Coucys appeared again. Seigneur from 1191 to 1242, he built or reconstructed castles and ramparts on six of his fiefs in addition to Coucy, including one at St. Gobain almost as large as that of Coucy. He took part in the slaughter of the Albigensian Crusade, fought in every other available war including, like his great-grandfather Thomas, one against the diocese of Reims growing out of a quarrel over feudal rights. He was accused of having pillaged its lands, cut down its trees, seized its villages, forced the doors of the cathedral, imprisoned the *doyen* in chains, and reduced the canons to misery.

When the Archbishop of Reims complained to the Pope in 1216, Enguerrand III too was excommunicated and all religious services in the diocese were ordered to be terminated if he should appear. A person under the ban was deprived of the sacraments and doomed to hell until such time as he made amendment and was absolved. In major cases only the bishop or in some cases the Pope could lift the ban. While it was in force the local priest was supposed to pronounce the curse upon the sinner before the parish two or three times a year in the name of the Father, Son, Holy Ghost, Virgin Mary, and all the Apostles and saints while the funeral knell tolled, candles were put out, and the cross and missals laid on the floor. Supposedly the guilty one was cut off from all social and occupational relationships, but the inconveniences for everyone resulting from this rule were such that his neighbors either resorted to throwing stones at his house or other measures to bring him to repentance, or ignored the ban. In Enguerrand III's case the cessation of all religious services was a fearful sentence upon the community, which brought him to settlement and absolution in 1219 after he had performed penance. But it did nothing to quench his civil ambitions, for he went on to build the great castle that cast its shadow over Paris.

His urgency in the construction was stimulated by expectation of a battle with his sovereign, for during the minority of Louis IX, the future St. Louis, Enguerrand III led a league of barons in opposition to the crown; even, as some say, aspired to the throne himself. He had inherited royal blood through his mother, Alix de Dreux, a descendant of Philip I. His *donjon*, designed to surpass the royal tower of the Louvre, was taken as a gesture of defiance and intent. The regency of the boy King's mother withstood the threat, but the Sire de Coucy remained a force to reckon with. He piled on property and international standing through marriages. His first and third wives were women of neighboring noble families who brought him additional estates in Picardy, and his second wife was Mahaut de Saxe, daughter of Henry the Lion, Duke of Saxony, granddaughter of Henry II of England and Eleanor of Aquitaine, niece of Richard the Lion-hearted, and sister of Otto of Saxony, subsequently Holy Roman Emperor. His daughter by one of these wives married Alexander II, King of Scotland.

In the constructions at Coucy he employed (as estimated from masons' marks) about 800 stonemasons, uncounted oxcarts to drag the stones from quarries to the hill, and some 800 other craftsmen such as carpenters, roofers, iron and lead workers, painters, and wood-carvers. Over the doorway of the *donjon* was carved in bas-relief the statue of an unarmored knight in combat with a lion, symbolizing chivalric courage. Walls of both castle and keep were decorated with painted borders and garlands of fantastic leaves, all on a scale to match the structure. Manteled chimneys, built into the walls, were a feature in every part of the castle. As distinct from a hole in the roof, these chimneys were a technological advance of the 11th century that by warming individual rooms, brought lords and ladies out of the common hall where all had once eaten together and gathered for warmth, and separated owners from their retainers. No other invention brought more progress in comfort and refinement, although at the cost of a widening social gulf.

Tucked into an interior angle of the second story was a small room with its own chimney, perhaps a boudoir for the Dame de Coucy, where from the window she could see a view stretching over the valley with here and there the bell tower of a village church poking up behind a clump of trees, and where, like the lady of Shalott, she could watch the people come and go on the road winding up from below. Except for this tiny chamber, the living quarters of the seigneur and his family were in that part of the castle least accessible from outside.

In 1206 the citizens of Amiens, Picardy's proud and prosperous capital, already a commune for a hundred years, acquired a piece of John the Baptist's head. As a fitting shrine for the relic, they determined to build the largest church in France, "higher than all the saints, higher than all the kings." By 1220, resources having been gathered, the noble vault of the cathedral was steadily rising. Within the same decade Enguerrand III built, alongside his *donjon*, a grandiose and magnificent chapel, larger than the Sainte Chapelle that St. Louis was to build in Paris a few years later. Vaulted and gilded and rich in carving and color, it glowed with stained-glass windows so beautiful that the greatest collector of the next century, Jean, Duc de Berry, tried to buy them for 12,000 gold écus.

Enguerrand III was now seigneur of St. Gobain, of Assis, of Marle, of La Fère, of Folembray, of Montmirail, of Oisy, of Crèvecoeur, of La Ferté-Aucoul and La Ferté-Gauche, Viscount of Meaux, Castellan de Cambrai. Long ago in 1095 the crown had retrieved sovereignty over the fief of Coucy from the Church; it was now held directly of the King, and its seigneur paid homage only to the King's person. During the 12th and 13th centuries the seigneur of Coucy, like the Bishop of Laon, coined his own money. Judged by the number of knights that royal vassals were obligated to provide at the King's summons, Coucy at this time was the leading untitled barony of the realm, ranking immediately behind the great dukedoms and counties which, except for homage owed to the French King, were virtually independent lordships. According to a record of 1216, the domain of Coucy owed 30 knights, in comparison to 34 for the Duke of Anjou, 36 for the Duke of Brittany, and 47 for the Count of Flanders.

In 1242 Enguerrand III was killed at the age of about sixty when in a violent fall from his horse the point of his sword was thrust through his body. His eldest son and successor, Raoul II, was soon afterward killed in battle in Egypt while on St. Louis' unhappy crusade of 1248–50. He was succeeded by his brother Enguerrand IV, a kind of medieval Caligula, one of whose crimes became the catalyst of a major advance in social justice.

On apprehending in his forest three young squires of Laon, equipped with bows and arrows but no hunting dogs for taking important game, Enguerrand IV had them executed by hanging, without trial or process of any kind. Impunity in such affairs was no longer a matter of course, for the King was Louis IX, a sovereign whose sense of rulership was equal to his piety. He had Enguerrand IV arrested, not by his peers but by *sergents* of the court, like any criminal, and imprisoned in the Louvre, although, in deference to his rank, not in chains.

Summoned to trial in 1256, Enguerrand IV was accompanied by the greatest peers of the realm—the King of Navarre, the Duke of Burgundy, the Counts of Bar and Soissons among others, grimly sensing a test of their prerogatives. Refusing to submit to investigation of the case as touching his person, honor, rank, and noble heritage, Enguerrand demanded judgment by his peers and trial by combat. Louis IX firmly refused, saying that as regards the poor, the clergy, "and persons who deserve our pity," it would be unjust to allow trial by combat. Customarily, non-nobles could engage a champion in such cases, but King Louis saw the method as obsolete. In a long and fiercely argued process, against the strenuous resistance of the peers, he ordered the Sire de Coucy to stand trial. Enguerrand IV was convicted, and although the King intended a death sentence, he was persuaded by the peers to forgo it. Enguerrand was sentenced to pay a fine of 12,000 livres, to be used partly to endow masses in perpetuity for the souls of the men he had hanged, and partly to be sent to Acre to aid in the defense of the Holy Land. Legal history was made and later cited as a factor in the canonization of the King.

The Coucy riches restored Enguerrand IV to royal favor when he lent King Louis 15,000 livres in 1265 to buy what was supposed to be the True Cross. Otherwise he continued a career of outrages into the 14th century and died at the ripe age of 75 in 1311, without issue though not without a bequest. He left 20 sous (equal to one livre) a year in perpetuity to the leprosarium of Coucy-la-Ville so that its inmates "will pray for us each year in the Chapel for our sins." Twenty sous at this time was equal to a day's pay of one knight or four archers, or the hire of a cart and two horses for twenty days, or, theoretically, the pay of a hired peasant for two years, so it may be presumed to have underwritten a reasonable number of prayers, though perhaps not adequate for the soul of Enguerrand IV.

When that unlamented lord, though twice married, died without heirs, the dynasty passed to the descendants of his sister Alix, who was married to the Count of Guînes. Her eldest son inherited the Guînes lands and title, while her second son, Enguerrand V, became the lord of Coucy. Raised at the court of Alexander of Scotland, his uncle by marriage, he married Catherine Lindsay of Baliol, the King's niece, and held the seigneury only ten years. He was followed in rapid succession by his son Guillaume and his grandson Enguerrand VI, who inherited the domain in 1335 and five years later was to father Enguerrand VII, last of the Coucys and the subject of this book. Through further marriages with powerful families of northern France and Flanders, the Coucys had continued to weave alliances of strength and influence and acquire lands, revenues, and a galaxy of armorial bearings in the process. They could display as many as twelve coats-of-arms: Boisgency, Hainault, Dreux, Saxony, Montmirail, Roucy, Baliol, Ponthieu, Châtillon, St. Pol, Gueldres, and Flanders.

The Coucys maintained a sense of eminence second to none, and conducted their affairs after the usage of sovereign princes. They held courts of justice in the royal style and organized their household under the same officers as the King's: a constable, a grand butler, a master of falconry and the hunt, a master of the stables, a master of forests and waters, and masters or grand stewards of kitchen, bakery, cellar, fruit (which included spices, and torches and candles for lighting), and furnishings (including tapestry and lodgings during travel). A grand seigneur of this rank also usually employed one or more resident physicians, barbers, priests, painters, musicians, minstrels, secretaries and copyists, an astrologer, a jester, and a dwarf, besides pages and squires. A principal vassal acting as *châtelain* or *garde du château* managed the estate. At Coucy fifty knights, together with their own squires, attendants, and servants, made up a permanent garrison of 500.

Outward magnificence was important as a statement of status, requiring huge retinues dressed in the lord's livery, spectacular feasts, tournaments, hunts, entertainments, and above all an open-handed liberality in gifts and expenditure which, since his followers lived off it, was extolled as the most admired attribute of a noble.

The status of nobility derived from birth and ancestry, but had to be confirmed by "living nobly"—that is, by the sword. A person was noble if born of noble parents and grandparents and so on back to the first armed horseman. In practice the rule was porous and the status fluid and inexact. The one certain criterion was function—namely, the practice of arms. This was the function assigned to the second of the three estates established by God, each with a given task for the good of the whole. The clergy were to pray for all men, the knight to fight for them, and the commoner to work that all might eat.

As being nearest to God, the clergy came first. They were divided between two hierarchies, the cloistered and secular, meaning in the latter case those whose mission was among the laity. Presiding over both hierarchies were the prelates—abbots, bishops, and archbishops, who were the equivalent of the secular *grands seigneurs*. Between the prelacy and the poor half-educated priest living on a crumb and a pittance there was little in common. The Third Estate was even less homogeneous, being divided between employers and workers and covering the whole range of great urban magnates, lawyers and doctors, skilled craftsmen, day laborers, and peasants. Nevertheless, the nobility insisted on lumping all non-nobles together as a common breed. "Of the good towns, merchants and working men," wrote a noble at the court of the last Duke of Burgundy, "no long description is necessary, for, among other things, this estate is not capable of great attributes because it is of servile degree."

The object of the noble's function, in theory, was not fighting for fighting's sake, but defense of the two other estates and the maintenance of justice and order. He was supposed to protect the people from oppression, to combat tyranny, and to cultivate virtue—that is, the higher qualities of humanity of which the mud-stained ignorant peasant was considered incapable by his contemporaries in Christianity, if not by its founder.

In his capacity as protector, the noble earned exemption from direct taxation by poll or hearth-tax, although not from the aids or sales taxes. These, however, took proportionately more from the poor than from the rich. The assumption was that taxpaying was ignoble; the knight's sword arm provided his service to the state, as prayers provided the clergy's and exempted them too from the hearth-tax. Justification for the nobles lay in the "exposure of their bodies and property in war," but in practice the rules were as changeable and diffuse as clouds in a windy sky. The tax status of the clergy, too, when it came to money for the defense of the realm, was the subject of chronic and fierce dispute.

Taxation like usury rested on principles that were anything but clearly defined and so muddled by ad hoc additions, exemptions, and arrangements that it was impossible to count on a definite amount of returns. The basic principle was that the King should "live of his own" under ordinary circumstances, but since his own revenues might not suffice for defense of the realm or other governmental purposes, his subjects could be taxed to enable him, as Thomas Aquinas neatly phrased it, "to provide for the common good from the common goods." This obligation derived from the deeper principle that "princes are instituted by God not to seek their own gain but the common good of the people."

A man born to the noble estate clung to the sword as the sign of his identity, not only for the sake of tax-exemption but for self-image. "Not one of us had a father who died at home," insisted a knight in a 13th century *chanson de geste;* "all have died in the battle of cold steel."

The horse was the seat of the noble, the mount that lifted him above other men. In every language except English, the word for knight—*chevalier* in French—meant the man on horseback. "A brave man mounted on a good horse," it was acknowledged, "can do more in an hour of fighting than ten or maybe one hundred could do afoot." The *destrier* or war-horse was bred to be "strong, fiery, swift, and faithful" and ridden only in combat. En route the knight rode his palfrey, high-bred but of quieter disposition, while his squire led the *destrier* at his right hand—hence its name, from *dexter*. In fulfilling military service, horse and knight were considered inseparable; without a mount the knight was a mere man.

Battle was his exaltation. "If I had one foot already in Paradise," exclaimed Garin li Loherains, the hero of a *chanson de geste*, "I would withdraw it to go and fight!" The troubadour Bertrand de Born, himself a noble, was more explicit.

> My heart is filled with gladness when I see
> Strong castles besieged, stockades broken and overwhelmed,
> Many vassals struck down,
> Horses of the dead and wounded roving at random.
> And when battle is joined, let all men of good lineage
> Think of naught but the breaking of heads and arms,
> For it is better to die than be vanquished and live. . . .
> I tell you I have no such joy as when I hear the shout
> "On! On!" from both sides and the neighing of riderless steeds,
> And groans of "Help me! Help me!"
> And when I see both great and small
> Fall in the ditches and on the grass
> And see the dead transfixed by spear shafts!
> Lords, mortgage your domains, castles, cities,
> But never give up war!

Dante pictured Bertrand in Hell, carrying his severed head before him as a lantern.

From ownership of land and revenues the noble derived the right to exercise authority over all non-nobles of his territory except the clergy and except merchants who were citizens of a free town. The *grand seigneur*'s authority extended to "high justice," meaning the power of life or death, while the lesser knight's was limited to prison, flogging, and other punishments of "low justice." Its basis and justification remained the duty to protect, as embodied in the lord's oath to his vassals, which was as binding in theory as theirs to him—and theirs was binding "only so long as the lord keeps his oath." Medieval political structure was ideally a contract exchanging service and loyalty in return for protection, justice, and order. As the peasant owed produce and labor, the lord in turn owed ministerial service to his overlord or sovereign, and counsel in peace as well as military service in war. Land in all cases was the consideration, and the oath of homage, made and accepted, was the seal binding both sides, including kings.

Not all nobles were *grands seigneurs* like the Coucys. A bachelor knight, possessor of one manor and a bony nag, shared the same cult but not the interests of a territorial lord. The total ranks of the nobility in France numbered about 200,000 persons in 40,000 to 50,000 families who represented something over one percent of the population. They ranged from the great dukedoms with revenues of more than 10,000 livres, down through the lord of a minor castle with one or two knights as vassals and an income under 500 livres, to the poor knight at the bottom of the scale who was lord of no one except those of servile birth and whose only fief was a house and a few fields equivalent to a peasant's holding. He might have an income from a few rents of 25 livres or less, which had to support family and servants and the knight's equipment that was his livelihood. He lived by horse and arms, dependent for maintenance on his overlord or whoever needed his services.

A squire belonged to the nobility by birth whether or not he obtained the belt and spurs of a knight, but legal process was often required to determine what other functions a gentleman might undertake without losing noble status. Could he sell wine from his vineyard, for instance?—a delicate question because the kings regularly sold theirs. In a case brought in 1393 to determine this question, a royal ordinance stated rather ambiguously, "It is not proper for a noble to be an innkeeper." According to another judgment, a noble could acquire license to trade without losing his status. Sons of noble fathers were known "who live and have long lived as merchants selling cloth, grain, wine and all other things of merchandise, or as tradesmen, furriers, shoemakers or tailors," but such activities would doubtless have lost them the privileges of a noble.

The rationale of the problem was made plain by Honoré Bonet, a 14th century cleric who made the brave attempt in his *Tree of Battles* to set forth existing codes of military conduct. The reason for the prohibition of commercial activity, he wrote, was to ensure that the knight "shall have no cause to leave the practice of arms for the desire of acquiring worldly riches."

Definition increasingly concerned the born nobles in proportion as their status was diluted by the ennoblement of outsiders. Like the grant of charters to towns, the grant of fiefs to commoners, who paid handsomely for the honor, was found by the crown to be a lucrative source of funds. The ennobled were men of fortune who procured the king's needs, or they were lawyers and notaries who had started by assisting the king at various levels in the administration of finance and justice and gradually, as the business of government grew more complex, created a group of professional civil servants and ministers of the crown. Called *noblesse de la robe* when elevated, as distinguished from nobility of the sword, they were scorned as parvenus by the ancestral nobles, who resented the usurping of their right of counsel, lost more or less by default.

In consequence, the heraldic coat-of-arms—outward sign of ancestry signifying the right to bear arms, which, once granted to a family, could be worn by no other—came to be an object almost of cult worship. At tournaments its display was required as evidence of noble ancestry; at some tournaments four were required. As penetration by outsiders increased, so did snobbery until a day in the mid-15th century when a knight rode into the lists followed by a parade of pennants bearing no less than 32 coats-of-arms.

Through disappearance by failure to produce a male heir or by sinking over the edge into the lower classes, and through inflow of the ennobled, the personnel of the nobility was in flux, even though the status was fixed as an order of society. The disappearance rate of noble families has been estimated at 50 percent a century, and the average duration of a dynasty at three to six generations over a period from 100 to 200 years. An example of the sinking process occurred in a family called Clusel with a small fief in the Loire valley. In 1276 it was headed by a knight evidently of too small resources to maintain himself in arms, who was reduced to the non-noble necessity of tilling his fields and operating his mill with his own hands. Of three grandsons appearing in local records, one was still a squire, one had become a parish priest, and the third a rent-collector for the lord of the county. After a passage of 85 years no member of the lineage was any longer referred to as a noble. In the case of another squire named Guichard Vert, who died as a young man in 1287, the family hovered on the edge. Guichard left two beds, three blankets, four bedsheets, two small rugs, one table, three benches, five coffers, two hams and a haunch of bacon in the larder, five empty barrels in the cellar, a chessboard, and a helmet and lance but no sword. Though without cash, he willed 200 livres to his wife to be paid in ten installments from his revenues of about 60 livres a year, and other income to found a chantry for his soul. He bequeathed gifts of cloth to friends and to the poor, and remitted two years' tax to his tenants, most of whom were already in arrears. Such a family, in physical conditions hardly distinguishable from a commoner's, would strain to keep its ties to the nobility, sending sons to take service as squires so that they might have access to gifts and pensions, or to enter the clergy in the hope of taking one of its many paths to riches.

A knight on the way down might pass an enterprising peasant on his way up. Having bought or inherited his freedom, a rent-paying peasant who prospered would add fields and tenants of his own, gradually leave manual labor to servants, acquire a fief from lord or Church, learn the practice of arms, marry the daughter of a needy squire, and slowly assimilate upward until he appeared in the records as *donicellus*, or squire, himself. The bailiff in the lord's service had greater opportunities to make himself rich and, if he had also made himself useful, was often rewarded by a fief with vassals and rents, perhaps also a fortified manor. He would begin to dress like a noble, wear a sword, keep hunting dogs and falcons, and ride a war-horse carrying shield and lance. Nothing was more resented by the hereditary nobles than the imitation of their clothes and manners by the upstarts, thus obscuring the lines between the eternal orders of society. Magnificence in clothes was considered a prerogative of the nobles, who should be identifiable by modes of dress forbidden to others. In the effort to establish this principle as law and prevent "outrageous and excessive apparel of divers people against their estate and degree," sumptuary laws were repeatedly announced, attempting to fix what kinds of clothes people might wear and how much they might spend.

Proclaimed by criers in the county courts and public assemblies, exact gradations of fabric, color, fur trimming, ornaments, and jewels were laid down for every rank and income level. Bourgeois might be forbidden to own a carriage or wear ermine, and peasants to wear any color but black or brown. Florence allowed doctors and magistrates to share the nobles' privilege of ermine, but ruled out for merchants' wives multicolored, striped, and checked gowns, brocades, figured velvets, and fabrics embroidered in silver and gold. In France territorial lords and their ladies with incomes of 6,000 livres or more could order four costumes a year; knights and bannerets with incomes of 3,000 could have three a year, one of which had to be for summer. Boys could have only one a year, and no *demoiselle* who was not the *châtelaine* of a castle or did not have an income of 2,000 livres could order more than one costume a year. In England, according to a law of 1363, a merchant worth £1,000 was entitled to the same dress and meals as a knight worth £500, and a merchant worth £200 the same as a knight worth £100. Double wealth in this case equaled nobility. Efforts were also made to regulate how many dishes could be served at meals, what garments and linens could be accumulated for a trousseau, how many minstrels at a wedding party. In the passion for fixing and stabilizing identity, prostitutes were required to wear stripes, or garments turned inside out.

Servants who imitated the long pointed shoes and hanging sleeves of their betters were severely disapproved, more because of their pretensions than because their sleeves slopped into the broth when they waited on table and their fur-trimmed hems trailed in the dirt. "There was so much pride amongst the common people," wrote the English chronicler Henry Knighton, "in vying with one another in dress and ornaments that it was scarce possible to distinguish the poor from the rich, the servant from the master, or a priest from other men."

Expenditure of money by commoners pained the nobles not least because they saw it benefiting the merchant class rather than themselves. The clergy considered that this expenditure drained money from the Church, and so condemned it on the moral ground that extravagance and luxury were in themselves wicked and harmful to virtue. In general, the sumptuary laws were favored as a means of curbing extravagance and promoting thrift, in the belief that if people could be made to save money, the King could obtain it when necessary. Economic thinking did not embrace the idea of spending as a stimulus to the economy.

The sumptuary laws proved unenforceable; the prerogative of adornment, like the drinking of liquor in a later century, defied prohibition. When Florentine city officials pursued women in the streets to examine their gowns, and entered houses to search their wardrobes, their findings were often spectacular: cloth of white marbled silk embroidered with vine leaves and red grapes, a coat with white and red roses on a pale yellow ground, another coat of "blue cloth with white lilies and white and red stars and compasses and white and yellow stripes across it, lined with red striped cloth," which almost seemed as if the owner were trying to see how far defiance could go.

To the *grands seigneurs* of multiple fiefs and castles, identity was no problem. In their gold-embossed surcoats and velvet mantles lined in ermine, their slashed and parti-colored tunics embroidered with family crest or verses or a lady-love's initials, their hanging scalloped sleeves with colored linings, their long pointed shoes of red leather from Cordova, their rings and chamois gloves and belts hung with bells and trinkets, their infinity of hats—puffed tam-o'shanters and furred caps, hoods and brims, chaplets of flowers, coiled turbans, coverings of every shape, puffed, pleated, scalloped, or curled into a long tailed pocket called a liripipe—they were beyond imitation.

When the 14th century opened, France was supreme. Her superiority in chivalry, learning, and Christian devotion was taken for granted, and as traditional champion of the Church, her monarch was accorded the formula of "Most Christian King." The people of his realm considered themselves the chosen objects of divine favor through whom God expressed his will on earth. The classic French account of the First Crusade was entitled *Gesta Dei per Francos* (*God's Deeds Done by the French*). Divine favor was confirmed in 1297 when, a bare quarter-century after his death, France's twice-crusading King, Louis IX, was canonized as a saint.

"The fame of French knights," acknowledged Giraldus Cambrensis in the 12th century, "dominates the world." France was the land of "well-conducted chivalry" where uncouth German nobles came to learn good manners and taste at the courts of French princes, and knights and sovereigns from all over Europe assembled at the royal court to enjoy jousts and festivals and amorous gallantries. Residence there, according to blind King John of Bohemia, who preferred the French court to his own, offered "the most chivalrous sojourn in the world." The French, as described by the renowned Spanish knight Don Pero Niño, "are generous and great givers of presents." They know how to treat strangers honorably, they praise fair deeds, they are courteous and gracious in speech and "very gay, giving themselves up to pleasure and seeking it. They are very amorous, women as well as men, and proud of it."

As a result of Norman conquests and the crusades, French was spoken as a second mother tongue by the noble estate in England, Flanders, and the Kingdom of Naples and Sicily. It was used as the language of business by Flemish magnates, by law courts in the remnants of the Kingdom of Jerusalem, by scholars and poets of other lands. Marco Polo dictated his *Travels* in French, St. Francis sang French songs, foreign troubadours modeled their tales of adventure on the French *chansons de geste*. When a Venetian scholar translated a Latin chronicle of his city into French rather than Italian, he explained his choice on the ground that "the French language is current throughout the world and more delightful to hear and read than any other."

The architecture of Gothic cathedrals was called the "French style"; a French architect was invited to design London Bridge; Venice imported dolls from France dressed in the latest mode in order to keep up with French fashions; exquisitely carved French ivories, easily transportable, penetrated to the limits of the Christian world. Above all, the University of Paris elevated the name of the French capital, surpassing all others in the fame of its masters and the prestige of its studies in theology and philosophy, though these were already petrifying in the rigid doctrines of Scholasticism. Its faculty at the opening of the 14th century numbered over 500, its students, attracted from all countries, were too numerous to count. It was a magnet for the greatest minds: Thomas Aquinas of Italy taught there in the 13th century, as did his own teacher Albertus Magnus of Germany, his philosophical opponent Duns Scotus of Scotland, and in the next century, the two great political thinkers, Marsilius of Padua and the English Franciscan William of Ockham. By virtue of the university, Paris was the "Athens of Europe"; the Goddess of Wisdom, it was said, after leaving Greece and then Rome, had made it her home.

The University's charter of privileges, dating from 1200, was its greatest pride. Exempted from civil control, the University was equally haughty in regard to ecclesiastical authority, and always in conflict with Bishop and Pope. "You Paris masters at your desks seem to think the world should be ruled by your reasonings," stormed the papal legate Benedict Caetani, soon to be Pope Boniface VIII. "It is to us," he reminded them, "that the world is entrusted, not to you." Unconvinced, the University considered itself as authoritative in theology as the Pope, although conceding to Christ's Vicar equal status with itself as "the two lights of the world."

In this favored land of the Western world, the Coucy inheritance in 1335 was as rich as it was ancient. Watered by the Ailette, the Coucys' land was called the *vallée d'or* (golden valley) because of its resources in timber, vineyards, grain crops, and a profusion of fish in the streams. The magnificent forest of St. Gobain covered more than 7,000 acres of primeval oak and beech, ash and birch, willow, alder and quivering aspen, wild cherry and pine. The home of deer, wolves, wild boar, heron, and every other bird, it was a paradise for the hunt. From taxes and land rents and feudal dues of various kinds increasingly converted to money, from tolls on bridges and fees for use of the lord's flour mill, wine press, and bread ovens, the annual revenue of an estate the size of Coucy would have been in the range of 5,000 to 6,000 livres.

Everything that had formed the fief since the tree trunks at Codiciacum was symbolized in the great lion platform of stone in front of the castle gate where vassals came to present rents and homage. The platform rested on three lions, *couchant*, one devouring a child, one a dog, and in between them, a third, quiescent. On top was a fourth lion seated in all the majesty the sculptor could evoke. Three times a year—at Easter, Pentecost, and Christmas—the Abbot of Nogent or his agent came to pay homage for the land originally granted to the monks by Aubry de Coucy. The rituals of the ceremony were as elaborate and abstruse as any in the royal crowning at Reims.

Mounted on a bay horse (or, according to some accounts, a palomino) with clipped tail and ears and a plow-horse's harness, the abbot's representative carried a whip, a seed bag of wheat, and a basket filled with 120 *rissoles*. These were crescent-shaped pastries made of rye flour, stuffed with minced veal cooked in oil. A dog followed, also with clipped ears and tail, and with a *rissole* tied around his neck. The agent circled a stone cross at the entrance to the court three times, cracking his whip on each tour, dismounted and knelt at the lion platform, and, if each detail of equipment and performance was exactly right so far, was allowed to proceed. He then mounted the platform, kissed the lion, and deposited the *rissoles* plus twelve loaves of bread and three portions of wine as his homage. The Sire de Coucy took a third of the offerings, distributed the rest among the assembled bailiffs and town magistrates, and stamped the document of homage with a seal representing a mitered abbot with the feet of a goat.

Pagan, barbarian, feudal, Christian, accumulated out of the shrouded past, here was medieval society—and the many-layered elements of Western man.

Chapter 2

Born to Woe: The Century

When the last of the Coucys was born, his country was supreme but his century was already in trouble. A physical chill settled on the 14th century at its very start, initiating the miseries to come. The Baltic Sea froze over twice, in 1303 and 1306–07; years followed of unseasonable cold, storms and rains, and a rise in the level of the Caspian Sea. Contemporaries could not know it was the onset of what has since been recognized as the Little Ice Age, caused by an advance of polar and alpine glaciers and lasting until about 1700. Nor were they yet aware that, owing to the climatic change, communication with Greenland was gradually being lost, that the Norse settlements there were being extinguished, that cultivation of grain was disappearing from Iceland and being severely reduced in Scandinavia. But they could feel the colder weather, and mark with fear its result: a shorter growing season.

This meant disaster, for population increase in the last century had already reached a delicate balance with agricultural techniques. Given the tools and methods of the time, the clearing of productive land had already been pushed to its limits. Without adequate irrigation and fertilizers, crop yield could not be raised nor poor soils be made productive. Commerce was not equipped to transport grain in bulk from surplus-producing areas except by water. Inland towns and cities lived on local resources, and when these dwindled, the inhabitants starved.

In 1315, after rains so incessant that they were compared to the Biblical flood, crops failed all over Europe, and famine, the dark horseman of the Apocalypse, became familiar to all. The previous rise in population had already exceeded agricultural production, leaving people undernourished and more vulnerable to hunger and disease. Reports spread of people eating their own children, of the poor in Poland feeding on hanged bodies taken down from the gibbet. A contagion of dysentery prevailed in the same years. Local famines recurred intermittently after the great sweep of 1315–16.

Acts of man no less than change in the climate marked the 14th century as born to woe. In the first twenty years, four ominous events followed one after another: the assault on the Pope by the King of France; the removal of the Papacy to Avignon; the suppression of the Templars; and the rising of the Pastoureaux. The most fateful was an assault on Boniface VIII by agents of Philip IV, King of France, surnamed the Fair. The issue was temporal versus papal authority arising from Philip's levy of taxes on clerical income without consent of the Pope. Boniface in response issued the defiant Bull *Clericos Laicos* in 1296 forbidding the clergy to pay any form of tax whatsoever to any lay ruler. He recognized in the growing tendency of prelates to hesitate between allegiance to their king and obedience to the Pope a threat to the papal claim to universal rule as Vicar of Christ. Despite formidable hostilities brought to bear on him by Philip the Fair, Boniface asserted in a second Bull, *Unam Sanctam*, in 1302, the most absolute statement of papal supremacy ever made: "It is necessary to salvation that every human creature be subject to the Roman pontiff."

Philip thereupon called for a council to judge the Pope on charges of heresy, blasphemy, murder, sodomy, simony and sorcery (including consorting with a familiar spirit or pet demon), and failure to fast on fast days. At the same time Boniface drew up a Bull to excommunicate the King, prompting Philip to resort to physical force. On September 7, 1303, agents of the King, aided by anti-papist Italian armed forces, seized the 86-year-old Pope in his summer retreat at Anagni near Rome with the intention of forestalling the excommunication and bringing him by force before a council. After three days' turmoil, Boniface was freed by the citizens of Anagni, but the shock of the outrage was mortal and within a month he was dead.

The assault on the Pope did not rally support for the cause of the victim and the fact that it did not was a measure of change. The tide was receding from the universality of the Church that had been the medieval dream. The all-embracing claim of Boniface VIII was obsolete before he made it. The indirect consequence of the "Crime of Anagni" was the removal of the papacy to Avignon, and in that "Babylonian Exile" demoralization began.

The move occurred when, under the influence of Philip the Fair, a French Pope was elected as Clement V. He did not go to Rome to take up his See, mainly because he feared Italian reprisals for the French treatment of Boniface, although the Italians said it was because he kept a French mistress, the beautiful Countess of Périgord, daughter of the

Count of Foix. In 1309 he settled in Avignon in Provence near the mouth of the Rhône. This was within the French sphere, though technically not in France since Provence was a fief of the Kingdom of Naples and Sicily.

Thereafter under six French popes in succession, Avignon became a virtual temporal state of sumptuous pomp, of great cultural attraction, and of unlimited simony—that is, the selling of offices. Diminished by its removal from the Holy See of Rome and by being generally regarded as a tool of France, the papacy sought to make up prestige and power in temporal terms. It concentrated on finance and the organization and centralization of every process of papal government that could bring in revenue. Besides its regular revenue from tithes and annates on ecclesiastical income and from dues from papal fiefs, every office, every nomination, every appointment or preferment, every dispensation of the rules, every judgment of the Rota or adjudication of a claim, every pardon, indulgence, and absolution, everything the Church had or was, from cardinal's hat to pilgrim's relic, was for sale. In addition, the papacy took a cut of all voluntary gifts and bequests and offerings on the altar. It received Peter's Pence from England and other kingdoms. It sold extra indulgences in jubilee years and took a special tax for crusades which continued to be proclaimed but rarely left home. The once great impulse had faded, and fervor for holy war had become largely verbal.

Benefices, of which there were 700 bishops' sees and hundreds of thousands of lower offices, were the most lucrative source of papal income. Increasingly, the popes reserved more and more benefices to their power of appointment, destroying the elective principle. Since the appointees were often strangers to the diocese, or some cardinal's favorite, the practice aroused resentment within the clergy. If an episcopal election was still held, the papacy charged a fee for confirming it. To obtain a conferred benefice, a bishop or abbot greased the palms of the Curia for his nomination, paid anywhere from a third to the whole of his first year's revenue as the fee for his appointment, and knew that when he died his personal property would revert to the Pope and any outstanding dues would have to be paid by his successor.

Excommunication and anathema, the most extreme measures the Church could command, supposedly reserved for heresy and horrible crimes—"for by these penalties a man is separated from the faithful and turned over to Satan"—were now used to wring money from recalcitrant payers. In one case a bishop was denied Christian burial until his heirs agreed to be responsible for his debts, to the scandal of the diocese, which saw its bishop lying unshriven and cut off from hope of salvation. Abuse of the spiritual power for such purposes brought excommunication into contempt and lowered respect for clerical leaders.

Money could buy any kind of dispensation: to legitimize children, of which the majority were those of priests and prelates;* to divide a corpse for the favorite custom of burial in two or more places; to permit nuns to keep two maids; to permit a converted Jew to visit his unconverted parents; to marry within the prohibited degree of consanguinity (with a sliding scale of fees for the second, third, and fourth degrees); to trade with the infidel Moslem (with a fee required for each ship on a scale according to cargo); to receive stolen goods up to a specific value. The collection and accounting of all these sums, largely handled through Italian bankers, made the physical counting of cash a common sight in the papal palace. Whenever he entered there, reported Alvar Pelayo, a Spanish official of the Curia, "I found brokers and clergy engaged in reckoning the money which lay in heaps before them."

The dispensation with most serious results was the one permitting appointment to a benefice of a candidate below the canonical age of 25 or one who had never been consecrated or never taken the required examination for literacy. Appointment of unfit or absentee clergy became an abuse in itself. In Bohemia on one occasion in the early 14th century, a boy of seven was appointed to a parish worth an annual income of 25 gulden; another was raised through three offices of the hierarchy, paying at each stage for a dispensation for non-residence and postponed consecration. Younger sons of noble families were repeatedly appointed to archbishoprics at 18, 20, or 22. Tenures were short because each preferment brought in another payment.

Priests who could not read or who, from ignorance, stumbled stupidly through the ritual of the Eucharist were another scandal. A Bishop of Durham in 1318 could not understand or pronounce Latin and after struggling helplessly with the word *Metropolitanus* at his own consecration, muttered in the vernacular, "Let us take that word as read." Later when ordaining candidates for holy orders, he met the word *aenigmate* (through a glass darkly) and this time swore in honest outrage, "By St. Louis, that was no courteous man who wrote this word!" The unfit clergy spread dismay, for these were the men supposed to have the souls of the laity in their charge and be the intermediaries between man and God. Writing of "incapable and ignorant men" who could buy any office they wanted from the Curia,

---

* Out of 614 grants of legitimacy in the year 1342–43, 484 were to members of the clergy.

the chronicler Henry of Hereford went to the heart of the dismay when he wrote, "Look . . . at the dangerous situation of those in their charge, and tremble!"

When Church practices were calculated at a money value, their religious content seeped away. Theoretically, pardon for sin could only be won through penitence, but the penance of a pilgrimage to Rome or Jerusalem had little meaning when the culprit could estimate the cost of the journey and buy an indulgence for an equivalent sum.

The popes—successors, as Petrarch pointed out, of "the poor fishermen of Galilee"—were now "loaded with gold and clad in purple." John XXII, a Pope with the touch of Midas who ruled from 1316 to 1334, bought for his own use forty pieces of gold cloth from Damascus for 1,276 gold florins and spent even more on furs, including an ermine-trimmed pillow. The clothing of his retinue cost 7,000 to 8,000 florins a year.

His successors Benedict XII and Clement VI built in stages the great papal palace at Avignon on a rock overlooking the Rhône, a huge and inharmonious mass of roofs and towers without coherent design. Constructed in castle style around interior courts, with battlements and twelve-foot-thick walls for defense, it had odd pyramidal chimneys rising from the kitchens, banqueting halls and gardens, money chambers and offices, rose-windowed chapels, a steam room for the Pope heated by a boiler, and a gate opening on the public square where the faithful gathered to watch the Holy Father ride out on his white mule. Here moved the majestic cardinals in their wide red hats, "rich, insolent and rapacious" in Petrarch's words, vying with each other in the magnificence of their suites. One required ten stables for his horses, and another rented parts of 51 houses to lodge all his retainers.

Corridors of the palace bustled with notaries and officers of the Curia and legates departing on or returning from their missions. Petitioners and their lawyers waited anxiously in anterooms, pilgrims crowded in the courtyards to receive the pontifical blessing, while through the halls passed the parade of the Pope's relatives of both sexes in brocades and furs with their attending knights and squires and retainers. The household of sergeants-at-arms, ushers, chamberlains, chaplains, stewards, and servants numbered about 400, all supplied with board, lodging, clothing, and wages.

Tiled floors were ornamented in designs of flowers, fantastic beasts, and elaborate heraldry. Clement VI, a lover of luxury and beauty who used 1,080 ermine skins in his personal wardrobe, imported Matteo Giovanetti and artists from the school of Simone Martini to paint the walls with scenes from the Bible. The four walls of Clement's own study, however, were entirely covered by scenes of a noble's secular pleasures: a stag hunt, falconry, orchards, gardens, fishponds, and a group of ambiguous nude bathers who could be either women or children depending on the eye of the beholder. No religious themes intruded.

At banquets the Pope's guests dined off gold and silver plate, seated beneath Flemish tapestries and hangings of silk. Receptions for visiting princes and envoys rivaled the splendors of any secular court. Papal entertainments, fetes, even tournaments and balls, reproduced the secular.

"I am living in the Babylon of the West," wrote Petrarch in the 1340s, where prelates feast at "licentious banquets" and ride on snow-white horses "decked in gold, fed on gold, soon to be shod in gold if the Lord does not check this slavish luxury." Though himself something of a lapsed cleric, Petrarch shared the clerical habit of denouncing at double strength whatever was disapproved. Avignon became for him "that disgusting city," though whether because of worldly corruption or the physical filth and smells of its narrow, overcrowded streets is uncertain. The town, crammed with merchants, artisans, ambassadors, adventurers, astrologers, thieves, prostitutes, and no less than 43 branches of Italian banking houses (in 1327), was not so well equipped as the papal palace for the disposal of sewage. The palace had a tower whose two lower stories contained exclusively latrines. Fitted with stone seats, these were emptied into a pit below ground level that was flushed by water from the kitchen drains and by an underground stream diverted for the purpose. In the town, however, the stench caused the ambassador from Aragon to swoon, and Petrarch to move out to nearby Vaucluse "to prolong my life."

More accessible than Rome, Avignon attracted visitors from all over Europe, and its flow of money helped to support artists, writers and scholars, masters of law and medicine, minstrels and poets. If corrupt, it was also Maecenas. Everybody scolded Avignon and everybody came there. St. Brigitta, a widowed Swedish noblewoman who lived in Rome and eloquently deplored the sins of the times, called the papal city "a field full of pride, avarice, self-indulgence, and corruption." But corruption takes two, and if the papacy sinned, it was not without partners. In the real world of shifting political balances and every ruler's constant need of money, popes and kings needed each other and made the necessary adjustments. They dealt in territories and sovereignties, men-at-arms, alliances, and loans. A regular method was the levy for a crusade, which allowed ecclesiastical income within each country to be taxed by its king, who soon came to regard it as a right.

The clergy were partners too. When prelates were gorgeously clad, the lower ranks would not long remain somber. Many were the complaints, like that of the Archbishop of Canterbury in 1342, that the clergy were dressing like laymen, in checkerboard squares of red and green, short coats, "notably scant," with excessively wide sleeves to show linings of fur or silk, hoods and tippets of "wonderful length," pointed and slashed shoes, jeweled girdles hung with gilt purses. Worse, ignoring the tonsure, they wore beards and long hair to the shoulders contrary to canonical rule, to the "abominable scandal among the people." Some kept jesters, dogs, and falcons, some went abroad attended by guards of honor.

Nor could simony stay isolated at the top. When bishops purchased benefices at the price of a year's income, they passed the cost down, so that corruption spread through the hierarchy from canons and priors to priesthood and cloistered clergy, down to mendicant friars and pardoners. It was at this level that the common people met the materialism of the Church, and none were more crass than the sellers of pardons.

Supposed to be commissioned by the Church, the pardoners would sell absolution for any sin from gluttony to homicide, cancel any vow of chastity or fasting, remit any penance for money, most of which they pocketed. When commissioned to raise money for a crusade, according to Matteo Villani, they would take from the poor, in lieu of money, "linen and woolen stuffs or furnishings, grain and fodder . . . deceiving the people. That was the way they gave the Cross." What they were peddling was salvation, taking advantage of the people's need and credulity to sell its counterfeit. The only really detestable character in Chaucer's company of Canterbury pilgrims is the Pardoner with his stringy locks, his eunuch's hairless skin, his glaring eyes like a hare's, and his brazen acknowledgment of the tricks and deceits of his trade.

The regular clergy detested the pardoner for undoing the work of penance, for endangering souls insofar as his goods were spurious, and for invading clerical territory, taking collections on feast days or performing burial and other services for a fee that should have gone to the parish priest. Yet the system permitted him to function because it shared in the profits.

The sins of monks and itinerant friars were more disturbing because their pretensions as men of God were higher. They were notorious as seducers of women. Peddling furs and girdles for wenches and wives, and small gentle dogs "to get love of them," the friar in a 14th century poem "came to our dame when the gode man is from home."

> He spares nauther for synne ne shame,
> For may he tyl a woman synne
> In priveyte, he will not blynne
> Er he a childe put hir withinne
> And perchance two at ones.

In the tales of Boccaccio, in the *fabliaux* of France, in all popular literature of the time, clerical celibacy is a joke. Priests lived with mistresses or else went in hunt of them. "A priest lay with a lady who was wed to a knight," begins one tale matter-of-factly. In another, "the priest and his lady went off to bed." In the nunnery where Piers Plowman served as cook, Sister Pernell was "a priest's wench" who "bore a child in cherry time." Boccaccio's rascally friars were invariably caught in embarrassing situations as victims of their own lechery. In real life their sinfulness was not funny but threatening, for when a friar failed so far in holiness how could he save souls? This sense of betrayal explains why the friars were so often the object of active hostility, sometimes even of physical assault, because, as a chronicle of 1327 stated simply, "they did not behave as friars ought."

According to the ideal of St. Francis, they were supposed to wander the world to do good, to walk barefoot among the poor and the outcasts bringing Christian love to the lowest, to beg for the necessaries of life in kind, never in money. By a supreme paradox, the Order that Francis founded on rejection of property attracted the support and donations of the wealthy because its purity seemed to offer assurance of holiness. Upon the approach of death, knights and noble ladies would have themselves clad in the Franciscan habit, believing that if they died and were buried in it, they could not go to hell.

The Order acquired lands and riches, built itself churches and cloisters, developed its own hierarchy—all the opposite of the founder's intent. Yet St. Francis had understood the process. Replying to a novice who wished to have a psalter, he once said, "When you have a psalter you will wish to have a breviary, and when you have a breviary you will sit in a chair like a great prelate and say to your brother, 'Brother, bring me my breviary.'"

In some monastic orders the monks had regular pocket money and private funds which they lent at interest. In some they had an allowance of a gallon of ale a day, ate meat, wore jewels and fur-trimmed gowns, and employed servants who in wealthy convents sometimes outnumbered the members. Enjoying the favor of the rich, the Franciscans preached to them and dined with them and took office in noble households as counselors and chaplains. Some still went barefoot among the poor, holding to their role, and were revered for it, but most now wore good leather boots and were not loved.

Like the pardoner, they bilked the villagers, selling them relics of inspired imagination. Boccaccio's Friar Cipolla sold one of the Angel Gabriel's feathers which he said had fallen in the Virgin's chamber during the Annunciation. As satire, this did not overreach the real friar who sold a piece of the bush from which the Lord spoke to Moses. Some sold drafts on the Treasury of Merit supposed to be stored in Heaven by the Order of St. Francis. Wyclif, on being asked what these parchments were good for, replied: "To covere mustard pottis." The friars were an element of daily life, scorned yet venerated and feared because they might, after all, have the key to salvation.

The satire and complaints survive because they are written down. They leave an impression of a Church so pervaded by venality and hypocrisy as to seem ripe for dissolution, but an institution so in command of the culture and so rooted in the structure of society does not readily dissolve. Christianity was the matrix of medieval life: even cooking instructions called for boiling an egg "during the length of time wherein you can say a Miserere." It governed birth, marriage, and death, sex, and eating, made the rules for law and medicine, gave philosophy and scholarship their subject matter. Membership in the Church was not a matter of choice; it was compulsory and without alternative, which gave it a hold not easy to dislodge.

As an integral part of life, religion was both subjected to burlesque and unharmed by it. In the annual Feast of Fools at Christmastime, every rite and article of the Church no matter how sacred was celebrated in mockery. A *dominus festi*, or lord of the revels, was elected from the inferior clergy—the curés, subdeacons, vicars, and choir clerks, mostly ill-educated, ill-paid, and ill-disciplined—whose day it was to turn everything topsy-turvy. They installed their lord as Pope or Bishop or Abbot of Fools in a ceremony of head-shaving accompanied by bawdy talk and lewd acts; dressed him in vestments turned inside out; played dice on the altar and ate black puddings and sausages while mass was celebrated in nonsensical gibberish; swung censers made of old shoes emitting "stinking smoke"; officiated in the various offices of the priest wearing beast masks and dressed as women or minstrels; sang obscene songs in the choir; howled and hooted and jangled bells while the "Pope" recited a doggerel benediction. At his call to follow him on pain of having their breeches split, all rush violently from the church to parade through the town, drawing the *dominus* in a cart from which he issues mock indulgences while his followers hiss, cackle, jeer, and gesticulate. They rouse the bystanders to laughter with "infamous performances" and parody preachers in scurrilous sermons. Naked men haul carts of manure which they throw at the populace. Drinking bouts and dances accompany the procession. The whole was a burlesque of the too-familiar, tedious, and often meaningless rituals; a release of "the natural lout beneath the cassock."

In daily life the Church was comforter, protector, physician. The Virgin and patron saints gave succor in trouble and protection against the evils and enemies that lurked along every man's path. Craft guilds, towns, and functions had patron saints, as did individuals. Archers and crossbowmen had St. Sebastian, martyr of the arrows; bakers had St. Honoré, whose banner bore an oven shovel argent and three loaves gules; sailors had St. Nicholas with the three children he saved from the sea; travelers had St. Christopher carrying the infant Jesus on his shoulder; charitable brotherhoods usually chose St. Martin, who gave half his cloak to the poor man; unmarried girls had St. Catherine, supposed to have been very beautiful. The patron saint was an extra companion through life who healed hurts, soothed distress, and in extremity could make miracles. His image was carried on banners in processions, sculpted over the entrance to town halls and chapels, and worn as a medallion on an individual's hat.

Above all, the Virgin was the ever-merciful, ever-dependable source of comfort, full of compassion for human frailty, caring nothing for laws and judges, ready to respond to anyone in trouble; amid all the inequities, injuries, and senseless harms, the one never-failing figure. She frees the prisoner from his dungeon, revives the starving with milk from her own breasts. When a peasant mother takes her son, blinded by a thorn in his eye, to the Church of St. Denis, kneels before Our Lady, recites an Ave Maria, and makes the sign of the cross over the child with a sacred relic, the nail of the Saviour, "at once," reports the chronicler, "the thorn falls out, the inflammation disappears, and the mother in joy returns home with her son no longer blind."

A hardened murderer has no less access. No matter what crime a person has committed, though every man's hand be against him, he is still not cut off from the Virgin. In the *Miracles of Notre Dame*, a cycle of popular plays performed in the towns, the Virgin redeems every kind of malefactor who reaches out to her through the act of repentance. A woman accused of incest with her son-in-law has procured his assassination by two hired men and is about to be burned at the stake. She prays to Notre Dame, who promptly appears and orders the fire not to burn. Convinced of a miracle, the magistrates free the condemned woman, who, after distributing her goods and money to the poor, enters a convent. The act of faith through prayer was what counted. It was not justice one received from the Church but forgiveness.

More than comfort, the Church gave answers. For nearly a thousand years it had been the central institution that gave meaning and purpose to life in a capricious world. It affirmed that man's life on earth was but a passage in exile on the way to God and to the New Jerusalem, "our other home." Life was nothing, wrote Petrarch to his brother, but "a hard and weary journey toward the eternal home for which we look; or, if we neglect our salvation, an equally pleasureless way to eternal death." What the Church offered was salvation, which could be reached only through the rituals of the established Church and by the permission and aid of its ordained priests. "*Extra ecclesiam nulla salus*" (No salvation outside the Church) was the rule.

Salvation's alternative was Hell and eternal torture, very realistically pictured in the art of the time. In Hell the damned hung by their tongues from trees of fire, the impenitent burned in furnaces, unbelievers smothered in foul-smelling smoke. The wicked fell into the black waters of an abyss and sank to a depth proportionate to their sins: fornicators up to the nostrils, persecutors of their fellow man up to the eyebrows. Some were swallowed by monstrous fish, some gnawed by demons, tormented by serpents, by fire or ice or fruits hanging forever out of reach of the starving. In Hell men were naked, nameless, and forgotten. No wonder salvation was important and the Day of Judgment present in every mind. Over the doorway of every cathedral it was carved in vivid reminder, showing the numerous sinners roped and led off by devils toward a flaming cauldron while angels led the fewer elect to bliss in the opposite direction.

No one doubted in the Middle Ages that the vast majority would be eternally damned. *Salvandorum paucitas, damnandorum multitudo* (Few saved, many damned) was the stern principle maintained from Augustine to Aquinas. Noah and his family were taken to indicate the proportion of the saved, usually estimated at one in a thousand or even one in ten thousand. No matter how few were to be chosen, the Church offered hope to all. Salvation was permanently closed to nonbelievers in Christ, but not to sinners, for sin was an inherent condition of life which could be canceled as often as necessary by penitence and absolution. "Turn thee again, turn thee again, thou sinful soul," spoke a Lollard preacher, "for God knoweth thy misgovernance and will not forsake thee. Turn thou to me saith the Lord and I shall receive thee and take thee to grace."

The Church gave ceremony and dignity to lives that had little of either. It was the source of beauty and art to which all had some access and which many helped to create. To carve the stone folds of an apostle's gown, to paste with infinite patience the bright mosaic chips into a picture of winged angels in a heavenly chorus, to stand in the towering space of a cathedral nave amid pillars rising and rising to an almost invisible vault and know this to be man's work in honor of God, gave pride to the lowest and could make the least man an artist.

The Church, not the government, sponsored the care of society's helpless—the indigent and sick, orphan and cripple, the leper, the blind, the idiot—by indoctrinating the laity in the belief that alms bought them merit and a foothold in Heaven. Based on this principle, the impulse of Christian charity was self-serving but effective. Nobles gave alms daily at the castle gate to all comers, in coin and in left-over food from the hall. Donations from all sources poured into the hospitals, favorite recipients of Christian charity. Merchants bought themselves peace of mind for the non-Christian business of making profit by allocating a regular percentage to charity. This was entered in the ledger under the name of God as the poor's representative. A Christian duty of particular merit was the donation of dowries to enable poor girls to marry, as in the case of a Gascon seigneur of the 14th century who left 100 livres to "those whom I deflowered, if they can be found."

Corporate bodies accepted the obligation to help the poor as a religious duty. The statutes of craft guilds set aside a penny for charity, called "God's penny," from each contract of sale or purchase. Parish councils of laymen superintended maintenance of the "Table of the Poor" and of a bank for alms. On feast days it was a common practice to invite twelve poor to the banquet table, and on Holy Thursday, in memory of Christ, the mayor of a town or other notable would wash the feet of a beggar. When St. Louis conducted the ceremony, his companion and biographer, the Sire de Joinville, refused to participate, saying it would make him sick to touch the feet of such villeins. It was not always easy to love the poor.

The clergy on the whole were probably no more lecherous or greedy or untrustworthy than other men, but because they were supposed to be better or nearer to God than other men, their failings attracted more attention. If Clement VI was luxury-loving, he was also generous and warm-hearted. The Parson among the Canterbury pilgrims is as benign and admirable as the Pardoner is repulsive, always ready to visit on foot the farthest and poorest house of his parish, undeterred by thunder and rain.

> To drawen folk to heaven with fairnesse
> By good ensample was his businesse.

Nevertheless, a wind of discontent was rising. Papal tax-collectors were attacked and beaten, and even bishops were not safe. In 1326, in a burst of anti-clericalism, a London mob beheaded the Bishop and left his body naked in the street. In 1338 two "rectors of churches" joined two knights and a "great crowd of country folk" in attacking the Bishop of Constance, severely wounding several of his retinue, and holding him in prison. Among the religious themselves, the discontent took serious form. In Italy arose the Fraticelli, a sect of the Franciscan Order, in another of the poverty-embracing movements that periodically tormented the Church by wanting to disendow it. The Fraticelli or Spiritual Franciscans insisted that Christ had lived without possessions, and they preached a return to that condition as the only true "imitation of Christ."

The poverty movements grew out of the essence of Christian doctrine: renunciation of the material world—the idea that made the great break with the classical age. It maintained that God was positive and life on earth negative, that the world was incurably bad and holiness achieved only through renunciation of earthly pleasures, goods, and honors. To gain victory over the flesh was the purpose of fasting and celibacy, which denied the pleasures of this world for the sake of reward in the next. Money was evil, beauty vain, and both were transitory. Ambition was pride, desire for gain was avarice, desire of the flesh was lust, desire for honor, even for knowledge and beauty, was vainglory. Insofar as these diverted man from seeking the life of the spirit, they were sinful. The Christian ideal was ascetic: the denial of sensual man. The result was that, under the sway of the Church, life became a continual struggle against the senses and a continual engagement in sin, accounting for the persistent need for absolution.

Repeatedly, mystical sects arose in an effort to sweep away the whole detritus of the material world, to become nearer to God by cutting the earth-binding chains of property. Embedded in its lands and buildings, the Church could only react by denouncing the sects as heretical. The Fraticelli's stubborn insistence on the absolute poverty of Christ and his twelve Apostles was acutely inconvenient for the Avignon papacy, which condemned their doctrine as "false and pernicious" heresy in 1315 and, when they refused to desist, excommunicated them and other associated sects at various times during the next decade. Twenty-seven members of a particularly stubborn group of

Spiritual Franciscans of Provence were tried by·the Inquisition and four of them burned at the stake at Marseille in 1318.

The wind of temporal challenge to papal supremacy was rising too, focusing on the Pope's right to crown the Emperor, and setting the claims of the state against those of the Church. The Pope tried to excommunicate this temporal spirit in the person of its boldest exponent, Marsilius of Padua, whose *Defensor Pacis* in 1324 was a forthright assertion of the supremacy of the state. Two years later the logic of the struggle led John XXII to excommunicate William of Ockham, the English Franciscan, known for his forceful reasoning as "the invincible doctor." In expounding a philosophy called "nominalism," Ockham opened a dangerous door to direct intuitive knowledge of the physical world. He was in a sense a spokesman for intellectual freedom, and the Pope recognized the implications by his ban. In reply to the excommunication, Ockham promptly charged John XXII with seventy errors and seven heresies.

In economic man, the lay spirit did not challenge the Church, yet functioned in essential contradiction. Capitalist enterprise, although it held by now a commanding place, violated by its very nature the Christian attitude toward commerce, which was one of active antagonism. It held that money was evil, that according to St. Augustine "Business is in itself an evil," that profit beyond a minimum necessary to support the dealer was avarice, that to make money out of money by charging interest on a loan was the sin of usury, that buying goods wholesale and selling them unchanged at a higher retail price was immoral and condemned by canon law, that, in short, St. Jerome's dictum was final: "A man who is a merchant can seldom if ever please God" (*Homo mercator vix aut numquam potest Deo placere*).

It followed that banker, merchant, and businessman lived in daily commission of sin and daily contradiction of the moral code centering upon the "just price." This was based on the principle that a craft should supply each man a livelihood and a fair return to all, but no more. Prices should be set at a "just" level, meaning the value of the labor added to the value of the raw material. To ensure that no one gained an advantage over anyone else, commercial law prohibited innovation in tools or techniques, underselling below a fixed price, working late by artificial light, employing extra apprentices or wife and under-age children, and advertising of wares or praising them to the detriment of others. As restraint of initiative, this was the direct opposite of capitalist enterprise. It was the denial of economic man, and consequently even more routinely violated than the denial of sensual man.

No economic activity was more irrepressible than the investment and lending at interest of money; it was the basis for the rise of Western capitalist economy and the building of private fortunes—and it was based on the sin of usury. Nothing so vexed medieval thinking, nothing so baffled and eluded settlement, nothing was so great a tangle of irreconcilables as the theory of usury. Society needed moneylending while Christian doctrine forbade it. That was the basic dichotomy, but the doctrine was so elastic that "even wise men" were unsure of its provisions. For practical purposes, usury was considered to be not the charging of interest per se, but charging at a higher rate than was decent. This was left to the Jews as the necessary dirty work of society, and if they had not been available they would have had to be invented. While theologians and canonists argued endlessly and tried vainly to decide whether 10, 12.5, 15, or 20 percent was decent, the bankers went on lending and investing at whatever rates the situation would bear.

Merchants regularly paid fines for breaking every law that concerned their business, and went on as before. The wealth of Venice and Genoa was made in trade with the infidels of Syria and Egypt despite papal prohibition. Prior to the 14th century, it has been said, men "could hardly imagine the merchant's strongbox without picturing the devil squatting on the lid." Whether the merchant too saw the devil as he counted coins, whether he lived with a sense of guilt, is hard to assess. Francisco Datini, the merchant of Prato, judging by his letters, was a deeply troubled man, but his agonies were caused more by fear of loss than by fear of God. He was evidently able to reconcile Christianity and business, for the motto on his ledger was "In the name of God and of profit."

Division of rich and poor became increasingly sharp. With control of the raw materials and tools of production, the owners were able to reduce wages in classic exploitation. The poor saw them now as enemies, no longer as protectors but as exploiters, as Dives, the rich man consigned to hellfire, as wolves, and themselves as lambs. They felt a sense of injustice that finding no remedy grew into a spirit of revolt.

Medieval theory intended that the lord or ruler should respond to charges of oppression by investigating and ordering the necessary reform to ensure that taxes fell equally on rich and poor. But this theory corresponded to reality no more than other medieval ideals, and because of this, wrote Philippe de Beaumanoir in 1280–83, "there have been acts of violence because the poor will not suffer this but know not how to obtain their right except by rising and seizing it themselves." They formed associations, he reported, to refuse to work for "so low a price as formerly but they will raise the price by their own authority" and take "certain pains and punishments" against those who do not join them. This seemed to Beaumanoir a terrible act against the common good, "for the common interest cannot suffer that work should stop." He advocated that such persons should be arrested and kept long in prison and afterward fined 60 sous each, the traditional fine for rupture of the "public peace."

The most persistent ferment was among the weavers and cloth-workers of Flanders, where economic expansion had been most intense. The textile industry was the automobile industry of the Middle Ages, and Flanders was a hothouse of the tensions and antagonisms brewed in urban society by capitalist development.

Once united by a common craft, the guild of masters, journeymen, and apprentices had spread apart into entrepreneurs and hired hands divided by class hatred. The guild was now a corporation run by the employers in which the workers had no voice. The magnates, who married into the nobility and bought country estates in addition to their city real estate, developed into a patrician class that controlled the government of the towns and managed it in their own interest. They founded churches and hospitals, built the great Cloth Halls, paved the streets, and created the canal system. But they made up the greater part of municipal expenses from sales taxes on wine, beer, peat, and grain, which fell most heavily on the poor. They favored each other in governing groups like the Thirty-nine of Ghent, named for life and serving in annual rotation of three parties of thirteen, or the twelve magistrates of Arras, who rotated among themselves every four months, or the oligarchy of the Hundred Peers of Rouen, which appointed the mayor and town councillors each year. The lower bourgeois who made fortunes and pressed upward could frequently penetrate the monopoly, but the artisans, despised as "blue nails" and vulnerable to unemployment, had no political rights.

Beneath the cry of protest much of medieval life was supportive because it was lived collectively in infinite numbers of groups, orders, associations, brotherhoods. Never was man less alone. Even in bedrooms married couples often slept in company with their servants and children. Except for hermits and recluses, privacy was unknown.

As nobles had their orders of chivalry, the common man had the *confrérie* or brotherhood of his trade or village, which surrounded him at every crux of life. Usually numbering from 20 to 100 members, these groups were associations for charity and social service as well as for entertainment and religious observance in lay life. They accompanied a member to the town gates when he went off on a pilgrimage and marched in his funeral when he died. If a man was condemned to be executed, fellow members accompanied him to the scaffold. If he drowned accidentally as in a case at Bordeaux, they searched the Garonne for three days for his body. If he died insolvent, the association furnished his shroud and the costs of the funeral and helped to support the widow and children. The furriers of Paris paid sick members three sous a week during incapacity for work and three sous for a week of convalescence. The associations' money came from dues scaled according to income and payable weekly, monthly, or quarterly.

The brotherhoods staged religious plays, furnished the music, and served as actors and stagehands. They held competitions, sports and games, awarded prizes, and invited the orator or preacher for special occasions. On feast days, after strewing the streets with flowers, the *confréries* joined in the processions, each marching in a body in the bright colors of its own costume, preceded by its banner and statue or portrait of its patron saint. Members were bound by rites and oaths; in some brotherhoods, they wore masks to conceal identity, making all within the group equal.

When the *confréries* donated church windows or commissioned murals, choir stalls, or illuminated books, the members could take pride in being patrons of art just like the nobles and rich magnates. Through their association they could buy merit as benefactors, adopting a hospital, distributing alms and food to the poor, or undertaking the charge of certain categories—as when the grocers of Paris supported the blind and the drapers supported prisoners in the city jail. The *confréries* provided a context of life that was intensely sociable, with the solace and sometimes the abrasions that sociability implies.

In 1320 the misery of the rural poor in the wake of the famines burst out in a strange hysterical mass movement called the Pastoureaux, for the shepherds who started it. Though less uprooted than the urban poor, the peasant too felt oppressed by the rich and was forever struggling against the lord's effort to grasp by one means or another more of the peasant's product or more of his services. Cases in manor courts going back to 1250 show peasants in concerted deliberate refusal to plow the lord's field, thresh his grain, turn his hay, or grind at his mill. Persisting year after year, despite fines and punishment, they denied bondage, disposed of land without consent, joined in bands to assault the bailiff or to rescue a fellow peasant from the stocks.

Oppression of the peasant by the landowner troubled the conscience of the time and evoked warnings. "Ye nobles are like ravening wolves," wrote Jacques de Vitry, a 13th century author of sermons and moral tales. "Therefore shall ye howl in hell . . . who despoil your subjects and live on the blood and sweat of the poor." Whatever the peasant amasses in a year, "the knight, the noble devours in an hour." He imposes illicit taxes and heavy exactions. De Vitry warned the great not to scorn the humble or inspire their hate for "if they can aid us, they can also do us harm. You know that many serfs have killed their masters or have burned their houses."

A prophecy current in the time of the famine foretold that the poor would rise against the powerful, overthrow the Church and an unspecified great monarchy, and after much bloodshed a new age of unity under one cross would dawn. Combining with vague talk of a new crusade and preached among the poor by an apostate monk and an unfrocked priest, the prophecy "as suddenly and unexpectedly as a storm" swept the peasants and rootless poor of northern France into a mass marching southward toward an imagined embarkation for the Holy Land. Gathering adherents and arms as they went, they stormed castles and abbeys, burned town halls and tax records, opened prisons, and when they reached the south threw themselves in concentrated assault upon the Jews.

Peasant indebtedness to Jews for loans to tide over bad times or enable the purchase of tools or a plow was of long standing. The peasants had thought the debt wiped out when Philip the Fair expelled the Jews in 1306, but his son Louis X brought them back on terms that made him a partner with a two-thirds share in the recovery of their debts. Exacerbating an old grudge, this drove the Pastoureaux, enthusiastically aided by the populace, to the slaughter of almost every Jew from Bordeaux to Albi. Despite the King's order that the Jews be protected, local authorities could not restrain the attacks and in some cases joined them.

That the Jews were unholy was a belief so ingrained by the Church that the most devout persons were the harshest in their antipathy, none more so than St. Louis. If the Jews were unholy, then killing and looting them was holy work. Lepers too were targets of the Pastoureaux on the theory that they had joined the Jews in a horrible compact to poison the wells, and their persecution was made official by a royal ordinance of 1321.

Menacing Avignon, attacking priests, threatening to seize Church property, the Pastoureaux spread the fear of insurrection that freezes the blood of the privileged in any era when the mob appears. Excommunicated by Pope John XXII, they were finally suppressed when he forbade anyone to provision them on pain of death and sanctioned the use of force against them. That was sufficient, and the Pastoureaux ended like every outbreak of the poor sooner or later in the Middle Ages, with corpses hanging from the trees.

In the woe of the century no factor caused more trouble than the persistent lag between the growth of the state and the means of state financing. While centralized government was developing, taxation was still encased in the concept that taxes represented an emergency measure requiring consent. Having exhausted every other source of funds, Philip the Fair in 1307 turned on the Templars in the most sensational episode of his reign. The result brought a curse, as his contemporaries believed, upon their country, and what people believe about their own time becomes a factor in its history.

No downfall was to be so complete and spectacular as that of this arrogant order of monastic knighthood. Formed during the crusades to be the sword arm of the Church in defense of the Holy Land, the Templars had moved from ideals of asceticism and poverty to immense resources and an international web of power outside the regular channels of allegiance. Tax exempt from the start, they had amassed riches as bankers for the Holy See and as moneylenders at lower interest rates than the Lombards and Jews. They were not known for charity and, unlike the Knights of St. John, supported no hospitals. With 2,000 members in France and the largest treasury in northern Europe, they maintained headquarters in the Temple, their formidable fortress in Paris.

Not only their money but their existence as a virtually autonomous enclave invited destruction. Their sinister reputation, grown from the secrecy of their rituals, supplied the means. In a pounce like a tiger's leap, Philip seized the Temple in Paris and had every Templar in France arrested on the same night. To justify confiscation of the Order's property, the main charge was heresy, in proof of which the King's prosecutors dragged into the light every dark superstition and fearful imagining of sorcery and Devil-worship that lay along the roots of the medieval mind. The Templars were accused by suborned witnesses of bestiality, idol-worship, denial of the sacraments; of selling their souls to the Devil and adoring him in the form of a huge cat; of sodomy with each other and intercourse with demons and succubi; of requiring initiates to deny God, Christ, and the Virgin, to spit three times, urinate, and trample on the cross, and to give the "kiss of shame" to the prior of the Order on the mouth, penis, and buttocks. To strengthen resolution for these various practices, they were said to drink a powder made from the ashes of dead members and their own illegitimate children.

Elements of witchcraft, magic, and sorcery were taken for granted in medieval life, but Philip's use of them to prove heresy in the seven-year melodrama of the Templars' trials gave them fearful currency. Thereafter charges of black arts became a common means to bring down an enemy and a favored method of the Inquisition in its pursuit of heretics, especially those with property worth confiscating. In Toulouse and Carcassonne during the next 35 years the Inquisition prosecuted 1,000 persons on such charges and burned 600. French justice was corrupted and the pattern laid for the fanatic witchcraft persecutions of subsequent centuries.

Philip bullied the first Avignon Pope, Clement V, into authorizing the trials of the Templars, and with this authority put them to atrocious tortures to extract confessions. Medieval justice was scrupulous about holding proper trials and careful not to sentence without proof of guilt, but it achieved proof by confession rather than evidence, and confession was routinely obtained by torture. The Templars, many of them old men, were racked, thumbscrewed, starved, hung with weights until joints were dislocated, had teeth and fingernails pulled one by one, bones broken by the wedge, feet held over flames, always with pauses in between and the "question" put again each day until confession was wrung or the victim died. Thirty-six died under the treatment; some committed suicide. Broken by torture, the Grand Master, Jacques de Molay, and 122 others confessed to spitting on the cross or some other variation of crime put into their mouths by the Inquisitors. "And he would have confessed that he had slain God Himself if they had asked him that," acknowledged a chronicler.

The process dragged on through prolonged jockeying over jurisdiction by Pope, King, and Inquisition while the victims, hung with chains and barely fed, were hauled in and out of their dungeons for further trials and humiliations. Sixty-seven who found the courage to recant their confessions were burned alive as relapsed heretics. After futile squirming by Clement V, the Templars' Order in France and all its branches in England, Scotland, Aragon, Castile, Portugal, Germany, and the Kingdom of Naples were abolished by the Council of Vienne in 1311–12. Officially its property was transferred to the Knights Hospitalers of St. John, but the presence of Philip the Fair sitting at the Pope's right hand at Vienne indicates that he was not left out of the arrangement. Afterward, indeed, the Knights of St. John paid him an enormous sum as a debt which he claimed from the Templars.

The end was not yet. In March 1314 the Grand Master, who had been the King's friend and godfather of his daughter, was conducted with his chief lieutenant to a scaffold erected in the plaza in front of the Cathedral of Notre Dame in Paris to reaffirm their confessions and be sentenced to life imprisonment by the papal legates. Instead, before the packed assembly of nobles, clergy, and commoners, they proclaimed their own and the Order's innocence. Despoiled of his final justification, the King ordered both men to be burned at the stake. As the faggots flamed next day, Jacques de Molay again proclaimed his innocence and cried aloud that God would be his avenger. According to the tradition that developed later, he called down a curse upon the King and his descendants to the thirteenth generation, and, in the last words to be heard as he burned to death, summoned Philip and Pope Clement to meet him before God's judgment seat within a year. Within a month Clement did in fact die, followed seven months later in November by Philip, in the midst of life, aged 46, from uncertain causes some weeks after a horseback accident. The legend of the Templar's curse developed, as most legends do, to explain strange coincidences after the event. The symptoms reported at Philip's deathbed have since been judged indicative of a cerebral stroke, but to awed contemporaries the cause was indubitably the Templar's curse that had floated upward with the smoke from the pyre in the red light of the setting sun.

As if carrying out the curse on Philip's posterity, the Capetian dynasty suddenly withered in the strange triplicate destiny of Philip the Fair's sons. Succeeding each other as Louis X, Philip V, and Charles IV, they reigned less than six years apiece and died aged 27, 28, and 33 respectively, each without leaving a male successor despite a total of six wives among them. Jeanne, the four-year-old daughter of the eldest brother, was passed over by her uncle, who had himself crowned as Philip V. After the event he convoked an assembly of notables from the three estates and the University of Paris, which duly approved his right on the principle, formulated for the occasion, that "a woman does not succeed to the throne of France." Thus was born the momentous Salic "Law" that was to create a permanent bar to the succession of women where none had existed before.

The death of the last of the three brothers in 1328 left the succession to the crown open, with results that led to the longest war—so far—in Western history. Three claimants were available—a grandson and two nephews of Philip the Fair. The grandson was the sixteen-year-old Edward III of England, son of Philip the Fair's daughter Isabel, who had married Edward II. She was generally believed to have connived with her lover in the murder of her husband the King, and to exercise a malign influence upon her son. His claim of direct lineage, vigorously put forward, met no welcomers in France not because it derived through a woman but because the woman in question was feared and disliked and in any case no one wanted the King of England on the throne of France.

The other two claimants, sons respectively of a brother and a half-brother of Philip the Fair, were Philip of Valois and Philip of Evreux. The first, a man of 35, son of an illustrious father, well known to the court and nobles of France, was easily the preferred choice and was confirmed as king by the princes and peers of France without overt opposition. As Philip VI he began the Valois line. Both of his rivals formally accepted the choice, Edward by coming in person to place his hands between those of Philip VI in homage for the Duchy of Guienne. The other Philip was recompensed by the Kingdom of Navarre and marriage to the bypassed Jeanne.

Though Philip VI maintained court in great state, he had not grown up expecting to be king and lacked something of the regal character. He seemed troubled by some uneasiness about his right to the crown, which was hardly soothed by his contemporaries' habit of referring to him as *le roi trouvé* (the found king) as if he had been discovered in the bulrushes. Or perhaps the lurking rights of his female cousins threatened him. He was dominated by his wife, the "bad lame Queen," Jeanne de Bourgogne, a malicious woman neither loved nor respected although she was a patron of the arts and of all scholars who came to court. Very devout like his great-grandfather St. Louis, though not his equal in intelligence or will, Philip was fascinated by the all-absorbing question of the Beatific Vision: whether the souls of the blessed see the face of God immediately upon entering Heaven or whether they have to wait until the Day of Judgment.

The question was of real concern because the intercession of the saints on behalf of man was effective only if they had been admitted into the presence of God. Shrines possessing saints' relics relied for revenue on popular confidence that a particular saint was in a position to make a personal appeal to the Almighty. Philip VI twice summoned theologians to debate the issue before him and fell into a "mighty choler" when the papal legate to Paris conveyed Pope John XXII's doubts of the Beatific Vision. "The King reprimanded him sharply and threatened to burn him like an Albigensian unless he retracted, and said further that if the Pope really held such views he would regard him as a heretic." A worried man, Philip wrote to the Pope that to deny the Beatific Vision was to destroy belief in the intercession of the Virgin and saints. Fortunately for the King's peace of mind, a papal commission decided after thorough investigation that the souls of the Blessed did indeed come face to face with the Divine Essence.

Philip's reign started well and the realm prospered. The effect of famine and epidemics was passing, evil portents were forgotten, perpetually contentious Flanders was brought back under French control by a victorious campaign in Philip's first year. The crown's relations with five of the six great fiefs—Flanders, Burgundy, Brittany, and, in the south, Armagnac and Foix—were reasonably firm. Only Guienne (or Aquitaine), which the Kings of England held as a fief of the Kings of France, was a perennial source of conflict. Here the English effort to expand pressed continually against the French effort to re-absorb the fief.

As the conflict came to a head, it brought about in 1338 a marriage that connected the Coucys with yet another reigning house, the Hapsburgs of Austria. This was the union from which Enguerrand VII was to be born. It was arranged by Philip VI himself, who was seeking allies in the coming struggle with England. In 1337 Philip had declared Guienne confiscated, whereupon Edward III announced himself the rightful King of France and prepared for war. Edward's renewed claim was not so much the reason for war as an excuse to resolve by war the endless conflict over the sovereignty of Guienne. While English forces landed in Flanders to prepare for the assault, both sides feverishly sought allies in the Low Countries and across the Rhine.

King Philip was concerned not only to gather allies but to ensure the loyalty of the strategically located barony of Coucy. As a rich prize, he obtained for Enguerrand VI the hand of Catherine of Austria, daughter of Duke Leopold I and granddaughter through her mother of the equally illustrious Amadeus V, Count of Savoy. The house of Savoy were autonomous rulers of a region extending from France to Italy astride the Alps, and themselves the center of a princely web of marriage threads connecting with crowns all over Europe—and beyond. One of Catherine's seven aunts was the wife of Andronicus III Paleologus, Emperor of Byzantium.

Marriages were the fabric of international as well as inter-noble relations, the primary source of territory, sovereignty, and alliance, and the major business of medieval diplomacy. The relations of countries and rulers depended not at all on common borders or natural interest but on dynastic connections and fantastic cousinships which could make a prince of Hungary heir to the throne of Naples and an English prince claimant to Castile. At every point of the loom sovereigns were thrusting in their shuttles, carrying the strand of a son or a daughter, and these, whizzing back and forth, wove the artificial fabric that created as many conflicting claims and hostilities as it did bonds. Valois of France, Plantagenets of England, Luxemburgs of Bohemia, Wittelsbachs of Bavaria, Hapsburgs of Austria, Visconti of Milan, the houses of Navarre, Castile, and Aragon, Dukes of Brittany, Counts of Flanders, Hainault, and Savoy were all entwined in a crisscrossing network, in the making of which two things were never considered: the sentiments of the parties to the marriage, and the interest of the populations involved.

Although the free consent of marriage partners was theoretically required by the Church, and the "I will" considered the doctrinal essence of the marriage contract made before a priest, practical politics overlooked this requirement, sometimes with unhappy results. Emperor Ludwig in betrothing his daughter before she had learned to talk, offered to speak for her and was later considered to have earned the judgment of God when she remained dumb all her life.

Rulers likewise paid no attention whatever—with predictable results—to the prohibition of consanguinity in marriage, whose risks were well understood and forbidden by the Church within the fourth degree. The prohibition was remembered only when it became desirable to break a betrothal that had become inconvenient or to discard an inconvenient spouse. For a fee or political favor proportionate to the rank of the petitioner, the Church invariably proved agreeable either to setting aside the consanguinity rule to permit a marriage, or recalling it as grounds for divorce.

To negotiate the financial terms of the Hapsburg-Coucy marriage required two treaties in 1337–38 between the King of France and the Duke of Austria. Duke Leopold gave his daughter a dowry of 40,000 livres, while King Philip assigned to her and her issue an annuity of 2,000 livres from the royal treasury. To Enguerrand VI the King made a gift of 10,000 livres plus promise of another 10,000 to acquit him of debts. Enguerrand in turn promised to settle 6,000 livres upon his wife and, what was of the essence to the King, to lead his vassals in the royal host in defense of the realm against Edward of England.

At its start, the war hardly boded a dangerous contest, since France was the dominant power of Europe whose military glory in her own eyes, as in others', far outshone that of England or any other country, and whose population of 21 million was five times England's of slightly more than 4 million. Nevertheless, possession of Aquitaine and alliance with Flanders gave Edward two footholds at the borders of France, and lent a force of more than mere words to the insolent challenge he addressed to "Philip of Valois who calls himself King of France." Neither party could know that they were opening a war that would outlast both of them, that would develop a life of its own, defying parleys and truces and treaties designed to stop it, that would drag on into their sons' lives and the lives of their grandsons and great-grandsons, and great-great-grandsons to the fifth generation, that would bring havoc to both sides and become, as its damage spread through Europe, the final torment of the closing Middle Ages.

Enguerrand VI had barely time to beget a child before he was summoned to war in 1339. In the north the English were advancing from Flanders and a party of 1,500 men-at-arms besieged the castle of Oisy belonging to the Coucys. So ardent was the defense of Enguerrand's vassals that the English were forced to withdraw, even though their leader was Sir John Chandos, who was to prove the most notable military figure on the English side. In revenge for his setback, he burned and sacked three other towns and smaller castles within the Coucy domain. Meanwhile Enguerrand VI had joined the King in the defense of Tournai on the Flemish border, and in 1340 while a rather feckless campaign was pursuing its way, his son, the seventh and last Enguerrand, was born.

Chapter 3

Youth and Chivalry

Although doubtless precious to his parents as firstborn son and heir of a great dynasty, the infant Enguerrand VII was probably not the adored object of the coddling and tenderness that babies are by nature supposed to inspire. Of all the characteristics in which the medieval age differs from the modern, none is so striking as the comparative absence of interest in children. Emotion in relation to them rarely appears in art or literature or documentary evidence. The Christ child is of course repeatedly pictured, usually in his mother's arms, but prior to the mid-14th century he is generally held stiffly, away from her body, by a mother who is aloof even when nursing. Or else the holy infant lies alone on the ground, swaddled or sometimes quite naked and uncovered, while an unsmiling mother gazes at him abstractedly. Her separateness from the child was meant to indicate his divinity. If the ordinary mother felt a warmer, more intimate emotion, it found small expression in medieval art because the attitudes of motherhood were preempted by the Virgin Mary.

In literature the chief role of children was to die, usually drowned, smothered, or abandoned in a forest on the orders of some king fearing prophecy or mad husband testing a wife's endurance. Women appear rarely as mothers. They are flirts, bawds, and deceiving wives in the popular tales, saints and martyrs in the drama, unattainable objects of passionate and illicit love in the romances. Occasionally motherhood may break through, as when an English preacher, to point a moral in a sermon, tells how a mother "that hath a childe in wynter when the childes hondes ben cold, the modur taketh hym a stree [straw] or a rusche and byddeth him warme itt, not for love of the stree to hete it . . . but for to hete the childes honds." An occasional illustration or carving in stone shows parents teaching a child to walk, a peasant mother combing or delousing her child's hair with his head in her lap, a more elegant mother of the 14th century knitting a child's garment on four needles, an acknowledgment from a saint's life of the "beauty of infancy," and from the 12th century *Ancren Riwle* a description of a peasant mother playing hide-and-seek with her child and who, when he cries for her, "leapeth forth lightly with outspread arms and embraceth and kisseth him and wipeth his eyes." These are isolated mentions which leave the empty spaces between more noticeable.

Medieval illustrations show people in every other human activity—making love and dying, sleeping and eating, in bed and in the bath, praying, hunting, dancing, plowing, in games and in combat, trading, traveling, reading and writing—yet so rarely with children as to raise the question: Why not?

Maternal love, like sex, is generally considered too innate to be eradicable, but perhaps under certain unfavorable conditions it may atrophy. Owing to the high infant mortality of the times, estimated at one or two in three, the investment of love in a young child may have been so unrewarding that by some ruse of nature, as when over-crowded rodents in captivity will not breed, it was suppressed. Perhaps also the frequent childbearing put less value on the product. A child was born and died and another took its place.

Well-off noble and bourgeois families bore more children than the poor because they married young and because, as a result of employing wet-nurses, the period of infertility was short. They also raised more, often as many as six to ten reaching adulthood. Guillaume de Coucy, grandfather of Enguerrand VII, raised five sons and five daughters; his son Raoul raised four of each. Nine out of the twelve children of Edward III and Queen Philippa of England reached maturity. The average woman of twenty, it has been estimated, could expect about twelve years of childbearing, with live births spaced out—owing to stillbirths, abortions, and nursing—at fairly long intervals of about thirty months. At this rate, the average of births per family was about five, of whom half survived.

Like everything else, childhood escapes a flat generalization. Love and lullabies and cradle-rocking did exist. God in his grace, wrote Philip of Novara in the 13th century, gave children three gifts: to love and recognize the person who nurses him at her breast; to show "joy and love" to those who play with him; to inspire love and tenderness in those who rear him, of which the last is the most important, for "without this, they will be so dirty and annoying in infancy and so naughty and capricious that it is hardly worth nurturing them through childhood." Philip advocated, however, a strict upbringing, for "few children perish from excess of severity but many from being permitted too much."

Books of advice on child-rearing were rare. There were books—that is, bound manuscripts—of etiquette, housewifery, deportment, home remedies, even phrase books of foreign vocabularies. A reader could find advice on washing hands and cleaning nails before a banquet, on eating fennel and anise in case of bad breath, on not spitting or picking teeth with a knife, not wiping hands on sleeves, or nose and eyes on the tablecloth. A woman could learn how to make ink, poison for rats, sand for hourglasses; how to make hippocras or spiced wine, the favorite medieval drink; how to care for pet birds in cages and get them to breed; how to obtain character references for servants and make sure they extinguished their bed candles with fingers or breath, "not with their shirts"; how to grow peas and graft roses; how to rid the house of flies; how to remove grease stains with chicken feathers steeped in hot water; how to keep a husband happy by ensuring him a smokeless fire in winter and a bed free of fleas in summer. A young married woman would be advised on fasting and alms-giving and saying prayers at the sound of the matins bell "before going to sleep again," and on walking with dignity and modesty in public, not "in ribald wise with roving eyes and neck stretched forth like a stag in flight, looking this way and that like unto a runaway horse." She could find books on estate management for times when her husband was away at war, with advice on making budgets and withstanding sieges and on tenure and feudal law so that her husband's rights would not be invaded.

But she would find few books for mothers with advice on breast-feeding, swaddling, bathing, weaning, solid-feeding, and other complexities of infant care, although these might seem to have been of more moment for survival of the race than breeding birds in cages or even keeping husbands comfortable. When breast-feeding was mentioned, it was generally advocated—by one 13th century encyclopedist, Bartholomew of England in his *Book on the Nature of Things* —for its emotional value. In the process the mother "loves her own child most tenderly, embraces and kisses it, nurses and cares for it most solicitously." A physician of the same period, Aldobrandino of Siena, who practiced in France, advised frequent cleaning and changing and two baths a day, weaning on porridge made of bread with honey and milk, ample playtime and unforced teaching at school, with time for sleep and diversion. But how widely his humane teaching was known or followed it is impossible to say.

On the whole, babies and young children appear to have been left to survive or die without great concern in the first five or six years. What psychological effect this may have had on character, and possibly on history, can only be conjectured. Possibly the relative emotional blankness of a medieval infancy may account for the casual attitude toward life and suffering of the medieval man.

Children did, however, have toys: dolls and doll carriages harnessed to mice, wooden knights and weapons, little animals of baked clay, windmills, balls, battledores and shuttlecocks, stilts and seesaws and merry-go-rounds. Little boys were like little boys of any time, "living without thought or care," according to Bartholomew of England, "loving only to play, fearing no danger more than being beaten with a rod, always hungry and hence disposed to infirmities from being over-fed, wanting everything they see, quick to laughter and as quick to tears, resisting their mothers' efforts to wash and comb them, and no sooner clean but dirty again." Girls were better behaved, according to Bartholomew, and dearer to their mothers. If children survived to age seven, their recognized life began, more or less as miniature adults. Childhood was already over. The childishness noticeable in medieval behavior, with its marked inability to restrain any kind of impulse, may have been simply due to the fact that so large a proportion of active society was actually very young in years. About half the population, it has been estimated, was under twenty-one, and about one third under fourteen.

A boy of noble family was left for his first seven years in the charge of women, who schooled him in manners and to some extent in letters. Significantly, St. Anne, the patron saint of mothers, is usually portrayed teaching her child, the Virgin Mary, how to read from a book. From age eight to fourteen the noble's son was sent as a page to the castle of a neighboring lord, in the same way that boys of lower orders went at seven or eight to another family as apprentices or servants. Personal service was not considered degrading: a page or even a squire as a grown man assisted his lord to bathe and dress, took care of his clothes, waited on him at table while sharing noble status. In return for free labor, the lord provided a free school for the sons of his peers. The boy would learn to ride, to fight, and to hawk, the three chief physical elements of noble life, to play chess and backgammon, to sing and dance, play an instrument, and compose, and other romantic skills. The castle's private chaplain or a local abbey would supply his religious education, and teach him the rudiments of reading and writing and possibly some elements of the grammar-school curriculum that non-noble boys studied.

At fourteen or fifteen, when he became a squire, the training for combat intensified. He learned to pierce the swinging dummy of the quintain with a lance, wield the sword and a variety of other murderous weapons, and know the rules of heraldry and jousting. As squire he led his lord's war-horse to battle and held it when the fighting was on foot. He assisted the seneschal in the business of the castle, kept the keys, acted as confidential courier, carried the purse and valuables on a journey. Book learning had little place in this program, although a young noble, depending on his bent, could make some acquaintance of geometry, law, elocution, and, in a few cases, Latin.

Women of noble estate were frequently more accomplished in Latin and other school learning than the men, for though girls did not leave home at seven like boys, their education was encouraged by the Church so that they might be better instructed in the faith and more fitted for the religious life in a nunnery, should their parents wish to dedicate them, with suitable endowment, to the Church. Besides reading and writing in French and Latin, they were taught music, astronomy, and some medicine and first aid.

The last of the Coucys entered a world in which movement was limited to the speed of man or horse, news and public announcements were communicated by the human voice, and light ended for most people with the setting of the sun. At dusk, horns were blown or bells rung to sound curfew or "cover fires," after which work was prohibited because a workman could not see to perform creditably. The rich could prolong time by torchlight and candles, but for others night was as dark as nature intended, and stillness surrounded a traveler after dark. "Birds, wild beasts and men without any noise did take their rest," wrote Boccaccio. "The unfallen leaves did hang upon the trees and the moist air abode in mild peace. Only the stars did shine to light his way."

Flowers covered the fields and forest floor and formed a cherished element of daily life. Wild flowers and garden flowers were woven into chaplets worn by noble men and women, strewn on floors and tables at banquets, and scattered in the streets before royal processions. Monkeys were common pets. Beggars were ubiquitous, most of them crippled, blind, diseased, deformed, or disguised as such. The legless dragged themselves along by means of wooden stumps strapped to their hands. Women were considered the snare of the Devil, while at the same time the cult of the Virgin made one woman the central object of love and adoration. Doctors were admired, lawyers universally hated and mistrusted. Steam was unharnessed, syphilis not yet introduced, leprosy still extant, gunpowder coming into use, though not yet effectively. Potatoes, tea, coffee, and tobacco were unknown; hot spiced wine was the favorite drink of those who could afford it; the common people drank beer, ale, and cider.

Men of the non-clerical classes had abandoned the gown for divided legs clad in tights. They were generally clean-shaven, although chin beards and mustaches came in and out of fashion. Knights and courtiers had adopted a fashion of excessively long pointed shoes called *poulaines*—which often had to be tied up around the calf to enable the wearer to walk—and excessively short tunics which, according to one chronicler's complaint, revealed the buttocks and "other parts of the body that should be hidden," exciting the mockery of the common people. Women used cosmetics, dyed their hair, plucked it to broaden their foreheads, and plucked their eyebrows too, although by these practices they committed the sin of vanity.

Fortune's Wheel, plunging down the mighty and (more rarely) raising the lowly, was the prevailing image of the instability of life in an uncertain world. Progress, moral or material, in man or society, was not expected during this life on earth, of which the conditions were fixed. The individual might through his own efforts increase in virtue, but betterment of the whole would have to await the Second Coming and the beginning of a new age.

Time, calendar, and history were reckoned by the Christian scheme. Creation of the world was dated 4,484 years before the founding of Rome, and modern history from the birth of Christ. Historical events thereafter were chronicled by papal reigns beginning with St. Peter's, which was fixed at A.D. 42–67. Current events were recorded in relation to religious holidays and saints' days. The year began in March—the month, according to Chaucer, "in which the world began, when God first made man." Officially it began at Easter, and because this was a movable feast falling anywhere within a period of thirty days, historical dating was imprecise. Hours of the day were named for the hours of prayer: matins around midnight; lauds around three A.M.; prime, the first hour of daylight, at sunrise or about six A.M.; vespers at six in the evening; and compline at bedtime. The reckoning of time was based on the movements of sun and stars, nature's time-keepers, which were familiar and carefully observed. About the time Enguerrand VII was born, the mechanical clock was coming into use on town-hall towers and in homes of the rich, bringing precision with all its possibilities for scientific observation.

People lived close to the inexplicable. The flickering lights of marsh gas could only be fairies or goblins; fireflies were the souls of unbaptized dead infants. In the terrible trembling and fissures of an earthquake or the setting afire of a tree by lightning, the supernatural was close at hand. Storms were omens, death by heart attack or other seizures could be the work of demons. Magic was present in the world: demons, fairies, sorcerers, ghosts, and ghouls touched and manipulated human lives; heathen superstitions and rituals abided among the country folk, beneath and even alongside the priest and sacraments. The influence of the planets could explain anything otherwise unaccounted for. Astronomy was the noblest science, and astrology, after God, the greatest determinant of affairs.

Alchemy, or the search for the philosopher's stone that would transmute base metals into gold, was the most popular applied science. At the end of that rainbow lay also the panacea for ills and the elixir of longevity. Inquiring minds investigated natural science through experiment and observation. A scholar of Oxford kept a seven-year record of the weather through the years 1337–44 and noted that the sound of bells heard more clearly or at a greater distance than usual was a sign of increased humidity and a prediction of rain. Mental depression and anxiety were recognized as an illness, although the symptoms of depression, despair or melancholy, and lethargy were considered by the Church the sin of *accidia* or sloth. Surveying by triangulation was practiced, and the height of walls and towers measured by a monk lying prone with the aid of a stick. Eyeglasses had been in use since the turn of the century, allowing old people to read more in their later years and greatly extending the scholar's life of study. The manufacture of paper as a cheaper and more plentiful material than parchment was beginning to make possible multiple copies and wider distribution of literary works.

Energy depended on human and animal muscle and on the gear shaft turned by wind or water. Their power drove mills for tanning and laundering, sawing wood, pressing olive oil, casting iron, mashing malt for beer and pulp for paper and pigment for paints, operating fullers' vats for finishing woolen cloth, bellows for blast furnaces, hydraulic hammers for foundries, and wheels for grindstones used by armorers. The mills had so augmented the use of iron that timberland was already being deforested to supply fuel for the forge. They had so extended human capacity that Pope Celestine III in the 1190s ruled that windmills must pay tithes. Unpowered tools—the lathe, brace and bit, spinning wheel, and wheeled plow—had also in the last century increased skills and powers of production.

Travel, "the mother of tidings," brought news of the world to castle and village, town and countryside. The rutted roads, always either too dusty or too muddy, carried an endless flow of pilgrims and peddlers, merchants with their packtrains, bishops making visitations, tax-collectors and royal officials, friars and pardoners, wandering scholars, jongleurs and preachers, messengers and couriers who wove the network of communications from city to city. Great nobles like the Coucys, bankers, prelates, abbeys, courts of justice, town governments, kings and their councils employed their own messengers. The King of England at mid-century kept twelve on hand who accompanied him at all times, ready to start, and were paid 3d. a day when on the road and 4s. 8d. a year for shoes. Befitting the greater majesty of France, the French King employed up to one hundred, and a *grand seigneur* two or three.

An average day's journey on horseback was about 30 to 40 miles, though it varied widely, depending on circumstance. A messenger on horseback, without riding at night, could cover 40 to 50 miles a day and about half as much on foot. In an emergency, given a good horse and good road (which was rare) and no load, he could make 15 miles an hour and, with changes of horse awaiting him, cover 100 miles a day. The great merchant cities of Venice and Bruges maintained a regular postal service between them so highly organized that it covered the 700 miles in seven days. Packtrains made about 15 to 20 miles a day; armies, when slowed by baggage wagons and retainers on foot, sometimes covered no more than 8 miles a day.

The length of France from Flanders to Navarre was generally reckoned a journey of 20 to 22 days, and the width, from the coast of Brittany to Lyon on the Rhône, 16 days. Travelers to Italy across the Alps usually went by way of the Mont Cenis pass from Chambéry in the territory of Savoy to Turin. Snowbound from November through May, the pass took 5 to 7 days to traverse. Traveling from Paris to Naples via this route took five weeks. The voyage from London to Lyon took about 18 days and from Canterbury to Rome about 30 days depending on the Channel crossing, which was unpredictable, often dangerous, sometimes fatal, and could take anywhere from three days to a month. One knight, Sir Hervé de Léon, was kept 15 days at sea by a storm and, besides having lost his horse overboard, arrived so battered and weakened "that he never had health thereafter." It was no wonder that, according to a ballad, when pilgrims took to sea for the voyage to Compostella or beyond, "Theyr hertes begin to fayle."

Except for galleys powered by oarsmen, ships were at the mercy of the weather, although rigging had been improved and the swinging stern rudder gave greater control. Maps and harbor charts were in use and the compass was allowing navigation to leave the coastline and merchant cargo to take the risk of crossing the open sea. As a result, larger ships capable of carrying 500 tons or more of cargo were being used for these voyages. Barge transportation by river and canal was much cheaper than packtrain, even given the tolls imposed by local lords at every convenient point. Along the busy Seine and Garonne, tolls succeeded each other every six or seven miles.

Wagons and peasants' two-wheeled carts were used for short hauls, but since roads were usually impassable by wheeled vehicles in winter and there was no connected system of roads and bridges, the mule train remained the essential carrier. Four-wheeled covered wagons drawn by three or four horses in tandem were available for ladies and the sick. Ladies who rode sat astride under flowing skirts, but the sidesaddle was to appear before the end of the century. For a knight to ride in a carriage was against the principles of chivalry and he never under any circumstances rode a mare.

Travelers stopped before nightfall, those of the nobility taking shelter in some nearby castle or monastery where they would be admitted indoors, while the mass of ordinary travelers on foot, including pilgrims, were housed and fed in a guest house outside the gate. They were entitled to one night's lodging at any monastery and could not be turned away unless they asked for a second night. Inns were available to merchants and others, though they were likely to be crowded, squalid, and flea-ridden, with several beds to a room and two travelers to a bed—or three to a bed in Germany, according to the disgusted report of the poet Deschamps, who was sent there on a mission for the French King. Moreover, he complained, neither bed nor table had clean linen, the innkeeper offered no choice of foods, a traveler in the Empire could find nothing to drink but beer; fleas, rats, and mice were unavoidable, and the people of Bohemia lived like pigs.

Given the hardships and the length of time consumed, people journeyed over long distances to an astonishing degree—from Paris to Florence, from Flanders to Hungary, London to Prague, Bohemia to Castile, crossing seas, alps, and rivers, walking to China like Marco Polo or three times to Jerusalem like the Wife of Bath.

What was the mental furniture of Enguerrand's class, the upper level of lay society? Long before Columbus, they knew the world was a globe, a knowledge proceeding from familiarity with the movement of the stars, which could be made comprehensible only in terms of a spherical earth. In a vivid image, it was said by the cleric Gautier de

Metz in his *Image du Monde*, the most widely read encyclopedia of the time, that a man could go around the world as a fly makes the tour of an apple. So far was the earth from the stars, according to him, that if a stone were dropped from there it would take more than 100 years to reach our globe, while a man traveling 25 leagues a day without stopping would take 7,157½ years to reach the stars.

Visually, people pictured the universe held in God's arms with man at its center. It was understood that the moon was the nearest planet, with no light of its own; that an eclipse was the passage of the moon between the earth and the sun; that rain was moisture drawn by the sun from the earth which condensed into clouds and fell back as rain; that the shorter the time between thunder and lightning, the nearer the source.

Faraway lands, however—India, Persia, and beyond—were seen through a gauze of fabulous fairy tales revealing an occasional nugget of reality: forests so high they touch the clouds, horned pygmies who move in herds and grow old in seven years, brahmins who kill themselves on funeral pyres, men with dogs' heads and six toes, "cyclopeans" with only one eye and one foot who move as fast as the wind, the "monoceros" which can be caught only when it sleeps in the lap of a virgin, Amazons whose tears are of silver, panthers who practice the caesarean operation with their own claws, trees whose leaves supply wool, snakes 300 feet long, snakes with precious stones for eyes, snakes who so love music that for prudence they stop up one ear with their tail.

The Garden of Eden too had an earthly existence which often appeared on maps, located far to the east, where it was believed cut off from the rest of the world by a great mountain or ocean barrier or fiery wall. In the earthly Paradise grow every kind of tree and flowers of surpassing colors and a thousand scents which never fade and have healing qualities. Birds' songs harmonize with the rustling of forest leaves and the rippling of streams flowing over jeweled rocks or over sands brighter than silver. A palace with columns of crystal and jasper sheds marvelous light. No wind or rain, heat or cold mars Paradise; no sickness, decay, death, or sorrow enters there. The mountain peak on which it is situated is so high it touches the sphere of the moon—but here the scientific mind intervened: that would be impossible, pronounced the 14th century author of *Polychronicon*, because it would cause an eclipse.

For all the explanations, the earth and its phenomena were full of mysteries: What happens to fire when it goes out? Why are there different colors of skin among men? Why do the sun's rays darken a man's skin but bleach white linen? How can the earth, which is weighty, be suspended in air? How do souls make their way to the next world? Where lies the soul? What causes madness? Medieval people felt surrounded by puzzles, yet because God was there they were willing to acknowledge that causes are hidden, that man cannot know why all things are as they are; "they are as God pleases."

That did not silence the one unending question: Why does God allow evil, illness, and poverty? Why did He not make man incapable of sin? Why did He not assure him of Paradise? The answer, never wholly satisfying, was that God owed the Devil his scope. According to St. Augustine, the fount of authority, all men were under the Devil's power by virtue of original sin; hence the necessity of the Church and salvation.

Questions of human behavior found answers in the book of Sidrach, supposedly a descendant of Noah to whom God gave the gift of universal knowledge, eventually compiled into a book by several masters of Toledo. What language does a deaf-mute hear in his heart? Answer: that of Adam, namely Hebrew. Which is worst: murder, robbery, or assault? None of these; sodomy is the worst. Will wars ever end? Never, until the earth becomes Paradise. The origin of war, according to its 14th century codifier Honoré Bonet, lay in Lucifer's war against God, "hence it is no great marvel if in this world there arise wars and battles since these existed first in heaven."

Education, so far as it would have reached Enguerrand, was based on the seven "liberal arts": Grammar, the foundation of science; Logic, which differentiates the true from the false; Rhetoric, the source of law; Arithmetic, the foundation of order because "without numbers there is nothing"; Geometry, the science of measurement; Astronomy, the most noble of the sciences because it is connected with Divinity and Theology; and lastly Music. Medicine, though not one of the liberal arts, was analogous to Music because its object was the harmony of the human body.

History was finite and contained within comprehensible limits. It began with the Creation and was scheduled to end in a not indefinitely remote future with the Second Coming, which was the hope of afflicted mankind, followed by the Day of Judgment. Within that span, man was not subject to social or moral progress because his goal was the next world, not betterment in this. In this world he was assigned to ceaseless struggle against himself in which he might attain individual progress and even victory, but collective betterment would only come in the final union with God.

The average layman acquired knowledge mainly by ear, through public sermons, mystery plays, and the recital of narrative poems, ballads, and tales, but during Enguerrand's lifetime, reading by educated nobles and upper bourgeois increased with the increased availability of manuscripts. Books of universal knowledge, mostly dating from the 13th century and written in (or translated from the Latin into) French and other vernaculars for the use of the layman, were literary staples familiar in every country over several centuries. A 14th century man drew also on the Bible, romances, bestiaries, satires, books. of astronomy, geography, universal history, church history, rhetoric, law, medicine, alchemy, falconry, hunting, fighting, music, and any number of special subjects. Allegory was the guiding concept. Every incident in the Old Testament was considered to pre-figure in allegory what was to come in the New. Everything in nature concealed an allegorical meaning relating to some aspect of Christian doctrine. Allegorical figures—Greed, Reason, Courtesy, Love, False-Seeming, Do-Well, Fair Welcome, Evil Rumor—peopled the tales and political treatises.

Epics of great heroes, of Brutus and King Arthur, of the "strong stryfe" of Greece and Troy, of Alexander and Julius Caesar, of how Charlemagne and Roland fought the Saracens and how Tristan and Iseult loved and sinned, were the favorites of noble households, though not to the exclusion of coarser stuff. The *fabliaux* or tales of common life, bawdy and scatological, were told in noble halls as well as taverns. The Ménagier of Paris, a wealthy bourgeois contemporary of Enguerrand VII, who at the age of sixty in 1392 wrote a book of domestic and moral instruction for his young wife, had read or possessed the Bible, *The Golden Legend*, St. Jerome's *Lives of the Fathers*, the works of St. Augustine, St. Gregory, Livy, Cicero, the *Roman de la Rose*, Petrarch's *Tale of Griselda*, and other less familiar titles. The Chevalier Geoffroy de La Tour Landry, a slightly older contemporary of Enguerrand, who in 1371 wrote a book of cautionary tales for his daughters, was as well acquainted with Sarah, Bathsheba, and Delilah as with Helen of Troy, Hippolyta, and Dido. If the Ménagier was too respectable to read Ovid, the Roman poet was well known to others. Aristotle was the basis of political philosophy, Ptolemy of "natural" philosophy, Hippocrates and Galen of medicine.

Contemporary writers rapidly found an audience. In Dante's lifetime his verse was chanted by blacksmiths and mule-drivers; fifty years later in 1373 the growth of reading caused the Signoria of Florence, at the petition of citizens, to offer a year's course of public lectures on Dante's work for which the sum of 100 gold florins was raised to pay the lecturer, who was to speak every day except holy days. The person appointed was Boccaccio, who had written the first biography of Dante and copied out the entire *Divine Comedy* himself as a gift for Petrarch.

In an Italian biographical dictionary at the end of the century, the longest articles were given to Julius Caesar and Hannibal, two pages to Dante, one page each to Archimedes, Aristotle, King Arthur, and Attila the Hun, two and a half columns to Petrarch, one column to Boccaccio, shorter mentions to Cimabue and Giotto, and three lines to Marco Polo.

For Enguerrand at age seven, the usual pattern was abruptly interrupted when his father was killed in the war against the English at about the time of the fatal Battle of Crécy in 1346, but whether in that or another engagement is uncertain.

When a fief owing an important number of fighting men to the King was left in the hands of a widow or minor heir, the question of control became crucial, the more so now when the kingdom was already at war. As governors of the barony of Coucy during Enguerrand's minority, the King appointed the chief of his Council, Jean de Nesles, Sire d'Offémont, a member of the old nobility, and another of the royal inner circle, Matthieu de Roye, Sire d'Aunoy, Master of the Crossbowmen of France, an office exercising command over all archers and infantry. Both were seigneurs of Picardy with lands not far from Coucy. Enguerrand's uncle, Jean de Coucy, Sire d'Havraincourt, was named his guardian and tutor or adviser. His mother, Catherine of Austria, left in a situation vulnerable to predatory ambitions, quickly concluded an agreement with the numerous brothers and sisters of her late husband who during his lifetime had held the property in common. They were confirmed in possession of various castles and manors, and Enguerrand VII, who had no brothers or sisters, was confirmed as successor to the major portion of the domain, including the territories of Coucy, Marle, La Fère, Boissy-en-Brie, Oisy-en-Cambrésis, and their towns and dependencies.

In 1348 or '49 Enguerrand's mother remarried, presumably by her own or her own family's choice, a fellow Austrian or German named Conrad de Magdebourg (also called Hardeck). Catherine bore no children of this marriage; within a year she and her husband were dead, victims of the great holocaust that was about to overtake Europe and leave Enguerrand an orphan.

During her lifetime Catherine was said to have taken great care of her son's education, wishing him to distinguish himself in "the arts, letters and sciences pertaining to his rank" and frequently reminding him of the "virtue and high reputation of his ancestors." Coming from a 16th century account of Enguerrand de Coucy, this statement may have been the kind of tribute routinely paid at that time to noble personages: equally well it could have had some basis in fact. Like other medieval childhoods, however, Enguerrand's is a blank. Nothing is known of him until his sudden emergence onto the pages of history in 1358 at the age of eighteen.

Of chivalry, the culture that nurtured him, much is known. More than a code of manners in war and love, chivalry was a moral system, governing the whole of noble life. That it was about four parts in five illusion made it no less governing for all that. It developed at the same time as the great crusades of the 12th century as a code intended to fuse the religious and martial spirits and somehow bring the fighting man into accord with Christian theory. Since a knight's usual activities were as much at odds with Christian theory as a merchant's, a moral gloss was needed that would allow the Church to tolerate the warriors in good conscience and the warriors to pursue their own values in spiritual comfort. With the help of Benedictine thinkers, a code evolved that put the knight's sword arm in the service, theoretically, of justice, right, piety, the Church, the widow, the orphan, and the oppressed. Knighthood was received in the name of the Trinity after a ceremony of purification, confession, communion. A saint's relic was usually embedded in the hilt of the knight's sword so that upon clasping it as he took his oath, he caused the vow to be registered in Heaven. Chivalry's famous celebrator Ramon Lull, a contemporary of St. Louis, could now state as his thesis that "God and chivalry are in concord."

But, like business enterprise, chivalry could not be contained by the Church, and bursting through the pious veils, it developed its own principles. Prowess, that combination of courage, strength, and skill that made a chevalier *preux*, was the prime essential. Honor and loyalty, together with courtesy—meaning the kind of behavior that has since come to be called "chivalrous"—were the ideals, and so-called courtly love the presiding genius. Designed to make the knight more polite and to lift the tone of society, courtly love required its disciple to be in a chronically amorous condition, on the theory that he would thus be rendered more courteous, gay, and gallant, and society in consequence more joyous. Largesse was the necessary accompaniment. An open-handed generosity in gifts and hospitality was the mark of a gentleman and had its practical value in attracting other knights to fight under the banner and bounty of the *grand seigneur*. Over-celebrated by troubadours and chroniclers who depended on its flow, largesse led to reckless extravagance and careless bankruptcies.

Prowess was not mere talk, for the function of physical violence required real stamina. To fight on horseback or foot wearing 55 pounds of plate armor, to crash in collision with an opponent at full gallop while holding horizontal an eighteen-foot lance half the length of an average telephone pole, to give and receive blows with sword or battle-ax that could cleave a skull or slice off a limb at a stroke, to spend half of life in the saddle through all weathers and for days at a time, was not a weakling's work. Hardship and fear were part of it. "Knights who are at the wars . . . are forever swallowing their fear," wrote the companion and biographer of Don Pero Niño, the "Unconquered Knight" of the late 14th century. "They expose themselves to every peril; they give up their bodies to the adventure of life in death. Moldy bread or biscuit, meat cooked or uncooked; today enough to eat and tomorrow nothing, little or no wine, water from a pond or a butt, bad quarters, the shelter of a tent or branches, a bad bed, poor sleep with their armor still on their backs, burdened with iron, the enemy an arrow-shot off. 'Ware! Who goes there? To arms! To arms!' With the first drowsiness, an alarm; at dawn, the trumpet. 'To horse! To horse! Muster! Muster!' As lookouts, as sentinels, keeping watch by day and by night, fighting without cover, as foragers, as scouts, guard after guard, duty after duty. 'Here they come! Here! They are so many— No, not as many as that—This way—that—Come this side—Press them there—News! News! They come back hurt, they have prisoners—no, they bring none back. Let us go! Let us go! Give no ground! On!' Such is their calling."

Horrid wounds were part of the calling. In one combat Don Pero Niño was struck by an arrow that "knit together his gorget and his neck," but he fought on against the enemy on the bridge. "Several lance stumps were still in his shield and it was that which hindered him most." A bolt from a crossbow "pierced his nostrils most painfully whereat he was dazed, but his daze lasted but a little time." He pressed forward, receiving many sword blows on head and shoulders which "sometimes hit the bolt embedded in his nose making him suffer great pain." When weariness on both sides brought the battle to an end, Pero

Niño's shield "was tattered and all in pieces; his sword blade was toothed like a saw and dyed with blood . . . his armor was broken in several places by lance-heads of which some had entered the flesh and drawn blood, although the coat was of great strength." Prowess was not easily bought.

Loyalty, meaning the pledged word, was chivalry's fulcrum. The extreme emphasis given to it derived from the time when a pledge between lord and vassal was the only form of government. A knight who broke his oath was charged with "treason" for betraying the order of knighthood. The concept of loyalty did not preclude treachery or the most egregious trickery as long as no knightly oath was broken. When a party of armed knights gained entrance to a walled town by declaring themselves allies and then proceeded to slaughter the defenders, chivalry was evidently not violated, no oath having been made to the burghers.

Chivalry was regarded as a universal order of all Christian knights, a trans-national class moved by a single ideal, much as Marxism later regarded all workers of the world. It was a military guild in which all knights were theoretically brothers, although Froissart excepted the Germans and Spaniards, who, he said, were too uncultivated to understand chivalry.

In the performance of his function, the knight must be prepared, as John of Salisbury wrote, "to shed your blood for your brethren"—he meant brethren in the universal sense—"and, if needs must, to lay down your life." Many were thus prepared, though perhaps more from sheer love of battle than concern for a cause. Blind King John of Bohemia met death in that way. He loved fighting for its own sake, not caring whether the conflict was important. He missed hardly a quarrel in Europe and entered tournaments in between, allegedly receiving in one of them the wound that blinded him. His subjects, on the other hand, said the cause was Divine punishment—not because he dug up the old synagogue of Prague, which he did, but because, on finding money concealed beneath the pavement, he was moved by greed and the advice of German knights to dig up the tomb of St. Adelbert in the Prague cathedral and was stricken blind by the desecrated saint.

As an ally of Philip VI, at the head of 500 knights, the sightless King fought the English through Picardy, always rash and in the avantgarde. At Crécy he asked his knights to lead him deeper into the battle so that he might strike further blows with his sword. Twelve of them tied their horses' reins together and, with the King at their head, advanced into the thick of the fight, "so far as never to return." His body was found next day among his knights, all slain with their horses still tied together.

Fighting filled the noble's need of something to do, a way to exert himself. It was his substitute for work. His leisure time was spent chiefly in hunting, otherwise in games of chess, backgammon, and dice, in songs, dances, pageants, and other entertainments. Long winter evenings were occupied listening to the recital of interminable verse epics. The sword offered the workless noble an activity with a purpose, one that could bring him honor, status, and, if he was lucky, gain. If no real conflict was at hand, he sought tournaments, the most exciting, expensive, ruinous, and delightful activity of the noble class, and paradoxically the most harmful to his true military function. Fighting in tournaments concentrated his skills and absorbed his interest in an increasingly formalized clash, leaving little thought for the tactics and strategy of real battle.

Originating in France and referred to by others as "French combat" (*conflictus Gallicus*), tournaments started without rules or lists as an agreed-upon clash of opposing units. Though justified as training exercises, the impulse was the love of fighting. Becoming more regulated and mannered, they took two forms: jousts by individuals, and melees by groups of up to forty on a side, either *à plaisance* with blunted weapons or *à outrance* with no restraints, in which case participants might be severely wounded and not infrequently killed. Tournaments proliferated as the noble's primary occupation dwindled. Under the extended rule of monarchy, he had less need to protect his own fief, while a class of professional ministers was gradually taking his place around the crown. The less he had to do, the more energy he spent in tournaments artificially re-enacting his role.

A tournament might last as long as a week and on great occasions two. Opening day was spent matching and seeding the players, followed by days set apart for jousts, for melees, for a rest day before the final tourney, all interspersed with feasting and parties. These occasions were the great sporting events of the time, attracting crowds of bourgeois spectators from rich merchants to common artisans, mountebanks, food vendors, prostitutes, and pickpockets. About a hundred knights usually participated, each accompanied by two mounted squires, an armorer, and six servants in livery. The knight had of course to equip himself with painted and gilded armor and crested helmet costing from 25 to 50 livres, with a war-horse costing from 25 to 100 livres in addition to his traveling palfrey, and with banners and trappings and fine clothes. Though the expense could easily bankrupt him, he might also come away richer, for the loser in combat had to pay a ransom and the winner was awarded his opponent's horse and armor, which he could sell back to him or to anyone. Gain was not recognized by chivalry, but it was present at tournaments.

Because of their extravagance, violence, and vainglory, tournaments were continually being denounced by popes and kings, from whom they drained money. In vain. When the Dominicans denounced them as a pagan circus, no one listened. When the formidable St. Bernard thundered that anyone killed in a tournament would go to Hell, he spoke for once to deaf ears. Death in a tournament was officially considered the sin of suicide by the Church, besides jeopardizing family and tenantry without cause, but even threats of excommunication had no effect. Although St. Louis condemned tournaments and Philip the Fair prohibited them during his wars, nothing could stop them permanently or dim the enthusiasm for them.

With brilliantly dressed spectators in the stands, flags and ribbons fluttering, the music of trumpets, the parade of combatants making their draped horses prance and champ on golden bridles, the glitter of harness and shields, the throwing of ladies' scarves and sleeves to their favorites, the bow of the heralds to the presiding prince who proclaimed the rules, the cry of poursuivants announcing their champions, the tournament was the peak of nobility's pride and delight in its own valor and beauty.

If tournaments were an acting-out of chivalry, courtly love was its dreamland. Courtly love was understood by its contemporaries to be love for its own sake, romantic love, true love, physical love, unassociated with property or family, and consequently focused on another man's wife, since only such an illicit liaison could have no other aim but love alone. (Love of a maiden was virtually ruled out since this would have raised dangerous problems, and besides, maidens of noble estate usually jumped from childhood to marriage with hardly an interval for romance.) The fact that courtly love idealized guilty love added one more complication to the maze through which medieval people threaded their lives. As formulated by chivalry, romance was pictured as extra-marital because love was considered irrelevant to marriage, was indeed discouraged in order not to get in the way of dynastic arrangements.

As its justification, courtly love was considered to ennoble a man, to improve him in every way. It would make him concerned to show an example of goodness, to do his utmost to preserve honor, never letting dishonor touch himself or the lady he loved. On a lower scale, it would lead him to keep his teeth and nails clean, his clothes rich and well groomed, his conversation witty and amusing, his manners courteous to all, curbing arrogance and coarseness, never brawling in a lady's presence. Above all, it would make him more valiant, more *preux;* that was the basic premise. He would be inspired to greater prowess, would win more victories in tournaments, rise above himself in courage and daring, become, as Froissart said, "worth two men." Guided by this theory, woman's status improved, less for her own sake than as the inspirer of male glory, a higher function than being merely a sexual object, a breeder of children, or a conveyor of property.

The chivalric love affair moved from worship through declaration of passionate devotion, virtuous rejection by the lady, renewed wooing with oaths of eternal fealty, moans of approaching death from unsatisfied desire, heroic deeds of valor which won the lady's heart by prowess, consummation of the secret love, followed by endless adventures and subterfuges to a tragic denouement. The most widely known of all such romances and the last of its kind was the *Châtelain de Coucy,* written about the time of Enguerrand VII's birth when the *chanson de geste* was dying out. Its hero was not a Seigneur de Coucy but a *châtelain* of the castle named Renault, modeled on a real individual and poet of the 12th century.

In the legend he falls madly in love with the Dame de Fayel and through an enormous series of maneuvers occupying 8,266 lines of verse is decoyed into the Third Crusade by the jealous husband, covers himself with glory, and when fatally wounded by a poisoned arrow, composes a last song and farewell letter to be dispatched after his death in a box with his embalmed heart and a lock of the lady's hair. Carried by a faithful servant, the box is intercepted by the husband, who has the heart cooked and served to his wife. On being informed what she has eaten, she swears that after such a noble food she will never eat again and dies, while the husband exiles himself in a lifelong pilgrimage to obtain pardon for his deed.

"Melancholy, amorous and barbaric," these tales exalted adulterous love as the only true kind, while in the real life of the same society adultery was a crime, not to mention a sin. If found out, it dishonored the lady and shamed the husband, a fellow knight. It was understood that he had the right to kill both unfaithful wife and lover.

Nothing fits in this canon. The gay, the elevating, the ennobling pursuit is founded upon sin and invites the dishonor it is supposed to avert. Courtly love was a greater tangle of irreconcilables even than usury. It remained artificial, a literary convention, a fantasy (like modern pornography) more for purposes of discussion than for every-day practice.

The realities were more normal. As described by La Tour Landry, his amorous fellow knights were not overly concerned with loyalty and *courtoisie*. He tells how, when he used to ride abroad with his friends as a young man, they would beg ladies for their love and if this one did not accept they would try another, deceiving the ladies with fair words of blandishment and swearing false oaths, "for in every place they would have their sport if they could." Many a gentlewoman was taken in by the "foul and great false oaths that false men use to swear to women." He tells how three ladies who were exchanging opinions of their lovers discovered that the senior Jean le Maingre, Sire de Boucicaut, was the favorite of each, he having made love to all, telling each he loved her best. When they taxed him with his falsity, he was in no way abashed, saying, "For at that time I spake with each of you, I loved her best that I spake with and thought truly the same."

La Tour Landry himself, a seigneur of substance who fought in many campaigns, emerges as a domestic gentleman who liked to sit in his garden and enjoy the song of the thrush in April, and loved his books. Contrary to chivalry, he had also loved his wife, "the bell and flower of all that was fair and good," and "I delighted me so much in her that I made for her love songs, ballads, roundels, verelays and divers new things in the best wise that I could." He does not think much of chivalry's favorite theme, that courtly love inspires knights to greater prowess, for though they say they do it for the ladies, "in faith they do it for themselves to win praise and honor." Nor does he ap-prove of love for its own sake, *par amours*, either before or after marriage, for it can cause all kinds of crime, of which he cites the *Châtelain de Coucy* as an example.

As suggested by a spectacular scandal of the time, Edward III's rape of the Countess of Salisbury, courtly love was the ideal of chivalry least realized in everyday behavior. Froissart, who believed in chivalry as St. Louis believed in the Trinity, expurgated the story, supposedly after careful inquiries, but more probably out of respect for his beloved first patron, Philippa of Hainault, Edward's Queen. He reports only that the King, on visiting Salisbury Castle after a battle in Scotland in 1342, was "stricken to the heart with a sparkle of fine love" for the beautiful Countess. After she repulsed his advances, Edward is reported (with some historic license) debating with himself about pur-suing his guilty passion in words that are a supreme statement of the chivalric theory of love's role: "And if he should be more amorous it would be entirely good for him, for his realm and for all his knights and squires for he would be more content, more gay and more martial; he would hold more jousts, more tourneys, more feasts and more revels than he had before; and he would be more able and more vigorous in his wars, more amiable and more trusting toward his friends and harsher toward his foes."

According to another contemporary, Jean le Bel, who had himself been a knight with few illusions before he took orders as a canon and became a chronicler, matters went rather differently. After sending the Earl of Salisbury to Brittany like Uriah, the King revisited the Countess and, on being again rejected, he villainously raped her, "stopping her mouth with such force that she could only cry two or three cries . . . and left her lying in a swoon bleeding from the nose and mouth and other parts." Edward returned to London greatly disturbed at what he had done, and the good lady "had no more joy or happiness again, so heavy was her heart." Upon her husband's return she would not lie with him and, being asked why, she told him what had happened, "sitting on the bed next to him crying." The Earl, reflecting on the great friendship and honor between him and the King, now so dishonored, told his wife he could live in England no more. He went to court and before his peers divested himself of his lands in such a manner that his wife should have her dowry for life, and then went before the King, saying to his face, "You have villainously dishonored me and thrown me in the dung," and afterward left the country, to the sorrow and wonder of the nobility, and the "King was blamed by all."

If the fiction of chivalry molded outward behavior to some extent, it did not, any more than other models that man has made for himself, transform human nature. Joinville's account of the crusaders at Damietta in 1249 shows the knights under St. Louis plunged in brutality, blasphemy, and debauchery. Teutonic knights in their annual forays against the unconverted natives of Lithuania conducted manhunts of the peasants for sport. Yet, if the code was but a veneer over violence, greed, and sensuality, it was nevertheless an ideal, as Christianity was an ideal, toward which man's reach, as usual, exceeded his grasp.

Chapter 4

War

dward III's first campaign in France, halted by the truce of 1342, had been inconclusive and without strategic result except for the naval battle fought off Sluys, the port of Bruges, in 1340. Here where the mouth of the Scheldt widens among protecting isles to form a great natural harbor, the French had assembled 200 ships from as far away as Genoa and the Levant for a projected invasion of England. The outcome of the battle was an English victory that destroyed the French fleet and for the time being gave England command of the Channel. It was won by virtue of a military innovation that was to become the nemesis of France.

This was the longbow, derived from the Welsh and developed under Edward I for use against the Scots in the highlands. With a range reaching 300 yards and a rapidity, in skilled hands, of ten to twelve arrows a minute in comparison to the crossbow's two, the longbow represented a revolutionary delivery of military force. Its arrow was three feet long, about half the length of the formidable six-foot bow, and at a range of 200 yards it was not supposed to miss its target. While at extreme range its penetrating power was less than that of the crossbow, the longbow's fearful hail shattered and demoralized the enemy. Preparing for the challenge to France, Edward had to make up for the disparity in numbers by some superiority in weaponry or tactics. In 1337 he had prohibited on pain of death all sport except archery and canceled the debts of all workmen who manufactured the bows of yew and their arrows.

Another new weapon, the gun, entered history at this time, but meekly and tentatively and much less effectively than the longbow. Invented about 1325, the first *ribaud* or *pot de fer*, as the French called it, was a small iron cannon shaped like a bottle which fired an iron bolt with a triangular head. When a French raiding force at the opening of the war sacked and burned Southampton in 1338, it brought along one *ribaud* furnished with three pounds of gunpowder and 48 bolts. In the next year the French manufactured more in the form of several tubes bound to a wheeled platform, with their touchholes aligned so that all could be fired at once. But they proved too small to fire a projectile with enough force to do serious damage. The English reportedly used some small cannon at Crécy without noticeable effect and definitely had them at the siege of Calais, where they proved powerless against the city's stone walls. Later, when cast in brass or copper and enlarged in size, they were useful against bridges and city or castle gates or in defense of these, but stone walls withstood them for another hundred years. Difficulties in re-loading, ramming the powder, inserting the projectile, and containing the gas until it built up enough explosive force, frustrated effective firing throughout the 14th century.

In the sea fight at Sluys, with Edward in personal command, the longbowmen dominated the English armament, with one ship of men-at-arms placed between every two ships of archers, plus extra ships of archers for reinforcements if need arose. Not naval power but the strength of soldiers and archers on board ship determined sea battle in this era. They operated from high-decked cogs of 100 to 300 tons fitted with fighting platforms or "castles" for the archers. The battle was "fierce and terrible," reports Froissart, "for battles on sea are more dangerous and fiercer than battles by land, for on the sea there is no recoiling or fleeing." Under the archers' attack the French were driven from their decks and, pursued by ill-luck and error, were engulfed in defeat.

No one dared tell the outcome of the battle to Philip VI until his jester was thrust forward and said, "Oh, the cowardly English, the cowardly English!" and on being asked why, replied, "They did not jump overboard like our brave Frenchmen." The King evidently got the point. The fish drank so much French blood, it was said afterward, that if God had given them the power of speech they would have spoken in French.

The English victory led nowhere at the moment because Edward could not deliver sufficient force on land. His various allies from the Low Countries, acquired at great expense in subsidies, were slipping away, having no basic interest in his goal. Even his father-in-law, Count William of Hainault, returned to a more natural attachment to France. With his own forces inadequate and his finances bankrupt, Edward was forced to accept the Pope's offer to arrange a truce. He withdrew, but only *pour mieux sauter*.

What was he really fighting for? What was the real cause of a war that was to stretch beyond imagining halfway into the next century? As in most wars, the cause was a mixture of the political, economic, and psychological. Edward wanted to obtain the ultimate sovereignty of Guienne and Gascony, that lower western corner of France remaining from the Duchy of Aquitaine which the marriage of Eleanor of Aquitaine had brought to his ancestor Henry II five generations before. The King of France still retained superior sovereignty under the formula of *superioritas et resortum,* which gave the inhabitants the right of appeal to the ultimate sovereign. Since his decisions were more than likely to go in their favor against their English overlord, and since the citizens, knowing this, exercised the right frequently, the situation was an endless source of conflict. To the English *superioritas et resortum* was politically and psychologically intolerable.

The situation was the more galling because of Guienne's importance to the English economy. With its fertile valleys, long coast, and network of navigable rivers all leading to the main port of Bordeaux, it was the greatest wine-exporting region in the world. England imported the wine and other products and sent back wool and cloth, taking on every transaction a handsome revenue from export taxes at Bordeaux and import taxes at English ports. Between Bordeaux and Flanders the same flourishing commerce was exchanged, arousing the envy of central France. To the French monarchy the English foothold within the realm was unacceptable. Every French king for 200 years had tried by war, confiscation, or treaty to regain Aquitaine. The quarrel was old and deep and bound for war as the sparks fly upward.

Edward III was fifteen years old when he ascended the throne in 1327, 25 when he embarked on war with France, and 34 at the time of the second attempt in 1346. Well built and vigorous with long-flowing golden hair, mustache, and beard, he was at the height of his energies, expansive and kingly, vain, gracious, willful, and no stranger to the worst in man. Having grown up under the vicious strife surrounding the murder of his father's favorites, the deposition and murder of his father, and the overthrow and hanging of his mother's lover, Mortimer, who had seized power, he seemed, as far as history knows, unscarred by the experience. He understood practical politics without possessing any larger sense of rulership. He had no great qualities apart from or ahead of his time, but shone in those qualities his time admired in a king: he loved pleasure, battle, glory, hunts and tournaments, and extravagant display. One analysis of his character contains the phrases "boyish charm" and "a certain youthful petulance," suggesting that the King of England too showed signs of the characteristic medieval juvenility.

When Edward launched his claim to be the rightful King of France, it is uncertain how seriously he took it, but as a device it was of incomparable value in giving him the appearance of a righteous cause. While desirable in any epoch, a "just war" in the 14th century was virtually a legal necessity as the basis for requisitioning feudal aids in men and money. It was equally essential for securing God on one's side, for war was considered fundamentally an appeal to the arbitrament of God. A "just war" had to be one of public policy declared by the sovereign, and it had to be in a "just" cause—that is, directed against some "injustice" in the form of crime or fault on the part of the enemy. As formulated by the inescapable Thomas Aquinas, it required a third criterion: right intention on the part of the participants, but how this could be tested, the great expounder did not say. Even more convenient than the help of God was the "right of spoil"—in practice, pillage—that accompanied a just war. It rested on the theory that the enemy, being "unjust," had no right to property, and that booty was the due reward for risk of life in a just cause.

The claim to the French crown gave an excuse of legality to any vassal of France whom Edward could recruit as an ally. If he, not Philip, were the rightful King of France, a vassal could transfer his homage on the ground that it had simply been misplaced. Allegiance in the 14th century was still given to a person, not a nation, and the great territorial lords of duchies and counties felt themselves free to make alliances as if almost autonomous. The Harcourts of Normandy and the Duke and other lords of Brittany, for various reasons, did just that. Edward's claim through his mother gave him the one thing that made his venture feasible—support within France and a friendly beachhead. He never had to fight his way in. In either Normandy or Brittany this situation was to last forty years, and at Calais, captured after the Battle of Crécy, it was to outlast the Middle Ages.

In Brittany the war centered upon the relentless feud between two rival claimants to the dukedom and two parties of the population, one supported by France and the other by England. As a result, France was perpetually endangered by the access given to the enemy. The Breton seacoast was open to English ships, English garrisons were on Breton soil, Breton nobles were openly allied to Edward. Brittany was France's Scotland, choleric, Celtic, stony, bred to opposition and resistance, and ready to use the English in its struggles against its overlord as the Scots used the French in theirs. Along its rockbound coast, in Michelet's words, "two enemies, earth and sea, man and nature, meet in eternal conflict." Storms throw up monstrous waves, fifty, sixty, eighty feet, whose foam flies as high as the church steeple. "Nature is atrocious here; so is man; they seem to understand each other."

The contestants for the dukedom were two relentless extremists, a man and a woman. In 1341 the last Duke had died, leaving a half-brother, Jean Comte de Montfort, and a niece, Jeanne de Penthièvre, as rival heirs. Montfort was the candidate and ally of England while Jeanne's claim was assumed by her husband, Charles de Blois, a nephew of Philip VI, who became the French candidate for the dukedom.

Given to the study of books as a child, Charles was an ascetic of exaggerated piety who sought spirituality by mortifying the flesh. Like Thomas à Becket, he wore unwashed clothes crawling with lice; he put pebbles in his shoes, slept on straw on the floor next to his wife's bed, and after his death was found to have worn a coarse shirt of horsehair under his armor, and cords wound so tightly around his body that the knots dug into his flesh. By these practices a seeker of holiness expressed contempt for the world, self-abasement, and humility, although he often found himself guilty of a perverse pride in his excesses. Charles confessed every night so that he might not go to sleep in a state of sin. He fathered a bastard son called Jehan de Blois, but sins of the flesh did not have to be eschewed, only repented. He treated the humble with deference, it was said, met the complaints of the poor with goodness and justice, and refrained from too heavy taxes. Such was his reputation for saintliness that when he undertook to walk barefoot in the snow to a Breton shrine, the people covered his path with straw and blankets, but he took another way at a cost of bleeding and frozen feet, so that for weeks afterward he was unable to walk.

His piety detracted not at all from his ferocious pursuit of the dukedom. He stated his claim below the walls of Nantes by having his siege engines hurl into the city the heads of thirty captured partisans of Montfort. His successful siege of Quimper was followed by a ruthless massacre of 2,000 civilian inhabitants of all ages and both sexes. According to then current laws of war, the besieged could make terms if they surrendered, but not if they forced a siege to its bitter end, so presumably Charles felt no compunctions. On this occasion, after he had chosen the place of assault, he was warned of rising flood waters, but refused to alter his decision, saying, "Does not God have empire over the waters?" When his men succeeded in taking the city before being trapped by the flood, the people took it for a miracle owed to Charles's prayers.

When Charles captured Jean de Montfort and sent him to Paris to be held prisoner by Philip VI, Montfort's cause was taken up "with the

courage of a man and the heart of a lion" by his remarkable wife.
Riding from town to town, she rallied the allegiance of dispirited
partisans to her three-year-old son, saying, "Ha, seigneurs, never
mourn for my lord whom you have lost. He is but one man," and
promising that she had riches enough to maintain the cause. She provisioned and fortified garrisons, organized resistance, "paid largely and
gave freely," presided over councils, conducted diplomacy, and expressed herself in eloquent and graceful letters. When Charles de Blois
besieged Hennebont, she led a heroic defense in full armor astride a
war-horse in the streets, exhorting the soldiers under a hail of arrows
and ordering women to cut short their skirts and carry stones and pots
of boiling pitch to the walls to cast down upon the enemy. During a
lull she led a party of knights out a secret gate, and galloped by a
roundabout way to take the enemy camp in the rear, destroyed half
their force, and defeated the siege. She devised feints and stratagems,
wielded her sword in sea fights, and when her husband escaped from
the Louvre in disguise only to die after reaching Brittany, she im-
placably continued the fight for her son.

When in 1346, Charles de Blois was finally captured by the English
party and taken to prison in England, his cause was pursued by his no
less implacable wife, the crippled Jeanne de Penthièvre. The pitiless
war went on. Its two chief protagonists met fates expressive of their
time, insanity and sainthood. The blows and intrigues, privations and
broken hopes of her life proved too much for the valiant Countess of
Montfort, who went mad and was confined in England while Edward
made himself guardian of her son. Shut up and forgotten in the castle
of Tickhill, she was to live on for thirty years.

Charles de Blois, after nine years as a prisoner, was to win his
liberty for a ransom variously reported as 350,000, 400,000, or 700,000
écus. Although he was ready at last to come to terms, his wife refused
to let him renounce her claim, so he renewed the struggle and was
eventually killed in battle. Afterward he was canonized, but the
process was nullified by Pope Gregory XI at the request of the younger
Jean de Montfort, who feared that as conqueror of a saint he would be
regarded by the Bretons as a usurper.

While famous exploits and great reputations were made in Brittany,
a different kind of struggle was fought for Flanders.

Trade and geography made Flanders a crucial stake in the Anglo-
French rivalry. Its towns were the leading commercial centers of 14th
century Europe, where Italian merchant bankers and moneylenders

made their northern headquarters, a sure sign of lucrative business. Wealth generated by the weaving industry enriched the magnates of the bourgeoisie, who enjoyed a luxury that had astonished Queen Jeanne, wife of Philip the Fair, when she visited Bruges. "I thought I would be the only queen here," she said, "but I find six hundred others."

Though a fief of France, Flanders was tied to England by wool as Gascony was by wine. "All the nations of the world," proudly wrote Matthew of Westminster, "are kept warm by the wool of England made into cloth by the men of Flanders." Unexcelled in Europe for its quality and colors, including heavy cloth for common use, the cloth of Flanders was sold as far away as the Orient and had achieved an economic success that made Flanders vulnerable to the disadvantages of a one-industry economy. In that situation lay the source of all the turbulence and uprisings of the previous hundred years, and also the lever that both France and England used in their contest for control of the region.

The Count of Flanders, Louis de Nevers, and the Flemish nobility were pro-French, while the merchants and working class and all who depended on the cloth industry were oriented toward England in self-interest if not sentiment. The feudal and natural tie with France predominated. Flemish cloth and French wine were exchanged in trade, the Count's court was patterned on that of France, the nobility intermarried, French prelates held high offices in Flanders, use of the French language was spreading, Flemish students went to schools and colleges in Laon, Reims, and Paris.

In Flanders at the beginning of the century, the despised commoners had inflicted upon French knighthood an unforgettable defeat. In 1302 the array of French chivalry in splendid armor rode north in support of Flemish urban magnates to crush a revolt of the workers of Bruges. In the clash at Courtrai, French foot soldiers and crossbowmen were about to overpower the Flemish workers—too soon. The knights, frantic for the charge and fearing to lose the honor of victory, ordered their own infantry to fall back, causing them to break ranks in confusion. Shouting their war cries and riding down their own men in wild disorder, the knights charged, ignoring the canals beneath their feet. Horses scrambled and fell, knights plunged into the water, a second wave piled upon the first. The Flemish infantry, armed with pikes, speared them like fish, and holding firm against all assault beat back the knights in a bloody massacre. Seven hundred gold spurs were stripped from knightly corpses after the battle and hung up in triumphant memorial in the church. The loss of so much French nobility caused royal commissioners afterward to scour the provinces for bourgeois and rich peasants prepared to pay for ennoblement.

The knighthood of France was not daunted by Courtrai nor was its contempt for the commoner-in-arms in any way altered. The battle was considered an accident of circumstance and terrain unlikely to be repeated. In that sense the conclusion was right. In another revolt and another clash 25 years later, the knights inflicted a terrible revenge at the battle of Cassel, where they butchered Flemish workers and peasants by the thousands. Yet the lost spurs of Courtrai were a valid omen of the rise of the common soldier armed with pike and a motive, and an omen, too, for the knights, which they ignored.

After the Count of Flanders had been re-established in power by French arms, Philip VI exerted pressure to tighten relations and isolate Flanders from England. Against this effort the industrial towns, led by Ghent, rose in revolt under Jacob van Artevelde, one of the most dynamic bourgeois figures of the 14th century. An ambitious merchant of the class that was pressing to take over political power from the nobility, he had noble pretensions of his own. His two sons called themselves *messire* and *chevalier*, and the oldest son and a daughter were married into the nobility. Gaining control of the insurrection, Artevelde defeated the Count's forces and forced him to flee to France in 1339, leaving the country under Artevelde's control.

Meanwhile Edward, as the supplier of wool for Flemish industry, was exerting pressure for an alliance that would give him a base from which to attack France. The Flemish cloth manufacturers favored the English alliance and Artevelde attached his fortunes to it. The obstacle of French sovereignty over Flanders was overcome when Edward assumed the title of King of France. In that capacity he signed a treaty with Artevelde in 1340 after the victory of Sluys, but the device was hollow and lasted only long enough to give Edward a springboard before Artevelde's ambition brought him down in ruin.

Artevelde was a man of brutal action who once, when he and a Flemish knight disagreed, smote him to the ground with a blow of his fist under the eyes of the King of England. Besides using Flemish funds to finance Edward's war, he violated Flemish sentiments of homage. He proposed that the King's eldest son, Edward, Prince of Wales, later known as the Black Prince, should supplant the Count of Flanders' eldest son, Louis de Male, as heir and future ruler of Flanders. This was too much for the good Flemish towns. To disinherit their natural lord in favor of the English prince, they stoutly told Artevelde, was "a thing they would surely never agree unto." Moreover the Pope, under King Philip's pressure, had already excommunicated them for deserting

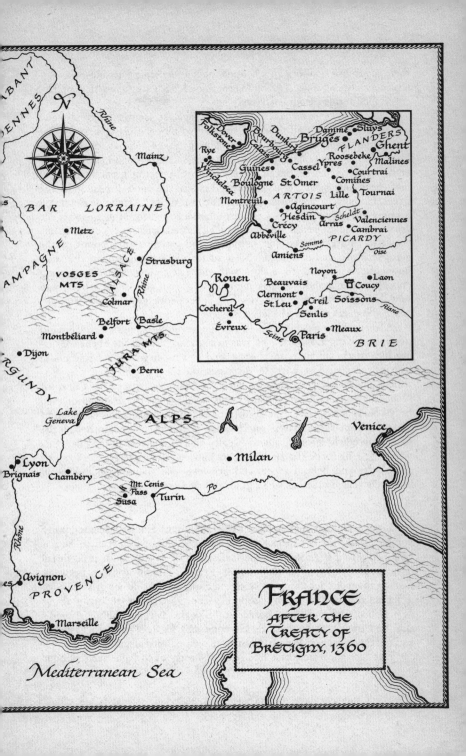

N

Brabant
Ardennes

Rhine

Mainz

BAR   LORRAINE

Metz

Champagne

VOSGES
MTS

ALSACE

Strasburg

Rhine

Colmar

Belfort   Basle

Montbéliard

Dijon

Burgundy

JURA MTS

Berne

Lake
Geneva

ALPS

Venice

Lyon

Milan

Brignais   Chambéry

Mt. Cenis
Pass

Po

Susa   Turin

Rhône

Avignon

PROVENCE

Marseille

Mediterranean Sea

Folkstone   Dover   Dunkirk   Damme   Sluys
Bourbourg   Bruges   FLANDERS   Ghent
Rye   Calais   Roosebeke
Winchelsea   Guines   Cassel   Ypres   Malines
Boulogne   St. Omer   Comines   Courtrai
Montreuil   ARTOIS   Lille   Tournai

Agincourt
Hesdin   Arras   Scheldt   Valenciennes
Crécy   Cambrai
Abbeville   Somme   PICARDY
Amiens   Oise

Rouen   Noyon   Laon
Beauvais   Coucy
Clermont   Creil   Soissons
Cocherel   St. Leu   Senlis   Aisne
Evreux   Seine   Paris   Meaux
BRIE

FRANCE
AFTER THE
TREATY OF
BRÉTIGNY, 1360

their sovereign, causing much uneasiness and damage to business. Resentment rose against Artevelde, combined with suspicion that he had embezzled funds for his own use.

"Then every man began to murmur against Jacques" (Jacob) and when he rode through Ghent, "trusting so much in his greatness that he thought soon to reduce them to his pleasure," angry crowds followed him to his house, demanding an accounting for all the revenues of Flanders. Then he began to fear and on entering his house, closed fast the gates, doors, and windows against the mob shouting in the street. Coming to the window "in great humilitie," Artevelde defended his nine years' governorship and promised a full account next day if the crowd would disperse. "Then they all cryed with one voyse, Come down to us and preche not so hyghe, and gyve us an account of the great treasure of Flaunders!" Now in terror, Artevelde shut the window and attempted to escape out the back door to an adjoining church, but the mob of 400 men broke down the doors, seized and slew him on the spot. Thus in July 1345 Fortune's Wheel brought down the great master of Flanders.

Afterward representatives of the Flemish towns hurried to England to appease King Edward, who was in a great wrath at the event. Assuring him of the alliance, they suggested a way in which his line could still inherit Flanders without dispossessing the rightful lord. Let Edward's eldest daughter, Isabella, then aged thirteen, marry the Count of Flanders' fourteen-year-old son Louis, who was in the communes' custody, "so that ever after the county of Flaunders shall be in the issue of your chylde." Edward was much taken with the scheme, although the prospective bridegroom, out of loyalty to France, was not. When Edward tried to force the betrothal on him two years later, the Count's escape, leaving behind an unwed princess, was to impinge indirectly but decisively on the life of Enguerrand de Coucy.

To contemporaries the power of the King of England seemed puny compared with that of the King of France; Villani referred to him as *"il piccolo re d'Inghilterra"* (the little King of England). It is doubtful if he actually intended to conquer France. Medieval wars between Europeans were not aimed at strategic conquest but rather at seizure of dynastic rule at the top by inflicting enough damage to bring about downfall of the opponent. Something like this was probably Edward's aim, and owing to his base in Guienne and his footholds in Flanders and northern France, it would not have seemed unrealizable.

The first abortive phase had been so costly as to have been ruinous if Edward had absorbed the cost; instead, he passed on the ruin to others. He had financed the war through loans underwritten by the great Florentine banking firms of the Bardi and Peruzzi. The sums, according to Villani, amounted to between 600,000 and 900,000 gold florins owed to the Bardi and two-thirds as much to the Peruzzi, secured on expected revenue from the wool tax. When this brought in too little and Edward could not repay, the drain on the Italian companies bankrupted them. The Peruzzi failed in 1343, the Bardi suspended a year later, and their crash brought down a third firm, the Acciaiuoli. Capital vanished, stores and workshops closed, wages and purchases stopped. When, by the malignant chance that seemed to hound the 14th century, economic devastation in Florence and Siena was followed first by famine in 1347 and then by plague, it could not but seem to the unfortunate people that the anger of God had been loosed upon them.

To raise an army for a second assault after being bankrupted by the first would have been impossible without the consent of the three estates represented in Parliament. Money was the crux. Raising money to pay the cost of war was to cause more damage to 14th century society than the physical destruction of war itself. The governing fact was that medieval organization by this time had passed to a predominantly money economy. Armed forces were no longer primarily feudal levies serving under a vassal's obligation who went home after forty days; they were recruited bodies who served for pay. The added expense of a paid army raised the cost of war beyond the ordinary means of the sovereign. Without losing its appetite for war, the inchoate state had not yet devised a regular method to pay for it. When he overspent, the sovereign resorted to loans from bankers, towns, and businesses which he might not be able to repay, and to the even more disruptive measures of arbitrary taxation and devaluation of the coinage.

Above all, war was made to pay for itself through pillage. Booty and ransom were not just a bonus, but a necessity to take the place of arrears in pay and to induce enlistment. The taking of prisoners for ransom became a commercial enterprise. Since kings could rarely raise sufficient funds in advance, and collection of taxes was slow, troops in the field were always ahead of their pay. Loot on campaign took the place of the paymaster. Chivalric war, like chivalric love, was, as Michelet said of the whole epoch, *double et louche* (a provocative phrase which could mean "double and squinting" or "equivocal" or "shady" in the sense of disreputable). The aim was one thing and the practice another. Knights pursued war for glory and practiced it for gain.

In 1344 the three estates in Parliament were informed by Edward of a breach of the truce by the King of France and asked to "show their opinion." The advice of Lords and Commons was "to end the war either by battle or honorable peace," and, once attempted, not to abandon the effort at letters or requests of the Pope or anyone else, "but to end the same by dint of the Sword." Clergy and Commons voted subsidies, and in 1345 Parliament authorized the King to require all landowners to serve in person or supply a substitute or a monetary equivalent. A man with £5 of income from land or rents was to supply an archer, a £10 income supplied a mounted spearman, £20 supplied two of these, income over £25 supplied a man-at-arms, meaning usually a squire or knight. Towns and shires were required to raise a given number of archers, and the system as a whole was to be administered by sheriffs and county officials.

Ships had to be requisitioned to carry men and horses and initial food for both. They also carried millstones and bake ovens, armorers and their forges, and extra materials to keep the bowmen supplied with arrows. Most ships were small, averaging 30 to 50 tons, with one large mast and a rectangular sail, although some ranged up to 200 tons. A medium-sized ship carried 100 to 200 men and 80 to 100 horses.

To fill out the ranks of "arrayed" or drafted foot soldiers, men were recruited by promise of loot, by pardons of those under sentence of outlawry, and by promoting anti-French feeling already aroused by French raids on Southampton, Portsmouth, and other south-coast towns. King Edward's assumption of the title of King of France was proclaimed to the people along with his messages on the justice of his cause and the wickedness of France. Under the ever-present fear of French invasion, warning beacons were planted along the coast, bodies of armed men and horses stationed at intervals, stores laid by, and small ships drawn close in to land or onto the beach—not without economic disruption.

In July 1346 the King was ready for his renewed attempt. Accompanied by his eldest son, fifteen-year-old Edward, Prince of Wales, he set sail for Normandy with 4,000 men-at-arms and 10,000 archers plus a number of Irish and Welsh foot soldiers. (Another force, sent earlier on the longer voyage to Bordeaux, had already engaged French forces along the frontiers of Guienne.) Guided by Godefrey d'Harcourt, who had been banished from France, the King's expeditionary force landed on the Cotentin Peninsula, where Harcourt promised rich opportunities for loot in the prosperous unwalled towns of his province. Although Edward "desired nothing so much as deeds of arms," according to Froissart, he also, in another case of medieval squinting, apparently welcomed Harcourt's promise that he would meet no resistance because the Duke of Normandy and his knights were fighting the English in Guienne and the people of Normandy were not used to war.

So fruitful proved Normandy that the English needed to make no further provision for their host, and so unwarlike that the inhabitants fled, leaving their houses "well-stuffed and granges full of corn for they wist not how to save and keep it. . . . Before that time they had never seen men of war nor they wist not what war or battle meant." At prosperous Caen, which was unwalled, the townspeople and a force of knights sent to the defense under the Constable, Comte d'Eu, offered a vigorous defense, but the English, drawing on prepared reinforcements, prevailed. The Constable was captured and, along with many other prisoners and wagons full of booty, was sent back to England to be held for a great ransom that was to have tragic consequences. "Burning, plundering and laying waste," the English advanced from town to town, gathering up rich draperies, jewels, plate, merchandise, livestock, and men and women as captives.

The sack of Normandy by an army led by the King of England himself was the prototype of all that was to follow. Organized in three corps or "battles," the invaders "overran, spoiled and robbed without mercy," finding so much booty that they "rode but small journeys and every day took their lodgings between noon and three of the clock." The soldiers "made no count to the King or his officers of what they did get; they kept that to themselves." While they moved along one side of the Seine toward Paris, King Philip, who had been at Rouen without taking action, followed them along the other side and re-entered Paris as Edward reached Poissy, twenty miles west of the city. Here, while the King of England kept the Feast of Our Lady in mid-August in robes of scarlet furred in ermine, his army burned and plundered surrounding villages. The flames at their gates struck the citizens of Paris with "stupefied amazement," wrote Jean de Venette, "and I who have written this saw all these deeds, for they could be seen from Paris by anyone who would ascend a turret."

Philip VI had meanwhile issued the *arrière-ban* or general summons to all capable of bearing arms in the war area. Based on the principle that all subjects owed their lives to "defense of country and crown," the general summons was supposed to be used only when the call to nobles had not or would not suffice to repel the enemy. It was issued, like all public announcements, by "public cry"—that is, by heralds riding forth to proclaim the order aloud in market place and village square. Individual letters also went to towns and abbeys, requisitioning the customary subsidies. Some towns still paid their service in bodies of foot soldiers, hastily assembled, untrained, and virtually useless; others paid in money, which permitted the hiring of more effective mercenaries.

Non-noble military contingents were furnished by towns and districts according to number of hearths and the relative prosperity or poverty of the community. In some regions every 100 hearths were obligated to pay for one soldier for one year. In poorer districts the obligation might be one soldier for every 200 or 300 hearths. The number of effectives raised at this rate was not large: in 1337, for example, Rouen supplied 200 men, Narbonne 150 crossbowmen, Nîmes 95 men-at-arms. In the light of these figures, the chroniclers' buxom references to tens of thousands shrivel to a more modest reality. Each levy from town, district, fief, or area of special status had to be negotiated separately at a different rate, for a different duration, and on the basis of different rights and privileges, causing endless disputes in the process. Lords of duchies and counties and great baronies like Coucy paid their own men through their own treasurer, although as the war stretched on they had to be recompensed by the King.

Knights and squires of noble estate received fixed rates of pay like other men. For banneret (a lord who led other knights under his banner), bachelor knight, and mounted squire the standard rate in the 1340s was respectively 20, 10, and 6 to 7 sous a day. A persistent problem was the need to make sure that a ruler was getting the count and quality he paid for. To this end a *montre* or review was held periodically, generally every month, by officials with watchful eye to see that a *valet* was not counted as a *gentilhomme*, that sound horses were not substituted for nags during the review and then withdrawn, and that pay was honestly distributed in coin and not in kind. In a loosely structured army, hierarchy of command was lacking. Apart from the King, who led in person, the permanent officials were the Constable, a kind of administrative chief of armed forces, and two Marshals of indeterminate function; otherwise, military decisions seem to have been reached by group council among the leaders.

Because of the necessity of donning armor with all its straps and buckles, battle was a more or less fixed engagement, arranged by the logic of approaching positions. The invention of plate armor early in the 14th century now supplemented chain mail, which was penetrable by the crossbow. While styles of armor varied and changed from one decade to the next, the basics were a suit of plate armor consisting of a chest piece, a skirt of linked hoops, and arm and leg pieces, all worn over a hauberk or shirt of chain mail and a leather or padded tunic, or a tight-fitting surcoat. Over the plate was worn a sleeveless jerkin embroidered with the coat-of-arms identifying the wearer. Chain mail covered the neck, elbows, and other joints; gauntlets of linked plates protected the hands. The helmet, formerly open over the face, now had the added protection of a visor hinged by removable pins at the brow or on the side. Weighing seven to eleven pounds, it was dark and stuffy inside, despite eye slits and ventilation holes. The weight of all the added protection was somewhat compensated by a smaller shield that allowed greater freedom of action.

"A terrible worm in an iron cocoon," as he was called in an anonymous poem, the knight rode on a saddle rising in a high ridge above the horse's backbone with his feet resting in very long stirrups so that he was virtually standing up and able to deliver tremendous swinging blows from side to side with any one of his armory of weapons. He began battle with the lance used for unhorsing the enemy, while from his belt hung a two-handed sword at one side and an eighteen-inch dagger on the other. He also had available, either attached to his saddle or carried by his squire, a longer sword for thrusting like a lance, a battle-ax fitted with a spike behind the curved blade, and a club-headed mace with sharpened, ridged edges, a weapon favored by martial bishops and abbots on the theory that it did not come under the rule forbidding clerics "to smite with the edge of the sword." The war-horse carrying this burden was itself armored by plates protecting nose, chest, and rump and caparisoned with draperies that got in the way of its legs. When his horse was felled, the knight, weighed down by his armor and tangled in weapons, shield, and spurs, was likely to be captured before he could manage to rise.

Tactics on the continent were simply the cavalry charge of knights followed by hand-to-hand fighting on foot, sometimes preceded or supplemented by archers and infantry, both of which the knights despised. In the Scottish wars, however, the English had found that foot soldiers equipped with the longbow and trained to keep a disciplined line could, by aiming at the horses, throw back a charge of mounted knights. A really useful discovery of this kind will take precedence over class disdain. Given the constant intercourse between France and England, the French must have seen the longbow in use, evidently without giving thought to its implications for themselves. French chivalry refused to concede a serious role in war to the non-noble, even though the Normans had once captured England by virtue of the archer who shot Harold through his eye.

The French too used archers and crossbowmen, usually hired companies of Genoese who made the crossbow a specialty, but when their blood was up, they hated to give the crossbow the scope for action that would take the edge off the clash of knights. Chivalry maintained that the combat of warriors must be personal and bodily; missiles that permitted combat at a distance were held in scorn. The first archer, according to a 12th century song, was "a coward who dared not come close to his foe." Nevertheless, when it came to fighting commoners as at Cassel in 1328, the French had given their crossbowmen the tactical scope that accounted for that victory.

The crossbow, made of wood, steel, and sinew, and pulled by aid of the archer's foot in a stirrup and a hook or winding handle attached to his belt, or by a complicated arrangement of winches and pulleys, shot a bolt of great penetrating power, but the bow was slow and cumbersome to wield and heavy to carry. The crossbowman usually carried about fifty bolts with him into action, and his equipment en route had to be transported by wagon. Owing to the long wind-up, the crossbow was in fact more useful in static situations such as clearing ramparts in sieges than in open battle. A charge of knights willing to take some losses could generally shatter the crossbowmen's line. Although its mechanical power when first invented had been frightening so that it was banned by the Church in 1139, the crossbow had continued in use for 200 years without threatening the knights' mailed dominion.

Protected by plate armor and the pride of chivalry, the noble felt himself invulnerable and invincible and became increasingly contemptuous of the foot soldier. He believed that commoners, being excluded from chivalry, could never be relied upon in war. As grooms, baggage attendants, foragers, and road-builders—the equivalent of engineer corps—they were necessary, but as soldiers in leather jerkins armed with pikes and billhooks, they were considered an encumbrance who in a sharp fight would "melt away like snow in sunshine." This was not simple snobbism but a reflection of experience in the absence of training. The Middle Ages had no equivalent of the Roman legion. Towns maintained trained bands of municipal police, but they tended to fill up their contingents for national defense with riff-raff good for nothing else. Abbeys had better use for their peasants than to employ their time in military drill. In any epoch the difference between a rabble and an army is training, which was not bestowed on foot soldiers called up by the *arrière-ban*. Despised as ineffective, they were ineffective because they were despised.

On August 26, 1346, the English and French armies met at Crécy in Picardy 30 miles inland from the coast. Like the clash in another

August in 1914, the battle opened an era of augmenting violence and disintegrating control. It had not been planned by the victors. Informed of the great host that was gathering around the French King in answer to his summons, Edward showed no desire for a confrontation, or at least not without first securing his retreat. Turning away from Paris, he marched northwestward toward the Channel coast, presumably making for Flanders, where he could be sure of ships. If that was his objective, it was not likely to make him King of France.

The French army by forced marches caught up with the English before they could reach the sea, but not before Edward, realizing he would have to fight, took up a good defensive position on a broad hill above the village of Crécy. So confident were the French nobles before the battle that they talked of whom they would take prisoner among their opponents, whose repute and combat records they knew from tournaments. Only King Philip was irresolute. "Mournful and anxious," he seemed to fear some further treason after the defections of Brittany and Harcourt, or some other hidden peril.

Camping too far from the enemy on the night before combat, his troops did not reach the battlefield until four P.M., with the sun in their faces and at the enemy's back. The crossbowmen were tired and complaining after the long march, and their bowstrings were wet from a sudden storm, whereas the English archers had protected their bowstrings by rolling them up under their helmets. What followed on the French side was a chaos of mindless audacity, bad luck, mistakes, indiscipline, and the knights' chronic disease of bravado, intent on proving valor devoid of tactical sense or organized plan.

Seized by last-minute advice to postpone action until the next day, Philip issued orders for the vanguard to turn back and the rear guard to halt, but he was not obeyed. Without giving the crossbowmen a chance to soften the English line, the forward knights plunged uphill against the enemy. Out of range of their targets and pierced by English arrows, the Genoese crossbowmen fell back, throwing down their bows. The King, who on sighting the English changed color "because he hated them," lost control of the situation. Seeing the Genoese flee, either he or his brother, the Count d'Alençon, shouted, "Slay these rascals who get in our way!" while his knights "in haste and evil order" slashed at the archers in their effort to cut a way through. Out of this terrible tangle in their own ranks, the French launched attack after attack upon the enemy but the disciplined line of England's longbowmen, stiffened by the long practice their weapon required, held firm and sowed confusion and death by their missiles. Then English knights advanced on foot, preceded by archers and supported by pikemen and murderous Welsh with long knives who went among the fallen and slew them on the ground. The Prince of Wales fought at the head of one battle group while King Edward retained command from a windmill on the hilltop. Through the failing light and on through darkness until midnight the melee continued until King Philip, wounded, was led away by the Count of Hainault, who said to him, "Sire, lose not yourself willfully" and, taking his horse's bridle, pulled him from the field. With no more than five companions, the King rode through the night to a castle whose seneschal, summoned to open his gate, demanded the name of the summoner. "Open your gate quickly," said the King, "for this is the fortune of France."

Dead upon the field lay some 4,000 of the French army, perhaps including Enguerrand de Coucy VI. Among the fallen were the greatest names of French and allied chivalry: the Count d'Alençon, brother of the King, Count Louis de Nevers of Flanders, the Counts of St. Pol and Sancerre, the Duke of Lorraine, the King of Majorca, and, most renowned of all, King John the Blind of Bohemia, whose crest of three ostrich feathers with the motto "*Ich dien*" was taken by the Prince of Wales and attached to his title thereafter. Charles of Bohemia, the blind King's son and future Emperor, less rash than his father, saw what was coming and escaped.

It was no lack of prowess that defeated the French and allied knights. They fought as valiantly as the English, for knights were much the same in all countries. England's advantage lay in combining the use of those excluded from chivalry—the Welsh knifemen, the pikemen, and, above all, the trained yeomen who pulled the longbow—with the action of the armored knight. So long as one side in the contest made use of this advantage while the other side did not, the fortunes of war were to remain unbalanced.

Pursuit for the strategic purpose of destroying the enemy's armed forces did not belong in the medieval lexicon of war. Evidently somewhat stunned by his own victory, Edward made no effort to pursue. Absorbed in the riches of conquest, the English spent the day after the battle in counting and identifying the dead, giving honorable burial to the noblest, and reckoning the ransoms of prisoners. Afterward, despite his claim to be King of France, Edward appeared to lose interest in Philip, who had taken refuge in Amiens. Keeping to the coast, the English marched north to assault Calais, the port opposite Dover where the Channel is narrowest. Here, blocked by a tenacious defense, they bogged down in a siege that was to last a year.

The defeat of French chivalry and of the supposedly most powerful sovereign in Europe started a train of reactions that were to grow more serious with time. Although it did not bring down the French monarchy nor bring it to terms, it did cause a crisis of confidence in the royal government, and a general resentment when the King once more had to resort to extraordinary taxation. From this date, too, began an erosion of belief in the nobles' performance of their function.

Philip had neither the instinct for rule possessed by Philip the Fair and St. Louis, nor councillors capable of reforming the military and financial customs to meet the new dangers that had come upon them. The provincial estates whose consent was required for new taxes were reluctant, like most representative bodies, to recognize crisis until it was underfoot. Given an inadequate and obsolete system, the King had to devise substitutes like the sales tax—called *maltôte* because it was so hated—or the equally unpopular salt tax; or else he fell back on devaluing the coinage. In disruption of prices, rents, debts, and credit, the effect of this subterfuge for taxation was regularly disastrous. "And in the year 1343 Philip of Valois made 15 deniers worth three," wrote one chronicler in sufficient comment.

Each time they were summoned to vote aids, the Estates voiced their loud discontent with fiscal abuses. Each time they made their grudging subsidies contingent on stated reforms, in the belief that better management by more honest men would enable the King once again to live of his own.

After Crécy and the loss of Calais, a new Estates General was summoned in 1347 to meet the King's desperate need of money for defense. Armed forces and a fleet had to be reconstructed against the danger of renewed invasion. Sharpened by the shame of steady defeats, the Estates' displeasure with the royal government was outspoken. "You should know," they told the King, "how and by what counsel you have conducted your wars and how you, by bad counsel, have lost all and gained nothing." If he had had good counsel, they said, no prince in the world "should have been able to do ill to you and your subjects." They reminded him how he had gone to Crécy and Calais "in great company, at great cost and great expense [14th century speakers and writers had an affinity for double statements] and how you were treated shamefully and sent back scurvily and made to grant all manner of truces even while the enemy were in your kingdom. . . . And by such counsel have you been dishonored." After this scolding, the Estates, acknowledging the need for defenses, promised subsidies, but on rather indefinite terms.

While besieging Calais, Edward still hoped to cement an alliance with Flanders by his daughter's marriage to the young Count Louis de

Male. The death at Crécy of the boy's father, Count Louis de Nevers, removed the main obstacle. But fifteen-year-old Louis, "who had been ever nourished among the noble men of France," would not agree and "ever he said he would not wed her whose father had slain his, though he might have half the whole realm of England." When the Flemings saw that their lord was "too much French and evil counseled," they put him in "courteous prison" until he should agree to accept their counsel, which greatly annoyed him, so that after several months in prison he gave the required promise. Released, he was allowed to go hawking by the river, but kept under such close surveillance lest he should steal away "that he could not piss without their knowledge." Under this treatment he finally agreed to wed.

Early in March 1347 the King and Queen of England with their daughter Isabelle came up from Calais to Flanders. The betrothal took place in great ceremony, the marriage contract was drawn, the wedding day fixed for the first week in April, and lavish gifts were prepared by the royal parents. Louis continued to go hawking daily by the river, making pretense that the marriage pleased him greatly, so that the Flemings relaxed their watch. But they misjudged their lord's outward countenance, "for his inward courage was all French."

In the same week that the marriage was to take place, he rode forth as usual with his falconer. Casting his hawk after a heron with the call "Hoie! Hoie!" he followed the flight until at some distance off he "dashed his spurs to his horse and galloped forth," not stopping until he was over the border in France, where he joined King Philip and told him how with "great subtlety" he had escaped the English marriage. The King was overjoyed and speedily arranged Louis' marriage with Margaret of Brabant, daughter of the Duke of Brabant, Flanders' neighbor on the east, who was closely allied to France. The insult to the English crown was sharp, and doubtless sharper to the fifteen-year-old bride. Her feelings could not have been soothed by a song written in her name and, according to Jean de Venette, sung everywhere in France with the refrain, "*J'ay failli à celui à qui je estoie donnée par amour*" (I have lost him whose love I was given to be). Four years later she revenged herself on a different bridegroom by jilting him in her turn almost at the church door. Either because these aborted betrothals gave her a taste for independence, or because she had a character notoriously willful, Isabelle of England was still unmarried when she met Enguerrand de Coucy VII thirteen years later.

The capture of Calais a few months after the Flemish marital fiasco was the single great result of the campaign. Philip had assembled a relief force and started toward the city, but, hampered by lack of money and the losses after Crécy, turned away without fighting. Waiting for the relief that never came and cut off from food, the citizens of Calais held out until, reduced to eating rats and mice and even excrement, they were starved into surrender. Recently wounded, their captain, Jean de Vienne, bare-headed and holding his sword reversed in token of submission, rode through the gate to hand over the keys of the city to the English. Walking behind him barefoot in their shirts were the six richest burghers with halters around their necks to signify the victor's right to hang them at will. In that somber scene, watched by the hollow-eyed, desolate survivors, a French cause was born: to retrieve Calais.

Exasperated by the prolonged resistance which had dragged him, against the medieval habit, through a winter's siege, Edward was in a furious mood and would have hung the six burghers but for Queen Philippa's moving plea for mercy. The drawn-out effort from August 1346 to August 1347 had soured his troops and exhausted his resources. Provisions, horses, arms, and reinforcements had to be brought from England, where the requisitioning of grain and cattle caused hardship, and the necessary mobilizing of ships wrecked commerce, reducing revenues from the wool-export tax. It has been estimated that some 32,000 combatants, plus the crews of ships and all the service troops needed for the siege, making a total of 60,000 to 80,000 men, were employed in the course of the Crécy-Calais campaign. The drain having reached its limits, Edward could not advance from his victory. The new foothold in France led nowhere but to acceptance of a truce running until April 1351.

If belligerents could make sober judgments during the course of a war, which they rarely can, the first ten years of the Anglo-French contest would have shown the English how inconclusive were their triumphs: to win a smashing naval victory, a smashing field victory, and a permanent foothold on the coast was still far from conquering France or its crown. But the taste of plunder, the gorgeous stuffs and rich ransoms flowing to England, and the glory and renown of Crécy cried by the heralds in public places had excited English blood. On their side, the French would now never stop short of the goal that the poet Eustache Deschamps was to make his refrain forty years later: "No peace until they give back Calais." Crécy and Calais ensured that the war would go on—but not yet, for Europe in 1347 stood on the edge of the most lethal catastrophe in recorded history.

Chapter 5

"This Is the End of the World": The Black Death

In October 1347, two months after the fall of Calais, Genoese trading ships put into the harbor of Messina in Sicily with dead and dying men at the oars. The ships had come from the Black Sea port of Caffa (now Feodosiya) in the Crimea, where the Genoese maintained a trading post. The diseased sailors showed strange black swellings about the size of an egg or an apple in the armpits and groin. The swellings oozed blood and pus and were followed by spreading boils and black blotches on the skin from internal bleeding. The sick suffered severe pain and died quickly within five days of the first symptoms. As the disease spread, other symptoms of continuous fever and spitting of blood appeared instead of the swellings or buboes. These victims coughed and sweated heavily and died even more quickly, within three days or less, sometimes in 24 hours. In both types everything that issued from the body—breath, sweat, blood from the buboes and lungs, bloody urine, and blood-blackened excrement—smelled foul. Depression and despair accompanied the physical symptoms, and before the end "death is seen seated on the face."

The disease was bubonic plague, present in two forms: one that infected the bloodstream, causing the buboes and internal bleeding, and was spread by contact; and a second, more virulent pneumonic type that infected the lungs and was spread by respiratory infection. The presence of both at once cause the high mortality and speed of contagion. So lethal was the disease that cases were known of persons going to bed well and dying before they woke, of doctors catching the illness at a bedside and dying before the patient. So rapidly did it spread from one to another that to a French physician, Simon de

Covino, it seemed as if one sick person "could infect the whole world." The malignity of the pestilence appeared more terrible because its victims knew no prevention and no remedy.

The physical suffering of the disease and its aspect of evil mystery were expressed in a strange Welsh lament which saw "death coming into our midst like black smoke, a plague which cuts off the young, a rootless phantom which has no mercy for fair countenance. Woe is me of the shilling in the armpit! It is seething, terrible . . . a head that gives pain and causes a loud cry . . . a painful angry knob . . . Great is its seething like a burning cinder . . . a grievous thing of ashy color." Its eruption is ugly like the "seeds of black peas, broken fragments of brittle sea-coal . . . the early ornaments of black death, cinders of the peelings of the cockle weed, a mixed multitude, a black plague like halfpence, like berries. . . ."

Rumors of a terrible plague supposedly arising in China and spreading through Tartary (Central Asia) to India and Persia, Mesopotamia, Syria, Egypt, and all of Asia Minor had reached Europe in 1346. They told of a death toll so devastating that all of India was said to be depopulated, whole territories covered by dead bodies, other areas with no one left alive. As added up by Pope Clement VI at Avignon, the total of reported dead reached 23,840,000. In the absence of a concept of contagion, no serious alarm was felt in Europe until the trading ships brought their black burden of pestilence into Messina while other infected ships from the Levant carried it to Genoa and Venice.

By January 1348 it penetrated France via Marseille, and North Africa via Tunis. Shipborne along coasts and navigable rivers, it spread westward from Marseille through the ports of Languedoc to Spain and northward up the Rhône to Avignon, where it arrived in March. It reached Narbonne, Montpellier, Carcassonne, and Toulouse between February and May, and at the same time in Italy spread to Rome and Florence and their hinterlands. Between June and August it reached Bordeaux, Lyon, and Paris, spread to Burgundy and Normandy, and crossed the Channel from Normandy into southern England. From Italy during the same summer it crossed the Alps into Switzerland and reached eastward to Hungary.

In a given area the plague accomplished its kill within four to six months and then faded, except in the larger cities, where, rooting into the close-quartered population, it abated during the winter, only to reappear in spring and rage for another six months.

In 1349 it resumed in Paris, spread to Picardy, Flanders, and the Low Countries, and from England to Scotland and Ireland as well as to

Norway, where a ghost ship with a cargo of wool and a dead crew drifted offshore until it ran aground near Bergen. From there the plague passed into Sweden, Denmark, Prussia, Iceland, and as far as Greenland. Leaving a strange pocket of immunity in Bohemia, and Russia unattacked until 1351, it had passed from most of Europe by mid-1350. Although the mortality rate was erratic, ranging from one fifth in some places to nine tenths or almost total elimination in others, the overall estimate of modern demographers has settled—for the area extending from India to Iceland—around the same figure expressed in Froissart's casual words: "a third of the world died." His estimate, the common one at the time, was not an inspired guess but a borrowing of St. John's figure for mortality from plague in Revelation, the favorite guide to human affairs of the Middle Ages.

A third of Europe would have meant about 20 million deaths. No one knows in truth how many died. Contemporary reports were an awed impression, not an accurate count. In crowded Avignon, it was said, 400 died daily; 7,000 houses emptied by death were shut up; a single graveyard received 11,000 corpses in six weeks; half the city's inhabitants reportedly died, including 9 cardinals or one third of the total, and 70 lesser prelates. Watching the endlessly passing death carts, chroniclers let normal exaggeration take wings and put the Avignon death toll at 62,000 and even at 120,000, although the city's total population was probably less than 50,000.

When graveyards filled up, bodies at Avignon were thrown into the Rhône until mass burial pits were dug for dumping the corpses. In London in such pits corpses piled up in layers until they overflowed. Everywhere reports speak of the sick dying too fast for the living to bury. Corpses were dragged out of homes and left in front of doorways. Morning light revealed new piles of bodies. In Florence the dead were gathered up by the Compagnia della Misericordia—founded in 1244 to care for the sick—whose members wore red robes and hoods masking the face except for the eyes. When their efforts failed, the dead lay putrid in the streets for days at a time. When no coffins were to be had, the bodies were laid on boards, two or three at once, to be carried to graveyards or common pits. Families dumped their own relatives into the pits, or buried them so hastily and thinly "that dogs dragged them forth and devoured their bodies."

Amid accumulating death and fear of contagion, people died without last rites and were buried without prayers, a prospect that terrified the last hours of the stricken. A bishop in England gave permission to laymen to make confession to each other as was done by the Apostles, "or if no man is present then even to a woman," and if no priest could be found to administer extreme unction, "then faith must suffice." Clement VI found it necessary to grant remissions of sin to all who died of the plague because so many were unattended by priests. "And no bells tolled," wrote a chronicler of Siena, "and nobody wept no matter what his loss because almost everyone expected death. . . . And people said and believed, 'This is the end of the world.' "

In Paris, where the plague lasted through 1349, the reported death rate was 800 a day, in Pisa 500, in Vienna 500 to 600. The total dead in Paris numbered 50,000 or half the population. Florence, weakened by the famine of 1347, lost three to four fifths of its citizens, Venice two thirds, Hamburg and Bremen, though smaller in size, about the same proportion. Cities, as centers of transportation, were more likely to be affected than villages, although once a village was infected, its death rate was equally high. At Givry, a prosperous village in Burgundy of 1,200 to 1,500 people, the parish register records 615 deaths in the space of fourteen weeks, compared to an average of thirty deaths a year in the previous decade. In three villages of Cambridgeshire, manorial records show a death rate of 47 percent, 57 percent, and in one case 70 percent. When the last survivors, too few to carry on, moved away, a deserted village sank back into the wilderness and disappeared from the map altogether, leaving only a grass-covered ghostly outline to show where mortals once had lived.

In enclosed places such as monasteries and prisons, the infection of one person usually meant that of all, as happened in the Franciscan convents of Carcassonne and Marseille, where every inmate without exception died. Of the 140 Dominicans at Montpellier only seven survived. Petrarch's brother Gherardo, member of a Carthusian monastery, buried the prior and 34 fellow monks one by one, sometimes three a day, until he was left alone with his dog and fled to look for a place that would take him in. Watching every comrade die, men in such places could not but wonder whether the strange peril that filled the air had not been sent to exterminate the human race. In Kilkenny, Ireland, Brother John Clyn of the Friars Minor, another monk left alone among dead men, kept a record of what had happened lest "things which should be remembered perish with time and vanish from the memory of those who come after us." Sensing "the whole world, as it were, placed within the grasp of the Evil One," and waiting for death to visit him too, he wrote, "I leave parchment to continue this work, if perchance any man survive and any of the race of Adam escape this pestilence and carry on the work which I have begun." Brother John, as noted by another hand, died of the pestilence, but he foiled oblivion.

The largest cities of Europe, with populations of about 100,000, were Paris and Florence, Venice and Genoa. At the next level, with more than 50,000, were Ghent and Bruges in Flanders, Milan, Bologna, Rome, Naples, and Palermo, and Cologne. London hovered below 50,000, the only city in England except York with more than 10,000. At the level of 20,000 to 50,000 were Bordeaux, Toulouse, Montpellier, Marseille, and Lyon in France, Barcelona, Seville, and Toledo in Spain, Siena, Pisa, and other secondary cities in Italy, and the Hanseatic trading cities of the Empire. The plague raged through them all, killing anywhere from one third to two thirds of their inhabitants. Italy, with a total population of 10 to 11 million, probably suffered the heaviest toll. Following the Florentine bankruptcies, the crop failures and workers' riots of 1346–47, the revolt of Cola di Rienzi that plunged Rome into anarchy, the plague came as the peak of successive calamities. As if the world were indeed in the grasp of the Evil One, its first appearance on the European mainland in January 1348 coincided with a fearsome earthquake that carved a path of wreckage from Naples up to Venice. Houses collapsed, church towers toppled, villages were crushed, and the destruction reached as far as Germany and Greece. Emotional response, dulled by horrors, underwent a kind of atrophy epitomized by the chronicler who wrote, "And in these days was burying without sorrowe and wedding without friendschippe."

In Siena, where more than half the inhabitants died of the plague, work was abandoned on the great cathedral, planned to be the largest in the world, and never resumed, owing to loss of workers and master masons and "the melancholy and grief" of the survivors. The cathedral's truncated transept still stands in permanent witness to the sweep of death's scythe. Agnolo di Tura, a chronicler of Siena, recorded the fear of contagion that froze every other instinct. "Father abandoned child, wife husband, one brother another," he wrote, "for this plague seemed to strike through the breath and sight. And so they died. And no one could be found to bury the dead for money or friendship. . . . And I, Angolo di Tura, called the Fat, buried my five children with my own hands, and so did many others likewise."

There were many to echo his account of inhumanity and few to balance it, for the plague was not the kind of calamity that inspired mutual help. Its loathsomeness and deadliness did not herd people together in mutual distress, but only prompted their desire to escape each other. "Magistrates and notaries refused to come and make the wills of the dying," reported a Franciscan friar of Piazza in Sicily; what was worse, "even the priests did not come to hear their confessions." A clerk of the Archbishop of Canterbury reported the same of English priests who "turned away from the care of their benefices from fear of death." Cases of parents deserting children and children their parents were reported across Europe from Scotland to Russia. The calamity chilled the hearts of men, wrote Boccaccio in his famous account of the plague in Florence that serves as introduction to the *Decameron.* "One man shunned another . . . kinsfolk held aloof, brother was forsaken by brother, oftentimes husband by wife; nay, what is more, and scarcely to be believed, fathers and mothers were found to abandon their own children to their fate, untended, unvisited as if they had been strangers." Exaggeration and literary pessimism were common in the 14th century, but the Pope's physician, Guy de Chauliac, was a sober, careful observer who reported the same phenomenon: "A father did not visit his son, nor the son his father. Charity was dead."

Yet not entirely. In Paris, according to the chronicler Jean de Venette, the nuns of the Hôtel Dieu or municipal hospital, "having no fear of death, tended the sick with all sweetness and humility." New nuns repeatedly took the places of those who died, until the majority "many times renewed by death now rest in peace with Christ as we may piously believe."

When the plague entered northern France in July 1348, it settled first in Normandy and, checked by winter, gave Picardy a deceptive interim until the next summer. Either in mourning or warning, black flags were flown from church towers of the worst-stricken villages of Normandy. "And in that time," wrote a monk of the abbey of Fourcarment, "the mortality was so great among the people of Normandy that those of Picardy mocked them." The same unneighborly reaction was reported of the Scots, separated by a winter's immunity from the English. Delighted to hear of the disease that was scourging the "southrons," they gathered forces for an invasion, "laughing at their enemies." Before they could move, the savage mortality fell upon them too, scattering some in death and the rest in panic to spread the infection as they fled.

In Picardy in the summer of 1349 the pestilence penetrated the castle of Coucy to kill Enguerrand's mother, Catherine, and her new husband. Whether her nine-year-old son escaped by chance or was perhaps living elsewhere with one of his guardians is unrecorded. In nearby Amiens, tannery workers, responding quickly to losses in the labor force, combined to bargain for higher wages. In another place villagers were seen dancing to drums and trumpets, and on being asked the reason, answered that, seeing their neighbors die day by day while their village remained immune, they believed they could keep the plague from entering "by the jollity that is in us. That is why we dance." Further north in Tournai on the border of Flanders, Gilles li Muisis, Abbot of St. Martin's, kept one of the epidemic's most vivid accounts. The passing bells rang all day and all night, he recorded, because sextons were anxious to obtain their fees while they could. Filled with the sound of mourning, the city became oppressed by fear, so that the authorities forbade the tolling of bells and the wearing of black and restricted funeral services to two mourners. The silencing of funeral bells and of criers' announcements of deaths was ordained by most cities. Siena imposed a fine on the wearing of mourning clothes by all except widows.

Flight was the chief recourse of those who could afford it or arrange it. The rich fled to their country places like Boccaccio's young patricians of Florence, who settled in a pastoral palace "removed on every side from the roads" with "wells of cool water and vaults of rare wines." The urban poor died in their burrows, "and only the stench of their bodies informed neighbors of their death." That the poor were more heavily afflicted than the rich was clearly remarked at the time, in the north as in the south. A Scottish chronicler, John of Fordun, stated flatly that the pest "attacked especially the meaner sort and common people—seldom the magnates." Simon de Covino of Montpellier made the same observation. He ascribed it to the misery and want and hard lives that made the poor more susceptible, which was half the truth. Close contact and lack of sanitation was the unrecognized other half. It was noticed too that the young died in greater proportion than the old; Simon de Covino compared the disappearance of youth to the withering of flowers in the fields.

In the countryside peasants dropped dead on the roads, in the fields, in their houses. Survivors in growing helplessness fell into apathy, leaving ripe wheat uncut and livestock untended. Oxen and asses, sheep and goats, pigs and chickens ran wild and they too, according to local reports, succumbed to the pest. English sheep, bearers of the precious wool, died throughout the country. The chronicler Henry Knighton, canon of Leicester Abbey, reported 5,000 dead in one field alone, "their bodies so corrupted by the plague that neither beast nor bird would touch them," and spreading an appalling stench. In the Austrian Alps wolves came down to prey upon sheep and then, "as if alarmed by some invisible warning, turned and fled back into the wilderness." In remote Dalmatia bolder wolves descended upon a plague-stricken city and attacked human survivors. For want of herdsmen, cattle strayed from place to place and died in hedgerows and ditches. Dogs and cats fell like the rest.

The dearth of labor held a fearful prospect because the 14th century lived close to the annual harvest both for food and for next year's seed. "So few servants and laborers were left," wrote Knighton, "that no one knew where to turn for help." The sense of a vanishing future created a kind of dementia of despair. A Bavarian chronicler of Neuberg on the Danube recorded that "Men and women . . . wandered around as if mad" and let their cattle stray "because no one had any inclination to concern themselves about the future." Fields went uncultivated, spring seed unsown. Second growth with nature's awful energy crept back over cleared land, dikes crumbled, salt water reinvaded and soured the lowlands. With so few hands remaining to restore the work of centuries, people felt, in Walsingham's words, that "the world could never again regain its former prosperity."

Though the death rate was higher among the anonymous poor, the known and the great died too. King Alfonso XI of Castile was the only reigning monarch killed by the pest, but his neighbor King Pedro of Aragon lost his wife, Queen Leonora, his daughter Marie, and a niece in the space of six months. John Cantacuzene, Emperor of Byzantium, lost his son. In France the lame Queen Jeanne and her daughter-in-law Bonne de Luxembourg, wife of the Dauphin, both died in 1349 in the same phase that took the life of Enguerrand's mother. Jeanne, Queen of Navarre, daughter of Louis X, was another victim. Edward III's second daughter, Joanna, who was on her way to marry Pedro, the heir of Castile, died in Bordeaux. Women appear to have been more vulnerable than men, perhaps because, being more housebound, they were more exposed to fleas. Boccaccio's mistress Fiammetta, illegitimate daughter of the King of Naples, died, as did Laura, the beloved—whether real or fictional—of Petrarch. Reaching out to us in the future, Petrarch cried, "Oh happy posterity who will not experience such abysmal woe and will look upon our testimony as a fable."

In Florence Giovanni Villani, the great historian of his time, died at 68 in the midst of an unfinished sentence: ". . . *e dure questo pistolenza fino a* . . . (in the midst of this pestilence there came to an end . . .)." Siena's master painters, the brothers Ambrogio and Pietro Lorenzetti, whose names never appear after 1348, presumably perished in the plague, as did Andrea Pisano, architect and sculptor of Florence. William of Ockham and the English mystic Richard Rolle of Hampole both disappear from mention after 1349. Francisco Datini, merchant of Prato, lost both his parents and two siblings. Curious sweeps of mortality afflicted certain bodies of merchants in London. All eight wardens of the Company of Cutters, all six wardens of the Hatters, and four wardens of the Goldsmiths died before July 1350. Sir John Pulteney, master draper and four times Mayor of London, was a victim, likewise Sir John Montgomery, Governor of Calais.

Among the clergy and doctors the mortality was naturally high because of the nature of their professions. Out of 24 physicians in Venice, 20 were said to have lost their lives in the plague, although, according to another account, some were believed to have fled or to have shut themselves up in their houses. At Montpellier, site of the leading medieval medical school, the physician Simon de Covino reported that, despite the great number of doctors, "hardly one of them escaped." In Avignon, Guy de Chauliac confessed that he performed his medical visits only because he dared not stay away for fear of infamy, but "I was in continual fear." He claimed to have contracted the disease but to have cured himself by his own treatment; if so, he was one of the few who recovered.

Clerical mortality varied with rank. Although the one-third toll of cardinals reflects the same proportion as the whole, this was probably due to their concentration in Avignon. In England, in strange and almost sinister procession, the Archbishop of Canterbury, John Stratford, died in August 1348, his appointed successor died in May 1349, and the next appointee three months later, all three within a year. Despite such weird vagaries, prelates in general managed to sustain a higher survival rate than the lesser clergy. Among bishops the deaths have been estimated at about one in twenty. The loss of priests, even if many avoided their fearful duty of attending the dying, was about the same as among the population as a whole.

Government officials, whose loss contributed to the general chaos, found, on the whole, no special shelter. In Siena four of the nine members of the governing oligarchy died, in France one third of the royal notaries, in Bristol 15 out of the 52 members of the Town Council or almost one third. Tax-collecting obviously suffered, with the result that Philip VI was unable to collect more than a fraction of the subsidy granted him by the Estates in the winter of 1347–48.

Lawlessness and debauchery accompanied the plague as they had during the great plague of Athens of 430 B.C., when according to Thucydides, men grew bold in the indulgence of pleasure: "For seeing how the rich died in a moment and those who had nothing immediately inherited their property, they reflected that life and riches were alike transitory and they resolved to enjoy themselves while they could." Human behavior is timeless. When St. John had his vision of plague in Revelation, he knew from some experience or race memory that those who survived "repented not of the work of their hands. . . . Neither repented they of their murders, nor of their sorceries, nor of their fornication, nor of their thefts."

Ignorance of the cause augmented the sense of horror. Of the real carriers, rats and fleas, the 14th century had no suspicion, perhaps because they were so familiar. Fleas, though a common household nuisance, are not once mentioned in contemporary plague writings, and rats only incidentally, although folklore commonly associated them with pestilence. The legend of the Pied Piper arose from an outbreak of 1284. The actual plague bacillus, *Pasturella pestis*, remained undiscovered for another 500 years. Living alternately in the stomach of the flea and the bloodstream of the rat who was the flea's host, the bacillus in its bubonic form was transferred to humans and animals by the bite of either rat or flea. It traveled by virtue of *Rattus rattus*, the small medieval black rat that lived on ships, as well as by the heavier brown or sewer rat. What precipitated the turn of the bacillus from innocuous to virulent form is unknown, but the occurrence is now believed to have taken place not in China but somewhere in central Asia and to have spread along the caravan routes. Chinese origin was a mistaken notion of the 14th century based on real but belated reports of huge death tolls in China from drought, famine, and pestilence which have since been traced to the 1330s, too soon to be responsible for the plague that appeared in India in 1346.

The phantom enemy had no name. Called the Black Death only in later recurrences, it was known during the first epidemic simply as the Pestilence or Great Mortality. Reports from the East, swollen by fearful imaginings, told of strange tempests and "sheets of fire" mingled with huge hailstones that "slew almost all," or a "vast rain of fire" that burned up men, beasts, stones, trees, villages, and cities. In another version, "foul blasts of wind" from the fires carried the infection to Europe "and now as some suspect it cometh round the seacoast." Accurate observation in this case could not make the mental jump to ships and rats because no idea of animal- or insect-borne contagion existed.

The earthquake was blamed for releasing sulfurous and foul fumes from the earth's interior, or as evidence of a titanic struggle of planets and oceans causing waters to rise and vaporize until fish died in masses and corrupted the air. All these explanations had in common a factor of poisoned air, of miasmas and thick, stinking mists traced to every kind of natural or imagined agency from stagnant lakes to malign conjunction of the planets, from the hand of the Evil One to the wrath of God. Medical thinking, trapped in the theory of astral influences, stressed air as the communicator of disease, ignoring sanitation or visible carriers. The existence of two carriers confused the trail, the more so because the flea could live and travel independently of the rat for as long as a month and, if infected by the particularly virulent septicemic form of the bacillus, could infect humans without reinfecting itself from the rat. The simultaneous presence of the pneumonic form of the disease, which was indeed communicated through the air, blurred the problem further.

The mystery of the contagion was "the most terrible of all the terrors," as an anonymous Flemish cleric in Avignon wrote to a correspondent in Bruges. Plagues had been known before, from the plague of Athens (believed to have been typhus) to the prolonged epidemic of the 6th century A.D., to the recurrence of sporadic outbreaks in the 12th and 13th centuries, but they had left no accumulated store of understanding. That the infection came from contact with the sick or with their houses, clothes, or corpses was quickly observed but not comprehended. Gentile da Foligno, renowned physician of Perugia and doctor of medicine at the universities of Bologna and Padua, came close to respiratory infection when he surmised that poisonous material was "communicated by means of air breathed out and in." Having no idea of microscopic carriers, he had to assume that the air was corrupted by planetary influences. Planets, however, could not explain the ongoing contagion. The agonized search for an answer gave rise to such theories as transference by sight. People fell ill, wrote Guy de Chauliac, not only by remaining with the sick but "even by looking at them." Three hundred years later Joshua Barnes, the 17th century biographer of Edward III, could write that the power of infection had entered into beams of light and "darted death from the eyes."

Doctors struggling with the evidence could not break away from the terms of astrology, to which they believed all human physiology was subject. Medicine was the one aspect of medieval life, perhaps because of its links with the Arabs, not shaped by Christian doctrine. Clerics detested astrology, but could not dislodge its influence. Guy de Chauliac, physician to three popes in succession, practiced in obedience to the zodiac. While his *Cirurgia* was the major treatise on surgery of its time, while he understood the use of anesthesia made from the juice of opium, mandrake, or hemlock, he nevertheless prescribed bleeding and purgatives by the planets and divided chronic from acute diseases on the basis of one being under the rule of the sun and the other of the moon.

In October 1348 Philip VI asked the medical faculty of the University of Paris for a report on the affliction that seemed to threaten human survival. With careful thesis, antithesis, and proofs, the doctors ascribed it to a triple conjunction of Saturn, Jupiter, and Mars in the 40th degree of Aquarius said to have occurred on March 20, 1345. They acknowledged, however, effects "whose cause is hidden from even the most highly trained intellects." The verdict of the masters of Paris became the official version. Borrowed, copied by scribes, carried abroad, translated from Latin into various vernaculars, it was everywhere accepted, even by the Arab physicians of Cordova and Granada, as the scientific if not the popular answer. Because of the terrible interest of the subject, the translations of the plague tracts stimulated use of national languages. In that one respect, life came from death.

To the people at large there could be but one explanation—the wrath of God. Planets might satisfy the learned doctors, but God was closer to the average man. A scourge so sweeping and unsparing without any visible cause could only be seen as Divine punishment upon mankind for its sins. It might even be God's terminal disappointment in his creature. Matteo Villani compared the plague to the Flood in ultimate purpose and believed he was recording "the extermination of mankind." Efforts to appease Divine wrath took many forms, as when the city of Rouen ordered that everything that could anger God, such as gambling, cursing, and drinking, must be stopped. More general were the penitent processions authorized at first by the Pope, some lasting as long as three days, some attended by as many as 2,000, which everywhere accompanied the plague and helped to spread it.

Barefoot in sackcloth, sprinkled with ashes, weeping, praying, tearing their hair, carrying candles and relics, sometimes with ropes around their necks or beating themselves with whips, the penitents wound through the streets, imploring the mercy of the Virgin and saints at their shrines. In a vivid illustration for the *Très Riches Heures* of the Duc de Berry, the Pope is shown in a penitent procession attended by four cardinals in scarlet from hat to hem. He raises both arms in supplication to the angel on top of the Castel Sant'Angelo, while white-robed priests bearing banners and relics in golden cases turn to look as one of their number, stricken by the plague, falls to the ground, his face contorted with anxiety. In the rear, a gray-clad monk falls beside another victim already on the ground as the townspeople gaze in horror. (Nominally the illustration represents a 6th century plague in the time of Pope Gregory the Great, but as medieval artists made no distinction between past and present, the scene is shown as the artist would have seen it in the 14th century.) When it became evident that these processions were sources of infection, Clement VI had to prohibit them.

In Messina, where the plague first appeared, the people begged the Archbishop of neighboring Catania to lend them the relics of St. Agatha. When the Catanians refused to let the relics go, the Archbishop dipped them in holy water and took the water himself to Messina, where he carried it in a procession with prayers and litanies through the streets. The demonic, which shared the medieval cosmos with God, appeared as "demons in the shape of dogs" to terrify the people. "A black dog with a drawn sword in his paws appeared among them, gnashing his teeth and rushing upon them and breaking all the silver vessels and lamps and candlesticks on the altars and casting them hither and thither. . . . So the people of Messina, terrified by this prodigious vision, were all strangely overcome by fear."

The apparent absence of earthly cause gave the plague a supernatural and sinister quality. Scandinavians believed that a Pest Maiden emerged from the mouth of the dead in the form of a blue flame and flew through the air to infect the next house. In Lithuania the Maiden was said to wave a red scarf through the door or window to let in the pest. One brave man, according to legend, deliberately waited at his open window with drawn sword and, at the fluttering of the scarf, chopped off the hand. He died of his deed, but his village was spared and the scarf long preserved as a relic in the local church.

Beyond demons and superstition the final hand was God's. The Pope acknowledged it in a Bull of September 1348, speaking of the "pestilence with which God is afflicting the Christian people." To the Emperor John Cantacuzene it was manifest that a malady of such horrors, stenches, and agonies, and especially one bringing the dismal despair that settled upon its victims before they died, was not a plague "natural" to mankind but "a chastisement from Heaven." To Piers Plowman "these pestilences were for pure sin."

The general acceptance of this view created an expanded sense of guilt, for if the plague were punishment there had to be terrible sin to have occasioned it. What sins were on the 14th century conscience? Primarily greed, the sin of avarice, followed by usury, worldliness, adultery, blasphemy, falsehood, luxury, irreligion. Giovanni Villani, attempting to account for the cascade of calamity that had fallen upon Florence, concluded that it was retribution for the sins of avarice and usury that oppressed the poor. Pity and anger about the condition of the poor, especially victimization of the peasantry in war, was often expressed by writers of the time and was certainly on the conscience of the century. Beneath it all was the daily condition of medieval life, in which hardly an act or thought, sexual, mercantile, or military, did not contravene the dictates of the Church. Mere failure to fast or attend mass was sin. The result was an underground lake of guilt in the soul that the plague now tapped.

That the mortality was accepted as God's punishment may explain in part the vacuum of comment that followed the Black Death. An investigator has noticed that in the archives of Périgord references to the war are innumerable, to the plague few. Froissart mentions the great death but once, Chaucer gives it barely a glance. Divine anger so great that it contemplated the extermination of man did not bear close examination.

Efforts to cope with the epidemic availed little, either in treatment or prevention. Helpless to alleviate the plague, the doctors' primary effort was to keep it at bay, chiefly by burning aromatic substances to purify the air. The leader of Christendom, Pope Clement VI, was preserved in health by this method, though for an unrecognized reason: Clement's doctor, Guy de Chauliac, ordered that two huge fires should burn in the papal apartments and required the Pope to sit between them in the heat of the Avignon summer. This drastic treatment worked, doubtless because it discouraged the attention of fleas and also because de Chauliac required the Pope to remain isolated in his chambers. Their lovely murals of gardens, hunting, and other secular joys, painted at Clement's command, perhaps gave him some refreshment. A Pope of prodigal splendor and "sensual vices," Clement was also a man of great learning and a patron of arts and science who now encouraged dissections of the dead "in order that the origins of this disease might be known." Many were performed in Avignon as well as in Florence, where the city authorities paid for corpses to be delivered to physicians for this purpose.

Doctors' remedies in the 14th century ranged from the empiric and sensible to the magical, with little distinction made between one and the other. Though medicine was barred by the Church from investigation of anatomy and physiology and from dissection of corpses, the classical anatomy of Galen, transferred through Arab treatises, was kept alive in private anatomy lessons. The need for knowledge was able sometimes to defy the Church: in 1340 Montpellier authorized an anatomy class every two years which lasted for several days and consisted of a surgeon dissecting a cadaver while a doctor of medicine lectured.

Otherwise, the theory of humors, along with astrology, governed practice. All human temperaments were considered to belong to one or another of the four humors—sanguine, phlegmatic, choleric, and melancholic. In various permutations with the signs of the zodiac, each of which governed a particular part of the body, the humors and constellations determined the degrees of bodily heat, moisture, and proportion of masculinity and femininity of each person.

Notwithstanding all their charts and stars, and medicaments barely short of witches' brews, doctors gave great attention to diet, bodily health, and mental attitude. Nor were they lacking in practical skills. They could set broken bones, extract teeth, remove bladder stones, remove cataracts of the eye with a silver needle, and restore a mutilated face by skin graft from the arm. They understood epilepsy and apoplexy as spasms of the brain. They used urinalysis and pulse beat for diagnosis, knew what substances served as laxatives and diuretics, applied a truss for hernia, a mixture of oil, vinegar, and sulfur for toothache, and ground peony root with oil of roses for headache.

For ills beyond their powers they fell back on the supernatural or on elaborate compounds of metallic, botanic, and animal substances. The offensive, like the expensive, had extra value. Ringworm was treated by washing the scalp with a boy's urine, gout by a plaster of goat dung mixed with rosemary and honey. Relief of the patient was their object—cure being left to God—and psychological suggestion often their means. To prevent pockmarks, a smallpox patient would be wrapped in red cloth in a bed hung with red hangings. When surgery was unavailing, recourse was had to the aid of the Virgin or the relics of saints.

In their purple or red gowns and furred hoods, doctors were persons of important status. Allowed extra luxury by the sumptuary laws, they wore belts of silver thread, embroidered gloves, and, according to Petrarch's annoyed report, presumptuously donned golden spurs when they rode to their visits attended by a servant. Their wives were permitted greater expenditure on clothes than other women, perhaps in recognition of the large fees doctors could command. Not all were learned professors. Boccaccio's Doctor Simon was a proctologist who had a chamber pot painted over his door to indicate his specialty.

When it came to the plague, sufferers were treated by various measures designed to draw poison or infection from the body: by bleeding, purging with laxatives or enemas, lancing or cauterizing the buboes, or application of hot plasters. None of this was of much use. Medicines ranged from pills of powdered stag's horn or myrrh and saffron to potions of potable gold. Compounds of rare spices and powdered pearls or emeralds were prescribed, possibly on the theory, not unknown to modern medicine, that a patient's sense of therapeutic value is in proportion to the expense.

Doctors advised that floors should be sprinkled, and hands, mouth, and nostrils washed with vinegar and rosewater. Bland diets, avoidance of excitement and anger especially at bedtime, mild exercise, and removal wherever possible from swamps and other sources of dank air were all recommended. Pomanders made of exotic compounds were to be carried on going out, probably more as antidote to the plague's odors than to its contagion. Conversely, in the curious belief that latrine attendants were immune, many people visited the public latrines on the theory that foul odors were efficacious.

Sewage disposal was not unprovided for in the 14th century, though far from adequate. Privies, cesspools, drainage pipes, and public latrines existed, though they did not replace open street sewers. Castles and wealthy town houses had privies built into bays jutting from an outside wall with a hole in the bottom allowing the deposit to fall into a river or into a ditch for subsequent removal. Town houses away from the riverbank had cesspools in the backyard at a regulated distance from the neighbor's. Although supposedly constructed under town ordinances, they frequently seeped into wells and other water sources. Except for household urinals, the contents of privies were prohibited from draining into street sewers. Public flouting of ordinances was more to blame for unsanitary streets than inadequate technology.

Some abbeys and large castles, including Coucy, had separate buildings to serve as latrines for the monks or garrison. The *donjon* at Coucy had latrines at each of its three levels. Drainage was channeled into vaulted stone ditches with ventilating holes and openings for removal, or into underground pits later mistaken by investigators of a more romantic period for secret passages and oubliettes. Under the concept of "noble" architecture, the 15th and later centuries preferred to ignore human elimination. Coucy probably had better sanitation than Versailles.

During the plague, as street cleaners and carters died, cities grew befouled, increasing the infection. Residents of a street might rent a cart in common to remove the waste, but energy and will were depressed. The breakdown in street-cleaning appears in a letter of Edward III to the Mayor of London in 1349, complaining that the streets and lanes of London were "foul with human fæces and the air of the city poisoned to the great danger of men passing, especially in this time of infectious disease." Removed as he probably was from the daily sight of corpses piling up, the King ordered that the streets be cleaned "as of old."

Stern measures of quarantine were ordered by many cities. As soon as Pisa and Lucca were afflicted, their neighbor Pistoia forbade any of its citizens who might be visiting or doing business in the stricken cities to return home, and likewise forbade the importation of wool and linen. The Doge and Council of Venice ordered burial on the islands to a depth of at least five feet and organized a barge service to transport the corpses. Poland established a quarantine at its frontiers which succeeded in giving it relative immunity. Draconian means were adopted by the despot of Milan, Archbishop Giovanni Visconti, head of the most uninhibited ruling family of the 14th century. He ordered that the first three houses in which the plague was discovered were to be walled up with their occupants inside, enclosing the well, the sick, and the dead in a common tomb. Whether or not owing to his promptitude, Milan escaped lightly in the roll of the dead. With something of the Visconti temperament, a manorial autocrat of Leicestershire burned and razed the village of Noseley when the plague appeared there, to prevent its spread to the manor house. He evidently succeeded, for his direct descendants still inhabit Noseley Hall.

St. Roch, credited with special healing powers, who had died in 1327, was the particular saint associated with the plague. Inheriting wealth as a young man, as had St. Francis, he had distributed it to the poor and to hospitals, and while returning from a pilgrimage to Rome had encountered an epidemic and stayed to help the sick. Catching the malady himself, he retreated to die alone in the woods, where a dog brought him bread each day. "In these sad times," says his legend, "when reality was so somber and men so hard, people ascribed pity to animals." St. Roch recovered and, on appearing in rags as a beggar, was thought to be a spy and thrown into jail, where he died, filling the cell with a strange light. As his story spread and sainthood was conferred, it was believed that God would cure of the plague anyone who invoked his name. When this failed to occur, it enhanced the belief that, men having grown too wicked, God indeed intended their end. As Langland wrote,

> God is deaf now-a-days and deigneth not hear us,
> And prayers have no power the Plague to stay.

In a terrible reversal, St. Roch and other saints now came to be considered a source of the plague, as instruments of God's wrath. "In the time of that great mortality in the year of our Lord 1348," wrote a professor of law named Bartolus of Sassoferrato, "the hostility of God was stronger than the hostility of man." But he was wrong.

The hostility of man proved itself against the Jews. On charges that they were poisoning the wells, with intent "to kill and destroy the whole of Christendom and have lordship over all the world," the lynchings began in the spring of 1348 on the heels of the first plague deaths. The first attacks occurred in Narbonne and Carcassonne, where Jews were dragged from their houses and thrown into bonfires. While Divine punishment was accepted as the plague's source, people in their misery still looked for a human agent upon whom to vent the hostility that could not be vented on God. The Jew, as the eternal stranger, was the most obvious target. He was the outsider who had separated himself by choice from the Christian world, whom Christians for centuries had been taught to hate, who was regarded as imbued with unsleeping malevolence against all Christians. Living in a distinct group of his own kind in a particular street or quarter, he was also the most feasible target, with property to loot as a further inducement.

The accusation of well-poisoning was as old as the plague of Athens, when it had been applied to the Spartans, and as recent as the epidemics of 1320–21, when it had been applied to the lepers. At that time the lepers were believed to have acted at the instigation of the Jews and the Moslem King of Granada, in a great conspiracy of outcasts to destroy Christians. Hundreds were rounded up and burned throughout France in 1322 and the Jews heavily punished by an official fine and unofficial attacks. When the plague came, the charge was instantly revived against the Jews:

> . . . rivers and fountains
> That were clear and clean
> They poisoned in many places . . .

wrote the French court poet Guillaume de Machaut.

The antagonism had ancient roots. The Jew had become the object of popular animosity because the early Church, as an offshoot of Judaism striving to replace the parent, had to make him so. His rejection of Christ as Saviour and his dogged refusal to accept the new law of the Gospel in place of the Mosaic law made the Jew a perpetual insult to the newly established Church, a danger who must be kept distinct and apart from the Christian community. This was the purpose of the edicts depriving Jews of their civil rights issued by the early Church Councils in the 4th century as soon as Christianity became the state religion. Separation was a two-way street, since, to the Jews, Christianity was at first a dissident sect, then an apostasy with which they wanted no contact.

The theory, emotions, and justifications of anti-Semitism were laid at that time—in the canon law codified by the Councils; in the tirades of St. John Chrysostom, Patriarch of Antioch, who denounced the Jews as Christ-killers; in the judgment of St. Augustine, who declared the Jews to be "outcasts" for failing to accept redemption by Christ. The Jews' dispersion was regarded as their punishment for unbelief.

The period of active assault began with the age of the crusades, when all Europe's intramural antagonisms were gathered into one bolt aimed at the infidel. On the theory that the "infidel at home" should likewise be exterminated, massacres of Jewish communities marked the crusaders' march to Palestine. The capture of the Holy Sepulcher by the Moslems was blamed on "the wickedness of the Jews," and the cry "HEP! HEP!" for *Hierosolyma est Perdita* (Jerusalem is lost) became the call for murder. What man victimizes he fears; thus, the Jews were pictured as fiends filled with hatred of the human race, which they secretly intended to destroy.

The question whether Jews had certain human rights, under the general proposition that God created the world for all men including infidels, was given different answers by different thinkers. Officially the Church conceded some rights: that Jews should not be condemned without trial, their synagogues and cemeteries should not be profaned, their property not be robbed with impunity. In practice this meant little because, as non-citizens of the universal Christian state, Jews were not allowed to bring charges against Christians, nor was Jewish testimony allowed to prevail over that of Christians. Their legal status was that of serfs of the king, though without reciprocal obligations on the part of the overlord. The doctrine that Jews were doomed to perpetual servitude as Christ-killers was announced by Pope Innocent III in 1205 and led Thomas Aquinas to conclude with relentless logic that "since Jews are the slaves of the Church, she can dispose of their possessions." Legally, politically, and physically, they were totally vulnerable.

They maintained a place in society because as moneylenders they performed a role essential to the kings' continuous need of money. Excluded by the guilds from crafts and trades, they had been pushed into petty commerce and moneylending although theoretically barred from dealing with Christians. Theory, however, bends to convenience, and Jews provided Christians with a way around their self-imposed ban on using money to make money.

Since they were damned anyway, they were permitted to lend at interest rates of 20 percent and more, of which the royal treasury took the major share. The increment to the crown was in fact a form of indirect taxation; as its instruments, the Jews absorbed an added measure of popular hate. They lived entirely dependent upon the king's protection, subject to confiscations and expulsions and the hazards of royal favor. Nobles and prelates followed the royal example, entrusting money to the Jews for lending and taking most of the profits, while deflecting popular resentment upon the agent. To the common man the Jews were not only Christ-killers but rapacious, merciless monsters, symbols of the new force of money that was changing old ways and dissolving old ties.

As commerce swelled in the 12th and 13th centuries, increasing the flow of money, the Jews' position deteriorated in proportion as they were less needed. They could not deal in the great sums that Christian banking houses like the Bardi of Florence could command. Kings and princes requiring ever larger amounts now turned to the Lombards and wealthy merchants for loans and relaxed their protection of the Jews or, when in need of hard cash, decreed their expulsion while confiscating their property and the debts owed to them. At the same time, with the advent of the Inquisition in the 13th century, religious intolerance waxed, leading to the charge of ritual murder against the Jews and the enforced wearing of a distinctive badge.

The belief that Jews performed ritual murder of Christian victims, supposedly from a compulsion to re-enact the Crucifixion, began in the 12th century and developed into the belief that they held secret rites to desecrate the host. Promoted by popular preachers, a mythology of blood grew in a mirror image of the Christian ritual of drinking the blood of the Saviour. Jews were believed to kidnap and torture Christian children, whose blood they drank for a variety of sinister purposes ranging from sadism and sorcery to the need, as unnatural beings, for Christian blood to give them a human appearance. Though bitterly refuted by the rabbis and condemned by emperor and pope, the blood libel took possession of the popular mind most rabidly in Germany, where the well-poisoning charge too had originated in the 12th century. The blood libel formed the subject of Chaucer's tale of a child martyr told by the Prioresse and was the ground on which many Jews were charged, tried, and burned at the stake.

Under the zeal of St. Louis, whose life's object was the greater glory and fulfillment of Christian doctrine, Jewish life in France was narrowed and harassed by mounting restrictions. The famous trial of the Talmud for heresy and blasphemy took place in Paris in 1240 during his reign, ending in foreordained conviction and burning of 24 cartloads of Talmudic works. One of the disputants in the case was Rabbi Moses ben Jacob of Coucy, intellectual leader of the northern Jewish community in the time of Enguerrand III.

Throughout the century the Church multiplied decrees designed to isolate Jews from Christian society, on the theory that contact with them brought the Christian faith into disrepute. Jews were forbidden to employ Christians as servants, to serve as doctors to Christians, to intermarry, to sell flour, bread, wine, oil, shoes, or any article of clothing to Christians, to deliver or receive goods, to build new synagogues, to hold or claim land for non-payment of mortgage. The occupations from which guild rules barred them included weaving, metalworking, mining, tailoring, shoemaking, goldsmithing, baking, milling, carpentry. To mark their separation, Innocent III in 1215 decreed the wearing of a badge, usually in the form of a wheel or circular patch of yellow felt, said to represent a piece of money. Sometimes green or red-and-white, it was worn by both sexes beginning between the ages of seven and fourteen. In its struggle against all heresy and dissent, the 13th century Church imposed the same badge on Moslems, on convicted heretics, and, by some quirk in doctrine, on prostitutes. A hat with a point rather like a horn, said to represent the Devil, was later added further to distinguish the Jews.

Expulsions and persecutions were marked by one constant factor —seizure of Jewish property. As the chronicler William of Newburgh wrote of the massacre of York in 1190, the slaughter was less the work of religious zeal than of bold and covetous men who wrought "the business of their own greed." The motive was the same for official expulsion by towns or kings. When the Jews drifted back to resettle in villages, market towns and particularly in cities, they continued in moneylending and retail trade, kept pawnshops, found an occupation as gravediggers, and lived close together in a narrow Jewish quarter for mutual protection. In Provence, drawing on their contact with the Arabs of Spain and North Africa, they were scholars and sought-after physicians. But the vigorous inner life of their earlier communities had faded. In an excitable period they lived on the edge of assault that was always imminent. It was understood that the Church could "justly ordain war upon them" as enemies of Christendom.

In the torment of the plague it was easy to credit Jewish malevolence with poisoning the wells. In 1348 Clement VI issued a Bull prohibiting the killing, looting, or forcible conversion of Jews without trial, which halted the attacks in Avignon and the Papal States but was ignored as the rage swept northward. Authorities in most places tried at first to protect the Jews, but succumbed to popular pressure, not without an eye to potential forfeit of Jewish property.

In Savoy, where the first formal trials were held in September 1348, the Jews' property was confiscated while they remained in prison pending investigation of charges. Composed from confessions extracted by torture according to the usual medieval method, the charges drew a picture of an international Jewish conspiracy emanating from Spain, with messengers from Toledo carrying poison in little packets or in a "narrow stitched leather bag." The messengers allegedly brought rabbinical instructions for sprinkling the poison in wells and springs, and consulted with their co-religionists in secret meetings. Duly found guilty, the accused were condemned to death. Eleven Jews were burned alive and the rest subjected to a tax of 160 florins every month over the next six years for permission to remain in Savoy.

The confessions obtained in Savoy, distributed by letter from town to town, formed the basis for a wave of accusations and attacks throughout Alsace, Switzerland, and Germany. At a meeting of representatives of Alsatian towns, the oligarchy of Strasbourg attempted to refute the charges but were overwhelmed by the majority demanding reprisal and expulsion. The persecutions of the Black Death were not all spontaneous outbursts but action seriously discussed beforehand.

Again Pope Clement attempted to check the hysteria in a Bull of September 1348 in which he said that Christians who imputed the pestilence to the Jews had been "seduced by that liar, the Devil," and that the charge of well-poisoning and ensuing massacres were a "horrible thing." He pointed out that "by a mysterious decree of God" the plague was afflicting all peoples, including Jews; that it raged in places where no Jews lived, and that elsewhere they were victims like everyone else; therefore the charge that they caused it was "without plausibility." He urged the clergy to take Jews under their protection as he himself offered to do in Avignon, but his voice was hardly heard against local animus.

In Basle on January 9, 1349, the whole community of several hundred Jews was burned in a wooden house especially constructed for the purpose on an island in the Rhine, and a decree was passed that no Jew should be allowed to settle in Basle for 200 years. In Strasbourg the Town Council, which opposed persecution, was deposed by vote of the guilds and another was elected, prepared to comply with the popular will. In February 1349, before the plague had yet reached the city, the Jews of Strasbourg, numbering 2,000, were taken to the burial ground, where all except those who accepted conversion were burned at rows of stakes erected to receive them.

By now another voice was fomenting attack upon the Jews. The flagellants had appeared. In desperate supplication for God's mercy, their movement erupted in a sudden frenzy that sped across Europe with the same fiery contagion as the plague. Self-flagellation was intended to express remorse and expiate the sins of all. As a form of penance to induce God to forgive sin, it long antedated the plague years. The flagellants saw themselves as redeemers who, by re-enacting the scourging of Christ upon their own bodies and making the blood flow, would atone for human wickedness and earn another chance for mankind.

Organized groups of 200 to 300 and sometimes more (the chroniclers mention up to 1,000) marched from city to city, stripped to the waist, scourging themselves with leather whips tipped with iron spikes until they bled. While they cried aloud to Christ and the Virgin for pity, and called upon God to "Spare us!", the watching townspeople sobbed and groaned in sympathy. These bands put on regular performances three times a day, twice in public in the church square and a third in privacy. Organized under a lay Master for a stated period, usually 33½ days to represent Christ's years on earth, the participants were required to pledge self-support at 4 pence a day or other fixed rate and to swear obedience to the Master. They were forbidden to bathe, shave, change their clothes, sleep in beds, talk or have intercourse with women without the Master's permission. Evidently this was not withheld, since the flagellants were later charged with orgies in which whipping combined with sex. Women accompanied the groups in a separate section, bringing up the rear. If a woman or priest entered the circle of the ceremony, the act of penance was considered void and had to be begun over again. The movement was essentially anti-clerical, for in challenge to the priesthood, the flagellants were taking upon themselves the role of interceders with God for all humanity.

Breaking out now in the German states, the new eruption advanced through the Low Countries to Flanders and Picardy as far as Reims. Hundreds of bands roamed the land, entering new towns every week, exciting already overwrought emotions, reciting hymns of woe and claims that but for them "all Christendom would meet perdition." The inhabitants greeted them with reverence and ringing of church bells, lodged them in their houses, brought children to be healed and, in at least one case, to be resurrected. They dipped cloths in the flagellants' blood, which they pressed to their eyes and preserved as relics. Many, including knights and ladies, clerics, nuns, and children, joined the bands. Soon the flagellants were marching behind magnificent banners of velvet and cloth of gold embroidered for them by women enthusiasts.

Growing in arrogance, they became overt in antagonism to the Church. The Masters assumed the right to hear confession and grant absolution or impose penance, which not only denied the priests their fee for these services but challenged ecclesiastical authority at its core. Priests who intervened against them were stoned and the populace was incited to join in the stoning. Opponents were denounced as scorpions and Anti-Christs. Organized in some cases by apostate priests or fanatic dissidents, the flagellants took possession of churches, disrupted services, ridiculed the Eucharist, looted altars, and claimed the power to cast out evil spirits and raise the dead. The movement that began as an attempt through self-inflicted pain to save the world from destruction, caught the infection of power hunger and aimed at taking over the Church.

They began to be feared as a source of revolutionary ferment and a threat to the propertied class, lay as well as ecclesiastical. The Emperor Charles IV petitioned the Pope to suppress the flagellants, and his appeal was augmented by the no less imperial voice of the University of Paris. At such a time, when the world seemed to be on the brink of doom, to take action against the flagellants who claimed to be under Divine inspiration was not an easy decision. Several of the cardinals at Avignon opposed repressive measures.

The self-torturers meanwhile had found a better victim. In every town they entered, the flagellants rushed for the Jewish quarter, trailed by citizens howling for revenge upon the "poisoners of the wells." In Freiburg, Augsburg, Nürnberg, Munich, Königsberg, Regensburg, and other centers, the Jews were slaughtered with a thoroughness that seemed to seek the final solution. At Worms in March 1349 the Jewish community of 400, like that of York, turned to an old tradition and burned themselves to death inside their own houses rather than be killed by their enemies. The larger community of Frankfurt-am-Main took the same way in July, setting fire to part of the city by their flames. In Cologne the Town Council repeated the Pope's argument that Jews were dying of the plague like everyone else, but the flagellants collected a great proletarian crowd of "those who had nothing to lose," and paid no attention. In Mainz, which had the largest Jewish community in Europe, its members turned at last to self-defense. With arms collected in advance they killed 200 of the mob, an act which only served to bring down upon them a furious onslaught by the townspeople in revenge for the death of Christians. The Jews fought until overpowered; then retreating to their homes, they too set their own fires. Six thousand were said to have perished at Mainz on August 24, 1349. Of 3,000 Jews at Erfurt, none was reported to have survived.

Completeness is rare in history, and Jewish chroniclers may have shared the medieval addiction to sweeping numbers. Usually a number saved themselves by conversion, and groups of refugees were given shelter by Rupert of the Palatinate and other princes. Duke Albert II of Austria, grand-uncle of Enguerrand VII, was one of the few who took measures effective enough to protect the Jews from assault in his territories. The last pogroms took place in Antwerp and in Brussels where in December 1349 the entire Jewish community was exterminated. By the time the plague had passed, few Jews were left in Germany or the Low Countries.

By this time Church and state were ready to take the risk of suppressing the flagellants. Magistrates ordered town gates closed against them; Clement VI in a Bull of October 1349 called for their dispersal and arrest; the University of Paris denied their claim of Divine inspiration. Philip VI promptly forbade public flagellation on pain of death; local rulers pursued the "masters of error," seizing, hanging, and beheading. The flagellants disbanded and fled, "vanishing as suddenly as they had come," wrote Henry of Hereford, "like night phantoms or mocking ghosts." Here and there the bands lingered, not entirely suppressed until 1357.

Homeless ghosts, the Jews filtered back from eastern Europe, where the expelled had gone. Two Jews reappeared in Erfurt as visitors in 1354 and, joined by others, started a resettlement three years later. By 1365 the community numbered 86 taxable hearths and an additional number of poor households below the tax-paying level. Here and elsewhere they returned to live in weakened and fearful communities on worse terms and in greater segregation than before. Well-poisoning and its massacres had fixed the malevolent image of the Jew into a stereotype. Because Jews were useful, towns which had enacted statutes of banishment invited or allowed their re-entry, but imposed new disabilities. Former contacts of scholars, physicians, and financial "court Jews" with the Gentile community faded. The period of the Jews' medieval flourishing was over. The walls of the ghetto, though not yet physical, had risen.

What was the human condition after the plague? Exhausted by deaths and sorrows and the morbid excesses of fear and hate, it ought to have shown some profound effects, but no radical change was immediately visible. The persistence of the normal is strong. While dying of the plague, the tenants of Bruton Priory in England continued to pay the heriot owed to the lord at death with such obedient regularity that fifty oxen and cattle were received by the priory within a few months. Social change was to come invisibly with time; immediate effects were many but not uniform. Simon de Covino believed the plague had a baneful effect upon morals, "lowering virtue throughout the world." Gilles li Muisis, on the other hand, thought there had been an improvement in public morals because many people formerly living in concubinage had now married (as a result of town ordinances), and swearing and gambling had so diminished that manufacturers of dice were turning their product into beads for telling paternosters.

The marriage rate undoubtedly rose, though not for love. So many adventurers took advantage of orphans to obtain rich dowries that the oligarchy of Siena forbade the marriage of female orphans without their kinsmen's consent. In England, Piers Plowman deplored the many pairs "since the pestilence" who had married "for greed of goods and against natural feeling," with result, according to him, in "guilt and grief . . . jealousy, joylessness and jangling in private"—and no children. It suited Piers as a moralist that such marriages should be barren. Jean de Venette, on the other hand, says of the marriages that followed the plague that many twins, sometimes triplets, were born and that few women were barren. Perhaps he in turn reflected a desperate need to believe that nature would make up the loss, and in fact men and women married immediately afterward in unusual numbers.

Unlike the dice transformed into prayer beads, people did not improve, although it had been expected, according to Matteo Villani, that the experience of God's wrath would have left them "better men, humble, virtuous and Catholic." Instead, "They forgot the past as though it had never been and gave themselves up to a more disordered and shameful life than they had led before." With a glut of merchandise on the shelves for too few customers, prices at first plunged and survivors indulged in a wild orgy of spending. The poor moved into empty houses, slept on beds, and ate off silver. Peasants acquired unclaimed tools and livestock, even a wine press, forge, or mill left without owners, and other possessions they never had before. Commerce was depressed, but the amount of currency was in greater supply because there were fewer people to share it.

Behavior grew more reckless and callous, as it often does after a period of violence and suffering. It was blamed on parvenus and the newly rich who pushed up from below. Siena renewed its sumptuary laws in 1349 because many persons were pretending to higher position than belonged to them by birth or occupation. But, on the whole, local studies of tax rolls indicate that while the population may have been halved, its social proportions remained about the same.

Because of intestate deaths, property without heirs, and disputed title to land and houses, a fury of litigation arose, made chaotic by the shortage of notaries. Sometimes squatters, sometimes the Church, took over emptied property. Fraud and extortion practiced upon orphans by their appointed guardians became a scandal. In Orvieto brawls kept breaking out; bands of homeless and starving brigands roamed the countryside and pillaged up to the very gates of the city. People were arrested for carrying arms and for acts of vandalism, especially on vineyards. The commune had to enact new regulations against "certain rascals, sons of iniquity" who robbed and burned the premises of shop-keepers and craftsmen, and also against increased prostitution. On March 12, 1350, the commune reminded citizens of the severe penalty in store for sexual relations between Christian and Jew: the woman involved would be beheaded or burned alive.

Education suffered from losses among the clergy. In France, according to Jean de Venette, "few were found in houses, villas and castles who were able and willing to instruct boys in grammar"—a situation that could have touched the life of Enguerrand VII. To fill vacant benefices the Church ordained priests in batches, many of them men who had lost their wives or families in the plague and flocked to holy orders as a refuge. Many were barely literate, "as it were mere lay folk" who might read a little but without understanding. Priests who survived the plague, declared the Archbishop of Canterbury in 1350, had become "infected by insatiable avarice," charging excessive fees and neglecting souls.

By a contrary trend, education was stimulated by concern for the survival of learning, which led to a spurt in the founding of universities. Notably the Emperor Charles IV, an intellectual, felt keenly the cause of "precious knowledge which the mad rage of pestilential death has stifled throughout the wide realms of the world." He founded the University of Prague in the plague year of 1348 and issued imperial accreditation to five other universities—Orange, Perugia, Siena, Pavia, and Lucca—in the next five years. In the same five years three new colleges were founded at Cambridge—Trinity, Corpus Christi, and Clare—although love of learning, like love in marriage, was not always the motive. Corpus Christi was founded in 1352 because fees for cele-brating masses for the dead were so inflated after the plague that two guilds of Cambridge decided to establish a college whose scholars, as clerics, would be required to pray for their deceased members.

Under the circumstances, education did not everywhere flourish.

Dwindling attendance at Oxford was deplored in sermons by the masters. At the University of Bologna, mourned Petrarch twenty years later (in a series of letters called "Of Senile Things"), where once there was "nothing more joyous, nothing more free in the world," hardly one of all the former great lecturers was left, and in the place of so many great geniuses, "a universal ignorance has seized the city." But pestilence was not alone responsible; wars and other troubles had added their scars.

The obvious and immediate result of the Black Death was, of course, a shrunken population, which, owing to wars, brigandage, and recurrence of the plague, declined even further by the end of the 14th century. The plague laid a curse on the century in the form of its own bacillus. Lodged in the vectors, it was to break out again six times over the next six decades in various localities at varying intervals of ten to fifteen years. After killing off most of those susceptible, with increasing mortality of children in the later phases, it eventually receded, leaving Europe with a population reduced by about 40 percent in 1380 and by nearly 50 percent at the end of the century. The city of Béziers in southern France, which had 14,000 inhabitants in 1304, numbered 4,000 a century later. The fishing port of Jonquières near Marseille, which once had 354 taxable hearths, was reduced to 135. The flourishing cities of Carcassonne and Montpellier shrank to shadows of their former prosperity, as did Rouen, Arras, Laon, and Reims in the north. The vanishing of taxable material caused rulers to raise rates of taxation, arousing resentment that was to explode in repeated outbreaks in coming decades.

As between landowner and peasant, the balance of impoverishment and enrichment caused by the plague on the whole favored the peasant, although what was true in one place often had an equal and opposite reaction somewhere else. The relative values of land and labor were turned upside down. Peasants found their rents reduced and even relinquished for one or more years by landowners desperate to keep their fields in cultivation. Better no revenue at all than that cleared land should be retaken by the wilderness. But with fewer hands to work, cultivated land necessarily shrank. The archives of the Abbey of Ramsay in England show that thirty years after the plague the acreage sowed in grain was less than half what it had been before. Five plows owned by the abbey in 1307 were reduced to one a century later, and twenty-eight oxen to five.

Hill farms and sections of poor soil were let go or turned to pasture for sheep, which required less labor. Villages weakened by depopulation and unable to resist the enclosure of land for sheep were deserted in increasing numbers. Property boundaries vanished when fields reverted to wasteland. If claimed by someone who was able to cultivate them, former owners or their heirs could not collect rent. Landowners impoverished by these factors sank out of sight or let castles and manors decay while they entered the military brigandage that was to be the curse of the following decades.

When death slowed production, goods became scarce and prices soared. In France the price of wheat increased fourfold by 1350. At the same time the shortage of labor brought the plague's greatest social disruption—a concerted demand for higher wages. Peasants as well as artisans, craftsmen, clerks, and priests discovered the lever of their own scarcity. Within a year after the plague had passed through northern France, the textile workers of St. Omer near Amiens had gained three successive wage increases. In many guilds artisans struck for higher pay and shorter hours. In an age when social conditions were regarded as fixed, such action was revolutionary.

The response of rulers was instant repression. In the effort to hold wages at pre-plague levels, the English issued an ordinance in 1349 requiring everyone to work for the same pay as in 1347. Penalties were established for refusal to work, for leaving a place of employment to seek higher pay, and for the offer of higher pay by employers. Proclaimed when Parliament was not sitting, the ordinance was reissued in 1351 as the Statute of Laborers. It denounced not only laborers who demanded higher wages but particularly those who chose "rather to beg in idleness than to earn their bread in labor." Idleness of the worker was a crime against society, for the medieval system rested on his obligation to work. The Statute of Laborers was not simply a reactionary dream but an effort to maintain the system. It provided that every able-bodied person under sixty with no means of subsistence must work for whoever required him, that no alms could be given to able-bodied beggars, that a vagrant serf could be forced to work for anyone who claimed him. Down to the 20th century this statute was to serve as the basis for "conspiracy" laws against labor in the long struggle to prevent unionization.

A more realistic French statute of 1351, applying only to the region of Paris, allowed a rise in wages not to exceed one third of the former level. Prices were fixed and profits of middlemen were regulated. To increase production, guilds were required to loosen their restrictions on the number of apprentices and shorten the period before they could become masters.

In both countries, as shown by repeated renewals of the laws with rising penalties, the statutes were unenforceable. Violations cited by the English Parliament in 1352 show workers demanding and employers paying wages at double and treble the pre-plague rate. Stocks were ordered set up in every town for punishment of offenders. In 1360 imprisonment replaced fines as the penalty and fugitive laborers were declared outlaws. If caught, they were to be branded on the forehead with F for "fugitive" (or possibly for "falsity"). New laws were enacted twice more in the 1360s, breeding the resistance that was to come to a head in the great outbreak of 1381.

The sense of sin induced by the plague found surcease in the plenary indulgence offered by the Jubilee Year of 1350 to all who in that year made the pilgrimage to Rome. Originally established by Boniface VIII in 1300, the Jubilee was intended to make an indulgence available to all repentant and confessed sinners free of charge—that is, if they could afford the journey to Rome. Boniface intended the Jubilee Year as a centennial event, but the first one had been such an enormous success, attracting a reported two million visitors to Rome in the course of the year, that the city, impoverished by the loss of the papacy to Avignon, petitioned Clement VI to shorten the interval to fifty years. The Pope of the joyous murals operated on the amiable principle that "a pontiff should make his subjects happy." He complied with Rome's request in a Bull of 1343.

Momentously for the Church, Clement formulated in the same Bull the theory of indulgences, and fixed its fatal equation with money. The sacrifice of Christ's blood, he stated, together with the merit added by the Virgin and saints, had established an inexhaustible treasury for the use of pardons. By contributing sums to the Church, anyone could buy a share in the Treasury of Merit. What the Church gained in revenue by this arrangement was matched in the end by loss in respect.

In 1350 pilgrims thronged the roads to Rome, camping around fires at night. Five thousand people were said to enter or leave the city every day, enriching the householders, who gave them lodging despite shortages of food and forage and the dismal state of the city's resources. Without its pontiff the Eternal City was destitute, the three chief basilicas in ruins, San Paolo toppled by the earthquake, the Lateran half-collapsed. Rubble and ruin filled the streets, the seven hills were silent and deserted, goats nibbled in the weed-grown cloisters of deserted convents. The sight of roofless churches exposed to wind and rain, lamented Petrarch, "would excite pity in a heart of stone." Nevertheless, famous saints' relics raked in lavish offerings, and Cardinal Anibaldo Ceccano, Legate for the Jubilee, administered an immense program of absolutions and indulgences to the crowds craving remission of sin. During Lent, according to Villani, who took a special interest in figures, as many as a million were in Rome at one time. The inpouring suggests either extraordinary recklessness and vigor so soon after the plague or a great need for salvation—or possibly that conditions did not seem as bad to participants as they seem in report.

The Church emerged from the plague richer if not more unpopular. When sudden death threatened everyone with the prospect of being carried off in a state of sin, the result was a flood of bequests to religious institutions. St. Germain l'Auxerrois in Paris received 49 legacies in nine months, compared to 78 in the previous eight years. As early as October 1348 the Council of Siena suspended its annual appropriations for religious charities for two years because these were so "immensely enriched and indeed fattened" by bequests. In Florence the Company of Or San Michele received 350,000 florins intended as alms for the poor, although in this case the directors of the company were accused of using the money for their own purposes on the grounds that the very poor and needy were dead.

While the Church garnered money, personal attacks on the clergy increased, stimulated partly by the flagellants, and partly by the failure of priests during the plague to live up to their responsibilities. That they died like other men was doubtless forgiven, but that they let Christians die without the sacraments or charged more for their services in the crisis, as many did, was violently resented. Even during the Jubilee the Roman populace, moved by some mysterious tremor of local hostility, jeered and harassed the Cardinal-Legate. On one occasion, as he was riding in a procession, he was shot at by a sniper and returned pale and trembling with an arrow through his red hat. Venturing out thereafter only with a helmet under his hat and a coat of mail under his gown, he departed for Naples as soon as he could, and died on the way—poisoned, it was said, by wine.

In England, where anti-clericalism was endemic, citizens of Worcester in 1349 broke down the gates of the Priory of St. Mary attached to the cathedral, attacked the monks, "chased the Prior with bows and arrows and other offensive weapons," and tried to set fire to the buildings. At Yeovil in the same year, when the Bishop of Bath and Wells held a thanksgiving service to mark the passing of the plague, it was interrupted by "certain sons of perdition" who kept the Bishop and congregation besieged in the church all night until rescue came.

Enriched by legacies, the friars' orders too reaped animus on top of that already felt for them. When Knighton reported the total demise of 150 Franciscans at Marseille, he added: "*bene quidem*" (a good thing), and of the seven friars who survived out of 160 at Maguelonne, he wrote: "and that was enough." The mendicant orders could not be forgiven for embracing Mammon and "seeking after earthly and carnal things."

The plague accelerated discontent with the Church at the very moment when people felt a greater need of spiritual reassurance. There had to be some meaning in the terrorizing experience God had inflicted. If the purpose had been to shake man from his sinful ways, it had failed. Human conduct was found to be "wickeder than before," more avaricious and grasping, more litigious, more bellicose, and this was nowhere more apparent than in the Church itself. Clement VI, though hardly a spiritual man, was sufficiently shaken by the plague to burst out against his prelates in a tirade of anger and shame when they petitioned him in 1351 to abolish the mendicant orders. And if he did, the Pope replied, "What can you preach to the people? If on humility, you yourselves are the proudest of the world, puffed up, pompous and sumptuous in luxuries. If on poverty, you are so covetous that all the benefices in the world are not enough for you. If on chastity—but we will be silent on this, for God knoweth what each man does and how many of you satisfy your lusts." In this sad view of his fellow clerics the head of the Church died a year later.

"When those who have the title of shepherd play the part of wolves," said Lothar of Saxony, "heresy grows in the garden of the Church." While the majority of people doubtless plodded on as before, dissatisfaction with the Church gave impetus to heresy and dissent, to all those seeking God through the mystical sects, to all the movements for reform which were ultimately to break apart the empire of Catholic unity.

Survivors of the plague, finding themselves neither destroyed nor improved, could discover no Divine purpose in the pain they had suffered. God's purposes were usually mysterious, but this scourge had been too terrible to be accepted without questioning. If a disaster of such magnitude, the most lethal ever known, was a mere wanton act of God or perhaps not God's work at all, then the absolutes of a fixed order were loosed from their moorings. Minds that opened to admit these questions could never again be shut. Once people envisioned the possibility of change in a fixed order, the end of an age of submission came in sight; the turn to individual conscience lay ahead. To that extent the Black Death may have been the unrecognized beginning of modern man.

Meantime it left apprehension, tension, and gloom. It accelerated the commutation of labor services on the land and in so doing unfastened old ties. It deepened antagonism between rich and poor and raised the level of human hostility. An event of great agony is bearable only in the belief that it will bring about a better world. When it does not, as in the aftermath of another vast calamity in 1914–18, disillusion is deep and moves on to self-doubt and self-disgust. In creating a climate for pessimism, the Black Death was the equivalent of the First World War, although it took fifty years for the psychological effects to develop. These were the fifty-odd years of the youth and adult life of Enguerrand de Coucy.

A strange personification of Death emerged from the plague years on the painted walls of the Camposanto in Pisa. The figure is not the conventional skeleton, but a black-cloaked old woman with streaming hair and wild eyes, carrying a broad-bladed murderous scythe. Her feet end in claws instead of toes. Depicting the Triumph of Death, the fresco was painted in or about 1350 by Francesco Traini as part of a series that included scenes of the Last Judgment and the Tortures of Hell. The same subject, painted at the same time by Traini's master, Andrea Orcagna, in the church of Santa Croce in Florence, has since been lost except for a fragment. Together the frescoes marked the start of a pervasive presence of Death in art, not yet the cult it was to become by the end of the century, but its beginning.

Usually Death was personified as a skeleton with hourglass and scythe, in a white shroud or bare-boned, grinning at the irony of man's fate reflected in his image: that all men, from beggar to emperor, from harlot to queen, from ragged clerk to Pope, must come to this. No matter what their poverty or power in life, all is vanity, equalized by death. The temporal is nothing; what matters is the after-life of the soul.

In Traini's fresco, Death swoops through the air toward a group of carefree, young, and beautiful noblemen and ladies who, like models for Boccaccio's storytellers, converse and flirt and entertain each other with books and music in a fragrant grove of orange trees. A scroll warns that "no shield of wisdom or riches, nobility or prowess" can protect them from the blows of the Approaching One. "They have taken more pleasure in the world than in things of God." In a heap of corpses nearby lie crowned rulers, a Pope in tiara, a knight, tumbled together with the bodies of the poor, while angels and devils in the sky contend for the miniature naked figures that represent their souls. A wretched group of lepers, cripples, and beggars (duplicated in the surviving fragment of Orcagna), one with nose eaten away, others legless or blind or holding out a cloth-covered stump instead of a hand, implore Death for deliverance. Above on a mountain, hermits leading a religious contemplative life await death peaceably.

Below in a scene of extraordinary verve a hunting party of princes and elegant ladies on horseback comes with sudden horror upon three open coffins containing corpses in different stages of decomposition, one still clothed, one half-rotted, one a skeleton. Vipers crawl over their bones. The scene illustrates "The Three Living and Three Dead," a 13th century legend which tells of a meeting between three young nobles and three decomposing corpses who tell them, "What you are, we were. What we are, you will be." In Traini's fresco, a horse catching the stench of death stiffens in fright with outstretched neck and flaring nostrils; his rider clutches a handkerchief to his nose. The hunting dogs recoil, growling in repulsion. In their silks and curls and fashionable hats, the party of vital handsome men and women stare appalled at what they will become.

Chapter 6

The Battle of Poitiers

ardly emerged from the plague, France moved toward a military debacle that was to release a flood of disruptive consequences and become a determining event in the life of Enguerrand de Coucy. The external agent was England, but the cause lay in the unsubdued autonomies of the seigneurial class, acted on by a King with a genius for misgovernment.

Jean II, who succeeded his father, Philip VI, in August 1350, could have served Machiavelli as model for Anti-Prince. Impolitic and impetuous, he never made a wise choice between alternatives and seemed incapable of considering consequences of an action in advance. Though brave in battle, he was anything but a great captain. Without evil intent, he was to foster disaffection to the point of revolt and lose half his kingdom and his person to the enemy, thereby leaving his country leaderless to meet its darkest hour of the age. His subjects with surprising forbearance named him Jean le Bon (John the Good), using the surname, it has been supposed, in the sense of "prodigal" or "careless" or being a good fellow. Or it may have referred to Jean's devotion to chivalric honor or to his alleged generosity to the poor, as illustrated by his once giving a purse to a servingmaid whose milk pails were knocked over by his greyhounds.

He came to the throne bent on taking the field to erase his father's defeats of the past decade, and on the first day of his reign notified all the principal lords of the realm to hold themselves ready to appear at his summons when "the time should come." The truce arranged after the fall of Calais and renewed during the Black Death was due to expire in April 1351. Inheriting an empty treasury, Jean had no money with which to pay an army, and could not move without first replenishing his funds and adapting his military resources. The need to learn something from the failures of Crécy and Calais was not lost on him, and he was groping with certain ideas for military reform.

His first act, however, within three months of becoming King, was to execute the Constable of France, Comte d'Eu, and sixteenth Comte de Guînes, a second cousin of Enguerrand VII, a man of powerful connections and "so courteous and amiable in every way that he was beloved and admired by great lords, knights, ladies and damsels." Captured by the English at Caen in 1345, D'Eu had been unable to raise the ransom fixed by King Edward. When it came to important captives, Edward never let himself be limited by the principle of chivalry that a knight's ransom should not be placed at a figure that would ruin him or exceed his revenue for one year. After four years of captivity, Comte d'Eu regained his liberty, supposedly in exchange for ceding to Edward his strategic castle and county of Guînes, adjoining Calais. On this suspicion, Jean had him beheaded upon his return to France without trial or public procedure of any kind. The King listened in silence to the pleas of D'Eu's friends for his life, offering no reply except to swear that "he would never sleep so long as the Comte de Guînes lived"; or according to another version replying in tears, "You shall have his body and we his head."

Jean could have chosen no better way to alienate the nobility whose support he needed than to execute a noble of D'Eu's rank and many friends without public explanation or trial by his peers. If D'Eu had indeed acted treasonably (the truth remains obscure), the King had every need to make plain the reasons for his act, but Jean was either too willful or too wooden-headed to understand the advisability of good public relations.

His next act made matters worse. He gave the office of Constable to his relative and favorite, Charles d'Espagne, who was said to be the object of the King's "dishonest affection," and to have persuaded Jean to murder Comte d'Eu so that he himself might have his office. Besides the prestige of military command second to the King, the Constable-ship had lucrative perquisites attached to the business of assembling the armed forces. Bestowal of the post on Charles d'Espagne, who was unpopular in the usual way of kings' favorites, added fury to the nobles' dismay at a time when the King had reason enough to fear their separatist tendencies. The episode was a divisive opening of the reign at a time when it most needed unity.

Jean's father, too, had been "*ung bien hastif homs*" (a very hasty man), and intermarriage for centuries with first cousins had left the Valois unstable. Jean retained Philip's uneasiness about the legitimacy of his claim to the crown and Philip's readiness, not without cause, to suspect treachery. In his capacity for sudden vindictiveness, he took after his mother, the lame Queen, who, despite her piety and good works, was called "a very cruel lady, for whomever she held in hate, he was dead without mercy." She was credited with having prodded her husband to the act that so appalled his time—the execution in 1343 of fifteen Breton lords who were his prisoners.

In the warfare of the 1340s, Jean had besieged the English at Aiguillon for four months without success, showing himself, according to report, resistant to any advice, obstinate, and "hard to move when he had taken an opinion." His most notable talent was for satisfying an exceptional avidity for money. He shared the Valois interest in arts and letters at least to the extent of commissioning French translations of the Bible and the Roman historian Livy and carrying books in his baggage when on campaign. As King he had his court painter, Girard d'Orléans, decorate his toilet stools, and he accumulated 239 tapestries made for his own use. His taste for luxury extended to everything but ministers, for he inherited from his father and kept in office a shady group, neither capable nor honest, who were despised by the nobles because they were of common birth and hated by the bourgeois for their avarice and venality. One of them, Simon de Buci, president of Parlement and member of the Secret Council, twice overreached himself in some way that required successive pardons. Robert de Lorris, the King's chamberlain and Master of Accounts, was restored to office after surviving a charge of treason and another of embezzlement. Jean Poilevain, who was imprisoned for peculation, prudently obtained a letter of pardon before his case was judged. As financiers for the King, men like these were a central source of disaffection with his regime.

Jean's first notable administrative act was a serious effort toward military coherence. It was becoming evident that the baronial right of independent withdrawal in the field, and independent response to the King's summons, crippled large military endeavor. Half feudal, half mercenary, not yet national, the ad hoc collection that was the 14th century army was too subject to the private interests of its components to be a reliable instrument. The Royal Ordinance of April 1351 was an attempt to introduce, as far as knightly terms allowed, principles of dependability and command.

By raising rates of pay to meet the inflation caused by the Black Death, the ordinance confirmed the fact that the warrior's function had become a trade for the poorer knights if not the grand seigneurs. The new rates under the ordinance were fixed at 40 sous (two livres) a day for a banneret, 20 sous for a knight, 10 for a squire, 5 for a valet, 3 for a foot soldier, 2½ for an armor-bearer or other attendant.

More significant was a provision designed to correct a critical fault on the medieval battlefield: the right of independent withdrawal. The new rule stipulated that every man in the host be subordinate to some captain and required an oath from all of the men "not to leave the company of their captain" without an order—that is, not to withdraw at will. An indication of how fragile was a commander's reliance on the force he could expect to deploy, the ordinance also required captains of companies to notify the chief of battalion that they would be present at a forthcoming battle.

The ordinance proved ineffective chiefly for lack of dependable revenue to support an organized army. Provisioning added to the cost of wages. While local peasantry, paid or pillaged, usually furnished food and horses' forage, a major expedition or siege or fleet at sea required organized supply of biscuit, smoked or salted meat and fish, wine, oil, and oats and hay for the horses. Ordinarily knights ate white bread made from wheat, meat in the form of beef, pork, and mutton, and drank wine daily. The common soldier received wine only on feast days or in active combat; otherwise he drank beer, ale, or cider, and ate rye bread, peas, and beans. Fish, cheese, olive oil, occasionally butter, salt, vinegar, onions, and garlic also figured in the rations. Poultry was so widely consumed and easily obtained that it was not recorded. Sugar, honey, mustard, spices, and almonds were kept for the wounded and sick and the privileged. On active duty, soldiers did not fast but were allotted fish as substitute for meat on the twelve "thin" days a month. The more continuous war became, as it did in the 14th century, the more organization and money it required.

The crown grasped for money by every means and favored the least scrupulous, which was debasing the coinage. Less directly obvious than aids and subsidies, it required no summoning of the Estates for consent. Coins called in were re-minted with a lower proportion of gold or silver and re-circulated at the old face value, with the difference being retained by the Treasury. Since the petty coins of daily use were those affected, the system reduced the real wages and purchasing power of the common people while bankers, merchants, and nobles, whose movable wealth was in large gold coins or gold and silver vessels and plate, were less affected. Under Jean II, manipulations were so frequent and erratic that they upset all values and succeeded in damaging and infuriating everyone except the manipulators themselves and those who could profit by holding back their gold. Abbot Gilles li Muisis of Tournai found the mysteries of the coinage even more obscure than the plague and was inspired to a famous verse:

> Money and currency are very strange things.
> They keep on going up and down and no one knows why;
> If you want to win, you lose, however hard you try.

In 1351, the first year of Jean's reign, the currency suffered eighteen alterations, and seventy in the course of the next decade.

The King's personal idea for improving the military arm was to found an order of chivalry modeled, like King Edward's recently founded Order of the Garter, on the Knights of the Round Table. Jean's Order of the Star was intended to rival the Garter, revive French prestige, and weld the splintered loyalty of his nobles to the Valois monarchy.

The orders of chivalry, with all their display and ritual and vows, were essentially a way of trying to secure a loyal body of military support on which the sovereign could rely. That was in fact the symbolism of the Garter, a circlet to bind the Knight-Companions mutually, and all of them jointly to the King as head of the Order. First broached with much fanfare in 1344, the Order of the Garter was originally intended to include 300 proved knights, starting with the most worthy of the realm. When formally established five years later, it was reduced to an exclusive circle of 26 with St. George as patron and official robes of blue and gold. Significantly, the statutes provided that no member was to leave the King's domain without his authority. The wearing of the Garter at the knee was further intended, in the words of the Order's historian, as a "Caveat and Exhortation that the Knights should not pusillanimously (by running away from Battle) betray the Valour and Renown which is ingrafted in Constancy and Magnanimity." Even knights of old knew fear and flight.

Since Jean's object was to be inclusive rather than exclusive, he made the Order of the Star open to 500 members. Established "in honor of God, of our Lady and for the heightening of chivalry and augmenting of honor," the full Order was to assemble once a year in a ceremonial banquet hung with the blazons of all its members. Companions were to wear a white tunic, a red or white surcoat embroidered with a gold star, a red hat, enameled ring of special design, black hose, and gilded shoes. They were to display a red banner strewn with stars and embroidered with an image of Our Lady.

At the annual banquet each would recite on oath all "the adventures that befell him in the year both shameful and honorable," and clerks would take down the recitals in a book. The Order would designate the three princes, three bannerets, and three knights who during the year had done the most in arms of war, "for no deed of arms in peace shall be taken into account." This meant no deed of private warfare as distinct from a war declared by the sovereign. Equally significant of the King's intention was the reappearance of the oath not to withdraw, worded more sternly than in the ordinance and more explicitly than in the Order of the Garter. Companions of the Star were required to swear they would never flee in battle more than four *arpents* (about 600 yards) by their own estimate, "but rather die or be taken prisoner."

While the purpose behind the orders was practical, the form was already nostalgic. War had changed since the 12th century romances from which men knew the legends of the 6th century Round Table, if it ever existed. The legends had shaped chivalry as the principle of order of the warrior class "without which the world would be a confused thing." But the quest of the Holy Grail was not an adequate guide to realistic tactics.

Chivalry's finest military expression in contemporary eyes was the famous Combat of the Thirty in 1351. An action of the perennial conflict in Brittany, it began with a challenge to single combat issued by Robert de Beaumanoir, a noble Breton on the French side, to his opponent Bramborough of the Anglo-Breton party. When their partisans clamored to join, a combat of thirty on each side was agreed upon. Terms were arranged, the site was chosen, and after participants heard mass and exchanged courtesies, the fight commenced. With swords, bear-spears, daggers, and axes, they fought savagely until four on the French side and two on the English were slain and a recess was called. Bleeding and exhausted, Beaumanoir called for a drink, eliciting the era's most memorable reply: "Drink thy blood, Beaumanoir, and thy thirst will pass!" Resuming, the combatants fought until the French side prevailed and every one of the survivors on either side was wounded. Bramborough and eight of his party were killed, the rest taken prisoner and held for ransom.

In the wide discussion the affair aroused, "some held it as a very poor thing and others as a very swaggering business," with the admirers dominating. The combat was celebrated in verse, painting, tapestry, and in a memorial stone erected on the site. More than twenty years later Froissart noticed a scarred survivor at the table of Charles V, where he was honored above all others. He told the ever-inquiring chronicler that he owed his great favor with the King to his having been one of the Thirty. The renown and honor the fight earned reflected the knight's nostalgic vision of what battle should be. While he practiced the warfare of havoc and pillage, he clung to the image of himself as Sir Lancelot.

With dazzling munificence, regardless of depleted finances, Jean launched the Order of the Star at an opening ceremony on January 6, 1352. He donated all the robes and staged a magnificent banquet in a hall draped with tapestries and hangings of gold and velvet decorated with stars and fleur-de-lys. Furniture was carved and gilded for the occasion. After a solemn mass, the revels grew so boisterous that a gold chalice was smashed and some rich draperies stolen. While the knights caroused, the English seized the castle of Guînes, whose absent captain was celebrating with his companions of the Star.

To their own undoing, the companions of the Star took seriously the oath not to flee from battle. In 1352, during the war in Brittany, a French force led by Marshal Guy de Nesle was caught in ambush at a place called Mauron by an Anglo-Breton force of about equal numbers. The French could have fled and saved themselves but that they were bound by their oath not to retreat. Though surrounded, they stood and fought until virtually all were killed or captured. So thick lay the dead on the field that the body of Guy de Nesle was not recovered until two days later. Seven French bannerets and 80 or 90 knights lost their lives not counting those captured, leaving so great a hole in the Order of the Star as, "with the great mischiefs and misfortunes that were to follow, caused the ruin of that noble company."

In France's misfortunes a young man of twenty, Charles, King of Navarre, grandson of Louis X, saw his opportunity. Whether he really aimed at the French crown, or at revenge for wrongs done him, or at stirring trouble for its own sake like Iago, is a riddle concealed in one of the most complex characters of the 14th century. A small slight youth with glistening eyes and a voluble flow of words, he was volatile, intelligent, charming, violent, cunning as a fox, ambitious as Lucifer, and more truly than Byron "mad, bad and dangerous to know." Seductive and eloquent, he could persuade his peers or sway a mob. He allowed himself the same unbridled acts of passion as Jean and other rulers, but, unlike Jean, he was a plotter, subtle, bold, absolutely without scruple, but so swerving and unfixed of purpose as to undo his own plots. His only constancy was hate. He is known to history as Charles the Bad.

Through his mother, daughter of Louis X, Charles of Navarre was more directly descended from the last Capets than Jean II, but his parents had renounced any claim to the crown when they acknowledged Philip VI. They had been compensated by the Kingdom of Navarre. The tiny mountain realm in the Pyrenees offered their son too little scope, but as Count of Evreux he held a great fief in Normandy where influence could be exerted. This became his main base of operations.

He was moved to action by jealousy and hatred of Charles d'Espagne, the new Constable, upon whom the King with rash favor had bestowed the county of Angoulême, which belonged to the house of Navarre. After infuriating Charles of Navarre by taking his territory, Jean, in fear of the result, tried to attach him by giving him his eight-year-old daughter, Jeanne, in marriage. Almost immediately he redoubled the first damage by withholding his daughter's dowry, which did not make a friend of his new son-in-law.

Charles of Navarre struck at the King through Charles d'Espagne. With no taste for half-measures, he simply had him assassinated, not without calculating that many nobles who equally hated the favorite would rally to the man who removed him. He did not kill with his own hands but through a party of henchmen led by his brother, Philip of Navarre, joined by Count Jean d'Harcourt, two Harcourt brothers, and other leading Norman nobles.

Seizing an occasion in January 1354 when the Constable was visiting Normandy, they broke into the room where he was sleeping naked (as was the medieval custom) and, with drawn swords gleaming in the light of their torches, dragged him from his bed. On his knees before Philip with hands clasped, Charles d'Espagne begged for mercy, saying "he would be his serf, he would ransom himself for gold, he would yield the land claimed, he would go overseas and never return." Count d'Harcourt urged Philip to have pity, but the young man, filled with his brother's rage and purpose, would not listen. His men fell upon the helpless Constable so "villainously and abominably" that they left his body pierced with eighty wounds. Galloping to where Charles of Navarre was waiting, they cried, "It is done! It is done!"

"What is done?" he asked for the record, and they answered, "The Constable is dead."

The audacity of the blow, as close to the King's person as it was possible to come, brought Charles of Navarre instantly to the forefront as a political factor. The King at once declared his Norman properties confiscated, but this would have to be made good by force.

Charles's contemporaries generally ascribed his act to hatred and revenge, but was it passion or calculation? While total absence of inhibition was characteristic of persons born to rule, bizarre bursts of violence were becoming more frequent in these years, perhaps as a legacy of the Black Death and a sense of the insecurity of life. In 1354 one of the periodic town-gown riots at Oxford exploded in such fury, with the use of swords, daggers, and even bows and arrows, that it ended in a massacre of students and the closing of the university until the King took measures to protect its liberties. In Italy in 1358 when Francesco Ordelaffi, tyrant of Forlì, known for a fearsome *subitezza* or quick temper, persisted in a last-ditch defense of his city against the papal forces, his son Ludovico dared to plead with him to yield rather than continue in war against the Church. "You are either a bastard or a changeling!" roared the infuriated father and, as his son turned away, drew a dagger and "stabbed him in the back so that he died before midnight." In a similar fit of ungovernable rage, the Count of Foix, who was married to a sister of Charles of Navarre, killed his only legitimate son.

The age had long been accustomed to physical violence. In the 10th century a "Truce of God" had been formulated to meet the craving for some relief from perpetual combat. During the truce, fighting was to be suspended on saints' days, Sundays, and Easter, and all non-combatants—clerks, peasants, merchants, artisans, and even animals—were to be left unharmed by men of the sword, and all religious and public buildings safeguarded. That was the theory. In practice, like other precepts of the Church, the Truce was a sieve that failed to contain human behavior.

In England coroners' rolls showed manslaughter far ahead of accident as cause of death, and more often than not the offender escaped punishment by obtaining benefit of clergy through bribes or the right connections. If life was filled with bodily harm, literature reflected it. One of La Tour Landry's cautionary tales for his daughters tells of a lady who ran off with a monk and, upon being found in bed with him by her brothers, they "took a knife and cut away the monk's stones and threw them in the lady's face and made her eat them and afterwards tied both monk and lady in a sack with heavy rocks and cast them into a river and drowned them." Another tale is of a husband who fetched his wife back from her parents' house, where she had fled after a marital quarrel. While lodged overnight in a town on the way home, the lady was attacked by a "great number of young people wild and infect with lechery" who "ravished her villainously," causing her to die of shame and sorrow. The husband cut her body into twelve pieces, each of which he sent with a letter to certain of her friends that they might be made ashamed of her running away from her husband and also be moved to take vengeance on her ravishers. The friends at once assembled with all their retainers and descended upon the town where the rape had occurred and slew all its inhabitants.

Violence was official as well as individual. Torture was authorized by the Church and regularly used to uncover heresy by the Inquisition. The tortures and punishments of civil justice customarily cut off hands and ears, racked, burned, flayed, and pulled apart people's bodies. In everyday life passersby saw some criminal flogged with a knotted rope or chained upright in an iron collar. They passed corpses hanging on the gibbet and decapitated heads and quartered bodies impaled on stakes on the city walls. In every church they saw pictures of saints undergoing varieties of atrocious martyrdom—by arrows, spears, fire, cut-off breasts—usually dripping blood. The Crucifixion with its nails, spears, thorns, whips, and more dripping blood was inescapable. Blood and cruelty were ubiquitous in Christian art, indeed essential to it, for Christ became Redeemer, and the saints sanctified, only through suffering violence at the hands of their fellow man.

In village games, players with hands tied behind them competed to kill a cat nailed to a post by battering it to death with their heads, at the risk of cheeks ripped open or eyes scratched out by the frantic animal's claws. Trumpets enhanced the excitement. Or a pig enclosed in a wide pen was chased by men with clubs to the laughter of spectators as he ran squealing from the blows until beaten lifeless. Accustomed in their own lives to physical hardship and injury, medieval men and women were not necessarily repelled by the spectacle of pain, but rather enjoyed it. The citizens of Mons bought a condemned criminal from a neighboring town so that they should have the pleasure of seeing him quartered. It may be that the untender medieval infancy produced adults who valued others no more than they had been valued in their own formative years.

Charles of Navarre by his outrageous act became the attraction for a growing group of nobles of northern France who were ready for a movement of protest against the Valois crown. The old condition of stress between barony and monarchy had been freshened by Philip's and Jean's violent reprisals against nobles whom they suspected of treachery, and by the military humiliations since Crécy. Landowners, hurt by the flight of labor and reduced revenue from their estates, tended to blame many of their troubles on the crown. They resented the financial pressures of the King and his despised ministers, and pressed for reform and more local autonomy. From his base in Normandy, Charles could become the focus of an adversary group, and he proclaimed that intention like a cock crowing.

"God knows it was I who with the help of God had Charles d'Espagne killed," he announced in a letter to Pope Innocent VI. He described his murder of the Constable as a righteous response to affronts and offenses, and expressed his devotion to the Holy See and his solicitude for the Pope's health. Charles was now prepared to offer himself as an agent of England in return for English aid to maintain his Norman possessions, and to this end he wanted to use the Pope as intermediary. In a letter to King Edward he wrote that by means of his castle and men in Normandy, he could do such harm to Jean II "as he shall never recover from," and he asked that English forces in Brittany be sent to his support.

Throughout that year, 1354, the future course of the century swayed between pressures for peace and others for continuing the war. Pope Innocent VI, who was aged and sickly, was trying urgently to bring about a settlement because he heard the sound of the infidel pounding at the gates. In 1353 the Turks had seized Gallipoli, key of the Hellespont, and thereby entered Europe. Christian energies must be united against them, which would be impossible if France and England renewed their war.

Pressed by the Pope and by their empty treasuries, Edward and Jean had entered negotiations for a permanent peace which neither really wanted. Edward had used up his credit with the English people for a war that neither fighting nor diplomacy could bring to an end. The English Third Estate was finding that the costs outweighed the spoils. In 1352 Parliament limited the King's powers of conscription. In April 1354 when the House of Commons was asked by the Lord Chamberlain, "Do you desire a treaty of perpetual peace if it can be had?" members unanimously cried, "Aye! Aye!"

On his side, Jean was trapped by fear of an arrangement between Charles of Navarre and England. Medieval intelligence channels rattled with the tale of his son-in-law's conspiracies. And while Charles was hostile, the King's ability to raise troops and taxes from Normandy was curtailed. Forced by humiliating necessity, he had to swallow his fury, cancel his confiscation of Charles's Norman fiefs, pardon him for the murder of Charles d'Espagne, and invite him to Paris for a ceremony of reconciliation. Charles came because all his life he could never resist another option, and perhaps because at 22 he was not as sure of himself as his acts proclaimed. With oaths and embraces and elaborate formulas, the pretense was carried out in March 1354 amid feelings between the two principals that need only be imagined.

The year teetered on the edge of peace. The war was almost settled by a treaty overwhelmingly to the advantage of England, but at the last minute France stiffened and refused. All that came of three years' parleys and the Pope's zeal for peace was an extension of the truce for one year while sparring was resumed. Once again Charles of Navarre treated with Edward and promised to meet the English at Cherbourg for a joint campaign.* Pope Innocent's hopes crashed in the collapse of the peace treaty. When he reproached the King of England for conspiring with Charles of Navarre against the King of France, Edward lied as easily as rulers of later times. "Speaking truly and swearing faithfully by the heart of God," he denied the charge in writing "on the word of a King" although the text of the correspondence exists.

In haste to renew the war, he proclaimed French perfidy and the righteousness of his cause in letters to the Archbishops of Canterbury and York which were read by heralds to the public. Sermons preached from the pulpit spread his tale of grievances. Edward understood public relations. By one device or another, funds were raised, consents wrung from Parliament, and fleets, men, and provisions assembled during the spring and summer of 1355. When on Midsummer's Day the truce expired without renewal, two expeditionary forces were ready to sail, one under the Black Prince for Bordeaux, one under the Duke of Lancaster for Normandy, where it was intended to link up with Charles of Navarre.

With fair winds speeding his several-score ships, Prince Edward reached Bordeaux in three or four days. He brought with him 1,000 knights, squires, and other men-at-arms, 2,000 archers, and a large number of Welsh foot soldiers. Now 24, strongly built, with a full mustache, the heir of King Edward was a hard and haughty prince who was to gain immortal renown as "the Flower of Chivalry." The reputation was helped by his having the good fortune to die before he was tarnished by the responsibilities of the throne. The French saw him as "cruel in manner" and as "the proudest man ever born of woman."

The object of the Prince's raid, extending 250 miles east to Narbonne and back to Bordeaux in October-November 1355, was not

---

* It was this deal, negotiated through England's envoy in Avignon, that was supposed to have earned him the title of Charles the Bad, although this is disputed by others who say it had been conferred by his Spanish subjects from the time he was eighteen. In fact the title was not contemporary and does not appear in the chronicles until the 16th century.

conquest but havoc, plus plunder. Never had the "famous, beautiful and rich" land of Armagnac known such destruction as was visited upon it in these two months. The havoc was not purposeless but intended, like military terrorism in any age, to punish or deter people from siding with the enemy. By sliding back into French allegiance, the inhabitants of Guienne were considered to be rebels against the King of England whom it was the Prince's duty to chastise. Such policy was bound to provoke hostility in and around the territory England wanted to hold, but the Prince, who was neither more nor less imaginative than most commanders, did not look into the future. With the addition of Gascon allies, he had collected a large force of about 9,000, consisting of 1,500 lances (three men—a knight and two attendants—to a lance), 2,000 archers, and 3,000 foot. He intended to demonstrate English might, convince local lords where their interest lay, and cut the French war potential by damaging a region which furnished the French King with rich revenues. Plunder would play its part both as profit and pay.

"Harrying and wasting the country," as the Prince wrote in matter-of-fact description to the Bishop of Winchester, "we burned Plaisance and other fine towns and all the lands around." After loading loot into the baggage wagons, rounding up cattle, slaughtering pigs and chickens, the company proceeded to the business of laying waste: burning granaries and mills, barns and haystacks, smashing wine vats, cutting down vines and fruit trees, wrecking bridges, and moving on. Bypassing Toulouse, they stormed and burned Mont Giscar, where many men, women, and children hitherto ignorant of war were maltreated and slain. The raiding party plundered Carcassonne for three days without attacking the citadel, "and the whole of the third day we remained for burning of the said city." The process was repeated at Narbonne. Strangely, the French offered no organized resistance, despite the presence of Marshal Jean de Clermont alongside the Count of Armagnac, the King's lieutenant in Languedoc. Beyond bringing people inside the city walls where possible, Armagnac failed to come out against the English except for an inconclusive skirmish on their way back.

His failure was probably owed to fear of a pounce at his back by his opulent neighbor and mortal enemy, Gaston, Count of Foix. The autonomies and rivalries of the great southern lords led to as unquiet relations with the King as with each other. Called "Gaston Phoebus" for his beauty and red-gold hair, Foix had ignored the summons of Philip VI for defense of the realm in the year of Crécy. He subsequently served as Lieutenant of Languedoc, but on becoming involved in a feud with King Jean had been imprisoned in Paris for eighteen months. Back in his domain in 1355, he entered into a deal of some kind with the Black Prince which spared his lands during the raid while he remained neutral. The virtual autonomy of such great lords drained away much of the strength of France.

The Prince's company returned to winter quarters at Bordeaux loaded down with carpets, draperies, jewels, and other spoils if not with glory. Where was prowess, where was valor, where the skills and feats of combat that were the warrior's pride? Robbing and slaying unarmed civilians called for no courage or strength of arms and hardly for the knightly virtues of the Round Table and the Garter. The Prince himself; his principal Gascon ally, the Captal* de Buch; his closest companion and adviser, Sir John Chandos; the Earls of Warwick and Salisbury, and at least three others of the company were charter members of the Order of the Garter, supposedly exemplars of magnanimity. Whether, when they lay down to sleep after a day's carnage, they felt any discrepancy between the ideal and the practice, no one knows. They left no such indication. To signify his right to punish, the Prince twice rejected a good price offered by towns to buy immunity from sack. His letters express only a sense of satisfied accomplishment. His raid had enriched his company, reduced French revenues, and proved to any wavering Gascons that service under his banner was rewarding. Yet even Froissart, the uncritical celebrator of knighthood, was moved to write, "It was an occasion for pity. . . ." As the war dragged on, the habituating of armed men to cruelty and destruction as accepted practice poisoned the 14th century.

Held up by contrary winds and by Charles of Navarre's sudden defection, the English force destined for Normandy did not sail until the end of October, already late for a campaign in the north. Its commander, Henry, Duke of Lancaster, called the "Father of Soldiers," was England's most distinguished warrior, who had not missed a battle in his 45 years. He was a veteran of the Scottish wars, of Sluys, of Calais and all the campaigns in France, and when his country was quiescent he rode forth in knightly tradition to carry his sword elsewhere. He had joined the King of Castile in a crusade against the Moors of Algeciras and journeyed to Prussia to join the Teutonic Knights in one of their annual "crusades" to extend Christianity over the lands of Lithuanian heathen.

---

* His title derived from the Latin *capitalis*, meaning chieftain.

Inheritor of enormous lands and fortune, Lancaster was in 1351 created the first English Duke outside the royal family, and subsequently built the palace of the Savoy as his residence in London. In 1352, while the truce still held between England and France, he was the star of a remarkable event in Paris. On returning from a season in Prussia, he had quarreled with Duke Otto of Brunswick and accepted his challenge to combat, which was arranged under French auspices. Given a safe-conduct, escorted by a noble company to Paris, magnificently entertained by King Jean, the Duke of Lancaster rode into the lists before a splendid audience of French nobility, but his mere reputation proved too much for his opponent. Otto of Brunswick trembled so violently on his war-horse that he could not put on his helmet or wield his spear and had to be removed by his friends and retract his challenge. The King covered the embarrassment to chivalry by a handsome banquet, at which he reconciled the two principals and offered Lancaster rich presents in farewell. Refusing them, the Duke accepted only a thorn from the Saviour's crown, which on returning home he donated to a collegiate church he had founded at Leicester.

As religious as he was martial, he wrote in French (still the language of the English court) a devotional book called the *Livre des sainctes médecines*, in which he used allegory to reveal the wounds of his soul—that is to say, his sins—to Christ, the Divine Physician. Each part of the body had an allegorical wound and each remedy a matching religious symbolism. Because the Duke was examining himself, a 14th century grand seigneur emerges as a real person who admires the elegance of his long pointed toes in the stirrup, and at jousts stretches out his legs for the notice of the ladies; who also reproaches himself for recoiling from the stench of the poor and the sick, and for extorting money, lands, and other property by exercising undue influence on his courts.

In the invasion of France in 1355, Lancaster was joined by King Edward. Making for Calais instead of Cherbourg, they landed on November 2, collected a force of 3,000 men-at-arms, 2,000 mounted archers, and about as many on foot, and set out ostensibly to seek battle with the King of France while raiding the Pas de Calais, Artois, and Picardy en route.

The King of France had "solemnly and publicly" issued the *arrière-ban* or general summons to all men between eighteen and sixty in May just before the truce ended. Perhaps owing to a poor response, it was repeated several times during the summer in Paris and all important places of the realm—"especially in Picardy," according to one chronicler. Since a general summons brought in persons of doubtful military value, the monarchy preferred to demand the cost of a given number rather than the men themselves, and tried to fix physical standards for those who served and send the rest home. Sorting them out to assemble a fighting force took time; doubtless also, owing to recent discontents, not a few nobles dragged their feet. By November the host that Jean led north to meet the English was incomplete.

Enguerrand de Coucy VII, aged fifteen, was a part of it. Nothing is reported of what he did, only that he was present among the "barons of Picardy" in the battalion of Moreau de Fiennes, a future Marshal of France. He was in distinguished company, with his guardian, Matthieu de Roye, Master of Crossbowmen, Geoffrey de Charny, known as the "perfect knight," and Marshal Arnoul d'Audrehem. The battalion also included the bourgeois of Paris, Rouen, and Amiens.

The campaign that was Enguerrand's first experience of war was no stuff for heroic legend. The French host was at Amiens on November 5–7 and had advanced northward to St. Omer by November 11, bypassing en route the English on the left who were simultaneously marching south to Hesdin. The armies sniffed and circled around each other, each King issuing invitations to the other to fight—"body to body or force against force," in the words of Jean's challenge—which each managed to decline in ornamental verbiage. If Jean, as the English chroniclers claimed, feared to seek pitched battle, Edward was no more eager. Jean's major military action was to burn or carry off provisions of the countryside so as to deprive the English of supply, at the cost of the local populace. Left to face a hungry winter robbed of their hard-earned harvests, the people experienced their own warrior class not as protectors but ravagers.

Jean's scorched-earth policy forced the English to fall back upon the coast for lack of food, wine, and beer. For four days they had no other drink but water, which seemed like starvation in an age that depended on wine or beer as an essential part of diet. The French had also taken care with letters and money to stimulate a Scottish diversion. News of a threat from the Scottish border plus the prospect of a winter on water caused Edward and Lancaster to re-embark after a campaign lasting no more than ten days.

Jean now faced the necessity of obtaining from an Assembly of the Three Estates a subsidy to pay his troops. Summoned by the King, the Estates of Langued'oil—that is, of northern France—met in Paris in December. Because, as a result of the tax-exemption of clergy and nobles, the Third Estate paid most of the taxes, it controlled the decision on how much aid to grant, and since it could use its leverage to exact reforms or privileges, the monarchy was never very happy on these occasions.

The offer made by the Estates of 1355 revealed the wealth of French resources and the national loyalty beneath the discontents, and also a profound mistrust of the King's government. The Estates agreed to support 30,000 men-at-arms for one year at an estimated cost of five million livres on condition that the funds were to be administered not by the King's treasury but by a committee of the Estates themselves which would pay the troops directly. The money was to be raised by a tax on everyone of all Estates and by a salt tax as well, at rates which had to be increased in the following year when the required sum was not produced. The new rates amounted to a tax of 4 percent on the incomes of the rich, 5 percent on the middle class, and 10 percent on the lowest taxable class. One result was a revolt of the "little against the great" in the textile city of Arras in northern Picardy. Though quickly suppressed, it was a signal of coming trouble.

Meanwhile, the restless scheming of Charles of Navarre produced the next explosion. He was trying to turn the eighteen-year-old Dauphin Charles against his father, and at the same time was encouraging the Norman lords to resist payment of aids to the King.

In April 1356 the Dauphin, in his capacity as Duke of Normandy, was entertaining Charles of Navarre and the leading Norman nobles at a banquet in Rouen when suddenly the doors were broken open and the King in helmet with many followers, preceded by Marshal d'Audrehem with drawn sword, burst in. "Let no one move or he is a dead man!" cried the Marshal. The King seized Navarre, calling him "Traitor," at which Navarre's squire Colin Doublel drew his dagger in the terrible act of *lèse majesté* and threatened to plunge it into the King's breast. Without flinching, Jean ordered his guards to "seize that boy and his Master too." He himself laid hold of Jean d'Harcourt so roughly that he tore his doublet from collar to belt, accusing him, and others present who had been in the party that murdered Charles d'Espagne, of treason. In horror, the Dauphin begged his father not to dishonor him by violence upon his guests, but was told by the King, "You do not know what I know"; these were wicked traitors whose crimes had been discovered. Charles of Navarre pleaded for mercy, saying he was the victim of false reports, but the King had him arrested with the others while the remaining guests fled, "climbing over walls in their terror."

Next morning, Jean d'Harcourt, Colin Doublel, and two other Norman lords were taken toward the gibbet, in two carts, the ignominious vehicle used for the condemned, accompanied by the King in person, dressed in full armor as if expecting attack. His nerves evidently working on him, Jean suddenly halted the procession in a field and ordered the prisoners decapitated on the spot. He allowed them no priest, for as traitors they were to die without being confessed, except for Colin Doublel, who was condemned for raising a weapon against the King rather than for treason. A substitute executioner was hastily located who took six blows to sever Harcourt's head. The four bodies, dragged the rest of the way to the gibbet, were hung up in chains and their heads stuck on lances, where they remained for two years. Charles of Navarre was imprisoned in the Châtelet in Paris and his estates in Normandy were again confiscated by the King.

When Welsh Fluellen in Shakespeare's *Henry V* speaks of the King's "cholers and his moods and his displeasures and his indignations and also being a little intoxicate in his brains," he might have been describing Jean le Bon. The King's principal victim, Jean d'Harcourt, had three brothers and nine children married into a network of families of northern France (a daughter subsequently married Raoul de Coucy, uncle of Enguerrand VII). The King succeeded in outraging the many connections of his victims without eliminating his real enemy, Charles of Navarre. Sympathy was aroused for the prisoner of the Châtelet, and popular songs were composed in his honor.

The affair of Rouen accomplished just what the King had tried to thwart—the reopening of Normandy to England. Jean d'Harcourt's brother Godefrey, the same who had led Edward III into Normandy ten years before, and Navarre's brother Philip appealed for English help to recover their estates, and when the English landed at Cherbourg in July 1356, both these lords took the oath of homage to Edward III as King of France. From Cherbourg the English under the Duke of Lancaster advanced toward contact with Brittany just at the time the Black Prince started out from Bordeaux on a new raid northward toward the heart of France. Events now moved toward the collision at Poitiers.

With English, Gascons, and reinforcements from home, the Prince marched north with a force of about 8,000. His object was to link up with Lancaster and spread damage on the way, taking plunder rather than towns, fortresses, or territory. Marching, fighting, and amassing loot, the Prince reached the Loire on or about September 3 and, finding the bridges destroyed, turned westward toward Tours, where he learned that a large French army was advancing toward him. He also received word that Lancaster had broken out of Normandy and was hastening toward a junction. But the Loire lay between them, and the country was alive with French men-at-arms. His men were now fatigued from many sharp fights, sated and burdened with plunder. After four days' hesitation which lost him a head start, the Prince turned southward again with clear intention to avoid pitched battle and bring his gains safely back to Bordeaux.

In the north Jean had first moved against Lancaster's force in Normandy and temporarily blocked it before turning to face the threat from the south. He had summoned a great mobilization for defense of the realm to rendezvous at Chartres in the first week of September. Stimulated by the enemy's presence on the Loire in the center of France, the nobles responded to the summons, whatever their sentiments toward the King. They came from Auvergne, Berry, Burgundy, Lorraine, Hainault, Artois, Vermandois, Picardy, Brittany, Normandy. "No knight and no squire remained at home," wrote the chroniclers; here was gathered "all the flower of France."

With the King were his four sons, aged fourteen to nineteen; the new Constable, Gautier de Brienne, who bore the title, Duke of Athens, from a defunct duchy founded in the crusades; the two Marshals; 26 counts and dukes, 334 bannerets, and nearly all the lesser lords. It was the largest French army of the century—a "great marvel," wrote an English chronicler, the "equal never seen of Nobility in arms." The actual number, given by chroniclers with individual abandon at anything up to 80,000, has been endlessly disputed and eventually brought to settle at around 16,000, about twice the size of the Black Prince's army.

It had no cohesion. The great seigneurs came at their own time, many late for the rendezvous, each with his own troop of 50, 100, or 150 under his own banner, and with his own household and baggage train and gold and silver vessels and plate for turning into ready cash when needed. The provisions of the ordinance of 1351 for discipline and order had borne few results. Owing to a quarrel over renewed taxation, bourgeois support was disaffected, causing the towns to withdraw their contingents. Froissart, on the other hand, reports that Jean dismissed the bourgeois forces when he crossed the Loire, "which was madness in him and in those who advised him."

With the might of France assembled, Jean was confident he could force the Prince back into Aquitaine, even back to England. Between September 8 and 13 the French army crossed the Loire at Orléans, Blois, and other points and pushed south in pursuit of the Anglo-Gascons. On September 12 the Black Prince was at Montbazon, five miles south of Tours, where he was met by the papal legates who had been endeavoring to make peace since early in the year. Besides writing to the Kings of England and France and to leading nobles of the two countries, urging them to negotiate, the Pope had dispatched the two cardinals in person to try to halt the hostilities.

The chief of the two was the aristocratic Cardinal Talleyrand de Périgord, a prelate *baldonzoso e superbo* (proud and haughty), as Villani called him. He was a son of the Count of Périgord and of the beautiful Countess reputed to have been Pope Clement V's mistress. At the age of six, perhaps too early to have a religious calling but not its income, he had been given the Pope's permission to receive the clerical tonsure and therefore the right to hold ecclesiastical benefices. A bishop at twenty-three, a cardinal at thirty, he had held at one time or another nine English benefices in London, York, Lincoln, and Canterbury, making him a principal target of English resentment.

From Cardinal Talleyrand, Prince Edward learned that the King of France counted on intercepting him and was preparing for pitched battle on September 14, and that the French army was daily enlarging as new units arrived. Though the Prince was not anxious to risk battle against fresh and superior numbers, he nevertheless rejected Talleyrand's proposal to negotiate a truce, perhaps because he was overconfident of being able to elude the enemy. The French were pushing hard, intending to outflank the Prince at Poitiers, where they would get across the road to Bordeaux and cut off his retreat. For four days more the armies continued on the march without making contact, the English barely ten or twelve miles ahead, the French gradually closing the gap.

On September 17 at a farm called La Chaboterie, three miles west of Poitiers, a French party led by Raoul de Coucy, Sire de Montmirail, uncle of Enguerrand VII and reputed one of the bravest knights of his time, sighted an English reconnaissance unit, and on its own initiative galloped to the attack. Whether Enguerrand was in the party is unrecorded, or even whether he was with the host. The domain of Coucy must certainly have sent its contingent, unless this was with the forces in Normandy opposing Lancaster. In the clash that now occurred, Raoul dashed so far forward that he reached the Prince's banner-bearer, fighting valiantly. Under the ardor of the French assault, the Anglo-Gascons reeled back, yet inexplicably, though they were far outnumbered, they recovered and overpowered the French. Many were killed and Raoul was captured, though ransomed soon afterward. Like so much else that happened at Poitiers, the outcome at La Chaboterie is difficult to explain.

Greedy for ransoms from the skirmish, the Anglo-Gascons pursued with such vigor that they were drawn three leagues from the field, with the result that the Prince, in order to rally and reassemble his forces, had to halt where he was and camp for the night though suffering greatly from lack of water.

On the following morning, Sunday, September 18, as the Prince's weary company resumed march just below Poitiers, his scouts from a crest of land saw a glitter of armor and the flutter of a thousand pennants as the French main body came into view. Knowing he was overtaken and battle now unavoidable, the Prince drew up his forces in the most favorable site he could find, on a wooded slope edged by vineyards and hedges and by a stream meandering through marshy land. Beyond the stream was a wide field traversed by a narrow road. The place was about two miles southeast of Poitiers.

Confident of victory in his superior strength, King Jean was held back from attack by Cardinal Talleyrand, who arrived with a great company of clerics to beg him to keep Sunday's "Truce of God" until next morning while allowing the Cardinal another chance to mediate. At a war council in the King's pavilion of scarlet silk, Marshal d'Audrehem and others ardent for battle, and conscious of the threat of the Duke of Lancaster at their rear, urged no delay. Against their advice, the King fatally agreed to the Cardinal's plea for delay. A proposal by Geoffrey de Charny for an arranged combat of 100 champions on each side was rejected by his companions lest it exclude too many from combat, glory, and ransoms. If either immediate battle or Charny's proposal had been adopted, the ultimate outcome might have been different.

When Cardinal Talleyrand hastened back to the English camp, he found the Prince was now amenable to, even anxious for, any arrangement that would get him out of danger with honor and spoils intact. Edward offered to restore free of ransom all prisoners he had taken during the two campaigns and all places he had occupied, and to agree to non-belligerency for seven years, during which he would pledge not to take up arms against the King of France. He even offered, according to the *Chronique des Quatre Premiers Valois*, to yield Calais and Guînes, though he certainly lacked the authority for such a surrender. His extraordinary concessions indicate his sense of a desperate situation and the realization that he could be starved out if the French chose to surround and invest him. Or, knowing that so inglorious a choice by the French was unlikely, he may have been playing for time to complete preparation of his archers' positions. This his men were already engaged in doing, and throughout the day of parleys they continued entrenching and setting up palisades.

King Jean agreed to consider the proposal. Cardinal Talleyrand and his clerics hurried back and forth on their mules, and the Prince's chief knights came under safe-conduct to parley in person. Hardly a battle of the endless war, except in Brittany, was not preceded by efforts to stop it that never succeeded. Arrogant in his confidence of victory, Jean accepted the offer on condition that the Prince of Wales would surrender himself and 100 of his knights as prisoners of the King of France. Such humiliation the Prince resolutely refused, having meanwhile improved his position among the woods and behind hedges. While Talleyrand still begged the King for the love of Christ to agree at least to a truce until Christmas, the day of parleys was over. The French council of war reconvened to determine a plan of attack.

Marshal Clermont advised blockade, the very action the Prince had feared. Rather than the folly of attacking the English in their protected position, he said the French should encamp around them and when they had no more food "they would depart from that place." This was the obvious and sensible course to adopt, but the dictates of chivalry forbade it. Met with scorn and fierce dispute by Marshal d'Audrehem, Clermont's proposal was rejected. Three knights who had reconnoitered the English lines came in to report that the only access to the enemy was a narrow passage permitting no more than four abreast to ride through. On the advice of Sir William Douglas, a Scot experienced against the English who was acting as the King's chief of tactics, the critical decision was taken for the main body to attack on foot. But rather than forgo altogether the cavalry charge of heavy armor, it was decided that the initial breakthrough of the archers' lines should be carried out by a task force of 300 of the elite of the army mounted on the strongest and swiftest war-horses. All three military chiefs, the Constable and both Marshals, were recklessly assigned to this body.

At sunrise on Monday, September 19, in bustle and clamor of arms with trumpets sounding, the French host was drawn up behind the mounted spearhead in the usual three battalions. They were deployed one behind the other, presumably for successive shocks, but precluded by this position from aiding one another on the flank. The nineteen-year-old Dauphin, who had never fought in war before, was nominal commander of the first battalion; Philippe d'Orléans, brother of the King, aged twenty and equally a novice, commanded the second; the King himself, the third. He was accompanied by a personal guard of nineteen others dressed exactly like him in black armor and white surcoat marked with fleur-de-lys. This was a prudent if not exactly knightly precaution, since in a battle in which a sovereign engaged, the enemy would do its utmost to capture him.

"On foot! On foot!" ordered Jean, and "he put himself on foot before all." It has been said that he took the decision to dismount in order to reduce the opportunity among his disunited forces for individual action or flight. Modern critics—for the debate has continued—have called it "suicidal folly"; others have considered it the only sensible and feasible decision because cavalry could not deploy en masse owing to the marshes, hedges, and ditches.

The knights dismounted, removed spurs, cut off the long pointed toes of their *poulaines*, and shortened their lances to five feet. The Oriflamme, fork-tongued scarlet banner of the Kings of France, was awarded to Geoffrey de Charny, "the perfect knight," to carry. Legend derived the banner from Charlemagne, who was said to have carried it to the Holy Land in response to an angel's prophecy that a knight armed with a golden lance from whose tip flames of "great marvel" burned would deliver the land from the Saracens. Embroidered with golden flames that gave it its name, the banner had been adopted by the monarchy from the Abbey of St. Denis along with the battle cry "Montjoie—St. Denis!" As the signal for advance or rally, the war cry signified allegiance to a particular lord. On that morning the King announced the royal cry as the cry for all. "You have cursed the English," he cried to the assembled ranks of chivalry, "and longed to measure swords with them. Behold them in your presence! Remember the wrongs they have done you and revenge yourselves for the losses and sufferings they have inflicted on France. I promise you we shall do battle with them, and God be with us!"

The Prince of Wales deployed two battalions in front for mutual support and one behind, with the archers in saw-tooth formation divided among the three. The four Earls—Warwick and Oxford, Suffolk and Salisbury—commanded the two front divisions, the Prince and Chandos the rear, with a body of 400 reserves at their side. The English had the advantage of terrain and a far greater advantage in being a coherent body, experienced together in two campaigns, professionally trained, and based on better management and organization. For overseas expeditions the English had to plan carefully and recruit selectively the ablest and strongest fighting material.

Yet even now, perhaps because of divided opinion among his advisors, the Prince essayed a movement to get away toward the road to Bordeaux. "For on that day," in the words of Chandos Herald, "he did not wish for combat, I tell you true, but wished without fail to avoid battle entirely." The movement of baggage wagons behind the hill, revealed by the fluttering pennants of their advance guard, was seen by Marshal d'Audrehem, who shouted, "Ha! Pursue! Charge, ere the English are lost to us!" The more sober Clermont still advised a surrounding action, precipitating a furious quarrel between the two Marshals on the very brink of battle. Audrehem accused his fellow of being "afraid to look on them" and of causing delay that would lose the day, to which Clermont replied with suitable insult. "Ha, *Maréchal*, you are not so bold but that your horse's nose will find itself in my horse's ass!" In this disunity the charge of the mounted spearhead was launched.

Warned of the assault, the Prince had halted the initial departure, reassembled, and in a fiery oration called upon his knights to fight for their King's claim to the French crown, for the great honor of victory, for rich spoils and eternal fame. He told them to trust in God and obey commands.

Attacking from the flank, Audrehem's squadron was caught and crushed under the piercing arrows of the archers, while Clermont, joined by the Constable, charged in the frontal attack he so mistrusted and was beaten back under flights of arrows so thick they darkened the air. Shooting from sheltered positions protected by dismounted knights and foot soldiers, the archers, at the express order of the Earl of Oxford, aimed for the horses' unarmored rumps. Stumbling and falling, the horses went down under their riders or reared back among those who followed, "making great slaughter upon their own masters." It was the frenzy of Crécy over again. Fallen knights could not raise their horses or rise themselves. In the melee that followed, amid call of trumpets, shouted battle cries, and screams of wounded men and horses, both Clermont and the Constable were killed, Audrehem was captured, and the greater part of the picked knights killed or taken prisoner.

Already the Dauphin's battalion was advancing on foot into the havoc. With Charles in the front lines were his two brothers, seventeen-year-old Louis, Duc d'Anjou, and sixteen-year-old Jean, future Duc de Berry. Tangled in the confusion of riderless horses and raging combat, many of the battalion fought on savagely, hand to hand, stabbing with shortened lances and hacking with battle-ax and sword. But with no hardened leader in command, only a boy witnessing debacle, the unit began to fall back. A shout of triumph from enemy throats signaled seizure of the Dauphin's standard. Whether on order of the King to save his sons, as later claimed, or at the decision of the four lords appointed as the princes' guardians, the greater part of the battalion withdrew from the field, falling back upon and infecting with failure the Duc d'Orléans' battalion. Instead of coming in with fresh force to give the hard-pressed English no pause, which at this stage might well have turned the tide, Orléans' battalion, swept up in the retreat, fled without striking a blow, retrieved its waiting horses, and galloped for the city.

"Advance," cried the King upon this successive disaster, "for I will recover the day or die on the field!" With Oriflamme flying and his youngest son, fourteen-year-old Philip, future Duke of Burgundy, at his father's side, this largest of the three battalions, awkward on foot in their iron cocoons, marched upon the bloody field. "Alack! We are undone!" cried an English knight, seeing them come. "You lie, miserable coward," stormed the Prince, "if you so blaspheme as to say that I, alive, may be conquered!" Each side fell upon the other with the strength and ferocity of desperation. Although a battle's outcome, it was said, could be told by the time the sixth arrow was loosed, now when the English archers had emptied their sheaves the issue wavered. In the pause before the new French assault, the archers had retrieved arrows from the wounds and dead bodies of the fallen; others now hurled stones and fought with knives. Had the third French assault been mounted, it is possible that at this stage, against a battered opponent, it might have prevailed.

The battle entered its seventh hour, a tossing mass of separate groups hammering each other, oblivious of any formation, except for the Prince and Chandos still holding command with the reserves on the hilltop. Pointing to where the Oriflamme flew, Chandos advised the Prince to attack the King's unit, for, he said, "Valor will not allow him to flee; he will fall into our power and victory will be ours." In what proved the decisive maneuver, the Prince ordered his D'Artagnesque ally, the Captal de Buch, to lead a small mounted force in attack upon the French rear while, with the mounted reserves and the unwounded from his own battalion, he summoned the army's last strength for a frontal offensive. "Sirs, behold me here! For God's mercy, think on striking! Advance, Banner, in the name of God and St. George!"

His trumpets sounded, and their echo, thrown back by the stone walls of Poitiers, rang through the woods "so that you would think the hills had called out to the valleys and that it had thundered in the clouds." The English charge, in whole or in part on horseback, rushed down upon the King's unit "like the wild boar of Cornwall." The battle reached climactic fury "and none so hardy" wrote Chandos Herald, "whose heart was not dismayed." "Beware, Father, to the right! Ware, to the left!" Philip cried as the blows descended. Knights grappled in personal combat, "each thinking of his own honor." Attacked by the Prince's charge in front and the Captal's horsemen from the rear, the French fought in ferocious despair. Bleeding from multiple wounds, Geoffrey de Charny was cut down and killed still holding the

Oriflamme. The King's guard, surrounding him in a mighty wedge, tottered under the assault. "Some, eviscerated, tread on their own entrails, others vomit forth their teeth, some still standing have their arms cut off. The dying roll about in the blood of strangers, the fallen bodies groan, and the proud spirits, abandoning their inert bodies, moan horribly." The slain piled up around the flailing battle-ax of the King, who with his helmet knocked off was bleeding from two wounds on his face. "Yield, yield," cried voices, "or you are a dead man!" In the midst of hoarse shouts and fierce contention to seize him, a French exile, Denis de Morbecque, banished for manslaughter and now serving the English, pressed forward and said, "Sire, I am a knight of Artois. Yield yourself to me and I will lead you to the Prince of Wales." King Jean handed him his glove and surrendered.

With the loss of the King, the remaining French forces disintegrated, those who could flying for the gates of Poitiers to escape capture. English and Gascons of all ranks pursued wildly, greed overmastering exhaustion, and scrambled for prisoners under the very walls of the city. Some of the French turned in flight and captured their pursuers.

The defeat swept France of its leadership. In addition to the King, the Constable and both Marshals, and the bearer of the Oriflamme, who were either dead or taken, the victors captured one fighting archbishop, 13 counts, 5 viscounts, 21 barons and bannerets, and some 2,000 knights, squires, and men-at-arms of the gentry. Too many to be taken back, most were released on a pledge to bring their ransoms to Bordeaux before Christmas.

The number of killed, a different figure in every account, was at least several thousand, of whom 2,426 were of the nobility. The fact that they equaled or outnumbered the captured was evidence of valiant fighting, but, unfortunately for France, the living who fled made a greater impression than the dead who fought. The *Grand Chronique* admits openly that battalions "fled shamefully and cravenly," and the *Chronique Normande* somberly concludes, "The mortality of this battle was not so great as the shame."

That was the great debris of Poitiers. Citizens watching from the city walls witnessed inglorious retirement and hectic flight, and their report spread throughout France. The retreat of Orléans' battalion which lost the day is hardly explicable except by the disaffected mood of nobles antagonized by the King. Certainly many were present that day who would not have grieved at misfortune to the monarchy, and it would have taken the shouts of only a few to induce panic. Whatever the cause, the effect was to deepen and spread mistrust of the noble estate and loosen confidence in the ordained structure of society.

Popular sentiment showed itself at once against lords returning to raise their ransoms. They were so "hated and blamed by the commoners," reports Froissart, that they had difficulty in gaining admittance to the towns and sometimes even to their own estates. Peasants of a village in Normandy belonging to the Sire de Ferté-Fresnel, seeing their seigneur come riding through with only a squire and a valet and without his sword, raised the cry, "Here is one of the traitors who fled from the battle!" They rushed upon the three riders, pulled the lord from his horse, and beat him up. He returned a few days later, better armed, to take vengeance, killing one villager in the process. Though this small outburst was quickly crushed, it was an omen. Many seigneurs returned to face gibes or sudden hostility and had trouble raising the traditional aid for the lord's ransom. To find the funds, many were forced to sell all their furnishings or free their serfs for payment. A residue of ruined knights was a by-product of Poitiers.

The cry of "Traitor!" was not a local voice only, but a bewildered people's explanation of the inexplicable. It was the eternal cry of conspiracy, of stab in the back. How else could the great King of France have been taken and the great host of French chivalry defeated by a handful of "archers and brigands" except by betrayal? A contemporary polemic in verse called "Complaint of the Battle of Poitiers" explicitly charges,

> The very great treason that they long time concealed
> Was in the said host very clearly revealed.

The author, an unknown cleric, accuses certain persons of having by "their cupidity sold secrets of the Royal Council to the English" and, on being discovered and "kicked out of the Council by the King," of conspiring to destroy him and his children. The flight of these false men, "treacherous, disloyal, infamous and perjured," was a planned betrayal; in them the nobility was dishonored and France too. They have denied God; they are men of pride, greed and haughty manners,

> Of bombast and vainglory and dishonest clothes,
> With golden belts and plumes on their heads
> And the long beard of goats, a thing for beasts.
> They deafen you like thunder and tempest.

The beard complained of, originally a mark of penitence, had lately been worn in narrow forked style as a worldy fashion and now became an object of satire linked with running away.

The "Complaint" has only praise for Jean II, who fought to the end with his little son beside him. In public opinion he became a hero. However inept as sovereign and captain, his personal valor, poignantly emphasized by the "little son," glorified him in the eyes of his subjects and gave France a focus for the recovery of honor. The "Complaint" hopes that God will send "good men of great power" to avenge the defeat and bring back the King, and concludes significantly:

> If he is well advised, he will not forget
> To lead Jaque Bonhomme and all his great company
> Who do not run from war to save their lives!

After the citizens of Poitiers had buried the bodies outside, the Mayor proclaimed mourning for the captured King and forbade celebration of any feast day or festival. In Languedoc the Estates General prohibited for the space of a year, so long as the King was not delivered, the wearing of gold, silver, or pearls, ornamented or scalloped robes and hats, and entertainment by minstrels and jongleurs. The Dauphin and his brothers, though judged unfavorably in comparison with young Philip, were not included in the blame of the nobles. Charles on his return to Paris "was received with honor by the people, grief-stricken by the capture of his father the King." They felt, according to Jean de Venette, that somehow he would bring about the King's release "and the whole country of France would be saved."

Why the flight? Why the defeat? To Villani in Italy the extraordinary event seemed "unbelievable"; Petrarch, learning about it in Milan on return from a journey, was no less stunned; the English themselves thought their victory a miracle, and succeeding generations have found it hard to fathom. Militarily, French numerical superiority was nullified by a failure of command. The 2,000 Genoese crossbowmen, according to some reports, were not even used, although others report the contrary. The comparative ineffectiveness of French archery throughout the century is a puzzle. Towns and villages of France maintained companies of archers who were encouraged by special privileges, and men of the Beauvaisis, adjoining Picardy, considered themselves in individual skill the best in the world. Yet they were never properly combined in action with knights and men-at-arms, because French chivalry scorned to share its dominance of the field with commoners.

Separatism in Normandy and Brittany, failure to resist the Black Prince's raid in Languedoc, and the intrigues and betrayals of Charles of Navarre were aspects of the disunity that lost the Battle of Poitiers. The right of independent withdrawal, which the Order of the Star and the ordinance of 1351 had tried to suppress, had not been yielded by the nobles in their own minds. The defeat at Poitiers was a pyrrhic triumph of baronial independence.

It was also, on the English side, a victory of generalship that made up for fatigue and inferior numbers. The Prince could give orders that were obeyed and, with moral leadership more secure than Jean's, and battalion chiefs on whom he could rely, could control what happened. He kept himself where he could view the battle and direct movements, he was served by toughened, experienced soldiers, and he had two essentials for winning: no possibility of retreat and a will that goaded men to the last ounce of fight. As a commander, in Froissart's words, he was "courageous and cruel as a lion."

Spent by combat and eager to bring his royal prize out of reach of any rescue attempt, the Prince made no further effort toward a juncture with Lancaster, but turned south at once for Bordeaux, dragging added baggage wagons filled with luxurious fittings including furred mantles, jewels, and illuminated books from the French camp. Released by the Dauphin after the defeat, the French nobles scattered to protect their own domains; none rallied to attempt a rescue of the King along the 150-mile march to Bordeaux. The Cardinals followed there to renew pressure for peace, and while terms of a settlement were under negotiation, English and Gascons engaged in a massive commerce of buying and selling prisoners and shares in ransoms with heated disputes over who had captured whom, and no little ill-will generated in the process. Complaints were heard that the archers had killed too many who might have been held for ransom. When the Prince proposed to take the King of France to England as a prisoner, the Gascons angrily claimed a share in his capture and had to be appeased by a payment of 100,000 florins, raised from a first offer of 60,000 they had spurned.

With the French King in their hands, the English were in a position to drive a crushing bargain. But though the French negotiators were prisoners themselves and the Dauphin at home was beleaguered by events in Paris, the French balked at the hard terms proposed. The winter passed with no agreement reached except for another truce to last two years. In May 1357, seven months after the battle, the Black Prince took King Jean with his son and other noble prisoners back to London, while in the aftermath of defeat the Third Estate grasped for control in Paris.

Chapter 7

Decapitated France:
The Bourgeois Rising
and the Jacquerie

Long exasperated by the anarchy of royal finance and the venality of royal ministers, the Third Estate of Paris seized upon the decapitation of the monarchy to try to impose some form of constitutional control. The summoning of an Estates General to grant money for defense in the crisis provided their opportunity. As soon as the 800 delegates could meet in Paris in October, the inexperienced Dauphin, humiliated and frightened by the defeat at Poitiers, had to report the battle's shameful outcome and ask the Estates for aids to deliver the King and defend the realm. The bourgeois, chief creditors of the state, made up half the delegates and listened coldly while King Jean's Chancellor, Pierre de la Forêt, supported the request. After voting themselves into a standing Committee of Eighty, including nobles and clergy, and allowing the rest gratefully to go home, the Estates prepared to confront the Dauphin with their demands. They asked to speak to him privately, believing that without his councillors he would be more easily cowed.

The major figure among them, who was to be the moving spirit of the coming eruption, was the Provost of Merchants, Etienne Marcel, a rich draper whose post was equivalent to that of Mayor of Paris. He had been the spokesman when the Estates of 1355 made manifest their mistrust of the royal government. Marcel represented the mercantile magnates of the Third Estate, the producers and businessmen of medieval society who over the last 200 years had achieved an influence, in practice if not in status, equal to that of the great prelates and nobles.

His first demand on behalf of the Estates was dismissal of the seven most notoriously venal of the royal councillors whose property was to be confiscated and who were to be barred forever from holding public office. In their place a Council of Twenty-eight, consisting of twelve nobles, twelve bourgeois, and four clerics, was to be appointed by the Estates, and on that understanding the Estates agreed to grant certain taxes in aid of the war. A final condition, which they would have done better to avoid, was the release from prison of Charles of Navarre.

They wanted him because his potential for trouble would put pressure on the Dauphin and because Navarre had an ally among them, a plotter like himself, who was the gray eminence of the reform movement. This was Robert le Coq, Bishop of Laon, a cleric of bourgeois origin and "dangerous" eloquence who through the avenue of the law had risen to favor and high office as King's Advocate under Philip VI and to the Royal Council under Jean II. He owned a library, large for its time, of 76 books, of which 48 dealt with civil and canon law, reflecting his concern with problems of government, and seven were collections of sermons used for models of the oratorical art. Style and language were a medieval preoccupation of which Le Coq made himself a master. Appointed Bishop of Laon, he had stage-managed the exquisite reconciliations of Jean II and Charles of Navarre, whose ambitions he saw as the chariot of his own. He wanted to be Chancellor and hated both the King for not giving him the office and the existing Chancellor for having it.

The Dauphin Charles, weakling though he seemed, possessed beneath his sickly exterior a hard core of resistance and a native intelligence, which came to his aid in adversity. Pale and thin, though not yet subject to the maladies that were later to be his portion, he had small, sharp eyes, thin lips, a long, thin nose, and an ill-proportioned body. He was anything but a libertine in appearance, although the two bastard sons credited to him by contemporaries must have been fathered, judging by their age, when he was fifteen or sixteen. Having neither taste nor capacity for military pursuits, he exercised his mind instead, which was useful for rulership, if not characteristic of the Valois. In fact there was gossip about his mother (who had been sixteen when she married Jean at thirteen) which suggested that her eldest son may not have been a Valois. He certainly resembled Jean in no way whatever.

For the moment, left to defend a crown amid the wreckage, Charles on the advice of his father's councillors rejected the Estates' demands and ordered them to dismiss. At the same time he removed himself from Paris as a precaution. Refusing to disperse, the standing committee assembled the day after he left, in November 1356, and listened to an inflammatory address by Robert le Coq denouncing royal misrule and specifying enlarged demands for reform. "Shame to him who speaks not forth," he cried, "for never was the time so good as now!"

The bid to limit the monarchy was now in the open. It might have been the French Runnymede if the challengers had been as cohesive as the English barons of 1215, but they were soon to split into factions.

The upper level of the Third Estate, made up of merchants, manufacturers, lawyers, office-holders, and purveyors to the crown, had nothing left in common with its working-class base except the fact of being non-noble. To overcome that barrier was every bourgeois magnate's aim. While climbing toward ennoblement and a country estate, he emulated the clothes, customs, and values of the nobles and on arriving shared their tax exemption—no small benefit. Etienne Marcel had an uncle who had paid the highest tax in Paris in 1313 and whose son bought a patent of nobility for 500 livres. Marcel's father- and brother-in-law, Pierre and Martin des Essars, starting from bourgeois origins in Rouen, had become enriched and ennobled in the service of Philip the Fair and Philip VI. As the crown's agents, they and their kind provisioned the royal households, commissioned their tapestries and books, purchased their jewels, fabrics, and works of art, served as their confidants and moneylenders, and held lucrative office as treasurers and tax-collectors. Pierre was able to give his daughter Marguerite, when she married Marcel, a princely dowry of 3,000 écus.

Nobles and clergy resented the royal favor shown and the opulence allowed to officials chosen from outside their ranks. Especially they hated the finance officers, "who travel in pomp and make fortunes greater than the dukes and marry their daughters to nobles and buy up the lands of poor knights whom they have cheated and impoverished . . . and appoint their own kind to offices whose numbers grow from day to day and whose salaries keep pace."

Between the official class and the mercantile bourgeois like Marcel, no love was lost, though they shared the enterprises of capitalism. When capitalism became feasible through the techniques of banking and credit, it became respectable. The theory of a non-acquisitive society faded, and accumulation of surplus wealth lost its odium—indeed, became enviable. In *Renart le Contrefait*, a satire of the time, the wealthy bourgeois enjoy the best estate of all: "They live in a noble manner, wear lordly garments, have falcons and sparrow hawks, fine palfreys and fine chargers. When the vassals must go to join the host, the bourgeois rest in their beds; when the vassals go to be massacred in battle, the bourgeois picnic by the river."

Chosen by the leading citizens, the Provost of Merchants and his fellow magistrates administered all the usual municipal functions and assigned daily duty to the police force, which was manned by the obligatory service of citizens in units of ten, forty, and fifty. Assisted by four deputies and a council of 24 clerics and laymen, the Provost was supposed to be on duty from seven A.M. every day except holy days. His seat was the Châtelet, which was also the city prison and was located on the right bank at the entrance to the Grand Pont, the only bridge leading over to the Ile de la Cité. Nearby the Châtelet was the City Hall on a large open square called the Place de Grève, where the unemployed came to be hired.

The city Marcel governed covered an area, by present landmarks, from approximately the Grands Boulevards on the right bank to the Luxembourg Gardens on the left, and east to west from the Bastille to the Tuileries. Everything beyond these boundaries was *faubourg* or countryside. The center of Paris was the Ile de la Cité in the middle of the Seine, on which stood the Cathedral of Notre Dame, the Hôtel Dieu or public hospital, and the royal palace built by St. Louis. The right bank, which had expanded beyond the old walls, was the side of commerce, industry, public markets, luxury trades, and wealthy residences, while the left bank, much smaller in populated area, was dominated by the University. According to a tax survey of the year 1292, the city at that time had 352 streets, eleven crossroads, ten squares, fifteen churches, and 15,000 taxpayers. Fifty years later, in Marcel's day, its total population after the Black Death was probably around 75,000.

Main streets were paved and wide enough to accommodate two carts or carriages, while the rest of the streets were narrow, muddy, and malodorous with a gutter running down the middle. For the average citizen the rule for elimination was "all in the street," and in lower-class quarters a pile of ordure usually lay at every doorway. Householders were supposed to carry the deposits to disposal pits and were reminded by repeated ordinances to pave and sweep their doorsteps.

Traffic jams blocked the narrow streets when pack mules with baskets hanging on either side met street vendors with their trays or porters bent under loads of wood and charcoal. Tavern signs on long iron poles further crowded the streets. Shop signs were gargantuan, the better to overwhelm customers, since shopkeepers were forbidden to call to buyers until after they had left the neighboring shop. A tooth-puller was represented by a tooth the size of an armchair, a glover by a glove with each finger big enough to hold a baby.

The noise of signs rattling in the wind competed with the cries of street vendors, the shouts of muleteers, the clatter of horses, and the announcements of public criers. Paris had six Master Criers appointed by the Provost, each with a number of assistants who were sent out to the crossroads and squares of the various quarters to announce official decrees, taxes, fairs and ceremonies, houses for sale, missing children, marriages, funerals, births, and baptisms. When the King's vintage was ready for sale, all the taverns had to close while public criers twice a day cried the royal wine. When deaths were announced, the criers rang bells as they moved along, calling in solemn tones, "Wake, you sleepers, pray God to forgive your trespasses; the dead cannot cry; pray for their souls as the bell sounds in these streets." Stray dogs howled to hear them.

Each trade occupied its own quarter—butchers and tanners around the Châtelet, money-changers, goldsmiths, and drapers on the Grand Pont, scribes, illuminators, and parchment- and ink-sellers on the left bank around the University. In the open shops worked bakers, soap-makers, fishmongers, hatters, cabinet-makers, potters, embroiderers, launderers, furriers, blacksmiths, barbers, apothecaries, and the myriad sub-specialties of the clothing and metal trades. Below the artisan class were day laborers, porters, and domestics. Named for their job or place of origin or some personal trait, they might be called Robert le Gros (the Fat), Raoul le Picard (of Picardy), Isabeau d'Outre-mer (from overseas), and Gautier Hors-du-sens (Crazy Walter).

In each quarter were public baths, providing either steam or hot water. A total of 26 were listed in the survey of 1292. Though considered dangerous to morality, especially of women, they were recognized as a contribution to cleanliness which the city took pains to keep from closing during a bad winter when fuel was costly. They were forbidden to admit prostitutes, vagabonds, lepers, or men of bad repute, or to open before dawn because of perils in the streets at night, but at daybreak the crier's voice was heard,

> Calling to you to bathe, Messire,
> And steam yourself without delay.
> Our water's hot and that's no lie.

As a capital city with a great university, Paris was host to a turbulent horde of students from all over Europe. They had privileged status not subject to local justice but only to the King, with the result that their crimes and disorders went largely unpunished. They lived miserably, overcharged for dirty rooms in dark neighborhoods. They sat on stools in cold lecture halls lit only by two candles and were perennially complained of for debauchery, rape, robbery, and "all other enormities hateful to God."

Though Oxford was growing as a center of intellectual interest, the University of Paris was still the theological arbiter of Europe, and the libraries of its separate faculties, some numbering up to a thousand volumes, augmented its glory. Added to these were the fine library of Notre Dame and no less than 28 booksellers, not counting open-air bookstalls. Here were "abundant orchards of all manner of books," wrote an enraptured English visitor; "what a mighty stream of pleasure made glad our hearts when we visited Paris, the paradise of the world!"

Water was supplied to the city at public fountains fed by aqueducts leading from the hills northeast of Paris. Windmills filled the *faubourgs,* where houses had room for gardens and vineyards, and abbeys stood amid cultivated fields. Produce entered the city mainly by riverboat to be laid out on market tables or sold from the trays of vendors. Beggars sat by church doors asking for alms, mendicant friars begged bread for their orders or for the poor in prison, jongleurs performed stunts and magic in the plazas and recited satiric tales and narrative ballads of adventure in Saracen lands. Streets were bright with colored clothes. Crimson, green, and particolored, being the most expensive, were reserved for nobles, prelates, and magnates. The clergy could wear color as long as their gowns were long and buttoned. At sundown the curfew bell rang for closing time, work ceased, shops were shuttered, silence succeeded bustle. At eight o'clock, when the Angelus bell signaled bedtime, the city was in darkness. Only the crossroads were lit by flickering candle or lamp placed in a niche holding a statue of Notre Dame or the patron saint of the quarter.

On Sundays all business was closed, everyone went to church, and afterward working people gathered in the taverns while the bourgeois promenaded in the *faubourgs.* On holidays it was a Paris custom to dine at a table set outside the front door. Houses were the characteristic high narrow urban type built side by side, sometimes with a courtyard between the front half and the back. They were half-timbered, with the spaces filled by clay or stone and each story cantilevered over the one below. The *hôtels* of nobles and magnates kept some elements of the fortified castle with conical towers and high walls. As a concession to urban life they had large glass-paned windows opening onto courtyards, and belvederes with many ornamental pinnacles on the roofs from which a watch could be maintained on all sides. The owner was made known by his coat-of-arms sculpted over the doorway. Streets had no inscribed names, so that people had to search for hours to find the place they wanted.

Indoors the noble residences were decorated with murals and tapestries, but furniture was meager. Beds, which served for sitting as well as sleeping, were the most important item. Chairs were few; even kings and popes received ambassadors sitting on beds furnished with elaborate curtains and spreads; otherwise, people sat on benches. Torches in wall sconces lit the rooms, and massive fireplaces were built into the walls. These wall chimneys "in the French fashion," as they were called in Italy, were the greatest luxury of middle-class homes. The only other warmth came from the oven and cooking fire and warming pans in bed at night. Like sanitation, heating was an arrangement that the age seems technologically equipped to have handled better than it did, were it not that man is as irrational about his comfort as about other activities. Fur coverlets, fur-lined clothes, or separate fur linings worn under tunics and robes substituted for active sources of heat. The furs of otter, cat, miniver, squirrel, and fox were less expensive than heavy wool cloth; ermine and marten adorned the rich.

Floors were strewn in summer with fragrant herbs and grasses and at other times by rushes or straw changed four times a year, or once a year in poorer homes, by which time it was filled with fleas and rank with dog droppings and refuse. A well-off merchant scattered violets and other flowers on his floor before a dinner party and decorated his walls and table with fresh greens bought in the market at early morning.

Rooms were few, servants slept where they could, privacy was nonexistent, which may have increased irritability. Whether it hampered or facilitated seduction is an open question. The two Cambridge students in Chaucer's Reeve's Tale were conveniently enabled to enjoy the favors of the Miller's wife and daughter because they were put to bed in the same room with the family. Even in greater homes guests slept in the same room with host and hostess.

Such was the Third Estate of Paris, from the poorest workman to the richest magnate, whom Marcel tried to mobilize in his struggle against the Dauphin. To make him submit, the Provost began to use the threat of strikes and popular violence. When the Dauphin tried to raise money by another devaluation of the coinage, arousing the wrath of Paris, "the Provost ordered all guilds and trades throughout the city to stop work and everyone to arm." Forced to cancel the edicts and left without funds, the Dauphin had no recourse but to recall the Estates and return to Paris to meet with them.

At this session, lasting a month from February to March 1357, all the proposed reforms, formulated in writing, were presented in a Grand Ordinance of 61 articles, the Magna Carta of the Third Estate. Written in French rather than Latin as if to emphasize a new voice, the ordinance set forth an ideal of "Good Government" as if its framers were trying to implement Lorenzetti's delectable vision under that name painted a few years earlier in Siena. In the painted city, citizens in gowns of gentle colors go harmoniously about their business, and mounted men-at-arms pass them by in mutual tolerance and benignity. In a distraught time, the Grand Ordinance was grasping for the same order and decency.

The framers had devised not a grand new scheme of government but rather a set of corrections of existing abuses into which were tossed three political fundamentals. These provided that the monarchy could levy no tax not voted by the Estates, that the Estates General had the right to assemble periodically at their own volition, and that a Grand Council of Thirty-six, twelve from each estate, was to be elected by the Estates to advise the crown.

The purge of King Jean's councillors was reaffirmed and the members of the new Grand Council "were abjured to forgo the habit of their predecessors of coming late to work and working very little." All officials were to be at work "every day at sunrise"; they were to be well paid, but lose their pay if they failed to appear early in the morning. The currency was not to be altered without the consent of the Estates, royal and princely expenditures were to be reduced, judicial cases in Parlement were to be speeded up, provincial bailiffs were not to hold two offices or engage in commerce, the summons to military service was to be issued only under specific conditions, nobles were not to leave the country without permission, and their private wars were sternly forbidden. Justice and charity for the poor were to be expedited, their property was not to be confiscated without just price, and their vehicles for never more than one day; the right of villagers to assemble and take arms against robbery and force was affirmed. Finally, the Estates undertook to raise taxes sufficient to pay 30,000 soldiers for one year, but the money was to be administered by the Estates, not through the crown.

Resisting and procrastinating, the Dauphin refused to sign the ordinance until he was browbeaten into it by Marcel's technique of bringing mobs released from work into the streets, increasing in numbers each day, and encouraged to shout, "To arms!" By this treatment the Dauphin's signature was obtained under the title of Regent, which the Estates required him to assume so that he could commit the monarchy. The new Council of Thirty-six was installed, while the ousted councillors hastened to Bordeaux to inform King Jean. Just before he was carried off to London, the King repudiated his son's signature and the entire ordinance.

During the summer of 1357 neither the Dauphin nor the Council was able to govern effectively while both sought support from the provinces. By making a royal progress through the country to show kingship still functioning, Charles had more success than Marcel. When the Estates reconvened in April with very few nobles present, it was clear that the nobility, resenting the terms of the Grand Ordinance, was withdrawing support. The reform movement was in trouble. Outside Paris the breakdown of authority was reaching catastrophe.

Its catalyst was the brigandage of military companies spawned by the warfare of the last fifteen years. These were the Free Companies who "write sorrow on the bosom of the earth" and were to become the torment of the age. Composed of English, Welsh, and Gascons released after Poitiers by the Black Prince, as soldiers customarily were to avoid further payment, they had acquired in the Prince's campaigns a taste for the ease and riches of plunder. Along with German mercenaries and Hainault adventurers, they gathered in groups of twenty to fifty around a captain and moved northward to operate in the area between the Seine and the Loire and between Paris and the coast. After the truce of Bordeaux they were joined by the forces of Philip of Navarre, by leftovers from the Duke of Lancaster's forces, and by experienced Breton captains and men-at-arms, masters of the art of exploiting a region. The refrain of the chronicles, *arser et piller* (burning and plundering), follows their kind down the century.

The loss of the King and of so many nobles eased their opportunity. In the year after the truce they swelled, merged, organized, spread, and operated with ever more license. Seizing a castle, they would use it as a stronghold from which to exact tribute from every traveler and raid the countryside. They would spy out a good town at one or two days' journey "and go by covert ways day and night and so enter the town unknown in the morning and set fire on some house; then they of the town would think it was done by some men of war and so fly away out of the town; and then these brigands would break up coffers and houses and rob and take what they list and fly away when they had done."

They imposed ransoms on prosperous villages and burned the poor ones, robbed abbeys and monasteries of their stores and valuables, pillaged peasants' barns, killed and tortured those who hid their goods or resisted ransom, not sparing the clergy or the aged, violated virgins, nuns, and mothers, abducted women as enforced camp-followers and men as servants. As the addiction took hold, they wantonly burned harvests and farm equipment and cut down trees and vines, destroying what they lived by, in actions which seem inexplicable except as a fever of the time or an exaggeration of the chroniclers.

Companies of this kind had existed since the 12th century and proliferated especially in Italy, where the nobility, more urban than elsewhere, left the profession of arms increasingly to mercenaries. Led by professional captains, the companies, sometimes numbering 2,000 to 3,000, were composed of exiles, outlaws, landless or bankrupt adventurers, Germans, Burgundians, Italians, Hungarians, Catalans, Provençals, Flemish, French, and Swiss, often splendidly equipped on horse and foot. In mid-century the outstanding captain was a renegade prior of the Knights of St. John called Fra Monreale, who maintained a council, secretaries, accountants, camp judges, and a gallows, and could command a price of 150,000 gold florins from Venice to fight Milan. In the single year of 1353 he extorted 50,000 florins from Rimini, 25,000 from Florence, and 16,000 each from Pisa and Siena. Invited to Rome by the revolutionary Cola di Rienzi, who wanted his wealth, Monreale overconfidently entered alone, was seized, tried as a public robber, and executed. He went to the block magnificently dressed in brown velvet embroidered in gold and had his own surgeon direct the ax of the executioner. Unrepentant at the end, he declared himself justified "in carving his way with a sword through a false and miserable world."

The most damaging aspect of the companies was that in the absence of organized armies they filled a need and became accepted. Philip VI, on learning how effectively a captain known only as Bacon had surprised and seized a castle, bought his services for 20,000 crowns and made him usher-at-arms, "ever well horsed, appareled and armed like an earl." Another, named Croquart, starting as a "poor page" in the Breton wars, rose by prowess to become a captain of brigands worth 40,000 crowns whose military repute caused him to be chosen as one of the English side in the Combat of Thirty. Afterward King Jean offered him a knighthood, a rich wife, and annual pay of 2,000 livres if he would enter the King's service. Preferring his independence, Croquart refused.

More brigand than mercenary, the companies in France, though basically English, attracted French knights ruined by the ransoms of Brittany and Poitiers who now shared in the ravaging of their own country. Lesser nobles reduced in revenue, younger sons and bastard sons, made themselves captains and found in the companies a living, a path to fortune, a way of life, a vent for the restless aggression once absorbed by the crusades.

The most notorious of the French was Arnaut de Cervole, a noble of Périgord called the "Archpriest" because of a clerical benefice he had once held. Wounded and captured at Poitiers, he had been released on paying his ransom, and on return to France in the anarchic months of 1357 made himself commander of a band which called itself frankly enough *Società dell' acquisito*. In collaboration with a lord of Provence named Raimond des Baux, the band grew to an army of 2,000 and the "Archpriest" into one of the great evildoers of his time. In the course of a raid Cervole launched through Provence in 1357, Pope Innocent VI felt so insecure in Avignon that he negotiated for immunity in advance. Cervole was invited to the papal palace, "received as reverently as if he had been the son of the King of France," and after dining several times with the Pope and cardinals, was given a pardon for all his sins—a regular item in the companies' demands—and the sum of 40,000 écus to leave the area.

His equal among the English was Sir Robert Knollys, "the man of few words," whom Froissart judged "the most able and skillful man-at-arms in all the companies." He too had risen from the ranks in the Breton wars and fought with the Thirty, gaining knighthood along the way. After service with Lancaster he remained to plunder Normandy with such skill and ruthlessness that he amassed in the year 1357–58 booty worth 100,000 crowns. During the next two years he established himself in the valley of the Loire, where he gained control of forty castles and burned and sacked from Orléans to Vézelay. In a raid through Berry and Auvergne his company left a trail of ravaged towns whose charred gables were known as "Knollys' miters." Such was the terror of his name that at one place, it was said, people threw themselves into the river at word of his approach.

Upon his informing King Edward that all the strongholds he had captured were at the King's disposal, Edward—who was pleased to share, like other rulers, in the benefits of banditry—handsomely pardoned Knollys for activities that violated the truce. Knollys was ultimately to earn high command and military renown on a level with Chandos and the Black Prince. In truce and war he passed back and forth from brigandage to service under the crown without missing a beat or changing his style. At the end of his career he retired with "regal wealth" and great estates to become a benefactor of churches and founder of almshouses and chantries. The French wrote him down as Sir Robert Canole, who "grievously harmed France all the days of his life."

In the anarchy after Poitiers, knights and brigands became interchangeable, bringing added popular hatred upon the estate of the sword, though not necessarily disrepute among their own kind. The "young, bold and amorous" Eustache d'Aubrecicourt, a knight of Hainault and companion of the Prince at Poitiers, turned brigand with such élan and material success that he won the love of the widowed Countess of Kent, a niece of the Queen of England and Hainault-born like himself. She sent him horses, gifts, and passionate letters which excited him to ever bolder if not more chivalrous exploits. He fastened a savage grip upon Champagne and part of Picardy until he was captured when French knights at last organized in defense. Greedy as he, they let him be ransomed for 22,000 gold francs, so that he promptly renewed his warfare. In command of 2,000 freebooters, he organized a traffic in seized castles, which were sold back to their owners at lucrative prices. In some way understandable to the 14th century, his use of the sword for robbery and murder carried no quality of dishonor to Isabelle of Kent, who was to marry her now wealthy hero in 1360.

In response to French complaints that the English companies were violating the truce, King Edward ordered them to disband, but his orders were neither meant nor taken seriously. While peace terms were still being negotiated, he was quite willing to let the companies keep up pressure on France. No less averse to fomenting trouble was Charles of Navarre. Though still in prison, he had agents, including his brother Philip, active in his behalf. Where the Navarrese joined forces with the English, the ravages were worst—deliberately so, some thought, as a means of applying pressure for Charles's release.

For defense against the companies, villages made forts of their stone churches, surrounding them with trenches, manning the bell towers with sentinels, and piling up stones to throw down upon the attackers. "The sound of church bells no longer summoned people to praise the Lord but to take shelter from the enemy." Peasant families who could not reach the church spent nights with their livestock on islands in the Loire or in boats anchored in mid-river. In Picardy they took refuge in underground tunnels enlarged from caves dug at the time of the Norman invasions. With a well in the center and air holes above, the tunnels could shelter twenty or thirty people with space around the walls for cattle.

At daylight the lookouts peered from the bell towers to see if the bandits had gone and they could return to the fields. Country families hastened with their goods to take refuge in cities, monks and nuns abandoned their monasteries, highways and roads were unsafe, robbers rose up everywhere, and enemies multiplied throughout the land. "What more can I say?" writes Jean de Venette in his catalogue of miseries. "Thence-forward infinite harm, misfortune and danger befell the French people for lack of good government and adequate defense."

A sympathizer of the Third Estate, Jean de Venette was a Carmelite prior and head of the Order in the 1360s at the time he was writing his chronicle. He blamed the Regent, who "applied no remedy," and the nobles, who "despised and hated all others and took no thought for the mutual usefulness of lord and men. They subjected and despoiled the peasants and villagers. In no wise did they defend their country from its enemies. Rather did they trample it underfoot, robbing and pillaging the peasants' goods" while the Regent "gave no thought to their plight."

The nobles were to blame also, as Jean de Venette saw it, for discord among the Estates General which caused the Estates to abandon the task they had begun. "From that time on all went ill with the kingdom, and the state was undone. . . . The country and whole land of France began to put on confusion and mourning like a garment because it had no defender or guardian."

Grief and wrath pervade too a Latin polemic called "Tragic Account of the Miserable State of the Realm of France" by an obscure Benedictine monk. Ashamed for once-proud France which let her King be captured "in the heart of the kingdom" and led without interference to captivity on foreign soil, he raised the crucial question of military discipline. "Where did you study [the art of war]? Who were your teachers? In what was your apprenticeship?" he asks the knights. "Was it while fighting under the banners of Venus, sucking sweetness like milk, abandoned to delights . . ." and so on in this vein until he suddenly concludes with the practical question, "Can the military art be learned in the games and hunts in which you pass your youth?"

The friar has censure left over for the common people, "whose belly is their God and who are the slaves of their women," and for the clergy, who receive the worst scolding of all. They are sunk in luxury, gluttony, pomp, ambition, anger, discord, envy, greed, litigation, usury, and sacks of silver and gold. Virtues die, vices triumph, honesty perishes, pity is stifled, avarice pervades, confusion overwhelms, order vanishes.

Was this merely the traditional monastic tirade upon the world, or a deeper pessimism that begins to darken the second half of the century?

King Jean's release was still unsettled. While treating the royal captive with elaborate honor, Edward was determined to squeeze from his triumph every last inch of territory and ounce of money that France could be made to yield. The great King of France, snatched from the field of Poitiers, was an extraordinary prize. Jean's entry into London as the Black Prince's prisoner in May 1357 occasioned one of the greatest celebrations ever seen in England and "great solemnities in all churches marvelous to think of." Such was the curiosity to see the French King that the procession took several hours to cross the town to the palace of Westminster. As the center of attention among the thirteen other noble prisoners, Jean was dressed in black "like an archdeacon or a secular clerk," and rode a tall white horse alongside the Prince on a smaller black palfrey. Past houses hung with captured shields and tapestries, over cobblestones strewn with rose petals, the procession moved through fantasies of pageantry that were the favorite art of the 14th century. In twelve gilded cages along the route, the goldsmiths of London had stationed twelve beautiful maidens, who scattered flowers of gold and silver filigree over the riders.

The éclat of the noble prisoners added chivalric distinction to the English court. Christmas and New Year's of the first winter were celebrated with extra pomp, including a splendid tournament held at night under torchlight. Housed in the Savoy, the new palace of the Duke of Lancaster, Jean was at liberty to receive visitors from France and enjoy all the pleasures of court life, although assigned a guard to prevent his escape or attempted rescue. Languedoc sent a delegation of nobles and bourgeois with a gift of 10,000 florins and the assurance that their lives, goods, and fortunes were dedicated to his delivery. Even Laon and Amiens sent money. The mystique of kingship possessed his subjects more than its responsibilities concerned the King.

In France's miserable hour, his accounts show expenses for horses, dogs, and falcons, a chess set, an organ, a harp, a clock, a fawn-colored palfrey, venison and whale meat from Bruges, and elaborate wardrobes for his son Philip and for his favorite jester, who received several ermine-trimmed hats ornamented with gold and pearls. Jean maintained an astrologer and a "king of minstrels" with orchestra, held a cockfight, commissioned books with fine bindings, and sold horses and wine he had received as gifts from Languedoc. The success of this venture led him to import more of both from Toulouse for sale as a profitable business. Reading through Jean's accounts in the archives 500 years later, Jules Michelet, France's most vivid if not most objective historian, said they made him sick.

Negotiations of terms for the ransom of the King and the conditions of a permanent peace treaty were obstructed by Edward's exorbitant demands. He wanted outright cession of Guienne, Calais, and all the former Plantagenet holdings in France, plus an enormous ransom of three million écus for Jean, in return for which he would give up his claim to the French crown. Under pressure of the papal delegates, the parleys dragged on while the French commissioners twisted and turned in agony. The one solution they never considered was to leave the King unransomed and go home. For one thing, this would have meant no peace treaty, and battered France had to have peace. More fundamentally, the King was a principle of order. Since the reign of St. Louis, who had used the royal authority to eliminate private wars, impose justice, and systematize taxes, the crown had come to be equated in the public mind with greater protection and law. All the back-sliding of his successors could not soil the kingship, and Jean, its careless representative, was yearned for as if he had been St. Louis.

The French provinces, believing royal power to be their last resource for defense against the companies, did not want to see the monarchy enfeebled. In August 1357 the Dauphin was emboldened to reinstate the dismissed councillors and defiantly to inform Marcel and the Council of Thirty-six that he intended to govern alone without their interference. Made an extremist by his frustrations, Marcel accepted an ally utterly incompatible with his purpose.

Into the turmoil of November 1357 stepped Charles of Navarre out of his prison near Cambrai in Picardy. Although a plot of his partisans was credited with effecting his escape or release, behind it the hand of Marcel and the mind of Robert le Coq were at work. Charles of Navarre was to be used as an alternative King against the Valois. He entered the capital "grandly accompanied" by nobles of Picardy and Normandy, among them "Monseigneur de Coussi." At seventeen, Enguerrand had been receiving the homage of vassals as their acknowledged lord. Probably sharing the anti-Valois sentiments of many nobles of the north, he would have been swept into the following of Charles of Navarre, although, with the remarkable political sense he was to display throughout his life, he did not stay there long.

With wonderful eloquence "seasoned by much venom," Charles of Navarre harangued a great assembly of Parisians, mentioning without actually pressing his claim to the crown, which he said was at least better than King Edward's. His challenge forced the Dauphin to re-enter Paris and recall the Estates, and within a month, when he had assembled "2,000" men-at-arms in the fortress of the Louvre, he too took to the people. Sending couriers through the city to assemble them, he spoke on horseback before a crowd gathered at the Halles on January 11, 1358, turning sentiment at once in his favor. Marcel's deputy, who tried to make himself heard in opposition, was drowned out in the shouting and turbulence. Intensely susceptible to the spoken word, people of the time responded to any Mark Antony and would listen for hours to the outdoor sermons of great preachers, which they regarded as a form of public entertainment.

Alarmed by the Dauphin's success, Marcel resorted to an act of violence in the unmistakable style of Charles of Navarre, and generally believed, after the event, to have been instigated by him. The pretext was the death of a citizen named Perrin Marc, who had murdered the Dauphin's treasurer and in turn had been forcefully taken from sanctuary in a church by the Dauphin's Marshal and hung. Assembling 3,000 artisans and tradesmen, armed and wearing the red-and-blue hoods of the popular party, Marcel marched at their head to the royal palace. Regnaut d'Acy, one of the Dauphin's councillors, encountered in the street, was recognized and greeted by shouts of "Death!" Before he could flee, he was struck down by so many blows that he died without uttering a sound.

On reaching the palace, Marcel mounted with part of his company to the Dauphin's chamber, where, while he made a show of protecting the prince, his men fell upon the Dauphin's two Marshals and slew them before his eyes. One was Jean de Clermont, son of the Marshal killed at Poitiers; it was he who had broken the church sanctuary. The other was Jean de Conflans, Sire de Dampierre, a former delegate to the Estates who had abandoned the reform party for the Dauphin. Every illuminated chronicle pictures the scene: the upraised swords of fiercely frowning men, the terrified Dauphin cowering on his bed, the bloodied bodies of the Marshals at his feet.

Their corpses were dragged to the courtyard of the palace and left there for all to see while Marcel hurried to the Place de Grève, where he addressed the crowd from a window of the city hall, asking their

1. *Coucy-le-Château as it would have appeared in the 14th century.*
From a 16th century engraving.

2. *The abandoned castle in later years.*
From Du Sommerard's Les Arts au Moyen Age, *1838-46.*

3. Fortune's wheel.
From a mid-14th century manuscript
of Roman de la Rose.

Erect figure, 1369

Shield quartered with arms of Austria,
field strewn with crowns (no date)

5. Chaucer's squire.
From the Ellesmere
manuscript, c. 1410.

Shield with Leopard of England, 1386

6. A 14th century
carriage (followed by
three horsemen wear-
ing Jews' hats). From
an illustrated Bible
showing Jacob's jour-
ney to Egypt. The
three horsemen are
Jacob's sons.

7. *View of Paris. From Froissart's* Chronicles, *Louis de Bruges copy, c. 1460.*

8. *A country village among the trees. From Bartholomew of England's* Book on the Nature of Things, *a manuscript of c. 1410.*

9. *Charles of Navarre. From a window in the Cathedral of Evreux.*

10. *Jean II. Portrait attributed to his court painter, Girard d'Orléans.*

11. The Black Prince. Effigy in Canterbury Cathedral.

12. English archers training with the longbow (the unpulled bows are the height of a man). From the Luttrell Psalter, late 13th century.

13. *View of London.*
From Poems of
Charles d'Orléans,
early 15th century.

14. The Last Judgment,
the Elect and the Damned.
From the Cathedral of
Bourges, west portal.

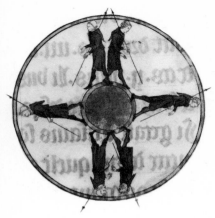

15. *The world as a globe. From* L'Image du Monde *by Gautier de Metz, a 14th century manuscript.*

16. *The child's education. From* Avis aus Roys, *a manual of instruction for French kings and princes, mid-14th century.*

17. *The pillage and burning of a town. From Froissart's* Chronicles, *Louis de Bruges copy, c. 1460.*

18. *A charivari. From* Roman de Fauvel, *an early 14th century manuscript.*

DOMINVS REGIT AE ET NICRIL MICRI DEERIT IN LOCO

19. *The fourth horseman of the apocalypse. "And Behold a pale horse, and he that sat upon him his name was Death . . ." (Revelation 6 : 8). Illustration for the Office of the Dead by Jean Colombe for the* Très Riches Heures *of the Duc de Berry, c. 1470.*

20. The Triumph of Death. *A detail from a fresco by Francesco Traini in the Camposanto, Pisa, c. 1350.*

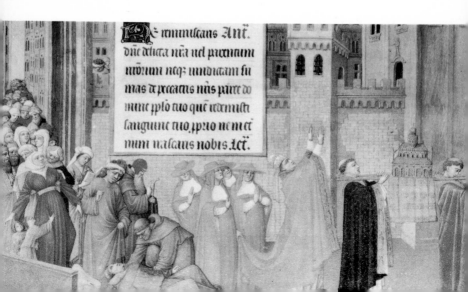

21. *Burial of the plague victims. From* Annales de Gilles li Muisis.

22. *Penitential procession led by the Pope during the plague (pictured in 14th century Rome although it purports to illustrate the 6th century plague under Gregory the Great). By Pol de Limbourg for the* Très Riches Heures *of the Duc de Berry, c. 1410.*

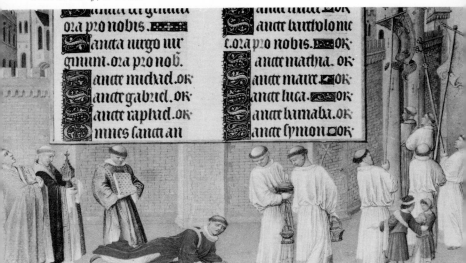

23. *A Cardinal. Detail from the Nine Hours Tapestries, French, late 14th century.*

24. *Knights. Seals of Amadeo V of Savoy (right) and Louis I, Duc d'Anjou.*

THE THREE ESTATES

25. Peasants. Labors of the Twelve Months. *Manuscript of Crescenzi li Rustican, c. 1460.*

26. *The slaughter of the Jacques on the bridge at Meaux. From Froissart's* Chronicles,
Louis de Bruges copy, c. 1460.

27. *Murder of the mar-*
shals. From the Grandes
Chroniques, *copy ex-*
ecuted for Charles V, c.
1375.

28. *The alaunt as war-dog, used against the horses of mounted brigands or men-at-war. From the 14th century manuscript* Tractatus de Pauli Sanctini Ducensis de re militari et machinis bellicis.

29. *The Battle of Sluys. From Froissart's* Chronicles, *Louis de Bruges copy, c. 1460.*

30. *Widowed Rome.*

31. *Florence, 15th century.*

endorsement of his deed. It had been done, he said, for the good of the kingdom and the removal of "false, wicked, and traitorous" knights. With one voice the mob shouted its approval and its adherence to the Provost "through life and death." Marcel promptly returned to the palace to present the Dauphin with that ever-justifying formula: the deed had been done "by the will of the people." The prince, he said, must show himself at one with the people by ratifying the act and pardoning everyone concerned.

"Grieving and dumbfounded," the Dauphin could read the warning of the sprawled bodies on the pavement. He prayed to the Provost that the people of Paris might be his good friends as he was theirs, and accepted from Marcel two lengths of red-and-blue cloth to make hoods for himself and his officers.

The terrible assault virtually upon his person had been designed to intimidate the Dauphin into accepting rule by the Council of the Estates. Instead it hardened the will beneath his deceptively feeble exterior. All he could do for the moment was to send his family for safety to the nearby fortress of Meaux on the Marne and remove himself to Senlis outside the capital. Once violence had been used against the monarchy, and against the nobility in the person of the Marshals, the conflict was to turn from political struggle to open strife with a decisive shift in the balance of forces. The murder of the Marshals cost Marcel what remained of support among the nobles for reform. It convinced them that their interests lay with the crown.

In May 1358 an act of the Dauphin-Regent precipitated the ferocious uprising of the peasantry called the Jacquerie, in which Enguerrand de Coucy at eighteen was swept into an active and visible role. Intending to undercut Marcel by blockading Paris, the Regent ordered the nobles along the valleys of waterborne commerce to fortify and provision their castles. According to one version, they seized the goods of their peasants for this purpose, provoking the uprising. According to another chronicler, the Jacques rose at the instigation of Marcel, who stirred them to believe that the Regent's order was directed against them as a prelude to new oppressions and confiscations. But the Jacques had reason enough of their own.

What was this peasant who supported the three estates on his back, this bent Atlas of the medieval world who now struck terror through the seigneurial class? Snub-nosed and rough in belted tunic and long hose, he can be seen in carved stone medallions and illuminated pages representing the twelve months, sowing from a canvas seed bag around his neck, scything hay bare-legged in summer's heat in loose blouse and straw hat, trampling grapes in a wooden vat, shearing sheep held between his knees, herding swine in the forest, tramping through the snow in hood and sheepskin mantle with a load of firewood on his back, warming himself before a fire in a low hut in February. Alongside him in the fields the peasant woman binds sheaves wearing a skirt caught up at the belt to free her legs and a cloth head-covering instead of a hat.

Like every other group, peasants were diverse, ranging in economic level from half-savage pauper to the proprietor of fields and featherbeds who could hoard money to send his son to the university. The general term for peasant was villein or *vilain*, which had acquired a pejorative tone, though harmlessly derived from the Latin *villa*. Neither exactly slave nor entirely free, the villein belonged to the estate of his lord, under obligation to pay rent or work services for use of the land, and in turn to enjoy the right of protection and justice. A serf was someone in personal bondage who belonged by birth to a particular lord, and, so that his children should follow him, was forbidden under a rule called *formariage* from marrying outside the domain. If he died childless, his house, tools, and any possessions reverted to the lord under the right of *morte-main*, on the theory that they had only been lent to the serf for his labor in life. Originally he owed, in addition to agriculture, every kind of labor service needed on an estate—repair of roads, bridges, and moats, supply of firewood, care of stables and kennels, blacksmithing, laundering, spinning, weaving, and other crafts for the castle. By the 14th century much of this was done by hired hands and the castle's needs were supplied by purchase from towns and peddlers, leaving a large part of the peasantry on a rent-paying basis with a certain number of days' work owed on the lord's fields.

Besides paying the hearth tax and clerical tithe and aids for the lord's ransom and knighting of his son and marriage of his daughter, the peasant owed fees for everything he used: for grinding his grain in the lord's mill, baking his bread in the lord's oven, pressing apples in the lord's cider press, settlement of disputes in the lord's court. At death he owed the heriot, or forfeit of his best possession to the lord.

His agricultural labor was supplied under rules that favored the seigneur, whose fields were plowed and seed sowed and hay cut and crops harvested and, in case of storm or pests, his harvest saved before the peasant could attend to his own. He had to drive his beasts to pasture and bring them home across the lord's fields rather than his own so that the lord should have the benefit of the manure. By these fees and arrangements, economic surplus was produced for the proprietors.

The system was aided by the Church, whose natural interests allied it more to the great than to the meek. The Church taught that failure to do the seigneur's work and obey his laws would be punished by eternity in Hell, and that non-payment of tithes would imperil the soul. The priest exerted constant pressure for tithes in kind—grain, eggs, a hen or a pig—and told the peasant these were a tax "owed to God." Everyday life was administered by the lord's bailiff, whose abuses and extortions were a constant source of complaint. The bailiff could levy an augmented tax, keeping a percentage for himself, or accuse a peasant of theft and accept a fee for letting him off.

Rents were generally reckoned in pennies earned by paid labor and sale of produce in the market. At harvest-time, men and women flocked to the grape-picking for extra cash and a few weeks' fun. Women were paid at half the rate of the men. The worst fear was famine, and local shortages were common because transportation was poor and yield, owing to inadequate fertilizer, low.

Possession of a plow which cost 10 to 12 livres and of a plow horse at 8 to 10 livres was the line between a peasant who prospered and one who just survived. Those too poor to afford a plow rented a communal one or turned the earth with hoe and spade. Perhaps 75 to 80 percent were below the plow line, of whom half had a few acres and some economic security while the rest lived on the edge of subsistence, cultivating tiny plots supplemented by paid work for the lord or for richer neighbors. The lowest 10 percent existed in misery on a diet of bread, onions, and a little fruit, sleeping on straw, living without furniture in a cabin with a hole in the roof to let out the smoke. Without even the tenure of serfs, they were a new agricultural proletariat created as the old manorial system was changing to a money basis.

What proportion of the peasantry was well off and what poor is judged by what they bequeathed, and since the poorest had nothing to leave, they remain mute. For no other class is that famous goal of the historian, *wie es wirklich war* (how it really was), so elusive. For every statement on peasant life there is another that contradicts it. It has been said that "bathing was common among the lower classes . . . even small villages had their public bath houses," yet the French peasant's contemporaries incessantly complained of his filth and foul smell. While the English of the time seem to agree that the French peasant was worse off than their own and frequently comment on his meatless diet, he is elsewhere recorded as regularly eating pork and fowl roasted on a spit. He also had access to eggs, salt fish, cheese, lard, peas, beans, shallots, onions, garlic, and some leaf vegetables grown in his kitchen garden, fruits cooked in juice or dried for winter, rye bread, honey, and beer or cider.

The middle group would own a bed for the whole family, a trestle table with benches, a chest, cupboard, wardrobe, iron and tin cooking pots, clay bowls and jugs, homemade baskets, wooden buckets and washtubs, in addition to farming tools. They lived in one-story, wood-framed houses with thatched roof and plaster walls made of various mixtures of clay, straw, and pebbles. Most such houses had Dutch doors to let light and air in and smoke out, some had tiny windows, the best had walled chimneys. Life expectancy was short owing to over-work, overexposure, and the afflictions of dysentery, tuberculosis, pneumonia, asthma, tooth decay, and the terrible rash called St. Anthony's Fire, which by constriction of the blood vessels (not then understood) could consume a limb as by "some hidden fire" and sever it from the body. In modern times the disease has been identified in some cases as erysipelas and in others as ergot poisoning caused by a fungus on rye flour kept too long over the winter.

The affluent few might own sixty to eighty acres, plow-horses and rope harness, sheep, pigs, cattle, stores of wool, hides, and hemp, and of wheat, oats, and corn, a boat and net for fishing in the river, a vine-yard, a woodpile, and vessels of copper, glass, and silver. Their homes contained, in the case of one comfortable peasant of Normandy, two featherbeds, one wooden bed, three tables, four skillets, two pots and other cooking utensils, eight sheets, two tablecloths, one towel or nap-kin, a lantern, two vats for trampling grapes, two barrels and two casks, a cart, a plow, two harrows, two hoes, two scythes, one spade, one sickle, three horse collars, and a pack saddle. Rich peasants are recorded who employed a dozen field hands and gave their daughters dowries of 50 gold florins plus a fur-trimmed mantle and fur bedcover.

Truer to the mass is the peasant who cries, in the French tale *Merlin Merlot*, "Alas, what will become of me who never has a single day's rest? I do not think I shall ever know repose or ease. . . . Hard is the hour when the villein is born. When he is born, suffering is born with him." His children go hungry, holding out their hands to him for food; his wife assails him as a poor provider. "And I, unhappy one, I am like a rooster soaked in the rain, head hanging and bedraggled, or like a beaten dog."

A deep grievance of the peasant was the contempt in which he was held by the other classes. Aside from the rare note of compassion, most tales and ballads depict him as aggressive, insolent, greedy, sullen, suspicious, tricky, unshaved, unwashed, ugly, stupid and credulous or sometimes shrewd and witty, incessantly discontented, usually cuck-olded. In satiric tales it was said the villein's soul would find no place in Paradise or anywhere else because the demons refused to carry it owing to the foul smell. In the *chansons de geste* he is scorned as inept in combat and poorly armed, mocked for his manners, his morals, even his misery. The name Jacques or Jacques Bonhomme to designate a peasant was used by nobles as a term of derision derived from the padded surplice called "*jacque*" which the peasant wore for protective armor in war. The knights saw him as a person of ignoble instincts who could have no understanding of "honor" and was therefore capable of every kind of deceit and incapable of trust. Ideally he should be treated decently, yet the accepted proverb ran, "Smite a villein and he will bless you; bless a villein and he will smite you."

An extraordinary passage from the tale *Le Despit au Vilain* breathes hatred with an intensity that seems more than mere storytell-ing. "Tell me, Lord, if you please, by what right or title does a villein eat beef? . . . And goose, of which they have plenty? And this troubles God. God suffers from it and I too. For they are a sorry lot, these villeins who eat fat goose! Should they eat fish? Rather let them eat thistles and briars, thorns and straw and hay on Sunday and pea-pods on weekdays. They should keep watch without sleep and have trouble always; that is how villeins should live. Yet each day they are full and drunk on the best wines, and in fine clothes. The great expen-ditures of villeins comes at a high cost, for it is this that destroys and ruins the world. It is they who spoil the common welfare. From the villein comes all unhappiness. Should they eat meat? Rather should they chew grass on the heath with the horned cattle and go naked on all fours. . . ." These tales were addressed to an upper-class audience. Was this what they wanted to hear, or was it a satire of their attitude?

In theory, the tiller of the soil and his livestock were immune from pillage and the sword. No reality of medieval life more harshly mocked the theory. Chivalry did not apply outside the knights' own class. The records tell of peasants crucified, roasted, dragged behind horses by the brigands to extort money. There were preachers who pointed out that the peasant worked unceasingly for all, often overwhelmed by his tasks, and who pleaded for more kindness, but all they could advise the victim was patience, obedience, and resignation.

In 1358 his misery had reached a peak. Brigands seized the seed grain out of his hand, stole his animals for their food, his carts for their loot, his tools and plowshares to forge their weapons. Yet the lords continued to demand fees and taxes and extra aids for their heavy ransoms, "and even for that hardly put themselves out to protect their vassals from attack." The common people "groaned," wrote Jean de Venette, "to see dissipated in games and ornaments the sums they had so painfully furnished for the needs of war." They resented the nobles' failure to use them in the fight against the enemy and felt less fear of them as the knights lost prestige in the defeats since Crécy and in the cowardice at Poitiers. Above all, they saw the complicity in lawlessness of the knight who, if he could not pay a brigand's demand for ransom, took service with his company for a year or two, "so easy it was to make out of a gentleman a brigand." No plan of revolution, but simple hate ignited the Jacquerie.

On May 28, 1358, in the village of St. Leu near Senlis on the Oise, a group of peasants held an indignation meeting in the cemetery after vespers. They blamed the nobles for their miseries and for the capture of the King, "which troubled all minds." What had the knights and squires done to liberate him? What were they good for except to oppress poor peasants? "They shamed and despoiled the realm, and it would be a good thing to destroy them all." Listeners cried, "They say true! They say true! Shame on him who holds back!"

Without further council and no arms but the staves and knives that some carried, a group of about 100 rushed in fierce assault upon the nearest manor, broke in, killed the knight, his wife, and children, and burned the place down. Then, according to Froissart, whose tales of the Jacquerie would have been obtained from nobles and clergy, "they went to a strong castle, tied the knight to a stake while his wife and daughter were raped by many, one after another before his eyes; then they killed the wife who was pregnant and afterward the daughter and all the children and lastly the knight and burned and destroyed the castle." Other reports say that four knights and five squires were killed on that night.

Instantly the outbreak spread, gathering adherents each day to join with torches and burning brushwood in the assault upon castles and manors. They came with scythes, pitchforks, hatchets, and any kind of implement that could be made a weapon. Soon thousands—ultimately, it was said, 100,000—were engaged in attacks covering the Oise valley, the Ile de France, and closer regions of Picardy and Champagne, and raging "throughout the seigneurie of Coucy, where there were great outrages." Before it was over more than "100" castles and manors in the territories of Coucy and Valois and the dioceses of Laon,

Soissons, and Senlis were sacked and burned and more than "60" in the districts of Beauvais and Amiens.

Forming no concerted defense, the nobles at the outset panicked and fled with their families to the walled towns, leaving their homes and all their goods. The Jacques continued killing and burning "without pity or mercy like enraged dogs." Surely, says Froissart, "never among Christians or even Saracens were such outrages committed as by these wicked people, such things as no human creature should dare think or see." The example he cites, taken from the antecedent chronicle of Jean le Bel, tells of a knight whom the Jacques "killed and roasted on a spit before the eyes of his wife and children. Then after ten or twelve of them violated the lady they forced her to eat some of her husband's flesh and then killed her." Repeated over and over in subsequent accounts, this one story became the mainstay of the atrocity tales.

In registered accusations after the event, the killings amount to a total of thirty (not including the roasted knight and lady), including one "spy" who had a trial before his execution. Destruction and looting were more practiced than murder. One group of Jacques made straight for the poultry yard, seized all the chickens they could lay hold of, fished carp out of the pond, took wine from the cellars and cherries from the orchard, and gave themselves a feast at the nobles' expense. As the insurgents organized, they supplied themselves from the castles' stores, burning furniture and buildings when they moved on. In districts where hatred for the clergy equaled that for the nobles, the Jacques warred on the Church; the cloistered trembled in their monasteries, the secular clergy fled to refuge in the towns.

A peasant leader arose in the person of one Guillaume Karle or Cale, described as a strong, handsome Picard of natural eloquence and experience in war, which was what the Jacques most needed. He organized a council which issued orders stamped by an official seal, and appointed captains elected by each locality, and lieutenants for squads of ten. His men fashioned swords out of scythes and billhooks and improvised armor of boiled leather. Cale adopted "Montjoie!" as his battle cry and ordered banners made with the fleur-de-lys, by which the Jacques wished to show they were rising against the nobles, not the King.

Cale's hope was to win the alliance of the towns in a joint action against the nobles; it was here that the two movements, peasant and bourgeois, came together. Few towns of the north "were not against the gentilhommes," according to the monk of St. Denis who wrote the

Chronicle of the Reigns of Jean II and Charles V, while at the same time many feared and despised the Jacques. Lesser bourgeois, however, saw the peasant rising as a common war of non-nobles against nobles and clergy. Towns like Senlis and Beauvais where the party of the red-and-blue hoods was dominant and radical, acted in solidarity with the Jacques, supplied food and opened their gates to them. Many of their citizens joined the peasant ranks. Beauvais, with the consent of mayor and magistrates, executed several nobles whom the Jacques had sent to them as prisoners. Amiens held trials condemning nobles to death in absentia.

Compiègne, on the other hand, which was Cale's major objective refused to surrender the nobles who had taken refuge there, shut its gates, and strengthened its walls. At Caen in Normandy, where the rising failed to take fire, an agitator for the Jacques, with a miniature plow pinned to his hat, toured the streets crying for sympathizers to follow him, but aroused no recruits and was later killed by three townsmen whom he had insulted.

According to letters of pardon after the event, individual bourgeois—butchers, coopers, carters, sergeants, royal officers, priests and other clerics—made themselves accomplices of the Jacques, especially in the looting of property. Even men of the gentry appear in the pardons, but whether they were moved by belief, opportunity for loot, excitement, or *force majeure* is uncertain. Knights, squires, and clerks accused of having led peasant bands always claimed afterward that they had been forced into service to save their necks, which may well have been true, for the Jacques felt painfully the lack of military leaders.

Their captains had little control. At Verberie a captain, on returning from a raid with a captured squire and his family, was surrounded by citizens howling death to the squire. "For god's sake, good sirs," the captain pleaded, "keep yourselves from such an act or you will be committing a crime." To this man the killing of a noble was still a fearsome thing, but not to the mob, who sliced off the squire's head on the spot.

As the rampage spread against all landowners' estates, the Jacques, when asked why they did these things, replied "that they knew not but they saw others do it and they thought they would thus destroy all the nobles and gentry in the world and there would be none any more." Whether or not the peasants really envisaged a world without nobles, the gentry assumed they did and felt the hot breath of annihilation. Seized by that terror the mass inspires when it overthrows authority, they sent for help from their fellows in Flanders, Hainault, and Brabant.

At a critical moment for Marcel, the rage of the Jacquerie offered him an added weapon, which he seized in a fatal choice that was to lose him the support of the propertied class. At his instigation, the estates of the hated royal councillors were made the targets of a band of Jacques organized in the environs of Paris under the command of two merchants of the capital. The properties of the King's chamberlain, Pierre d'Orgement, and of those two inveterate peculators, Simon de Buci and Robert de Lorris, were sacked and destroyed. Breaking into the castle of Ermenonville, one of the many benefits of royal favor bestowed on Robert de Lorris, a combined force of bourgeois and Jacques cornered the owner inside. On his knees before his enemies, he was forced to take an oath to disown the "gentry and nobility" and swear loyalty to the commune of Paris.

Compromised by murder and destruction, Marcel had mounted the tiger. The royal family at Meaux was the next target of the band from Paris. Enlarged as they marched along the Marne by bands of Jacques coming ·from many places and by many paths, the combined group numbering "9,000" reached Meaux on June 9 "with great will to do evil." Prospects of rape and death filled the fortress called the Market of Meaux, where the Dauphin's wife, sister, and infant daughter with some 300 ladies and their children were guarded by a small company of lords and knights. The Mayor and magistrates of Meaux, who had sworn loyalty to the Dauphin and promised to allow no "dishonor" to his family, crumbled before the invaders. Either in fear or in welcome, the citizens opened the gates and set out tables in the streets with napkins and bread, meat and wine. On approaching a town, the marauding Jacques customarily let it be known that they expected such provisions. Pouring into the city, the fearful horde filled the streets with "savage cries" while the ladies in the fortress, say the chroniclers, trembled in anguish.

At that moment, knighthood errant galloped to the rescue in the persons of that glittering pair, the Captal de Buch and Gaston Phoebus, Count of Foix. Although one owed fealty to England and the other to France, they were cousins who were riding home together from a "crusade" in Prussia, where they had gone to keep themselves occupied during the truce after Poitiers. Neither was a friend of the Valois, but noble ladies in danger were every knight's cause, and these two from the south did not share the initial paralysis of the northerners under the onslaught of the Jacques. Nor had either been involved in the shame of

Poitiers. Learning of the peril at Meaux, they hastened to the relief with a company of forty lances (120 men), reaching the Market of Meaux on the same day the commoners entered the city. Connected by a bridge to the city, the fortress, surrounded by walls and towers, was situated on a strip of land between the river and a canal.

At the head of twenty-five knights in bright armor with pennants of argent and azure displaying stars and lilies and couchant lions, the Captal and the Count rode through the portcullis onto the bridge. In its narrow confines where superiority of numbers could not be mustered, the commoners unwisely chose to fight. Wielding weapons from horseback, the knights cut down their opponents, trampling them, toppling bodies into the river, forcing the rest back across the bridge, and opening the way to carnage. Despite some hard hand-to-hand fighting, the "small dark villeins poorly armed" recoiled before the lances and axes of the mailed warriors and, succumbing to terrorized retreat, were butchered. The knights charged, hacking furiously, killing the commoners like beasts, until exhausted from the slaughter.

"Several thousand" were slain, according to the chroniclers' impossible figures, which testify nevertheless to an appalling toll. Fleeing remnants were chased through the countryside and exterminated. The knights lost but a few, one with an arrow through his eye. Their fury, growing by what it fed on, was unleashed in vengeance upon the town, which was put to pillage and flames. Houses and even churches were sacked, leaving nothing of value behind; the Mayor was hanged, many of the citizens massacred, others imprisoned, others burned inside their houses. Meaux burned for two weeks and was afterward condemned for *lèse majesté* and suppressed as an independent commune.

Meaux was the turning point. Gaining courage from the conquest, French nobles of the area joined in desolating the surrounding country, wreaking more damage on France, said Jean de Venette, than had the English. From there, the suppression of the Jacquerie followed, and in its train the fall of Marcel.

Charles of Navarre led the counter-action in Picardy and the Beauvais region, pushed thereto by the nobles of his party. They went to him saying that "if those who are called Jacques continue for long they will bring the gentry to nothing and destroy everything." As one of the great nobles of the world, he must not suffer his own kind to be so reduced. Knowing that he could gain the crown, or the power he wanted, only with the support of the nobility, Charles was persuaded. With a force of several hundred including the "baron de Coussi," he marched against the Jacques gathered at Clermont under Guillaume

Cale. Cale sensibly ordered his army of several thousand to fall back upon Paris for the support and aid of the city, but the Jacques, eager for a fight, refused to obey. Cale then deployed them in the traditional three battalions, of which two, led by archers and crossbowmen, were stationed behind a line of baggage wagons. The third, of 600 horsemen poorly mounted and many without arms, was held in support.

Sounding trumpets and shouting battle cries, with tattered banners flying, the peasants faced the enemy. Surprised by this organized resistance, Navarre preferred guile and treachery. He invited Cale to parley, and upon this invitation from a king, Cale's common sense apparently deserted him. Considering himself an opponent in war to whom the laws of chivalry applied, he went to the parley without a guard, whereupon his royal and noble opponent had him seized and thrown into chains. The capture of their leader by such easy and contemptuous treachery drained the Jacques' confidence and hope of success. When the nobles charged, the commoners succumbed like their fellows at Meaux and suffered equal slaughter. Only a few who hid among the brush escaped the swords of the searching horsemen. Surrounding villages handed over fugitives to the nobles. Pursuing the attack elsewhere in the region, Navarre and his company massacred "3,000" more peasants, including 300 burned alive in a monastery where they had taken refuge. To consummate his victory, Charles of Navarre beheaded Guillaume Cale after reportedly crowning him, in wicked mockery, King of the Jacques with a circlet of red-hot iron.

As the savage repression swept north, its new leader emerged in Enguerrand de Coucy, whose domain had been at the center of the storm. The Jacques were never able to reassemble, says Froissart, because "the young sire de Coucy gathered a great number of gentlemen who put an end to them wherever they found them without pity or mercy." That so young a man should have taken the leadership bespeaks a strong personality, but nothing more about him can be learned from the episode. The *Chronique Normande* and other accounts also mention his hunting down peasants through hamlets and villages and hanging them from trees while his neighbor the Comte de Roussi hung them from the doors of their cottages. The totality of what is known is fixed by the 19th century authority Père Denifle: "It was chiefly Enguerrand VII, the young seigneur de Coucy, who, at the head of the gentry of his barony, completed the extermination of the Jacques."

Reinvigorated by the blood of Meaux, the nobles of that region finished off the Jacquerie between Seine and Marne. "They flung themselves upon hamlets and villages, putting them to the flame and pursuing poor peasants in houses, fields, vineyards and forest to be miserably slaughtered." By June 24, 1358, "20,000" Jacques had been killed and the countryside converted to a wasteland.

The futile rising was over, having lasted, despite its long shadow, less than a month, of which two weeks were taken up by the repression. Nothing had been gained, nothing changed, only more death. Like every insurrection of the century, it was smashed, as soon as the rulers recovered their nerve, by weight of steel, and the advantage of the man on horseback, and the psychological inferiority of the insurgents. Reckless of consequence, the landowners, who were already suffering from the shortage of labor after the plague, let revenge take precedence over self-interest.

Within the next month the struggle in Paris came to a climax and an end. Since the day after Poitiers, Marcel had kept men at work extending the walls, strengthening the gates, building moats and barriers. Now fully enclosed and fortified, the capital was the key to power. From Vincennes on the outskirts, the Regent with assembled nobles was probing for an entry; Marcel, who had lost sight of every purpose but overpowering the Regent, was planning to deliver the capital to Charles of Navarre; the eel-like Navarre was negotiating with both sides and was in contact with Navarrese and English forces outside the walls.

At a mass meeting staged for him by Marcel in the Place de Grève, he told the crowd that "he would have been King of France if his mother had been a man." Planted demonstrators responded with shouts of "Navarre! Navarre!" While the majority, shocked by the disloyalty, remained silent, he was elected by acclamation Captain of Paris. His acceptance of the office on the side of the people alienated many of his noble supporters, for they did not wish to be "against the gentry." Probably at this time Enguerrand de Coucy fell away from the Navarrese party, for he soon afterward appeared in opposition to it.

Under Marcel too the ground was breaking away like ice in a river. His connivance with the Jacques frightened many of the "good towns" and, more seriously, caused the disaffection of the upper bourgeois in his own city. In the chaos and scarcities and disruption of trade, they veered toward the Regent as the only focus in the desperate need for authority. Paris was coming apart in furious factions, some for fighting to the end behind Marcel, some for deposing Navarre, some for admitting the Regent, all fired by hatred of the English, who were ravaging the outskirts with daily atrocity. With his support waning,

Marcel was reduced to the naked need of armed force. On July 22, in the act that turned sentiment against him, he allowed Charles of Navarre to bring a band of English men-at-arms into the city. Aroused and armed Parisians fell upon them with such effect that they had to be locked up in the fortress of the Louvre for protection.

Meanwhile the prosperous bourgeois feared that if the Regent succeeded in taking the city by force instead of surrender, all citizens alike would be subjected to punishment and plunder. Unable to force Marcel to yield the city, they determined to dispose of him on the theory that "it was better to kill than be killed." Amid cabals and enemies and inexplicable events, the citizens were easy prey to whispers of treachery on the part of the Provost.

On July 31 the end came when Marcel appeared at the Porte St. Denis and ordered the guards to deliver the keys of the gate to officers of the King of Navarre. The guards refused, shouting betrayal of the city. Weapons flashed, and a draper named Jean Maillart, evidently pre-equipped, unfurled the royal banner, mounted his horse, and raised the royal battle cry "Montjoie–St. Denis!" Crowds took up the cry, clashes and confused alarms erupted. Marcel next appeared across the city at the Porte St. Antoine, where he again demanded the keys and met the same response, which was led by a certain Pierre des Essars, a knighted bourgeois and cousin by marriage of both Maillart and Marcel. In a rush upon the Provost, the guards of St. Antoine struck him down, and when the bloodstained weapons had lifted and the melee had cleared, the body of Etienne Marcel lay trampled and dead in the street.

Two of his companions were also killed, and others of his party were stripped, beaten, and left naked under the walls. "Then the people rushed off to find others to treat the same way." More of the Provost's partisans were murdered and dumped naked in the streets. While Charles of Navarre escaped to St. Denis, the royalist faction took control and two days later, on August 2, 1358, opened the city to the Regent.

He at once proclaimed a pardon for the citizens of Paris except for close associates of Marcel and Navarre, who were executed or banished, and their confiscated property turned over to the Regent's party. But the spirit of the blue-and-red hoods remained strong enough to cause angry demonstrations when more of Marcel's adherents were arrested. The situation was sullen and dangerous. On August 10 the Regent issued a general amnesty and ordered nobles and peasantry to pardon each other so that the fields might be cultivated and the harvest brought in. The extermination of the Jacques was making itself felt.

With Marcel's death the reform movement was aborted; the

glimpse of "Good Government" was to remain only a glimpse. After Artevelde and Rienzi, Marcel was the third leader of a bourgeois rising within a dozen years to be killed by his own followers. The people of France on the whole were not ready for an effort to limit the monarchy. They blamed all their troubles—heavy taxes, dishonest government, debased coinage, military defeats, banditry of the companies, the fallen condition of the realm—on the crown's evil councillors and the caitiff nobles, not on the King, who had fought bravely at Poitiers, or even on the Dauphin. No political movement sprang from Marcel's bones. The right of the Estates General to convene at will was lost, the provisions of the Grand Ordinance largely, though not entirely, discarded. The crown was left free for the period of royal absolutism that history held in waiting.

Though the Regent held Paris, he was ringed by enemies. From St. Denis, Charles of Navarre announced open defiance and renewed his alliance with King Edward. "Very grievous and cruel," the undeclared warfare of Navarrese and English companies intensified, individual groups were fighting back, the land was prey to local battles and raids, the besieging of castles and burning of villages. Caught up in the havoc, "the young Sire de Coucy carefully guarded his castle and territory," with the aid of two redoubtable warriors. One was his former guardian Matthieu de Roye, who on one occasion forced the surrender of and took prisoner an entire English company of 300. The other was the governor of Coucy's domain, a "hard and valiant knight" called the Chanoine de Robersart, who "made himself more feared by the English and Navarrese than anyone else, for he chased them many times."

Enguerrand's own feat was to destroy the castle of Bishop Robert le Coq, who was attempting to carry Laon over to the camp of Charles of Navarre. The particulars are unrecorded except for the fact that the Sire de Coucy "did not like the said Bishop." Otherwise, by paying wages to his men-at-arms and allowing no one to remain outside the walls, he kept the brigands at bay, although they succeeded in capturing the neighboring castle of the Comte de Roussi, "causing great scarcity" in the district. Through untilled fields and charred villages, scarcity was stalking France.

Chapter 8

Hostage in England

All this time efforts in London to conclude a permanent peace treaty had not succeeded. When the French balked at the terms of a settlement reached in 1358, Edward responded by raising his demands. In March 1359 when the truce was about to expire, King Jean yielded, trading half his kingdom for his own release. By the Treaty of London he surrendered virtually all of western France from Calais to the Pyrenees, and agreed to an augmented and catastrophic ransom of 4 million gold écus, payable at fixed installments, to be guaranteed by the delivery of forty royal and noble hostages, of whom Enguerrand de Coucy was designated as one. In case of obstruction to the transfer of ceded territories, Edward retained the right to send armed forces back to France, whose cost was to be borne by the French King.

Desperate for peace though France was, shame and anger rose when the terms became known. Dragged to maturity in the grim years since Poitiers, the Dauphin had learned greater stewardship than his father. Neither he nor his Council was prepared to yield what the King of France had agreed to. Facing a fearful choice between accepting the treaty and renewal of the war, they summoned the Estates General with a request for "the most substantial notable and wise men" bearing full powers to represent the communes.

In this somber hour, one of the darkest in French history, the few delegates who braved the bandit-infested roads to come to Paris were in earnest. When the text of the Treaty of London was read to them on May 19, they deliberated briefly and made their response to the Dauphin without dispute. It was for once laconic. "They said the Treaty was displeasing to all the people of France and intolerable, and for this they ordered war to be made on England."

Edward prepared to launch a supreme effort to consummate victory. He laid the cause to French "perfidy" in rejecting the treaty, thus establishing grounds for a "just war" and allowing bishops to offer indulgences in aid of recruitment. Determined to assemble an expeditionary force that should lack nothing to make it invincible, he spent all summer gathering the components. An immense convoy of 1,100 ships carrying 11,000 to 12,000 men and more than 3,000 horses (to be joined by as many more at Calais) was assembled, with 1,000 carts and some four-horse wagons for the baggage train, plus tents, forges, hand mills, horseshoes and nails, bows and arrows, arms and armor, cooking utensils, initial stocks of wine and food, leather boats for fishing in the rivers, not forgetting, for the hunt, thirty falconers with hawks, sixty couple of hounds, and sixty of harriers.

By the time the King embarked, taking with him his four eldest sons, it was the end of October, ensuring a winter campaign. All military experience, including his own, knew this to be ruinous to a force away from its home base, but the impetus of great preparations is hard to halt, and possession of many garrisons in France gave Edward confidence in a quick victory.

England's fortunes were at the crest. A dynamic King had attracted the aid of an extraordinary group of able soldiers—Chandos, Knollys, Sir Walter Manny, Sir Hugh Calveley, the Captal de Buch, and not least the Prince of Wales—such a group "as the Starres have an influence to produce at one time more than another." Success was tangible. "A woman who did not possess spoil from France," wrote the chronicler Walsingham, "garments, furs, bed covers, silver vessels and cloth of linen, was of no account." Ebullience had reached a perfect moment in 1350 when King Edward sailed forth to meet a Spanish challenge. On board the cog *Thomas* in August, as described by Froissart, the King, in a black velvet doublet and round beaver hat "which became him well," sat in the forecastle enjoying talk and song with the Prince and a group of nobles. "The King was that day, as I was told by those present, as joyous as ever he was in his life and ordered the minstrels to play before him an Almaine dance which Sir John Chandos had lately introduced." He commanded Sir John to dance and sing with the minstrels, "which delighted him greatly," while from time to time he glanced up at the lookout on the mast who was watching for sight of the Spaniards. Needless to say, when sighted, they were met and conquered, confirming Edward's boast to be "Lord of the Sea."

From Calais in 1359 the English set out for Reims, where Edward intended to be crowned King of France. Trailing an enormous baggage train said to cover two leagues, they crossed Picardy in three separate lines of march in order to spread their foraging, and even so found scant provisions in a country already devastated by the companies. Horses starved, pace slowed, rain fell daily, progress contracted to three leagues a day. Worst of all, Edward's goal of decisive battle eluded him. The English marched through a deliberately created vacuum. No glittering armed force came out to meet them. The French concentrated their defense in fortified towns and castles that could withstand attack.

Avoidance of pitched battle—the strategy that was to save France—evolved, like most military innovations, from defeat, ignominy, and paucity of means. The person who perceived what the situation demanded was the Regent, a ruler who harkened to necessity, not glory.

In respect of his hostile brother-in-law of Navarre, the Regent's position had improved, because in August Charles of Navarre had deserted his alliance with Edward and, in yet one more elaborate ceremony of reconciliation, promised to be "a good friend to the King of France, to the Regent and the kingdom." Though his promise was widely thought to be inspired by God, the King of Navarre could not live without plotting, and within months was engaged in a new plan to dispose of the Dauphin.

Edward reached Reims in the first week of December, presumably expecting the city to admit him after what was to have been his victorious advance. Forewarned of his intention, Reims had been strengthening its walls during the long preparation and remained stubbornly closed, forcing the English into a siege. The French had emptied the countryside of everything that could serve the enemy and had destroyed buildings that could shelter him. At the gates of Reims, Edward saw the monastery of St. Thierry, which he had intended to use as his headquarters, burning before his eyes. Foiled of provisions as they had been of battle, and reduced by cold and hunger, the English were forced to lift the siege after forty days. They headed south for the rich land of Burgundy, looting and destroying for two months until Edward allowed himself to be bought off for 200,000 moutons d'or by the then Duke of Burgundy, Philip de Rouvre.

As he turned toward Paris in March, Edward learned with fury and vows of vengeance of a savage French raid carried out in that month on Winchelsea, on the south coast of England. Its ultimate object was the rescue of King Jean, which would have spared France his ruinous ransom. As originally planned, the raid was also intended, by "making a show of remaining there," to frighten the English into withdrawing forces from France in self-defense. Costs were raised by the major towns. A bold ship captain named Enguerrand Ringois of Abbeville, renowned for his courage and indomitable character at the siege of Calais, was chosen as naval commander. The land forces, numbering 2,000 knights, archers, and foot soldiers from Picardy and Normandy, suffered from the usual absence of single command. They were led by a triumvirate of nobles who were at odds with each other. Pierre des Essars, the man who had disposed of Etienne Marcel, led a body of Parisian volunteers.

Rumor preceding the attack had caused Jean to be moved on March 1 from Lincolnshire to a castle nearer London and subsequently to the Tower of London itself. Despite reconnoitering of the coasts, the French, misled by false information, landed on the south coast on March 15. Seizing Winchelsea without difficulty, they made no effort to establish a foothold, but plunged into the usual frenzy of pillage, murder, and rape, including massacre of a group of citizens attending mass in the church. While alarm flew over the countryside, the French sacked the neighboring town of Rye, then met and repelled a hastily assembled force of 1,200 English who came against them. Fearing greater reinforcements, they decided against the "show of remaining there" and, returning to the beachhead after a 48 hours' invasion, re-embarked in the light of the burning town.

England was thrown into a panic by news that the enemy were "riding over the country, slaying, burning, destroying and doing other mischief," and that worse might be expected "unless they be speedily and manfully opposed." While that proved unnecessary, the panic left a persistent fear of invasion that was to exert some restraint on future activities against France. Otherwise the raid, bravely planned and badly led, accomplished nothing except to provoke Edward's wrath and reprisals on discovering that the French could act as viciously in his realm as the English did in France.

Surrounding Paris early in April, the English sent heralds to challenge the defenders to battle, but the Dauphin, relying on Marcel's improved fortifications, forbade any response. After a week of burning and killing outside the walls failed to provoke a fight, Edward turned away, baffled as he had been at Reims, though not yet ready to give up. He took the road for Chartres, not for the coast. For the past two months papal legates had been shuttling between the Dauphin and the English, attempting to reopen negotiations, always blocked by Edward's refusal to reduce his terms. The Dauphin himself had sent envoys with peace proposals. Seeing "how the realm could not long endure the great tribulation and poverty" the English were inflicting, "for the rents of the lords and churches were nigh lost in every part," he and his Council offered to settle on the basis agreed to in 1358 before Edward had raised his demands. The Duke of Lancaster advised

Edward to accept, for if he persisted he might have to make war "all the days of your life" and might "lose in one day what it has taken us twenty years to win."

The anger of the heavens supported the Duke. On Monday, April 13, a "foul dark day" of mist and bitter cold, as the army camped on the approach to Chartres, a violent hailstorm struck with the force of a cyclone, followed by cloudbursts of freezing rain. Horses and men were killed by the prodigious hailstones, tents were torn up by the wind, the baggage train was dragged through mud and floods, and scores died of the fearful cold, "wherefor unto thys day manye men callen it Black Monday." In half an hour Edward's army took a beating that human hands could not have inflicted and that could hardly be taken as other than a celestial warning. Black Monday brought to a head all the faults of the six months' campaign—the vulnerability of the English army, the foiling of decisive battle, the incapacity to take a major walled town or capital city, the vaguely perceived knowledge, of which Lancaster had a glimmer, that France could not be conquered by pillage, nor by siege, town by town, fortress by fortress. In the long run, this was what would condemn the war to drag on for a hundred years—the fact that, short of a fluke like the capture of a king at Poitiers, medieval armies had no means of achieving a decisive result, much less unconditional surrender.

Yielding to Heaven's warning and Lancaster's counsel, Edward appointed commissioners to treat with the French on revised peace terms. They met at the little village of Brétigny about a league's distance from Chartres, where the twenty years' war was at last brought to an end— as it then seemed.

Signed May 8, 1360, the Treaty of Brétigny covered a maze of legal and territorial details in 39 articles, five letters of confirmation, and multiple rhetoric as eternal as lawyers. Basically it was a return to the original settlement of 1358. King Jean's ransom was put back to 3 million gold écus and Edward's excess territorial demands were abandoned, to that extent marking his last campaign as a failure and a waste. But the basic cession of Guienne and Calais to the King of England free of homage was confirmed, plus the transfer of other territories, towns, ports, and castles between the Loire and the Pyrenees and in the region of Calais, representing in all about a third of France, the largest gain ever recorded in western Europe up to that time. Edward renounced the crown of France and all territorial claims not granted in the treaty.

To ensure fulfillment, the earlier provision for forty hostages representing the greatest in the realm was renewed, again including Enguerrand de Coucy. As lord of the greatest stronghold in northern France and a center of resistance to the English, he was deliberately selected in the belief that the peace would be better kept if such men were hostages.

The group was headed by the four "Fleurs-de-Lys" or royal princes—namely, the King's two sons, Louis and Jean (future Ducs d'Anjou and de Berry); his brother, the Duc d'Orléans; and the Dauphin's brother-in-law, Louis II, Duc de Bourbon. The Counts d'Artois, d'Eu, de Longueville, d'Alençon, de Blois, de St. Pol, d'Harcourt, de Grandpré, de Braisne, and other *grands seigneurs* and notable fighters including Matthieu de Roye, Coucy's former guardian, made up the list. King Jean was to be returned as far as Calais, where he would remain until a first payment of 600,000 écus was made on his ransom and a preliminary transfer of territories had taken place. He would then be liberated with ten of his fellow prisoners from Poitiers and replaced by forty hostages of the Third Estate—the real source of money—four from Paris and two from each of eighteen other towns. Thereafter, sovereignty of towns and castles was to be transferred, and the remainder of the ransom paid, 400,000 at a time, in six installments at six-month intervals, with one fifth of the hostages released upon each delivery.

The Treaty of Brétigny was "too lightly given to the great grief and prejudice of the kingdom of France" in the judgment of the anonymous chronicler of the *Quatre Valois,* of whom nothing is known except that he was a citizen of Rouen. Fortresses and good towns were given up, he wrote, that "could not have easily been conquered," which was true enough, but the treaty was excused on the ground that it was necessary to deliver the King.

Delivering France from the companies was even more urgent. In an appendix to the treaty, Edward forbade on pain of banishment any further acts against the peace by English men of war, but there was no firm intent behind the provision and it brought France no surcease. In fact the Treaty of Brétigny opened the period of the companies' greatest flourishing, as a swarm of newly discharged soldiers in groups labeled the *Tard-Venus* (Late-Comers) scavenged on the heels of their predecessors and gradually swelled the ranks of the mercenary armies.

Efforts to raise the ransom were stretched to the extreme. Towns, counties, and noble domains assessed themselves, among them the house of Coucy, which contributed 27,500 francs. Sales taxes of twelve pence in the pound were levied on Paris and the surrounding country, to be paid by nobles and clergy and "all persons capable of paying." When returns were meager, recourse was had to the Jews, who were invited back on a grant of twenty years' residence for which they were to pay twenty florins each on re-entry and seven florins annually thereafter.

Jean himself sold his eleven-year-old daughter Isabelle in marriage to the nine-year-old son of the rich and rampant Visconti family of Milan for 600,000 gold florins. The alliance of the King of France with an upstart Italian tyrant was almost as great a wonder as the defeat of Poitiers. To obtain the princess, Galeazzo Visconti, the bridegroom's father, offered half the money cash down and half in return for a territorial dowry. The marriage was to take place in July, immediately following betrothal as was customary, but had to be postponed when the princess fell ill of a fever. What anxiety must have hovered over a daughter's sickbed, on which so much gold depended!

At that time the plague had re-appeared in Savoy and Lombardy in the first outbreak of what was to be a major recurrence in the following year. After escaping to country villas for the summer months while thousands died in Milan and corpses rotted in sealed houses, the Visconti brothers returned as the plague abated, and sent throughout Italy for jewels, silks, and gorgeous raiment in preparation of the wedding. Guests were assured it "would be the greatest that Lombardy had ever seen." The French princess, having recovered, was dispatched to Milan via Savoy regardless of risk, and duly married in mid-October in festivities of "imperial" luxury lasting three days. A thousand guests with all their retainers converged upon the city for the occasion. The opulent show put on by the Visconti—and paid for by their subjects—only underlined what was widely seen as a humiliation for France. "Who could imagine," wrote Matteo Villani, considering the greatness of the crown of France, "that the wearer of that crown should be reduced to such straits as virtually to sell his own flesh at auction?" The fate of the King's daughter seemed to him "truly an indication of the infelicity of human affairs."

King Jean meanwhile had been waiting in English custody at Calais since July along with his youngest son, now called Philip the Bold. The surname of the future Duke of Burgundy was earned at a banquet given by King Edward for the prisoners of Poitiers, in the course of which the young prince jumped up from the table in a fury and struck the master butler, crying, "Where did you learn to serve the King of England before the King of France when they are at the same table?" "Verily, cousin," commented Edward, "you are Philip the Bold." In 1361, on the death of Philip de Rouvre, King Jean took over the duchy of Burgundy for his youngest son who was to make it a fateful inheritance.

On October 24, 1360, a first payment of 400,000 écus on Jean's ransom, collected mostly in the north, was delivered to the English at Calais. The Visconti gold was so entangled in complex financial deals, dowries, and exchanges between Jean and Galeazzo that it seems not to have assisted the ransom. Though less than the stipulated sum, the 400,000 was accepted, and the peace treaty, with some modifications, thereupon formally ratified as the Treaty of Calais. The signature of Enguerrand de Coucy as one of the chief hostages was added to the document. After jointly swearing with Edward to keep the peace perpetually according to the terms of the treaty, the two Kings parted, and Jean after four years' imprisonment returned at last to his ravaged country.

Four days after his liberation, on October 30, the party of French hostages in the custody of King Edward and his sons sailed for England. Some were to stay for ten years, some to return in two or three, some to die in exile. Among their varying fates, Enguerrand's was unique: he was to become the son-in-law of the King of England.

Immortality traveled with him across the Channel. Whether on the same ship or another of the convoy, a young clerk of bourgeois family from Valenciennes in Hainault was journeying to England to present an account he had written of the Battle of Poitiers to Queen Philippa of England, his countrywoman, in hopes of obtaining her patronage. By name Jean Froissart, aged 22 or 23, he succeeded in pleasing the Queen and, with her encouragement, began collecting material for the chronicle that was to make him the Herodotus of his age. Consciously the celebrator of chivalry, he wrote with intent that "the honorable and noble adventures and feats of arms, done and achieved by the wars of France and England, should notably be inregistered and put in perpetual memory." Within those confines, no more complete and vivid chronicle exists. Crystallized in the "perpetual memory" Froissart achieved for them, the nobles of his time forever ride, brilliant, avaricious, valiant, cruel. If, as Sir Walter Scott complained, Froissart had "marvelous little sympathy" for the "villain churls," that was a condition of the context.

The convoy carrying the hostages contained an extraordinary concentration of the primary actors of the day. Among them was another observer who had immortality to bestow. Humanity was Geoffrey Chaucer's subject, and all of 14th century society—except the lowest —his scope. Twenty years old at this time, born in the same year as Enguerrand de Coucy, he had accompanied the English army to France as a member of the household of the King's second son, Lionel, Duke of Clarence. While in a foraging party outside Reims, he had been captured by the French and ransomed by King Edward for £16, which compared favorably with the £6 13s. 4d. paid in compensation for Lord Andrew Lutterall's dead horse and with the £2 paid to ransom the average archer. No documentary evidence attests to Chaucer's presence on the return voyage to England, but since the Duke of Clarence sailed with the hostages, it is more than likely that Chaucer, as a member of his retinue, accompanied him.

In due time Coucy was to meet and know Chaucer and become a friend and patron of Froissart, although there is nothing to show whether the three young men made contact during the voyage. Some time afterward, however, while eagerly observing everyone who might be material for his history, Froissart took notice of his future patron. At a court festivity in England when elaborate dances and singing preceded the banquet, he observed how "the young lord de Coucy shined in dancing and caroling whenever it was his turn. He was in great favor with both the French and English, for whatever he chose to do he did well and with grace and all praised him for the agreeable manner in which he addressed everyone." In the talents that a stylish young nobleman was supposed to show, Enguerrand was clearly an accomplished performer who, not surprisingly, attracted attention.

Pursuit of adventures under Mars and Venus was supposed to be the business of a young knight's life. "If at arms you excel," advises the God of Love in the *Roman de la Rose*, "you will be ten times loved. If you have a good voice, seek no excuse when asked to sing, for good singing gives pleasure." Dancing and playing the flute and strings also aid the lover on his way to a lady's heart. He should likewise keep his hands, nails, and teeth clean, lace his sleeves, comb his hair, but use no paint or rouge, which are not fitting even for women. He should dress handsomely and fashionably and wear fresh new shoes, taking care that they fit so well that "common folk will discuss how you got them on and where you entered them." He should finish off with a garland of flowers, which costs little.

How far Enguerrand conformed to this ideal cannot be said, for no portrait exists, which is not exceptional since, except for royal personages, the art of portraiture was hardly yet practiced. The 14th century seems to have been interested in individual appearance and character traits only in the case of ruling figures or an occasional oddity like Bertrand Du Guesclin. Other people are undifferentiated by chronicles and illustrators and become personalities only through their deeds. For Enguerrand de Coucy two clues to appearance exist; one that he was tall and strong, as his figure was described under a rain of blows in his last battle; the other that he may have been dark and, in maturity, saturnine, as he appears in a portrait painted more than 200 years after his death. Since the portrait was commissioned by a Celestine monastery which Enguerrand had founded, some tradition of the founder's looks may have survived to instruct the artist, but the face portrayed could just as well have been imaginary.

The most vivid description of all is non-specific; yet in his singing and dancing, elegant horsemanship, charm of manner, and lover's talents, it is impossible not to see the young Enguerrand de Coucy in the Squire of the *Canterbury Tales*. Which is not to say that Chaucer, who saw knights and squires every day during his career at court, had Enguerrand particularly in mind when he drew the sparkling portrait in the Prologue. Nevertheless it fits.

> A lovyere and a lusty bacheler
> With lokkes crulled [curled] as they were leyd in presse,
> Of twenty yeer of age he was, I gesse.
> Of his stature he was of evene lengthe,
> And wonderly deliver, and great of strengthe.
> And he had been sometime in chevachye,
> In Flaundres, in Artoys, and Picardye,
> And born him wel, as of so litel space,
> In hope to stonden in his lady grace.
> Embroudered was he as it were a mede
> Al ful of fresshe floures whyte and rede.
> Singing he was or floytinge [fluting] all the day;
> He was as fresh as is the month of May.
> Short was his goune, with sleves long and wyde.
> Wel coude he sitte on hors and faire ryde.
> He coude songes make and wel endyte,
> Jouste and eek daunce, and wel purtreye and wryte.
> So hote he lovede that by nightertale [nighttime]
> He sleep namore than dooth a nightingale.

Headed by the four "Lilies," Anjou, Berry, Orléans, and Bourbon, the hostages in their silks and parti-colors, "embroidered like a field of flowers," brought no less splendor to England than the prisoners of Poitiers whom they replaced. They were required to live at their own expense—considerable in the case of the Duc d'Orléans, who had sixteen servants with him and a total retinue of over sixty. Handsomely entertained with banquets and minstrels and gifts of jewels, the hostages moved about freely and joined in hunting and hawking, dancing and flirting. French and English chivalry took pride in treating one another courteously as prisoners, however greedy the ransom—in contrast to Germans, who, according to Froissart's scornful report, threw their prisoners "in chains and irons like thieves and murderers to extort a greater ransom."

Coucy would not have felt alien in England. His family possessed lands there inherited from his great-grandmother Catherine de Baliol, although these had been confiscated during the war by King Edward and handed over as a munificent reward to the captor of the King of Scotland.

English and French, like English and Americans of a later day, shared a common culture and, among nobles, a common language, the legacy of the Norman Conquest. At about the time the hostages arrived, the use of French by the upper class was beginning to be replaced by the national speech of the commoners. Before the Black Death, French had been the language of the court, Parliament, and the lawcourts. King Edward himself probably did not speak English with any fluency. French was even taught in the schools, much to the resentment of the bourgeois, whose children, according to a complaint of 1340, "are compelled to leave the use of their own language, a thing which is known in no other country." When many clerics who could teach French were eliminated by the Black Death, children in the grammar schools began learning their lessons in English—with both profit and loss, in the opinion of John of Trevisa. They learned grammar more quickly than before, he wrote, but, lacking French, they were at a disadvantage when they "scholle passe the se and travayle in strange londes."

Because of its island limits and earlier development of parliamentary power, England was more cohesive than France, with a greater national feeling, enhanced by growing antagonism to the papacy. Now with the ransoms of two kings, Jean of France and David of Scotland, the triumphs in battle and the territorial gains, England had turned the tables on William the Conqueror. Yet beneath the pride and glory and flow of cash, the effects of war were gnawing at the country.

The plunderers of France brought home the habit of brigandage. Many in the invasion forces had been outlaws and criminals to begin with who had joined up for a promised pardon. Others were made lawless and violent by the approved daily practice in France. Returning home, some formed companies in imitation of their fellows who had stayed in France. "Arrayed as for war," they robbed and assaulted travelers, took captives, held villages for ransom, killed, mutilated, and spread terror. A statute of 1362 instructed justices to gather information "on all those who have been plunderers and robbers beyond the seas and are now returned to go wandering and will not work as they were used to do."

In the spring of 1361, twelve years since the passing of the great plague, the dreaded black swellings reappeared in France and England, bringing "a very great mortality of hasty death." An early victim was the Queen of France, Jean's second wife, who died in September 1360 ahead of the main epidemic. The *Pestis Secunda*, sometimes called the "mortality of children," took a particularly high toll of the young, who had no immunity from the earlier outbreak, and, according to John of Reading, "especially struck the masculine sex." The deaths of the young in the Second Pest halted repopulation, haunting the age with a sense of decline. In the urge to procreate, women in England, according to *Polychronicon*, "took any kind of husbands, strangers, the feeble and imbeciles alike, and without shame mated with inferiors."

Because the pneumonic form was absent or insignificant, the death rate as a whole was less than that of the first epidemic, although equally erratic. In Paris 70 to 80 died daily; at Argenteuil, a few miles away where the Oise joins the Seine, the number of hearths was reduced from 1,700 to 50. Flanders and Picardy suffered heavily, and Avignon spectacularly. Through its choked and unsanitary quarters the plague swept like flames through straw. Between March and July 1360 "17,000" were said to have died.

Though less lethal, the Second Pest carried a more terrible burden than the first in the very fact of its return. Thereafter people lived in fear, repeatedly justified, of another recurrence, just as they lived in fear of the brigands' return. At any time either the phantom that "rises like black smoke in our midst" or the steel-capped horsemen could appear, with death and ruin at their heels. A sense of overhanging disaster weighed on the second half of the century, expressed in prophecies of doom and apocalypse.

The most celebrated of these was the "Tribulation" of Jean de la Roquetaillade, a Franciscan friar incarcerated at Avignon because of his preaching against corrupt prelates and princes. Like Jean de Venette, he sympathized with the oppressed against the mighty, lay and clerical. From his cell in 1356, the year of Poitiers, he prophesied that France would be brought low and all Christendom be vexed by troubles: tyranny and robbers would prevail; the lowly would rise against the great, who "shall be cruelly slain by the commons"; many women would be "defiled and widowed" and their "haughtiness and luxury shall wither"; Saracens and Tatars would invade the kingdoms of the Latins; rulers and peoples, outraged by the luxury and pride of the clergy, would combine to strip the Church of its property; nobles and princes would be cast down from their dignities and suffer unbelievable afflictions; Anti-Christ would appear to spread false doctrines; tempests, floods, and plagues would wipe out most of mankind and all hardened sinners, preparing the way for renewal.

These were the concerns and real currents of the time. Like most medieval doom-sayers, however, Roquetaillade predicted debacle as the prelude to a better world. In his vision, the Church, purified by suffering, chastisement, and true poverty, would be restored, a great reformer would become Pope, the King of France against all custom would be elected Holy Roman Emperor and rule as the holiest monarch since the beginning of time. He and the Pope together would expel the Saracens and Tatars from Europe, convert all Moslems, Jews, and other infidels, destroy heresy, conquer the world for the universal church, and, before they died, establish a reign of peace that would last a thousand years until the Day of Judgment and the End.

The hostages did not escape the plague. A high-ranking victim was Count Guy de St. Pol, a knight of great virtue, "very devout and merciful to the poor," who abhorred the lusts and corruptions of the world, fasted unsparingly, and had maintained virginity until agreeing to marriage. The bourgeois hostages of Paris, Rouen, and several other towns were likewise victims. The great Duke of Lancaster, probably the richest man in the kingdom, was not proof; he too died of the plague, leaving his title and vast inheritance to his son-in-law, John of Gaunt, third son of King Edward. How and where the hostages were housed and whether chivalric courtesy allowed them escape to country retreats is not recorded. In 1357, eight years after the first plague, London was reported still one-third empty, but, though uncrowded, its sanitation was still careless enough to elicit repeated ordinances requiring citizens to clean their premises. Though it was against the law to empty chamber pots into the streets, their contents and kitchen garbage were often flung out of windows, more or less aimed at the gutters, which carried a steady current of water. Barns for keeping horses, cattle, pigs, and chickens were located inside the walls as well as outside, causing many complaints about accumulating piles of manure. At about this time London's aldermen organized a system of hired "rakers" to carry the piles away in dump carts or in dung boats on the Thames.

For the hostages, prospects were not carefree. Their hope of return depended on regular payments of the King's ransom, which already lagged. Collection of money was slowed by the plague and was anyway hard to come by in the ashes left by the companies. The case of Bux-eaul, a town in Burgundy, was typical of many. According to a royal ordinance of 1361, plague and massacre had reduced its fifty or sixty hearths to ten and these "have been pillaged and ruined by our enemies so that little or nothing remains to them wherefore some of the inhabitants have left the place and are still leaving from day to day"; and because of these things, the survivors if required to pay customary taxes "would have to flee and leave the place and become poor beggars"; therefore it was ordained that the town should pay one tax a year instead of two and be freed of all heriot.

The desolation of churches sacked by the enemy was a subject of constant appeals to the bishops. Candles cannot be lit at mass because the winds blow through for lack of window glass; collapse threatens without funds for maintenance; roofs leak, rain falls on the altar. Abbots and abbesses wander in search of subsistence; prelates who would have blushed to appear in public without retinues of horsemen and servants "are now under the necessity of going on foot in humiliation followed by a single monk or valet and subsisting on the most frugal diet." Universities suffered from lack of attendance and fees. Montpellier declared itself "destitute of lecturers and auditors because in the said *studium* where formerly a thousand students used to dwell, scarcely 200 are to be found today."

To the shocked eyes of Petrarch, sent by Galeazzo Visconti to congratulate King Jean on his liberation, France was "a heap of ruins." Petrarch was an inveterate complainer who raised every complaint to an extremity, whether it was the iniquity of doctors, the smells of Avignon, or the decadence of the papacy. But even if exaggerated, his account of France as he saw it in January 1361 was tragic enough. "Everywhere was solitude, desolation and misery; fields are deserted, houses ruined and empty except in the walled towns; everywhere you see the fatal footprints of the English and the hateful scars still bleeding from their swords." In royal Paris, "shamed by devastation up to her very gates . . . even the Seine flows sadly as if feeling the sorrow of it, and weeps, trembling for the fate of the whole land."

Petrarch presented the King with two rings from Galeazzo, one a huge ruby as a gift, one torn from Jean's hand at Poitiers which Galeazzo had somehow redeemed. Afterward he treated the court to a Latin oration on the Biblical text of Manasseh's return from Babylon, with felicitous references to the mutability of Fortune as shown by Jean's marvelous restoration out of captivity. The King and the Prince, Petrarch wrote in the voluminous correspondence of which he carefully kept copies, "fixed their eyes on me" with great interest, and he felt that his discussion of Fortune especially aroused the attention of the Dauphin, "a young man of ardent intelligence."

Personal misfortunes, apart from those of his country, had afflicted the Dauphin. In October 1360 his three-year-old daughter, Jeanne, and her infant sister, Bonne, his only children, had died within two weeks of each other, though whether of the plague, like the Queen, is not stated. At the double burial the Dauphin was seen "so sorrowful as never before he had been." He himself had been afflicted by an illness which caused his hair and nails to fall out and rendered him "dry as a stick." Gossip attributed it to poison administered by Charles of Navarre, which it may well have been, for the symptoms are those of arsenic poisoning. The King of Navarre had once again turned inimical. In December 1359 when the English were at Reims, perhaps fearing that Edward might indeed gain the crown, he had plotted a coup of his own. Armed men were to enter Paris by several gates, combine forces to seize the Louvre, enter and kill the Dauphin and his Council, then spread through the city, seizing strong points before the Parisians could assemble. His ultimate purpose as usual remains mysterious. Betrayed to the Dauphin, the plot fractured relations between them and left Charles of Navarre prowling in hostility as before.

Not only payment of the ransom but fulfillment of the territorial terms controlled the hostages' fate. Too lightly, as the chronicler said, sovereignties had been disposed of at Brétigny, with no account taken of the fact that territories on paper represented people on the ground. Something had happened to these people during two decades of war. The citizens of the seaport of La Rochelle implored the King not to give them up, saying they would rather be taxed up to half their property every year than be turned over to English rule. "We may submit to the English with our lips," they said, "but with our hearts never." Weeping, the inhabitants of Cahors lamented that the King had left them orphans. The little town of St. Romain de Tarn refused to admit the English commissioners within its gates, although it reluctantly sent envoys to take the oath of homage next day at a neighboring place.

For all his countrymen who equated the English with the brigands and hated them helplessly in their hearts, Enguerrand Ringois of Abbeville, the naval commander of the raid on Winchelsea, spoke through his acts. As citizen of a ceded town, he adamantly refused to take the oath of allegiance to the King of England. Persisting against all threats, he was transferred to England, held in a dungeon without recourse to law or friends, and finally taken to the cliffs of Dover, where he was given the choice between taking the oath or death on the wave-washed rocks below. Ringois threw himself into the sea.

Like Pope Boniface's claim to total papal supremacy, the terms of Brétigny were obsolete. It was too late to transfer provinces of France like simple fiefs; unnoticed, the inhabitants had come to feel themselves French. Between the happening of a historical process and its recognition by rulers, a lag stretches, full of pitfalls.

The fate of the hostages was caught up in it. With the ransom in arrears and trouble arising over the ceded territories, their exile stretched ahead to no visible horizon. They were not being returned in fixed numbers every six months as planned, nor being replaced by substitutes, because few could be found willing to go and Edward made difficulties over the names proposed. In November 1362 the four impatient royal Dukes, who had expected to be released a year earlier, negotiated a treaty of their own with Edward by which they promised to deliver 200,000 florins due on the ransom and certain additional territories belonging to the Duc d'Orléans in return for their freedom and that of six other hostages. They were to stay in Calais on parole until delivery had been fulfilled. Never averse to taking a little extra, Edward was willing to let them go on these terms, but King Jean insistently refused his consent unless his cousin the Comte d'Alençon, the Comte d'Auvergne, and the Sire de Coucy were released in place of three of those named by the "Lilies." Since Jean's choices were greater nobles than the other three, Edward in his turn refused consent. Correspondence flowed, the royal Dukes dispatched urgent and angry appeals, finally King Jean, who had by now left his unhappy country for Avignon, lost interest and yielded. Coucy as a result remained in England. More than ever, after the departure of the royal Dukes, he was the object of Edward's and his daughter's interest.

Events took a startling turn when King Jean himself, for whose recovery his country had sacrificed so much, voluntarily returned to captivity in England. The motivations of this curious monarch are not readily understood 600 years later; only the train of circumstance is clear.

On regaining the throne, King Jean's first effort to cope with his country's tormentors proved to be another Poitiers in miniature. To stem the "Great Company" of *Tard-Venus* who were overrunning central France, he had hired one of their own kind, the "Archpriest," Arnaut de Cervole, and, in addition, dispatched a small royal army of 200 knights and 400 archers under the Count of Tancarville, lieutenant of the region, and the renowned Jacques de Bourbon, Count de la

Marche, a great-grandson of St. Louis, who had saved King Philip's life at Crécy. Both had been wounded and captured at Poitiers without having their appetite for offensive warfare in the least diminished. On April 6, 1362, against the advice of Arnaut de Cervole, the two valorous knights ordered an attack at Brignais, a height held by the *Tard-Venus* near Lyon. The brigands let loose an avalanche of stones upon the royal host, cracking helmets and armor, felling horses, and shattering the attack as the English archers had done at Poitiers. Then on foot, with shortened lances, they finished off the business. Jacques de Bourbon and with him his eldest son and his nephew were killed, and the Count of Tancarville and many other rich nobles captured and held for ransom. Otherwise the brigands made no use of their victory other than to continue brigandage. Lyon purchased artillery, strengthened its walls, and maintained guards with lanterns at night; the countryside suffered as before.

The King's response to Brignais was to leave for Avignon, where he was to stay for nearly a year. Amid military chaos and every other affliction of his realm, his purpose in going was to resume the crusade that had been broken off twenty years ago by the Anglo-French war. Though he could neither protect his own land, raise his ransom, nor redeem the fifty to sixty hostages who stood for him in exile, he felt concerned to redeem his father's unfulfilled vow to take the cross. Froissart gives him the realistic motive of intending by the crusade to draw out of his realm the pillaging companies, but adds oddly that he "preserved this purpose and intent to himself." Perhaps Jean genuinely considered crusade the proper role of the "Most Christian King"; perhaps he saw it compensating for his recent humiliations; perhaps France's troubles were too much for him and he wanted an excuse to get away.

The King also had in mind a project of uniting to France the territory of Provence—which included Avignon—by marrying its Countess, Joanna, Queen of Naples, the most complicated heiress of the century. Halfway through an active connubial career, she was at this time twice a widow, once, as widely believed, by her own hand. Since Naples was a fief of the papacy, her marriage had to be approved by the Pope. As a Frenchman, Innocent VI was expected to be amenable.

Jean's other project, crusade, was the supreme goal of this earnest and pious Pope who, for its sake, had tried so persistently to make peace between France and England. Worn out by ten years of discord and struggle to curb the worldliness of prelates, and finally by plague and brigands, Innocent died in September 1362, while Jean was on his way to Avignon. His successor, Urban V, though also a French native, saw the absorption of Provence by France as a threat to papal independence and disapproved the marriage. But he preached the crusade, actively supported by the titular King of Jerusalem, Pierre de Lusignan, King of Cyprus, who had arrived in Avignon to promote it.

The Latin Kingdom of Jerusalem by this time was no more than a memory; the last European settlers of Syria had retreated to Cyprus, and Europeans now came only to trade. When commerce with Moslems flourished, zeal for their massacre declined. Holy war had lost its thrust with the lessening of European unity, with too frequent use of crusade against internal heretics, and lately with loss of population in the plague. The infidel, like the heretic, was still feared by Christianity as a figure of genuine menace. Crusade still had its devout propagandists, but as a common impulse the zeal had faded. For the Church it had become largely a device for raising money; for nobles and kings the tradition survived as part of the chivalric code and had recently received a new impulse from the threat of the Turks on the shores of Europe. The difficulty was that crusade now suffered from the same necessity as the state: no longer composed of self-financed volunteers, it required paid armies and money to pay them.

The Kings of Cyprus and France spent all winter and spring at Avignon discussing possibilities with the Pope. On Good Friday the crusade was proclaimed. Jean was named Captain-General and took the cross along with the Count of Tancarville and other companions of the recent battering at Brignais. That marked the peak of the enterprise. King Edward, on being visited by the King of Cyprus, excused himself "graciously and right sagely," and after arousing no greater response at other courts of Europe, the King of Cyprus was forced to let crusade lapse for the present.

Having failed in his projects at Avignon, Jean was obliged to face the unpleasantness of home. He rode through his distressed realm at a leisurely pace, reaching Paris in July 1363. Here he found that the Regent and Council had disallowed the private treaty between the royal hostages and Edward, on the grounds that it gave too much away. Worse, the Duc d'Anjou had absconded, breaking his parole. Newly married before going as a hostage, he had gone to Boulogne to meet his wife, with whom he was said to be much in love, and refused to return to Calais. Jean considered his son's act a "felony" upon the honor of the crown. Combined with arrears in ransom, cancellation of the "hostages'" treaty, to which he had assented, and non-fulfillment of other cessions, it brought his own honor into disrepute and left him no way out, so he claimed, but to return to captivity.

Even for the 14th century, this reasoning, in the face of political realities, seemed extreme. Jean's Council and the prelates and barons of France "conseled him sore to the contrary" and told him his plan was "a great folly," but he insisted, saying that if "good faith and honor were to be banished from the rest of the world, they should still be found in the hearts and words of princes." He departed a week after Christmas, crossing the Channel in midwinter.

His going was an amazement to his contemporaries. Jean de Venette, who loved neither kings nor nobles, suggested he went back for *"causa joci"* (reasons of pleasure). Historians have offered him every excuse: that he returned to avert war, or, counting on personal relations, to persuade Edward to reduce the ransom, or persuade him to call off the renewed hostilities of the King of Navarre. If these were his reasons, none was accomplished. If it was honor that took him back, what of kingship? What did he owe to the kingdom that needed its sovereign, to the citizens who were being squeezed of their last penny to pay his ransom, to the memory of Ringois of Abbeville? Who can say what made Jean return? Perhaps it was no medieval reason, but the human tragedy of a man who, knowing himself inadequate for the task he was born to, sought the enforced passivity of prison.

He arrived in London in January 1364, was greeted with lavish entertainments and processions, fell ill of an "unknown malady" in March, and died in April, aged 45. Edward gave him a magnificent funeral service at St. Paul's during which 4,000 torches each twelve feet high and 3,000 candles each weighing ten pounds were consumed. Afterward his body was returned to France for burial in the royal basilica of St. Denis. King Jean had found the permanent passivity of the grave.

A million florins were still owed on his ransom, leaving the hostages unreleased. Some used the safe-conducts given them from time to time and did not return, despite repeated summonses. Some bought their freedom from Edward with shares of their own territories. Others simply disappeared, by one means or another. Anjou's younger brother, Jean, Duc de Berry, managed so shrewdly and made so many excuses while on leave that he retained liberty and honor too. Matthieu de Roye, on the other hand, perhaps because his reputation as a fighter kept him well guarded, was still a hostage after twelve years. Enguerrand de Coucy was to be released under special circumstances in 1365:

Chapter 9

Enguerrand and Isabella

Isabella of England, second child and eldest daughter of King Edward and Queen Philippa, was the favorite of her father, whose marriage diplomacy on her behalf had five times failed to produce results. Since the last failure, when she was nineteen, she had been allowed to live independently, an over-indulged, willful, and wildly extravagant princess who was 33 in 1365, eight years older than Enguerrand de Coucy.

As a baby she had lain in a state cradle, gilded and crested, lined with taffeta, and furnished with a coverlet made of 670 skins although she was born in June. A special dressmaker appointed to the infant made her a robe of Lucca silk with four rows of "garnitures" edged with fur to wear at her mother's *relevailles*, or first reception after the birth. The Queen for the occasion wore a robe of red and purple velvet embroidered with pearls, and received the court reclining on a state bed equipped with a gigantic spread of green velvet measuring seven and one half by eight ells* and embroidered with an all-over pattern of merman and mermaid holding the shields of England and Hainault. All her ladies of the chamber and the whole of her household, from chancellor and treasurer down to kitchen maid, wore new clothes ordered for the occasion. Ostentation was the duty of princes.

The first three royal children—Edward, Isabella, and Joanna—had their own household together, with their own chaplains, musicians, a noble governor and governess, three waiting damsels for Isabella and two for Joanna, a staff of esquires, clerks of pantry and butlery, chief cook, valets of larder and kitchen, valets de chambre, water-carriers, candle-bearers, porters, grooms, and other attendants. They were served on silver, slept on silk-upholstered beds, and had fur-trimmed

* If the unit was the Flemish ell of 27 inches, the coverlet would have measured 17 by 18 feet; if it was the English ell of 45 inches, the dimensions would have been 28 by 30 feet.

robes of scarlet and gray cloth with buttons of gold and silver thread. Their wardrobes were replenished for state festivities and at Christmas, Easter, and All Saints' Day, when all who could afford to wore new clothes. When Isabella and Joanna rode their palfreys from London to Westminster, each led by a valet at the bridle, their almoners walked alongside, distributing alms to the poor and to the prisoners of Newgate. For their attendance at a tournament when they were aged ten and nine, eighteen workmen were employed for nine days to embroider their robes under the supervision of the King's armor-bearer, using eleven ounces of gold leaf in the process. The material life of the 14th century survives in the diligent bookkeeping, itemized down to the minutest transaction on parchment rolls.

At the age of twelve Isabella's favored position was marked by her having seven ladies-in-waiting compared to Joanna's three. All seven, with Isabella, are reported arriving in Canterbury for a tournament in 1349 during the Black Death, wearing masks, presumably against contagion, although these did not help to prevent the death of her favorite attendant, Lady de Throxford. Curiously undeterred by the plague, the court held the elaborate ceremonial of the Order of the Garter as usual in 1349, with the Queen, Isabella, and 300 ladies present at the jousts and festivities. Ladies of the Garter wore the same robes as the men, embroidered with blue and silver garters and the Order's motto, and furnished to them annually at royal expense.

When Isabella was three years old, the King had proposed her marriage to Pedro, son of the King of Castile, but negotiations fell through, perhaps fortunately because the prospective bridegroom was later to win unpleasant renown as Pedro the Cruel. Replacing her sister, Joanna was on her way to marry this prince when she died of the plague at Bordeaux in 1348. A second match for Isabella with the son of the Duke of Brabant was held up owing to consanguinity, and while the Pope was considering dispensation, she was betrothed instead to the reluctant Louis of Flanders and all but reached the altar before the celebrated jilting. Two years later King Edward failed to bring off a match with Charles IV of Bohemia, the elected but not yet consecrated Emperor, then a widower.

Then came the episode of Isabella's retaliation. In 1351 when she was nineteen, the King announced her coming marriage to Bérard d'Albret, son of Bernard-Ezi, Sire d'Albret, a great lord of Gascony and Edward's chief lieutenant there. Whether the choice was the King's or his daughter's is moot. Though not a ruling family, the d'Albrets were an extensive and powerful clan, straddling homage to both England and France, whom Edward was disposed to keep friendly. In the year of the betrothal he bestowed a pension of £1,000 on Bernard-Ezi, recalling his loyal service in resisting both "the threats and the blandishments" of the King of France.

While union with the d'Albrets for a king's eldest daughter was no diplomatic triumph, it was advantageous at a time when Edward was doing everything to strengthen his hold on Guienne. He said as much in the marriage announcement, which spoke of his desire "to kindle in the lord of Albret and his posterity a closer attachment to our royal house, and to bind them more intimately to us"—exactly the motive that was to reappear in the case of Coucy. At the same time, the King seemed reluctant to let Isabella go, describing her as "our very dear eldest daughter whom we have loved with a special affection." In settling on her a portion of 4,000 marks and an annual revenue of £1,000, he added the unusual provision—almost an inducement to her to change her mind—that in case anything prevented the marriage, the sums would revert not to the King, but to Isabella herself.

To carry the princess and her retinue of knights and ladies to Bordeaux, five ships were ordered by the direct method of furnishing a royal officer with a warrant to arrest five suitable vessels in "all ports and places" from the mouth of the Thames westward. The bride's trousseau included robes of cloth of gold and Tripoli silk and a mantle of Indian silk lined in ermine and embroidered all over with leaves, doves, bears, and other devices worked in silver and gold. For another robe of crimson velvet, the elaborate embroidery fashionable at the time required thirteen days' work by twenty men and nine women. For gifts, Isabella brought 119 chaplets made of silk entwined with pearls surmounted by a golden Agnus Dei standing on a green velvet band wrought with flowers and leaves. But these marvelous contrivances were never to be worn—or at least not as intended. At the water's edge Isabella changed her mind and came home. Was it desire to jilt as she had been jilted? Or reluctance to assume a lower rank? Or perhaps memory of her sister's death on an earlier marriage voyage to Bordeaux? Or was the whole affair a contrivance to acquire revenues and a new wardrobe?

Bérard d'Albret was said to be so wounded by the bride's defection that he renounced his inheritance in favor of a younger brother and put on the corded robe of a Franciscan friar. According to other evidence, however, he married a Dame de St. Bazeille, received certain territories from the King of France in 1370, and adopted a shield with the strange device of a head of Midas supported by two lions—which suggests interests the reverse of Franciscan poverty.

Not at all put out by Isabella's waywardness, her father continued to endow her with fiefs and revenues, manors, castles, priories, wardships, farms, and gifts of costly jewelry. Her expenditures continued to outrace his gifts. When she bought silver buckles on credit, let her servants' wages fall into arrears, pawned her jewelry up to the value of 1,000 marks, the King complacently paid her debts, and in 1358, when she was 26, assigned her a regular income of another £1,000 a year, which was duly paid as long as he lived. Six years later he gave her the wardship of a rich minor, Edmund Mortimer, Earl of March, which Isabella sold back to the Earl's mother for another £1,000 a year, with the stiff proviso that if quarterly payments were late by so much as a single day, the penalty would be double payment for that quarter.

At what point during Enguerrand de Coucy's five-year sojourn in England Isabella first became interested in him is nowhere told, but concerning her choice of him the chronicler Ranulph Higden stated forthrightly that "only for love she wished to be betrothed." It may be that after all her years of single independence she really did fall in love or, at her father's suggestion, was willing enough, even pleased, to marry a young attractive rich French lord of ancient lineage and great estates. Edward was clearly pleased by the match and may have been its instigator. Holding a great foothold in France on the borders of Picardy, he would naturally wish to put the hinterland of Calais in allied hands and nullify, in case of renewed hostilities, a strong French opponent. He still thought in terms of wooing the allegiance of great French nobles, the more so because disputes continued to arise over the transfer of French territories. Whether to win over Enguerrand, or because he had taken a personal liking to him, Edward had already in 1363 restored him to full possession of the lands in Yorkshire, Lancashire, Westmoreland, and Cumberland inherited from his great-grandmother.

How Enguerrand felt about his marriage is a blank. Since his sovereign and his prospective father-in-law were now at peace, no conflict of loyalty was involved. The comradeship of chivalry still held nobles together in a trans-national bond that closed over as soon as the temporary enmity of war was terminated. The material advantages of the match, in freeing him from hostageship and bringing money and power too, were obvious. How he felt about the lady herself, who did not easily fit the role of virginal demoiselle merging into submissive wife, was another question.

Isabella's life as an independent woman in a court of the usual amorous license could hardly have been sheltered or innocent. Ladies of the court were not reticent. Joan, widowed Countess of Holland, called the Fair Maid of Kent, whom the Black Prince married in 1361, was considered "the fairest lady in all the kingdom of England" and "the most amorous." She wore daring and extravagant clothes copied from the dresses of the "*bonnes amies* of the brigands of Languedoc." At tournaments, to the scandal of the people, there often came groups of questionable ladies, "the most costly and lovely but not the best of the kingdom," dressed "in divers and wonderful male attire as if they were part of the tournay." Wearing divided and parti-colored tunics, short capes, and daggers in pouches, riding fine coursers and palfreys, they exhibited a "scurrilous wantonness" that "neither feared God nor blushed at the scorn of the crowd."

No female iniquity was more severely condemned than the habit of plucking eyebrows and the hairline to heighten the forehead. For some reason a particular immorality was attached to it, perhaps because it altered God's arrangements. Demons in purgatory were said to punish the practice by sticking "hot burning awls and needles" into every hole from which a hair had been plucked. When a hermit was frightened by a dream about a lady suffering this treatment, an angel comforted him saying, "She had well deserved the pain."

As satirized by Jean de Meung through the mouth of the Duenna in the *Roman de la Rose*, the concerns of a 13th to 14th century lady were not peculiar to the Middle Ages. If her neck and bosom were lovely, she should wear a decolletage; to add color to her face she should use ointments daily, but in secret so that her lover does not know; if aware of bad breath, she should not talk with her mouth too close to others; she should laugh prettily and cry gracefully, eat and drink daintily, and take care not to get drunk or sleep at table. She should go to church, weddings, and parties in her best clothes to let herself be seen and gain renown, lifting her gown to show her fine foot and opening her mantle like a peacock's tail to reveal the beautiful form beneath. She should spread her nets for all men in order to snare one, and if she hooks several, should take care they do not meet. She should never love a poor man because she will get nothing from him and might be tempted to give him something, nor love a stranger, for he may have a vagabond heart, unless of course he offers her money or jewels. While pretending to be won by love alone, she should accept all gifts and encourage presents to her servants, maid, sister, and mother, for many hands get more booty and they can press her lover to get her gowns or other pledges out of pawn.

The insistence on money may have been exaggerated by the author, but satire is a wrapping of exaggeration around a core of reality. Certainly in Isabella's case money was of the essence. She was said to have always in her retinue two or three goldsmiths, seven or eight embroiderers, two or three cutlers, and two or three furriers who were kept busy filling her needs.

If Isabella had any love affairs by the age of 33, they did not reach recorded gossip, but, judging by example, they are not unimaginable. The high-born maiden of seventeen who seduced the elderly, gouty Guillaume de Machaut for the renown of having that celebrated poet and musician as her lover was said to have been Agnes of Navarre, sister of Charles the Bad. Whoever she was, she insisted that Machaut publicize their affair in songs and poems and in a long, lush, embarrassing verse narrative called *Livre du Voir Dit* (*True Tale*). She teased and kissed and gave the bemused poet the little gold key to the *clavette* or chastity belt that guarded her "precious treasure." All the time, as he discovered later, she was regaling her young circle with accounts of the affair's progress and mocking her lover, as Boccaccio was mocked by his mistress Fiammetta, bastard daughter of the King of Naples.

Medieval girls, like boys, became adults in their mid-teens. Marriage was generally consummated at fourteen or thereafter, although in the case of the highborn it might be legally concluded in infancy or childhood. Another young girl, the fifteen-year-old heroine of Deschamps's poem *"Suis-je belle?"*, clearly inspired by Agnes of Navarre, also had control of the key to her "treasure," although this probably represented a literary echo of Agnes rather than a common possession. Often spoken of as if it were familiar, the chastity belt rests on only the faintest factual support in the Middle Ages and was then probably more of a literary conceit than an item of customary use. Believed to have evolved from the Moslem practice of infibulation, which involved attaching a padlock to the labia, it is said to have been imported to Europe with other luxuries through the crusades. An occasional actual model exists, but non-literary evidence such as lawsuits does not appear until the Renaissance and later times. As a device of rabid male possessiveness, the chastity belt afflicted medieval women less than their successors.

Deschamps's luscious damsel details her charms in each stanza—sweet red mouth, green eyes, dainty eyebrows, round chin, white throat, firm high breasts, well-made thighs and legs, fine loins and fine "cul de Paris"—following each with the refrain *"Suis-je, suis-je, suis-je belle?"* (Am I, am I, am I not fair?). She is a male vision of the amorous girl, but Agnes and the taunting Fiammetta were real enough, though both are known, as are virtually all medieval women, only through the pens of men. What is rare is a woman's account of herself. The anguished Héloïse in the 12th century and the feminist Christine de Pisan in the later 14th speak out, and both are bitter, although that does not necessarily establish a rule. In individuals as in nations, contentment is silent, which tends to unbalance the historical record.

Given the non-privacy of medieval life, little about sexual habits was likely to be hidden from the unmarried girl, noble or otherwise. That the Chevalier de La Tour Landry really designed his tales of carnality for the moral edification of his motherless daughters need not be taken at face value, but it is interesting that this was his excuse. His book covers lechery, fornication, and rape, with examples drawn from Lot's daughters, the incest of Tamar, and cases nearer home, such as the lady who loved a squire and contrived to be with him by telling her husband she had vowed divers pilgrimages so that he let her go where she list, or another lady who was told by a knight that if she were wise and good she would not "come to men's chambers by nights darkly without candle nor to coll and kiss men in her bed alone as she did." Life in the castle was evidently easy-going. Knights and ladies stayed up late, "singing, playing and japing and making such noise they could not have heard thunder," and "when one of the men held his hand under one of the women's clothes," he had his arm broken by the angry husband.

Entertainment was not only the recital of lofty epics of chivalrous if tedious adultery. The coarse comic *fabliaux* in quick rhymed couplets, satiric, obscene, often cruel or grotesque, were told for laughs like dirty stories of any age, to noble as well as bourgeois audiences. Often written by court poets in parody of the romances, they treated sex more as pratfall than ennoblement, and their recital or reading aloud was as welcome in the castle as in town, tavern, and probably cloister.

Isabella could well have listened to the tales of Jean de Condé, poet in her lifetime at her mother's native court in Hainault. His style is illustrated by a story about a game of truth-telling played at court before a tournament. A knight, asked by the Queen if he has fathered any children, is forced to admit he has not, and indeed he "did not have the look of a man who could please his mistress when he held her naked in his arms. For his beard was . . . little more than the kind of fuzz that ladies have in certain places." The Queen tells him she does not doubt his word, "for it is easy to judge from the state of the hay whether the pitchfork is any good." In his turn, the knight asks, "Lady, answer me without deceit. Is there hair between your legs?" When she replies, "None at all," he comments, "Indeed I do believe you, for grass does not grow on a well-beaten path."

Life's basic situation in the *fabliaux* is cuckoldry, with variations in which an unpleasing lover is tricked or humiliated instead of the husband. While husbands and lovers in the stories are of all kinds, ranging from sympathetic to disgusting, women are invariably deceivers: inconstant, unscrupulous, quarrelsome, querulous, lecherous, shameless, although not necessarily all of these at once. Despite their more realistic characters, the *fabliaux* were no more true to life than the romances, but their antagonism to women reflected a common attitude which took its tone from the Church.

Woman was the Church's rival, the temptress, the distraction, the obstacle to holiness, the Devil's decoy. In the *Speculum* of Vincent de Beauvais, greatest of the 13th century encyclopedists and a favorite of St. Louis, woman is "the confusion of man, an insatiable beast, a continuous anxiety, an incessant warfare, a daily ruin, a house of tempest," and—finally the key—"a hindrance to devotion." Vincent was a Dominican of the severe order that bred the Inquisitors, which may account for his pyramid of overstatement, but preachers in general were not far behind. They denounced women on the one hand for being the slaves of vanity and fashion, for monstrous headdresses and the "lascivious and carnal provocation" of their garments, and on the other hand for being over-industrious, too occupied with children and housekeeping, too earthbound to give due thought to divine things.

Theology being the work of males, original sin was traced to the female. Had not a woman's counsel brought first woe by causing Adam to lose Paradise? Of all mankind's ideas, the equating of sex with sin has left the greatest train of trouble. In Genesis, original sin was disobedience to God through choosing knowledge of good and evil, and as such the story of the Fall was an explanation of the toil and sorrow of the human condition. In Christian theology, via St. Paul, it conferred permanent guilt upon mankind from which Christ offered redemption. Its sexual context was largely formulated by St. Augustine, whose spiritual wrestlings set Christian dogma thereafter in opposition to man's most powerful instinct. Paradoxically, denial became a source of attraction, giving the Church governance and superiority while embedding its followers in perpetual dilemma.

"Allas, allas, that ever love was sinne!" cried the Wife of Bath. What ages of anxiety and guilt are condensed into that succinct lament, even if the speaker herself does not seem to have been greatly incommoded by what she lamented. Indeed, through her, the century's most forthright celebration of sex was given to a woman. More than in some later times, the sexuality of women was acknowledged in the Middle Ages and the marital debt considered mutual. Theologians bowed to St. Paul's dictum, "Let the husband render to his wife what is due her, and likewise the wife to the husband," but they insisted that the object must be procreation, not pleasure.

To divide the amative from the procreative, as if by laying a flaming sword between the two, was another daring command contrary to human habit. Christianity in its ideas was never the art of the possible. It embraced Augustine's principle that God and Nature had put delight in copulation "to impel man to the act," for preservation of the species and the greater worship of God. Using copulation for the delight that is in it and not for the end intended by nature was, Augustine ruled, a sin against nature and therefore against God, the ordainer of nature. Celibacy and virginity remained preferred states because they allowed total love of God, "the spouse of the soul."

The struggle with carnality left many untouched; others were tortured by it all their lives. It did not inhibit Aucassin from preferring Hell to Paradise "if I may have with me Nicolette my sweet love." Nor did it inhibit creation of the *Roman de la Rose*, the monumental bible of love written in two sections fifty years apart during the 13th century. Begun in the courtly tradition by one author, it was expanded in a cynical and worldly version and at inordinate length by another. When 21,780 lines of elaborate allegory finally wind to an end, the Lover wins his Rose in an explicit description of opening the bud, spreading the petals, spilling "a little seed just in the center," and "searching the calyx to its inmost depths."

Petrarch on the other hand, after twenty years of literary mooning over Laura while fathering elsewhere two illegitimate children, succeeded in his forties, "while my powers were unimpaired and my passions still strong," in throwing off the bad habits of an ardent temperament which he "abhorred from the depths of my soul." Though still subject to "severe and frequent temptations," he learned to confess all his transgressions, pray seven times a day, and "fear more than death itself that association with women which I once thought I could not live without." He had only to recollect, he wrote to his brother the monk, "what woman really is," in order to dispel desire and retrieve his normal equanimity. "What woman really is" referred to the clerical doctrine that beauty in women was deceptive, masking falsehood and physical corruption. "Wheresoever Beauty shows upon the face," warned the preachers, "there lurks much filth beneath the skin."

The nastiness of women was generally perceived at the close of life when a man began to worry about hell, and his sexual desire in any case was fading. Deschamps as a poet began in good humor and ended with a rancid tirade against women, the *Miroir de Mariage*, in which marriage appears as a painful servitude of suffering, sorrow, and jealousy—for the husband. Through 12,000 verses, he ground out all the conventional clerical accusations of woman—as wanton, quarrelsome, capricious, spendthrift, contradictory, over-talkative, and so demanding that she exhausts her husband by her amorous desires. Since Deschamps elsewhere describes himself as a comfortably married man, this great pile of dead wood represented his atonement, as the end approached, for having enjoyed women and the pleasures of the flesh.

Doctrine tied itself into infinite knots over the realities of sex. If the sacrament of marriage was holy, how could sexual pleasure within marriage be sinful? If enjoyment was venial sin, at what point did it become concupiscence, or immoderate desire, which was mortal sin? Was bearing a child outside marriage, though procreative, more sinful than intercourse only for pleasure within marriage? Was a chaste or virgin marriage, though non-procreative, more holy than marital intercourse? What if a man slept with his wife when she was pregnant or after menopause when procreation could not be the purpose? Or, being tempted by another woman, slept with his wife to "cool off" illicit desire: that is, committed one sin to avoid another? Or departed on crusade without his wife's consent or without taking her along, which was anti-procreative, yet in the interests of the Church? These were questions that concerned the dialecticians probably more than the average person.

Like usury, sex defied doctrinal certitude, except for the agreed-upon principle that any sexual practice contrary to the arrangements and ends "ordained by nature" was sinful. The covering term was sodomy, which meant not only homosexuality but any use, with the same or opposite sex, of the "unfit" orifice or the "unfit" position, or spilling the seed according to the sin of Onan, or auto-erotic emission, or intercourse with beasts. All were sodomy, which, by perverting nature, was rebellion against God and therefore counted as the "worst of sins" in the category of lechery.

Marriage was the relationship of the sexes that absorbed major interests. More than any other, it is the subject on the minds of the Canterbury pilgrims and its dominant theme is who, as between husband and wife, is boss? In real life too the question of obedience dominates the manual of conduct composed by the Ménagier of Paris for his fifteen-year-old wife. She should obey her husband's commandments and act according to his pleasure rather than her own, because "his pleasure should come before yours." She should not be arrogant or answer back or contradict him, especially in public, for "it is the command of God that women should be subject to men . . . and by good obedience a wise woman gains her husband's love and at the end hath what she would of him." She should subtly and cautiously counsel him against his follies, but never nag, "for the heart of a man findeth it hard to be corrected by the domination and lordship of a woman."

Examples of the terrible fate that meets carping and critical wives are cited by the Ménagier and also by La Tour Landry, who tells how a husband, harshly criticized by his wife in public, "being angry with her governance, smote her with his fist down to the earth," then kicked her in the face and broke her nose so that she was disfigured ever after and "might not for shame show her visage." And this was her due "for her evil and great language she was wont to say to her husband."

So much emphasis is repeatedly placed on compliance and obedience as to suggest that opposite qualities were more common. Anger in the Middle Ages was associated with women, and the sin of Ire often depicted as a woman on a wild boar, although the rest of the seven Vices were generally personified as men.* If the lay view of medieval woman was a scold and a shrew, it may be because scolding was her only recourse against subjection to man, a condition codified, like everything else, by Thomas Aquinas. For the good order of the human family, he argued, some have to be governed by others "wiser than themselves"; therefore, woman, who was more frail as regards "both vigor of soul and strength of body," was "by nature subject to man, in whom reason predominates." The father, he ruled, should be more loved than the mother and be owed a greater obligation because his share in conception was "active," whereas the mother's was merely "passive and material." Out of his oracular celibacy St. Thomas conceded that a mother's care and nourishment were necessary in the upbringing of the child, but much more so the father's "as guide and guardian under whom the child progresses in goods both internal and external." That women reacted shrewishly in the age of Aquinas was hardly surprising.

Honoré Bonet posed the question whether a queen might judge a knight when she was governing the kingdom in the king's absence. No, he answered, because "it is clear that man is much nobler than woman, and of greater virtue," so that a woman cannot judge a man, the more so since "a subject cannot judge his lord." How, in these circumstances, the queen governed the kingdom is not explained.

The apotheosis of subjection was patient Griselda, whose tale of endurance under a husband's cruel tests of her marital submission so

---

* In one 14th century illuminated manuscript, Pride was a knight on a lion, Envy a monk on a dog, Sloth a peasant on a donkey, Avarice a merchant on a badger, Gluttony a youth on a wolf, Ire a woman on a boar, and Luxury (instead of the standard Lechery) a woman on a goat.

appealed to male authors that it was retold four times in the mid-14th century, first by Boccaccio, then in Latin by Petrarch, in English by Chaucer in the Clerk's Tale, and in French by the Ménagier. Without complaint, Griselda suffers each of her children to be taken away to be killed, as her husband informs her, and then her own repudiation and supposed divorce, before all is revealed as a test, and she willingly reunites herself with the odious author of her trials.

The Ménagier, a kindly man at heart, thought the story "telleth of cruelty too great (to my mind) and above reason" and felt sure "it never befel so." Nevertheless, he thought his wife should be acquainted with the tale so that she will "know how to talk about all things like unto the others." Medieval ladies depended on stories, verbal games, and riddles for their amusement, and a well-bred young married woman would need to be equipped to discuss the abject Griselda and her appalling husband. In the end, Chaucer too was ashamed of the story and in his envoy hastened to advise noble wives,

> Let noon humilitee your tonge naille . . .
> Ne suffreth nat that men yow doon offence . . .
> Ne dreed hem nat, do hem no reverence . . .
> Be ay of chere as light as leefe on linde,
> And lat him care and wepe and wringe and waille!

Married love, despite the formula of courtly romance, was still a desired goal to be achieved after, rather than before, the tying of the knot. The task devolved upon the wife, whose duty was to earn her husband's love and "gain in this world that peace which may be in marriage," by constant attention, good care, amiability, docility, acquiescence, patience, and no nagging. All the Ménagier's wise counsels on this matter can be rolled into one: "No man can be better bewitched than by giving him what pleaseth him." If the Third Estate, which he represented, laid greater stress on married love than did the nobility, it was doubtless because the more continuous proximity of a bourgeois husband and wife made amiable relations desirable. In England connubial contentment could win the Dunmow Flitch—a side, or flitch, of bacon awarded to any couple who could come to Dunmow in Essex after a year of marriage and truthfully swear that they never quarreled and did not regret the marriage and would do it over again if given the chance.

While the cult of courtly love supposedly raised the standing of noble ladies, the fervid adoration of the Virgin, which developed as a cult at the same time, left little deposit on the status of women as a whole. Women were criticized for gossip and chatter, for craving sympathy, for being coquettish, sentimental, over-imaginative, and over-responsive to wandering students and other beggars. They were scolded for bustling in church, sprinkling themselves with holy water at every turn, saying prayers aloud, kneeling at every shrine, paying attention to anything but the sermon. Cloistered nuns were said to be melancholy and irritable, "like dogs who are chained up too much." Nunneries were a refuge from the world for some, the fate of others whose families offered them as gifts to the Church, the choice of a few with a religious calling, but generally available only to those who came with ample endowment.

Evidence from poll and hearth taxes indicates that women's death rate was higher than men's between the ages of twenty and forty, presumably from childbearing and greater vulnerability to disease. After forty the death rate was reversed, and women, once widowed, were allowed to choose for themselves whether to remarry or not.

In everyday life women of noble as well as non-noble class found equality of function, if not of status, thrust on them by circumstance. Peasant women could hold tenancies and in that capacity rendered the same kinds of service for their holdings as men, although they earned less for the same work. Peasant households depended on their earnings. In the guilds, women had monopolies of certain trades, usually spinning and ale-making and some of the food and textile trades. Certain crafts excluded females except for a member's wife or daughter; in others they worked equally with men. Management of a merchant's household—of his town house, his country estate, his business when he was absent—in addition to maternal duties gave his wife anything but a leisured life. She supervised sewing, weaving, brewing, candle-making, marketing, alms-giving, directed the indoor and outdoor servants, exercised some skills in medicine and surgery, kept accounts, and might conduct a separate business as *femme sole*.

Some women practiced as professors or doctors even if unlicensed. In Paris in 1322 a certain Jacoba Felicie was prosecuted by the medical faculty of the University for practicing without their degree or the Chancellor's license. A witness testified that "he had heard it said that she was wiser in the art of surgery and medicine than the greatest master or doctor or surgeon in Paris." At the University of Bologna in the 1360s the faculty included Novella d'Andrea, a woman so renowned for her beauty that she lectured behind a veil lest her students be distracted. Nothing is said, however, of her professional capacity.

The *châtelaine* of a castle more often than not had to manage alone when her husband was occupied elsewhere, as he generally was, for the sun never set on fighting in the 14th century. If not fighting, or attending the King, he was generally being held somewhere for ransom. In such case his wife had to take his place, reach decisions and assume direction, and there were many besides Jeanne de Montfort who did so. Marcia Ordelaffi, left to defend Cesena while her hot-tempered husband (he who had stabbed his son) held a second city against the papal forces, refused all offers to negotiate despite repeated assaults, mining of walls, bombardment day and night by stones cast from siege engines, and the pleas of her father to surrender. Suspecting her councillor of secretly arranging a surrender, she had him arrested and beheaded. Only when her knights told her that collapse of the citadel would allow no escape from death and that they proposed to yield with or without her consent did she agree to negotiate, on condition that she conduct the parley herself. This she did so effectively that she obtained safe-conduct for herself and her family and all servants, dependents, and soldiers who had supported her. She was said to fear only the wrath of her terrible husband—not without cause, for, despite all the talk of *courtoisie*, lords of chivalry, no less than the bourgeois, were known to beat their wives. In a case of particular brutality and high rank, the Count of Armagnac was accused of breaking his wife's bones and keeping her locked up in an effort to extort property.

Woman's status in the 14th century had one explicit female exponent in Christine de Pisan, the only medieval woman, as far as is known, to have earned a living by her pen. Born in 1364, she was the daughter of Thomas of Pisano, a physician-astrologer with a doctor's degree from the University of Bologna who was summoned to Paris in 1365 by the new King, Charles V, and remained in his service. Christine was schooled by her father in Latin, philosophy, and various branches of science not usual in a woman's education. At fifteen, she married Etienne Castel of Picardy, one of the royal secretaries. Ten years later, she was left alone with three children when her husband, "in the flower of his youth," and her father died within a few years of each other. Without resources or relatives, she turned to writing to earn the patronage that must henceforth be her livelihood. She began with poetry, recalling in ballades and rondeaux her happiness as a wife and mourning her sorrows as a widow. Though the forms were conventional, the tone was personal.

> No one knows the labor my poor heart endures
> To dissimulate my grief when I find no pity.
> The less sympathy in friendship, the more cause for tears.

> So I make no plaint of my piteous mourning,
> But laugh when I would rather weep,
> And without rhyme or rhythm make my songs
> To conceal my heart.

The plaintive note (or perhaps more sympathy than Christine pretended) loosened the purses of nobles and princes—whose status was reflected in patronage of the arts—and enabled Christine to undertake studies for a flow of didactic prose works, many of them adapted or translated from other authors, as was the common practice of the time. No subject deterred her: she wrote a large volume on the art of war based on the Roman classic *De re militari* by Vegetius; a mythological romance; a treatise on the education of women; and a life of Charles V which remains an important and original work. Her own voice and interest are strongest when she writes about her own sex, as in *La Cité des dames* on the lives of famous women of history. Though translated from Boccaccio's *De claris mulieribus*, Christine makes it her own in the prologue, where she sits weeping and ashamed, wondering why men "are so unanimous in attributing wickedness to women" and why "we should be worse than men since we were also created by God." In a dazzling vision, three crowned female figures, Justice, Faith, and Charity, appear to tell her that these views of the philosophers are not articles of faith "but the mists of error and self-deception." They name the women of history who have excelled—Ceres, donor of agriculture; Arachne, originator of spinning and weaving; and various heroines of Homeric legend, the Old Testament, and Christian martyrology.

In a passionate outcry at the close of the century in her *Epistle to the God of Love*, Christine again asks why women, formerly so esteemed and honored in France, are now attacked and insulted not only by the ignorant and base but also by nobles and clergy. The *Epistle* is a direct rejoinder to the malicious satire of women in Jean de Meung's continuation of the *Roman de la Rose*, the most popular book of the age. A professional writer with a master's degree in Arts from the University of Paris, Jean de Meung was the Jonathan Swift of his time, a satirist of the artificial conventions in religion, philosophy, and especially chivalry and its central theme of courtly love. Nature and natural feeling are his heroes, False Seeming (hypocrisy) and Forced Abstinence (obligatory chastity) his villains, whom he personifies as mendicant friars. Like the clerics who blamed women for men's desires, or like the policeman who arrests the prostitute but not the customer, Jean de Meung, as a male, blamed women for humanity's departure from the ideal. Because courtly love was a false glorification of women, he made women personify its falsity and hypocrisy. Scheming, painted, mercenary, wanton, Meung's version of woman was simply the male fantasy of courtly love in reverse. As Christine pointed out, it was men who wrote the books.

Her protest was to provoke a vociferous debate between antagonists and defenders of Jean de Meung in one of the great intellectual controversies at the turn of the century. Meanwhile her melancholy flute still sounded in poetry.

> It is a month today
> Since my lover went away.
> My heart remains gloomy and silent;
> It is a month today.
> "Farewell," he said, "I am leaving."
> Since then he speaks to me no more.
> It is a month today.

As shown by the sumptuous bindings of surviving copies, her works were in large demand by wealthy nobles. At the age of 54 she retired to a convent in grief for the condition of France. She lived for another eleven years to write a poem in praise of the figure who, to posterity, stands out above all others of her time—another woman, Joan of Arc.

Fixed as they were in the pattern of female nature conceived for them by men, it was no accident that women often appeared among the hysterical mystics. In the uncontrollable weeping of English Margery Kempe there is a poignancy that speaks for many. She began to weep while on a pilgrimage to Jerusalem when "she had such great compassion and such great pain at seeing the place of Our Lord's pain." Thereafter her fits of "crying and roaring" and falling on the ground continued for many years, once a month or a week, sometimes daily or many times a day, sometimes in church or in the street or in her chamber or in the fields. The sight of a crucifix might set her off, "or if she saw a man or beast with a wound, or if a man beat a child before her, or smote a horse or other beast with a whip, if she saw it or heard it, she thought she saw our Lord being beaten or wounded." She would try to "keep it in as much as she could, that people might not hear it to their annoyance, for some said that a wicked spirit vexed her or that she had drunk too much wine. Some banned her, some wished her in the sea in a bottomless boat." Margery Kempe was obviously an uncomfortable neighbor to have, like all those who cannot conceal the painfulness of life.

On July 27, 1365, at Windsor Castle, Isabella of England and Enguerrand de Coucy were married amid festivity and magnificence. The finest minstrels in the realm played for the occasion. The bride was resplendent in jewels received as her wedding present from her father, mother, and brothers, at a cost of £2,370 13s. 4d. Her dowry, considerably increased over the d'Albret marriage-portion, was an annual pension of £4,000. The King's gift to Enguerrand was no less valuable: he was released from his role as hostage without payment of ransom.

Four months later, in November, the couple received the King's leave to return to France, evidently given with some reluctance, for the letter refers to a repeated request "to go into France to visit your lands, possessions and estates." Isabella being already pregnant, the King's letter promised that all children male or female born to her abroad would be capable of inheriting lands in England and considered "as fully naturalized as though they were born in the realm."

To the customary ringing of church bells vigorously pulled to induce the saints to ease labor, a daughter was born at Coucy in April 1366 and christened Marie. Before a month had passed, Isabella with husband and infant was hurrying back to England. A lady of rank and in delicate condition would travel in a four-wheeled covered wagon with cushioned seats, accompanied by her furniture, bed linen, vessels and plate, cooking pots, wine, and with servants going on ahead to prepare lodgings and hang tapestries and bed curtains. Even with such comforts, to brave the Channel crossing and the bumpy land journey with a newborn baby seems peculiar and reckless haste or a desperate affection for home. Throughout her married life, Isabella never put down roots at Coucy-le-Château, and instantly rushed back to her father's court whenever her husband departed on some expedition. Perhaps she was unhappy in the great walled castle on the hill, or did not feel at home in France, or more likely could not live without the indulgence and royal surroundings of her youth.

Edward's determination to attach Coucy as firmly as possible to England was acted on as soon as Enguerrand and his wife returned. On May 11, 1366, the Chancellor informed the nobles and commons in Parliament, in the presence of Edward, "how the King had married his daughter Isabella to the Lord de Coucy, who had handsome estates in England and elsewhere; and for the cause that he was so nearly allied to him, it were fitting that the King should enhance and increase him in honor and name, and make him an earl; and thereupon he requested that advice and assent." Lords and Commons duly consented, leaving to the King the choice of what lands and title to confer. Enguerrand was named to the vacant earldom of Bedford with a revenue of 300 marks a year, and as Ingelram,* Earl of Bedford, he appears thereafter in English records. To complete the honors, he was inducted into the Order of the Garter.

At the same time Isabella received yet another £200 of annual revenues, which promptly disappeared down the bottomless drain of her expenditures. She seems to have been one of those people for whom spending is a neurosis, for within a few months of her return, the King paid £130 15s. 4d. to discharge her debts to merchants for silk and velvet, taffetas, gold cloth, ribands and linen, and another £60 to redeem a jeweled circlet she had pawned.

Sometime before Easter of 1367, which fell on April 18, the Coucys' second daughter was born in England, within a year of the first. Named Philippa for her grandmother the Queen, the infant received from her royal grandparents an elaborate silver service of six bowls, gilded and chased, six cups, four water pitchers, four platters, and 24 each of dishes, salt cellars, and spoons costing a total of £239 18s. 3d.

In further enlargement of his fortune, Enguerrand now acquired the equivalent of an earldom in France, helped thereto by the not disinterested hand of his father-in-law. A fellow hostage, and neighbor in France, was Guy de Blois et de Châtillon, Count of Soissons, a nephew of both Philip VI and Charles de Blois of Brittany, who despite his great family and connections, had so far been unable to buy his liberty. As the price of his release, an arrangement was now reached by which, with the consent of King Charles of France, he ceded his county of Soissons to Edward, who in turn presented it to Coucy in lieu of the £4,000 provided by Isabella's dowry. The great domains of Coucy and Soissons, constituting a sizable portion of Picardy, were now joined in the hands of a son-in-law of the King of England. With a territorial title diluting the once proud austerity of the Coucy motto, Enguerrand was now Count of Soissons, and as such returned with his wife and daughters to France in July 1367.

---

* Judging by the diverse spelling of proper names on either side of the Channel, pronunciation of the common language must have been close to mutually unintelligible. Chaucer's Prioresse spoke French

> After the scole of Stratford atte Bowe,
> For Frensh of Paris was to hir unknowe.

Chapter 10

Sons of Iniquity

In the seven years of Coucy's absence in England, the havoc wrought by the Free Companies, spreading through France, Savoy, Lombardy, and the papal dominions, had become a major fact of European affairs. Not a passing phenomenon nor an external force, the companies had become a way of life, a part of society itself, used and joined by its rulers even as they struggled to throw them off. They ate at society from within like Erysichthon, the "tearer up of earth," who, having destroyed the trees in the sacred grove of Demeter, was cursed by the goddess with an insatiable appetite and finally devoured himself attempting to satisfy his hunger.

Discipline and organization made the companies more useful as fighting forces than knights bent on glory and unacquainted with the principle of command. Rulers employed them, as when Amadeus VI, Count of Savoy, contracted with one of the worst of the captains to crush the partisans of an opponent by use of terrorism within his own dominions. Whether employed or living by adventure, they made pillage pay the cost. Life by the sword became subordinate to its means; the means became the end; the climate of the 14th century succumbed to the brute triumph of the lawless.

In France during the transfer of territories, despite the renewed orders of King Edward, many bands refused to demobilize or evacuate their fortresses. Discharged from regular employment, like bees from a broken hive, they created small hives around a particular captain and joined the host of *Tard-Venus*. Finding mercenary employment combined with brigandage profitable, they spread, attracting into their ranks those who quickly relapse into lawlessness when the social contract breaks down. While the lower ranks came from the debris of town and country and from the cast-offs of every occupation including the Church, the leaders came from the top—lords who found a life of gain by the sword irresistible, or losers of the knightly class whom the companies themselves had uprooted. Unable to live adequately off ruined lands, they joined the mercenaries rather than follow a life without the sword. "Unbridled in every kind of cruelty," in the words of the Pope's excommunication in 1364, they seemed to defenseless people like another plague, to be attributed to the planets or God's wrath.

In France they were called *écorcheurs* (skinners) and *routiers* (highwaymen), in Italy *condottieri* from the *condotta* or contract that fixed the terms of their employment as mercenaries. They extorted a systematized income from vulnerable towns in the form of *appatis*, a forced tribute to buy freedom from attack, of which the terms were put in writing by clerks. They drew into their service from ordinary life notaries, lawyers, and bankers to handle their affairs, as well as clerks, blacksmiths, tanners, coopers, butchers, surgeons, priests, tailors, laundresses, prostitutes, and often their own legal wives. They dealt through regular brokers who sold their plunder, except for particular arms or luxuries they wished to keep, such as jewels and women's gowns or steel for swords or, in one case, ostrich plumes and beaver hats. They became installed in the social structure. When Burgundy was occupied by the "Archpriest" Arnaut de Cervole in 1364, young Duke Philip treated him with respect, calling him his adviser and companion, and making over to him a castle and several noble hostages as security until he could raise 2,500 gold francs to buy his departure. To raise the sum, Philip adopted the usual expedient of taxing his subjects, another cause of bitterness against the lords.

Bertucat d'Albret, of the same family as Isabella's rejected bridegroom, was one of the notable great lords who were more *pillard* than seigneur. Years later, in old age, he sighed for the days "when we would leap upon rich merchants from Toulouse or La Riolle or Bergerac. Never did a day fail to bring us some fine prize for our enrichment and good cheer." His friend and fellow Gascon, Seguin de Badefol, often called "King of the Companies," replaced the five hats in his father's coat-of-arms with five bezants, or gold coins, indicating his major interest. Aimerigot Marcel, who after thirty years as a brigand was to end on the scaffold, boasted of his takings in silks from Brussels, skins from the fairs, spices coming from Bruges, rich fabrics from Damascus and Alexandria. "All was ours or ransomed at our will. . . . The peasants of Auvergne supplied us in our castle, bringing wheat and flour and fresh bread, hay for the horses, good wine, beef and mutton, fat lambs and poultry. We were provisioned like kings. And when we rode forth the country trembled before us."

Popular hatred credited the companies with every crime from eating meat in Lent to committing atrocities upon pregnant women which caused death to unborn and unbaptized children. Three quarters of France was their prey, especially the wine-growing areas of Burgundy, Normandy, Champagne, and Languedoc. Walled towns could organize resistance, turning back the violence upon the countryside, which was repeatedly devastated, creating a vagabond population of destitute peasants, artisans seeking work, priests without parishes.

The companies did not spare churches. "Insensible to the fear of God," wrote Innocent VI in a pastoral letter of 1360, "the sons of iniquity . . . invade and wreck churches, steal their books, chalices, crosses, relics and vessels of the divine ritual and make them their booty." Churches where blood had been spilled in combat were considered profaned and prohibited from sacramental use until they had gone through a long bureaucratic process of reconciliation. Nevertheless, papal taxes continued, and incumbents of ruined benefices were often reduced to penury, and deserted, not infrequently to join their persecutors. "See how grave it has become," mourned Innocent in the same letter, "when those charged with divine grace . . . participate in rapine and despoliation, even in the shedding of blood."

With clergy and knights joining the sons of iniquity, the average man felt himself living in an age of rapine and powerless to control it. "If God Himself were a soldier, He would be a robber," said an English knight named Talbot.

One chain still held: the necessity of absolution. Fear of dying without it was so ingrained that ghosts were believed to be the souls of the unshriven who had returned to seek absolution for their sins in life. No matter how far the brigands had separated themselves from other rules, they insisted on the formula if not the substance of forgiveness. In theory a man who met death in a "just war" would go straight to Heaven if he had repented of his sins, but a knight guilty of the sin of rapine would have to prove penitence by restitution of his gains. Making no pretense of just war, much less given to restitution, the companies were content to extort absolution by force, like a bag of gold. When negotiating ransoms or quittances with their captives, even those they had maimed or tortured, they would make it a condition of release that the victims solicit absolution for them or urge the Pope to lift his excommunication.

Innocent's successor, Urban V, issued two Bulls of Excommunication in 1364, *Cogit Nos* and *Miserabilis Nonullorum*, which were supposed to have the effect of prohibiting any cooperation with or provisioning of the companies, and which offered plenary indulgence to all who died in combatting them. If the ban disturbed the brigands, it did not restrain them.

The outstanding professional among the *Tard-Venus*, one whom Coucy was destined to meet in combat, was Sir John Hawkwood, who first appeared by name as leader of one of the companies besieging Avignon in 1361. His origin was the kind that sent many into the companies. As the second son of a minor landowner and tanner by trade, he left home when his elder brother inherited the manor along with £10, six horses, and a cart, leaving the younger son landless with a portion of £20 10s. Listed among the English army in France in the 1350s, Hawkwood was "still a poor knight who had gained nothing but his spurs" when he joined the *Tard-Venus* after Brétigny. He was then about 35. By the time he was diverted by papal gold from Avignon to Italy, he commanded the White Company of 3,500 mounted men and 2,000 foot whose white flags and tunics and highly polished breastplates gave the company its name. On their first appearance in Lombardy they spread terror by their fury and license, and as time went on, "nothing was more terrible to hear than the name of the English." They gained the reputation of *perfidi e scelleratissimi* (perfidious and most wicked), although it was conceded that "they did not roast and mutilate their victims like the Hungarians."

Hired by one or another of the Italian city-states in their chronic wars, Hawkwood could soon command the highest price for his services. However ruthless his methods—and they inspired the proverb "an Italianized Englishman is a devil incarnate"—he spent no time on mere brigandage, but contracted his company to whatever power had the capacity to pay, on either side in any war. He fought for Pisa against Florence and vice versa, for the papal forces against the Visconti and vice versa, and on leaving the service of the Visconti, correctly turned back to Galeazzo the castles the White Company had conquered. War was business to Hawkwood, provided that his contracts exempted him from fighting against the King of England. When he died after 35 years in Italy, rich in lands, pensions, and renown, he was buried in the cathedral of Florence and commemorated by Uccello's equestrian fresco over the door. National pride in the year of his death reclaimed him; at the personal request of Richard II, his body was returned to England for burial in his native town.

In Italy the companies were used virtually as official armies in public wars. In France they were out of control. The only effective counter-force would have been a permanent army, which was not yet within the vision of the state nor within its financial capacity. The only feasible strategy against the companies was to pay them to go somewhere else. Since the King of Hungary was appealing for help against the Turks, a concerted effort to drain off the menace in a crusade was made in 1365 by the Pope, the Emperor, and the King of France.

The person nominated by the former Regent, now Charles V, to lead the crusade was a strange new captain as rough as his Breton name, which the French rendered De Clequin or Kaisquin or Clesquy until fame settled on Bertrand Du Guesclin. Flat-nosed, dark-skinned, short, and heavy, "there was none so ugly from Rennes to Dinant." So begins Cuvelier's rhymed epic designed to create a French hero to rival Chandos Herald's panegyric of the Black Prince. "Wherefore his parents hated him so sore that often in their hearts they wished him dead. Rascal, Fool, or Clown they were wont to call him; so despised was he as an ill-conditioned child that squires and servants made light of him." The parents were poor nobility. The uncouth son, unspoiled by tournaments, learned to fight in the guerrilla warfare of Brittany in the service of Charles of Blois, becoming skilled in the tactics of ambush and ruse, the use of disguise, spies, secret messengers, smoke clouds to hide movements, bribes of money and wine, torture and killing of prisoners, and surprise attacks launched during the "Truce of God." He was intrepid as he was unscrupulous, fierce with the sword but ever ready to use stratagem; hard, tricky, and ruthless as any *écorcheur*.

Born between 1315 and 1320, he did not become a knight until he was over 35 and had won local renown in the defense of Rennes. His bold capture of a fortress from the Navarrese, witnessed by the Regent, began his prominence in the royal service. Though Charles V was not a fighter himself, he had a fighting purpose. Through all the years since the Treaty of Brétigny, his single silent overriding aim was to frustrate the renunciations of territory that would have dismembered the realm. Having no wish to lead a host in battle, he knew he needed a military leader, and found one in this "hog in armor," the first effective commander comparable to the Black Prince or Sir John Chandos to appear on the French side.

In 1364, the opening year of Charles's reign, Du Guesclin led the French to victory, then defeat, in two historic battles. In the first at Cocherel in Normandy against the forces of Charles of Navarre, the numbers were small but the outcome was large, for it led to the elimination of Navarre's chronic threat to Paris. The battle was even more notable for the capture of Navarre's cousin, the Captal de Buch, whom Charles afterward liberated without asking ransom in the hope of winning over this heart of turbulence to the French side. The second battle five months later, at Auray on the rocky Breton coast, was decisive for the war in Brittany. Charles of Blois, the French candidate for the dukedom, was killed and Du Guesclin taken prisoner. This was the last clash of the rival Dukes of Brittany, leaving the English candidate, Jean de Montfort, in possession, although by the terms of the Treaty of Brétigny the dukedom remained a French fief. The defeat was in fact turned by Charles V into a source of advantage. By means of a huge pension, he persuaded Blois's widow to yield her claim, thus ending the running war and the bleeding of French strength. Charles V was one who preferred not to fight where he could buy.

Du Guesclin, after being ransomed, did not fall from favor. His rise had been predicted by astrology and the prophecies of Merlin, which may have appealed to Charles, who, for all his astuteness, was a devotee of astrology, as was Du Guesclin. Besides keeping an astrologer at hand on all his campaigns, Bertrand was also married to one, a lady trained in the subject and famed for her occult powers. The King's interest was more scientific. Like most rulers, he employed a court astrologer who advised on propitious times for action and carried out confidential missions; but going beyond that, Charles commissioned translations of astrological works and founded a college of astrology at the University of Paris which he equipped with library, instruments, and royal scholarships.

In 1365 he summoned to his court Thomas of Pisano, a doctor of astrology from the University of Bologna whose imaginative if somewhat risky talents must have suited the King because he kept him on at a salary of 100 francs a month. It is not impossible that Charles's perpetual illnesses may have owed something to a medicine containing mercury prepared for him by Thomas, for which the doctor was much blamed. Undeterred, Thomas went on to an experiment "unique and ineffable," of which the object was to expel the English from France. Out of lead and tin, he fashioned hollow images of nude men, filled them with earth collected from the center and four corners of France, inscribed the foreheads with the names of King Edward or one of his captains, and, when the constellations were right, buried them face down while he recited spells to the effect that this was perpetual expulsion, annihilation, and burial of the said King, captains, and all adherents.

When it came to removing the companies, a more practical method was through crusade in Hungary. The Emperor Charles IV, anxious to repel the Turks, came himself to Avignon with an offer to underwrite the costs of the journey and guarantee the revenues of Bohemia for three years to pay the mercenaries. His appearance at mass with Urban V on Whitsunday, Emperor and Pope sitting side by side, at peace for the first time in living memory, cast a spell of hope over the occasion. Urban announced that the tithes of the French clergy would be turned over to the King of France to enable him to finance his share of the enterprise. Despite all the promised money, and Paradise too—for excommunication would be lifted by crusade—the mercenaries viewed the prospect of Hungary with the greatest distaste, asking "why should they go so far to make war?" But pressed by the strength of sentiment for their departure and given Arnaut de Cervole, one of their own, as leader replacing Du Guesclin, some were persuaded. From various places, various bodies set forth in the summer of 1365 for a rendezvous in Lorraine within the Empire.

The rest was fiasco. The brigands' terrible repute roused the population of Alsace to desperate resistance. Despite Arnaut's assurances that he had no designs on the country and wanted only to water his horses in the Rhine, the citizens of Strasbourg refused to let them cross the bridge, and the Emperor was forced by his subjects to appear with an army to bar the way. The companies' own reluctance more than the people's resistance turned them back within a month. In the meantime a new enterprise had need of them in Spain.

The Anglo-French war had not really been ended in Brétigny; it had moved down to Spain to take sides in a struggle for the crown between Pedro the Cruel, King of Castile, whose oppressions had aroused a revolt, and his illegitimate brother Don Enrique of Trastamare, eldest of his father's ten bastards and leader of the opposition. The issue affected the balance of forces swirling around Languedoc, Aquitaine, and Navarre. Since Pedro was supported by the English and had furthermore abandoned and reputedly murdered his wife, who was a sister of the Queen of France, and since Don Enrique was the protégé of the French, whose accession would place an ally on an important throne, the struggle sucked in the former antagonists. Furthermore, Don Pedro was an enemy of the Pope, who had excommunicated him for refusing to obey a summons to Avignon to answer charges of wicked conduct.

The Spanish cockpit offered, under the guise of a crusade against the Moors of Granada, an ideal outlet and perhaps a grave for the companies. Du Guesclin as the appointed leader had persuaded twenty-five captains of the most dangerous companies, including Hugh of Calveley and Eustache d'Aubrecicourt and others who had been his opponents at Auray, to follow him to Spain. High pay was promised, but the men of the companies had no intention of crossing the Pyrenees without a grip on hard cash. The confrontation by which it was obtained, told with relish in Cuvelier's epic, is a microcosm of the 14th century, even though it has been said of Cuvelier that "the tyranny of rhyme left him little leisure for accuracy."

Marching to Avignon instead of directly to Spain, the companies camped within sight of the papal palace across the Rhône at Villeneuve. There the Pope sent a trembling cardinal to tell them "that I who have the power of God and all the saints, angels and archangels, will excommunicate the whole company if they do not go from hence without delay." Met courteously by Du Guesclin and the "learned, wise and prudent knight" Marshal d'Audrehem, veteran of Poitiers, the cardinal was asked if he had brought any money; he tactfully replied that he had been sent to learn their purpose in coming to Avignon.

"Sir," responded d'Audrehem, "you see before you men who for ten years have committed many evil deeds in the realm of France, who are now on their way to fight the miscreants in Granada," and whose leaders were conducting them there "so that they should not return again to France." Before leaving, each was a suppliant for absolution, therefore the Holy Father was begged "to release us from all our sins and from punishment of the grievous and weighty crimes which all of us have committed since infancy, and besides, that for our voyage he would present us with 200,000 francs."

"Changing his face," the cardinal replied that, though their numbers were great, he thought he could assure them of absolution, but not the money. "Sir," quickly intervened Bertrand, "we must have all that the Marshal has asked, for I tell you that there are many here who care little for absolution; they would rather have the money." Adding that "we are leading them to where they can rightfully pillage without doing harm to Christian people," he urged that unless their demands were met, the men could not be managed, and the longer they waited, the sorrier it would be for Villeneuve.

Hastening back over the bridge, the cardinal told the Pope first about the companies' request for absolution, saying that he had brought their confession of crimes. "They have . . . committed all the evil that one could do and more than one could tell; so they beg for mercy and pardon of God and full absolution from you."

"They shall have it," said the Pope without hesitation, "provided that they then leave the country." Then the additional matter of 200,000 francs was laid before him. From his window Urban could see the men-at-arms seizing livestock, chickens and geese, good white bread, and everything they could carry away. Summoning a council for advice on how to raise the money, he adopted the suggestion that it be raised from a tax on the bourgeois of Avignon, "so that the treasures of God might not be diminished." When the money thus collected was brought to Du Guesclin by the Provost of Avignon along with the absolutions signed and sealed, Du Guesclin asked if it had come from the papal treasury. On being told that it had been contributed by the commons of Avignon, he denounced the avarice of Holy Church "very irreverently" and swore he would not accept a penny unless it came from the clergy; all the taxed money must be restored to the people who had paid it. "Sir," said the Provost, "God grant you a happy life; the poor people will be greatly rejoiced." The money was duly returned to the people and replaced by 200,000 francs from the papal treasury, for which the Pope quickly indemnified himself by imposing a tithe on the clergy of France.

On the English side, image-making was at work too, notably by Chandos Herald, who celebrated the Black Prince's rule of Aquitaine at this time as "seven years of joy, peace and pleasantness," when in fact it was the reverse. The Prince's arrogance and extravagance were arousing in his Gascon subjects a fury of resentment and a turning toward France. Imbued with ideals of largesse and the nobility of bankruptcy, the Prince was indifferent to any balance between income and expenditure. He made up the gap by taxes which alienated the loyalty and allegiance he was supposed as viceroy to promote. "Since the time that God was born, never was open house kept so handsomely and honorably." He fed "more than fourscore knights and full four times as many squires"—some 400 people—at his table every day, maintained a huge retinue of squires, pages, valets, stewards, clerks, hawkers, and huntsmen; held banquets, hunting parties, and tournaments, and would himself be served by none but a knight wearing golden spurs. His wife, the beauteous Joan, outdid her sister-in-law Isabella in sumptuous fabrics, furs, jewels, gold, and enamel. The Prince's reign, Chandos Herald enthusiastically reported, was marked by "liberality, high purpose, good sense, moderation, righteousness, reason, justice and restraint." Except for the first two, the Prince had none of these qualities.

Du Guesclin's warriors went off to Spain, where they fought with such effect and dispatch that Don Pedro fled, Don Enrique was crowned King, and the companies, of whom too few found a grave, returned all too soon to France. The interests of England, however, renewed the struggle. Don Pedro appealed to the Black Prince, who, moved by eagerness for war and glory, took up his cause. He was moved, too, by the need to break a Franco-Castilian alliance which, owing to a strong Spanish fleet, threatened English communication with Aquitaine and heightened the persistent English fear of invasion. Finances, as always, were crucial. Don Pedro swore to repay all costs when he had regained the throne, and the Black Prince, though advised not to rely on a man so stained by villainies, refused to forgo the battle. With Du Guesclin and the French companies again supporting Don Enrique, the war was reopened in 1367 and the outcome reversed.

At the Battle of Najera in April 1367 the English won a victory famous in medieval annals, and the French suffered another of the defeats that were undercutting not only the renown but the fact of military supremacy. Don Enrique had been advised by Du Guesclin and Marshal d'Audrehem not to risk a pitched battle against the Prince and "the best fighting men on earth," but rather to cut off their supplies and "to famish them without striking a blow"—the same advice given and ignored by the French at Poitiers. For various reasons of terrain, weather, and because it would have seemed ignoble to the new King's Spanish following, the advice was impractical and the result catastrophic. Don Enrique fled, Don Pedro was restored, and Bertrand Du Guesclin a second time taken prisoner. Although inclined to hold him, the Prince let himself be stung by Bertrand's taunt that he was keeping him "out of fear," and agreed to let him be ransomed at a stiff price of 100,000 francs.

If glory was lost at Najera, the defeat, like that of Auray, was not without advantage, for only battered remnants of the companies returned to France. For this relief Du Guesclin received the credit, so that, as Deschamps was to write, all the prayers of the common people were lavished upon him. Further relief resulted from the deaths of the bandit leader Seguin de Badefol and the "Archpriest"—the former poisoned at dinner by Charles of Navarre to avoid paying him, and the latter assassinated by his own followers. The respite, however, was short. When Don Pedro, as predicted, defaulted on his debts, the Black Prince, hard-pressed by angry unpaid troops, "encouraged them underhand" to filter back into France to supply themselves there by the usual forceful means. Small in numbers but war-hardened and formidable, Anglo-Gascon bands made their way into Champagne and Picardy, "where they did so much damage and wicked acts as caused great tribulation."

For the Prince, the glory of Najera quickly turned sour; the victory for him was the peak of Fortune's Wheel—all the rest was to be downward. His pride alienated the Gascons, for "he did not value a knight at one button, nor a burgher nor a burgher's wife, nor any common folk." When he transferred the burden of Don Pedro's debts to the people of Guienne in the form of annual hearth taxes in 1367–68, Gascon lords rebelled and re-opened negotiations with Charles V for a return to French allegiance. A cause and an instrument for upsetting the Treaty of Brétigny was now in the French King's hands.

Chapter 11

The Gilded Shroud

Such was the France to which Coucy returned in 1367. His own domain, judging by a major step he took in the following year, suffered from the shortage of labor that was afflicting landowners everywhere since the Black Death. Picardy, in the path of English penetration from the start, had suffered not only from invaders but also from the Jacquerie and the ravaging of the Anglo-Navarrese. Rather than pay the repeated taxes that followed upon French defeats, peasants deserted to nearby imperial territory in Hainault and across the Meuse.

To hold labor on the land, Coucy's rather belated remedy was enfranchisement of the serfs, or non-free peasants and villagers, of his domain. From "hatred of servitude," his charter acknowledged, they had been leaving, "to live outside our lands, in certain places, freeing themselves without our permission and making themselves free whenever it pleased them." (A serf who reached territory outside his lord's writ and stayed for a year was regarded as free.) Except for the charter issued to Coucy-le-Château in 1197, Coucy's territory was late in the dissolution of serfdom, perhaps owing to former prosperity. Free peasants were already in the majority in France before the Black Death. Abolition had occurred less from any moral judgment of the evils of servitude than as a means of raising ready money from rents. Though the paid labor of free tenants was more expensive than the unpaid labor of serfs, the cost was more than made up by the rents, and, besides, tenants did not have to be fed on the job, which had amounted to an important expense.

Coucy's charter of August 1368 took the form of a collective grant of freedom to 22 towns and villages of his barony in return for specific rents and revenues from each, "in perpetuity to us and our successors." The sums ranged from 18 livres for Trosly down to 24 sous for Fresnes (still extant villages, as are most in the list), and 18 pence per hearth for Courson. The wording, though swollen by lawyers' superfluity in every line, is a clear and precise picture of medieval tenure, unlike the dense tangle that has been made of the subject ever since.

"By general custom and usage," it states, all persons who live in the barony of Coucy "are our men and women by *morte-main* and *formariage*" except if they are clerics or nobles or others "who hold of us by oath and homage." Because of the many who have departed, "our said land was left in great part uncultivated, unworked and reverted to wasteland, for which the said land is greatly reduced in value." In the past the inhabitants had requested their freedom from his father, offering certain revenues in perpetuity, "of which thing our dear and well-beloved father whose soul is with God took counsel and found it would greatly profit him to destroy and render null the said custom, taking the profit offered to him"; but before he could accomplish the request, he died. Being fully informed of these things, and having come of age and in full control of his lands, and since the same request has been made of him and payments offered "more profitable and honorable than the said *morte-mains* and *formariages* are or could be in the future"; and since by ending their servitude "the people will be more abundant and the land cultivated and not allowed to revert to waste, and in consequence more valuable to us and to our successors"; therefore, let it be known that, having taken "great deliberation on these said matters and well ascertained our rights and profits, we do destroy and render null . . . and free of all *morte-mains* and *formariages* each of them in perpetuity and for always, whether clergy or any other estate, without retaining servitude or power to renew servitude to any of them now or in the future by us or our successors nor by any other persons whatsoever." Rent and revenues to be received from the said places will be joined "to our heritage and fief and barony which we hold of the King," who will be asked to approve and confirm the deed. Royal confirmation was duly received three months later.

Landowners in general, especially the less prosperous with holdings too small to allow a margin of revenue, had suffered economically more than the peasantry from the disasters of the past twenty years. Servile labor, lost through the plague, could not be replaced, since free men could not be turned back into serfs. Mills, granaries, breweries, barns, and other permanent equipment had to be rebuilt at the cost of the owner. Expenses of ransom and upkeep as a prisoner during two decades of largely lost battles, even if the cost was passed on to towns and peasants, were a drain on revenues, although Coucy, whom fortune always favored, did not suffer from this particular blight. Besides having been spared ransom, he received 1,000 francs from the King of France in June 1368 to reimburse him for his expenses as hostage and repair damages caused by the war to his domain. Charles V, too, was wooing the lord of Coucy and Soissons.

If ties between lord and dependent were weakened by the transfer to a paid basis, the revenue from rents gave the wealthier nobles greater goods and comforts and freedom of residence. They were building great *hôtels* in Paris and acquiring urban interests. The center of attraction was now the King's new residence called St. Pol, a collection of houses which he had assembled and converted into a palace with seven gardens and a cherry orchard on the eastern edge of the city near the present Place de la Bastille. Twelve galleries connected its buildings and courtyards; topiary figures adorned the gardens, lions were kept in the menageries and nightingales and turtledoves in the aviary.

Charles reigned in a time of havoc, but in all such times there are unaffected places filled with beauty and games, music and dancing, love and work. While clouds of smoke by day and the glow of flames by night mark burning towns, the sky over the neighboring vicinity is clear; where the screams of tortured prisoners are heard in one place, bankers count their coins and peasants plow behind placid oxen somewhere else. Havoc in a given period does not cover all the people all the time, and though its effect is cumulative, the decline it drags behind takes time before it is recognized.

At Coucy's level, men and women hawked and hunted and carried a favorite falcon, hooded, on the wrist wherever they went, indoors or out—to church, to the assizes, to meals. On occasion, huge pastries were served from which live birds were released to be caught by hawks unleashed in the banquet hall. At the turret of the castle where the lord's flag flew, a watchman was stationed with a horn to blow at the approach of strangers. He blew also for the hour of rising at sunup or cockcrow, after which matins were chanted by the chaplain, followed by mass in the chapel. In the evening minstrels played with lutes and harps, reed pipes, bagpipes, trumpets, kettle drums, and cymbals. In the blossoming of secular music as an art in the 14th century, as many as 36 different instruments had come into use. If no concert or performance was scheduled after the evening meal, the company entertained each other with song and conversation, tales of the day's hunting, "graceful questions" on the conventions of love, and verbal games. In one game the players wrote verses, more or less impolite, on little rolls of parchment, which were passed around and, when read aloud, supposedly revealed the character of the reader.

At such evenings grand seigneurs liked to preserve the old custom of lighting rooms by means of torches held by servants, instead of wall sconces, because it satisfied a sense of grandeur. They built their "follies," of which the most elaborate were the mechanical practical jokes devised by Count Robert of Artois at the château of Hesdin. Statues in his garden squirted water on visitors when they walked past or squawked words at them like parrots; a trapdoor dropped the passer-by onto a featherbed below; a room, on the opening of the door, produced rain or snow or thunder; conduits under certain pressures "wet the ladies from below." When the château passed into the posses-sion of Philip of Burgundy, the devices were kept in working order by a resident artist.

In Picardy, for more general enjoyment, the swan festival was held in July and August, when all three estates joined to chase the young swans raised in local ponds and canals and not yet able to fly. Led by the clergy, followed by nobles, bourgeois, and commoners in order, everyone went out in boats accompanied by music and illuminations. Participants were forbidden to kill what they caught. For sport only, the chase lasted several days interspersed with festivities.

Because life was collective, it was intensely sociable and dependent on etiquette, hence the emphasis on courteous conduct and clean fingernails. There was much washing of hands both before and after meals, even though knives and spoons were in use and forks, though rare, were not unknown. An individual basin was brought to the lord and a washroom provided at the entrance to the banquet hall where several people at a time could wash their hands at a series of small water jets and dry them on a towel. For the lord's and lady's baths, which were frequent, hot water was brought to a wooden tub in the bedroom, in which the bather sat and soaked or, in the case of one illustrated gentleman, bathed in a tub in his garden looking ineffably smug under the loving attentions of three ladies. For lesser residents, a room for communal bathing was generally arranged near the kitchen.

Two meals a day were customary for all, with dinner at ten A.M. and supper at sundown. Breakfast was unknown except possibly for a piece of dry bread and glass of wine, and even that was a luxury. Fine dressing could not be suppressed despite ever-renewed sumptuary laws which tried especially and repeatedly to outlaw the pointed shoes. Even when stuffed at the toe to make them curl up or tied at the knee with chains of gold and silver, the *poulaines* produced a mincing walk that excited ridicule and charges of decadence. Yet the upper class remained wedded to this particular frivolity, which grew ever more elegant, made sometimes of velvet sewn with pearls or gold-stamped leather or worn with a different color on each foot. Ladies' surcoats for the hunt were ornamented with bells, and bells hung too from belts, which were an important item of clothing because of all the equipment they carried: purse, keys, prayer book, rosary, reliquary, gloves, pomander, scissors, and sewing kit. Undershirts and pants of fine linen were worn; furs for warmth were ubiquitous. In the trousseau of the unfortunate Blanche de Bourbon, who unwisely married Pedro the Cruel, 11,794 squirrel skins were used, most of which were imported from Scandinavia.

In church, nobles often left the moment mass was over, "scarcely saying a Paternoster within the Church walls." Others more devout carried portable altars when they traveled and contributed alms set by their confessors for penance, although the alms amounted on the whole to far less than they spent on clothes or the hunt. Devout or not, all owned and carried Books of Hours, the characteristic fashionable religious possession of the 14th century noble. Made to order with personal prayers inserted among the day's devotions and penitential psalms, the books were marvelously illustrated, and not only with Bible stories and saints' lives. In the margins brimming with burlesque, all the comic sense, fantasy, and satire of the Middle Ages let itself go. Buffoons and devils curl and twist through flowering vines, rabbits fight with soldiers, trained dogs show their tricks, sacred texts trail off into long-tailed fantastical creatures, bare-bottomed monks climb towers, tonsured heads appear on dragons' bodies. Goat-footed priests, monkeys, minstrels, flowers, birds, castles, lusting demons, and imaginary beasts twine through the pages in bizarre companionship with the sanctity of prayer.

Often in religious observance the sacred mixed with the profane. When mass was celebrated for rulers, complained a bishop, they held audience at the same time, "busying themselves with other things and paying no attention to the service nor saying their prayers." The sacrament of the Eucharist celebrated in the mass, in which the communicant, by partaking of the body and blood of Christ, is supposed to share in the redeeming sacrifice of the cross and in God's saving grace, was the central rite of Christianity and the prerequisite for salvation. Clouded by the metaphysics of transubstantiation, it was little understood by the ordinary layman, except for the magical powers believed to reside in the consecrated wafer. Placed on cabbage leaves in the garden, it kept off chewing insects, and placed in a beehive to control a swarm, it induced the pious bees, in one case, to build around it a complete chapel of wax with windows, arches, bell tower, and an altar on which the bees placed the sacred fragment.

Even so, communion and confession, which were supposed to be observed every Sunday and holy day, were on the average practiced hardly more than the obligatory once a year at Easter. A simple knight, on being asked why he went not to mass, so important for the salvation of his soul, replied, "This I knew not; nay, I thought that the priests performed their mass for the offerings' sake." For northern France it has been estimated that about 10 percent of the population were devout observers, 10 percent negligent, and the rest wavered between regular and irregular observance.

At the moment of death, however, people took no chances: they confessed, made restitutions, endowed perpetual prayers for their souls, and often deprived their families by bequests to shrines, chapels, convents, hermits, and payments for pilgrimages by proxy.

King Charles, according to his admiring biographer Christine de Pisan, daughter of Thomas the astrologer, was zealous in piety. He made the sign of the cross as soon as he awoke and spoke his first words of the day to God in his prayers. When combed and dressed, he was brought his breviary, recited the canonical hours with his chaplain, celebrated high mass in his chapel at eight A.M. with "melodious song" and low mass afterward in his private oratory. Then he held audience for "all manner of people, rich and poor, ladies and damsels, widows and others." On fixed days he presided over matters of state at the Council. He lived consciously with "majestic regularity" to show that the dignity of the crown must be maintained by solemn order. After midday dinner he listened to the minstrels play sweetly "to rejoice the spirit," and then for two hours received ambassadors, princes, and knights, often such a crowd that "in his great halls one could hardly turn around." He listened to reports of battles and adventures and news of other countries, signed letters and documents, assigned duties, and distributed and received gifts. After an hour's rest, he spent time with the Queen and his children—a son and heir was born in 1368 and afterward a second son and two daughters—visited his gardens in summer, read and studied in winter, talked with his intimates until supper, and after the evening's entertainment, retired. He fasted one day a week and read the Bible through each year.

Whatever his true paternity, Charles possessed to the full the Valois passion for acquisitions and luxury. He was already reconstructing Vincennes for a summer palace and would soon build or acquire three or four more. He employed the famous chef Taillevent, who served up roasted swan and peacocks reconstructed in all their feathers with gilded beaks and feet and resting on appropriate landscape made of spun sugar and painted pastry. He collected precious objects and gem-studded reliquaries to house the piece of Moses' rod, the top of John the Baptist's head, the flask of Virgin's milk, Christ's swaddling clothes, and bits and pieces of various instruments of the crucifixion including the crown of thorns and a fragment of the True Cross, all of which the royal chapel possessed. At his death he was to own 47 jeweled gold crowns and 63 complete sets of chapel furnishings including vestments, altarpieces, chalices, liturgical books, and gold crucifixes.

Thirty years old in 1368, two years older than Enguerrand de Coucy, the King was pale, thin, and grave, with a long sinuous prominent nose, sharp eyes, thin closed lips, sandy hair, and carefully controlled feelings. Through a hard school, he had learned to keep his thoughts to himself, so that he was accused of being subtle and secret. He had recovered from the severe headaches, toothaches, dyspepsia, and other ailments which afflicted him during his regency, but still suffered from a malady—perhaps gout—of the right hand or arm and a mysterious fistula and abscess of the left arm, probably from tuberculosis, but supposed to be the result of the attempt by Charles of Navarre to poison him in 1358. A learned physician from Prague, sent to him by his uncle the Emperor, treated the poison, but told him that if ever the abscess should cease oozing, Charles would die after fifteen days in which he would have time to settle his affairs and attend to his soul. Not surprisingly, the King lived under a sense of urgency.

As a man of inquiring mind, interested in cause and effect, and in philosophy, science, and literature, he formed one of the great libraries of his age, which was installed in the Louvre, where he maintained a second residence. The library's rooms were paneled in carved and decorated cypress, stained-glass windows were screened by iron wire against "birds and other beasts," and a silver lamp was kept burning all night so that the King could read at any time. Not knowledge only but the spread of knowledge concerned him. He commissioned Nicolas Oresme, a learned councillor of advanced and scientific mind, to explain the theory of stable currency in simple language; it was this kind of statecraft that earned him the title of Charles le Sage (the Wise). He commissioned translations into French of Livy, Aristotle, and Augustine's *City of God* "for the public utility of the realm and all Christendom," and owned many other classics, works of the church fathers, and Arab scientific treatises in French translation. The library was eclectic, ranging from Euclid, Ovid, Seneca, and Josephus to John of Salisbury, the *Roman de la Rose,* and a then current best seller, Sir John Mandeville's *Travels.* It contained the various 13th century encyclopedias of universal knowledge, a collection of works on the crusades and on astrology and astronomy, 47 Arthurian and other romances, codes, commentaries and grammars, works of philosophy, theology, contemporary poetry, and satire—in all, according to an inventory of 1373, over 1,000 volumes, ultimately the nucleus of the national library of France. When reproached for spending too much time with books and clerks, Charles answered, "As long as knowledge is honored in this country, so long will it prosper."

His three brothers were all compulsively acquisitive: Louis d'Anjou, eldest of the three, for money and a kingdom; Jean de Berry for art; Philip of Burgundy for power. Tall, robust, and blond like his father, Anjou was headstrong, vain, and driven by insatiable ambition. Berry, sensual and pleasure-loving, was the supreme collector, whose square common pug-nosed face and thick body consorted oddly with his love of art. Philip of Burgundy had Berry's coarse heavy features but greater intelligence and an overweening pride. Each put his own interests above the kingdom's, each was given to conspicuous consumption to enhance and display his prestige, and each was to produce through his patronage works of art unsurpassed of their kind: the Apocalypse series of tapestries made for Anjou, the *Très Riches Heures* and *Belles Heures* illuminated for Berry by the brothers Limbourg, and the statues of the Well of Moses and the Mourners sculpted by Claus Sluter for Burgundy.

Never did princely magnificence display itself more noticeably than on two occasions in 1368–69 in which Coucy shared. His brother-in-law, Lionel, Duke of Clarence, a widower and father at 29, came to Paris in April 1368 on his way to Milan to marry Violante Visconti, the thirteen-year-old daughter of Galeazzo.* Accompanied by a retinue of 457 persons and 1,280 horses (perhaps the extras were for gifts), he was lodged in a suite especially decorated for him at the Louvre. His sister, the Dame de Coucy, and Enguerrand came to Paris to meet him and to join in the feasts and honors with which the King and his brothers during the next two days overwhelmed their late enemy.

Another conspicuous guest was Enguerrand's cousin and the bride's uncle Amadeus VI of Savoy, called "the Green Count" from the occasion of his knighthood at nineteen when he had appeared in a series of tournaments wearing green plumes, green silk tunic over his armor, green caparisons on his horse, and followed by eleven knights all in green, each led into the lists by a lady in green leading her champion's horse by a green cord. Amadeus yielded to no one in ostentation. While in Paris, where the shops were displaying their finest goods for the occasion, the Green Count enjoyed a shopping spree, leaving orders for jeweled necklaces, table knives, boots, shoes, plumes, spurs, and straw hats. He gave the King a "chapel" of rubies and large pearls costing 1,000 florins and bestowed three gold francs on Guil-

---

* His name was Giovanni or Gian Galeazzo, but the shorter form is used to distinguish him from his son, Gian Galeazzo the younger.

laume de Machaut for a romance presented to him by the poet. He took home to his wife four lengths of cloth of Reims costing 60 francs and a *jaquette* lined with 1,200 squirrel skins.

Dinners and suppers, dancing and games at St. Pol and the Louvre crowded Clarence's visit, including an elaborate banquet which cost the Duke of Burgundy 1,556 livres. All the abundant species of game, fish, and fowl then inhabiting the woods and rivers, as well as domestic meats especially fattened for the table, were available for eating. Forty kinds of fish and thirty different roasts appear among the recipes of the time. On Clarence's departure the King presented him and his suite with gifts valued at "20,000" florins, part of a routine of gift-giving that, besides exhibiting the status of the giver, was useful to the receiver, who could turn the gifts into cash by pawning.

The acme of ostentation awaited in Milan. To have bought a daughter of the King of France for his son and now a son of the King of England for his daughter was a double triumph for Galeazzo Visconti and one more marvel in the notoriety of the Vipers of Milan, so called from the family device of a serpent swallowing a struggling human figure, supposedly a Saracen. Two Visconti ruled jointly in Lombardy—Galeazzo and his more terrible brother, Bernabò. Murder, cruelty, avarice, effective government alternating with savage despotism, respect for learning and encouragement of the arts, and lusts amounting to sexual mania characterized one or another of the family. Lucchino, an immediate predecessor, had been murdered by his wife, who, after a notable orgy on a river barge during which she entertained several lovers at once including the Doge of Venice and her own nephew Galeazzo, decided to eliminate her husband to forestall his same intention with regard to her. The debaucheries of Matteo, eldest brother of Bernabò and Galeazzo, were such that he endangered the regime and was disposed of by his brothers in 1355, the year after their accession, "dying like a dog without confession."

War with the papacy, from which they had seized Bologna and other fiefs of the Holy See, was the Visconti's major activity. When excommunicated by the Pope in the course of the war, Bernabò compelled the legate who brought him the Bull of Excommunication to eat it, including silken cord and seals of lead. He was supposed to have had four nuns burned and an Augustinian monk roasted alive in an iron cage for no known reason unless it was malice toward the Church.

Greedy, crafty, cruel, and ferocious, given to paroxysms of rage and macabre humor, Bernabò was the epitome of the unbridled aristocrat. If any of his 500 hunting dogs was not in good condition, he would have the keepers hanged and all poachers as well. The *Quare-*

sima, a forty-day program of torture attributed to Bernabò and his brother, supposedly issued as an edict on their accession, was a catalogue so lurid as to make one hope it was intended to frighten, rather than for actual use. With the *strappado,* the wheel, the rack, flaying, gouging of eyes, cutting off of facial features and limbs one by one, and a day of torture alternating with a day of rest, it was supposed to terminate in death for "traitors" and convicted enemies.

In his personal habits Bernabò was dedicated "to an astonishing degree to the vice of lust, so that his household appeared to be more the seraglio of a sultan than the habitation of a Christian prince." He fathered seventeen children by his wife, Regina, said to be the only person who could approach him in his mad moods, and more than that number of illegitimate children by various mistresses. When Bernabò rode through the streets, all citizens were obliged to bend the knee; he would frequently say he was God on earth, Pope and Emperor in his own domain.

Bernabò ruled in Milan, his brother Galeazzo in the ancient city of Pavia twenty miles away. More than 100 towers darkening Pavia's narrow streets testified to the incessant strife of Italian towns. Galeazzo's great square castle, just completed in 1365, was built into the northern wall of the town, overlooking gardens and fruitful countryside. Called by the chronicler Corio with patriotic pride "the first palace of the universe," and by a later admirer "the finest dwelling place in Europe," it was built of rose-red brick baked from Lombard clay, and boasted 100 windows surrounding a magnificent courtyard. Petrarch, who for eight years was an ornament of the Visconti court, described its crown of towers "rising to the clouds," where "in one direction could be seen the snowy crest of the Alps and in the other the wooded Apennines." On a balcony overlooking the moat, the family could dine in summer, refreshed by the sight of water and a view of gardens and forested park rich in game.

A less melodramatic tyrant than his brother, Galeazzo was sober in personal habits and devoted to his wife, the "good and gentle" Blanche of Savoy. He wore his red-gold hair long, in braids or loose, or "sometimes resting on his shoulders in a silken net or garlanded with flowers," and he suffered grievously from gout—"the malady of the rich," as it was called by the Count of Flanders, who suffered from it too.

The wedding of Lionel of England and Violante Visconti was to be held in Milan, leading city of Lombardy and inland rival of Venice and Genoa. As the center for trade below the Alps, it had dominated northern Italy for a thousand years. Its marvels, recorded by a friar of the previous century, included 6,000 fountains for drinking water, 300 public ovens, ten hospitals of which the largest accommodated 1,000 patients two to a bed, 1,500 lawyers, forty copyists of documents, 10,000 monks of all orders, and 100 armorers manufacturing the famous Milanese armor. By mid-14th century it was subject to the general habit of deploring decadence in comparison with the good simple days of yore. Men were reproved for extravagant fashions, especially if foreign—tight garments "in the Spanish manner," monstrous spurs like the Tatars', adornment with pearls after the French fashion. Women were reproved for frizzled hair and gowns that bared their breasts. Milan had so many prostitutes, it was said, that Bernabò taxed them for revenue to maintain the city walls.

On arrival in Milan, Lionel was accompanied, in addition to his own suite, by 1,500 mercenaries of the White Company, which had switched from the Pope's service to that of the Visconti. Eighty ladies all dressed alike—as was customary to enhance the pageantry of great occasions—in gold-embroidered scarlet gowns with white sleeves and gold belts, and sixty mounted knights and squires also uniformly dressed came in the train of Galeazzo to greet him. In addition to a dowry for his daughter so extensive that it took two years to negotiate, Galeazzo paid expenses of 10,000 florins a month for five and a half months for the bridegroom and his retinue.

The stupendous wedding banquet, held outdoors in June, left all accounts gasping. Its obvious purpose was to testify to "the Largeness of Duke Galeas his soul, the full satisfaction he had in this match and the abundance of his coffers." Thirty double courses of meat and fish alternated with presentation of gifts after each course. Under the direction of the bride's brother, Gian Galeazzo the younger, now seventeen and father of a two-year-old daughter, the gifts were distributed among Lionel's party according to rank. They consisted of costly coats of mail, plumed and crested helmets, armor for horses, surcoats embroidered with gems, greyhounds in velvet collars, falcons wearing silver bells, enameled bottles of the choicest wine, purple and golden cloth and cloaks trimmed with ermine and pearls, 76 horses including six beautiful little palfreys caparisoned in green velvet with crimson tassels, six great war-horses in crimson velvet with gold rosettes, and two others of extra quality named Lion and Abbott; also six fierce strong *alaunts* or war-dogs, sometimes used with cauldrons of flaming pitch strapped to their backs, and twelve splendid fat oxen.

The meats and fish, all gilded,* paired suckling pigs with crabs,

---

* With a paste of powdered egg yolk, saffron, and flour sometimes mixed with real gold leaf.

hares with pike, a whole calf with trout, quails and partridges with more trout, ducks and herons with carp, beef and capons with sturgeon, veal and capons with carp in lemon sauce, beef pies and cheese with eel pies, meat aspic with fish aspic, meat galantines with lamprey, and among the remaining courses, roasted kid, venison, peacocks with cabbage, French beans and pickled ox-tongue, junkets and cheese, cherries and other fruit. The leftover food brought away from the table, from which servants customarily made their meal, was enough, it was said, to feed a thousand men. Among those who shared the feast were Petrarch, an honored guest at the high table, and both Froissart and Chaucer among the company, although it is doubtful if the two young unknowns were introduced to the famous Italian laureate.

Never did Fortune's Wheel come down with such a crash; never was vainglory so reprimanded. Four months later, while still in Italy, the Duke of Clarence died of an undiagnosed "fever," which naturally raised cries of poison, although, since it destroyed the influential alliance that Galeazzo had bought at such enormous expense, the cause was more likely the delayed effect of all those gilded meats in the heat of the Lombardy summer. Violante's fate was no happier. She was next married to a half-mad sadist, the seventeen-year-old Marquis of Montferrat, who was given to strangling boy servants with his own hands. After his violent death she married a first cousin, one of Bernabò's sons, who came to a violent end at the hands of her brother. She died at 31, three times a widow.

Twelve months after the Visconti wedding, Enguerrand de Coucy was an envoy of the King at a wedding of greater political significance and no less splendor. Charles V had outmaneuvered the King of England to win for his brother Philip of Burgundy the same heiress that King Edward wanted for his son Edmund. She was Marguerite of Flanders, daughter and heir of Louis de Male, Count of Flanders, he who had once run away from union with Isabella. Edward had been negotiating for this lady of large expectations for five years, even to the point of pledging Calais and 170,000 livres to her father. But since the principals were related within the fourth degree of consanguinity, as hardly any two royal persons in Europe were not, a papal dispensation was needed. Determined to keep England and Flanders apart, Charles exploited the utility of a French Pope. Urban V refused the dispensation to Edmund and Marguerite and, after a decent interval, granted it to Philip and Marguerite, who were related in the same degree. The uniting of Burgundy and Flanders, so great a coup for France, carried the seed of a monstrous birth, for it created a state that was to contend with the parent and in the next century give England revenge in the darkest stage of the war.

To please Marguerite's passion for jewels, the Duke of Burgundy sent throughout Europe for diamonds, rubies, and emeralds, and bought, as the prize of the collection, a pearl necklace from Enguerrand de Coucy for 11,000 livres.

Three enormous coffers of precious objects preceded Philip's arrival in Ghent for the wedding. Through gifts and feasts to both nobles and burghers, processions and tournaments, escorting and meeting guests at the frontiers, and liveries made especially for the occasion, the Duke made every effort to win over and impress the Flemish. Ostentation for Philip was political, part of the process of building a state by prestige. He himself was always gorgeously dressed, affecting a hat with plumes of ostrich, pheasant, and "bird of India," and another of gold ribbons and damask imported from Italy. A man of strenuous temperament, he spent days at a time hunting, often sleeping outdoors in the forest, played energetic tennis, and was the most restless traveler of the day, moving from place to place as often as one hundred times a year. Many of his journeys were pilgrimages, with a portable reliquary and rosary carried wherever he went. He attended mass almost as assiduously as the King, meditated alone like the King in a private oratory, and did not fail to make his religious offerings conspicuous. After his marriage, he presented the Virgin's statue in the Cathedral of Tournai with a robe and mantle of cloth of gold lined with miniver and brilliantly embroidered with his and his wife's coats-of-arms.

Riding into Ghent resplendent in color and bells and richly draped horses, the nobility gathered for the wedding. "Especially," reports Froissart, "the good Sire de Coucy was there, who made the finest showing at a festivity and knew better than any other how to conduct himself, and for that the King sent him." Bit by bit the picture builds of a striking figure, one who stood out in manners and appearance among his peers.

The amount the rich could squander on occasions like these in a period of repeated disasters appears inexplicable, not so much with regard to motive as with regard to means. Where, in the midst of ruin and decline and lowered revenues from depopulated estates and towns, did all the money come from to endow the luxury? For one thing, money in coin was not vulnerable to plague like human life; it did not disappear, and if stolen by brigands it re-entered circulation. In a reduced population the amount of hard cash available was proportionately greater. Probably too, in spite of the plague's heavy mortality, the capacity to produce goods and services was not reduced, because so much of the population at the beginning of the century had been surplus. In proportion to the surviving rich, goods and services may have actually increased.

Ostentation and pageantry to raise the ruler's image above his peers and excite the admiration and awe of the populace was traditionally the habit of princes. But now in the second half of the 14th century it went to extremes, as if to defy the increased uncertainty of life. Conspicuous consumption became a frenzied excess, a gilded shroud over the Black Death and lost battles, a desperate desire to show oneself fortunate in a time of advancing misfortune.

The sense of living in a time of affliction was expressing itself in art in a greater emphasis on human drama and human emotion. The Virgin becomes more anguished in sorrow for her dead son; in the Narbonne Altarpiece painted at this time, she is pictured swooning in the arms of her supporters. In another version by the Rohan Master, all humanity's bewildered suffering is concentrated in the face of John the Apostle, who, as he supports the swooning mother at the foot of the cross, turns grief-stricken eyes to God as if to ask, "How could you let this happen?"

Boccaccio felt the shadows closing in and turned from the good-humored, life-loving *Decameron* to a sour satire on women called *Il Corbaccio (The Crow)*. Once the delight of his earlier tales, woman now appears as a greedy harpy, concerned only with clothes and lovers, ready to consort in her lechery with servant or black Ethiopian. Following *The Crow*, he chose another dispiriting theme on the fall from fortune of great figures in history who through pride and folly were reduced from happiness and splendor to misery.

"Such are the times, my friend, on which we are fallen," agreed Petrarch in a letter to Boccaccio of 1366. The earth, he wrote, "is perhaps depopulated of true men but was never more densely populated with vice and the creatures of vice."

Pessimism was a normal tone of the Middle Ages, because man was understood to be born doomed and requiring salvation, but it became more pervasive, and speculation about the coming of Anti-Christ more intense, in the second half of the century. *Speculatores* or scouts existed, it was believed, who watched for signs that would tell of the coming of "last things." The end was awaited both in dread and in hope, for Anti-Christ would finally be defeated at Armageddon, ushering in the reign of Christ and a new age.

Chapter 12

Double Allegiance

s events moved toward the re-opening of war between France and England, Enguerrand was caught by his English marriage on the prongs of a forked allegiance. He could neither take up arms against his father-in-law, to whom he owed fealty for his English lands, nor, on the other hand, fight against his natural liege lord, the King of France.

King Charles was pressing hard on the issue of sovereignty raised by the Gascon lords. Taking pains to prepare an elaborate justification for resuming hostilities, the King asked for legal opinions from eminent jurists of the universities of Bologna, Montpellier, Toulouse, and Orléans, who not surprisingly returned favorable replies. Draped in the law, Charles summoned the Black Prince to Paris to answer the complaints against him. "Fiercely beholding" the messengers, the Prince fittingly replied that he would gladly come, "but I assure you that it will be with helmet on our head and 60,000 men in our company." Thereupon Charles promptly proclaimed him a disloyal vassal, pronounced the Treaty of Brétigny void, and declared war as of May 1369.

As this situation developed, lords who held lands of both kings "were sore troubled in their myndes . . . and specially the lorde of Coucy, for it touched him gretly." In the awkward predicament of owing allegiance to two lords at war with each other, a vassal, according to Bonet, should render his military service to the lord of his first oath and send a substitute to fight for the other—an ingenious but expensive solution. Coucy could not be compelled by King Edward to fight against his natural liege, but it was clear enough that if he fought for France, his great holdings as Earl of Bedford, and possibly Isabella's too, would be confiscated.

His first plan was to leave in pursuit of a Hapsburg inheritance from his mother which lay across the Jura on the Swiss side of Alsace and had been withheld from him by his cousins Albert III and Leopold III, Dukes of Austria. Although Coucy's claim has been disputed and the circumstances are confused, he himself clearly had no doubts of his right. His seal of 1369 bears a shield quartered with the arms of Austria in the same fashion that Edward quartered his arms with those of France to represent his claim to the French crown. Faceless and barely two inches high, the tiny figure on the seal expressed by its unusual stance the same haughtiness as the Coucy motto. Unlike the typical noble's seal of a galloping knight with upraised sword, the Coucy figure stands erect, in mail with closed visor, austere and stern, holding in its right hand a lance planted on the ground and in its left the shield. Such a standing figure, rarely used, implied regency or royal descent, and appeared in Coucy's time on the arms of the Dukes of Anjou, Berry, and Bourbon. In one form or another, sometimes with a crest of plumes descending upon the shoulders, the upright immobile figure remained on Coucy's seals throughout his lifetime.

With a small body of knights and mixed Picard-Breton-Norman men-at-arms, Coucy entered Alsace in imperial territory in September 1369. At about this time Isabella returned to England with her daughters, either to protect her revenues or because her mother was dying at Windsor, or both. The death of good Queen Philippa in August 1369 had historic effect in that it turned Froissart back to France and French patrons—of whom Coucy was to be one—and to a French point of view in the unfolding chronicle.

In Alsace, Coucy had contracted with the Count of Montbéliard, at a price of 21,000 francs, for his aid against the Hapsburg Dukes. In a manifesto to the towns of Strasbourg and Colmar, he disclaimed any hostile intention against them and stated the case of his inheritance. Thereafter, as the evidence dims, it is clear only that the project aborted. Some say that the Dukes of Austria recruited a powerful enemy of Montbéliard to immobilize his forces, others that Coucy was recalled by an urgent message from Charles V on September 30 requiring his service in the war against England. Forced to a decision, he was evidently able to make an acceptable case for his neutrality to the King, for at that point he vanishes, and for the next two years, except for a single reference, his history is blank.

The single reference places him in Prague, from where he dated a legal document of January 14, 1370, endowing an annuity of 40 marks sterling drawn from his English revenues on his senseschal, the Chanoine de Robersart. A journey to Prague would have been a natural effort to enlist the Emperor's influence upon the Hapsburgs in behalf of his inheritance. Froissart was later to say that Coucy had "oftentimes" complained of his rights to the Emperor, who acknowledged their justice but professed inability to "constrain them of Austria, for they were strong in his country with many good men of war."

After a documentary hiatus of 22 months, the next piece of evidence places Coucy in Savoy, where from November 1371 he was actively engaged with his cousin the Green Count against that nobleman's inexhaustible supply of antagonists. In 1372–73 both together fought in Italy in the service of the Pope against the Visconti.

Since the fall of the Roman Empire, power had moved out of Italy, leaving political chaos in a land of cultural wealth. Italy's cities throve in art and commerce, her agriculture developed greater skills than elsewhere, her bankers accumulated capital and a monopoly of finance in Europe, but the incessant strife of factions and the rending struggle for control between papacy and empire, Guelf and Ghibelline, brought Italy to the age of despots out of a craving for order. City-states, once the parents of republican autonomy, succumbed to Can Grandes, Malatestas, Visconti, who ruled by no title but force. Servile to tyrants —except for Venice, which kept its independent oligarchy, and Florence its Signoria—Italy was compared by Dante to both a slave and a brothel. No people talked more about unity and nationhood, and had less, than the Italians.

Partly as a result of these conditions foreign *condottieri* found a ready foothold in Italy. Bound by no loyalties, serving for gain rather than fealty, they nourished wars for their own benefit and protracted them as long as they could, while the hapless population suffered the effects. Merchants and pilgrims had to engage armed escorts. City gates were shut at night. The prior of a monastery near Siena moved all his possessions two or three times a year into the walled town "for fear of these companies." A merchant of Florence, passing by a mountain village taken over by brigands, was set upon and though he cried aloud for help and the whole village heard him, no one dared come to his aid.

Yet even when roads are lawless and assault is normal, ordinary life has the same persistence as the growth of weeds. The great maritime republics of Venice and Genoa still brought to Europe the cargoes of the East, the Italian network of banking and credit still buzzed with invisible business, the weavers of Florence, the armorers of Milan, the glassblowers of Venice, the artisans of Tuscany still pursued their crafts under red-tiled roofs.

In mid-14th century the central political fact of Italy was the desperate effort of the Avignon papacy to maintain control of its temporal base in the Papal States. To govern this great band of middle Italy from outside the country was in fact impossible. The cost of the attempt was a series of ferocious wars, blood and massacre, oppressive taxation, alien and hated governors, and steadily increasing hostility to the papacy within its homeland.

Inevitably the effort to reconquer the Papal States collided with the expansion of Milan under the Visconti who had seized Bologna, a papal fief, in 1350 and threatened to become the dominant power of Italy. When the papal forces succeeded in regaining Bologna, Bernabò Visconti in an epic rage forced a priest to pronounce anathema upon the Pope from the top of a tower. Rejecting papal authority altogether, he seized ecclesiastical property, forced the Archbishop of Milan to kneel to him, forbade his subjects to pay tithes, seek pardons, or have any other dealings with the Curia, refused to accept papal appointees to benefices in his domain, tore up and trampled on papal missives. When he ignored a summons to Avignon to be sentenced for debaucheries, cruelties, and "diabolic hatred" of the Church, Urban V excommunicated him as a heretic in 1363 and, in one of the century's more futile gestures, preached crusade against him. Hostile to the Avignon papacy for its worldliness, rapacity, and its very existence in the French orbit, Italians regarded Urban as no better than a French tool, and paid no attention to his call.

Born Guillaume de Grimoard of a noble family of Languedoc, Urban was a sincerely devout man, a former Benedictine monk, who genuinely desired to restore the credibility of the Church and revive papal prestige. He reduced multiple benefices, raised the educational standards for priests, took stern measures against usury, simony, and clerical concubinage, forbade the wearing of pointed shoes in the Curia, and did not endear himself to the College of Cardinals. He had not been one of them but a mere Abbot of St. Victor's in Marseille when elected. His elevation over higher-ranking candidates, including the ambitious Talleyrand de Périgord, had been owed only to the inability of the cardinals to agree on one of themselves, but the public thought this astonishing departure outside their own group must have been inspired by God. According to Petrarch, pursuing his favorite theme, only the Divine Spirit could have caused such men as the cardinals to suppress their own jealousies and ambitions and open the way for elevation of a Pope who would return the papacy to Rome.

This Urban intended to do as soon as he should have firm control over the patrimony of St. Peter. Among the devout everywhere, the yearning for return to Rome was an expression of their yearning for a purifying of the Church. If the Pope shared that sentiment, he also recognized that return was the only means of controlling the temporal base, and he understood the necessity of terminating what the rest of Europe saw as French vassalage. It was clear that the longer the papacy remained in Avignon, the weaker became its authority and the less its prestige in Italy and England. Over the violent objections of the cardinals, and the resistance of the King of France, Urban was determined upon return.

In Italy, Bernabò was not the only enemy of priests. Francesco Ordelaffi, despot of Forlì, responded to excommunication by causing straw-stuffed images of the cardinals to be burned in the market place. Even Florence, though allied on and off with the papacy out of need to resist Milan, was anti-clerical and anti-papal in spirit. The Florentine chronicler Franco Sacchetti excused Ordelaffi's vicious mutilation of a priest on the ground that he had not acted from the sin of avarice and that it would be a good thing for society if all priests were treated in the same way.

In England they had a saying, "The Pope has become French and Jesus English." The English were increasingly resentful of the papal appointment of foreigners to English benefices, with its accompanying drain of English money outside the country. In their growing spirit of independence, they were already moving toward a Church of England without being aware of it.

In April 1367 Urban carried out the great removal, sailing from Marseille over the wailing of the cardinals, who are reported to have shrieked aloud, "Oh, wicked Pope! Oh, Godless brother! Whither is he dragging his sons?" as if he were taking them into exile instead of out of it. Reluctant to leave the luxuries of Avignon for the insecurity and decay of Rome, only five of the college in the first instance accompanied him. The greater part of the huge administrative structure was left at Avignon.

Urban's first landfall was at Leghorn, where Giovanni Agnello, the Doge of Pisa, an "odious and overbearing" ruler, came to meet him escorted by Sir John Hawkwood and 1,000 of his men-at-arms in their glittering mail. At the sight, the Pope trembled and refused to disembark. It was not a propitious omen for return to the Eternal City.

The malign spirit of the 14th century ruled over the return. Only when he had assembled a temporal army and an imposing escort of Italian nobles was the Holy Father able to enter the capital city of Christendom, now sadly disheveled. Dependent formerly on the immense business of the papal court, Rome had no thriving commerce like that of Florence or Venice to fall back on. In the absence of the papacy it had sunk into poverty and chronic disorder; the population dwindled from over 50,000 before the Black Death to 20,000; classical monuments, tumbled by earthquake or neglect, were vandalized for their stones; cattle were stabled in abandoned churches, streets were pitted with stagnant pools and strewn with rubbish. Rome had no poets like Dante and Petrarch, no "invincible doctor" like Ockham, no university like Paris and Bologna, no flourishing studios of painting and sculpture. It did harbor one notable holy figure, Brigitta of Sweden, who was kind and meek to every creature, but a passionate denouncer of the corruption of the hierarchy.

For a moment in 1368, the arrival of the Emperor in Lombardy to make common cause with the Pope against the Visconti seemed to augur well. But little came of his effort, and the feuds and rivalries resumed. In 1369 the ancient goal of reunion with the Eastern Church seemed almost at hand when the Byzantine Emperor, John V Paleologus, came to Rome to meet Urban in a magnificent ceremony at St. Peter's. He hoped to obtain Western help against the Turks in return for rejoining the Roman Church, but this project too fell apart when the churches could not agree on ritual.

Harassed by renewed revolt in the Papal States, threatened by a massing of Bernabò's troops in Tuscany, defeated and disillusioned, Urban crept back to Avignon in September 1370. In deserted Rome, Brigitta of Sweden predicted his early death for betraying the Mother of Churches. Within two months he died, like King Jean of an unspecified illness. Perhaps its name was despair.

In electing a successor, the cardinals thought to play safe with a thorough Frenchman of great baronial family, the former Cardinal Pierre Roger de Beaufort, who took title as Pope Gregory XI. He was a pious and modest priest of 41, bothered by some debilitating ailment from which he "endured much pain," who, it was believed, would have no spirit for the perils of Rome. Though a nephew of the superb Clement VI, who had made him a cardinal at age nineteen, Gregory did not have his uncle's lordly ways, nor his prestige, nor any particularly visible strength of character. The cardinals had overlooked, however, the sometimes transforming effect of supreme office.

As soon as he was enthroned, Gregory, like his predecessor, felt the force of the call to Rome, both in the cries of the religious and in the political necessity of leaving Avignon and returning the papacy to its home base. Reluctant and indecisive by nature, he might have preferred a quiet life, but as Supreme Pontiff he felt a sense of mission. He could not move to Italy, however, until the Papal States were made safe against the Visconti. For this purpose Urban had organized a Papal League of various powers to declare war upon Milan, which Gregory now inherited. In 1371 when Bernabò seized further fiefs of the Holy See, the need for action was compelling.

In the same year, Amadeus of Savoy, the Green Count, entered Piedmont, where his territory adjoined Milan, in pursuit of a local war against one of his vassals. He was accompanied by his cousin Enguerrand de Coucy, whom he appointed his Lieutenant-General for Piedmont.

Enguerrand crossed the snowbound Alps with a company of 100 lances some time between November and March in the winter of 1371–72. Though impassable in the 20th century in winter, the alpine passes were negotiated in all seasons by medieval travelers, with the aid of Savoyard mountaineers as guides. People of the Middle Ages were less deterred by physical hazards than their more comfortable descendants. Monks of the local hospices and local villagers, exempted from taxes for their service, kept paths marked and strung ropes along the ridges. They guided parties of loaded mules and pulled travelers on the *ramasse*, a rough mattress made of boughs with ends tied together by a rope. Travelers wore snow goggles or hats and hoods cut like masks over their faces. A cardinal's party with a train of 120 horses was seen crossing in one November with the horses' eyelids closed by the freezing snow. The bodies of travelers overcome by storm, or who had failed to reach a hospice by nightfall, were regularly cleared away by the guides in spring.

From their trans-alpine perch, the Counts of Savoy exercised control of the passes with great effect. The Green Count, Amadeus VI, was a strong-willed enterprising prince whose father and Coucy's maternal grandmother had been brother and sister. Seventeenth of his dynasty, brother-in-law of the Queen of France, founder of two orders of chivalry, leader of the crusade which had expelled the Turks from Gallipoli in 1365 and restored the Emperor of Byzantium to his throne, Amadeus despised mercenaries as "scoundrels" and "nobodies"— and hired them nonetheless. On occasion he was not above bribing them to betray their previous contracts. For operations in Piedmont against the Marquis of Saluzzo in 1371, he engaged the dreaded and brutal Anachino Baumgarten with his German-Hungarian company of 1,200 lances, 600 *briganti*, and 300 archers. In the face of this threat, Saluzzo turned for support to Bernabò Visconti, who sent him reinforcements.

At this point Coucy entered Piedmont as leader of the Savoyard campaign. Clearly well schooled in standard practice, Coucy is reported "wasting" Saluzzo's territory and sending to Amadeus for more men so as to strip the country more effectively. These tactics, designed

ITALY
IN 1360

to induce surrender, rapidly succeeded. Coucy's conquest of three towns and siege of a fourth provoked a counter-offensive by Bernabò in behalf of his ally. In reaction Amadeus joined the Papal League against the Visconti, to the extreme distress of his sister Blanche, who was married to Galeazzo Visconti. In recognition of the 1,000 lances Amadeus promised to engage at his own expense, the Pope named him Captain-General of the league forces in western Lombardy.

In the ensuing struggle, the parties were entangled in a web of relationships more important to themselves than to posterity. Connected by marriage or vassalage or treaty in one way or another, the belligerents shifted in and out of alliances and enmities like chess pieces playing a gigantic game, which may account for the strangely insubstantial nature of the fighting. The war was further conditioned by the use of mercenaries, who, having no loyalties at all, shifted overnight even more easily than their principals. The lord of Mantua started as a member of the league and abandoned the Pope to join Bernabò. Sir John Hawkwood, starting in the pay of Bernabò, abandoned him to join the league. The Marquis of Montferrat, heavily besieged by Galeazzo, subsequently married his daughter, the widowed Violante. Amadeus and Galeazzo, reluctant enemies linked by common devotion to Blanche, felt more threatened by Bernabò than by each other, and ultimately came to a private understanding. The war that engaged Enguerrand de Coucy in Lombardy for the next two years was a snake pit of wriggling fragments.

At Asti, focus of the Savoyard campaign, Coucy found himself in August 1372 facing Sir John Hawkwood's White Company, then in the pay of the Visconti. Each of Hawkwood's men, as described by Villani, was served by one or two pages who kept his armor bright so that it "shone like a mirror and thus gave them a more terrifying appearance." In combat their horses were held by the pages while the men-at-arms fought on foot in a compact round body with each lance, pointed low, held by two men. "With slow steps and terrible outcry, they advanced upon the enemy and very difficult it was to break or disunite them." However, Villani adds, they did better at night raids on villages than in open combat, and when successful "it was more owing to the cowardice of our own men" than to the company's valor or moral virtue.

Troubled by gout and having no taste anyway for personal combat, Galeazzo had sent his 21-year-old son in nominal command of the siege of Asti. Called the Count of Vertu from the title acquired by his childhood marriage to Isabelle of France, Gian Galeazzo was tall and well built with the reddish hair and striking good looks of his father, though his intellectual rather than his physical qualities were what impressed most observers. The only son of devoted parents, educated in statecraft but untried in war, the young Visconti, himself the father of three, was accompanied by two guardians under orders from his father and mother to keep him from being killed or captured, which, they noted, "are frequent events in war." All too dutifully the guardians prevented Hawkwood from the frontal assault he wanted to make, causing him, in exasperation, to strike his tents and leave the camp. In consequence, the Savoyards were able to relieve the city. When Bernabò halved Hawkwood's pay in penalty, he deserted to the papal forces. Shortly afterward Baumgarten, the Savoyard mercenary, deserted to the Visconti.

For the Savoyards, the relief of Asti, if something less than a brilliant military victory, opened the way for the march on Milan. Gian Galeazzo, returning without glory from his first essay in arms, came back to Pavia in time to be present at the death of his 23-year-old wife, Isabelle of France. She died in the birth of their fourth child, a son who survived her only seven months.

Enguerrand's role at Asti, though not chronicled, must have been prominent and possibly decisive in some way, for the Pope immediately empowered his legate, the Cardinal of St. Eustache, "to contract and make treaties, alliances and agreements with Enguerrand, Lord of Coucy, on behalf of the Church," with the object of giving him command of papal troops which the Cardinal was conducting to Lombardy. A first payment to Coucy of 5,893 florins was authorized through a banker of Florence, "to be received by hand," on condition that if Coucy failed to carry out strictly the terms of his agreement with the Cardinal, he must reimburse the papal treasury by 6,000 florins.

At 20 florins per lance per month, the usual mercenary rate, the sum indicates that the force assigned to Coucy numbered 300 lances, rather than the 1,000 originally promised by the Pope. Three hundred lances was a normal-size company in the contracts of the time, which ranged from 60 or 70 to 1,000 lances, of three mounted men each, plus mounted archers, foot soldiers, and servants.

In December the Pope formally appointed Coucy Captain-General of the papal company operating in Lombardy against the "sons of damnation." The appointment reflected Gregory's impatience with Amadeus, who had undertaken to advance on Milan from the west, but was still in Piedmont, defending his own territory against Visconti forces. Coucy's mission was to join Hawkwood, now in papal employ, who had retired to Bologna after changing sides, and was already marching westward again toward the hoped-for envelopment of Milan. Coucy was to proceed with him toward a junction with Amadeus which would complete the envelopment.

In February 1373 Amadeus at last entered Milanese territory, having reached a pact of neutrality with Galeazzo. The hand of his sister Blanche was clearly active in ending the unhappy family situation in which her husband's lands were being ravaged by her brother. In their agreement Amadeus promised not to molest Galeazzo's territory, in return for Galeazzo's promise not to give aid to Bernabò against him. Galeazzo thus took himself halfway out of the war, leaving Amadeus free to proceed against Bernabò without fear of attack on his rear.

By January 1373 Coucy had joined Hawkwood somewhere east of Parma, from which they continued to move toward Milan. On February 26, just as they were approaching their goal, the Pope in an astonishing about-face instructed Coucy to provide a safe-conduct to the Visconti brothers to appear in Avignon before the end of March.

Gregory had been taken in by an offer of the Visconti to negotiate, which was merely Bernabò's device for gaining time to assemble his forces. While still rejoicing in his enemies' anticipated submission, Gregory wrote to commend Coucy for acting "bravely and forcefully to foster the interests of the Church in Italy," and to thank him for that uncommon commodity, his "undivided loyalty." Two days later, discovering himself deceived by the Visconti, the Pope expressed his pain and astonishment that Coucy had "entertained peace proposals from the enemies of the Church." He was ordered to listen to no further propositions of this kind, but to carry out his mission in the assurance that the Pope was resolved "never to negotiate." In letters to all concerned, Gregory beseeched more energetic action to effect the junction.

Coucy and Hawkwood, after crossing the Po in April, reached the hill town of Montichiari about forty miles east of Milan. By this time Amadeus had circled Milan to the north and after a long pause, supposedly caused by agents of Bernabò poisoning his provisions, had proceeded to a point no more than fifty miles distant from Coucy and Hawkwood. Here he came to a stop, evidently to prepare a defensive position against the advance of 1,000 lances under Bernabò's son-in-law, the Duke of Bavaria, who was said to be approaching.

Between the two arms of the papal forces, Bernabò had constructed dikes on the river Oglio which could be opened to flood the plain and prevent the enemy's passage. He had called for reinforcements from Galeazzo to block the threatened envelopment and "requite in good earnest" the Sire de Coucy and Giovanni Acuto, as the

Italians called Hawkwood. While precluded from fighting his brother-in-law of Savoy, Galeazzo considered himself free to act against the other arm of the enemy, that is, against Coucy and Hawkwood. He sent his son at the head of a combined force of Lombards and Baumgarten's mercenaries, numbering altogether more than 1,000 lances plus archers and many foot soldiers. Gian Galeazzo, who was kept informed of the enemy's strength and route by the lord of Mantua, advanced confidently in the knowledge of numerical superiority.

At Montichiari the Coucy-Hawkwood force numbered 600 lances and 700 archers besides some hastily assembled *provisionati* or peasant infantry. Seeing himself vastly outnumbered, Coucy is said to have handed the baton of command to Hawkwood on the grounds of his greater experience and knowledge of Italian warfare, but the course of events supports a contrary version—that he himself launched the attack with the *furia francesca* for which his countrymen were known. As the forces clashed, men-at-arms "tangled so heavily against one another that it was a marvel to behold." Beaten back with heavy losses, Coucy would have been overcome but for Hawkwood, who, according to Froissart, "came to his aid with five hundred because the lord of Coucy had wedded the kynge of England's daughter and for none other cause." Though taking heavy punishment, they managed to retreat to the hilltop while Visconti's mercenaries, believing victory won, broke apart in the customary rampage of looting. Men of the companies always presented a problem of control. Gian Galeazzo was inexperienced and Baumgarten was either complacent or not present in person. He is not mentioned in accounts of the battle.

Seizing their chance, Coucy and Hawkwood regrouped their battered numbers and charged down upon Gian Galeazzo. Unhorsed, with lance beaten from his hand and helmet from his head, he was saved only by the valiant fighting of his Milanese men-at-arms, who covered his escape from the field but were themselves overcome before the mercenaries could be reassembled. In an upset as astonishing in miniature as Poitiers, the inferior papal force triumphed and bore from the field the Visconti banners and 200 prisoners including thirty high-ranking Lombard nobles good for rich ransoms. The Pope pronounced the victory a miracle, and its report, traveling swiftly to France, endowed Coucy with sudden fame. In the small world of his time, fame was easily won; more important was what he learned. Coucy never again indulged himself in that reckless attack for which French knighthood as a whole had so great an affinity.

Militarily, Montichiari had little impact. It led to no junction with Savoy because the Coucy-Hawkwood force, bloodied and depleted, judged it rash to try to break through, and withdrew instead to Bologna, to the great distress of the Pope. He kept pleading for the junction with Savoy to crush Bernabò, that "Son of Belial." He promised Hawkwood that delayed payments would soon be made, and covered Coucy with compliments on his "loyal and careful good judgment, remarkable honesty and well-known prudence." Recognizing "by the test of experience your great decisiveness and foresight," the Pope renewed Coucy's commission as Captain-General in June. Hawkwood, whose company was the mainstay of the force, was not one to give action without pay, and his unpaid men were growing rebellious. Passing through Mantua, they inflicted such injury and thievery upon the citizens as caused the lord of Mantua to complain to the Pope, who in turn begged Coucy to restrain the "forces of the Church" from committing further damage. The danger if not the irony of using brigands to restore papal authority was becoming apparent.

By a brave fight through a narrow pass, the Count of Savoy broke out of his position and was able to advance and join Coucy and Hawkwood at Bologna, from where, all together, they marched westward again in July. Again at Modena the mercenaries aroused the fury of the citizens, which the Pope almost tearfully begged Coucy to appease, especially as Modena belonged to the Papal League. Reaching Piacenza in August 1373, the papal forces laid siege to the city, but the effort petered out when Amadeus fell ill. From that point, under heavy rains flooding rivers, assaults by Bernabò's troops, and general lack of enthusiasm, the offensive disintegrated.

As captain of a force now thoroughly disorganized and compromised, Coucy saw little future in the papal war. On the grounds of long absence from his wife and children and his estate, and the need to care for his affairs in his own war-torn country, he applied for leave to return to France. Gregory graciously granted the release on January 23, 1374, with further fulsome tributes to Coucy's loyalty, devotion, decisiveness, "great honesty," and other virtues "with which you have been endowed by the Almighty." Considering that Coucy was abandoning the cause, the excess of flattery may have been meant to cover an absence of cash, for the money due him was not paid by the papal treasury until many years later.

His departure may have been given added impetus by the recurrence of the Black Death in Italy and southern France in 1373–74. Under its influence, Gregory's war effort dwindled away. Discouraged by illness, Amadeus concluded a separate peace with Galeazzo and abandoned the Pope once his own interests in Piedmont were preserved. Galeazzo on his part, fearing that Bernabò's policies would lead to destruction, was equally ready to separate from his brother. Bernabò was said to have been so enraged by the reconciliation with Savoy that he attempted to assassinate his sister-in-law Blanche as its agent. Forced to make peace with the Pope for the time being, he secured favorable terms in a treaty of June 1374 by bribing papal councillors. Nothing had been accomplished by either side in the war because no combatant but the Pope—who could not make his will effective—had fought for anything fundamental, and war is too unpleasant and costly a business to be sustained successfully without a cause.

For Gian Galeazzo his second discomfiture was enough. He never again took command of troops in battle. A skillful statesman who was to bring the Visconti empire to the peak of its power, Gian Galeazzo remained a melancholy man, oppressed perhaps by the inability to govern without trickery and violence, and saddened by family tragedies. After the loss of his wife and infant son, his eldest son died at the age of ten and his second son at thirteen, leaving him with an adored only daughter who was not to escape an unhappy fate.

With the third advent of the plague, contagion was more strictly controlled if no better understood. While it raged in Milan, Bernabò ordered every victim to be taken out of the city and left to die or recover in the fields. Any person who nursed a plague patient was to be strictly quarantined for ten days; priests were to examine their parishioners for symptoms and report to a special commission under pain of death for failure; anyone who brought the disease into the city was subject to the death penalty and confiscation of property. Venice denied entry to all ships suspected of carrying infection, but with the flea and rat not yet implicated, the precautions, though groping in the right direction, failed to stop the carrier. At Piacenza, where Coucy's war effort ended, half the population died, and at Pisa, where the plague lasted two years, it was said to have wiped out four fifths of the children. The most famous death of 1374 was Petrarch's at age seventy, not of plague but peacefully in a chair with his head and arms resting on a pile of books. His old friend Boccaccio, soured and ill, followed a year later.

In the Rhineland, unconnected with the plague, a new hysteria appeared in the form of a dancing mania. Whether it sprang from misery and homelessness caused by heavy spring floods of the Rhine that year, or whether it was the spontaneous symptom of a disturbed time, history does not know, but the participants were in no doubt. They were convinced that they were possessed by demons. Forming circles in streets and churches, they danced for hours with leaps and screams, calling on demons by name to cease tormenting them or crying that they saw visions of Christ or the Virgin or the heavens opening. When exhausted they fell to the ground rolling and groaning as if in the grip of agonies. As the mania spread to Holland and Flanders, the dancers appeared with garlands in their hair and moved in groups from place to place like the flagellants. They were chiefly the poor—peasants, artisans, servants, and beggars, with a large proportion of women, especially the unmarried. Sexual revels often followed the dancing, but the dominant preoccupation was exorcism of devils. In the agony of the times, people felt a demonic presence, and in their minds nothing pointed more surely to Satan's handiwork in society than the fashion for wearing pointed shoes, which they had so often heard denounced in sermons. Something slightly insane about this crippling frivolity made it in the common mind the mark of the Devil.

Hostility to the clergy marked the dancers as it had the flagellants. In their anxiety to suppress a craze which menaced them, priests performed as many exorcisms as they could while the public watched, sharing in the presence of demons. Processions and masses were held to pray for the sufferers. The frenzy died out within a year, although it was to reappear on and off over the next two centuries. Whatever its cause, it testified to a growing submission to the supernatural, of which the Pope took notice. In August 1374 he announced the right of the Inquisition to intervene in trials for sorcery, heretofore considered a civil crime. Because sorcery was made to work by the aid of demons, Gregory claimed it lay within Church jurisdiction.

On his return home, Coucy found his native country gaining the advantage in the war for the first time in thirty years. France now had a King who, if no captain, was a purposeful leader with a definite war aim—recovery of the ceded territories. During Coucy's absence in Italy, England had lost most of these territories, and her three greatest soldiers as well: Sir John Chandos, the Captal de Buch, and the Black Prince. Had Coucy been present and active during this period of his country's recovery, instead of neutralized by his English marriage, he might well have taken the primary role that went to Du Guesclin. As it was, Charles V, whose constant effort was to win support of the great territorial barons on whom he had to depend, made a special attempt to re-attach him. The title of Sire de Coucy, according to a saying of the time, was held in the general estimation "as high as that of King or prince."

On Enguerrand's return, he was summoned directly to the King, who feasted him and asked for all the news of the papal war. From Paris Enguerrand went home to rejoin his wife, "and if they had a great meeting together there was reason enough," assumed Froissart, "for they had not seen each other for a great while." Marital reunion was followed by a notable honor offered to Coucy when in November 1374 Charles V appointed him Marshal of France, sending a knight under the royal banner to bring him the insignia of office. Still constrained by his double allegiance, Coucy felt obliged to decline the baton. The King nevertheless assigned him an annual pension of 6,000 francs on August 4, 1374, of which he received a first payment of 1,000 francs in November.

Far from clouding his name, Coucy's departure from France rather than take part in the war, and his steadfast neutrality thereafter, were considered the epitome of honor on both sides, and served him well by protecting his estates from English attack. During Knollys' raid through Picardy of 1370, "the land of the lord of Coucy abode in peace, nor was there any man or woman of it that had any hurt the value of a penny if they said they belonged to the lord of Coucy." If they were robbed before their identity was made known, they were paid back by double the amount. A French knight, the Chevalier de Chin, took rather unchivalric advantage of this known immunity by carrying a banner bearing the Coucy arms into a furious scrimmage in Picardy in 1373. He caused great marvel among the English at the sight of his banner, for they said, "How is it that the Lord Coucy hath sent men hither to be against us when he ought to be our friend?" Yet such was the confidence in his honor that they did not believe the banner and forbore to take reprisals against his land "nor burn nor do any damage there."

Charles's planned strategy was avoidance of major battle while exerting scattered military action at every vulnerable point, with as much pressure as possible concentrated on Aquitaine. To recover Castile as an ally, he sent Du Guesclin back to Spain in 1369 with spectacular result. In a "marvelous grete and ferse batayle" near Toledo the two half-brothers Don Enrique and King Pedro fought with awful ax strokes hand to hand, "each cryinge theyre cryes," until Pedro was overcome and captured. Froissart always prefers the noble version, but, according to a Spanish and possibly better-informed chronicler, the capture was effected less honorably. Surrounded and trapped in a castle, Pedro conveyed an offer to Du Guesclin of six fiefs and 200,000 gold dobles if he would convey him to safety. Feigning acceptance, Bertrand led the King out secretly and promptly turned him over to Enrique. Confronted by his brother, Pedro "set his hand on his knife and would have slayne him without remedy," had not an alert French knight seized him by the leg and turned him upside down, whereupon Enrique killed him with a plunge of his dagger, and recovered the crown.

For France the result was the invaluable addition of Castilian sea power, and for England a renewed fear of invasion that cramped her effort overseas. Thereafter one mischance after another befell the English cause. The Black Prince was invalided by a contagious dysentery that spread among the English and Gascons and, in his case, gave way by a cruel irony to dropsy. With swollen limbs, he was "weighed down by so great infirmity of body that he could scarcely sit upon his horse," and as he grew heavier and weaker could not mount and was confined to bed. For the paragon of battle, the man of action and incomparable pride, to be incapacitated at 38 by a humiliating disease was maddening, the more so when the situation he commanded was deteriorating. The Prince fell into rage and ill-temper. Before these came to a tragic climax, the next mischance arose.

In the wind of national feeling, French nobles were answering the crown, turning back transferred castles, forming small forces of 20, 50, or 100 men-at-arms to recover towns and strongholds in ceded territories. In one such skirmish early in 1370 at Lussac between Poitiers and Limoges, Sir John Chandos, seneschal of the region, with a company of about 300 clashed with a French force at a hump-backed bridge over the river Vienne. Dismounting to fight on foot, he marched to meet his enemies "with his banner before him and his company about him, his coat of arms upon him . . . and his sword in his hand." Slipping on the dew-moistened ground of early morning, he fell and was struck by an enemy sword on the side of his blind eye so that he failed to see the blow coming. The sword penetrated between nose and forehead and entered the brain. For some unexplained reason, he had not closed his visor. Stunned to extra ferocity, his men beat off the enemy and, after blows and bloodshed, turned directly to tears with all the facility of medieval emotion. Gathering around the unconscious body of their leader, they "wept piteously . . . wronge their handes and tare their heeres," crying, "Ah, Sir John Chandos, flowre of chivalry, unhappily was forged the glaive that thus hath wounded you and brought you in parell of dethe!"

Chandos died the next day without recovering consciousness, and the English in Guienne said "they had lost all on that side of the sea."

As the architect and tactician of English victories at Crécy, Poitiers, and Najera, Chandos was the greatest captain of his side if not of both sides. Although the French rejoiced at the enemy's loss, there were some "right noble and valiant knights" who thought it a common loss, for an interesting reason. Chandos, they said, was "so sage and so imaginatyve" and so trusted by the King of England that he would have found some means "whereby peace might have ensued between the realms of England and France." Even knighthood knew the craving for peace.

A few months later the Black Prince came to his last act of war. Territories were slipping from his hands, gnawed by forces under the Duc d'Anjou, the King's energetic lieutenant in Languedoc, and by other forces under Du Guesclin. In August 1370 Charles's policy of piecemeal negotiation with towns and nobles regained Limoges, whose Bishop, although he had taken the oath of fealty to the Black Prince, easily allowed himself to be bought back by the Duc de Berry, lieutenant for the central region. For a price of ten years' exemption from excise taxes, the magistrates and citizens were glad to go along. Limoges raised the fleur-de-lys over its gates, and after due ceremony Berry departed, leaving a small garrison of 100 lances, too small to avert what was to follow.

Enraged by the "treason" and vowing to make the city pay dearly for it, the Black Prince determined to make an example that would prevent further defections. Commanding from a litter, he led a strong force, including two of his brothers and the elite of his knights, to assault Limoges. Miners tunneled under the walls, propping them with wooden posts which when fired caused sections of the wall to collapse. Plunging through the gaps, the men-at-arms blocked the city's exits and proceeded on order to the massacre of the inhabitants regardless of age or sex. Screaming with terror, people fell on their knees before the Prince's litter to beg for mercy, but "he was so inflamed with ire that he took no heed to them" and they passed under the sword. Despite his order to spare no one, some great personages who could pay ransom were taken prisoner, including the Bishop, upon whom the Prince cast "a fierce and fell look," swearing to cut off his head. However, by a deal with the Prince's brother John of Gaunt, the Bishop escaped to Avignon, carrying with him the fearful tale.

The knights who watched or participated in the slaughter were no different in kind from those who wept so piteously for Chandos, but the obverse of facile emotion in the 14th century was a general insensitivity to the spectacle of pain and death. Chandos was bewailed because he was one of themselves, whereas the victims of Limoges were outside chivalry. Besides, life was not precious, for what was the body, after all, but carrion, and the sojourn on earth but a halt on the way to eternal life?

In customary punishment, Limoges was sacked and burned and its fortifications razed. Though the blood-soaked story, spreading through France, doubtless cowed resistance for the moment, it fostered in the long run the hatred of the English that fifty years later was to bring Joan of Arc to Orléans.

A hero's career ended in the vengeful reprisal at Limoges. Too ill to govern, the Prince turned the rule of Aquitaine over to John of Gaunt, and at the same time suffered the death of his eldest son, Edward, aged six. In January 1371 he left Bordeaux never to return. With his wife and second son, Richard, he went home to six more years of the helpless life of an invalid.

With France now holding the initiative, England's military strategy was mainly negative. The object of Sir Robert Knollys' savage raid through northern France in 1370 was to do as much injury as possible in order to damage the French war effort and hold back French forces from Aquitaine. His forces could rob villages and burn ripe wheat in the fields as they marched, but could take no fortified places nor provoke frontal battle. Without prospect of either ransoms or glory, his knights grew disaffected as they neared Paris, yet their threat was sufficiently alarming to cause the appointment of Du Guesclin as Constable in October.

A record of being four times taken prisoner suggests either a rash or an inept warrior, but Bertrand was not a reckless plunger of the type of Raoul de Coucy. On the contrary, he was cautious and wily, and a believer in wearing down the enemy by deprivation and attrition, which was why Charles chose him. His first act was to conclude a personal pact with a formidable fellow Breton, one-eyed Olivier de Clisson, called "the Butcher" from a habit of cutting off arms and legs in battle. The Breton team and its adherents harassed and pursued Knollys, and when his company was split by the defection of discontented knights, defeated it in combat on the lower Loire. Snapping and biting here and there, or buying off English captains too strongly installed, Du Guesclin's forces liberated piece by piece the ceded territories.

Crucial advantage was won at sea in June 1372 by the Castilians' defeat of an English convoy off La Rochelle. The English ships were bringing men and horses to reinforce Aquitaine and—more critically— £20,000 in soldiers' pay, said to be enough to support 3,000 combatants for a year. Informed by his spies of the expedition, Charles called upon his alliance with King Enrique. The Castilian galleons of 200 tons propelled by 180 oars manned by free men, not chained criminals, were more maneuverable than the square-rigged English merchantmen, which could not tack but only sail before the wind. The Spaniards were commanded by a professional admiral, Ambrosio Boccanegra, whose father had been admiral for Don Pedro but, with a sharp eye for the Wheel of Fortune, had changed sides at the right moment. The English commander was the Earl of Pembroke, a son-in-law of King Edward, aged 25 with a bad moral reputation and no known naval experience. Sailing into the bay, his ships were rammed by the Castilians, who sprayed the English rigging and decks with oil which they ignited by means of flaming arrows. From high poops or "castles" taller than the enemy's, they threw stones down upon the English archers. In a two-day battle the English ships were burned, routed, and sunk. Among other losses, the vessel carrying the money was sent to the bottom.

Loss of the money weakened England's hold of Aquitaine, which depended on payment of troops. Castilian control of the sea endangered communication with Bordeaux and, worse, opened the way to French raids on English shores. With just that in mind Charles was at this time developing a naval base and shipbuilding yards at Rouen, where the largest ships could ride up the Seine with the tide. Rather than wait to be attacked at home, the aging King Edward, now sixty, swore to go overseas himself "with such puissance that he would abide to give battle to the whole power of France."

Assembling another fleet by the usual method of "arresting" merchant ships with their own masters and crews, and taking with him the ailing Black Prince and John of Gaunt, King Edward sailed with a large force at the end of August 1372, ready to brave the Castilians, only to be defeated by the weather. Contrary winds that prevailed for nine weeks repeatedly turned back the fleet or held it in port until it was too late in the year to go. The King had to give up the attempt at a cost of enormous expenditure in provisions and equipment, in pay and maintenance of mariners and men-at-arms, in cessation of trade and economic loss to the shipowners, and, not least, in growing discontent with the war.

Medieval technology could raise marvels of architecture 200 feet in the air, it could conceive the mechanics of a loom capable of weaving patterned cloth, and of a gearshaft capable of harnessing the insubstantial air to turn a heavy millstone, but it failed to conceive the fore-and-aft rig and swinging boom capable of adapting sails to the direction of the wind. By such accident of the human mind, war, trade, and history are shaped.

The naval fiasco led indirectly to the tragic fate of England's third great soldier, the Captal de Buch. While Edward's fleet floundered offshore, the French were recovering La Rochelle and its hinterland, and in the course of these combats the Captal was taken. He was caught at night by a Franco-Castilian landing party under the command of Owen of Wales, a protégé of France claiming to be the true Prince of Wales. Though the Captal fought mightily by torchlight, he was overpowered. Contrary to chivalric custom, Charles held him in prison in the Temple in Paris without privilege of ransom. The fate of the Captal became the wonder and dismay of knighthood.

Political purpose was more important to Charles V than the chivalric cult. He had never forgiven the Captal's defection after the Battle of Cocherel in 1364, when the Captal at first turned French, in response to Charles's grant of large revenues, and then relapsed. His heart belonged to his companion in arms, the Black Prince, and when war was renewed in 1369, he repudiated his homage to the King of France, gave back the properties, and rejoined the English. Charles was now determined to keep him out of action.

Although King Edward offered to exchange three or four French prisoners with ransoms worth 100,000 francs, Charles refused absolutely to let the intrepid Gascon be ransomed, even though he had been the rescuer of Charles's wife and family at Meaux. While the Captal languished, French nobles pleaded with the King not to let a brave knight die in prison, but Charles said he was a strong warrior who, if free to fight again, would recover many places. Therefore he would release him only if he would "turn French," which the Captal refused to do. On being once more petitioned by a group of which Coucy was this time the spokesman, the King reflected a little and asked what he might do. Coucy replied, "Sir, if you asked him to swear he would never again take up arms against the French, you could release him and it would be to your honor."

"We will do it if he will," said the King, but the gaunt and weakened Captal said "he would never take such an oath if he had to die in prison." Left to that choice, never again to know his sword, his horse, or his freedom, he succumbed to depression, wanted neither to eat nor drink, gradually sank into coma, and died after four years in prison in 1376.

Following Edward's aborted expedition, the English made one more effort. A new army was assembled which probably numbered about 4,000 to 5,000 men despite the chroniclers' "10,000" and "15,000." Led by John of Gaunt, Duke of Lancaster, without his father or elder brother, both now unfit for war, the army crossed to Calais in July 1373 with the stated purpose of marching to the relief of Aquitaine. It was the longest and strangest march of the war.

Although supposedly seeking decisive battle, in which the English usually prevailed, Lancaster did not take the direct route southward, where he would have encountered Du Guesclin's forces on the way. Instead he took the long way around, behind Paris, in a protracted raid of pillage that led down through Champagne and Burgundy, across the central highlands of Auvergne, and eventually, after five months and almost 1,000 miles, to Aquitaine. Probably the intention of the famous, if indirect, offensive was to spread damage like Knollys, with the added purpose of distracting the French from organizing a possible invasion of England. Perhaps Lancaster simply wanted a wider opportunity to find knightly adventure and the plunder necessary to make up the pay which the state could not furnish.

Covering eight or nine miles a day in the usual three lines of march, the better to live off the country and gather loot, the army inflicted wanton damage in order to provoke, through the complaints of the inhabitants, the combat of French knights. This failed, owing to Charles's strict prohibition and because the population was encouraged to take refuge inside fortified towns. Lancaster's march stretched out into the cold and rains of autumn; provisions dwindled, horses starved and died, discomfort grew into hardship and hardship into privation. The Duke of Burgundy's men, following on the army's heels, picked off stragglers, local resistance accounted for more losses, in the south Du Guesclin laid ambushes. November was met on the wind-swept shelterless plateau of Auvergne, knights without horses plodded on foot, some discarded rusted armor, some as they entered Aquitaine were seen to beg their bread. Of the wasted army that stumbled into Bordeaux at Christmastime, half the men and almost all the horses had perished.

Enough were left to hold the old Aquitaine, now reduced to its original boundaries, but not to regain what had been lost. By 1374 the Treaty of Brétigny had been nullified in fact as well as name. Except for Calais, England was left with no more than she had held before Crécy. The English had no way of holding territory without the financial means to maintain an army abroad nor, once war had broken out, could they hold ceded regions whose population had become hostile.

Nor could military superiority conquer an opponent who refused decisive battle. In August 1374 King Edward declared his readiness to conclude a truce.

For both sides the time had come. Charles V, by using his head, and Du Guesclin, by his unorthodox tactics, had combined to forge a strategy based on recognition of the possible—the direct antithesis of combat for honor, chivalry's central principle. While contemporary chroniclers and propagandists tried to make of Du Guesclin the "Tenth Worthy" and Perfect Knight, and Charles's biographer Christine de Pisan insisted on eulogizing him for everything but his real contribution, it was in truth the non-chivalric qualities of these two hard-headed characters that brought France back from ruin. Charles had succeeded in his war aim, but at the cost of a ravaged and exhausted country. After some stalling, he agreed to send envoys to a peace parley at Bruges.

Chapter 13

Coucy's War

No peace treaty was reached at Bruges because the English were determined to retain their former possessions in France under their own sovereignty, while Charles V was equally determined to regain the sovereignty of Guienne yielded at Brétigny. His lawyers argued that the yielding of sovereignty had been invalid because it violated the sacred oath of homage, therefore the Black Prince and the King of England had been guilty of rebellion comparable to that of Lucifer against God. While this satisfied Charles's life-long care to exhibit a lawful case, it failed to impress the English. To avoid total waste of the parley, which had been conducted at great expense and rival magnificence by the Dukes of Burgundy and Lancaster (Burgundy received 5,000 francs a month in expenses), a one year's truce beginning in June 1375 was agreed upon, with an undertaking to resume negotiations in November.

Left unemployed by the truce, the companies in France reverted to plundering the people they had lately liberated. More than a year earlier, in January 1374, the royal government had attempted by a sweeping ordinance to bring the units under control. The ordinance provided for a system of authorized companies at fixed rates of pay under captains appointed by the crown who would be required to forswear pillage and be held responsible, under pain of stated penalties, for the conduct of their men. It was a conscientious effort, but the Free Companies proved too much a part of the military system to be either uprooted or domesticated. Their brigandage continued.

"Greatly troubled" by this situation, the King took counsel with his advisers on what he might do. They "bethought them of the Sire de Coucy." He was to be a new Pied Piper who could lead the brigands out of France in a foreign war—his own.

Coucy's case against the Dukes of Austria and his determination to pursue it were well known. He could serve France in this matter, unhindered by his ties to England. The proposal was put to him by Bureau de la Rivière and Jean le Mercier, the King's Chamberlain and Treasurer, that if he would take into his service the companies of some 25 captains from many parts of France and lead them against the Hapsburg Dukes, the King would provide 60,000 livres toward their pay and the expenses of the compaign. Especially he was to remove the hard-bitten Bretons, followers of Du Guesclin and Clisson, who had been committing terrible ravages since the end of official war.

Coucy's experience of mercenaries in Lombardy was enough to teach him the dangers and undependability of such a command, even though it promised him extraordinary aid toward his own purpose. He was now 35, rich enough to loan money in that year to the Duc de Berry but not to finance a campaign against the Hapsburgs out of his own resources. He agreed to undertake the great riddance.

Among the captains recruited to Coucy's banner were the Constable's brother, Olivier du Guesclin, who had been occupying and devastating the lands of the Duc de Berry, and his cousin Sylvestre Budes, chief of a Breton company which had been the bane of the Pope and the scourge of Avignon, where it plundered even the wheat sent by the King to relieve a famine in 1375. In vain the Pope had pleaded, negotiated, paid, excommunicated. He now paid the Bretons 5,000 francs and agreed to revoke the excommunication if they would go with Coucy. "Great terror" spread through Burgundy as they moved northward up the left bank of the Rhône; runners reported their advance, towns and villages sent out heralds to recruit help. Like fierce summer locusts, the Bretons, joined by other companies, swept through Champagne in July, into Lorraine in August, and into Alsace, which was part of the Hapsburg domain within the Empire, in September.

Knights of Picardy, Artois, Vermandois, and Hainault came with their squires and men-at-arms to "advance themselves in honor" in Coucy's enterprise. "Honor" in the lexicon of chivalry meant combat against other knights, anticipated in this case against the Austrians. The elasticity of the human mind allowed honor to be unaffected by partnership with mercenaries and brigands. Among the recruits were Raoul de Coucy, Enguerrand's uncle, the Vicomtes de Meaux and d'Aunay and other seigneurs, and not least that celebrated and busy warrior Owen of Wales. Son of a father executed by the King of England, Owen had been brought up at the court of Philip VI. Described as high-spirited, haughty, bold, and bellicose, he had fought at Poitiers, in the Lombard wars of the 1360s, for and against the Dukes of Bar in Lorraine, as a free-lance in Spain, and with Du Guesclin in the campaigns of the 1370s, during which he had returned from leading a naval raid on the Channel Islands to capture the Captal de Buch.

In 1375 Owen was fresh from action at the successful siege of St. Sauveur-le-Vicomte on the coast of Normandy, where for the first time cannon had been used with notable effect. Forty "engines" great and small, projecting balls of iron and leather as well as stone, failed to bring down the walls but so harassed the defenders that they could not continue resistance. "They were so covered by the engines that they did not dare go into the town or outside the castle but stayed in the towers." Even there one ball penetrated a room where an English captain lay sick in bed and rolled around the walls several times "as if the thunder itself had entered his chamber," convincing him his last hour had come, before it crashed through the floor to the room below.

Under contract with Coucy dated October 14, 1375, the prodigious Owen was to lead 400 men at a pay of 400 francs a month plus another 100 francs for his lieutenant, Owen ap Rhys. He was to take second place to no other captain and make no other alliance until released, while Coucy in turn was to make no peace without Owen's agreement. Any town or fortress taken by Owen was to be yielded to Coucy, but he could retain booty and prisoners worth less than 200 francs in ransom. Of those worth more than that, Coucy was to receive one sixth of the value, and in the event of the Duke of Austria himself being captured, Owen was required to deliver him to Coucy in return for payment of 10,000 francs.

The enterprise became a magnet for restless swords, attracting from their annual Prussian sport 100 knights of the Teutonic Order. The ink on the Truce of Bruges was hardly dry before English knights too came riding to the rendezvous, attracted by the leadership of the King of England's son-in-law. Well armed, on fine horses with silver bridles, wearing sparkling cuirasses and helmets and magnificent long surcoats, the English, supposedly numbering "6,000," cast their fearful reputation over Coucy's entire army with the result that their opponents were to identify them all as *Engländer*.

The total number, though vague, evoked awed estimates of forty, fifty, sixty, even one hundred thousand. Estimated by the number of captains, it was probably somewhere around 10,000, comparable to the army Du Guesclin led to Spain. An Alsatian chronicle mentions 16,000 knights "in helmets and hoods." The pointed helmets and cowl-like hoods on heavy cloaks worn against the cold were noticed by all observers. Called *Gügler* (from the Swiss-German for cowl or point), the hoods gave their name to what became known as the Gügler War.

Before leaving, Coucy took care for the future of his soul in case he met death. On a grand scale befitting his rank, he endowed two masses "every day and in perpetuity" at the Abbey of Nogent-sous-Coucy for himself, his ancestors, and his successors. His instructions, like most of their kind, were precise and specific, leaving nothing to choice. The prayers were to be said in front of the image of Notre Dame in the chapel, already designated as the site for his and his wife's tombs. One hundred livres a year were assigned for the upkeep of the monks and the augmentation of Divine service. The money was to be taken from "perpetual" rents and from the *taille* due to Coucy from particular towns, specified to the exact penny, 50 livres from one, 45 livres and 10 sous from another, 4 livres and 10 sous from a third. Like his contemporaries, Coucy counted on a perpetuity without change. He further donated to the monks of Nogent for their sole use the rights to the fish in the river Ailette over a given distance from the Rue de Brasse to the Pont St. Mard.

Solid and everlasting, Coucy's bequest did not exhibit the urgency of some donors. The Captal de Buch in a will of 1369, the year he abandoned French fealty, evidently felt the need of immediate sanction: he left 40,000 gold écus for 50,000 masses, all to be said within a year of his death, plus perpetual lamps and additional pious legacies.

These endowed chantries, ranging up to periods of thirty or fifty years or perpetuity, and usually including the relatives of the donor, provided employment to the clergy and income to the churches. Unattached priests with no other function could make a living from the commissions and otherwise lead, as was popularly supposed, an idle and dissolute life. The Princess of Wales maintained three priests whose only duty was to say prayers for her deceased first husband.

While his assembled forces plundered Alsace for six weeks through October and into November, Coucy still had not taken command. His delay is the first puzzle among many that cannot be unraveled in this strange winter war because of gaps and contradictions in the record. Did he postpone deliberately to add to the chance of depleting the companies through the hardships of winter? The fact that Du Guesclin too, in 1365, did not begin his march across the Pyrenees until December suggests a pattern. But Coucy was clearly intending to fight it out with his mother's cousin Leopold, not merely to lead the companies on a goose-chase over the Jura and lose them somewhere in the mountain snows.

At the end of September he had written to the Duke of Brabant, imperial Vicar in Alsace, informing him of his intention to reclaim

Brisgau, Sundgau, and the small county of Ferrette, and had received an assurance that no imperial action would be taken to oppose his efforts to obtain justice. Further to make a case for a just war and distinguish himself from a mere captain of mercenaries, Coucy also wrote to the towns of Strasbourg and Colmar in Alsace disclaiming any threat against them, stating his claim against his cousin, urging them not to take alarm but to aid him in obtaining his rights, and offering to explain his case further if they wished. This elicited no answer, since beneath the city walls the companies were already doing their worst.

If the cry of horror in the local chronicles is evidence, never was carnage worse than in Alsace. Forty villages in the Sundgau were robbed and wrecked, 100 inhabitants of Wattwiller killed without mercy, men and women seized to serve the brigands' needs, the Franciscan monastery of Thann burned to the ground, the convent of Schoenensteinbach so ruined that it was abandoned and its lands not cleared again for twenty years. The companies exacted their usual tribute, which the rich paid in money, horses, and fine fabrics, and the poor in shoes, horseshoes, and nails. When questioned as to the purpose of their campaign, some captains reportedly replied that they had come for "60,000 florins, sixty stallions fit for combat, and sixty garments of gold cloth." The Bishop and magistrates of Strasbourg paid 3,000 florins to ransom the city from attack. In one place where a band of combative villagers succeeded in killing twenty of the enemy billeted among them, they suffered such cruelties in retaliation that audacity gave way to despair and they fled, abandoning their homes.

At the outset, the captains in Coucy's pay had endeavored to maintain discipline, and some hanged culprits almost daily in an effort to stop the disorders. Against men habituated to lawless force, violent punishment failed to bring the violence under control.

In the face of invasion, Leopold adopted the same strategy as had Charles V: he ordered the Alsatians to destroy everything that could aid, shelter, or feed the enemy and to retreat with their goods and provisions within walled towns and castles. Like Charles, he ordered the fortifying of towns and castles capable of defense, the razing of others, and the burning of outlying villages. On paper such orders are easily assumed; in practice, it would have been agony for a peasant to destroy or see destroyed the product of his labor, the slim margin of his life for another year. To what extent these drastic measures were actually carried out is hard to judge.

Lacking sufficient force to confront Coucy's numbers, Leopold withdrew into the fortress of Breisach across the Rhine and counted on exciting the resistance of the self-reliant Swiss to repel the enemy from further advance. He had painful reason to know the capacity for combat of his Swiss subjects.

Whether real or legendary, William Tell's defiance of the Austrian bailiff Gessler at the start of the century personified the struggle against Hapsburg tyranny. Twice thereafter in the last sixty years the Swiss had humiliated the Hapsburg cavalry. At Morgarten and Laupen in 1315 and 1339 the victories of the man on the ground over the mounted knight had made military history. At Morgarten in the forest Canton of Schwyz, the Swiss, concealed above a mountain pass, hurled down boulders and tree trunks on the knights as they rode through the narrow defile, and then charged upon the scrambled mass and slew them "like sheep in the hurdles." They gave no quarter, for they expected no ransom, and they carried the field because it was they and not their foe who had chosen where to fight. The knights claimed terrain as the cause of defeat, and in fact the disadvantage of cavalry in the mountains, where it could not charge, was an element, no less than the defiant spirit of the cantons, in the ultimate gain of Swiss independence.

At Laupen on an open hillside, no excuse of terrain could explain away the result. There the city levy of Berne, joined by mountain men of the Forest Cantons, advanced under the command of a local knight and took their position upon a hill requiring ascent by the Hapsburg knights. In the clash the Swiss, though surrounded, formed a "hedgehog" phalanx that stood its ground and withstood penetration. While they engaged the knights in hand-to-hand combat, inflicting terrible wounds with their halberds—a combination of ax and pike—their reserve fell upon the nobles from behind and crushed them. Seventy crested helms and 27 noble banners were carried from the field. Though a generation had passed since then, the Güglers might have taken warning.

The Swiss responded meagerly to Leopold's summons for defense against Coucy. They hated the Hapsburg more than they feared the invaders. The three Forest Cantons in the center of the country refused action. Led by Schwyz, boldest of the three and patronym of the future nation, they said they had no interest in sacrificing themselves to defend Leopold's territory against the Sire de Coucy, who had never offended them. They would remain "spectators of this war," except to defend themselves against the victor if he pushed his enterprises too far. Zürich, however, along with Berne, Lucerne, and Solothurn agreed to defend the Aargau, the region adjoining Alsace along the river Aar, because it touched their borders and was their "boulevard."

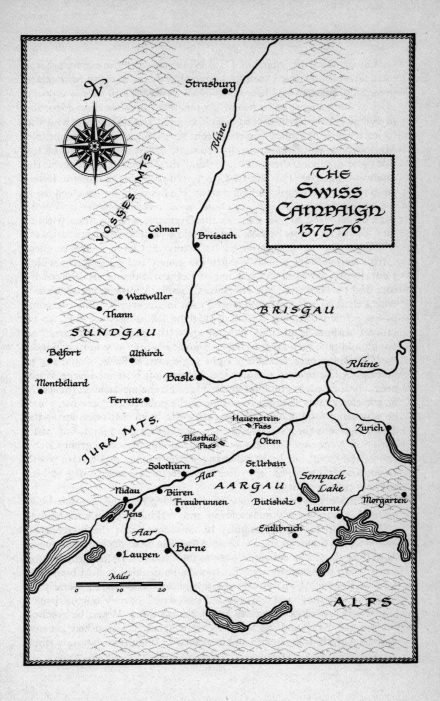

THE
SWISS
CAMPAIGN
1375~76

Strasburg

Rhine

N

LOSGES MTS.

Colmar

Breisach

BRISGAU

Wattwiller

Thann

SUNDGAU

Belfort

Altkirch

Montbéliard

Basle

Rhine

Ferrette

Zurich

JURA MTS.

Hauenstein Pass

Blasthal Pass

Olten

Solothurn

Aar

St. Urbain

AARGAU

Sempach Lake

Nidau

Büren

Fraubrunnen

Butisholz

Lucerne

Morgarten

Jens

Entlibruch

Aar

Laupen

Berne

Miles

0   10   20

ALPS

On or about St. Martin's Day, November 11, Coucy with 1,500 men arrived in Alsace to take command. By now, with winter approaching, the area had been thoroughly ravaged until no more provisions or forage were to be found. At this juncture a startling distortion of events occurs in the record which, coming from Froissart, who was to learn much of Coucy's history from his own mouth, is inexplicable. Mutinous captains, according to Froissart, called a meeting to accuse Coucy of deceiving them. "How's this?" they cried. "Is such as this the duchy of Austria? The Sire de Coucy told us it was one of the fattest lands of the world and we find it poor. He has shabbily deceived us. If we were across the Rhine, we could never return before we were all dead or captured by our enemies the Germans, who are men without pity. Let us return to France, and cursed be he who advances further!"

Suspecting he was about to be betrayed, Coucy spoke to them softly, saying, "Sirs, you have taken my money and my gold for which I am deeply indebted to the King of France, and you are obliged by oath and by faith to acquit yourselves loyally in this enterprise. Otherwise I shall be the most dishonored man in the world." But the companies refused to move, growling that the Rhine was too wide to be crossed without ships, they did not know the roads beyond, and "no one should take men-at-arms out of a good country as you have done."

The Rhine, which makes a right angle turn at Basle, would not in fact have to be crossed to enter the Aargau, but it loomed large, if not precisely located, in common knowledge. To the mercenary, the world he traveled in was as vague in outline as the political purpose for which he was being used. Coucy tried to persuade them that once across the dark mountains they saw ahead they would find good land, but without avail. A message from Leopold at this point offered to grant Coucy one of the territories he had demanded, the county of Ferrette worth 20,000 francs a year, but the offer was rejected because Coucy and his advisers considered it too small.

In Froissart's version, Coucy on discovering that the men would go no further was "greatly melancholy" and, "taking counsel with himself as a wise and far-seeing knight," he considered that the mercenaries might well sell him to the Duke of Austria in lieu of promised wages, "and if he should be delivered over to the Germans he would never be freed." After consulting with his friends, he decided he had better return to France. With only two companions he departed secretly at night "in disguise," and had traveled two days' journey out of danger before any but close associates knew he had gone. When he reached France, the King and his brothers were "greatly astonished because they thought him in Austria and it seemed to them that they saw three ghosts." Asked to give an account of himself, Coucy had no trouble in explaining the affair, "for he was an eloquent speaker and had a true excuse." He told the King and Dukes everything that had occurred "so that it might be seen that he was in the right and the companies to blame."

The fact that nothing of the kind happened illustrates the problem of medieval records. Coucy and the companies did indeed go forward into the Aargau, leaving Alsace on St. Catherine's Day, November 25, and marching to Basle, where they paraded around the city for three days in a display of strength, presumably to discourage any opposition to their advance over the Jura. The Bishop of Basle gave them free passage, it was said, out of hatred for Berne.

At close hand, the purple darkness of the Jura was seen to be pines covering a low range that did not rise above tree level. Riding along a stream that rushed toward France in the opposite direction, the hooded men-at-arms crossed over the crest, forced the passes at Hauenstein and Blasthal, descended among the valley hamlets, robbing and destroying as they went, until they came to the Aar, a wide tributary of the Rhine marking the frontier of the Aargau. Meeting little resistance, because lords of the region fled before the invaders to take refuge with Leopold, they seized castles and the ancient wooden bridge at Olten.

Urgently summoned by Leopold, the Bernese had advanced to meet the enemy, but seeing the nobles abandon the territory, they had turned in disgust and marched home. All Aargau in a fright abandoned arms and villages for refuge in the towns, leaving the Güglers masters of the countryside. Infuriated by the Bernese disobedience, Leopold laid ruthless waste in front of the enemy. His agents burned fields and harvests, felled trees, and left such a wake of misery that little villages were hard pressed that winter to fight off the wolves that came out of the forest. The embittered people mocked the Austrians who "lay across the Rhine, safe as in a coffer." They accused Count Rudolph of Nidau and other local lords of opening the way to the torrent that would devastate the cantons.

Coucy's men-at-arms swept up what they could find. Dividing themselves into three groups they spread out farther and farther into the Aargau as hunger and plunder drove them. Coucy made his headquarters less than five miles east of the river in the Abbey of St. Urbain, set with its back to a crescent of pine-covered hills and looking out over a wide sweep of meadow land. According to the abbey's records, he stayed there eighteen days. The more important cities of the Aargau had been made pledges for the unpaid portion of his mother's dowry. Had he been able to take these cities, his personal goal might have been gained, but the scattering of his forces and the strength of walls against men prevented it. He could do no better than Edward had in France. Even the small town of Büren in the Aar valley withstood a siege he conducted in person, although its lord, the Count of Nidau, reaped the punishment of his double-dealing when he put his head out of a window and was killed by an enemy arrow.

In December's cold the companies, hunting in small parties to spread their foraging, penetrated to the frontiers of Zürich and Lucerne. Their thinning out made them vulnerable at the same time that their crimes were arousing Swiss defiance. In Schwyz, near the lake of Sempach, in the mountain district of Entlibuch, a stalwart peasantry, proud of ancient privileges, assembled a body of several hundred for action. Stirred by their example, the young men of Lucerne, against city orders, climbed over the walls at night to join them, along with others from surrounding towns. On December 19 the group, numbering about 600, surrounded the small town of Buttisholz, where a company of "3,000" Güglers was billeted. The Swiss attacked, slew 300, and burned others alive in a church where they had taken refuge. The rest were put to flight. Triumphantly the men of Entlibuch, with captured arms and trophies, rode back to their mountains. Seeing them pass, a noble who had not fought called mockingly from his castle to a mountaineer riding the war-horse and wearing the helmet and cuirass of a dead knight, "Noble sir of noble blood, should villeins wear such arms?" The Entlibucher shouted back, "Sir, today we have so mixed the blood of nobles and horses that one cannot be told from the other." On the site of the skirmish a monument was raised commemorating the *Niederlage der Gügler.*

Berne, city of the Bear, took fire from the news. Within six days a force of Bernese and citizens of nearby towns, including Nidau and Laupen, was assembled under the leadership of Berne's chief magistrate. On Christmas night the troop surprised a company of Bretons at Jens fifteen miles away and left another 300 Güglers dead, evidently with minor loss to themselves, for they were ready to march out again the next night.

Their objective this time was the Abbey of Fraubrunnen, where no less an enemy than Owen of Wales was quartered with a large company. Carrying the banner of the Bear, the citizens marched through the night of the 26th in intense cold, and surrounded the abbey before dawn. With loud yells and flaming torches they fired the buildings and fell upon the sleeping "English," killing many before they woke. The rest sprang to their weapons in a desperate defense: cloisters once accustomed to ceremonial silence rang with the shouts and clang of battle, the contenders fought "stab for stab and blow for blow," smoke and flames filled every building of the abbey, Owen swung his sword with "savage rage," the Bernese leader, Hannes Rieder, was killed, but his men forced the Güglers to flight. "And those who fled were slain and those stayed were burned up." Owen escaped, leaving 800 of his men dead. The Swiss too suffered heavy losses, but the survivors carried glory back to Berne. Among the captured banners still displayed in the city is a red-and-white one, stained and torn, said to be Coucy's.* Was he at Fraubrunnen in person? His presence is nowhere mentioned but is not impossible.

Berne decreed an annual distribution of alms in thanksgiving; songs and chronicles celebrated the victory over the dreaded companies which had so long harassed Christendom. Ballads told how the "Knight of Cussin set out to seize castle and town," with "forty thousand lances in their pointed hats"; how he "thought the land was all his and brought his kinsmen of England to help him with body and goods"; how "Duke Yfo of Wales came with his golden helm"; how the Bishop of Basle treacherously promised to serve the Gügler, and how at last when Duke Yfo came to Fraubrunnen,

> The Bear roared "You shall not escape me!
> I will slay, stab and burn you";
> In England and France the widows all cried,
> "Alas and woe!
> Against Berne no one shall march evermore!"

For posterity, Coucy's role was recorded more soberly, if inexactly, in Latin on a stone pillar erected at Fraubrunnen:

> Seeking again the dowry of the beloved wife
> Which the Austrian brother gave, Coucy, the English leader,
> Led across the sea the standards of strong cohorts—
> A knight attacking foreign fields far and wide.
> In this place, on this ridge, the people of Berne
> Destroyed the enemy camp and slaughtered many men
> In this unjust war. Thus may Omnipotent God
> Protect the Bear from the open [attacks] and secret stratagems
> Of the enemy.

---

* The Historical Museum of Berne describes the banner as a 15th century reproduction of the original. Bernard Aucien suggests that it may have been captured in 1388 when the Swiss regained Nidau which had been ceded to Coucy at the close of the Aargau campaign.

The voice of an aroused pride and confidence sounds in these war songs and memorials. The fights at Buttisholz, Jens, and Fraubrunnen in Christmas week of 1375, although they did not destroy the Güglers, were greater in significance than in size. They re-energized the Swiss struggle against the Hapsburgs and propelled it toward the decisive battle at Sempach in Schwyz eleven years later in which Leopold was to be killed and the Hapsburg hold over the cantons all but broken, although it took another century before independence of the Confederation was definitely won. As catalyst, Coucy's expedition played an unhappy role in the growth of a nation, not unlike the Black Prince's massacre at Limoges. But if the clashes he generated confirmed the fighting capacity of commoners when engaged in their own cause, the lesson did not apply beyond the Swiss and, to some extent, the Flemish. Other attempts like the Jacquerie in the recurring civil struggles of the 14th century were smashed.

After Fraubrunnen, Coucy was forced to turn back to France. Against Leopold's refusal to fight he could not regain his inheritance, nor could he hold the companies any longer in a scorched and empty country in freezing weather and in the sunken morale left by defeats at the hands of the populace. Like Edward, like Lancaster, like every invader of his time, he had set out to live off the country with no chain of supply, and he met no different result. The gloomy repetitions of history were never more apparent than in the Gügler War. Habit has an especially tenacious grip when, as in the Middle Ages, the pace of change is slow.

The exit through Alsace in January was dogged by hunger and cold. Men dropped by the way or deserted, starving horses were left to die, harness and armor abandoned. The strong continued to pillage. Cities closed their gates against the ravagers and in one case, with the aid of the Virgin Mary, added the humiliation of another defeat. The citizens of Altkirch, resolved to do battle against a Gügler company which was preparing an assault, were waiting on the walls for the signal to begin combat when the night sky was suddenly illuminated by colored lights like an aurora borealis. Convinced that their patron, the Holy Virgin, was manifesting her aid, the emboldened citizens charged to the offensive. With equal but opposite effect on the enemy, the heavenly intervention spread consternation and put the Güglers to flight.

Further on, at Wattwiller, within a day's ride of Leopold's castle at Breisach, a treaty was signed on January 13 between Coucy and the Dukes of Austria by which they ceded to him the fief of the deceased

Count of Nidau, including the town of Büren, in return for his renouncing his other claims. Whether Coucy on his way out still represented a sufficient threat to extract this settlement, or whether it had been negotiated earlier as the price of his departure, is unrecorded. In any event, he did not go home empty-handed.* The companies straggled back through January and February. Coucy had succeeded in keeping them out of France for almost six months, longer than Du Guesclin had removed them to Spain in 1365.

King Charles in February promptly commissioned him, together with Marshal Sancerre and Olivier de Clisson and several knights who had served with the Güglers, to command operations against their former associates who had resumed pillage in Champagne. The Sire du Coucy, "knight banneret with two knights bachelor and seven squires of his house," and Marshal Sancerre were each to have 200 men-at-arms, and Clisson 100, in the pay of the King, to lead "against several companies just returned from the borders of Germany." Evidently they applied successful pressure. By March the Breton companies reappeared along the Rhône and in May were hired by the Pope for renewed war in Italy.

The Anglo-French peace conference in Bruges, reconvened in December 1375 in the presence of dukes, cardinals, Constable Du Guesclin, and other grand personages, spent itself in more legalities, more displays, jousts, fetes, and banquets, and attracted even more people than the previous parley, until an epidemic of some kind subdued its pleasures. The dispute over territories and sovereignty became further complicated by Charles's demand that Edward pay reparations for damages caused by the war. No agreement was reached except to extend the truce for another year. Again Charles, now anxious for a "good peace," bethought him of the Sire de Coucy, whose connections in England "well fitted him to treat of peace between the two Kings."

At the time of Coucy's expedition against Austria, the restless Isabella had gone home as usual to England, leaving France several months before her husband's departure. Judging by various gifts, grants, and subsidies showered on her by King Edward, she still exercised a spell upon her father. Now in his dotage, Edward was equally subject to the spell of a beautiful and vulgar mistress, Alice Perrers, to

---

* According to Swiss sources, the cession was not made until ten years later when Leopold wanted Coucy's support against the Swiss in the struggle that led to Sempach.

whom he gave the late Queen's robes and jewels and who paraded through London on her way to a tournament in a triumphal chariot under the title of "Lady of the Sun." Isabella on her previous visit had not shared residence at court with the supplanter of her mother, but on this occasion her scruples were vanquished by filial affection, or possibly expectation of largesse. The King paid her debts and expenses and servants' wages and granted pardons to three separate criminals for whom she interceded, including one for "breach of the peace" in killing the servant of another man. The record does not tell why she was interested. She was presented "by the King's own hand" with a hooded robe of scarlet cloth cut in the style of the robes of the Garter "with hood and sleeves furred and turned up with ermine"; a second of the same for St. George's Day; and at Christmas an ermine-trimmed velvet robe each for herself and her daughter Philippa. (Marie, as heiress to the Coucy domain, remained in France.)

As King Edward's granddaughter, eight-year-old Philippa was a distinct personage who had been betrothed since the age of four to Robert de Vere, ninth Earl of Oxford, then aged ten. In consequence of this alliance she bore the title of Countess of Oxford and shared with her mother in the bounty of the autumnal monarch. As the year turned, Edward gave Isabella a complete set of chapel furnishings and two saddles, one of red velvet embroidered with gold violets and one ornamented with suns of gold and copper. She hunted at Windsor, joined in archery with twelve ladies, each presented by the King with an ornamental bow, and doubtless with some reluctance returned to France in January 1376 when Coucy came back from the Aargau. By April she was quite ready to go home again. In that month Coucy asked the King of France for permission to visit England with his wife.

Since his return from the Aargau, Coucy's friends had been urging him to become wholly French. They argued, according to Froissart, that he need not necessarily lose his English lands if it came to a choice, because the King of England could not expect him to give up his far greater French domain, especially since he was French "by name, blood, arms and extraction." Since he knew himself esteemed by the French King and felt grateful to him for financing the Austrian expedition, and doubtless too because he had no wish, in case of renewed war, to be left again in an enforced and difficult neutrality, Coucy was drawing close to a decision. But first he clearly hoped to resolve the matter of his English lands and revenues on the forthcoming visit. His English wife, in view of her unfading attachment to home, would surely have energetically opposed a renunciation of her country. Nevertheless, that choice was clearly in her husband's mind upon accepting his new assignment.

"And seeing that he was regarded as one of the wisest and most prudent of nobles . . . in whom one could not want more of all good and all loyalty, it was said to him, 'Sire de Coucy, it is the intention of the King and his Council that you belong with us in France and that you can aid and counsel us in treating with the English. Therefore we ask you that you make this voyage covertly and wisely, as you know how to do, and that you discover from the King of England and his Council on what terms peace can be made between them and us.' And so he hastened upon the voyage."

Chapter 14
England's Turmoil

Coucy arrived in England in April 1376 just at the moment when English discontent came to a head in the first impeachment by Parliament of ministers of the crown. In the historic session called the Good Parliament the monarchy discovered that it had drained the cup of public confidence in a government that could neither win the war nor end it.

The failure to conclude peace at Bruges had brought to a climax public resentment of corrupt royal officials, a profitless war, military mismanagement, and waste or embezzlement of the people's tax money. These were the same ills that twenty years earlier had generated the French Third Estate's challenge to the monarchy. They found the same opportunity to make themselves felt when the English crown needed a new subsidy to prepare for the prospective end of the truce a year hence. Parliament was summoned for April, and as members gathered, London reverberated with "a great murmur of the people."

The Sire and Dame de Coucy, who had been welcomed "joyously" at court on their arrival, found themselves in the midst of wrath and crisis surrounding the royal family and focusing on Isabella's brother, John of Gaunt, otherwise known as the Duke of Lancaster. In place of the sick Prince and senile King, he was the key figure in the royal government who was now held to blame for all that had gone wrong.

Seventy-four knights of the shire and sixty town burgesses made up the Commons of the Good Parliament. Acting with some support from the Lords, they demanded redress of 146 grievances before they would consent to a new subsidy. Their primary demand was the dismissal of venal ministers together with the King's mistress, who was generally credited with being both venal and a witch. In addition they wanted annual Parliaments, election rather than appointment of members, and a long list of restraints upon arbitrary practices and bad government. Two of their strongest discontents were directed not against the government, but against abuses of a foreign Church hierarchy and the demands of a laboring class grown disobedient and disorderly. These issues, too, were great with significance: one was to lead to the ultimate break with Rome and the other, much sooner, to the Peasants' Revolt.

The strenuous and jubilant England Coucy had known in the aftermath of Poitiers had grown sadly disgruntled. Pride of conquest and wealth of ransoms had thinned like smoke, buoyant energy and confidence were sunk in quarrels and frivolity, the widened empire had shriveled, English fleets were swept ignominiously from the Channel, bellicose Scots on the border—whom Edward had been fighting even longer than he had the French—were as unsubdued as ever. England's heroes—Henry of Lancaster, Chandos, the Prince of Wales—were dead or dying; the good Queen was replaced by a strumpet who was believed to have established her dominion over the King by restoring his sexual potency through the enchantments of a friar skilled in the black arts. The once exuberant Edward who had looked down on victory from the windmill at Crécy was now a foolish infatuated old man "not stronger in mind than a boy of eight." The high tide of success had turned to loss, with every loss paid for by disrupted trade and renewed taxes. A fifty-year reign of incessant warring was coming to a close in a rising sense of wasted effort and misrule.

England by now had caught the contagion of lawlessness which the war had spread upon the continent. Soldiers, returning with the habit but no longer the fruits of pillage, formed small bands to live by robbery, or as retainers of lords and knights who returned to find their demesnes impoverished as a result of the Black Death. A whole generation, from the sack of Caen at Edward's first landing to the raid in the Aargau, had accustomed itself to brigandage and resorted to it easily at home. According to a complaint in Parliament, companies of men and archers, sometimes under a knight, "do ride in great routs in divers parts of England," and take possession of manors and lands, ravish women and damsels and bring them into strange counties, "beat and maim and slay the people for to have their wives and their goods," hold them prisoner for ransom, and "sometimes come before the justices in their sessions in such guise with great force whereby the justices be afraid and not hardy to do the law." They commit riots and "horrible offenses" whereby the realm is in great trouble, "to the great mischief and grievance of the people." Royal justice made no serious effort to restrain them because the King was dependent for military forces on the same nobles who were responsible for the disorders.

The resulting breakdown of justice was a major cause of the Commons' anger. In the *Vision of Piers Plowman*, which first appeared in 1377, the figure of Peace petitioning against Wrong, in the person of a King's officer who has carried off his horses and grain and left a tally on the King's Exchequer in payment, complains that he cannot bring him to law because "he maintaineth his men to murder mine own." Private lawlessness equally was on the rise. "Tell me," asked the Bishop of Rochester, a sympathizer of the Commons, "why, in England, so many robberies remain unpunished when in other countries murderers and thieves are commonly hanged? In England the land is inundated by homicides and the feet of men are swift to the shedding of blood."

Outlawry among free peasants had increased because their command of higher wages, as a result of depopulation, brought them in constant conflict with the law. The Statute of Laborers, in a world that believed in fixed conditions, still held grimly to pre-plague wage levels, blind to the realities of supply and demand. Because the provisions against leaving one employment for a better were impossible to enforce, penalties were constantly augmented. Violators who could not be caught were declared outlaws—and made lawless by the verdict. Free peasants took to the nomadic life, leaving a fixed abode so that the statute could not be executed against them, roaming from place to place, seeking day work for good wages where they could get it, resorting to thievery or beggary where they could not, breaking the social bond, living in the classic enmity to authority of Robin Hood for the Sheriff of Nottingham.

It was now that Robin Hood's legend took on its great popularity with the people, if not with the country gentlemen and solid merchants of the Commons. They complained bitterly how "out of great malice" laborers and servants leave at will, and how "if their masters reprove them for bad service or offer to pay them according to the said statutes, they fly and run suddenly away out of their service and out of their country . . . and live wicked lives and rob the poor in simple villages in bodies of two and three together."

To keep them on the land, the lords offered many concessions, and towns welcomed the wanderers to fill the shortage of artisans, so that they grew aggressive and independent. They were most angry and seditious, and haughty about food, according to Langland, when their fortunes prospered. "They deign not to dine on day-old vegetables . . . penny ale will not do, nor a piece of bacon," but rather fresh-cooked meat and fried fish, "hot-and-hot for the chill of their maw." Joining with villeins and artisans, they learned the tactics of association and strikes, combined against employers, subscribed money for "mutual defense," and "gather together in great routs and agree by such Confederacy that everyone shall aid the other to resist their Lords with a strong hand." A generation ready to revolt against oppression was taking shape.

Return of the Black Death in 1374–75 in the same epidemic that had hastened Coucy's departure from Lombardy thinned more hearths and reduced the tax yield. The recurring outbreaks were beginning to have a cumulative effect on population decline as they did on the deepening gloom of the century. In the poll tax of 1379 four villages of Gloucestershire were recorded as making no returns; in Norfolk six centuries later, five small churches within a day's visit of each other still stood in deserted silence on the sites of villages abandoned in the 14th century. As before, however, mortality was erratic and there was no lack of land-hungry younger sons, poor relations, and landless tenants ready to take over ownerless property and keep land in cultivation.

Religious unrest was also disturbing the public mind and found its voice in an Oxford theologian and preacher, John Wyclif. Seen through the telescope of history, he was the most significant Englishman of his time. The materialism of the Church and the worldliness of its representatives were old complaints common to all Europe, but they were sharpened in England by antagonism to a foreign papacy. As elsewhere in Europe, there was a deep craving to detemporalize the Church and clear the way to God of all the money and fees and donations and oblations that cluttered it. In Wyclif the political and spiritual strains of English protestantism met and were fused into a philosophy and a program.

Master of Balliol when he was 36, he stimulated anti-clericalism and gained attention by his stirring sermons. On the issue of secular versus spiritual authority, he carried further the dangerous thoughts of Marsilius of Padua and William of Ockham and found himself champion of the English struggle against the supremacy of papal law over the King's courts and against the payment of revenues to the papacy. As King's chaplain in the 1360s he formulated ideas very attractive to the government on the relationship of church and state. In 1374 he served as the King's envoy in the effort to reach a settlement with the Pope.

In the year of Coucy's visit Wyclif metaphorically nailed his thesis to the door in the form of a treatise, *De Civili Dominio* (*On Civil Authority*), which proposed nothing less than the disendowment of the temporal property of the Church and the exclusion of the clergy from temporal government. All authority, he argued, derived from

God, and in earthly matters belonged to the civil powers alone. By logical progression and in harsh polemic filled with references to the "stinking orders" of the friars and "horned fiends" of the hierarchy, his theories were soon to lead him to the radical proposition that the priesthood should be disestablished as the necessary mediator between man and God.

Wyclif's peculiar achievement was to express both national interest and popular feeling. For decades Parliament had complained bitterly of the income withdrawn from England by foreign holders of rich benefices like the haughty Cardinal Talleyrand de Périgord. The amount was said to be twice the revenues of the crown, and Church property in England was estimated at a third of the land of the realm. The selling of papal letters of authority by impostors was a wide abuse extended by a regular business in forged papal seals. Immunity of the clergy from civil justice, leaving a lay complainant without redress, was another cause of resentment. Most of all, people minded the unfitness of priests. When a priest could purchase from diocesan authority a license to keep a concubine, how should he have better access to God than the ordinary sinner? Priestly susceptibility was such that when a man confessed adultery, the confessor was not allowed to ask the name of the partner lest he be inclined to take personal advantage of her frailty.

The venality if not lechery of the parish priest was usually a result of his being underpaid, which led to the necessity of selling his services; even the Eucharist might be withheld unless the communicant produced an offering, which made a mockery of the ritual. Judas, it was said, sold the body of Christ for thirty pieces of silver; now priests did it daily for a penny. Frivolity was another complaint: vicars were scolded by their bishops for throwing candle drippings from the upper choir stalls on the heads of those below, or conducting "detestable" parodies of the Divine service "for the purpose of exciting laughter and perhaps of generating discord." Worldly clerics were censured in 1367 for wearing short tight doublets with long fur- or silk-lined sleeves, costly rings and girdles, embroidered purses, knives resembling swords, colored boots, and even that mark of the Devil, slashed and curling pointed shoes.

Great prelates of noble family were as lordly as their lay peers, dressing their retinues in uniform and traveling with squires, clerks, falconers, grooms, messengers, pages, kitchen servants, carters, and porters. Charity was gone from them, wrote Langland; bishops of the Holy Church once apportioned Christ's patrimony among the poor and needy "but now Avarice keeps the key"; Charity was once found "in a friar's frock, but that was afar back in St. Francis's lifetime." His fellow poet John Gower, speaking "for all Christian folk," denounced absentee priests, and bishops who added to their great incomes by taking bribes from rich adulterers, and arrogant cardinals in their red hats "like a crimson rose opening to the sun; but that red is the color of guilty pride."

When, from denouncing such priests, Wyclif reached the point of denying the validity of the priesthood itself as necessary to salvation, he was to strike at the foundation of the Church and its interpretation of Christ's role. From that point he moved ineluctably to the heresy of denying transubstantiation, for without miraculous power the priest could not transform the bread and wine into the true body and blood of Christ. From there the rest followed—the non-necessity of the Pope, rejection of excommunication, confession, pilgrimages, worship of relics and saints, indulgences, treasury of merit. All were to be swept away under Wyclif's broom.

In replacement he offered the Bible in English, translated by his disciples, that it might bring religion to the people in a form they could understand without need of the priest and his meaningless Latin doggerel. No other act of a religious reformer would cut more sharply into the thousand-year establishment of the Christian Church, but this was still some years ahead. In the seventies the movement of dissent called Lollardy, from a word applied to Flemish mystics meaning "mumbler," was preparing the way. While Lollardy was greatest among the common people and lower clergy, it spread, too, among knights and some great nobles who resented the clergy's hold on political power. The Earl of Salisbury removed all statues of saints from his chapel, earning the title of "derider of images, scoffer at sacraments," and there were others called "hatted knights" who refused to uncover when the host was carried through the streets.

Wyclif's ideas and the crown's needs fitted together like sword and sheath, accounting for the strange alliance that made him a protégé of John of Gaunt. His theory of disendowment, which maintained that nobles could repossess the lands their ancestors had bequeathed to the Church, put a doctrinal floor under Gaunt's desire to plunder the rich ecclesiastical establishment. What Henry VIII succeeded in doing a century and a half later, John of Gaunt already had in mind in 1376. Meanwhile the losses of territory in France, for which the clerical Chancellor, William of Wykeham, Bishop of Winchester, and his fellow ecclesiastics in office were held responsible, served to oust them from government. The Lords in Parliament resolved in 1371 that none but laymen "who could answer for their misdeeds in the King's courts" could henceforth hold the offices of Chancellor, Treasurer, Barons of the Exchequer, and Clerks of the Privy Council.

The adverse tide in France was not stemmed by the change. Merchants and landed gentry were not happy to see the money squeezed from them in taxes dissipated in the *horribles expenses et incredibiles* of the Duke of Lancaster and his suite at Bruges. The envoys spent their time—according to the censorious monk of St. Albans, Thomas Walsingham, who hated Lancaster because of his anti-clerical policy—in "rioting . . . revelling and dancing" at a cost of £20,000. If Walsingham's *Chronicon Angliae* is suspect for its animus, it is also invaluable for vivid information about a hectic time.

The people's loyalty was severely tried, too, by purveyance—that is, the King's right when traveling to commandeer supplies for a number of miles on either side of the road, and also for the provisioning of the army. Purveyors "seize on men and horses in the midst of their field work . . . on the very bullocks at the plough" so that "men make dole and murmur" at the King's approach. What had been a nuisance was raised in wartime to economic tyranny. Nobles in charge of military organization profiteered on war contracts, as did royal purveyors and the clerks who made payments from Exchequer funds. Coastal towns suffered from the billeting of troops while they awaited transportation overseas. Trade declined owing to the disruption of shipping, ransoms no longer flowed in a golden stream to nourish the economy, and such ransoms as did come in were kept by the crown to pay English troops and release English prisoners. Installments on King Jean's ransom had reached only three fifths of the total when King Charles stopped payment on the renewal of war and, indeed, demanded return of the money as reparations. By now England was growing poorer, not richer, from the war.

When Parliament met in 1376, the Commons, which existed only as an ad hoc body for purposes of consenting to taxes, gathered itself for political action. First it sought strength by association with the Lords, who represented the permanent Parliament and contained a strong anti-Lancaster faction prepared to challenge the Duke. A council of twelve, consisting of four bishops, four earls, and four barons, was drawn from the Lords to act in concert with the Commons. The lay leader of the group was Coucy's former ward, the young Earl of March, who was married to Philippa, daughter of Lancaster's elder brother, the late Duke of Clarence. She stood in line to the crown after the dying Black Prince and his nine-year-old son, Richard. Consequently her husband believed he had reason to fear the Duke of Lancaster, who was popularly credited with a wicked uncle's designs on the crown.

Lancaster indeed had his sights fixed on a crown, but it was the crown of Castile by right of his marriage to a daughter of the defunct Pedro the Cruel. He already styled himself King of Castile—or Monsieur d'Espagne—and probably had no serious intention of usurping his nephew's rights; what he wanted was to end the war with France so that he could mobilize England's forces to gain the Spanish throne. As President of the Royal Council, he was the real head of the government; he controlled his father, the King, by alliance with Alice Perrers and gained a reputation as a libertine by openly maintaining a mistress of his own, Katherine Swynford, widow of a knight killed in Aquitaine, whom he later respectably married and by whom he fathered the Tudor line. He lived in the splendid Savoy Palace on the bank of the Thames and enjoyed its terraces, rose gardens, magnificent collection of jewels, and the rest of the inheritance of his first wife's father, the first Duke of Lancaster; in short, he possessed all the attributes of power and riches necessary for unpopularity and was widely considered to be a villain. The reputation, like his older brother's as a paragon of chivalry, was probably overdrawn.

Popular excitement as Parliament convened was heightened by the arrival of the Prince of Wales, who had himself carried to Westminster from his country estate to be present during the session. His purpose, in the shadow of death, was to obtain assurance from Lords and Commons of fealty to his son, but the public believed he had come to support the Commons against his brother, the Duke, whose ambitions he was believed to fear. In fact the Prince's arrogant temperament was not one likely to welcome interference with the monarchy, but what counts is not so much the fact as what the public perceives to be the fact. Because the challengers in Parliament believed the Prince to be their supporter, they drew assurance and strength from his presence.

The tumultuous assembly was held at Westminster, with the Commons meeting in the chapter house of the abbey and the Lords in the White Chamber of the palace nearby. As Earl of Bedford, Coucy could have taken his place among the Lords at the opening ceremony on April 28, but there is no evidence that he did.

Taking the offensive, the Commons for the first time in its history elected a Speaker in the person of a knight of Herefordshire, Sir Peter de la Mare, who not accidentally was seneschal of the Earl of March. Critical moments often produce men to match the need; Sir Peter proved to be a man of courage, perseverance, and, in Walsingham's partisan judgment, a "spirit lifted up by God." On behalf of the whole House he brought charges of malfeasance against two of the King's ministers, Lord Latimer, the Chamberlain, and Sir Richard Lyons, a rich merchant and member of the Royal Council who acted as the King's chief agent with the commercial community, and also against Alice Perrers, who, it was said, "has yearly up to 3,000 pounds from the King's coffers. The realm would greatly profit by her removal."

Latimer was a great noble and Knight of the Garter, a veteran of Crécy, Auray, and of Lancaster's long march, a former Constable of Dover and Warden of the Cinque Ports. He and Lyons were accused by the Speaker of amassing immense fortunes by schemes and frauds to cheat the revenue, including the acceptance of 20,000 pounds from the King in repayment for a loan of 20,000 marks, the mark being worth two thirds of the pound.

One by one, members of the Commons, speaking in turn at a lectern in the center of the chamber, added their charges and complaints. The King's councillors, they said, had grown rich at the cost of impoverishing the nation; they had deceived the King and wasted his revenues, causing the repeated demands for fresh subsidies. The people were too poor and feeble to endure further taxation. Let Parliament discuss instead how the King might maintain the war out of his own resources.

Infuriated by the presumption of what he called "these low hedge-knights," Lancaster threatened in private "to give them such a fright that they shall not provoke me again." He was warned by an adviser that the Commons "have the countenance of the Prince your brother" and the support of the Londoners, who would not allow them to be touched. Biding his time, the Duke visited the Commons next day under a guise so gracious that members stared at him in amazement, but they were not diverted from pursuing the charges against Latimer and Lyons. They summoned as witnesses two former Treasurers and other officials, demanded to examine the public accounts, and conducted the proceedings as a formal trial. When all the evidence had been heard, the Commons cried with one voice, "Lord Duke, now you can see and hear that Lord Latimer and Richard Lyons have acted falsely for their own advantage for which we demand remedy and redress!"

When Latimer demanded to know by whom and by what authority he was being indicted, Sir Peter de la Mare supplied the historic answer that the Commons as a body would maintain all their charges in common. At one stroke he created the constitutional means for impeachment and removal of ministers. Lyons thought to spike the process by sending the Black Prince a bribe of £1,000 concealed in a barrel of sturgeon. The Prince sent it back, but the King, in more comfortable cynicism, accepted a similar bribe with the jest that he was only taking back his own.

Parliament found the charges proved. The two accused ministers and four subordinates, including Latimer's son-in-law, Lord Nevill, steward of the King's household, were judged guilty, dismissed from office and condemned to fines and imprisonment, although Latimer was shortly released on bail provided by a group of his friends. Even Alice Perrers was removed on charges of meddling in the law by sitting alongside judges on the bench and overawing them into decisions in favor of her friends. Miserably the King had to acquiesce in her banishment from court.

The petitions of reform were accepted in the King's name by John of Gaunt, who for the time being considered that he had insufficient support in the Lords to do otherwise. Besides annual Parliaments, the Commons demanded election of members by the "better folk" of the shires rather than by appointment of the sheriff. The petition for enforcement of the Statute of Laborers, with provisions for arrest and punishment of violators, reflected the growing antagonism between employer and worker. Likewise the growing antagonism to the papacy appeared in the petition for the exclusion of papal tax-collectors and prohibition of the export of money. No petition was made for peace, probably because the Commons believed the recent ill-fortunes in war had been due to the incompetent and corrupt leadership they were now replacing.

To contain John of Gaunt—or "bell the cat," as it appeared in Langland's fable—and to maintain the reforms once Parliament had dispersed, a new Council was named of nine lords and prelates including the ex-Chancellor, William of Wykeham, and the Archbishop of Canterbury, Simon of Sudbury, a rather pedestrian character of non-noble birth. The youth of the Council was characteristic of the early age at which men exercised power. Apart from Wykeham and Sudbury, six of the seven other members, including William Courtenay, Bishop of London, were under the age of 34, two of these under 30, and one, the Earl of March, was 25. Their opponent, the great Duke of Lancaster, was 36, born in the same year as Coucy.

Just as Parliament reached the peak of its accomplishment, the Prince fell into a fatal phase of his disease, complicated by dysentery. He grew so weak that he several times fainted and was thought to be dead. His chambers filled with doctors and surgeons, with the weeping and groaning of his followers and visits of the royal family for the final leave-taking. His sister Isabella and the Sire de Coucy came to the bedside to add their tears. John of Gaunt came, and the two younger brothers, Edmund of Langley, future Duke of York, something of a nonentity, and Thomas of Woodstock, unpleasant, violent, and ill-fated. In a parent's sad survival, the King came amid "great lamentation" and "no one there could keep from tears in great desolation at the circumstances and the sorrow of the King taking leave of his son forever," the fifth of his adult children to go before him.*

The doors of the Prince's room were opened so that old comrades and all who had served him could attend the passing, and "each one sobbed heartily and wept very tenderly," and he said to all, "I commend you to my son, who is very young and little, and pray you, as you have served me, to serve him loyally." He asked the King and Lancaster to swear an oath of support, which they gave without reserve, and all the earls, barons, and bachelors swore it too, and "of lamentation and sighing, of crying aloud and sorrowing, there was a great noise."

On the day before the end, the Prince's last will was completed, adding to the detailed arrangements already made. Though death was but the flight of the soul from its bodily prison, it was customarily accompanied by the most precise care for bequests, funeral, tombstone, and every other aspect of earthly remains, as if anxiety of what was to come sharpened reluctance to leave the world. The Prince's instructions were unusually detailed: his bed furnishings, including hangings embroidered with the deeds of Saladin, were left to his son, his warhorses were specifically disposed, his funeral procession was designed to the last trumpet, his tomb effigy ordered, with curious ambivalence, to show him "fully armed in the pride of battle . . . our face meek and our leopard helm placed beneath the head."

Attendant bishops urged the dying man to ask forgiveness of God and of all those he had injured. In a last flare of arrogance he refused, then, as the end approached, joined his hands and prayed pardon of God and man. But he could not sustain meekness. When Sir Richard Stury, a Lollard knight who had been among those dismissed from the King's household by the Good Parliament, and who at some point had evidently fallen foul of the Prince, came to "make his peace," the Prince said bitterly, "Come, Richard, come and look on what you have long desired to see." When Stury protested his good will, the Prince replied, "God pay you according to your deserts. Leave me and let me

---

* The others were Lionel, dead in Italy, Joanna in the Black Death, and two daughters, Margaret, married to the Earl of Pembroke, and Mary, married to the Duke of Brittany.

see your face no more." Begged by his confessors not to die without forgiving, he remained silent and only under pressure muttered at last, "I will do it." A few hours later, on June 8, 1376, he died aged 46.

As Earl of Bedford and member of the family, Coucy rode in the mile-long funeral procession with King Edward and the Prince's brothers behind the hearse drawn by twelve horses. On the monument at Canterbury, where the Prince desired to be buried, were inscribed verses in French on the traditional theme of the evanescence of earthly power: how in life the deceased had great nobility, lands, houses, treasure, silver and gold, but now of all bereft, with beauty gone and flesh wasted, he lies alone, reminding the passerby,

> Such as thou art, so once was I,
> As I am now, so shalt thou be.

Encased in armor, the effigy speaks differently: in what little can be seen of the face under a drooping mustache and close-covering helmet, there is no glimpse of Christian humility.

Left between a doddering King and a child heir, with only the hated regent Lancaster at the helm, the nation indulged in grief exaggerated by fear. At a time when defeats at sea had revived fears of French invasion, the English felt bereft of their protector, "for while he lived," wrote Walsingham, "they feared no inroad of any enemy, even as when he was present they feared no warlike encounter." Had the Prince lived and kept his health, he could have averted the troubles that were to arise under a child king, but not the social unrest nor the ebbing of victory. Although Walsingham reproached "thou untimely too-eager Death," death may not have been untimely, for, unlike his father, the Prince died while he still reflected the image of a hero. Froissart called him "the Flower of Chivalry of all the world" and the chronicler of the *Quatre Premiers Valois* acknowledged him "one of the greatest knights on earth, having renown above all men." Charles V held a requiem mass for his late enemy in the Sainte Chapelle, attended by himself and the ranks of French nobility.

What was it in the Black Prince that everyone admired? Comrades in chivalry felt pride in him because he represented their image of themselves; the massacre of Limoges was nothing to them. The people of England mourned him because his marvelous capture of a king at Poitiers and his other conquests had dressed them in greatness. Though his famous victory in Spain had proved ephemeral, his empire in Aquitaine had collapsed, and his prowess faded in disease, yet he represented that emotional choice a people makes to satisfy its craving for a leader.

The death of the Prince was the turning point in favor of John of Gaunt. While still in session, Parliament took the precaution of having the boy Richard presented to them in person to be confirmed as heir apparent. This being done, the memorable session closed on July 10, having lasted 74 days, the longest of any Parliament up to that time. Its spectacular accomplishment was wiped away the moment it dispersed. With no permanent organization or autonomous means of reassembly, the Commons ceased to exist as a body as soon as members scattered to shire and town. Its reforms had not been enacted as statutes and, like the reforms of the French Grand Ordinance, were simply rendered null by the hand that regained effective power. By favors or threats, Lancaster won over or neutralized the leading lords of the opposition, except for the Earl of March, who was compelled to resign as Marshal. His place was taken by his onetime ally Sir Henry Percy, who went over to the Duke.

The Lords' absence of political principle was the key to the collapse. Lancaster declared the entire parliamentary session invalid, reinstated Lord Latimer and his associates, dismissed the new Council and recalled the old, arrested and imprisoned without trial Sir Peter de la Mare when he attempted a protest, banished Bishop William of Wykeham from court and seized his temporal properties. When, sealing his control, he brought back Alice Perrers to reweave her spell over the King, the bishops who had acted with the Commons "were like dumb dogs unable to bark."

Except for impeachment, the work of the Good Parliament left hardly a constitutional trace. Yet in expressing so forcefully, and for its brief moment effectively, the will of the middle class, the role of the Commons strongly impressed the nation and taught an experience of political action that took root.

Witness to England's turmoil, Coucy returned to France in the summer or fall of 1376. Given the crisis during his visit, he is unlikely to have obtained a clear statement of what peace terms England was prepared to accept, but he would certainly have brought back a report of a torn and vulnerable nation. He is reported by Froissart to have advised Charles V not to wait for the King of England to offer combat when the truce should end, but to seek him out in his own territory because "the English are never so weak or so easy to defeat as at home."

Before Coucy left England, King Edward fell ill of a great malady and "all his physicians despaired and did not know how to care for him or what medicines to give him." Although he recovered spontaneously, the end of the reign was clearly approaching and with it the moment for Coucy's decision. Whether Isabella returned with him to France or remained with her sinking father is uncertain. Out of respect for his father-in-law, Coucy took no overt action at this time, but immediately on his return he accepted a diplomatic mission to the Count of Flanders in the interests of France against England. By now Coucy was a member of the Royal Council, clearly relied on by Charles V for his perspicacity and diplomacy. The King's anxieties had been increased by the mental illness of Queen Jeanne who in 1373 was afflicted "so that she lost her mind and her memory." After many prayers and pilgrimages by her husband who was devoted to her, she recovered her health and senses and was named, in the event of the King's death, guardian of the Dauphin. She was to be assisted by a Regency Council of fifty composed of prelates, ministers of crown and Parlement, and ten of the "most notable and sufficient" bourgeois of Paris. Twelve of the Council were to be in constant service of the Queen. As a member of the Council, Coucy received an annual wage of 1,000 francs in addition to payments of 500 francs a month on his annual pension of 6,000 francs. At about this time his daughter Marie, heiress of his domain, joined the household of the Queen who took charge of her education along with that of the Dauphin and his brothers and sisters. In April 1377 the records show a payment to Coucy of 2,000 francs, to be deducted from his pension, for furnishing his several castles with crossbows against the event of renewed war.

Still trying to avert that last calamity, Charles again delegated Coucy as diplomat to re-open negotiations with England, this time without benefit of the royal Dukes, to spare their expensive presence. Over the next six months, from January to June 1377, the parleys met variously at Boulogne, Calais, and halfway between at Montreuil on the coast. As the only lay noble in a group of ministers, Coucy had as his chief colleague Bureau de la Rivière, the Chamberlain, along with two ecclesiastical ministers, the Bishops of Laon and Bayeux, and various members of the Council.

The English envoys, representing adherents of both Lancaster and the late Prince, were men with whom Coucy was very likely acquainted, from his recent visit to England if not before. Varying from one meeting to another, they included the guardian of the heir to the throne, Sir Guichard d'Angle, a gallant and admired Gascon, long a campaigner with the Black Prince; the Lollard knight Sir Richard Stury, whom Lancaster had reinstated in office; Lord Thomas Percy, a veteran of the French wars and brother of Sir Henry Percy; the Earl of Salisbury; and lastly a trusted servant of the court connected with Lancaster's entourage, Geoffrey Chaucer.

Recently appointed to the well-paid and important post of Comptroller of the Wool Customs for the port of London, Chaucer was a successful civil servant whose other life as a poet had bloomed in an astonishing break with precedent: in 1369 he had written a long poem of courtly love, *The Book of the Duchess*, not in French appropriate to its subject and audience, but in unliterary and still unstable English. Though he was well acquainted with French, from which he had translated the *Roman de la Rose*, something in the ambience of his time prompted Chaucer to work in the same language as his gaunt and penniless contemporary, the street cleric Langland, who called himself "Long Will."

In different circumstances from Langland, Chaucer enjoyed a grant from the King of a daily pitcher of wine and was married to Katherine Swynford's sister Philippa, a relationship that had brought them both into the ducal household. *The Book of the Duchess* was a graceful elegy for Gaunt's first wife, Blanche, a well-beloved lady who had died at the age of 27 after bearing seven children. Though its choice of language was considered peculiar, its author lost no favor for that. In 1373 he was sent on a diplomatic mission to Italy to negotiate a commercial treaty with the Doge of Genoa and to conduct "secret business" in Florence. It was the year of Boccaccio's lectures in Florence on Dante. Chaucer returned steeped in new material, but his epic of *Troilus and Criseyde*, adapted from Boccaccio, had to wait while he was dispatched to treat of peace with France.

Poets and writers served frequently as ambassadors because their rhetorical powers conferred distinction on the elaborate speeches required on these occasions. Petrarch had served the Visconti as envoy or at least as ornamental figurehead of a mission. Boccaccio negotiated for Florence with the Pope, and the poet Deschamps acted for Charles V and his successor. Diplomacy was a ceremonial and verbose procedure with great attention paid to juridical detail and points of honor, which may have been one reason why it so often failed to produce agreement.

The prolonged parleys of 1377 acquainted Coucy with every pivot in the complex relationship of England and France. Offers and counter-offers and intricate bargains were discussed concerning Scotland, Castile, Calais, a proposed new dynasty for Aquitaine under a son of Edward III who would renounce his ties to England, or failing that, a partition, or an exchange of fiefs as complicated as a game of jack-straws. As always since the war began, nuncios of the Pope added their intensive efforts at mediation. Although the French held the upper hand, the English out of weakness and indecision could not be brought to accept any settlement, even a proposed match between Prince Richard and King Charles's seven-year-old daughter Marie.

The first parley broke up without progress and reconvened a month later. Twice the truce, due to expire April 1, was prolonged for a month to keep the negotiations alive. The envoys treated earnestly in long working sessions. What was Coucy's role, what Chaucer's? Their words have vanished; no record was kept because the discussions, especially regarding the marriage, were secret. Charles's instructions to his envoys stated that "The King does not wish the marriage to be broached on his part, but if the English mention it, you may listen to what they say and afterwards report to the King."

The French offered many proposals, including title to twelve cities of Aquitaine (which England already held), if Edward would give back Calais and all that he had taken in Picardy; either that, they said, "or else nothing." Stubbornly the English refused, believing that as long as they held their foothold in northern France they could yet return and regain their losses.

England's domestic situation during the parleys erupted in a new crisis. Lancaster had suppressed but far from settled English discontents. A new Parliament, sufficiently packed by the Duke to elect his steward as Speaker, obediently granted subsidies in January. The bishops were not so amenable and Wyclif was their target. He had not yet voiced his denial of the Eucharist and the priesthood, but his statement of civil dominion and disendowment was heresy enough. Although his call for reform of clerical abuses and his anti-papism had support among the clergy, they were not going to wait passively to be disendowed. Archbishop Sudbury and Bishop Courtenay of London summoned Wyclif to a convocation in February to answer for his heretical preaching. The recurring struggle of centuries between crown and Church, was now played out again in an uproarious fracas at St. Paul's Cathedral.

Lancaster hoped to discredit the bishops with the laity. He assigned four Masters of Theology to Wyclif's defense and proceeded himself in company with the Marshal, Sir Henry Percy, and their armed retinues to attend the hearings at St. Paul's. A crowd of aroused citizens filled the cathedral, angered by rumors that Lancaster was planning to extend the Marshal's jurisdiction over the city's traditional right to maintain public order. Bishop Courtenay was popular with the Londoners, the Duke was not. Anger rose when the armed guard shoved people aside to make way for the Duke and Marshal, followed by a loud quarrel when Courtenay refused the Duke's demand for a chair for Wyclif. The young and vigorous Bishop, himself the son of an earl and a descendant of Edward I, was not about to take orders inside his own precincts.

"I will make you bend, you and all the rest of the bishops," growled Lancaster. The crowd moved and shouted in menace, Lancaster threatened to arrest the disturbers, Courtenay told him if he did so in the cathedral he would be excommunicated. "A little more of this," the Duke was heard to mutter, "and I will have you dragged out of the church by the hair of your head." The crowd's rage exploded, the Duke and Marshal judged it wise to withdraw, Wyclif had not even spoken. Lancaster had succeeded in breaking up the proceedings, which was his object, but at a cost of turning popular sentiment ever more against himself, not against the bishops.

London seethed, and on news that Percy had arrested a citizen for slandering the Duke, boiled over. A mob gathered in a lynching mood to rush the Savoy Palace, and on its way fell upon a priest who spoke insultingly of Peter de la Mare and beat him to death, as Marcel's mob had murdered a hapless victim of its rage twenty years before. Warned while dining on oysters at the Savoy, Lancaster and Percy escaped by boat down the Thames to take refuge in the honored halls of the Princess of Wales and her son, where none would venture to assault them. Meanwhile Bishop Courtenay, also warned and fearing a catastrophe for which he might be blamed, had hastened to the Savoy Palace and succeeded in quieting the mob.

After flight and humiliation, Lancaster required that his authority be restored by a formal apology from the city. The Princess pleaded with the citizens to be reconciled with the Duke for her sake; the King's sovereignty was invoked; the authorities of London exacted the release of Peter de la Mare as the price of their apology; the clergy regained the offices of Chancellor and Treasurer. Factions were deepened and the state further torn by the affair.

In the excitement at St. Paul's, the matter of Wyclif had not been tested. The English prelates, caught between clerical interest and national sentiment, might have been content to let the matter drop, but the papacy was not. In May, Gregory XI issued five Bulls addressed to the English episcopacy and to the King and the University of Oxford, condemning Wyclif's errors and demanding his arrest. All discussion of his heretical doctrines was to be suppressed and all who supported them removed from office. An issue full of danger was added to all the other sources of strife. The new Parliament was strongly anti-papal; the King, babbling of hawks and hunting instead of attending to the urgent needs of his soul, was dying. For the moment, while England waited uneasily for the change of reign, the bishops held the proceedings against Wyclif in abeyance.

In France the negotiators held a final meeting in May at Montreuil in the ancient walled castle whose western ramparts faced the sea. The Chancellors of both countries took part, Pierre d'Orgement for France and the Bishop of St. David's for England. Terms were discussed at length in open session, which Charles wanted so that his final offer should be formally submitted and receive a firm answer. He did not get it. While generous in what it left in English hands, his offer withheld sovereignty over any part of France and insisted on Calais. Concealing rejection in evasion, the English said they lacked final authority and would have to submit the terms to their King. As the event shortly proved, the French must at this point have started preparing for belligerent action. While the talks petered out, the little Princess Marie died in Paris, eliminating the proposed marriage. The parley broke up with no place or date agreed upon for another meeting and no prolongation of the truce.

By the time the English envoys reached home, King Edward too had died, on June 23, the penultimate day of the truce. The jubilee year of his reign had passed virtually unnoticed and his death excited hardly more attention. He died deserted by the minions of power, including Alice Perrers, who was said to have stripped the rings from the King's fingers as she departed. A ten-year-old child mounted the throne, initiating the divisive time that was to spread its wreckage over the next century and confirm Langland's warning from Holy Writ, "Woe is the land with a youth for its king!"

Isabella de Coucy, summoned from France in April by couriers on "business of extreme urgency,"* was at her father's side when he died. Shortly before the end, she dispatched couriers to Coucy with news and "important questions" to be settled. On June 26, even before her father's funeral, she requested and received permission to return to France, evidently with urgent matters to discuss.

The problem for Coucy was more than simply one of allegiance; it was aggravated by great revenues, by bonds of kinship of great importance in that day, and by the oath of fellowship in the Order of the Garter. To repudiate fealty, kinship, and fellowship was no light thing.

---

* It is not entirely clear whether the couriers were sent *to* her in France or *by* her from England to her husband in France.

Other lords, like the Captal de Buch and Clisson, had transferred their loyalty from one side to another, but they were generally Gascons or Bretons or Hainaulters who did not feel themselves basically French or English. Coucy's own seneschal, the valiant Chanoine de Robersart, turned English while he was in England with Coucy in the 1360s. After swearing homage to Edward III, he coolly returned with Lancaster's army to ravage Picardy, which a few years earlier he had fought with such verve to defend. He was, however, a native of Hainault.*

Plainly, Coucy could play no great part in his country's affairs if he maintained neutrality as before. He not only needed to take sides; he doubtless wanted to take sides. National feeling had swelled in the years of French recovery. Writers gloried in the many cities of Picardy, Normandy, and Aquitaine retaken by Charles V. "Not Roland, not Arthur nor Oliver," exclaims the knight in the *Songe du Vergier,* a political allegory of 1376, "ever did such deeds of arms as you have done by your wisdom, your power and your prayers!" (and, the author might have added, by Charles's persuasive use of money). "When you came to the throne the horns and pride of your enemies reached up to heaven. Thanks to God, you have broken their horns and profoundly humiliated them."

Out of the polarity of war, a sense of French nationhood developed against the foil of England. In a dialogue between a French and an English soldier written about 1370 by the future Cardinal Pierre d'Ailly, the Englishman declares that Normandy at least should belong to England and that they are within their rights in this matter. "Hold your peace!" cries the Frenchman. "That is not true. You can hold nothing this side of the sea except by tyranny; the sea is and ought to be your boundary." That was a new idea. Homage and dynastic marriages were still the form of loyalty, but country was becoming the determinant. No longer could a French noble like Harcourt have so guiltlessly joined and guided the English in invasion of his native land. No longer could Coucy straddle loyalty across the Channel.

Two months after King Edward's death, Coucy addressed to Richard II a formal renunciation of "all that I hold of you in faith and homage." Dated August 26, 1377, and presented to Richard by several lords and squires sent by Coucy to witness the delivery, the letter recalled the "alliance" he had had with "my most honored and re-

---

* Robersart settled in England with three sons and founded a line that terminated some 200 years later in Amy Robsart, the ill-fated wife of Queen Elizabeth's favorite, Robert Dudley, Earl of Leicester.

doubted lord and father, the King lately deceased (on whom God have mercy)," and continued:

> Now it has happened that war has arisen between my natural and sovereign lord, on the one part, and you on the other, at which I grieve more than at anything that could happen in this world, and would it could be remedied, but my lord has commanded and required me to serve him, and acquit myself of my duty, as I am bound to do; whom as you know well I ought not to disobey; so I will serve him to the best of my power as I ought to do.
>
> Wherefore, most honorable and puissant lord, in order that no one may in any wise speak or say a thing against me, or against my honor, I acquaint you with the aforesaid things and return to you all that I may hold from you in faith or homage.
>
> And also, most honored sire, my most honored lord and father above named was pleased to ordain and place me in the most noble company and Order of the Garter; so let it please your most noble and puissant lordship to provide in my place whomsoever you may please, and therein hold me excused.

The double allegiance was broken. In becoming "a good and true Frenchman," Coucy had chosen a nationality, even if the word did not yet exist. Only one thing was remarkable about the choice: that he parted with his wife along with his English lands and fealty. It has generally been said that he felt obliged to part with her in order to be free to choose France, but this would have been necessary only if Isabella had refused to be reconciled to the loss of their English estates. On renunciation of allegiance, the properties would be subject to confiscation. Everything known about Isabella suggests that this was the determining factor. Her compulsive extravagance, her neurotic dependence on home and on her father's indulgence—which she may have hoped to transfer onto her brothers and nephew—her insecurity in France make it likely that the separation was her choice, whether or not it was also her husband's.

What Coucy felt for his vain, spoiled, selfish, willful wife—love, hate, or indifference—no evidence tells. Judging by what is known of her temperament, she was not a lovable Plantagenet, of whom history records few. In any event, she returned to and remained in England with her younger daughter, Philippa, who had always lived there. All her husband's English estates, "manors, hamlets, honours, domains, towns, lands, tenements, animals, provender, goods and chattels" were forfeited to the crown and cautiously delivered to a trusteeship for Isabella consisting of the Archbishop of York, two bishops, and four other commissioners. Since women were not precluded from owning property in their own right, the arrangement indicates that her brothers mistrusted her habits. The terms provided that the revenues would be paid to her by the trustees "as long as she remains in England."

Isabella's indeterminate status as neither wife nor widow lasted only two years. In April 1379 she died in unknown circumstances at the age of 47. All of Coucy's lands in England were eventually settled on his daughter Philippa.

The French renewed belligerency the instant the truce expired. In combination with the Spanish fleet, they launched a series of raids on England's south coast even before they learned of King Edward's death. In an effort to keep that event secret from them during the transfer of power, the English had "stopped incontinent all the passages of the kingdom, letting no one issue from the realm." The organization required to close all exits must have been considerable, but proved futile since the French had already started.

Under the command of Admiral Jean de Vienne, the French and Spaniards landed at Rye opposite Boulogne on June 29 and subjected it to 24 hours of savagery—burning, looting, killing men, women, and children and carrying off girls to the ships in deliberate emulation of the English savagery inflicted on the towns of France. In the flames, a church of "wonderful beauty" (according to Walsingham) was destroyed. Despite the insistence of a group of French knights who wanted to hold Rye as a permanent base—a kind of Calais in England —the Admiral refused. Occupation was not the French object but destruction and terror to bring the English to a peace treaty, and to prevent reinforcements for Calais, where the French were planning a major attack.

Meeting little effective resistance, the French continued down the south coast, attacking Folkestone, Portsmouth, Weymouth, Plymouth, Dartmouth, and marching ten miles inland to burn Lewes, where they scattered and slaughtered a body of 200 defenders led by the local prior and two knights. After sailing away, they returned a month later to devastate the Isle of Wight off Southampton. The dread that haunted the English out of a dark atavistic terror of ancient Danish raiders and conquering Normans was brought to awful reality.

Weakness of defense was not due to any false sense of security. These were the same towns attacked by the French in previous raids. Moreover in the last six months, as the truce waned, royal decrees had been raising the blackest specters of French invasion, but in the disarray of the time few defense measures had been taken. When the invader came, the fate of the towns did not greatly excite the nobles' protective efforts. Sir John Arundel, a knight of later infamy, successfully defended Hampton with 400 lances, but not until the citizens at his demand had put up the money in good coin to engage them.

When Lancaster's castle of Pevensey on the Sussex coast was endangered, the Duke was reported by the ever-hostile Walsingham to have refused to send defenders, with the callous remark, "Let the French burn it. I am rich enough to rebuild it." The remark sounds invented and as such breathes the same malice toward the nobles as animated another clerical chronicler, Jean de Venette—and for the same reason: failure of the knights to defend the land and people against their enemies. It was no accident that out of these invaded counties, Kent and Sussex, the Peasants' Revolt was to come.

Chapter 15

The Emperor in Paris

The most spectacular if not the most significant event of the decade in France was the visit to Paris of the Holy Roman Emperor, Charles IV, in December to January 1377–78. Coucy's notable social presence was again called on, as it had been for the wedding of the Duke of Burgundy, to lend his quality of grace and splendor to the escort of nobles for the visitor. In the jeweled glow of the occasion's majestic pageantry, Charles V's reign came to its zenith. The public was awed and gratified by the splendid ceremonies, and the propaganda value for Valois prestige probably equaled the incalculable expense.

Although Charles V was the third generation of Valois on the throne, he was not entirely free of uneasiness about the legitimacy of the title, the more so because of doubts about his own paternity. For private and for state reasons, his constant effort was to enhance the dignity of the crown. Politically his purpose in arranging the visit was to isolate England by tightening his ties with his uncle the Emperor, and he also had questions of territorial transfer and marital arrangements to discuss with him. Emotionally the kinship was important to him, although he knew his uncle to be calculating and slippery when it came to the test. Above all, he would have an occasion for the kind of grandiose public ceremony so important to medieval rule.

In theory the Holy Roman Emperor exercised a temporal sway matching the spiritual rule of the Pope over the universal community under God. Although vestiges of the imperial prestige remained, neither theory nor title any longer corresponded to existing reality. Imperial sovereignty in Italy was hardly more than a sham; it was dwindling on the western fringe of the empire in Hainault, Holland, and Luxemburg, and retreating in the east before the growing nationhood of Bohemia, Hungary, and Poland. Its core was a haphazard federation of German principalities, duchies, cities, leagues, margraves, archbishoprics, and counties under shifting and overlapping sovereignties. Hapsburgs and Luxemburgs, Hohenstaufens, Hohenzollerns, Wittelsbachs, and Wettins despoiled each other in endless wars; the *Ritter* or knight lived by robbing the merchant; every town believed its prosperity depended on the ruin of its rival; within the towns, merchants and craft guilds contended for control; an exploited peasantry smoldered and periodically flamed in revolt. The Empire had no political cohesion, no capital city, no common laws, common finances, or common officials. It was the relic of a dead ideal.

As theoretic lay leader of the Christian community, the Emperor was an elected sovereign currently drawn from the Luxemburg rulers of Bohemia. Charles IV's family ties with France, the preferred home of his father, John the Blind, were close. He had been brought up at the French court from the age of seven, had married a sister of Philip VI, and his own sister Bonne had married Philip's son Jean II. Though slightly hunchbacked and sallow of skin, he had been handsome in his prime, with long black hair and beard and lustrous black eyes. Now 61, he had outlived three wives, wedded a fourth, and married off seven or eight of his offspring into an intricate network of Hungarian, Bavarian, and Hapsburg dynasties. Seemingly affable and meek, he was quick and firm in decision, but restless and never still. He was given to whittling willow branches as he listened apparently abstracted to petitioners and advisers, and then made to each a reply "full of wisdom." He spoke and wrote Czech as well as French, Italian, German, and Latin, all equally proficiently. In being cerebral and shrewd, he was like his nephew Charles V, both being the opposite of irrational, intemperate fathers.

Charles IV was astute enough to recognize that the Empire of his title was not that of Charlemagne. His central concern was the Kingdom of Bohemia, whose territorial enlargement and cultural enrichment he pursued with effect that earned him the title "Father of His Country." He himself represented the nationalist tendencies that were making his imperial title obsolete.

While the Emperor's welcome was being prepared, Coucy entered the war with England, not in his home territory of Picardy but in Languedoc against the Gascons, under the leadership of the Duc d'Anjou, Governor of Languedoc. Like Lancaster also a king's brother, Anjou was driven by ambition for a crown of his own. In joining him, Coucy forged the connection that within a few years was to draw him into Anjou's fateful pursuit of the crown of Naples.

After two months of siege and skirmish in Gascony, Coucy returned to Paris to serve as an escort to the Emperor. The welcoming party that was to greet him at Cambrai on the Hainault border included, besides Coucy, the King's two chief advisers, Rivière and Mercier, and many nobles, knights, and squires, making in all a party of 300 resplendent horsemen. On December 22, they rode forward a league from the city to meet the advancing guests. Two hundred of Cambrai's leading townsmen and clergy, headed by the Bishop, rode with them through ranks of archers and commoners stationed at the gates. The Emperor in a furred winter cloak of gray on a gray horse, together with his eldest son, Wenceslas, King of the Romans, was escorted into the city, where he dismounted with some difficulty, being afflicted by gout, and accompanied the Bishop to prayers in the church.

His primary purpose in coming, he told the French lords afterward at dinner, was to visit King Charles and his Queen and their children whom he wished to see "more than any other creatures in the world." When he had accomplished this and presented his son to them, he would die with a quiet mind whenever God wished to take him. The Emperor was in fact in the last year of his life, and perhaps anticipating death, as people did in a time of few remedies or cures, he may have undertaken the uncomfortable journey more from a desire to revisit the Paris of his youth than for political advantage.

At each town in his progress through Picardy and the Ile de France, delegations met him in ceremonial welcome and presented gifts of meat, fish, bread, wines, and wagonloads of hay and oats, paid for by the King. On each occasion the Emperor was careful to state that he was a guest in a city of the King of France, while his hosts took pains that no bells should be rung or other rituals allowed that might signify imperial supremacy. The Emperor's choice of a gray horse was a gesture to mark the distinction from an entry into a town of the Empire, when he customarily rode a white horse. The emphasis placed by the authorized French chronicle on these points of protocol shows that the matter was much on the mind of the French King. Charles V wanted to build up the visit as a showcase for his claim of a just war, but not to leave his people under any illusions about the Emperor as overlord or universal monarch. The elaborate courtesies and festivities he arranged were a measure of the great significance he attached to the visit. In the semi-official chronicle of his reign, no less than eighty pages of detailed account were devoted to it.

At Compiègne near Paris, the Emperor was welcomed by the Duc de Bourbon, brother of the Queen, with a retinue in new liveries of parti-colored white and blue. At Senlis the welcomers were the Dukes of Berry and Burgundy and the Archbishop of Sens with a suite of 500 all dressed alike in gray and black, the knights in velvet and the squires in silk of the same colors. Enjoying this spectacle, the viewer would spread word of the occasion's grandeur, but its unhappy hero, whose gout took a turn for the worse, had to forgo a planned banquet and proceed the rest of the way by means of the Dauphin's litter harnessed to two mules and two horses.

At the Abbey of St. Denis, three archbishops, ten bishops, and the entire Royal Council awaited the Emperor for the visit to the royal mausoleum, where he had to be lifted from his litter and carried into the church to pray devoutly at the tomb of St. Louis. Expressing himself as "madly desirous" to see the famous treasure and relics of St. Denis, the Emperor was shown the preserved body of the saint, who, having been martyred by decapitation on the hill of Montmartre (hence its name), had walked with his head in his hands to the site where he laid the head down and founded the abbey. The Emperor gazed for a long time at the relics and the jeweled crown of St. Louis and the royal tombs, especially of Philip VI, his onetime brother-in-law.

His entry into Paris, for which the King had planned to present him with a black war-horse, had to be made instead in the Queen's litter. The Provost's Guard and 2,000 merchants, magistrates, and citizens of Paris, all on horseback and uniformly dressed in parti-colored gowns of white and violet, were waiting to escort him to the meeting with the King. Gout or not, this ceremony had to be equestrian. Lifted to the saddle, the Emperor, with his son alongside, awaited the parade advancing toward them from the old palace on the Ile de la Cité. Not for a generation had Paris witnessed such a royal procession. Particular care had been taken that, in spite of great crowds, everyone should be able to see. Guards with mace and sword were placed at every intersection along the route, and, warned by criers a day in advance, people were forbidden to cross the Rue St. Denis. Street barriers were erected and sergeants given precise orders as to where and when pedestrians and riders could or could not cross.

First came Marshal Sancerre and his guard wearing two swords each and ruffled hats, followed by the King's trumpeters flourishing bright pennants from their silver trumpets. The four dukes—Berry, Burgundy, Bourbon, and the Duc de Bar, husband of the King's sister and future father-in-law of Marie de Coucy—rode two by two, followed by twelve counts, including Coucy as Count of Soissons, and a long parade of prelates, nobles, judges, councillors, and officers of the royal household, each group uniformly dressed according to function.

Chamberlains wore parti-colored velvet or silk in two shades of scarlet, stewards were in velvet of sky blue and fawn, grooms of the King's armor in blue damask, ushers in blue and red, butlers in white and fawn satin, chefs and squires of the kitchen in fur-lined silk surcoats with pearl buttons, valets de chambre in black striped in white and gray, wine stewards in brown stripes over red.

Last came the scrawny long-nosed King riding a white palfrey and wearing a fur-lined scarlet mantle and beaked hat "after the ancient manner." The length of the procession took half an hour to leave the palace, and because of the press of people, it was even longer before the two sovereigns came face to face. Both doffed their hats as they met. Taking care not to rub against the painful legs of his uncle, Charles placed himself between the Emperor and Wenceslas, and so they rode three abreast back through the city to the palace.

Seated in a gold-draped chair in the courtyard where once Provost Marcel had dumped the bodies of the murdered Marshals, the Emperor heard an address of welcome by his host, and afterward in their chambers "they removed their hats and spoke together with great friendship and joy of meeting." The next days were filled with banquets, conferences, gift-giving by the goldsmiths of Paris of their finest art, and special services and viewing of relics in the Sainte Chapelle, so richly decorated and lighted that "it was a marvel to see." In between, the sovereigns held private talks, one lasting three hours "without even the Chancellor present," as the Chancellor's chronicler took care to note, "and what they said no one knows."

The state dinners drew on all the resources of the 14th century to delight, amaze, and glut the guests. So many torchbearers stood like living candlesticks against the pillars of the great stone hall that "one could see as well as if it were day." So many courses and dishes were served that for once there were "too many to tell," and indeed too many for the ailing guest of honor. The King had ordered four courses of ten pairs of dishes in each, but thoughtfully eliminated one course of ten to reduce the time the Emperor would have to sit at table. As it was, he would have had to partake of thirty pair of such dishes as roast capons and partridges, civet of hare, meat and fish aspics, lark pasties and rissoles of beef marrow, black puddings and sausages, lampreys and savory rice, entremet of swan, peacock, bitterns, and heron "borne on high," pasties of venison and small birds, fresh- and salt-water fish with a gravy of shad "the color of peach blossom," white leeks with plovers, duck with roast chitterlings, stuffed pigs, eels reversed, frizzled beans—finishing off with fruit wafers, pears, comfits, medlars, peeled nuts, and spiced wine.

So well ordered was the service for 800 guests at the banquet of January 6 that the low tables were served at the same time and with the same dishes as the high, and all alike were set with gold and silver plate. The crowned heads and guests of highest rank sat at five tables on raised platforms, each under an individual canopy of cloth of gold, with the Emperor, King, and Archbishop of Reims at a marble table in the center. Cloth of gold adorned with fleurs-de-lys made the tablecloths and festooned pillars and windows. Tapestries covered the walls between. Coucy sat with the Duc de Bourbon at the table of the nine-year-old Dauphin "to keep him company and guard him from the great multitude." Young Marie de Coucy was among the "great ladies" attending the Queen. At late refreshment after entertainment by minstrels, the Duc de Berry and his brother of Burgundy served wine and spices to the King and Emperor, but whether on horseback, as was often the custom of noble servitors, the exhausted chronicler fails to say. On a previous visit by the Emperor to the Count of Savoy in 1365, mounted nobles had served platters of food poised on the ends of lances especially fitted with brackets for the purpose. Whatever its moral limitations, chivalry required a strong wrist.

For the grand climax, all 800 guests moved to the Hall of Parlement, where the spectacle presented to them, representing the taking of Jerusalem by the First Crusade, was a triumph of the stagecraft in which the 14th century excelled. Artificers at banquets, as described in Chaucer's Franklin's Tale, could bring bodies of water into the hall, make boats row up and down, grim lions appear, flowers spring from meadows, grapevines grow, and a castle seemingly made of stone vanish, or "thus it seemed to every manne's sight." At a banquet given in Coucy's time by a certain Vidame de Chartres, the ceiling painted like a sky opened to allow the dinner to descend on machines resembling clouds, which raised the dishes again when they had been emptied. An artificial storm lasting half an hour accompanied dessert, dropping a rain of scented water and a hail of sweetmeats.

In the miracle plays and mysteries staged for the populace, realism was the desired effect. A system of weights and pulleys resurrected Jesus from the tomb and lifted him to a ceiling of clouds. Angels and devils were made to appear magically through trapdoors; Hell opened and closed its monstrous mouth, and Noah's flood inundated the stage from casks of water overturned backstage while stone-filled barrels turned by cranks resounded with thunder. When John the Baptist was decapitated, the actor was whisked away so cunningly in exchange for a fake corpse and fake head spilling ox blood that the audience shrieked in excitement. Actors playing Jesus sometimes remained tied to the cross reciting verses for three hours.

More completely than any other medium, the stage mirrored medieval life. Developing out of liturgical plays performed at the church door, drama had left the church for the street, where it was produced by guilds and *confréries* on wheeled platforms with different scenes drawn along in succession. The plays traveled from town to town, attracting all of society as audience—peasants and bourgeois, monks and students, knights and ladies, and the local seigneur in a front-row seat. For a major performance, criers went out to inform the public a day in advance. Subject matter was religious, but manner was secular, designed for entertainment. Every mystery of the Christian story, and its central mystery of salvation through the birth and death of Christ, was made physical and concrete and presented in terms of everyday life—irreverent, bloody, and bawdy. The shepherds who watched by night were portrayed as sheep-stealers, pathos in the sacrifice of Isaac was played to the hilt, the favorite comic relief was the on-stage donkey for Balaam's ass or for the Virgin to ride on the Flight into Egypt or for the Three Kings in lieu of camels. The "hin-han" brayed by the actor inside the donkey's skin and the turds dropped from a lifted tail evoked howls of delight even when the donkey bore Jesus into Jerusalem.

Sex and sadism were relished in the rape of Dinah, in the exposure of Noah naked and drunk, the sins of the Sodomites, the peeping of the Elders at Susanna, and all the varieties of torn flesh in the martyrdom of saints. Scenes of torture in revolting realism were regular theatrical fare, as if a violent time bred enjoyment of violence. Nero slitting open the belly of his mother to see where he came from was performed with the aid of gory entrails, supplied by the local pork butcher, spilling from the victim. *Schadenfreude* was not peculiar to the Middle Ages, but it was a dark variety indeed, induced by plague and successive calamities, that found expression in gruesome scenes of the tortures on the cross, with the soldiers shown spitting on the Redeemer of man.

In an age of anxiety, the *Miracles of Notre Dame,* a series of plays originating in the second half of the century, supplied what comfort faith in divine omnipotence could offer. No wretch so poor or wicked, no misery or injustice but could be remedied by the miraculous intervention of the Holy Virgin. The most vulnerable figure of society, a wronged woman, seduced and deserted or falsely accused of crime, was usually the central figure. In one play a long-barren woman whose prayers to the Virgin have at last brought her a son is exhausted by the pains of childbirth and falls asleep while bathing her baby. When he drowns in the tub, the mother is accused of child-murder and condemned to the stake. In response to her husband's prayers, Notre Dame descends from Heaven to comfort him, and when the mother, about to be burned, begs for one last look at her child, he is restored to life in her arms.

Guilty passions, faithless spouses, agonies of childbirth, frail nuns and pregnant abbesses, adulterous queens, cruel deaths of children made up the plots. All humanity—proud cardinals and beggars, bailiff and butcher's wife, Jews, innkeepers, riotous students, knights, woodcutters, midwives, village fools—were the characters. The Virgin befriended and forgave them all, even the mother of a Pope who is so swollen with pride that she thinks herself greater than the Mother of God. After appropriate punishment, she too receives grace.

God in the plays was costumed in a white robe with gilt wig and beard and gilded face, angels had gilded wings, Herod had a black beard and Saracen's robes, devils and demons wore grisly masks, horns, forked tails, and body suits covered with horsehair. Often they ran through the audience to pinch and frighten the spectators.

Apocalypse, never far out of mind, was enacted in the Day of Judgment and the Harrowing of Hell when Christ goes down to lead Adam and the prophets out to Paradise. Anti-Christ appears at his appointed time, traditionally fixed at three and a half years before the Last Judgment. Born of Satan's seduction of a woman of Babylon, and instructed in all the demonic arts, he gains such power that kings and cardinals pay him homage until he is overthrown at Armageddon in the triumph of good over evil. The saved are separated from the damned, and angels empty the vials of wrath.

A Lollard preacher in England, seeking to justify the 14th century stage, said that men and women seeing the Passion of Christ and his saints would be moved to "compassion and devotion, weeping bitter tears, not scorning God but worshiping." Seeing how the Devil moved people to lechery and pride and made them his servants to bring them to Hell, they would be converted to "good living," therefore the playing of miracles "turneth men to bileve and not perverteth." Perhaps unconvinced by his own argument, he added reasonably that men must have some recreation and it was better, or at least less evil, that they took it in the playing of miracles than by other "japes."

The siege of Jerusalem played before the Emperor broke away from previous subject matter to present for the first time the re-enactment of a historical event. Its technical marvels and verve of staged battle were breathtaking. The crusaders' ship, complete with mast, sail, and flying banners, was propelled down the hall so "lightly and softly" as actually to seem to be moving on water. Knights, wearing the correct heraldry if not costumes of nearly 300 years before, poured from the ship to assault the reconstructed battlements of Jerusalem. From a painted Moslem tower a muezzin chanted the wailing Arabic prayer. Saracens in turbans flashed wicked scimitars, crusaders were thrown from siege ladders, the onlookers gazed in wonder, stirred by the beauty and excitement to enthusiasm for a new crusade—which indeed was the purpose of the performance. The leading propagandist of crusade, Philippe de Mézières, was much admired by the King, who had appointed him a member of the Royal Council and tutor of his son.

Next day provided still another wonder. A specially constructed boat, fitted like a residence with halls, chambers, fireplaces, chimneys, and a court bed, was provided to convey the royal party half a mile down the river to the new palace of the Louvre. The Emperor was visibly impressed. Charles showed him the reconstructions by which he had transformed the old fortress into a "true royal palace"—windows and wide staircase, chapels, gardens, frescoes, paneled rooms, as well as the original weapons room, where arrows were fashioned and women feathered the shafts. After dinner the faculties of the University were presented to the Emperor, who responded in Latin to a formal address by the University's chancellor.

Charles's ultimate purpose, the apotheosis of his case against England, was reached the following day at a state assembly attended by fifty of the imperial party and about the same number of leading French personages—royal Dukes, prelates, peers including Coucy, knights, and members of the Council. According to the chronicler, the King was motivated by "the lies the English were spreading in Germany," but more fundamentally he seems always to have been seeking some ultimate justification. He would lay before his uncle, perhaps as a father figure, the concessions he had offered for the sake of peace and let him judge of their sufficiency.

Charles spoke for two hours, tracing the ancient quarrel down the centuries from Eleanor of Aquitaine to the Treaty of Brétigny and rehearsing the intricate legalities under which the treaty had been voided and war renewed in 1369. If the speech was a tour de force of legal and historical argument, the Emperor's response was a masterpiece of ornate formula. He spoke of loyalty and kinship, and the depth of his and his son's and his subjects' devotion which entitled them to be considered the defenders of the King's honor and realm, brothers and children—let them indeed be called "allies." Yet, when examined, the substance was shadowy. If, in the end, the speech—and the entire visit—produced no concrete alliance, the imposing verbal effect may have been what Charles of France wanted.

He did not stint in further courtesies and gift-giving, exchanging with the Emperor presents of enameled goblets and jeweled daggers set with rubies and diamonds, sapphires and pearls. Princely magnificence, Charles considered, was best displayed by jewels, tapestries, and the goldsmith's art. His uncle was not embarrassed to ask for an exquisite Book of Hours, and when Charles set two before him, one large and one small from which to choose, the Emperor, preferring not to select, kept both. Sensibility had its hour when he visited the Queen and her mother, the dowager Duchess of Bourbon, whose sister Beatrice had been his first wife. Tears flowed freely in mutual memory although Beatrice had been dead for thirty years and her place filled by three wives since. The last day was spent in sylvan pleasure at Vincennes, where at the edge of the noble forest on the bank of the river the King had built his favorite country manor, called Beauté-sur-Marne. Furnished in luxury and comfort with beautiful tapestries, a Flemish organ, and turtledoves cooing in the courtyard, it was lauded by the poet Deschamps as "Of all places pleasant and agreeable, / Gay and lovely for joyous living."

Departing by way of Reims, the Emperor was escorted to the frontiers of the kingdom by Coucy and attendant nobles. Possibly hastened by the exertions of so much ceremonial, his death followed ten months later in November 1378.

The memorable visit, even if devoid of practical effect, honored and enhanced the crown of France. Although royal powers were undefined, and the Council's authority unformulated, and the institutions of royal government always in flux, Charles V's sense of the crown's role was firm: kingship depended on the King's will. The sovereign was not above the law; rather, his duty was to maintain the law, for God denied Paradise to tyrants. Sanction derived in theory from the consent of the governed, for kings and princes, as a great theologian, Jean Gerson, was to remind Charles's successor, "were created in the beginning by the common consent of all." As Charles knew well, the cult of monarchy was the basis of the people's consent. He deliberately fed the cult while at the same time he was the first to show that rulership could be exercised "from the chamber" independent of personal leadership in battle.

In the bright apogee of 1378, France was not immune from trouble. War had come back to Brittany and Normandy; Charles of Navarre, as venomous as ever after twenty years, was again in dangerous league with the English; heresy and sorcery were on the rise, testifying to needs unsatisfied by the Church.

For all its dominance, there never was a time when the Church was not resisted somewhere by dissent. In the distracted 14th century, when God seemed hostile to man or else hidden behind ecclesiastical counting of coins and selling of benefices, the need for communion with God was never greater, nor less satisfied by His appointed agents. A Church preoccupied with war in Lombardy and revenues in Avignon and the mundane necessities of maintaining its position was not ministering to popular need. The friars' movements had been the last effort for reform from within, and when they, too, succumbed to the lure of endowments, the seekers of spiritual comfort increasingly sought it outside the Church in the mystical sects.

The Beghards, or Brethren of the Free Spirit, who claimed to be in a state of grace without benefit of priest or sacrament, spread not only doctrinal but civil disorder. One of the sects of voluntary poverty that perennially rose against the establishment, they had flourished for over a century in Germany, the Low Countries, and northern France, sometimes fading or driven underground by persecution but re-stimulated in the 14th century by the worldliness of Avignon and the mendicant orders. Because the Free Spirits believed God to be in themselves, not in the Church, and considered themselves in a state of perfection without sin, they felt free to do all things commonly prohibited to ordinary men. Sex and property headed the list. They practiced free love and adultery and were accused of indulging in group sex in their communal residences. They encouraged nudity to demonstrate absence of sin and shame. As "holy beggars," the Brethren claimed the right to use and take whatever they pleased, whether a market woman's chickens or a meal in a tavern without paying. This included the right, because of God's immanence, to kill anyone who forcibly attempted to interfere.

If the Brethren's habits came to be less pure than their precepts, the impulse was nevertheless religious. They were in search of personal salvation, not social justice. Medieval heresies were concerned with God, not man. Poverty was embraced not only in imitation of Christ and the Apostles but in deliberate contrast to the avarice that corrupted men of property. To be without property was to be without sin. Dissent was not a denial of religion but an excess of piety in search of a purer Christianity. It became heresy by definition of the Church, which recognized in the mystics' renunciation of property the same threat as in Wyclif's disendowment.

In monk-like robes deliberately ragged, the Brethren of the Free

Spirit cluttered the towns like sparrows, preaching, begging, interrupting church services, scorning monks and priests. Drawn from clerks, students, dissenting clergy, and from the propertied class, especially women, they were articulate and usually literate. Women, out of their frustrations and search for ecstasy, were prominent among the mystics. In the Béguines they had a sect of their own, a lay order that followed its own religious rule of good works and, when nunneries had no room, provided a place for unmarried women and widows, or, as a bishop wrote in criticism of the Béguines, a retreat from the "coercion of marital bonds." Members joined the Béguines by taking an oath of dedication to God before a parish priest or other cleric, but the movement was never quite sanctioned by the Church. At street meetings the Béguines read the Bible translated into French.

While the Brethren of the Free Spirit admitted both sexes, its two major gospels were written or formulated by women, one a shadowy figure known only as Schwester Katrei, the other named Marguerite Porete, who wrote *The Mirror of Free Souls* and was excommunicated and burned along with her book in 1310. Following her, the daughter of a rich merchant of Brussels known as Bloemardine attracted fervent disciples by her preaching. In 1372 the movement was condemned by the Inquisition, its books were burned in Paris on the Place de Grève, and a woman leader of the French group, Jeanne Dabenton, was burned at the stake together with the corpse of a male associate who had died in prison. Like the heresy of the Spiritual Franciscans, the sect of the Free Spirit persisted and spread in spite of the Inquisition.

Apocalypse was in the air. The Duc d'Anjou in 1376, in the course of authorizing an annual corpse for dissection by the medical faculty of Montpellier, took notice that the population was so reduced, owing to epidemics and wars, that "it may be diminished to ever greater extent and the world brought to nothing." Under the influence of malign and capricious events, overwrought minds turned to magic and the supernatural. The Inquisitor of France, on inquiring of the Pope in 1374 if he should take cognizance of sorcerers, was authorized by Gregory XI to pursue them vigorously. Since early in the century the papacy had been taking an increasingly punitive view of recourse to the supernatural, especially during the hyperactive reign of John XXII. In a series of Bulls in the 1320s, Pope John had equated sorcerers with heretics and authorized their punishment as such, since they had made a "pact with Hell," forsaking God and seeking the aid of the Devil. He ordered their books of magic lore to be sought out and burned. Despite his alarm, prosecuted cases were few until the second half of the century, when sorcery and its links to demonology took on new life and were met by new efforts at repression. In 1366 the Council of Chartres ordered anathema to be pronounced against sorcerers every Sunday in every parish church.

Demonology and the black arts were the opposite of heresy, not more pious than the Church but impious, seeking communion with the Devil, not God. Adepts in their rites worshiped Lucifer arrayed as the King of Heaven and believed that he and the other fallen angels would recapture Heaven while the Archangel Michael and his fellows would take their places in Hell. A pact with the Devil offered pleasure without penitence, enjoyment of sexuality, riches, and earthly ambitions. If the price was eternal hellfire, that was what many could expect anyway at the Day of Judgment. Though old and indigenous, demonology was never more than an aberration, but insofar as it offered an alternative answer, it was seen by the Church as dangerous.

The problem was to distinguish between diabolic and lawful magic powers. Respectable sorcerers claimed that their images of wax or lead acquired potency through being baptized and exorcised, that their mysteries were consecrated by celebration of the mass, that God was invoked to compel the obedience of demons—indeed, that God flowed from their arts, as proved by the fulfillment of wishes. Theologians disallowed such pretensions. Even if it was only to recover a straying lover or cure a peasant's sick cow, sorcerers were offering aid outside the approved channel of prayer, priests, and saints. As the times darkened, all magic and witchcraft came to be taken as an implied contract with Satan.

Women turned to sorcery for the same reasons they turned to mysticism. In Paris in 1390 a woman whose lover had jilted her was tried for taking revenge by employing the magical powers of another woman to render him impotent. Both were burned at the stake. In the following year two more women were condemned on charges of *maleficiam* or doing evil. Since confessions in trials for sorcery were extracted by torture, they tended to reflect the accusations of diabolic power drawn up by the prosecutors, and since the accused were likely to be cranks or fanatics or otherwise disturbed, they did not hesitate to claim the powers imputed to them. They admitted to consorting with demons and to pacts with the Devil for lust or revenge, to diabolic rites and flights through the night to copulate with the Devil in the shape of a monstrous black cat or goat with flaming eyes or a gigantic man with black skin, a huge phallus, and eyes like burning coals. The Devil was a Gothic satyr with horns and cloven hoofs, fierce teeth and claws, a sulfurous smell and sometimes ass's ears. The lore developed as much from the minds of the prosecutors as from the hallucinations of the accused, and together they laid the ground for the rage against witch-craft that was to explode upon the next century.

The clear voice of common sense spoke through the King's ad-viser in philosophy, Nicolas Oresme, who despised both astrology and sorcery. A man of scientific spirit though a bishop, he was a mathe-matician and astronomer and translator of the *Politics* and *Ethics* of Aristotle. One of his books began with the sentence, "The earth is round like a ball," and he postulated a theory of the earth's rotation. Refuting the powers ascribed to sorcerers, he denied that they could invoke demons, although he did not rule out the existence of demons. Not all things, he wrote, could be explained by natural causes; some marvels or extraordinary strokes of fortune must be the work of angels or demons, but he preferred to look for a natural and rational explana-tion. Magicians, he pointed out, were adept at using aids to favor illu-sions—darkness, mirrors, drugs, or gases and fumes that could be made to give rise to visions. The basis for illusion was likely to be an abnor-mal state of mind induced by fasting or by frightening phenomena. A man ahead of his time, Oresme suggested that the source of demons and specters could be the disease of melancholy. He also made the point that evidence for sorcery was derived from confessions under torture, and that many miracles were fraudulently devised by the clergy to increase offerings to their churches.

Oresme proves the frailty of generalization. He was highly es-teemed by the same King in whose employ the astrologer Thomas of Pisano fashioned wax images to destroy the English.

Scientific spirit could not dispel the sense of a malign influence upon the times. As the century entered its last quarter, the reality and power of demons and witches became common belief. The theological faculty of the University of Paris in a solemn conclave at the end of the century declared that ancient errors and evils, almost forgotten, were emerging with renewed vigor to infect society. They drew up a statement of 28 articles to disprove, not the power of the black arts, but their lawfulness. No less emphatically they rejected the incredulity of those who questioned the existence and activity of demons.

Unorthodoxy, as always, made disproportionate noise. Heresy and sorcery, though increasingly significant, were not the norm. In 1378 the real danger to the Church emerged from within.

Chapter 16

The Papal Schism

In Italy the war for control of the Papal States had renewed itself in 1375. During the temporary peace, Italian hatred of the papacy's mercenaries and French legates had not subsided but swelled. The agents of a French Pope ruled with the contempt of colonial governors for natives. When the nephew of the Abbot of Montmayeur, legate in Perugia, was seized by desire for the wife of a Perugian gentleman and, breaking into her chamber, would have ravished her by force, the lady, seeking escape by the window to an adjoining house, lost her footing, fell to the street, and was killed. In response to a delegation of outraged citizens who demanded justice against his nephew, the Abbot said carelessly, "*Quoi donc!* [What then!] Did you suppose all Frenchmen were eunuchs?" The tale spread from city to city, feeding the antagonism of which Florence now made herself the champion.

Establishment of a strong papal state at her borders was felt by Florence as a threat, heightened by the incursion into Tuscany of Hawkwood during a lapse in papal pay. Forced to buy him off at a huge cost of 130,000 florins, the Florentines believed he had been encouraged to come against them by the Pope. Anti-papism now pervaded Florentine politics in a wild swing of the perpetual feud of Guelf and Ghibelline. Described in exasperation by a later French Governor of Genoa, this ancient roil kept Italians at each other's throats out of inherited, witless animosity.

> For with no other quarrel of land or seigneury, they have only to say, "You are Guelf and I am Ghibelline; we must hate each other," and for this reason only and knowing no other, they kill and wound each other every day like dogs, the sons like the fathers, and so year by year the malice continues and there is no justice to remedy it. . . . And from this come the despots of this country, elected by the voice of the

people, without reason or right of law. For as soon as one party prevails over the other and is the stronger, then those who see themselves on top cry "Long live so-and-so!" and "Death to so-and-so" and they elect one of their number and kill their adversary if he does not flee. And when the other party regains the advantage, they do the same and in the fury of the people, from which God protect us, all is torn to pieces.

Until now, popular antagonism toward the papal party represented by the Guelfs had not reached the point of taking up arms against the Church. When during a food scarcity in 1374–75 papal legates embargoed the export of grain from the Papal States to Florence, passions reached the point of belligerence. Under the slogan *Libertas* inscribed in gold on a red banner, Florence organized a revolt of the Papal States in 1375 and formed a league against the papacy, joined by Milan, Bologna, Perugia, Pisa, Lucca, Genoa, and all the various potentates who had territorial ambitions in the Papal States.

To one chronicler it seemed "as if these times are under the rule of a planet which produces strife and quarreling." In an Augustinian monastery near Siena, he recorded, "the monks murdered their Prior with a knife," and in a neighboring abbey, after intramural fighting, "six brethren were turned out." Because of quarreling among the Carthusians, the General of the order came and moved them all to other houses. "It was no better among kinsfolk by blood. . . . The whole world was fighting. In Siena there was no one who kept his word, the people disagreed with their leaders and agreed with no one, and truly the whole world was a valley of shadows."

The revolt brought into action an individual destined to be the catalyst of new calamity. Robert of Geneva, the Pope's Legate in Italy, was a cardinal of 34 who shrank from no force to regain control of the papal patrimony. A brother of the Count of Geneva, a descendant of Louis VII and cousin of Charles V, a relative of the Counts of Savoy and of half the sovereign houses of Europe, he shared the lack of inhibition characteristic of so many princes. He was lame and squinting, and described as either squat and fat or handsome and well formed, depending on partisanship in the coming schism. Imposing and autocratic in manner, he was sonorous of voice, eloquent with tongue and pen, cultivated and well read in several languages, sophisticated and artful in his management of men.

To reconquer the Papal States, he persuaded Gregory XI to hire the Bretons, worst of the mercenary bands, with the extra incentive of removing them from the vicinity of Avignon. Crossing the Alps into Lombardy in May 1376, they spread terror across Italy with swords blessed and consecrated by the Cardinal Legate. They failed, however, to take Bologna, keystone of the Papal States, and suffered several defeats by the Florentines, to the wrath of their employer. With the fury of a conqueror defied, Cardinal Robert determined to set an example by atrocity and found his occasion at Cesena, a town near the east coast between Ravenna and Rimini. When the Bretons who were quartered there seized supplies without paying for them, they provoked an armed rising of the citizens. Swearing clemency by a solemn oath on his cardinal's hat, Cardinal Robert persuaded the men of Cesena to lay down their arms, and won their confidence by asking for fifty hostages and immediately releasing them as evidence of good will. Then summoning his mercenaries, including Hawkwood, from a nearby town, he ordered a general massacre "to exercise justice." Meeting some demurral, he insisted, crying, *"Sangue et sangue!"* (Blood and more blood!), which was what he meant by justice.

He was obeyed. For three days and nights beginning February 3, 1377, while the city gates were closed, the soldiers slaughtered. "All the squares were full of dead." Trying to escape, hundreds drowned in the moats, thrust back by relentless swords. Women were seized for rape, ransom was placed on children, plunder succeeded the killing, works of art were ruined, handicrafts laid waste, "and what could not be carried away, they burned, made unfit for use or spilled upon the ground." The toll of the dead was between 2,500 and 5,000. From the sacked city, 8,000 refugees fled to Rimini begging for alms. A generation later the great preacher Bernardino of Siena still made audiences tremble with the tale of horror.

"Not to be held entirely infamous," Hawkwood, it was said, sent a thousand women to safety in Rimini and allowed some men to escape. Carrying out the solution threatened by Solomon, he was also reported to have cleft in half a nun over whom two of his soldiers were fighting. On the whole, however, he had more relish for money than for killing, and shortly after the massacre of Cesena he abandoned the papal employ, where pay was slack, for more lucrative contracts offered by Florence and Milan. To make employment of the great mercenary permanent, Bernabò Visconti gave one of his illegitimate daughters by a favorite mistress in marriage to Hawkwood with a dowry of 10,000 florins. The political resources of a prince with 36 living children were far-reaching.

For his remaining two decades Hawkwood lived in riches and respect, elected Captain of Florence by the Signoria, and paid for his services, or for immunity, by almost all the city-states of central and northern Italy. He bequeathed to Italy an example of successful rapine to inspire Italian *condottieri*—Jacopo del Verme, Malatesta, Coleoni, Sforza—who were soon to replace the foreign captains.

Robert of Geneva, who became for Italy the "Man of Blood" and "Butcher of Cesena," never attempted to excuse or extenuate his action. As far as he was concerned, the citizens were rebels like those of Limoges to the Black Prince. His resort to terror, resounding through Italy, did not enhance the authority of the Church. "People no longer believe in the Pope or Cardinals," wrote a chronicler of Bologna on the massacre, "for these are things to crush one's faith."

Meanwhile, Florence was excommunicated by the Pope, who invited non-Florentines to prey upon the commerce of the outlaw. Her caravans could be seized, debts could not be collected, clients were not bound to keep their contracts. Florence retaliated by expropriating ecclesiastical property and forcing local clergy to keep churches open in defiance of the ban. Popular sentiment was so aroused that the Committee of Eight who directed strategy were called the Eight Saints, and the conflict with the papacy came to be known in Italian annals as the War of the Eight Saints.

By now both sides had reason to want to end the war. Besides drastic effect on Florentine commerce, the excommunication had divisive effects on the league. To hold the multiple rivalries of Italian city-states in cohesion for long was impossible. For the papacy to maintain control of the Papal States from Avignon was equally impossible, and a new danger was added when Florence offered inducements to Rome to join the league. It was as apparent to Gregory as to his predecessor that necessity was calling the papacy home. A clamorous voice at his elbow was adding force to the summons.

Since June 1376, Catherine of Siena, who was to be canonized within a century of her death and ultimately named patron saint of Italy along with Francis of Assisi, had been in Avignon exhorting the Pope to signal reform of the Church by returning to the Holy See. Already at 29 a figure with an ardent following and an insistent voice, she was revered for her trances and raptures and her claim to have received, while in ecstasy after communion, the stigmata of the five wounds of Christ on hands, feet, and heart. While these remained visible only to her, such was her repute that Florence commissioned her as ambassador to negotiate reconciliation with the Pope and a lifting of the interdict. Catherine's larger mission in her own mind was apostleship for all humanity through her own total incorporation with God and Jesus, and through a cleansing and renewing of the Church. Her authority was the voice of God speaking directly to her, and preserved in the *Dialogues* dictated to her secretary-disciples and believed by them to have been "given in person by God the Father, speaking to the mind of the most glorious and holy virgin, Catherine of Siena . . . she being the while entranced and actually hearing what God spoke in her."

Behind the trances were extreme austerities of fasting and deprivations of sleep and comfort. The more extreme in such practices, the more a person was removing himself from material life. (According to La Tour Landry, "To eat once a day is the life of an angel; twice a day the right life of men and women; more than that the life of a beast"). Catherine was reported to have lived on hardly more than a little raw lettuce, and if forced to eat, to turn her head away and spit out what she had chewed or cause herself to vomit lest any food or liquid remain in her stomach. She had practiced asceticism since the age of seven, when she saw her first visions, perhaps not unconnected with being the youngest of 23 children. Thereafter she stubbornly secluded herself from the worldly commotion of a large family in a dyer's household, and dedicated her virginity to Christ.

The ecstasies of the union were very real to Catherine, as they were to many women who escaped the marital bond by entering religious life. Christ confirmed her betrothal, Catherine wrote, "not with a ring of silver but with a ring of his holy flesh, for when he was circumcised just such a ring was taken from his holy body." Taught to read at the age of twenty by a Dominican sister of noble family, Catherine read the Song of Songs over and over, repeating in her prayers the sigh of the bride, "May he kiss me with the kiss of his mouth," and was rewarded when Jesus appeared to her and bestowed upon her "a kiss which filled her with unutterable sweetness." After her prolonged prayers to be fixed in "perfect faith" and to become an instrument for the salvation of erring souls, Jesus took her for his bride in a ceremony performed by his Holy Mother and attended by St. John, St. Paul, and St. Dominic, with music from David's harp.

As a tertiary or non-cloistered member of the Dominicans, Catherine threw herself into the care of humanity, seeking out prisoners, the poor, and the sick, tending the plague victims of 1374 among whom two of her siblings and eight nieces and nephews died. In an extreme episode she sucked pus from the cancerous sore of a hospital patient as if acting out the mystics' insistence on direct contact with the wounds of Christ as the source of spiritual experience.

In the words of the German mystic Johannes Tauler, Catherine's contemporary, it was necessary "to press one's mouth to the wounds of the crucified." The blood that flowed from the wounds, from the thorns, from the flagellation, obsessed religious fanatics. It was a sacred bath to cleanse sin. To drink it, to wash the soul with it was salvation. Tauler dwelt on the subject for so long in his thoughts that he felt he must have been present at the source. He calculated the number of lashes and knew that Jesus had been tied so tightly to the column that the blood spurted from his nails; that he had been whipped on the back and then on the chest until he was one great wound. St. Brigitta in her revelations saw his bloody footsteps when he walked and how, when crowned with thorns, "his eyes, his ears, his beard ran with blood; his jaw distended, his mouth open, his tongue swollen with blood. His stomach was pulled in so that it touched his spine as if he had no more intestines."

Catherine herself hardly ever spoke of Christ, her bridegroom, without mentioning blood—"blood of the Lamb," "the keys of the blood," "blood filled with eternal divinity," "drinking the blood of the heart of Jesus." *Sangue* was in every sentence; *sangue* and *dolce* (blood and sweet) were her favorite words. Words poured from her in a torrent unhindered by need of pen. Even her devoted confessor, Raymond of Capua, a cultivated nobleman and future General of the Dominican Order, sometimes fell asleep under the redundant flow. That so much of Catherine's talk was preserved was owed to the astonishing capacity of medieval scribes to record verbatim the prolix speech of the period. Speech was customarily filled with repetition to allow time for the listener to absorb what was being said. Information and learning were still largely acquired through listening to heralds, sermons, orations, and reading aloud, and for that very reason, scribes, before the age of printing, were far better trained to take down the spoken word than at any time since.

As word spread of Catherine's visions and fasting, people came to see her in her trances. Between raptures, in moods of earthly and warm-hearted common sense, she settled civil quarrels and converted notorious rascals to penitence and faith. She acquired fame and worshipful disciples to whom she felt as a mother, calling them to her, as she put it, "as a mother calls a child to her breast." They in turn called her *Mamma*. From 1370 on, she took an increasing part in public life, exhorting rulers, prelates, town councils, and individuals in effusive letters of political and spiritual advice.

Her influence lay in her absolute conviction that God's will and hers were one. "Do God's will and mine!" she commanded Charles V in a letter urging crusade, and to the Pope in the same tone she wrote, "I demand . . . that you set forth to fight the infidels!" Next to re-form, "holy sweet crusade" was her incessant theme. Gregory himself, in all the letters of his pontificate, was an advocate of crusade, not only for defensive war against the Turks, but as a means of reconciling France and England and draining the mercenaries from Europe. While Catherine pleaded for peace at home, crying, "Woe, woe, peace, peace, for God's sake . . . ," she implored all the potentates no less heartily to visit war upon the infidel. For her, crusade had an exalted religious value in itself. This was Christians' work for the greater glory of God, and the more earnest its advocates, like Catherine and Philippe de Mézières, the more ardent their summons to war.

"Be a man, Father, arise! . . . No negligence!" she hectored the Pope. Hawkwood was likewise exhorted to rise against Christ's ene-mies instead of tormenting Italy with misery and ruin. In a letter ad-dressed to "Messer Giovanni condottiere," delivered in person by Father Raymond, she wrote, "Therefore I pray you sweetly, since you delight so much in making war and fighting, make no more war upon Christians because it offends God." Rather, she told him, go to fight the Turks so that, "from being the servant and soldier of the Devil, you might become a manly and true knight."

Catherine's favorite admonition was "Be manly!" In her devotions, the Virgin Mary hardly appeared, all Catherine's passion being ab-sorbed by the Son. Yet in worldly affairs she often appealed to femi-nine influence, writing not to Bernabò Visconti but to his strong-minded wife, Regina; not to the King of Hungary but to his dominant mother, Elizabeth of Poland. Of the Duc d'Anjou, whom she envi-sioned as leader of the crusade, she begged that he (of all people) de-spise the pleasures and vanities of this world and unite himself to the cross and the passion of Jesus in holy war. When she visited him and the Duchess in person, the Duke, who among his other ambitions was quite prepared to lead a crusade, accepted the mission.

In Avignon she was oppressed by the atmosphere of sensuality and "stench of sin," and by the curiosity of the grand ladies who poked and pinched her body to test her trances after communion or even pierced her foot with a long needle. To the Pope, whom she addressed in a familiar version of Holy Father as "my sweet papa" (*dolce babbo mio*), she poured out all her themes in endless letters and in public and private audiences in which Raymond of Capua acted as interpreter because Catherine spoke in the Tuscan dialect and the Pope in Latin. Let him begin reform through the appointment of worthy priests, she demanded, let him pacify Italy not by arms but by mercy and pardon, let him return to Rome not with armed guard and sword but with cross in hand like the Blessed Lamb, "for it seems to me that Divine Goodness is preparing to change furious wolves into lambs . . . and I will bring them humiliated to your bosom. . . . Oh, Father, peace for the love of God!"

All the suffering under the "furious wolves" of her time spoke through her voice, and all the craving for religious reform. For most people reform meant relief from ecclesiastical extortions. In Germany in 1372 papal tax-collectors were seized, mutilated, imprisoned, some even strangled, and the clergy of Cologne, Bonn, and Mainz pledged themselves not to pay the tenth demanded by Gregory XI. In parishes wrecked by the mercenaries, the tithes reduced priests to penury. Many deserted, leaving villages without communion or sacraments, and empty churches to rot or be used for barns. Some priests supplemented their too meager pay by occupation as taverners or horse-dealers or other work disallowed for the clergy as *inhonesta*.

In the upper ranks, property and worldly offices absorbed the prelates, to the neglect of care for the diocese. Because the Church could offer to ambitious men a career of power and riches, many who entered it were more concerned with material than with spiritual reward. "Fear of God is thrown away," lamented Brigitta in Rome, "and in its place is a bottomless bag of money." All the Ten Commandments, she said, had been reduced to one: "Bring hither the money."

Conscious of its failings, the Church issued streams of orders reproving profane dress, concubinage, lack of zeal, but it was tied to the things of Caesar and could not reform at the root without destroying its vested interests. It had become dependent on the financial system developed in the exile at Avignon, and while everyone acknowledged the need of reform, the hierarchy was bound, in the nature of things, to resist it. Even Catherine in a moment of clarity knew reform could not come from within. "Do not weep now," she said to Father Raymond when he burst into tears at some new scandal for the Church, "for you will have still more to weep for" when in the future not only laymen but clerics would rise against the Church. As soon as the Pope attempted reform, she said, the prelates would resist, and the Church "will be divided, as it were by a heretical pestilence."

Catherine herself was never heretical, never disillusioned, never disobedient. The Church, the papacy, the priesthood, the Dominican order were her home, and their sanctity her foundation. She scolded, but from within the fold. Disenchantment among the clergy itself produced the great heretics, Wyclif and, in the next generation, Jan Hus.

Catherine's appeals gave Gregory XI the strength to resist the pressures exerted by the French King and cardinals against return of the papacy to Rome. Charles V insisted that "Rome is wherever the Pope happens to be," and sent his brothers, the Dukes of Anjou and Burgundy, to try to dissuade the Pope. In the same effort, the cardinals argued against going to Rome just when the Kings of France and England, "so long divided by a war which destroys the whole world," were conducting peace parleys that required his aid. Gregory was unmoved. Despite somber presentiments, he believed that only his presence could hold Rome for the papacy, and when Rome promised submission if he would return, he could postpone no longer.

Confounding all expectations of his French birth and feeble health, he departed in September 1376 despite a fearful storm that damaged his ships as if in warning. At the last moment his aged father, Count Guillaume de Beaufort, in the unrestrained physical gesture of the time, threw himself prone before his son in a plea to stay. Gregory stepped over his parent, murmuring unfilially from the Psalms, "It is written that thou shalt trample on the adder and tread down the basilisk." One of his bishops, going by land, wrote, "Oh God, if only the mountains would move and block our way."

Owing to the insecurity of the region, Rome was not entered until January 1377, and fifteen months later, in March 1378, Gregory died. In the interval he had struggled as helplessly as his predecessor, Urban V, in the turmoil of Italian politics. Beset by difficulties and ceaselessly goaded by the French cardinals to return to Avignon, he was said to have agreed, but, feeling the approach of death, deliberately waited to die in Rome in order that the election of a new Pope should take place there and keep the papacy where it belonged. His worthy intention precipitated the crisis that was to damage the medieval Church beyond repair.

The schism had nothing to do with doctrine or religious issue. Sixteen cardinals were present in Rome for the conclave, of whom one was Spanish, four were Italian, and eleven were divided between two hostile French parties of Limousins and Gallicans. Since neither French party was prepared to elect a Pope from the other, hectic canvassing for votes took place in which Robert of Geneva, leader of the Gallicans, was active even before Gregory was dead. When the necessary two-thirds majority could not be assembled for any one of the cardinals, sentiment gathered for an outsider as a compromise candidate who could ensure that neither French party would triumph over the other. He was Bartolomeo Prignano, Archbishop of Bari and Vice-Chancellor of the Curia, a Neapolitan of lowly birth, short, stout, swarthy, hard-working, and apparently unassuming. Through long service in Avignon he was considered a pliable protégé by both French groups. Although a strong opponent of simony and corruption, with the excitable temper of the south Italian, he was thought by the cardinals, as their social inferior, to be governable and, above all, amenable to a return to Avignon.

On Gregory's death, the citizens of Rome, seeing at last a chance to end the reign of French popes, sent a deputation of important citizens to the Vatican to urge the election of a "worthy man of the Italian nation," specifically a Roman. The College contained two Romans, Cardinal Tebaldeschi of St. Peter's, "a good saintly man" but aged and infirm, and Cardinal Orsini, considered too young and inexperienced. Both were unwanted by their colleagues for the very reason that they *were* Roman.

Clearly expecting trouble on this score, the French cardinals moved their households with all their valuables, plate, jewels, money, and books, and the papal treasury, into the Castel Sant'Angelo, and demanded security measures by the city to assure public order and protect them against violence and insults. Taking no chances, Cardinal Robert of Geneva donned a coat of mail; the Spanish Cardinal Pedro de Luna dictated his will. Because the cardinals gave no pledge of a Roman, rumor spread that a French-dominated Pope would mean return of the papacy to Avignon. Public excitement rose and threatening crowds gathered as the cardinals, surrounded by "many strong soldiers and warlike nobles," entered the Vatican for the conclave. Beneath the windows they could hear the populace howling, *"Romano lo volemo!* [We want a Roman!] *Romano! Romano!"* The specter of the deaths of Cola di Rienzi and Jacob van Artevelde, lynched by the mob, rose to the surface.

In fear for their lives, the cardinals resorted to dressing the trembling old Cardinal Tebaldeschi, over his protests, in the miter and cope to be exhibited on the throne as elected Pope for long enough to allow his colleagues to escape from the Vatican to fortified places outside the city. As the bells of St. Peter's pealed amid clash and confusion, word of the hoax was learned. The crowd's shrieks turned to *"Non le volemo!*" and "Death to the cardinals!" Swords were drawn and drunks who had broken into the papal cellars grew rough and uproarious.

Next day, April 9, the cardinals announced the election of the Archbishop of Bari as Urban VI and, under heavy guard, escorted him on a white palfrey amid "angry faces" on the traditional ride to the Lateran. Notice of the election and enthronement was conveyed to the six cardinals remaining in Avignon, with no suggestion of possible invalidity by reason of intimidation. On the contrary, in the first weeks of the new reign the cardinals treated Urban's pontificate as so much an accomplished fact that they showered him with the usual petitions for benefices and promotions for their relatives.

Papal power, raising him to authority over the high-born cardinals, went instantly to Urban's head. From a humble unspectacular official totally unprepared for the papal throne, he was transformed overnight into an implacable scourge of simony, moved less by religious zeal than by simple hatred and jealousy of privilege. He publicly chastised the cardinals for absenteeism, luxury, and lascivious life, forbade them to hold or sell plural benefices, prohibited their acceptance of pensions, gifts of money, and other favors from secular sources, ordered the papal treasurer not to pay them their customary half of the revenue from benefices but to use it for the restoration of churches in Rome. Worse, he ordered these princes of the Church to restrict their meals to one course.

He berated them without tact or dignity, his face growing purple and his voice hoarse with rage. He interrupted them with rude invective and cries of "Rubbish!" and "Shut your mouth!" He called Cardinal Orsini a *sotus* (half-wit), and moved to strike the Cardinal of Limoges, only stopped by Robert of Geneva, who pulled him back, crying, "Holy Father, Holy Father, what are you doing?" He accused the Cardinal of Amiens, when acting as mediator between France and England, of accepting money from both sides and prolonging discord to keep his purse filled, causing that Cardinal to rise and with "indescribable haughtiness" to call His Holiness a "liar."

Carried away by self-assertion, Urban plunged into the secular affairs of Naples, announcing that the kingdom was badly governed because the ruler, Queen Joanna, was a woman, and threatening to put her in a nunnery or depose her because of failure to pay the dues of Naples as a papal fief. This gratuitous quarrel, which he pursued with venom, was to provide a base for his enemies.

The feelings of the men who had raised Urban over their own heads probably cannot be adequately described. Some thought that the delirium of power had made the Pope *furiosus et melancholicus*—in

y senfuinent les lamentacions Salmon pour au
enites merneilles a sui auenues on pelermage
De ce monde z les epistres pour ce par sui baillees
et enuoiees à tresexcellent z trespuissant prince e

1. *An entire illuminated page from a manuscript of 1409* (Dialogues de **Pierre**
Salmon). *The subject is Charles VI in the royal palace in Paris receiving a book.*
Flowers bloom in pots on the window sills below.

2,3. The Effects of Good Government, in the City and in the Country. *Fresco by Ambrogio Lorenzetti, c. 1340s, in the Palazzo Pubblico, Siena.*

4. *The Battle of Poitiers. From* Froissart's Chronicles, *copy executed for Louis de Bruges, c. 1460.*

5. *Deer hunt (with ladies riding pillion). From* Hours of Marguerite d'Orléans, *c. 1425.*

6. A victorious captain (Guidoriccio da Fogliano).
Fresco by Simone Martini, 1328, in the Palazzo Pubblico, Siena.

7. Banquet for
the Emperor.
Given by Charles
V for the Emperor
Charles IV and his
son Wenceslas,
showing the
pageant of the
First Crusade.
From the Grandes
Chroniques, exe-
cuted for Charles
V, mid-14th
century.

8. *Departure for Mahdia cam-*
paign. From Froissart's Chronicles,
Harleian copy (below).

9. Bal des Ardents. *From Froissart's* Chronicles, *Louis de Bruges copy, c. 1460.*

short, mad. Rages and insults might have been borne, but not interference with revenue and privilege. When Urban flatly refused to
return to Avignon as arranged, the crisis came. Rather than try, as once
before with an obstreperous Pope, any half-measure requiring him to
sign "Capitulations" of his authority, the cardinals decided on the fatal
course of removal. Since there was no procedure for ousting a Pope for
unfitness, their plan was to annul the election as invalid on grounds that
it had been conducted under duress from mob violence. Unquestion-
ably they had been terrified when they elected Urban, but equally
clearly they had decided to elect him before a threat was heard.

The first hints of an invalid election were circulated in July 1378,
and the cardinals began assembling military support through the Duke
of Fondi, a nobleman of the Kingdom of Naples. In the meantime, the
Romans and their armed forces rallied to Urban, who had won their
support by his refusal to go back to Avignon. He reinforced his position by concluding peace with Florence and lifting the interdict, to the
jubilation of the people. His messenger bearing the olive branch for
once made the papacy popular with the Florentines. Lines were being
drawn. Guarded by the Breton mercenaries of Sylvestre Budes, who
had been with Coucy in Switzerland, the cardinals moved out of Rome
to the papal summer resort at Anagni. Here on August 9 they issued a
Declaration to all Christendom pronouncing Urban's election void on
the ground that it had been conducted in "fear of their lives" to the
sound of "tumultuous and horrible voices." After declaring the Holy
See vacant, they rejected in advance any arbitration by an Ecumenical
Council on the grounds that only a Pope could call a Council. In a
further manifesto, they anathemetized Urban as "Anti-Christ, devil,
apostate, tyrant, deceiver, elected-by-force."

Repudiation of a Pope was so fateful an act that it is impossible to
suppose the cardinals envisaged a schism. Rather, they acted in the
belief that by withdrawing in a body from the Curia, they could compel Urban to resign, or at worst depose him by force of arms. In a test
of strength Budes's company, acting as their military arm, had already
defeated a company of the Pope's Roman supporters in a skirmish in
July.

The cardinals moved first to secure the support of Charles V. All
the information received by the King of France was heavily weighted
against Urban, and his political interest at any rate leaned in the same
direction. He summoned a council of prelates and doctors of law and
theology on September 11 to listen to the cardinals' envoys make their
case. After two days of deliberation, the council soberly advised the
King to abstain from a precipitous decision one way or another on "so

high, perilous and doubtful" an issue. If this was hedging, it was also a well-advised caution which Charles did not follow. Though he did nothing overt, later developments indicate that he must have conveyed assurance of support to the cardinals—the major error of policy-making in his record.

After further legal preparation and efforts to obtain approval from the University of Paris, which was not forthcoming, the cardinals moved to Fondi, inside the territory of Naples, and in a conclave of September 20 elected a new Pope from among their number. Seeking, in the circumstances, a forceful and decisive man they made an incredible choice. The person elected, enthroned, and crowned as Clement VII all on the same day was Robert of Geneva, the "Butcher of Cesena."

The election of an Anti-Pope was bound to be divisive, and the interests of the papacy might have been supposed to dictate a choice as acceptable as possible to Italians. To elect the man feared and loathed throughout Italy suggests an arrogance of power almost as mad as the behavior of Urban. Perhaps by this time the 14th century was not quite sane. If enlightened self-interest is the criterion of sanity, in the verdict of Michelet, "no epoch was more naturally mad." Dominated by the French, the College of Cardinals was unconcerned about Italian feelings and so threatened by curtailment of its revenues in the name of reform that even the three* Italian cardinals gave tacit consent to the vote. This was the end product of the exile in Avignon. Only a profound materialism and cynicism could have permitted the placing of Robert of Geneva in the chair of St. Peter. The complaints of the reformers could have had no more telling proof.

"Oh, unhappy men!" cried Catherine, voicing the Italian reaction, "you who were to nourish yourselves at the breast of the Church, to be as flowers in her garden, to shed forth sweet perfume, to be as pillars to support the Vicar of Christ and his bark, as lamps for the enlightenment of the world and diffusion of the faith . . . you who were angels upon earth, have turned to the way of devils. . . . What is the cause? The poison of selfishness destroys the world." If her rich imagery was mixed, it was also a measure of the reverence felt for the great ones of the Church and the corresponding sense of betrayal. With the native common sense that often broke through her verbal rhapsodies, Catherine gave no credit to the cardinals' claim of having elected Urban under duress.

Far from resigning, Urban created an entirely new College of

---

* The fourth, the aged Cardinal Tebaldeschi, had died.

Cardinals within a week and hired a company of mercenaries under one of the first Italian *condottieri*, Alberigo da Barbiano, to maintain his See by force of arms. War on schismatics gave Catherine a new holy cause. "Now is the time for new martyrs," she encouraged Urban. "You are the first who have given your blood; how great is the fruit you will receive!" And so it proved, initially. In a battle against the forces of his rival, commanded by Sylvestre Budes and the Count of Montjoie, Clement's nephew, Urban's forces were victorious. They regained the Castel Sant'Angelo and took prisoner the two enemy captains, with the result that Clement had to flee Rome and take refuge with Joanna of Naples. So hostile was the populace, however, crying "Death to the Anti-Christ! Death to Clement and his cardinals! Death to the Queen if she protects them!" that he was forced to leave. With no safety for him anywhere in Italy, he returned with his cardinals to Avignon in April 1379.

With one Pope and College of Cardinals in Rome and another Pope and College in Avignon, the schism was now a terrible fact. It was to become the fourth scourge—after war, plague, and the Free Companies—of a tormented century. Since the election at Fondi, every sovereign power had taken sides, often with divisive effect between ruler and clerics, or clerics and people. Charles V recognized Clement officially in November 1378 and issued a proclamation forbidding obedience to Urban by anyone, cleric or lay, within the realm. He rejected settlement by an Ecumenical Council as advocated by the University of Paris, because he wanted no solution that might prove contrary to French interest. The University, profoundly troubled, was forced to comply.

England, in natural opposition to France and a French Pope, remained loyal to Urban; Scotland of course took the other side. Flanders, though a fief of France, remained Urbanist largely because the Count of Flanders was following a pro-English policy in the war. The Emperor Charles IV died just in time to be spared a decision, but his son and successor, Wenceslas, so recently and lavishly entertained in Paris, declared for Urban and carried most of the Empire with him, except for certain areas such as Hainault and Brabant closely linked to France. The stand taken by the new Emperor, followed by Hungary, Poland, and Scandinavia, was a bitter disappointment to Charles V, who had thought his own decision would draw other sovereigns in its wake, leaving Urban isolated and forced to resign.

Charles's old ally Don Enrique, King of Castile, also died before taking sides, and his son, Juan I, though heavily pressed by Charles V to support Clement, preferred to maintain "neutrality," saying that, while faithful to the French alliance, he could not go against the conscience of his subjects. Common people, nobility, clerics, learned men, he wrote, were all Urbanist. "What government, O wise prince," he pointedly inquired of Charles, "has ever succeeded in triumphing over public conscience supported by reason? What punishments are available to subjugate a free soul?" During a career of more than ordinary Spanish confusion, Juan I from time to time sent out signals of serious thought about the relationship of ruler to subject. Unfortunately, Charles was already demonstrating that he could indeed frustrate "public conscience supported by reason." Neutrality in the schism, in which Pedro IV of Aragon also tried to take refuge, was illusory. Political pressures forced both Spanish Kings and eventually Portugal, too, to opt for Clement.

Urban's actions after his repudiation grew more savage, irrational, and uncontrolled than before. He excommunicated Joanna of Naples for her support of Clement and declared her deposed in favor of one of her many throne-hungry relatives, Charles of Durazzo. Urban thereby plunged his papacy into a remorseless conflict. He quarreled with Catherine of Siena over this issue, and when she died of self-willed privation shortly afterward in 1380, he lost what had been the warmest voice in his support. He devoted infinite devices to the advancement of a worthless nephew, Francesco Prignano, and when Charles of Durazzo refused to grant the nephew certain favors, Urban resorted to arms. On being besieged by Charles of Durazzo, the Pope mounted four times a day to the battlements to excommunicate the besiegers. If he had not been mad before, the cardinals' challenge had unhinged him now.

Increasingly alienated by his wildness and vindictiveness, two of Urban's cardinals defected to Clement, but most felt they had no choice but to remain with Urban rather than accept a return to French subjection. Burdened with a crazed Pope, they planned a kind of regency council to govern for him while holding him in protective custody, but Urban learned of the plot and arrested the six cardinals involved. While they were being tortured to extract confessions of conspiracy, he was reported by an observer to have walked up and down beneath the windows, reading his breviary in a loud voice while listening to the cries of the victims. Five were executed for conspiracy. The sixth, an English cardinal named Adam Easton, spared through the intervention of Richard II, survived to testify to what he had witnessed. As the years passed, Urban became as hated and vilified as his rival. With two such men claiming leadership of Holy Church, it seemed as if God had good reason to repent of His house on earth.

Of all the "strange evils and adversities" predicted for the century, the effect of the schism on the public mind was among the most damaging. When each Pope excommunicated the followers of the other, who could be sure of salvation? Every Christian found himself under penalty of damnation by one or the other Pope, with no way of being sure that the one he obeyed was the genuine one. People might be told that the sacraments of their priest were not valid because he had been ordained by the "other Pope," or that the holy oil for baptism was not sanctified because it had been blessed by a "schismatic" bishop. In disputed regions, double bishops might be appointed, each holding mass and proclaiming the ritual of the other a sacrilege. The same religious order in different countries might have divided allegiance, with its monasteries under two competing priors and its abbeys torn by strife. When, as in Flanders, political and economic rivalries caused a city to ally itself with the French under Clement, loyal Urbanists, fearing to live under Anti-Christ, left their homes, shops, and trades to move to a diocese of the "true" persuasion.

Though no religious issue had created the schism, once it became an accomplished fact, partisans were divided by the same hatred as marked the later religious wars. To Honoré Bonet in France, Urban appeared as the falling star to whom was given the key to the "bottom-less pit" in St. John's vision of the Apocalypse. The "smoke of a great furnace" arising from the pit to darken the sun was the schism darkening the papacy. The accompanying "locusts and scorpions" were the "traitorous Romans" who, by terrorizing the conclave, had forced the false election.

Since papal revenue was cut in half, the financial effect of the schism was catastrophic. To keep each papacy from bankruptcy, simony redoubled, benefices and promotions were sold under pressure, charges for spiritual dispensations of all kinds were increased, as were chancery taxes on every document required from the Curia. Sale of indulgences, seed of the Reformation, became financially important. Instead of reform, abuses multiplied, further undermining faith. When a French bishop or abbot died, according to the Monk of St. Denis who wrote the *Chronicle of the Reign of Charles VI*, the tax-collectors of Avignon descended like vultures to carry off his goods and furnishings on pretext of making up arrears in clerical tithes. "Everywhere the service of God was neglected, the devotion of the faithful diminished, the realm was drained of money, and ecclesiatics wandered here and there overcome with misery."

Legates of each Pope no longer strove for peace between France and England, but worked openly for one side or another because each of the principals sought military support to eliminate his rival. Meanwhile their mutual vituperation and unedifying struggle over the body of the Church degraded Christendom. The Church was pulled this way and that, sorrowed the Monk of St. Denis, "like a prostitute found at the scene of a debauch." She became "a subject for satire and object of laughter for all peoples of the world, and they made up songs about her every day."

More than anyone else, Charles V was responsible for allowing the schism to take hold, for Clement would have had no footing without the support of France. He acknowledged his debt as soon as he became Pope by a grant to the King of a third of the taxes on the French clergy. In the end Charles's choice was to blight all he had accomplished for the recovery of France. Thinking only of retrieving a French papacy under French influence, he had assumed that his candidate could be imposed. Though surnamed the Wise, he was not immune from the occupational disease of rulers: overestimation of their capacity to control events.

No one was a more ardent Clementist than the King's brother Anjou, for reasons of his own ambition. The moment the Duke learned of Clement's election, he had it proclaimed through the streets of Toulouse to the accompaniment of mass in the cathedral and Te Deum sung in all the churches. Speaking of the new Pope as a "close relative, the issue like myself of the house of France," he ordered obedience to the new papacy by Languedoc, sent money to the cardinals, and envoys to gather support in Florence, Milan, and Naples. When Clement suffered defeat by Urban's forces and lost Italy, he applied to Anjou for military support. Anjou's asking price was a kingdom.

By agreement between them confirmed in a Bull of April 17, 1379, Anjou was to reconquer the Papal States in Italy and keep the greater part of them (with the exception of Rome and Naples) for himself as a Kingdom of Adria, so called from the Adriatic, along whose shores it was to lie. Bestriding the Apennines, the kingdom was to include Ferrara, Bologna, Ravenna, the Romagna, the March of Ancona, and the duchy of Spoleto. It was to be a fief of the Holy See paying an annual sum to the papacy of 40,000 francs; every three years Anjou was to give the Pope a white palfrey in token of vassalage. The Bull expressly provided that Adria and Naples should never be united under one ruler. Anjou was to be allowed a delay of two years to assemble finances and forces, but if within two months after the two years he had not yet led an expedition into Italy or sent a "capable general" in his place, the agreement would become void.

Adria was a kingdom in the clouds. If in all their battles papal forces had never succeeded in regaining control of the patrimony, there was no reason to suppose that a French prince would succeed where they had failed. But overestimation of its powers affected French policy more and more from this time on; feasibility restrained it less and less. In the meantime, Anjou's aid was urgently needed to maintain Queen Joanna on the throne of Naples, Clement's only base in Italy. In order that he have a vested interest in coming to her defense, Anjou was named—as her distant cousin—the childless Queen's heir. By naming the same person as future King of Naples and putative King of Adria, Clement was arranging exactly the single rulership he had banned, but perhaps he never expected Anjou to achieve both. With Naples beckoning, Anjou's destiny now lay in Italy, where it would soon draw Coucy with it.

To rally the French public to Clement, once royal policy was committed to him, required more than mere fiat. Through April and May of 1379 a series of public assemblies was held in Paris to impress upon notables and citizens the invalidity of Urban's election. The Cardinal of Limoges, he who had nearly suffered Urban's blow, came to tell in person all that had happened and swear with hand on heart, calling on God, angels, and saints as witnesses to his sincerity, that the cardinals had voted for Urban "under fear of death." In contrast, he said, Clement had been chosen under the right and proper conditions necessary to the election of a true pontiff. Following him, Charles V rose to say that all conscientious scruples about accepting Clement must now be eased, for it was clear that a man of such authority and wisdom as the Cardinal of Limoges would not "damn his soul for love or hate of a living person." At further meetings, further cardinals confirmed the version of duress with solemn oaths.

Formal assent was obtained from an imposing group assembled at the Château de Vincennes on May 7 in the presence of the King and Anjou and the Sire de Coucy, among other leading nobles, ministers, prelates, and masters of theology. After each cardinal in turn was again asked by the King to declare on his conscience all he knew of the circumstances, in order to clear all hesitant minds of doubt and "fortify their faith," the assembly, with hidden anguish in many hearts, voted unanimously in favor of the new Pope. A week later for the benefit of the public a great ceremony was held in the plaza of Notre Dame, where on a platform especially erected for the occasion the four cardinals supported by the Duc d'Anjou proclaimed the advent of Clement VII and declared schismatic anyone who refused obedience.

The University of Paris remained unreconciled. Masters of Theology, less affected by the compromises of worldly office, did not bend so easily as bishops. To them the succession of St. Peter was a serious matter. Under extreme pressure from the crown, they formally accepted Clement on May 30, but the acquiescence was sullen, not unanimous, and a precursor of trouble. Two years later, after the death of Charles V, all four faculties passed a resolution in favor of a General Council to put an end to the schism, and appealed to the crown to summon one. Although authority to convene was uncertain, fifteen such councils had been held so far in the history of the Church to settle grave issues of doctrine. The University's appeal in 1381, presented by a master of theology, Jean Rousse, was necessarily addressed to the hostile ears of the Duc d'Anjou, then Regent. As a fearsome example to quiet all such talk, he had Rousse arrested and imprisoned in the Châtelet. The insult to clergy and University created a scandal, not appeased when Rousse's release was secured only at the cost of an order by Anjou prohibiting any discussion of a council or a papal election.

Alienated and dismayed, prominent doctors of theology fled to Rome to join Urban. Others too were leaving. Students and faculty of Urbanist countries, unable to remain under Clementist obedience, departed for universities in Italy, the Empire, and Oxford. "The sun of knowledge" in France, said a departing master, "has suffered an eclipse." At this time the decline of the University of Paris as a great cosmopolitan center began.

In England the schism brought Wyclif to the turning point that led to protestantism. At first he welcomed Urban as a reformer, but as the financial abuses of both Popes grew more flagrant, he came to regard both as Anti-Christs and the schism as the natural end of a corrupted papacy. Since the moment the Church allowed penance to be commuted by money, he believed, nothing but evil had been the result. Despairing of reform from within after the schism, he came in 1379 to a radical conclusion: since the Church was incapable of reforming itself, it must be brought under secular supervision. He now saw the King as God's Vicar on earth from whom bishops derived their authority and through whom the state, as guardian of the Church, could compel reform. Going beyond the abuses of the Church to attack the theory, Wyclif was now prepared to sweep away the entire ecclesiastical superstructure—papacy, hierarchy, orders. Having rejected the divine authority of the Church, it was now that he came to his rejection of its essence—the power of the sacraments, specifically of the Eucharist.

In a culminating heresy, he transferred salvation from the agency of the Church to the individual: "For each man that shall be damned shall be damned by his own guilt, and each man that is saved shall be saved by his own merit." Unperceived, here was the start of the modern world.

When he had preached disendowment of the Church's temporal property, Wyclif had had powerful friends, but when he rejected the sacerdotal system, his patrons, fearing heresy and the jaws of Hell, withdrew. In 1381 a council of twelve doctors of the University of Oxford was to pronounce eight of his theses unorthodox and fourteen heretical, and to prohibit him from further lecturing or preaching. Though his voice was silenced, his work spread through dissemination of the Bible in English. The entire Scripture of some three quarters of a million words was translated from the Latin by Wyclif and his Lollard disciples in the dangerous business of opening a direct pathway to God, bypassing the priest. In the future fierce reaction after the Peasants' Revolt, when Lollardy was harried as the brother of subversion, and mere possession of a Bible in English could convict a man of heresy, the making of multiple copies of the manuscript Bible was a labor of risk and courage. In view of 175 copies that still survive and the number that must have been destroyed during the persecution and lost over the centuries, many hundreds must have been laboriously and secretively copied out by hand. Wyclif died in 1384, and the current of protest, as persecution intensified, ran on underground. When Jan Hus was burned at the stake for heresy by the Council of Constance in 1415, Wyclif's bones were ordered dug up and burned at the same time. Even riddled by the schism, the Church was still in control. The cracking of old and famous structures is slow and internal, while the façade holds.

With Europe polarized between two papacies, and the Church politicized by the rivals' struggle for secular support, it became harder to heal the schism each year that it lasted. All thoughtful men recognized how it was damaging society and tried to find the means of reunification, but in the schism, as in the war, vested hostilities kept the breach open. Ecumenical Council, advocated by the University of Paris and many individuals, was the obvious solution. As a challenge to their supremacy, however, both Popes adamantly rejected it. The hateful rift in Christendom was to last for forty years. According to a popular saying toward the end of the century, no one since the beginning of the schism had entered Paradise.

Part Two

Chapter 17

Coucy's Rise

Now "wholly French" once more, Coucy served as the King's right arm through the closing efforts of the reign. Though only 41, Charles V felt time pressing. In February 1378 his Queen, Jeanne de Bourbon, who was the same age as he, died of childbed fever after the birth of a daughter, Catherine. Three weeks later, the last to survive of her previous five daughters died, leaving of her eight children only two sons and the newborn to outlive her. The King "sorrowed long and marvelously" from his wife's death "and so did many other good people, for the Queen and he loved each other as much as loyal married people can." A month later came the death—precipitating the schism—of Pope Gregory XI, with whom Charles had been closely associated, followed in November by the death of his uncle the Emperor and shortly afterward by the passing of his longtime ally King Enrique of Castile. In all these losses Charles cannot but have felt the advancing shadow of his own limited time, and with it an urgency to leave his kingdom whole and at peace before he too departed.

To that end he must close the three portals of danger represented by the persistent betrayals of Charles of Navarre, by the alliance of the Duke of Brittany with England, and by the continuing war with England itself. Coucy's strategic territory, his military and diplomatic talents, and that evident dependability which Gregory XI had found notable made him a fulcrum of the King's effort. His first task was to conduct a campaign to eliminate Charles of Navarre from Normandy once and for all.

On learning that Navarre had again secretly negotiated to re-open Normandy to the English, Charles V swore to drive his faithless vassal out of every town and castle he held there. Legality was at hand in the person of Navarre's two sons, in whose name the Navarrese fiefs in Normandy could be taken over. Since their mother, the King's sister, was dead, Charles V could claim their guardianship by an argument that would admit of no dispute: they were both in his custody at the court of France at the time. Why their father allowed this to happen is unclear, unless he intended it as some devious camouflage of his dealings with England.

Legal evidence of Navarre's treason was provided when his chamberlain, Jacques de Rue, arrived in Paris with letters for the two sons. Under interrogation, De Rue testified freely—without torture, as the King took care to have stated in the authorized chronicle—that Charles of Navarre planned to poison the King of France right after Easter through a steward of the royal bakery. Taking advantage of the ensuing disarray and succession of a minor, he would then open hostilities by seizing French strongholds along the Seine while the English landed in Normandy.

This story was easily believable of a prince who had already attempted the life of his other brother-in-law, the Count of Foix, in a melodrama infused with all the lurid glitter of the 14th century. Foix had married the flirtatious Agnes, Navarre's sister, but, as a man of "impetuous passions," had not ceased his gallantries, with the result that Agnes departed in umbrage to take refuge with her brother. The brothers-in-law were already at odds in a quarrel over money. When Agnes' fifteen-year-old son, Gaston, came to plead with her to return, she refused to go unless the request came from her husband. Charles of Navarre then gave his nephew a bag of powder to take home, telling him that it would cause his father to desire the reconciliation, but that he must keep the agent secret or it would not work. On Gaston's return to Foix, the bag of powder was discovered by his bastard brother Yvain, and shown to the Count, who fed it to one of his dogs, which promptly expired in painful convulsions.

Restrained from killing his heir and only legitimate son on the spot, the Count locked him up while all of Gaston's household who had gone with him to Navarre were examined and fifteen of them executed. Meanwhile Gaston, realizing that his uncle had conspired to have him commit parricide, gave way to despair, refusing all food. On being informed of this situation while he was paring his nails with a knife, the Count of Foix rushed to his son's cell, seized him by the throat saying, "Ha, traitor, why dost thou not eat?" and accidentally cut him across the jugular with the knife that was still in his hand. The boy turned on his side without a word and, the wound proving fatal, died the same day. One more mortal sin was added to the already overburdened record of Charles of Navarre.

Corroboration of Navarre's "crimes and treasons" against the King of France was supplied when codes to his ciphered correspondence were taken from a second arrested counselor, Pierre du Tertre. All the collected evidence, and signed confessions by the two counselors, were made public in their formal trial, conducted with utmost solemnity before a great assembly of magistrates, clerics, notaries, merchants, and visitors to Paris. Upon sentence of death, both counselors were executed. Their headless bodies were hung on the gibbet and their severed limbs on the four principal gates of Paris. A public record was thus established to justify Charles of Navarre's Norman subjects in transferring their allegiance to his son.

The Normandy campaign was already under way. At the first report of Navarre's treason, the King had assembled an army at Rouen and "sent hastily for the Sire de Coucy and the Sire de Rivière," whom he put in command under the nominal leadership of the Duke of Burgundy. Fearful of English landings, he instructed them to conquer Navarre's towns and castles, especially those nearest the coast, as speedily as possible either by force or by negotiation. Bureau de la Rivière, the King's Chamberlain, with whom Coucy was to be so closely associated in this campaign and afterward, belonged to the group of bourgeois-born councillors derisively called Marmosets by the King's brothers in reference to the little stone grotesques that peered from the cornices and pillars of churches. He was a courteous and gracious official, highly esteemed by Charles V, who had given him controlling power in the Regency council he had established in case he should die while the Dauphin was still a minor.

The combination of Coucy and Rivière reflected the combined military and political strategy to be employed. Against walled towns, siege was slow and costly. For rapid conquest everything depended on a negotiated surrender, but this could be achieved only by a credible show of force and in most cases initial combat. To add to the persuasion of force, Charles of Navarre's two sons were taken along "to show to the whole country that the war was in behalf of these children for their inheritance."

Bayeux, "a handsome and strong city" at the base of the Cotentin peninsula where an English landing might be expected (ten miles from a later landing place renamed Omaha Beach), was the first major objective. Bringing up their forces below the walls and exhibiting the young heir of Navarre as the rightful lord, Coucy and Rivière warned the citizens "in impressive language" that if the town were taken by storm "they would all be slaughtered and the place re-peopled by another set of inhabitants." The problem in each case was that the captains of Navarrese garrisons, who might be charged with treason to their

Prince or dishonored if they surrendered without making a defense, had not the same motive to yield as the citizens. And since captains generally shut themselves up in the citadel if besiegers won, thus escaping the slaughter and plunder visited upon the populace, they preferred to risk a siege rather than to surrender.

At Bayeux, the garrison was overruled. Influenced by the rights of Navarre's sons and the persuasions of their Bishop, the townspeople asked for a three-day truce to negotiate terms, always an intricate business which had to be put in writing with signed and sealed copies delivered to each side. When this was completed, Coucy and Rivière entered the city to take possession in the name of the King of France. After replacing the magistrates with their own appointees and leaving in place a garrison to prevent rebellion, they moved forward up the peninsula toward the next stronghold. Successive towns and castles, bombarded both "by arms and words," were taken without much loss of time, although not without active siege measures, mining of walls, and sharp combats with killed and wounded on both sides. In the interests of haste, Coucy and Rivière readily granted favorable terms and allowed determined partisans of Navarre to depart if they chose to go. Working effectively with Rivière, Coucy displayed a capacity he shared with the King for cool pursuit of policy, grafted in Coucy's case upon a man of action.

Charles of Navarre himself, under attack in the south by the King of Castile, was not present, and because of contrary winds no more than a few of his English allies arrived. One group succeeded in occupying Cherbourg, but was hemmed in there by a French siege. Elsewhere, Navarrese captains faced a hard choice, because if they chose to resist they could hope for little help, while if they yielded, Normandy would be lost to the King of Navarre. Evreux, the heart of his Norman possessions, manned by his strongest garrison and a loyal population, gave Coucy and Rivière their hardest fight. "Every day they made assault," and so tightly encircled the town that it was forced to capitulate. The fall of Evreux delighted the King who came to Rouen to greet the victors who "had so well sped." Only Cherbourg, which the English could supply by sea, withstood prolonged sieges commanded at different times by Du Guesclin and Coucy, and remained in English hands.

With that exception, by the end of 1378 Charles of Navarre had lost all his estates in Normandy. Walls and fortifications were razed so that his strongholds could not again be held by enemies of France. In the south, the seigneury of Montpellier, his last possession in France, was taken from him by the Duc d'Anjou. Scotched at last after thirty years of compulsive plotting, Charles of Navarre was left to live out a destitute and friendless decade in his mountain kingdom so much too narrow for his soul. So might Satan have been penned in a sheepfold.

Famous knights who were to be Coucy's companions in future ventures took part in episodes of the Normandy campaign, among them the late Queen's brother, the good-tempered if unremarkable Louis, Duc de Bourbon; also the energetic new Admiral, Jean de Vienne; and, most notably, one-eyed Olivier de Clisson, who brought a Breton company to Coucy's aid at the siege of Evreux. Whether at this time or some other, these two disparate personalities joined in the special comradeship of brotherhood-in-arms, a formal arrangement in which the partners drew up terms of mutual aid and equal division of profits and ransoms.

Clisson came of a turbulent family embattled on both sides in Brittany. His father, discovered in dealings with Edward III, had been beheaded by Philip VI, who had him arrested in the middle of a tournament, thrown in prison, and conducted almost naked to his execution without trial. The victim's wife was said to have carried her husband's severed head from Paris to Brittany to display before her seven-year-old son and exact his oath of vengeance and eternal hate for France. Then in an open boat, storm-tossed and starving, they escaped to England, where Edward, who was making every effort to win the loyalty of the Bretons, showered favor and properties on the widow and son.

Olivier was brought up at the English court along with the young Jean de Montfort, his Duke, whose jealousy and dislike he reciprocated. While he displayed a noble's haughty manners, reinforced by an inflated opinion of himself, Clisson was called at one time "the churl" for his coarse language. Pursuing his vowed revenge, he fought against the French with incredible ferocity at Reims, Auray, Cocherel, and Najera in Spain. He wielded a two-handled ax with such force that it was said "no one who received his blows ever got up again," although he failed to avert the enemy ax that cut through his helmet and took out his eye. In the course of the war in Brittany, Montfort enraged Clisson by favoring Sir John Chandos, and when he rewarded Chandos with a town and castle, Clisson denounced the Duke in terrible wrath, assaulted and razed the castle intended for Chandos, and used the stones to reconstruct his own.

Charles V had returned to him the lands confiscated from his father and wooed him with gifts, even sending him venison "as to a friend." Whether it was these material persuasions or, as Olivier claimed, the arrogance of the English toward the French that he could no longer suffer, he turned French in 1369 and redirected his ferocity against his former associates. It reached a peak when he learned that his squire, wounded and captured by the English, had been killed as a prisoner on being discovered to belong to Clisson. Olivier swore a great oath never "by the Mother of God throughout this year, neither in the morning nor in the evening, to give quarter to any Englishman. . . ." The following day, though lacking siege engines, he attacked an English stronghold with such fury and took it with such slaughter that no more than fifteen defenders were left alive. After locking them up in a tower room, Olivier ordered them released one by one, and as each came through the door he struck off his head with a single blow of a great ax and thus, with fifteen heads rolling at his feet, avenged his squire.

The cool-headed Coucy and the savage Breton must have found a complement in each other, for these two powerful barons, according to Clisson's biographer, "remained always in the most perfect harmony." At this time Coucy had just lost in shocking circumstances his companion from the Swiss campaign, Owen of Wales. While Coucy was in Normandy, Owen was conducting the siege of Mortagne on the coast at the mouth of the Gironde. Arising early on a clear and lovely morning, he sat on a stump in his shirt and cloak, viewing the castle and countryside, as was his habit, while having his hair combed by his Welsh squire, James Lambe. This man had recently been taken into his service as a compatriot who brought him tidings of his native land and told him "how all the country of Wales would gladly have him to be their lord." Standing behind his master on the still morning before others were abroad, James Lambe plunged a Spanish dagger into Owen's body, "stabbing him clean through so that he fell down stark dead."

The assassin's hand was certainly hired by the English, possibly to remove a focus of agitation on the Welsh border, or, as contemporaries believed, in reprisal for the miserable death in prison of the Captal de Buch, originally captured by Owen. If so, it was a surprisingly dishonorable blow upon an unarmed man, as recognized by the English captain inside besieged Mortagne to whom Lambe reported his deed. "He shook his head and beheld him right felly and said, 'Ah, thou has murdered him. . . . But that this deed is for our profit . . . we shall have blame thereby rather than praise.' " On the French side, Charles V, though terribly angered, did not altogether regret the removal of Owen, a freebooter not guiltless of nefarious deeds of his own. His murder reflected a new kind of animosity growing out of the war. Suborned assassination within the brotherhood of knights was an innovation of the 14th century.

Halfway through the Normandy campaign Coucy had been sent to strengthen the defense of the frontier with Flanders, where new dangers threatened. The Count of Flanders, whose boyhood loyalty had been so strongly French when he ran away from Isabella, had long since been brought by economic interests to favor the English. He appeared as a threat when he gave asylum to the Duke of Brittany, who had repudiated French vassalage and rejoined the English. King Charles now decided to rid himself of the problem of Brittany once and for all by confiscating the dukedom from Montfort on grounds of "felony" toward his sovereign. In the belief that most Breton nobles were pro-French, he planned to unite the dukedom with the crown of France under Montfort's rival Jeanne de Penthièvre, but instead of suppressing the Breton nest of hornets, he succeeded only in arousing it.

In December 1378, at a ceremonial Court of Justice with the King seated in "royal majesty," Montfort was tried before the peers of the realm—in absentia, since he ignored the summons. The twelve lay and twelve ecclesiastical peers of France were an elastic body in which successive barons of Coucy sometimes figured and sometimes did not. Froissart specifically refers to Enguerrand VII as a "peer of France," and on this occasion he was one of four barons seated "on the fleur de lys" along with the peers of royal blood and a superabundance of eighteen prelates including four "mitred" abbots. The royal usher, after summoning Montfort aloud three times—at the entrance to the chamber, at the Marble Table in the courtyard, and at the gate of the palace—duly reported back that "he is not there." The Procurator then read the indictment, citing the Duke's treasons, crimes, "injuries and vexations," including the murder of the priest sent to summon him. (After the Visconti fashion, Montfort had the messenger drowned in the river with the summons tied around his neck.) Following a juridical argument at enormous length of the rights and claims to the dukedom, Montfort's title was declared null, and the King announced Brittany's union with the crown.

Charles's error was at once made clear by a rebellious outburst in the independent-minded duchy, even among the pro-French party. The endless quarrel came alive again, and since Montfort was conniving with the Count of Flanders and both of them with England,

Charles feared the possibility of a new invasion across the northern frontier. In this situation, the domain of Coucy guarding the northern gateway came into focus.

In February 1379 the King sent his Treasurer, Jean le Mercier, and an official with the title of Visitor General of Royal Property to survey the barony of Coucy with instructions "to look and advise and report the estate of the said seigneur." In March, after receiving Mercier's report, Charles went himself on a week's tour of Coucy-le-Château and other castles and towns of the domain. Evidently ailing, the King watched from his litter the "joyous chase of deer" in hunts organized in his honor. Whether Enguerrand was present to welcome his sovereign is nowhere recorded, and the absence of mention suggests he may have been in the north assembling forces for defense, or in Normandy at the siege of Cherbourg.

The King was, however, accompanied by the court poet Eustache Deschamps, who immediately produced a ballade extolling the marvels of the barony. A master of the verbal acrobatics of the French verse of his time, yet a realist and satirist at heart, Deschamps described himself as the "King of Ugliness" with the skin of a boar and the face of a monkey. He had entered royal service from humble birth as a simple messenger, advancing to usher-at-arms, bailiff, and *châtelain* of royal properties and, in the next reign, Steward of Water and Forests and ultimately *Général des finances*. Ready to turn out poetry for any occasion—a total of 1,675 ballades, 661 rondeaux, 80 virelais, 14 lays, and miscellaneous pieces—he now described in verse the "strongholds for men of valor" in Coucy's many castles of St. Gobain, St. Lambert and La Fère, the parks of Folembray, the lovely manor St. Aubin, the falcons' chase of herons, the famous *donjon*:

> Who would know a land of great delight
> Where lies the heart of the realm of France,
> With fortress strong of marvelous might,
> Tall forests and lakes of sweet *plaisance*,
> Songs of birds, parks orderly as a dance.
>   Must to Coucy turn his steps.
> There he will find the *nonpareille*
> Whence comes the cry, "*Coucy à la merveille!*"

It has been surmised that Charles had in mind the eventual purchase of Coucy, placing the crown in control of the greatest stronghold of the north. Purchase of great fiefs was not unprecedented; Coucy himself had thus indirectly acquired Soissons. Yet how he might have been adequately compensated for so great an estate or why he would be expected to comply with the King's desire remains obscure. The fact that he had no son and only a single female heir, the other being irrevocably English, may have been a consideration.

The marriage of Marie, sole heiress to the barony, was then being negotiated. At thirteen she was one of three candidates, along with Yolande de Bar, a niece of the King, and Catherine of Geneva, a sister of Pope Clement, who were prospects for the recently widowed son of the King of Aragon. Such places were not left empty for long. Eight days after the death of his wife, the Spanish prince dispatched envoys to Coucy, to the Duc d'Anjou as Yolande's uncle, and to the Count of Geneva, with instructions to arrange matters as soon as possible with any one of the three. When Yolande was chosen, Marie afterward married Yolande's brother Henri de Bar, eldest son of the Duc de Bar and of Marie de France, sister of Charles V. Alliance with the heir to a great duchy on the borders of Lorraine maintained the high level of the Coucys' marital connections.

Whether Enguerrand was influenced by this new royal connection or by pride in his success in Normandy, he created at this time his own Order of Chivalry called, in the grand manner of the Coucys, the Order of the Crown. As indicated by Deschamps, who celebrated the order in a poem, the Crown was meant to symbolize not only grandeur and power but the dignity, virtue, and high conduct that surround a king. The points of its circle were the "twelve flowers of authority": Faith, Virtue, Moderation, Love of God, Prudence, Truth, Honor, Strength, Mercy, Charity, Loyalty, and Largesse "shining on all below." After 1379, Coucy's seals display a patterned background of tiny crowns and a standing figure holding a crown— with some now uncertain significance—upside down. However elevated in name, the Order was democratic in spirit: it admitted ladies, demoi- selles, and squires to membership.

In 1379 Isabella de Coucy died in England leaving Enguerrand free to remarry. Less precipitate than the Prince of Aragon, or too oc- cupied in urgent affairs, he did not fill her place for seven years. Noth- ing came of the King's visit to his barony at the time, but the crown's interest remained active.

A new reign in England brought the English no better fortunes in the war. The easy mastery of the Channel that Edward III had once enjoyed was lost, thanks to Charles's steady alliance with the sea power of Castile and his own program of shipbuilding. When a force led by the Duke of Lancaster finally succeeded in landing near St. Malo in Brittany, the situation of Cherbourg was reversed. Held by the French, St. Malo defied siege and wore out the Duke until he went home in a cloud of failure. "And the commons of England began to murmur against the noblemen, saying how they had done all that season but little good." Unsuccessful war stimulated more than murmur. While Lancaster was bogged down in Brittany, English merchant ships were harassed and captured with impunity by French and Scottish pirates. When the merchants complained, the nobles and prelates of the King's Council replied only that defensive action was up to Lancaster and his fleet.

At this, a rich alderman and future Mayor of London, John Philpot, Master of the Grocers' Company, assembled a private force of ships with a thousand sailors and men-at-arms and went forth to battle the pirates, several of whom he captured together with their prize ships. When, after a triumphant welcome in London, he was summoned by the Council to answer for acting without the King's leave, his hot reply summed up the growing exasperation of the Third Estate with the less than adequate performance by the Second. He had spent his money and risked his men, Philpot said, not to shame the nobles or win knightly fame, but "in pity for the misery of the people and country which, from being a noble realm and dominion over other nations, has through your supineness been exposed to the ravages of the vilest race. Since you would not lift a hand in its defense, I exposed myself and my property for the safety and deliverance of our country." Even if Philpot and his fellow merchants were primarily concerned with the safety and deliverance of their trade, his complaint of the country's defenders was none the less valid.

With ill-success on both sides in the war, both desired peace. Reopening of hostilities in Brittany had counterbalanced for France her success in Normandy, and the schism raised the temperature of hostility everywhere. Aware of failing health, Charles V did not want to leave the quarrels with Brittany and England a burden upon his son. The parleys after King Edward's passing had closed without result and evidently in bad feeling. To avoid mutually irritating debates, it was proposed to convene separately the next time: the English at Calais and the French twenty miles away at St. Omer, with the Archbishop of Rouen acting as go-between. Postponed by the schism, this plan was adopted for a renewed effort in September 1379.

Coucy, Rivière, and Mercier with one or two others were the French plenipotentiaries at this parley, and they were also delegated to meet with the Count of Flanders at Arras in the hope of inducing him to mediate a settlement with the Duke of Brittany. Before they could accomplish anything, the Count was caught up by a local revolt that, surmounting every repression and involving every faction, was to plunge Flanders into ruinous civil war.

The rising of the men of Ghent had no connection with the workers' insurrection that had seized control of Florence in the previous year. Although separate and spontaneous, the events in the two cloth cities initiated a whirlwind of class war over the next five years arising both from the accumulated miseries of the working class and from a new strength resulting from the disruptions of the Black Death. In Florence, Flanders, Languedoc, Paris, England, and back to Flanders and northern France, insurrections succeeded each other without visible link, except in the last phase. Some were urban, some rural; some arose from desperation, some from strength; but all were precipitated by one factor: oppressive taxes.

At Ghent, where the weavers were in greatest strength, the Count invited trouble when he levied a tax on the city to pay for a tournament. Led by the cry of an angry tradesman that tax money must not be squandered "on the follies of princes and the upkeep of actors and buffoons," the citizens refused to pay. The Count, playing on the commercial rivalry of the cities, secured the support of Bruges by a promise to build a canal connecting it to the sea, to the advantage of its commerce and the detriment of Ghent. When 500 diggers began work on a channel to divert the river Lys, Ghent dispatched its militia to the attack, and from that point on, the conflict enlarged itself like a cell dividing. Of Flanders' fierce tribulations that now began, Froissart wrote, "What shall they say that readeth this or heareth it read, but that it was the work of the Devil?"

At the opposite end of France at the same time, revolt erupted in Languedoc, where famine, oppression, war, and taxes had left a trail of misery under the harsh rule of the Duc d'Anjou. Impatient, bold, and habitually forcing events, Anjou exercised virtually sovereign power over a region amounting to a quarter of the realm. He swallowed its revenues whole, without distinguishing what was applied to his personal use from what was applied to the defense of Languedoc or the kingdom. To make up for fewer hearths as a result of the plague, the tax per hearth was raised each year, but the people obtained no benefit in better defense. Bandit companies still penetrated their valleys, still forced their villages to buy respite from pillage. In 1378, food taxes on consumption were added to those on sales, falling most heavily on the poor. When tax-collectors began the practice of house searches, like agents of the Inquisition, outrage was piled on misery.

"How can we live like this?" protesting groups cried as they gathered before the Virgin's statue to implore her aid. "How can we feed ourselves and our children when already we cannot pay the heavy taxes laid on us by the rich for their own comfort?" Riots and disorders spread and reached revolt in July 1379 when Anjou's Council levied a heavy new tax of twelve francs per hearth without convoking the Estates, merely asking the assent of the municipal councils. The Duke himself was absent at the time, conducting the war in Brittany. The wrath of his overburdened subjects burst with extraordinary violence against all in authority: royal officials, nobles, and the upper bourgeois of the town councils, whom the common people held responsible for the new tax. "Kill, kill all the rich!" was the cry, as reported by a seigneur of Clermont afterward. "Seigneurs and other good men of the country and towns," he said, "went in great fear of death" and in that other fear inspired by all revolts, "that if this infamous insolence of the common people was not rigorously suppressed, worse would follow."

At Le Puy, Nîmes, Clermont, and other towns, the people formed armed mobs, looted rich households, murdered officials, and committed acts of savagery—even, it was reported, "cut open bodies with their knives and ate like animals the flesh of baptized men." In October the commotion reached a climax in Montpellier when five of Anjou's councillors were killed and eighty others reportedly massacred. The insurgents sent out emissaries in an effort to raise a general revolt, but lacking the solid industrial base and traditions of the Flemish struggle, the rising quickly flared and was soon suppressed. Clement VII, dependent on Anjou's control of Languedoc for his support, instantly sent Cardinal Albano, a native of Languedoc, to calm the people and warn them of the terrible punishment for *lèse-majesté*. Already afraid of their rebellion, the leaders were persuaded to submit to the King's mercy.

The fate of Montpellier was deliberately dramatized for punitive effect. On the day of the return of the Duc d'Anjou in January, a vast procession of citizens over the age of fourteen was led through the city gate by the Cardinal, along with surviving officials, ecclesiastics, monks, faculty, and students of the university. Lined up on both sides of the road, they fell on their knees crying "Mercy!" as the Duke and his men in armor rode by. Along the way were stationed magistrates in gowns of office without mantles, hats, or belts, women in unadorned dress, citizens with halters around their necks, and, finally, all the children under fourteen, each group falling to its knees in turn to cry "Mercy!" The keys to the city's gates and the knocker of the great bell were humbly submitted. During the next two days, at Anjou's command, all arms were surrendered and the chief buildings turned over to his men-at-arms.

Then from a platform erected in the main square the Duke announced the ferocious sentence: 600 individuals condemned to death—one third to be hung, one third beheaded, one third burned, all their property to be confiscated, and their children sentenced to perpetual servitude. One half the property of all other citizens was to be confiscated and a fine levied of 6,000 francs plus the cost of the Duke's expenses caused by the outbreak. The walls and gates of the city were to be razed, the university to lose all its rights, properties, and archives.

A great outcry greeted the sentence, the Cardinal and prelates pleaded "very lovingly" for pity on the people, the university wept, women and children knelt and wailed. On the following day a reduced sentence was announced, remitting most of the penalties. The whole performance had been for effect. A letter of Charles V to the Cardinal, dated two months earlier, had stated his intention to be merciful, but the power of the crown to punish required demonstration.

The events in Languedoc had one far-reaching result: in exhibiting the distress of his subjects, they left the King with a guilty conscience, which could have serious consequences at a medieval deathbed. For the time being, conscious of the avarice and oppressions of his brother and the unpopularity they reflected on the crown, Charles reduced the hearth tax and recalled Anjou as Governor of Languedoc. Unhappily, his replacement, after an interim under Du Guesclin, was the Duc de Berry, whose rule of pure acquisitiveness undiluted by any political sense proved, if anything, more rapacious than his brother's.

In April 1379, Coucy and Rivière with several new colleagues went once more in quest of peace to a parley at Boulogne. They were empowered to make new concessions of territory and sovereignty and again to offer a marriage, in the person of Charles's baby daughter, Catherine, to Richard II. Through six parleys in the last six years the mirage of peace had mocked its seekers. In the same period, except for French success in Normandy, continuance of war had brought no advantage to either side but rather, through increasing antagonism and suspicion, had made the war harder to end.

The English came to the parley in divided mind, partly to try what diplomacy could gain, partly to maintain a holding operation while they prepared another assault. Montfort's rebellion had given them another opportunity to re-enter France and regain the territories they thought of as theirs. Ever since Charles's repudiation of the Treaty of Brétigny and the reverses that followed, they had hated the French for falsely and wrongfully, as they saw it, dispossessing them of their property. Defense of their own countrymen might be lackadaisical, but in combat overseas, where plunder offered, there was no lack of will to fight, only lack of money. Other means being exhausted, funds for an expedition to Brittany were raised in 1379 by a graduated poll (or head) tax, a new device designed to cover clergy and peasants at lower income levels than before. Calculated, with the usual vagueness about population figures, to bring in £50,000, it produced only £20,000, all of it invested in a fleet commanded by Sir John Arundel.

Delayed until winter by lack of wind and then by threat of a French raid, Arundel took part of his force to Southampton to guard against an enemy landing and, while there, to conduct himself indistin-guishably from the enemy. Besides robbing the countryside, he quartered his men-at-arms and archers in a convent, allowing them to violate at will the nuns and a number of poor widows who lived there, and to carry them off to the ships when ready to sail. Arundel was the man who had demanded money in hand before he would defend the south-coast towns against earlier French raids. If Walsingham may be believed, he used it for ostentation as extreme as his brutality. He is said to have embarked with a wardrobe of 52 suits embroidered in gold, and horses and equipment to the value of £7,000.

Sailing in December, his convoy was caught by a violent storm during which he ordered the kidnapped women thrown overboard to lighten the ships, maltreated the crew, and having struck down the pilot, was fittingly wrecked on the rocks of the Irish coast. Twenty-five ships with all equipment and all but seven survivors were lost. Arundel's body, rolling in the waves, was washed up three days later. Driven back by the storm, the remainder of the fleet never made the crossing and the tax money was accordingly wasted.

Already in 1378 the Commons had complained of the drain of money in a war in which they no longer perceived a national interest. Although war provided business and a living to many besides the nobles, the Commons protested that it was the King's affair and that he had spent £46,000 for the maintenance of Calais, Cherbourg, Brest, and other places "for which the Commons ought in no way to be charged." The government replied that the good-keeping of these "barbicans" overseas was the safeguard of the realm, "otherwise we should never find rest nor peace with our enemies for then they would push hot war to the thresholds of our houses which God forbid." The argument was not likely to persuade the south-coast towns, which continued to suffer hot war pushed to their thresholds by savage French and Castilian raids. In August 1380 even London was to tremble when an audacious Castilian force sailed fifteen miles up the Thames to sack Gravesend and leave it in flames.

In answer to the Commons, the Royal Council claimed that the footholds in France gave the King "convenient gates and entrances toward his enemies to grieve them when he is ready to act." It was a revealing statement of the intentions of the war party headed by the new King's youngest uncle, the Earl of Buckingham. A proud, fierce, intolerant young man of 25, he was a late version of the 12th century Bertrand de Born, who had once so feelingly exhorted his fellow knights, "Never give up war!"

In March 1380 the English renewed promises of aid to Montfort, but realization was postponed while the alternatives of peace were tested at Boulogne. At this parley Coucy and his fellow envoys offered new cessions and adjustments and the entire county of Angoulême as dowry for Catherine, but the English remained suspicious. They believed that the French offer was a ruse to prevent their coming to Montfort's aid. But basically, English reluctance to make peace was simply a desire to go on fighting, now strongly reinforced by the fact of the schism.

Pope Urban, not yet in his mad stage, was exercising every pressure to prevent Richard's marriage to a French princess and encourage a marriage to Wenceslas' sister, Anne of Bohemia, which would weld England and the Empire in an Urbanist axis. When there was only one Pope, England was anti-papal, but the existence of two made it necessary to take sides. Richard's advisers rejected the French marriage, negotiations were ruptured, and two years later the King of England married Anne of Bohemia. In the final irony for Charles, it was the schism, for which he was responsible, that frustrated his goal of peace. "All the witte of this worlde," Langland wrote in epitaph,

> Can nought conforem a pees bytwene the pope and his enymys;
> Ne bitwene two Cristene kynges, can no wighte pees make,
> Profitable to ayther people.

Nor could Charles find a settlement in Brittany. Coucy and others were sent on several missions, evidently in search of a formula, and a Breton Assembly of the Three Estates pleaded movingly for a pardon of their Duke, but Charles mistrusted Montfort too much to restore him. Montfort on his part would make no peace with the sovereign who had confiscated his dukedom. For others, particularly Du

Guesclin, the situation was a tangle of conflicting loyalties. Reluctant to fight his Breton compatriots, and subjected to a whispering campaign by his enemies at court, Du Guesclin left Brittany to lead a campaign against the Free Companies in Auvergne. Here, while besieging a castle, he suddenly fell ill and died in July 1380. While his burial was taking place in the royal mausoleum at St. Denis with honors "as though he had been the King's son," a new English expedition under Buckingham was already on its way. With the enemy at hand, and war or unrest in Brittany and Flanders, France was without a Constable.

At urgent councils held to decide Du Guesclin's successor, Coucy and Clisson were the leading candidates. Because of the "great repute" he had won in Normandy and the "great favor" in which the King held him, Coucy was offered the appointment, the highest and most lucrative lay office of the realm.

As chief military officer, the Constable outranked the royal princes; an attack upon his person was considered a crime of *lèse-majesté*. He was responsible for cohesion of the armed forces, and for tactical command when the King did not take the field. With control of recruitment, enrollment, provisioning, and all other arrangements for war, his opportunities for enlarging his fortune were immense. If the King was not engaged, the Constable's banner flew over captured towns; all booty theoretically belonged to him, except for money and prisoners reserved to the King and for artillery reserved to the Master of Crossbows. In addition to a fixed salary of 2,000 francs a month in peace as in war, he was paid upon the outbreak of hostilities a sum equal to one day's pay for every man-at-arms under contract. Even if this was intended for military expenses, it offered the recipient considerable scope. And apart from its profits, the Constableship had become, with the widening of war, a post of real function.

For reasons that remain enigmatic, Coucy declined the appointment. The reason he gave the King was that in order to hold Brittany, the Constable should be someone well known to, and familiar with, the Bretons—such as Clisson, whose appointment Coucy advised. His excuse, by itself, seems unconvincing. Clearly the problem of Brittany was crucial; nevertheless, if a settlement had to be reached with Montfort, Coucy himself, as Montfort's former brother-in-law, was more likely to achieve it than Clisson, Montfort's mortal enemy. Coucy and Montfort had both been married to daughters of Edward III, and though both wives were dead, the link established a relationship of importance in the Middle Ages, and in fact determined the choice of Coucy as mediator in the next reign.

Something is missing from Coucy's explanation. It is improbable that, like Dante's Pope, he made "the grand refusal" from a sense of inadequacy to the task. Modesty was certainly not a mark of the Coucys, and Enguerrand VII, judging by his seals and his Order of the Crown, held himself very highly. He accepted without hesitation all other assignments—battle, diplomacy, secret missions, foreign war, domestic governance—that crowded upon him, including the final one that was to cost his life. He was one of the nobility forced by the growing complications of public affairs to become statesmen, not merely swordsmen on horseback. Coucy's rank, prowess, and territorial importance would have warranted military command in any case, but other qualities were making him indispensable to the crown. Intelligence, tact, skills of rhetoric, and a noticeable level-headedness were coming to be more useful than the traditional mindless impetuosity of the knight in the iron cocoon.

Why then did he refuse the Constableship? The fact that Marshal Sancerre, to whom it was offered next, likewise refused it suggests some motive common to both, perhaps connected with the King's failing health. Charles V was, in fact, within two months of his death, and the advancing shadow may have been apparent. With the Dauphin a minor and the prospect of the King's three rapacious, ambitious, and mutually hostile brothers vying for control of the Regency, the Constableship may have appeared likely to be politically dangerous for the occupant. Coucy could lose more than he might gain from it. Unlike Clisson, who was to accept the post, he avoided making enemies, nor, with his great lands and ancient ancestry, did he need the office for power and position.

Upon his refusal, the King appointed him Captain-General of Picardy and gave him the town, castle, and seigneury of Mortaigne on the northern frontier between Tournai and Valenciennes to ensure that this outpost would be held in strong hands. He was also named to the Regency Council for the Dauphin, on whose account Charles was increasingly troubled since the death of the Queen. Owing to the royal Dukes' resistance to Clisson, the Constableship was left for the moment unfilled.

On the day Coucy took command of Picardy, July 19, 1380, the Earl of Buckingham landed at Calais and, with a force known from paymasters' records to number 5,060, began a march of devastation and plunder through the region for which Coucy was now responsible. To raise the cost of the expedition, the English crown had resorted to a tithe on the clergy and an export tax on wool and hides, but as the proceeds were not yet in hand, the King had to pawn the crown jewels for £10,000, which was sufficient only for the start. Thereafter the men-at-arms were to be paid from pillage en route. Because naval losses had reduced shipping, the expeditionary force had to cross "little by little," taking two weeks for the whole force to complete the one or two days' sail across the narrow neck of the Channel to Calais. The much longer sail directly to Brittany was precluded.

Buckingham's raid was to prove virtually a replica of Lancaster's seven years before—an open-eyed walk into privation, hunger, and ultimate futility. The strategic objective was to bring support to Montfort in Brittany and regain England's footholds there. Buckingham, however, like Lancaster before him, instead of going directly toward his objective, took a long way around to the east through Champagne and Burgundy, in quest of combat and booty. Since the same tactics brought the same results as before, the question arises: Why this mad persistence?

Thomas of Buckingham himself is part of the answer. Aggressive and ruthless by temperament and "wonderfully overbearing" in manner in the same way as his brother the Black Prince, Buckingham resented Lancaster's arrogation of power and saw himself carrying on the valor and glory of his father and eldest brother. Englishmen still felt themselves to be living in the triumphant era of Poitiers and Najera. "The English," said Clisson after he left them, "are so proud of themselves and have had so many good days [at war] that they think they cannot lose."

England's most experienced soldier, Sir Robert Knollys, and other famous knights such as Lord Thomas Percy and Sir Hugh Calveley accompanied Buckingham to France. What beckoned them and younger men was personal opportunity for clash of arms, for reputation and profits, and for whatever punishment they could inflict upon France. For poor knights, squires, and yeomen, war was livelihood; as Buckingham argued, "They can better live in war than in peace, for in lying still there is no advantage." Most knights went to war to "advance themselves," as they put it. National strategic aim was not in their minds, and Brittany hardly more than an excuse.

With a force half men-at-arms and half archers, the English rode through Artois and northern Picardy keeping close order in case of French attack. "They shall have battle before they finish their march!" Coucy assured French knights who brought him intelligence of the enemy's route, although he knew well enough that battle was enjoined by the King. Charles V was not to be swerved from his philosophy of war. Not being a fighter himself, he was not prevented by personal pride from employing the lessons of experience, nor did he hesitate to hurt the pride of chivalry by reminders of past defeats. His own initiation into war on the awful day of Poitiers had left a permanent mark. If a mystique of success enveloped the English in the conviction that "they could not lose," Charles suffered from the opposite psychology. From the major clashes of the early part of the war, he had concluded that the delivery of armed force could not be reliably directed and that war was too important to be left to the chances of battle.

From headquarters at Péronne on the Somme, Coucy issued a general summons to all knights and squires of Artois and Picardy. The documents show him moving from place to place, at Hesdin, Arras, Abbeville, and St. Quentin, holding reviews and deploying units for defense of towns, "for he was anxious that no loss should be suffered from any negligence on his part." How far Coucy, as a man of the sword, agreed with the King's policy is moot; he carried out orders to avoid battle while following Buckingham's march, even when it left a trail of burning villages through his own domain, but certain actions show that he shared the knights' impatience to break through the agony of restraint.

Parties of French knights kept close to the English line of march to hamper foraging, and this proximity opened tempting opportunities for combat. Although one report describes the French as *immobilis quasi lapis* (immovable as stones), skirmishes were unavoidable, from which on the whole they did not carry off the honors. In one case, a fierce fight lasting an hour on horse and foot, the English took eighteen prisoners from a French party of thirty; in another the French, perceiving the enemy stronger, sounded retreat and fled. "The horses felt the effect of the spurs and very opportunely did these lords find the barriers [of their town] open," but not before fifteen had been captured. Another party of thirty English, "seeking to perform some deed of arms," set forth at dawn with their foragers, but were meanly frustrated of their main purpose when a group of important French lords escaped them. "God!" they cried, "what fortunes would have been ours if we had taken them, for they would have paid us 40,000 francs."

When the countryside was stripped, the English demanded food from the towns under threat of attack. Refused by Reims, secure behind its walls, they retaliated by burning sixty surrounding villages within a week. Discovering several thousand sheep herded into ditches outside the city walls, the English sent men to drive them out under cover of their archers, who shot so keenly that no one from Reims dared to venture out or even appear on the bulwarks. Under renewed threat by the English to burn the fields of ripe grain, the citizens now delivered to them sixteen loads of bread and wine.

In this manner Buckingham advanced to Burgundy, where 2,000 French knights and squires had assembled in a mood to throw off the King's restraints and fight. The leading nobles of the realm—Bourbon, Coucy, the Duc de Bar, the Comte d'Eu, Admiral Jean de Vienne—were present under the command of Philip the Bold, Duke of Burgundy. Armed head to foot and with battle-ax in his hand, the Duke in bellicose spirit reviewed his forces. Heralds rode out from both sides with challenges to deeds of valor. Still the King from his chamber prohibited battle unless the French found themselves in decisive superiority. Burgundy did not dare defy his wishes, but the restraints broke when an English squire was killed in a fracas. In answer to the enemy's challenge, a body of knights, including Coucy, engaged the English in a strenuous fight outside the gates of Troyes. The outcome was inconclusive, Buckingham moved on, the French followed, pleading with the King not to let the enemy slip through their hands. Charles replied only, "Let them alone; they will destroy themselves."

At the Loire the French had gathered the advantage in numbers. Coucy and his companions were determined, "whether the King willed it or not," to give battle before the English crossed the Sarthe into Brittany. Meanwhile Charles, negotiating while the armies marched, had persuaded the city of Nantes, key to Brittany and pro-French, not to admit the English and to declare loyalty to France without reference to Montfort. In the first week of September the English crossed the Sarthe and in that week Charles entered his last illness. The secretion from the abscess on his arm dried up, heralding death, and physicians and patient accepted the signal. Moved by litter to his favorite château of Beauté on the Marne, Charles sent for his brothers and brother-in-law—excepting Anjou, whom he hoped to keep at a distance from the Royal Treasury—and prepared to make dispositions for the journey of his soul.

Philip the Bold hastened to Paris, and Coucy likewise because of his responsibility as a member of the Regency Council. Anjou, who was kept apprised of events by partisans in Paris, hurried up from Languedoc, whether wanted or not.

The King suffered physically in his last days, but his mental anguish was heavier. Two things weighed on his conscience: his part in the schism and the questionable legality of his taxation. He had stretched temporary grants by the Estates into ten years of continuous taxes, and though he had used them for defense of the realm and the "public weal," he had filled the royal coffers in the process and bought the allegiance of nobles with the people's tax money. How would he answer to God? He had raised France from a "heap of ruins"; he had canceled—except for Calais—the English conquests made in the time of his father and grandfather; he had uprooted Navarre permanently from Normandy; and if peace had receded from his grasp, he had, by the steady pursuit of national purpose, justified the loyalty of all who had felt themselves French in the hour of choice.

But had he bought recovery at the price of the people's misery? The uprising in Languedoc had revealed the cost, and Charles was aware, through tax-collectors' reports, of angry mutterings closer to home. Oppression of his subjects reacted upon the fate of his soul, for a sovereign's illegal taxes could arouse the Divine wrath, and the complaints of those he had wronged would follow him to the judgment seat. In his own time the unknown author of the allegory *Songe du Vergier* (Dream of the Woodsman) branded as tyrants all princes who burdened their subjects with "taxes impossible to bear," and theologians warned rulers that they should cancel all exactions and make restitution to great and small if they hoped for salvation. That hope dictated the King's last act.

Within hours of death, fully dressed and laid on a chaise-longue before a perturbed group of prelates, seigneurs, and councillors representing the three estates, the King in a fading voice spoke first of the schism. He insisted in a troubled and rambling defense that he had sought to follow "in this as in all else, the surest road," that "if ever rumor should say that the Cardinals acted under the inspiration of the Demon, you may be sure that no consideration of kinship dictated my choice but solely the statements of the said Cardinals and the advice of prelates, clerics and my councillors"; finally, that he would obey a decision of a General Council of the Church and "God could not reproach me if in my ignorance I acted contrary to a future decision of the Church." It was the declaration of a very worried man.

At the door of death in the Middle Ages, the trembling traveler, more often than not, felt required to repudiate what he had done in life. When it came to taxes, the most conscientious sovereign of his time repudiated the exercise of kingship. He announced the terms of an ordinance to "abate and abolish" the hearth taxes, "as from here on, and it is our pleasure, wish and order by these same letters, that they shall no longer be current in our kingdom and that from now on our said people and subjects shall not pay any of them but shall be quit and discharged."

Other, indirect taxes existed, but the hearth tax was the basic property tax on which the financial system rested. To decree that it should "no longer be current" was to deceive the people and deprive his successors—supposing the decree were to be carried out—of the means of governing. Charles's act was not an aberration. Sovereigns before him had been known to cancel taxes and return subsidies illegally exacted, and deathbed donors regularly made restitutions and established foundations that, if carried out, would bankrupt their families. Charles had amassed a huge fortune for his son, but by 1380 the theory that the King could live of his own domain was a ragged fiction. A regular financial footing, as Charles knew all too well, was government's greatest need. In the chill of death, his soul's need was stronger.

The King received extreme unction, commended to his brothers his twelve-year-old son, and urged on them with his last breath the lifting of taxes: "Take them off as speedily as you can." Bureau de la Rivière, kneeling in tears at the bedside, embraced the King; the room was emptied of the sobbing crowd so that his last moments should be in peace. He died on September 16, 1380, and his last ordinance was proclaimed the next day. Between public rejoicing and the conflicting sentiments of the late King's brothers, an explosive situation was created.

In Brittany in the same month Buckingham received an ambiguous welcome. Montfort, whose whole life was spent balancing enemies, intriguing, fighting, quarreling, and making treaties with everyone, was a habitual double-dealer. Charles being dead, he was prepared to make peace with the new King, and opened negotiations with the French while at the same time signing a compact of many oaths with Buckingham to jointly besiege Nantes. But the reluctance of Breton nobles to support an attack on their countrymen decided their lord to choose France. Coucy, warmly in favor of a reconciliation with Brittany, was one of the negotiators who concluded a treaty with Montfort in January 1381. Buckingham, who was not kept informed by his ally, found towns and castles closed to him and provisions withdrawn inside their walls. Through the winter months his wasted army wandered from place to place, often lacking food and shelter. Finally told by Montfort that he must leave, he and his companions took ship for England in March 1381. Except for individual knighthoods and ransoms and some fruits of pillage collected en route, Buckingham and his fellows had accomplished no military purpose, "to their great discomfort and the discomfort of the whole English nation."

Both nations under boy kings now suffered the rule of ambitious and contending uncles who, wearing no crown, exercised power without responsibility. War receded; internal stress reached the bursting point.

Chapter 18

The Worms of the Earth
Against the Lions

Let him go to the Devil! He lived long enough," cried a workingman on the death of the King. "It would have been better for us if he had died ten years ago!" Within a few months of the King's death, France experienced the explosion of working-class revolt that had already swept through Florence and Flanders. In addition to oppressive taxes, a rising rancor of the poor against the rich and a conscious demand by the lowest class for greater rights in the system supplied the impulse. Concentration of wealth was moving upward in the 14th century and enlarging the proportion of the poor, while the catastrophes of the century reduced large numbers to misery and want. The poor had remained manageable as long as their minimum subsistence could be maintained by charity, but the situation changed when urban populations were swelled by the flotsam of war and plague and infused by a new aggressiveness in the plague's wake.

As the masters became richer, the workers sank to the level of day labor, with little prospect of advancement. Membership in the guilds was shut off to the ordinary journeyman and reserved under complicated requirements and fees for sons and relatives of the master class. In many trades, work was farmed out to workers in their homes, often at lower wages to their wives and children, whose employment was forbidden in the guilds. Obligatory religious holidays, which numbered 120 to 150 a year, kept earnings down. Although forbidden to strike and, in some towns, to assemble, workers formed associations of their own to press for higher wages. They had their own dues and treasuries and connections across frontiers through which jobs and lodgings could be secured for members, and which doubtless served as channels of agitation.

Self-consciousness as a class—the "people"—was growing. Christ was often portrayed as a man of the people and shown in frescoes and carvings surrounded by an artisan's or peasant's tools—hammer, knife, ax, and wool-carder's comb—instead of by the instruments of the Crucifixion. In Florence, the workers called themselves *il popolo di Dio*. "*Viva il popolo!*" was the cry of the revolt of the Ciompi in 1378. As the greatest industrial center of the day, Florence was the natural starting place of insurrection.

The Ciompi were the lowest class of workers unaffiliated with any guild, but while the revolt came to be called after them, artisans of all levels and degrees below the major craft guilds were involved in the rising. They worked at fixed wages, often below subsistence level, for sixteen to eighteen hours a day, and their wages might be withheld to cover waste or damage to raw materials. The alliance of the Church with the great was plain enough in a bishop's pastoral letter declaring that spinners could be excommunicated for wasting their wool. Workers could be flogged or imprisoned or suffer removal from the list of employables or have a hand cut off for resistance to employers. Agitators for the right to organize could be hung, and in 1345 ten wool-carders had been put to death on this charge.

In the outbreak of 1378, after a storm of violence throughout the city, the workers rushed up the steps of the Signoria's palazzo to present their demands. They wanted open access to the guilds, the right to organize their own unions, reform of the system of fines and punishments, and, most significantly, the right "to participate in the government of the City." In an era without guns or tear gas, mobs inspired immediate terror. Although the city hall was well supplied with means of defense, the Signoria were "frightened men," and capitulated. The workers installed a new government based on labor's representation in the guilds. It lasted 41 days before it began to crumble under internal stress and the counter-offensives of the magnates. Reforms gained in the revolt slowly eroded, and by 1382 the major guilds had reasserted their control, if not their confidence. Thereafter the fear of another proletarian outbreak contributed to the decline of republican government and the rise of the Medici as the dominant ruling family.

The weavers of Ghent had greater staying power. At Ypres and Bruges the original revolt had been suppressed by the Count of Flanders with fearful vengeance of burning and hanging. But the Gantois, through sieges, truces, treacheries, and brutal retaliations on both sides, had maintained their war despite blockade and near starvation. Ghent's struggle was not in fact class war, though it came to be perceived as such. Rather it was a stubborn defense of town autonomy against the Count, crisscrossed by the strife of social and religious factions. It was a complex of rivalries between towns, between trades, and among different levels within a trade. The weavers oppressed the lower-class fullers with as much animus as they directed against the Count.

In France, the King's deathbed promise of abolition of taxes aroused a fever of impatience for its fulfillment. Anger at taxes continually levied in the name of fighting the English had reached outrage when Buckingham raided the countryside unopposed and the people saw their money go, as it seemed, for nothing. In fact, as a result of funds spent by Charles V on improved defenses, towns and castles were better able to withstand the enemy than in the miserable years after Poitiers. But this did not lessen the burden on the lowest taxable class nor the resentment of the independent towns at having to pay for what was considered to be the King's business. Such was this feeling that Laon refused to open its gates to Coucy as Captain-General of Picardy and refused also to send him a company of thirty archers he had demanded. The towns of Picardy balked at further payments. At St. Quentin and Compiègne, crowds rioted, burned tax offices, assaulted tax-collectors and chased them out of town.

In Paris, the government was half paralyzed by the scramble for power around the throne. As eldest uncle, Anjou held the title of Regent, and used it to seize as much of the Treasury as he could for the purpose of pursuing the kingdom that beckoned him in Italy. Aware of his brothers' predatory habits, the late King had arranged for the Regency to end when his son was fourteen, but he had died two years too soon. He had named his brother Burgundy and his wife's brother Bourbon as guardians of his son. With Anjou as Regent, they were to rule with a Council of Twelve. Bourbon, who had no ambitions and held aloof from cabals, was known as "the Good Duke" in nice distinction to the paternal uncles, but he had less influence than they because he was not of the blood royal.

Pulled apart by their separate interests—Burgundy in Flanders, Anjou in Italy, Berry in a passion for collecting—the paternal uncles had no common interest in the integrity of the realm. Their only cohesion was in desire to remove the hands of the late King's ministers from the controls. Meanwhile, amid their discords, they found time to divide up his magnificent library of a thousand volumes. Anjou took 32 carefully chosen books with silk and enameled bindings and golden clasps, among the most beautiful in the collection, including one entitled *The Government of Princes*.

Clisson was named Constable and the coronation was hastened to strengthen the authority of the regime. A disgraceful scene marred the monarchy's sacred ceremony on November 4. At the banquet table, Anjou and Burgundy, who detested each other, engaged in a physical scramble for the seat of honor next to the new King. Amid tumult of partisans' and prelates' dismay, a Council was hastily convened which decided in favor of Burgundy as premier peer of France, whereupon Anjou seized the seat anyway, only to be shoved out of it by Philip the Bold, who sat down in his place. In this sorry exhibition, the reign began.

Its sovereign, twelve-year-old Charles VI, was a handsome, well-built boy, tall and fair like his grandfather, with an inexpressive face, mirror of a shallow soul. "Shining and polished arms pleased him more than all the jewels in the world," and he adored the rituals of chivalry. These were never more fittingly displayed than at the coronation banquet when Coucy, Clisson, and Admiral de Vienne, magnificently mounted on horses caparisoned in cloth of gold down to the ground, served the King's dishes from horseback. To give the King's entry into Paris the greatest possible *éclat*, three days of splendid festivities with music by minstrels were held in squares hung with tapestries. "New marvels," in the form of artificial fountains running with milk, wine, and clear water, were constructed to amaze the people.

They did not suffice. The summoning of an Estates General for November 14 to provide a substitute for the hearth tax intensified public anxiety at the prospect of a new levy. Excited clusters of artisans discussed their grievances in the streets, secret meetings were held at night, assemblies gathered to denounce the government, the people were "inflamed and agitated by an ardent desire to enjoy liberty and free themselves from the yoke of subsidies."

When the Chancellor, Miles de Dormans, Bishop of Beauvais, informed the Estates that the King needed aids from the people, the predictable explosion came. A crowd of commoners rushed upon a meeting of merchants, who, though opposed to the aids, were not prepared to force the issue.

"Know, citizens, how you are despised!" cried a cobbler in passionate oratory to his followers. All the bitterness of the little against the great was expressed in his denunciation of the "endless greed of seigneurs" who "would take from you, if they could, even your share of daylight." They crush the people with their exactions, more each year. "They do not wish us to breathe or to speak or to have human faces or mix with them in public places. . . . These men to whom we render forced homage and who feed on our substance have no other thought but to glitter with gold and jewels, to build superb palaces and invent new taxes to oppress the city." He poured scorn on the cowardice of the merchants, citing in comparison the stalwart citizens of Ghent who at that very moment were in arms against their Count because of taxes.

If the cobbler's eloquence was owed in part to embellishment by the Monk of St. Denis, who recorded it, that only serves to indicate the sympathy of many monastic chroniclers with the plight of the people. In his famous prophecy, the friar Jean de Roquetaillade had seen the day coming when "the worms of the earth will most cruelly devour the lions, leopards and wolves . . . and the little and common folk will destroy all tyrants and traitors."

For the cobbler and his 300 companions, that day was at hand. Screaming and brandishing knives, they forced the Provost of Merchants to carry their demand for tax abolition to Anjou and the Chancellor. At the Marble Table in the palace courtyard, the Provost pleaded for a lifting of the "intolerable burden." With "terrible shouts" the crowd confirmed his words, swearing they would pay no more but die a thousand times rather than suffer "such dishonor and shame." These unexpected words appear frequently in the protests, as if to add the dignity of knightly formula. The poor no less than the great needed to feel themselves acting nobly.

Anjou, in smooth and soothing words of pity for the poor, promised to obtain by the next day the King's assent to abolition of taxes. During the night the people listened to dangerous counsels about challenging the sovereignty of nobles and churchmen. They believed, according to the chronicler of St. Denis, "that the government would be better directed by them than by their natural lords." Whether this revolutionary sentiment was in fact in the minds of the people or only feared to be by the chronicler, it was certainly in the air.

When the frightened government confirmed abolition next day, the relief was all too quick. In a frenzy of triumph and unspent wrath, the people rushed to rob and assault the Jews, the one section of society upon whom the poor could safely vent their aggression. The assault was instigated, it was said, by certain nobles in the crowd who saw a way of wiping out their debts. While some of the crowd raced through the city to seize tax coffers and destroy the registers, the main body, with nobles participating, rampaged through the Jewish quarter to cries of "*Noël! Noël!*" (referring to the birthday of Christ). They broke down doors, looted goods and documents, carried off valuables, pursued Jews through the streets to throw those they could catch into the river, and seized numbers of children for forced baptism. Most of the Jews fled for refuge to the dungeons of the Châtelet, but ten bodies, including a rabbi's, were recovered after the carnage. The pogroms spread to Chartres, Senlis, and other cities. As the symptom of a disturbed society, the persecutions continued off and on over the next decade until the crown was forced to decree yet another expulsion of the Jews in 1394.

For the moment, the crown's need of money dictated an effort through Hugues Aubriot, Provost of Paris, to take the Jews under royal protection. Aubriot, a contentious figure and notorious libertine, sent out heralds ordering restoration of everything stolen from the Jews including the kidnapped children. "Very few obeyed the order," and the Provost's snatching of souls from Christian baptism was to be a charge against him in his coming downfall.

By edict of November 16, the government, as promised, abolished "henceforth and forever all taxes, tithes, *gabelles,* by which our subjects are much grieved, quitting and remitting all aids and subsidies which have been imposed for the said wars since our predecessor, King Philip, until today." This stroke of fiscal suicide reflected momentary panic rather than serious intention. Aside from Charles V, most rulers governed by impulse in the 14th century.

In search of other money, the government immediately appealed to the provincial Estates for voluntary aids, with generally meager results. At the Estates of Normandy, when one member proposed to vote a grant, the assembly cried with one voice, "Nothing! Nothing!" At Rouen and Amiens, the people "were all of one will" against it. "By God's blood, it shall never pass!" shouted a bourgeois orator to a protest meeting in the pig market of Sens. Opinion was general that the King's treasure was enough for his needs and that more money would only go into greater extravagances by the nobles. While some districts voted aids, the major result of summoning the provincial Estates was to spread discussion and excite resistance.

Divided interests in the Third Estate complicated the struggle. The petty bourgeois were seeking to wrest control from the ruling oligarchy of merchants and masters of guilds, and both parties used the rising agitation of the working class for their own ends. They had inflammable tinder in the unhappy ranks of the unskilled and in dispossessed peasants, driven into the cities by the wars, who created a reservoir of anger and misery.

The late King's ministerial structure, like the financial, was soon riddled by the uncles' efforts to remove his councillors. Bureau de la Rivière, whom Charles V had loved and wished to have buried at his feet, was accused of treason by a spokesman of the Dukes but was saved when Clisson threw down his glove in the presence of the whole court and no one dared take up the awful challenge. In fear of reprisals, Rivière afterward left office, d'Orgement and Mercier were eventually pushed out, and another of the former councillors, Jean de La Grange, Cardinal of Amiens, found good reason to depart.

La Grange was disliked by the young King, who had been led by the Cardinal's enemies to believe that he kept a familiar demon. On one occasion when Charles was ten, he had crossed himself at the Cardinal's approach, crying, "Flee from the Devil! Throw out the Devil!"—to the considerable annoyance of that prince of the Church. On learning that the young King, on his accession, had said to a friend, "This is the moment to revenge ourselves on this priest," Cardinal La Grange put his treasure in safekeeping and fled to Avignon, never to return.

The sensational fall of the Provost of Paris added to the sense of crumbling authority. Hugues Aubriot was a man in his sixties who had won the favor of Philip of Burgundy by extravagant banquets and gifts, and the favor of the bourgeois by construction of the first sewers and by vigorous repair of walls and bridges. But he was marked for destruction by the clergy, whom he openly insulted, and by the University, which he scorned as that "nursery of priests" and whose privileges he combatted and members he arrested on any pretext. It was said that he reserved two dungeons in the Châtelet expressly for scholars and clerics. At the funeral of Charles V, when Aubriot refused to allow the University to take precedence in the procession, a furious fracas broke out between the Provost's sergeants and the scholars, ending with many of the University wounded and 36 thrown in jail. "Ha, that rabble!" Aubriot exclaimed. "I am sorry that nothing worse happened to them."

Aubriot's intervention in the case of the Jews gave the University its handle for revenge. Accused of heresy, sodomy, and being a false Christian, and, specifically, of "profaning the sanctity of baptism" by returning the Jewish children, he was brought to trial before the Bishop of Paris in May 1381. Besides charges of voicing contempt for the Eucharist, failure to take communion at Easter, and public disrespect of the clergy, he was accused of neglect of a virtuous wife, of buying virgins, and having "recourse to sorcery that his passions might triumph," of imprisoning husbands to have freedom with their wives, of cohabiting bestially with women against nature and having carnal relations with Jews.

Convicted, but spared a death sentence by Burgundy's influence, he was exposed on a wooden platform in front of the cathedral, where, on his knees and hatless, he was obliged to beg for absolution and vow an offering of candles for the baptized Jews he had returned to their parents. Absolved by the Bishop and Rector of the University, he was then condemned to perpetual penitence in prison on bread and water. His removal, contributing to the weakening of government, left the people of Paris readier to rise.

Coucy during these uneasy happenings remained in the Royal Council on good terms with the Dukes, each of whom desired his support. One of Anjou's first acts as Regent, on September 27, had been to confirm Coucy in lifetime possession of Mortaigne on the Channel, bestowed on him by the late King. In addition to grand estate, Coucy clearly possessed a personal power of attraction and a faculty for not making enemies. In the great game of "who's in, who's out," he was always able to work with whoever held power, perhaps owing to political sophistication gained from the circumstances of his marriage. After accomplishing the treaty of peace with the Duke of Brittany in January 1381, he was sent once more as ambassador to the English at Montreuil to negotiate a dispute over terms of the truce. Later in the year, documents show him paying spies for information on Calais, Guînes, and other English fortresses. While charged with defense of the frontier, he was recalled to Paris in May to advise Anjou on his projects in Italy.

Spoiling for a kingdom, Anjou needed money. Informed of the treasure stored by Charles V at Melun for the use of his son, Anjou laid hold of it by the direct expedient of threatening to execute the guardian of the fund. The Monk of St. Denis, however, does not vouch for this story because "one never knows the truth about these things that take place in the shadow." Whatever Anjou obtained, it was not enough. He continued pressing for aids through 1381, winning a few grants here and there, but generally meeting sullen resistance.

While France smoldered, true revolt erupted in June 1381 in England, not of the urban class but of the peasants. In a country whose economy was largely rural, they were the working class that mattered. The third poll tax in four years, to include everyone over the age of fifteen, was the precipitant. Voted in November 1380 by a subservient Parliament to finance Lancaster's ambitions in Spain, the collection brought in only two thirds of the expected sum, not least because tax commissioners were easily bribed to overlook families or falsify their numbers. A second round of collecting became necessary, which could have been foreseen as an invitation to trouble if the lords and prelates and royal uncles of Richard's government had paid attention to the constant complaints of rural insubordination. They did not, and brought upon themselves the most fearful challenge of the century.

At the end of May, villages in Essex on the east coast just above London refused payment; the resistance spread with some evidence of planning, and burst into violence in Kent, the adjoining county south of the Thames. Peasants mingled with yeomen from the French wars armed themselves with rusty swords, scythes, axes, and longbows blackened by age, and triumphantly stormed a castle where a runaway villein had been imprisoned. Electing Wat Tyler, an eloquent demagogue and veteran of the wars, as their commander-in-chief, they seized Canterbury, forced the mayor to swear fealty to "King Richard and the Commons," and liberated from the Archbishop's prison the ideologue of the movement, John Ball. He was a vagrant priest, scholar, and zealot who had been wandering the country for twenty years, frequently hauled in by the authorities for prophesying against Church and state and preaching radical doctrines of equality.

Although the poll tax was the igniting spark, the fundamental grievance was the bonds of villeinage and the lack of legal and political rights. Villeins could not plead in court against their lord, no one spoke for them in Parliament, they were bound by duties of servitude which they had no way to break except by forcibly obtaining a change of the rules. That was the object of the insurrection, and of the march on the capital that began from Canterbury.

As the Kentishmen swept forward to London, covering the seventy miles in two days, the Essex rebels marched southward to meet them. Abbeys and monasteries on the way were a special object of animosity because they were the last to allow commutation of servile labor. In the towns, artisans and small tradesmen, sharing the quarrel of the little against the great, gave aid and food to the peasants. As the sound of the rising spread to other counties, riots and outbreaks widened.

The "mad multitude" on its march from Kent and Essex opened prisons, sacked manors, and burned records. Some personally hated landlords and officials were murdered and their heads carried around on poles. Others, in fear of death, fled to hide in the same woods where villein outlaws frequently hid from them. Certain lords were forced by the rebels to accompany them "whether they would or not," either to supply needed elements of command or the appearance of participation by the gentry.

At the same time, peasant spokesmen swore to kill "all lawyers and servants of the King they could find." Short of the King, their imagined champion, all officialdom was their foe—sheriffs, foresters, tax-collectors, judges, abbots, lords, bishops, and dukes—but most especially men of the law because the law was the villeins' prison. Not accidentally, the Chief Justice of England, Sir John Cavendish, was among their first victims, along with many clerks and jurors. Every attorney's house on the line of march reportedly was destroyed.

If the Jacquerie 23 years earlier had been an explosion without a program, the Peasants' Revolt arose out of a developing idea of freedom. Though theoretically free, villeins wanted abolition of the old bonds, the right to commute services to rent, a riddance of all the restrictions heaped up by the Statute of Laborers over the past thirty years in the effort to clamp labor in place. They had listened to Lollard priests, and to secular preachers moved by the evils of the time, and to John Ball's theories of leveling. "Matters cannot go well in England," was his theme, "until all things shall be held in common; when there shall be neither vassals nor lords, when the lords shall be no more masters than ourselves. . . . Are we not all descended from the same parents, Adam and Eve?"

Wyclif's spirit, which had dared deny the most pervasive authority of the time, was abroad. What had happened in the last thirty years, as a result of plague, war, oppression, and incompetence, was a weakened acceptance of the system, a mistrust of government and governors, lay and ecclesiastical, an awakening sense that authority could be challenged—that change was in fact possible. Moral authority can be no stronger than its acknowledgment. When officials were venal—as even the poor could see they were in the bribing of tax commissioners—and warriors a curse and the Church oppressive, the push for change gained strength.

It was encouraged by the preachers' castigation of the powerful. "The tournaments of the rich," they said, "are the torments of the poor." They regularly denounced "evil princes," "false executors who increase the sorrows of widows," "wicked ecclesiastics who show the worst example to the people," and, above all, nobles who empty the purses of the poor by their extravagance, and disdain them for "lowness of blod or foulenesse of body," for deformed shape of body or limb, for dullness of wit and uncunning of craft, and deign not to speak to them, and who are themselves stuffed with pride—of ancestry, fortune, gentility, possessions, power, comeliness, strength, children, treasure—"prowde in lokynge, prowde in spekyng, . . . prowde in goinge, standynge and sytting." All would be drawn by fiends to Hell on the Day of Judgment.

On that day of wrath, said the Dominican John Bromyard in terms that spoke directly to the peasant, the rich would have hung around their necks the oxen and sheep and beasts of the field that they had seized without paying for. The "righteous poor," promised a Franciscan friar, "will stand up against the cruel rich at the Day of Judgment and will accuse them of their works and severity on earth. 'Ha, ha!' will say the others, horribly frightened, 'These are the folk formerly in contempt. See how they are honored—they are among the sons of God! What are riches and pomp to us now who are abased?' "

If the meek were indeed the sons of God (even if they too were scolded by the preachers for greed, cheating, and irreverence), why should they wait for their rights until the Day of Judgment? If all men had a common origin in Adam and Eve, how should some be held in hereditary servitude? If all were equalized by death, as the medieval idea constantly emphasized, was it not possible that inequalities on earth were contrary to the will of God?

At its climax on the outskirts of London, the Peasants' Revolt came to the edge of overpowering the government. No measures had been taken against the oncoming horde, partly from contempt for all Wills and Cobbs and Jacks and black-nailed louts, partly from mediocre leadership and lack of ready resources. Lancaster was away on the Scottish border, Buckingham was in Wales, and the only organized armed forces were already embarking at Plymouth for Spain under the command of the third brother, Edmund of Cambridge. Except for 500 or 600 men-at-arms in the King's retinue, the crown controlled no police or militia; London's citizens were unreliable because many were in sympathy and some in active connivance with the rebels.

Twenty thousand peasants were camped outside the walls demanding parley with the King. While they promised him safety, they shouted for the heads of Archbishop Sudbury and Sir Robert Hailes, the Chancellor and Treasurer, whom they held responsible for the poll tax, and for the head, too, of the arch "traitor," John of Gaunt, symbol of misgovernment and a failing war. John Ball harangued them with a fierce call to cast off the yoke they had borne for so long, to exterminate all great lords, judges, and lawyers and gain for all men equal freedom, rank, and power.

In agitated council, the government could find no course but to negotiate. Richard II, a slight fair boy of fourteen, accompanied by his knights, rode out to meet the insurgents and hear their demands: abolition of the poll tax and of all bonds of servile status, commutation at a rate of four pence an acre, free use of forests, abolition of the game laws—all these to be confirmed in charters sealed by the King. Everything the rebels asked was conceded in the hope of getting them to disperse and go home.

Meanwhile, partisans had opened the city's gates and bridges to a group led by Wat Tyler, who gained possession of the Tower of London and murdered Archbishop Sudbury and Sir Robert Hailes. Balked of Gaunt, they flung themselves upon his palace of the Savoy and tore it apart in an orgy of burning and smashing. At Wat Tyler's order, it was to be not looted but destroyed. Barrels of gunpowder found in storage were thrown on the flames, tapestries ripped, precious jewels pounded to bits with ax heads. The Temple, center of the law with all its deeds and records, was similarly destroyed. Killing followed; Lombards and Flemings (hated simply as foreigners), magnates, officials, and designated "traitors" (such as the rich merchant Sir Richard Lyons, who had been impeached by the Good Parliament and restored by Lancaster) were hunted down and slain.

In the hectic sequence of events, only Richard moved in a magic circle of reverence for the King's person. Perched on a tall war-horse before the peasants, a charming boy robed in purple embroidered with the royal leopards, wearing a crown and carrying a gold rod, gracious and smiling and gaining confidence from his sway over the mob, he granted charters written out and distributed by thirty clerks on the spot. On this basis, many groups of peasants departed, believing in the King as their protector.

While in London, Sir Robert Knollys, the Master of War, was urgently assembling an armed force, Wat Tyler, inflamed by blood and conquest, was exhorting his followers toward a massacre of the ruling class and a takeover of London. He was no longer to be satisfied by the promised charters, which he suspected were hollow, and he knew he would never be included in any pardon. He could only go forward toward a seizure of power. According to Walsingham, he boasted that "in four days' time all the laws of England would be issuing from his mouth."

He returned to the camp at Smithfield for another meeting with the King, where he put forth a new set of demands so extreme as to suggest that their purpose was to provoke rejection and provide a pretext for seizing Richard in person: all inequalities of rank and status were to be abolished, all men to be equal below the King, the Church to be disendowed and its estates divided among the commons, England to have but one bishop and the rest of the hierarchy to be eliminated. The King promised everything consistent with the "regality of his crown." Accounts of the next moments are so variously colored by the passions of the time that the scene remains forever obscure. Apparently Tyler picked a quarrel with a squire of the King's retinue, drew a dagger, and in a flash was himself struck down by the short sword of William Walworth, Mayor of London.

All was confusion and frenzy. The peasants drew their bows; some arrows flew. Richard, with extraordinary nerve, ordering no one to follow, rode forward alone, saying to the rebels, "Sirs, what is it you require? I am your captain. I am your King. Quiet yourselves." While he parleyed, Knollys' force, hastily summoned, rode up and surrounded the camp in mailed might with visors down and weapons gleaming. Dismayed and leaderless, the peasants were cowed; Wat Tyler's head displayed on a lance completed their collapse, like that of the Jacques at the death of Guillaume Cale.

Ordered to lay down their arms and assured of pardons to encourage dispersal, they trailed homeward. Leaders, including John Ball, were hanged and the rising elsewhere in England was suppressed— with sufficient brutality, if not the wild massacre that had taken place in France after the Jacquerie. Except for scattered retribution, the English revolt, too, was over within a month, defeated more by fraud than by force. The pardons issued in the King's name were revoked without compunction, and the charters canceled by a landowners' Parliament on the grounds that they had been issued under duress. To a deputation from Essex who came to remind the King of his promise to end villeinage, Richard replied, "Villeins ye are, and villeins ye shall remain."

The assumptions of autocrats are often behind the times. Economic forces were already propelling the decline of villeinage, and commutation continued, despite the crushing of the revolt, until the unfree peasant gradually disappeared. Whether the revolt hastened or delayed the process is obscure, but the immediate outcome encouraged complacency in the ruling class, beginning with the King. Perhaps intoxicated by success, Richard developed all the instincts of absolutism except the toughness to quell his opponents, and was to end as the victim of one of them. The military saw no need for improvement; the Church was stiffened against reform. Alarmed by the Lollards' leveling doctrines, the privileged class turned against them. In Gower's "Corruptions of the Age," the poet denounced them as breeders of division between church and state sent into the world by Satan. Lollardy went underground, long postponing the Protestant separation.

In these "days of wrath and anguish, days of calamity and misery," the laboring men's revolt seemed to many but one more tribulation signifying, like the Black Death, the anger of God. An anonymous

poet, associating the rising of the peasants with an earthquake that
occurred in 1382 and with the "pestilens," concluded that these three
things

> Beeth tokenes of grete vengaunce and wrake
> That schulde falle for synnes sake.

Even the French raids on the English coast could be taken, as the monk
Walsingham suggested, as the Lord "calling men to repentance by
means of such terrors." Seen in these terms, revolt conveyed no political significance. "Man cannot change," a Florentine diarist wrote at
this time, "that which God, for our sins, has willed."

How much impact the insurrection in England had on revolutionary sentiment abroad is uncertain. With or without it, war and its
attendant demon, taxes, would have supplied enough fuel for discontent. Yet war could hardly have failed to give employment and spread
money—to armorers, carters, grain dealers, bakers, horse-breeders, and
a hundred other trades besides the archers, foot soldiers, and servants in
the army. Contemporaries are silent on the subject of war as economic
stimulus, but very vocal about its unequal burden on the poor. "It
should be an established principle," wrote Villani, "that war ought not
to be paid for out of the purses of the poor but rather by those to
whom power belongs."

This was not a principle recognized by the Duc d'Anjou, whose
pursuit of money provoked a new wave of insurrection in France
beginning in February of 1382. His projected inheritance of the Kingdom of Naples had just been jeopardized by the overthrow of Queen
Joanna by a rival. Against the advice of Coucy, who was summoned
again from Picardy for consultation, Anjou was bent on leading an
army to Italy. At a meeting with the Provost of Merchants and principal bourgeois in January 1382, he seems to have wrung consent for a
new sales tax on wine, salt, and other merchandise. In fear of popular
reaction, the edict was issued secretly and the bidding for the lucrative
post of tax-collector was held behind closed doors in the Châtelet.
Many came willingly enough to bid, but hesitated to make the public
announcement. No less apprehensive, the court remained at Vincennes
outside the walls.

When tradesmen and travelers spread news of the new tax, an outcry of angry refusal was voiced in riots at Laon, Amiens, Reims, Orléans, and Rouen, as well as in Paris. As spokesman for the bourgeois of

the capital, Jean de Marès, an aged, respected, and eloquent advocate who had served under every King since Philip VI, tried in vain to persuade Anjou to rescind the order. Shopkeepers locked out tax-collectors who came to evaluate their merchandise; citizens seized arms, rang the tocsin, and rampaged through tax offices. That the agitation was heated by "the example of the English," and even by "letters and messages from the Flemings" was common belief. Concerted action, however, was less a fact than a fear of the ruling class.

The riots burst into violence at the end of February in Rouen, capital of Normandy. Here the tax on wine injured important vintners who wished to excite popular resistance without compromising themselves. They harangued artisans and poor workers of the cloth trade about the shame of submitting to the tax while distributing free wine among them. To shouts of "*Haro!*" against the government, "*Haro!*" against tax-collectors (an obscure cry implying rebellion), a company of 200 intoxicated drapers rushed for the city hall to ring the tocsin. So began the famous Harelle.

Gathering adherents, the drapers sacked the houses of the rich, broke open coffers, threw furnishings into the streets, smashed windows and wine barrels, and let the contents flow after drinking all they could hold. Priests, pawnbrokers, Jews, and the houses of all former mayors were attacked, while the tocsin rang all night. The rich fled for refuge to monasteries, and a few royal officials and tax-collectors were killed. The chief of the drapers' guild, a fat, simple-witted character called, for his bulk, Jean le Gras, was dragged against his will to leadership of the mob and paraded through the streets on a throne, thus compromising the upper bourgeois in spite of their effort to remain behind the scenes.

In climactic assault, the rioters, joined by many of the better class, attacked the Abbey of St. Ouen, hated for its large land holdings and the privileges it maintained against the town. Doors were smashed with axes, rent registers and charters burned, and the Abbé forced to sign remittances of all dues owed by the town. The fact that these documents were formulated in proper legal language testifies to the role of the upper bourgeois in the affair. Afterward, in a solemn if not sober assembly in the market place, the crowd petitioned their fat "King" to declare them "free of the yoke of taxes," while some "laughed and shook their heads" at the performance.

Fearing royal punishment, the upper bourgeois sent delegates to Vincennes to plead for pardon. The Royal Council, fearing in its turn the spread of rebellion to other towns, advised the boy King to conceal his wrath and "appease the people who were very riotous." With appropriate display of the sacred aura of kingship, Charles VI was sent to Rouen, where the town's leaders, evidently nervous of the agitation they had unleashed, promised a fixed sum in aids in return for the King's pardon. Underneath the temporary lid, the struggle was unresolved, and wrath on both sides only awaited another chance.

In the same moment that Rouen was subdued, Paris rose. No one had yet ventured to proclaim the new levy in public until one herald, on being offered a bonus, rode into the market place and, having won all ears by announcing a reward for the return of gold plate stolen from the palace, then cried out the new tax and, setting spurs to his horse, galloped away. As the news sped through the streets, people gathered in angry groups, vowing with "terrible oaths" never to pay, and plotting resistance. Arrests of the agitators brought in porters, tinkers, candle-makers, pastry cooks, knife-grinders, cowl-makers—the small tradesmen, artisans, and servants of Paris. Next morning, March 1, when a tax-collector was seen to demand payment from a woman vendor of watercress at Les Halles, the market people fell upon him and killed him.

In an instant Paris was in an uproar. People ran through the *quartiers* calling on their neighbors to arm "for the liberty of the country" and rousing them with fierce yells and threats. "If you do not arm as we do," cried one, "we will kill you right here in your own house!" Then, in "terrible tumult," the crowd broke into the Hôtel de Ville in the Place de Grève, where they seized 3,000 long-handled mallets normally used by the police. Mounted with cylindrical heads of lead and wielded with both hands, these had been stored by Hugues Aubriot in case of need against the English, and now gave their name to the insurgents as Maillotins.

So armed, they inspired extra terror. While they were absorbed in rampage throughout the right bank, nobles, prelates, and officials, hurriedly filling carts with their valuables, escaped to Vincennes. Belatedly, the Maillotins closed the gates, fastened street chains, and posted guards to block the exodus of the rich, even bringing back some whom they caught. They hunted down notaries, jurists, and everyone connected with taxes, invaded churches to drag tax-collectors from sanctuary, seized one from the altar of St. Jacques, where he was clinging in terror to a statue of the Virgin, and cut his throat. Records everywhere were burned, the Jewish quarter looted as always. "Turn Christian or we will kill you!" a Jewish woman was ordered. "She said she would rather die," an onlooker testified, "so they killed and robbed her." The Jews again sought shelter in the Châtelet, but were turned away by officials in fear of the Maillotins. Of some thirty persons murdered the first day, half were Jews.

The upper bourgeois were anxious both to contain the rising and to use it to force concessions from the crown. They quickly mobilized a militia to resist both the rebels and armed intervention by the King. Squads were stationed at street crossings and scouts sent up into church towers to watch for the approach of men-at-arms. "They soon showed themselves so strong," wrote Buonaccorso Pitti, a Florentine banker in Paris, that the Maillotins in time obeyed them, with the result that the bourgeois were able to use the armed rebels in their own struggle against the crown.

Following so closely on events in Rouen, the uprising in Paris deepened fears of a conspiracy of revolt. The court decided to parley. Coucy, known for his tact and persuasiveness, was sent with the Duke of Burgundy and the Chancellor to the Porte St. Antoine to hear the insurgents' demands. Jean de Marès acted as mediator. The Parisians insisted on an abolition of all levies since the coronation, plus amnesty for all acts of riot, and the release of four bourgeois arrested earlier for having advised against Anjou's tax. The royal negotiators, until they could return with an answer, granted release of the four prisoners as a gesture of appeasement—with contradictory results. Without waiting to hear more, the mob stormed the Châtelet and other prisons, opening every cell and dungeon, releasing inmates so broken or emaciated that they had to be carried to the hospital wards of the Hôtel Dieu. All records of trials and convictions were destroyed in bonfires.

The most celebrated prisoner of Paris, Hugues Aubriot, was among the liberated. Mounted on a "little horse," the former Provost was escorted to his home by the Maillotins, who begged him to become their leader. In every rising, the same need was felt and the same effort made to persuade or force someone of the governing class to take charge and give orders. Aubriot wanted no part of it. During the night, while the insurgents caroused "in eating, drinking and debauches," he managed to leave Paris, and when in the morning they found him gone, a great cry was raised that the city was betrayed.

The bourgeois pressed for a solution, anxious that "the hot imprudence of the lowest people should not be turned to the detriment of men of substance." Ready to subdue Paris by whatever means, the crown agreed to everything except pardon for those guilty of breaking into the Châtelet—but its intent was no more honest than Richard II's. On receiving the royal letters confirming the agreement, the bourgeois leaders alertly noted that the language of the remittance was ambiguous and the document, instead of being sealed in green wax on silk, was sealed in red wax on parchment, denying it the quality of perpetuity.

Despite popular rage at this duplicity, the court was stiffening. Other towns where protest had erupted were found to have been acting not in concert but independently, thus subject to local suppression. Armed force was gathering at Vincennes and fear of punishment spreading in Paris. The court was able to force the city's leaders to yield forty fomenters of the revolt, of whom fourteen were publicly executed to the great indignation of the populace. According to the Monk of St. Denis, others were secretly drowned in the river by royal order. Gaining security, the Dukes sent the King back to Rouen on March 29 to impose reprisals held in abeyance. In a miserable exhibition of ritual joy at the royal approach, the people, in festival clothes of blue and green, were lined up in organized plea for clemency, crying *"Noël, Noël, Vive le Roi!"* which did not suit the Duke of Burgundy. To induce the proper mood for heavy fines, he ordered his men-at-arms to ride among the people with drawn swords telling them "to cry rather for Mercy, *la hart au col*" (with a rope around the neck), signifying the right of the King to hang or spare them at will.

For a gift of money to the King and the Duke, all the silver and gold plate of the *confréries* and their candlesticks and incense boxes were sold. Royalty was not mollified. Despite the original pardon, twelve of the rioters were executed, the tocsin bell taken down, the chains for closing streets removed, fines imposed, Rouen's charter of liberties revoked, and its administration turned over from the independent guilds to a royal bailiff. Cowed by the example, the Estates of Normandy voted a sales and a salt tax and a tax on income. In suppression of revolt, the crown was finding a way to fill its treasury and, more significantly, an opportunity to cancel town charters and extend royal power.

The wrath of Paris was still far from subdued, and dangerous events in Ghent augmented the fear that a general rising, if not yet concerted, might become so. The cry of solidarity, *"Vive Gant! Vive Paris no' mere!"* was being heard in towns from the Flemish border to the Loire.

In Ghent, the White Hoods of Jacob van Artevelde's day reappeared. A people's militia was organized and a captain found in Artevelde's son Philip, a small, sharp-eyed man of aggressive energy and "insinuating eloquence," chosen largely for the aura of his name. Forced by circumstance, if not preference, to depend on the common people, he ordered that all classes would be heard in counsel, "the poor like the rich," and all would be fed alike. When 30,000 had eaten no bread for two weeks, he forced abbeys to distribute their stores of grain and merchants to sell at fixed prices. Traditionally, the turmoils of Flanders had divided the Count, the nobility, the urban magnates and guilds in shifting alignments against each other, but this time they began to see in the sustained rebellion of Ghent the red vision of revolution and closed ranks under the Count to suppress it.

Reduced by hunger, the city agreed to a parley in April 1382. The Count, confident of mastery, demanded that all the Gantois from fifteen to sixty should come bareheaded in their shirts with halters around their necks halfway to Bruges, where he would determine how many would be pardoned and how many put to death. At a meeting in the market place, the starving townsmen were told these terms by their deputies and offered three courses of action—to submit, to starve, or to fight. The third was chosen: an army of 5,000 of those best fit to fight was mobilized and launched against Bruges, headquarters of the Count's party. The result was one of the stunning upsets of the century.

The militia of Bruges, no less confident against their old rivals than the Count, caroused through the night and staggered forth on the morrow, May 5, shouting and singing in drunken disorder. In vain the Count and his knights endeavored to hold them back for orderly advance. A blast of stone and iron cannonballs followed by an assault of the Gantois mowed them down. Panic and flight could not be stemmed and seem rather easily to have swept the Flemish knights into the retreat. Louis de Male, the Count, was unhorsed and, despite efforts to rally his forces after dark by lantern light, avoided capture only by changing clothes with his valet and escaping on foot to refuge in a poor woman's hut. "Do you know me?" he asked. "Oh yes, Monseigneur, I have often begged at your gates." Found by one of his knights, he called for a horse and, provided with the indignity of a peasant's mare, rode bareback into Lille, a less happy journey than when long ago he had galloped briskly away from marriage with Isabella.

Ghent was provisioned and joined in her triumph by other cities under the cry "*Tout un!* (All one)." Having taken possession of Bruges and 500 of its most notable bourgeois as hostages, Philip van Artevelde declared himself Regent of Flanders. All the towns surrendered to his rule, "and there he made new mayors and aldermen and new laws." He adopted a noble's trappings of command: trumpets heralded his approach, a pennon displaying three silver hats preceded him in the streets, minstrels played at his door. He wore scarlet and miniver and dined off the Count's silver plate, seized as booty.

Once again, as in the days of his father, the interests of England and France were at stake. Louis de Male appealed for French aid to his son-in-law and heir, the Duke of Burgundy. Artevelde offered alliance to England. The English Commons favored it for the sake of the wool trade, and because the Flemish, like themselves, were Urbanist in the schism. Pope Urban declared an expedition in aid of Flanders to be a crusade, which meant that clerical tithes could be used toward the cost. Despite this advantage, the English nobility hesitated to ally themselves with rebels, and while they hesitated, their opportunity was lost.

In April the Duc d'Anjou had departed for Italy, having amassed, by whatever means, enough money to recruit 9,000 men and furnish himself with pavilions and equipment "the most sumptuous that any lord had ever commanded." The crown had less success in a renewed demand for aids from Paris. The King at this time was at Meaux on the Marne. Hoping that a settlement might be reached if he placated Paris by his presence, the Council decided to send Coucy to negotiate with the Parisians, "for he knew better how to manage them than any other."

Accompanied by no other lords but only by members of his household, Coucy entered the hostile city, where he appears to have been well regarded and well received. He went to his own residence, recently acquired, a *hôtel* called the Cloître St. Jean off the Place de Grève.* Summoning certain leaders for a conference, he reproved them "wisely and prudently" for their wickedness in killing officials of the King and breaking open his prisons. For this the King could make them pay dearly if he wished, but he did not desire to do so because he loved Paris as his birthplace and because, it being the capital of the kingdom, he was "unwilling to destroy its well-intentioned inhabitants." Coucy said he had come to make up the quarrel between the citizens and their sovereign and would entreat the King and his uncles "mercifully to pardon them for their evil deeds."

The citizens answered that they had no wish to make war against the King but that the taxes must be repealed, at least as regards Paris. When exempted, they would be ready to assist the King "in any other manner." Pouncing on this, Coucy asked, "In what manner?" They said they would pay certain sums into the hands of a chosen receiver

---

* The hotel, called Rieulet or Nieulet in some contemporary manuscripts, was located in the now non-existent Rue St. Jean-en-Grève, which ran from the present Hôtel de Ville to the Rue de Rivoli. The residence was listed as sold to Raoul de Coucy, "*conseiller du Roi*," in 1379, probably an error for Enguerrand, who in a charter of 1390 referred to it as "*nôtre hostel à Paris*."

every week for support of the soldiers. When Coucy asked how much they would pay, they replied, "Such a sum as we shall agree upon."

Coucy managed smoothly by "handsome speeches" to obtain a preliminary offer of 12,000 francs on condition of a pardon. This was accepted by the King, but the conditions for his re-entering Paris testified to the court's nervousness: the people were to lay down their arms, open the gates, leave the street chains down at night so long as the King was in the city, and send six or seven notables to Meaux as hostages. Submitted to an Assembly in Paris, the conditions were angrily rejected by the Maillotins, who demanded with threats and curses that the merchants join in their opinion. With greatest reluctance, six bourgeois carried this refusal to Meaux, under the pressure, as they told the court, of the great fury of the people. The government decided on force. Men-at-arms were sent to occupy the bridges upstream to cut off the supply of food to the city, while others were let loose to pillage the *faubourgs*, committing such excesses "as by an enemy upon an enemy." Preparing for assault of Paris, nobles collected empty wagons "to carry away plunder from the said city if occasion offers." The Parisians fastened the street chains, distributed arms, and mounted a watch on the walls.

Moderate parties on both sides, led by Coucy for the crown and Jean de Marès for the city, still worked for a settlement. Their combined eloquence and influence gained the people's consent to a tax of 80,000 francs to be collected by their own receivers and distributed directly to troops on active service, untouched by royal uncles or treasurers. Paris was to receive in exchange a general pardon and the King's written promise that the aids would not be used as a precedent for new taxes, and that he would hold no malice against Paris in the future. If any trust in a royal pardon still remained, it was because of a quality of sacredness in an anointed king and a profound need to perceive him—as opposed to the lords—as the people's protector.

At this moment Ghent's startling victory over the Count of Flanders intervened, frightening the propertied class and giving the court urgent reason to settle with Paris. With Anjou gone to Italy and Berry dispatched as Governor of Languedoc, the Duke of Burgundy was in control, and his dominant purpose now was to employ French force for the retrieval of his heritage in Flanders. Terms with Paris were hastily concluded.

The King re-entered the capital only for a day, to the great displeasure of the citizens. Rouen erupted again when tax-collectors set up their tables in the Cloth Hall but the rising was quickly suppressed by the royal governor with the aid of an armed galley in the river. Southern France too was in turmoil, spread by bands of dispossessed peasants and vagabond poor. The Monk of St. Denis called them the *désespérés* and *crève-de-faim* (the hopeless and starving), but locally they were called the Tuchins. Some say the name derives from *tue-chien* (kill-dog), meaning people reduced to such misery that they ate dogs as in times of famine; others, that it derived from *touche*, meaning, in the local patois, the *maquis* or brush where the dispossessed took refuge.

Through the uplands of Auvergne, as well as in the south, the Tuchins, in bands of 20, 60, or 100, organized a guerrilla warfare against established society. They preyed upon the clergy—hated for their tax exemptions—ambushed travelers, held lords for ransom, attacking all, it was said, who did not have callused hands. Like the Mafia of Sicily, they originated out of misery to prey upon the rich, but, on becoming organized, were used by the rich in local feuds and brigandage. Towns and seigneurs hired them in their war against the crown's officers, who were called the "eaters." The unrest in Languedoc was to reach the force of insurrection in the following year.

In all these evils, the upper class felt the rising tide of subversion. The rioters of Béziers in Languedoc were reported in a plot to murder all citizens having more than 100 livres, while forty of the plotters planned to kill their own wives and marry the richest and most beautiful widows of their victims. The English peasants seemed to one chronicler "like mad dogs . . . like Bacchantes dancing through the country." The Ciompi were "ruffians, evil-doers, thieves . . . useless men of low condition . . . dirty and shabby," and the Maillotins were viewed as their brothers. The weavers of Ghent were credited with intent to exterminate all good folk down to the age of six.

The source of all subversion, the focus of danger, was seen to lie in Ghent.

Conscious of all that hung upon the outcome, the French prepared for an offensive in strength in Flanders. Rebellion of the lower class against the upper, danger of an English alliance with Artevelde, the hostile allegiance of Flanders to the Urbanist cause in the schism were involved. Coucy was among the first designated for the army, which he joined with a retinue of three other knights banneret, ten knights bachelor, 37 squires, and ten archers, subsequently enlarged to 63 squires and 30 archers. His cousin Raoul, Bastard of Coucy, son of his uncle Aubert, was his second in command, though listed as a squire. In the sullen atmosphere, it took six months before an adequate and well-equipped force was assembled, and it was November before the march began. Many advised against starting on the edge of winter, but anxiety to forestall the English carried the enterprise forward through days of rain and leaden cold.

The army's strength, wildly and variously reported at figures up to 50,000, probably numbered about 12,000—large enough to require foot soldiers, as was often necessary, to cut down hedges and trees to widen the line of march.

The King, now fourteen, rode with the army accompanied by his uncles Burgundy, Bourbon, and Berry and the foremost lords of France—Clisson, Sancerre, Coucy, Admiral de Vienne, the Counts de la Marche, d'Eu, Blois, Harcourt, and many notable seigneurs and squires. The scarlet Oriflamme, reserved for urgent occasions or war against the infidel, was carried for the first time since Poitiers to emphasize the character of holy war—which was somewhat embarrassed by the fact that if the enemy was Urbanist, so was the King's ally Louis of Flanders. Unpopular in any case because of his dealings with the English, Louis was coldly treated throughout the campaign.

Hostility lay at the army's back. French towns and populace, sympathetic to Ghent, withheld or hampered supplies and continued to resist the payment of aids. The Duke of Burgundy, if not the King, was denounced aloud. In Paris, the Maillotins swore on their mallets an oath of collective resistance to tax-collectors. They began to forge helmets and weapons at night, and plotted to seize the Louvre and the great *hôtels* of Paris so that these could not be used as strongholds against them. They were restrained from action, however, by the counsel of Nicolas de Flament, a cloth merchant who had been associated with Etienne Marcel in the killing of the two Marshals in 1358. He advised waiting until it was seen whether the men of Ghent prevailed; then the right moment would come. At the same time, commoners rioted at Orléans, Blois, Châlons, Reims, Rouen, voicing such sentiments as showed that "the Devil was entered into their heads to have slain all noblemen."

On reaching the river Lys at the border of Flanders, the royal army found the bridge across to Comines destroyed by the enemy and all boats removed. The river's banks were marshy and muddy; 900 Flemings waited on the other side under the command of Artevelde's lieutenant, Peter van den Bossche, standing with battle-ax in hand. Coucy had advised crossing farther east at Tournai so as to be in contact with supplies from Hainault, but Clisson had insisted on the more direct route and was now greatly vexed, acknowledging that he should have taken Coucy's advice.

While foragers were sent for timber and fence rails to repair the bridge, a party of knights was guided to three sunken boats, which were hauled up and rigged by ropes to both banks at a spot concealed from the Flemings. By this means, nine at a time, an adventurous force of knights and squires was ferried across while the main force diverted the Flemings' attention by fire of crossbows and "bombards" or small portable cannon. Fearing to be discovered, yet determined "to gain reputation as valiant men-at-arms," the adventurers, joined by Marshal Sancerre, continued crossing until 400 had reached the other side. No varlet was permitted to accompany them.

Deciding to seize Comines at once, they buckled their armor, raised their banners, and marched into the open in battle formation, to the extreme anxiety of the watching Constable, whose "blood began to tremble in fear for them." "Ah, by St. Ives, by St. George, by Our Lady, what do I see over there? Ha, Rohan! Ha, Beaumanoir! Ha, Rochefort, Malestroit, Lavalle," Clisson cried, naming each banner as he recognized it. "What do I see? I see the flower of our army outnumbered! I would rather have died than witnessed this. . . . Wherefore am I Constable of France if without my counsel you put yourself in this adventure? If you lose, the fault shall be laid to me and it shall be said that I sent you thither." He proclaimed that all who wished should now join the force on the other side and issued frantic orders to hasten repair of the bridge. With darkness falling, the Flemings were ordered by their leader not to attack, and the French for the same reason halted. Unsheltered in a cold wind, with their feet in mud and rain running down their helmets, they remained in armor through the night, keeping up their spirits by staying alert against attack.

At daybreak both sides advanced, the French shouting the war cries of many absent seigneurs to make their numbers seem larger. Again Clisson suffered unrestrained agonies of anxiety, bewailing his inability to cross over with all his army. In the event, when the clash came, the long French spears tipped with Bordeaux steel outreached the Flemings' weapons, pierced their thin mail, and gained the ascendancy. Peter van den Bossche was struck down, wounded in head and shoulder, but was carried to safety. While the Flemings fought in despair and village bells rang to summon help, the French finished repair of the bridge. Clisson's force thundered across, routed the defenders, and completed the capture of Comines. Flemings were chased and killed in streets and fields, in mills and monasteries where they sought shelter, and in neighboring towns. In a moment the pillagers were scouring the country and finding rich plunder, for—trusting in the Lys—the Flemings had not removed their goods or cattle to the walled towns.

Upon the King's entry into Comines, the upper bourgeois of Ypres and neighboring towns overthrew Artevelde's governors and sent deputies to the French with terms of surrender. On their knees before Charles VI, twelve rich notables of Ypres offered to turn over their town to him permanently in return for peaceful occupation. The King was pleased to accept at a price of 40,000 francs, which was immediately pledged. Malines, Cassel, Dunkirk, and nine other towns followed suit at a further payment of 60,000 francs. Although the terms of surrender supposedly exempted towns from pillage, the Bretons could not be restrained. Rather than encumber themselves with furs, fabrics, and vessels, they sold their loot cheap to the people of Lille and Tournai, "caring only for silver and gold." Business, like a jackal, trotted on the heels of war.

At Ghent, some fifty miles to the north, Philip van Artevelde summoned from the vicinity every man capable of bearing arms, assuring them they would defeat the French King and win independent sovereignty for Flanders. For months his envoys had been pressing England, but though a herald had come with terms of a treaty, no ships filled with soldiers followed. Even so, he had another ally: winter was closing in. If he had fortified his position and stayed on the defensive, he could have left it to winter and scarcity to defeat the invaders. But the threat of an internal rising by the Count's party which might turn over Bruges to the French forced Artevelde into action, even though he still held the principal citizens of Bruges as hostages. Perhaps he was moved not by fear but overconfidence; perhaps he simply miscalculated.

Armed with bludgeons and iron-pointed staves, with large knives in their belts and iron caps on their heads, a formidable force of "40,000" or "50,000" Flemings (in reality, probably under 20,000) was collected, led by 9,000 of Ghent on whom Philip relied most. Carrying the banners of towns and trades, they marched south to meet the enemy. Scouts reported their approach to the French, who took up a position between the hill and the town of Roosebeke a few miles from Passchendaele, where history held another bloodshed in waiting for 1916. As an Urbanist, Louis de Male was forced by the French to withhold his division from the order of battle so they should not have to fight alongside a heretic and schismatic. In rain and cold the King's army awaited the conflict impatiently, "for they were very discomfited at being out in such weather."

At the final war council on the eve of combat, an extraordinary decision was taken: that Clisson should resign his office for the day of battle to be near the King's person, and be replaced as Constable by Coucy. Very agitated and pleading that he would be thought a coward by the army, Clisson begged the King for a reversal. The bewildered boy, after a long silence, consented, "for you see further in this matter than I do or those who first proposed it."

What lay behind the proposal is unspoken in the chronicles; the only clue is Clisson's fit of anxiety at the Lys. In a man who could cut off fifteen heads without a twinge, it reflected unusual tension and must have persuaded his equally tense colleagues to turn to Coucy and the extreme expedient of changing Constables in midstream. Win or lose, fighting against other knights changed nothing fundamental, but in this fight the nobles felt their order itself endangered. The sentiment is reflected by Froissart in many variations of his statement that if the French King and "noble chivalry" had met defeat in Flanders, all nobles would have been "dead and lost in France" and "commoners would have rebelled in divers countries to destroy all the nobility."

Artevelde on the eve of battle now favored the defensive and advised standing in place against the enemy. He had the advantage of terrain, having taken up a good position on the hill, and he believed the French in their impatience and discomfort would grow reckless or careless or even turn back. He was overruled by men still in the pride of their earlier victory over the Count at Bruges and eager for a fight. Accepting the decision, Artevelde ordered the army to give no quarter and take no prisoners other than the King, "for he is but a child who acts only as instructed. We shall bring him to Ghent and teach him to speak Flemish." As for tactics, he commanded the men to keep always in a compact body "so that none may break you," and for greater solidarity to hold their weapons with arms intertwined. They were to confound the enemy with the heavy fire of the crossbows and bombards they had used at Bruges and then, advancing shoulder to shoulder, overcome the French line by the sheer weight and solidity of their ranks.

In the tension of the night before combat, Flemish guards reported shouts and clang of arms from the French camp, as if the enemy were preparing a night attack. Others thought it was "the devils of hell running and dancing about the place where the battle was to be because of the great prey they expected there."

On the morning of November 29, 1382, two hostile halves of society moved toward each other through a mist "so thick it was almost night." With their horses held at the rear, the French advanced on foot and, contrary to custom, in silence without battle cries, all eyes on the dark mass ahead. Descending the hill in close order with staves upright, the Flemings appeared like a moving forest. They opened with a massive fire of crossbows and bombards, then charged with lowered staves and the force of "enraged boars." The French plan was for the King's battalion under the Constable to hold the center while two stronger wings—of which one was commanded by Bourbon and Coucy—closed in on the enemy from either side. Under the force of the Flemish charge, the French center gave way and in the turmoil the Bourbon-Coucy battalion found itself blocked.

"See, good cousin," cried Bourbon (as reported by his contemporary biographer), "we cannot advance to attack our enemies except through our Constable's ranks."

"Monseigneur, you say true," answered Coucy, here credited with devising a plan of action on the spot. "And it seems to me that if we were to advance as a wing of the King's battalion and take the hill we should have a good day's fight at God's pleasure."

"Fair cousin, that is good advice," Bourbon agreed, and so, as 14th century military history is written, they went up the hill and took the enemy from behind with terrible blows of lance, ax, and sword, and "whoever saw the Sire de Coucy break through the press and strike the Flemings, cutting and killing, he will forever remember a valiant knight." In the respite afforded by this attack, the Constable's battalion recovered and returned, along with the other wing, to the fray. Heavy battle-axes and maces cut through Flemish helmets with a noise "as loud as all the armorers of Paris and Brussels working together." Compressed ever more tightly by the French, the Flemings were so squeezed against each other that the inner ranks could not raise arms or weapons; even breathing became difficult—they could neither strike nor cry out.

As French lances pierced and axes hacked at the solid mass of bodies, many of whom lacked helmet or cuirass, the dead piled up in heaps. French foot soldiers, penetrating between the men-at-arms, finished off the fallen with their knives, "with no more mercy than if they had been dogs." Under the attack of the Bourbon-Coucy wing, the Flemish rear turned and fled, throwing away their weapons as they ran. Philip van Artevelde, fighting in the front ranks, tried to rally them, but from his position could exercise no effective command. He lacked the assurance of the Black Prince at Poitiers to retain control from a hilltop above the battle. Borne backward by the mass as the rout spread, he was trampled and killed under the feet of his own forces, as was his banner-bearer, a woman named Big Margot.

Bourbon and Coucy, mounting their horses, led their battalion in pursuit of the fugitives, and in a fierce fight routed 3,000 Flemings from a wood where they had gathered for a final defense. The debacle was complete. While their battalion pursued and killed as far as Courtrai, Coucy and Bourbon rode back to Roosebeke, where the King "welcomed them joyously and praised God for the victory which, through their efforts, He had given." The battle was over in the space of two hours. Many Flemish bodies were found without wounds, crushed to death under their companions' pressure, but so many thousands were killed by French weapons that "the ground was inundated by blood." The number of dead "miscreants" was reported in figures of fantasy, but agreement was general that few of the Flemish army survived. Fit only to be the "prey of dogs and crows," the bodies were left unburied, so that for days afterward, the stench of the battlefield was insupportable.

While being divested of his armor in his scarlet pavilion, the King expressed a wish to see Artevelde dead or alive. For a reward of 100 francs, searchers found his body, which was taken before the victors, who stared at it for a while in silence. The King gave it a little kick, "treating it as a villein." Then it was taken away and "hanged upon a tree." Artevelde's image was subsequently woven into a tapestry depicting the battle, which the Duke of Burgundy commissioned and used as a carpet because he liked to walk on the commoners who had attempted to overthrow the ordained order.

The sack of Courtrai was merciless, in revenge for defeat in the Battle of the Spurs eighty years before. Citizens fled vainly to cellars and churches to escape the soldiers; they were dragged into the streets and killed. On his knees Louis de Male begged mercy for the town, but was ignored. Every house was ransacked and even nobles of the town and their children carried away for ransom. The Duke of Burgundy, with a Valois eye for the best, dismounted the cathedral clock, finest in Flanders, and transported it by ox wagon to Dijon (where it still is). When the King departed, Courtrai was set on fire at his command, "so that it should be known ever after that the French King had been there." Clisson, restored to his normal ferocity, was thought to have had a hand in the order.

The totality of victory had one major exception. Ghent, the main objective, was never taken. At first news of their army's defeat, the people were stunned and despairing, so that if the French had come to their gates in the several days after the battle "they would have suffered them to enter without resistance." But medieval war had a tendency to stop short of political objective. Weary of cold and rain, occupied with profit and revenge in the immediate aftermath of Roosebeke, and confident that Ghent would surrender on demand, the French did not go north.

Peter van den Bossche, despite his wounds, had himself carried to Ghent and re-inspirited the city, insisting the war was not over, that the French would not come in winter, and with new men in a new season "we shall do more than we ever did before," even without English help. The English, as soon as they heard of the Flemish defeat, broke off negotiations and were "not greatly displeased" by the outcome. Had it gone otherwise, they feared the "great pride of the commoners" would have encouraged a new rising in their own country.

Afterward, when the French attempted a parley, Ghent, as "hard and proud" as if it had won the victory, refused absolutely to yield to the Count of Flanders but only to the direct suzerainty of the King of France. The Count, and more especially Philip of Burgundy, the heir apparent, rejected that arrangement. By this time at the end of December it was too late to begin a siege. Having restored authority in the rest of Flanders, though they failed to convert it to Pope Clement, the French were ready to go home. They had business to settle with Paris.

In the first week of January 1383 the royal army halted outside Paris and sent for the Provost and magistrates to assure the capital's submission. With armed forces at hand, and strengthened by the victory of Roosebeke, the crown had greater authority than in the year before, and was prepared to use it. Breton and Norman companies were deployed in a semi-circle around Paris, champing on the brink of pillage. A huge force of Parisians, in a desperate show of the strength which they had long prepared, marched out armed with crossbows, shields, and mallets and assumed battle formation beyond Montmartre. Warily, the crown sent a delegation including the Constable and Coucy to appraise their strength and ask why they advanced thus combatively. The commoners replied that they wished the King to view their strength, which, being very young, he had never seen. They were sternly ordered to return and lay down their arms if they wished the King to enter Paris. Subdued since the verdict of Roosebeke, their spirit did not match their show; they turned back without resistance. The royal army was nevertheless notified to appear in the guise of war, not peace—that is, in armor—for the entry into Paris.

Coucy and Marshal Sancerre were sent to open the city by taking down the solid gates from their hinges and removing street chains. The gates were thrown into the streets that the King might ride over them—

"to trample the pride of the city," as the Monk of St. Denis sadly acknowledged. Alarm and anger rose among the citizens, who posted guards at night and said, "There will be no peace yet. The King has destroyed and pillaged the land of Flanders and he will do the same in Paris." To dampen trouble, heralds proclaimed to the people that no sack nor harm would come to them. On the day of entry, the bourgeois, represented by the Provost of Merchants, the magistrates, and 500 notables, came forward in festival clothes in the ritual plea for pardon. As they knelt, the King and his nobles, Coucy among them, flanked by men-at-arms with lances poised, rode past them through the shorn gates into the city.

Men-at-arms were immediately posted at all bridges and at squares where the people were accustomed to gather. Houses where soldiers were to lodge were required to keep their doors open. Everyone possessing arms was ordered to bring them in a sack to the Louvre, from where they were removed to Vincennes.

Arrests began at once, with special attention to the bourgeois notables, in whom the crown recognized its real opponents. Jean de Marès and Nicolas de Flament were among 300 substantial citizens arrested. Two rich merchants, a draper and a goldsmith, were executed at once, and thirteen more within a week. Nicolas de Flament, spared in 1358, went to the block now. All the bourgeois who had served in the city militia during the revolt were summoned one by one before the Council to be sentenced to heavy fines. Free to take revenge, the King's government continued to impose convictions, fines, and executions for the next six weeks. "They cut off heads," recorded the Ménagier de Paris, "three and four at a time," to a total of more than 100, not counting those executed in other rebel towns.

The seal of conquest was the re-imposition of a sales tax of twelve pence in the livre on all merchandise, plus extra on wine and salt—the same tax that had provoked the revolt of the Maillotins and that the Parisians had been refusing to pay for the past year. A week later, before a full assembly of the governing class of the city, the King's ordinance was read revoking the privileges and franchises of Paris. The proud rights of self-government and chartered liberties, hard-won by the towns through the High Middle Ages, were being drained off and absorbed by a central government. In Paris the offices of Provost of Merchants and of the magistrates were suppressed and their jurisdictions taken over by the crown. The major trades were deprived of autonomy, as at Rouen, and subjected henceforward to supervisors appointed by the Provost of Paris. The police squads formerly maintained by the Provost of Merchants were abolished and the defense of Paris taken into the hands of the King. Meetings of *confréries*, as possible breeders of trouble, and all public assemblies except for attendance at church were forbidden. Participants in illicit meetings were to be treated as "rebel and disobedient," subject to the death penalty and confiscation of property.

The trial of Jean de Marès followed. He had not left Paris like other notables, the Monk of St. Denis recalled, but for more than a year had contained and moderated the fury of the people and striven to mediate between the court and the city. For that the hatred of the Dukes pursued him. A train of informers was brought forward to support the charge that he had counseled the rebels to take up arms. He was convicted, condemned to death, stripped of gown and hood, and carried in a cart with twelve others to the place of execution at Les Halles. Placed above the others in the cart, "so that he should be viewed by all," he cried to the crowd collected in the streets, "Where are those who have condemned me? Let them come forward to justify my conviction if they can." The people sorrowed for him, but none dared to speak.

Told by the executioner to beg mercy of the King that he might be pardoned for his crimes, Marès replied that he had done nothing for which to beg pardon, "but from God alone I shall beg mercy and ask Him humbly to forgive me my sins." After words of farewell to the people, who were all in tears, he turned to his death.

Not yet done, the crown summoned a mammoth assembly in the courtyard of the Marble Table on March 1, anniversary of the Maillotins' revolt. One person from every house in Paris was required to attend, without head covering. Charles VI, attended by his uncles and Council, sat on a platform while Pierre d'Orgement as Chancellor read in the King's name a harsh accusation of all the crimes committed by the people of Paris since the death of Charles V. After speaking of the executions, he cried in a terrible voice, "It is not finished!" The people knew their roles. Wails of fear rose from the crowd. With disordered clothes and hair, the wives of imprisoned men stretched out their arms to the King, imploring mercy in tears. The proud uncles and the King's younger brother, Louis, knelt to beg for the relief of civil rather than criminal punishment—civil meaning fines. Orgement announced that the King, obeying his natural goodness and the pleas of his kin, consented to a general pardon, revocable if ever the Parisians returned to their evil ways. The convicted would be released from prison and pain of death but not from payment of fines. Some men of ample property were fined amounts equal to all they owned in money, houses, and land, reducing them to ruin.

Similar punitive measures were taken at Amiens, whose ancient charter was revoked, at Laon, Beauvais, Orléans, and other cities. The immense sums collected in fines amounted to 400,000 francs from Paris and a comparable figure from the provinces. Much of it went to enrich the uncles, to pay the Constable and other royal officials who had received no salaries for the past two years, and to reimburse nobles, including Coucy, for expenses of the Flanders campaign. Coucy received 13,200 francs and a pledge of one third of the aids levied on his domain to cover the expense of fortifying his towns and castles.

Strangely, in view of his role in removing the gates, Coucy retained a favorable image in Paris. A saying was recorded among the people that "the Sire de Coucy had not feared to remonstrate with the King and tell him that if he destroyed his own country he would be reduced to plying the workman's spade." The prophecy picturing the King doing a peasant's work captured the public mind and was to have a long and curious life.

The authority of the lions was regained in full. Paris did not recover a Provost of Merchants for thirty years; Rouen never recovered the liberties it had enjoyed before the Harelle. Where insurgency had won momentary control, it was because of the absence of organized and ready forces of public order. The state had no arrangements for meeting revolution, although, by contrast, the role of suppression was as formalized as a ceremonial rite.

Except in Ghent, insurgency could not retain a grip because it, too, had no prepared role and its ranks were divided. The poor provided the explosive force, but became the agents of the merchant class, whose interests were not theirs. The towns themselves failed in their aim because they were each other's enemies. Ghent maintained its struggle for two more years until, on the death of Louis de Male, its liberties were restored by the Duke of Burgundy to consolidate his heritage. Elsewhere, communal liberties and autonomy were lost or reduced. The process that had operated in Etienne Marcel's revolt continued: to the extent that the towns lost, the monarchy gained, while through financial support the crown increasingly made partners of the nobility.

After the storm, the lower class was seen as more dangerous, more suspect. It gained recognition as a dynamic rather than passive section of society, by some in fear, by others in sympathy. "Therefore the innocent must die of hunger with whom these great wolves daily fill their maw," wrote Deschamps. "This grain, this corn, what is it but the blood and bones of the poor folk who have plowed the land? Wherefore their spirit crieth on God for vengeance. Woe to the lords, the councillors and all who steer us thus, and woe to all who are of their party, for no man careth now but to fill his bags."

The wave of insurrection passed, leaving little change in the condition of the working class. Inertia in the scales of history weighs more heavily than change. Four hundred years were to elapse before the descendants of the Maillotins seized the Bastille.

Chapter 19
The Lure of Italy

The lure of a foothold in Italy exerted the same pull on the French as a foothold in France exerted on the English. From the time the Duc d'Anjou crossed the Alps in 1382, the Angevin claim to the Kingdom of Naples drew France southward, creating a habit of intervention that was to persist on and off for 500 years. Its pattern was laid at the start, when Anjou's expedition encountered misfortune almost at once and sent repeatedly throughout the year 1383 for reinforcement under the Sire de Coucy.

Angevins had ruled the Kingdom of Naples and Sicily since Charles of Anjou, younger brother of St. Louis, had been placed on the throne by papal influence in 1266. Sicily was absorbed by Aragon at the end of the century, but the Angevin dynasty retained the mainland portion, covering the entire lower half of Italy south of Rome, the largest domain on the peninsula.* Flourishing in commerce and culture, it enjoyed the civilized reign of King Robert, the "new Solomon" whose literary approval Petrarch came to seek. Boccaccio followed because he preferred residence in the "happy, peaceful, generous, and magnificent Naples with its one monarch" to his native republican Florence "devoured by innumerable cares." Robert built his palace, Castel Nuovo, on the water's edge facing Naples' incomparable bay, where ships of Genoa, Spain, and Provence came to trade. Nobles and merchants added their palazzos alongside, bringing down Tuscan artists to fill them with frescoes and sculpture. Under just laws and a stable currency, with security of roads, hostels for traveling merchants, festivities, tournaments, music, and poetry, Robert's reign, which ended in 1343, was said to be "something like Paradise." Citizens could journey unarmed through Calabria and Apulia "except for a wooden club to defend themselves against dogs."

---

* The name Sicily remained attached to the Kingdom of Naples, causing confusion which should be resolutely ignored.

The blight of the 14th century descended after the good King's death. Robert's talents petered out in his granddaughter and successor, Joanna, whose four ill-fated efforts to bolster the female succession by marriage brought turmoil culminating in the schism. The conflict of popes made Naples a battlefield. When Joanna opted for Clement and, at his instigation, named Anjou her heir, the furious Urban declared her deposed as a heretic and schismatic and crowned another Angevin descendant, Charles, Duke of Durazzo, as rightful King of Naples. Elevated from an obscure Albanian principality to a great Mediterranean kingdom, this prince took the throne as Charles III.

A small, fair-haired man said to resemble Robert in courage and geniality as well as love of learning, Charles of Durazzo did not let his good nature inhibit his struggle against Joanna. Within two months he had defeated her forces, established himself in the Castel Nuovo, and imprisoned the Queen in the hope of coercing her to appoint him her heir and thus legitimize his conquest. To put on the garment of legitimacy is the first aim of every coup. When Joanna refused to acknowledge him and Anjou entered Italy on his way to her aid, Charles did not hesitate. He had the Queen strangled in prison and her corpse exposed in the cathedral for six days before burial so that no doubt should be left of her death.

Anjou came by way of Avignon, where he, in turn, was crowned King of Naples, Sicily, and Jerusalem, including Provence, by Pope Clement, and his rival, Charles of Durazzo, was simultaneously excommunicated. Despite his persuasive arts, Anjou had been unable during the insurrections in France to collect enough funds to take him all the way to Naples and had tried in vain to persuade the Royal Council to finance his venture as a national war. Now, as sovereign of Provence, he minted huge quantities of coin and enriched his troops by allowing them freedom to loot his new subjects on the pretext of punishment for their recent rebelliousness. He collected additional money and forces from Pope Clement and was joined in his enterprise by that energetic nobleman, Amadeo, the Green Count of Savoy, who contributed 1,100 lances at a cost to Anjou of 20,000 ducats a month.

Replenished and leading an army of 15,000 "gorged with booty," Anjou crossed into Lombardy followed by 300 pack mules and unnumbered baggage wagons. The Green Count's equipment included an enormous green pavilion ornamented with twelve shields bearing the arms of Savoy in red and white, an emerald silk surcoat embroidered with the red-and-white device, twelve saddle-and-bridle sets all in green, and four others ornamented with "Hungarian ribbon knots" for his immediate retinue, and green shoes, hoods, and tunics for his pages.

When, before leaving, certain of his barons objected to the venture on various grounds, he silenced them, saying with unhappy clairvoyance, "I will fulfill what I have promised even if it means my death." Many notable lords joined under his banner "for love of the prowess and largesse they admired in him."

In Milan, Visconti wealth supplied the largest portion of Anjou's funds just as it had a very large portion of his father's ransom, in exchange for the same kind of goods. Anjou's seven-year-old son, Louis, was offered in betrothal to Bernabò's daughter Lucia. For the prospect of a daughter as future Queen of Naples, Bernabò paid 50,000 florins—roughly equivalent to the annual income of about 100 bourgeois families*—plus an additional sum from Gian Galeazzo. Anjou was using every means to collect resources adequate for the fitting display of a king en route to his kingdom.

In plumed helmets and sumptuous pomp, loaded with gifts and honors, he and Amadeo and their knights left Milan, followed by such numbers of men and wagons as "seemed like an army of Xerxes." They headed east for the difficult route down the Adriatic coast, because Florence, which opposed both Anjou and Durazzo, did not want the embarrassment—nor the pillaging—of their passage and had raised 6,000 men to block the road through Tuscany. According to the Monk of St. Denis—who, like his fellow monk Walsingham, took a sour view of marauding dukes—Anjou and his nobles flattered themselves that through them the Lilies of France would spread afar "the sweet perfume of glory." As they rode, they celebrated their enterprise in song and verse and "fabulous recitals" of French valor.

Although Anjou had proclaimed his intention to "promote the fate of the Church by the force of chivalry"—that is, by force of arms—he failed to exert that force against Urban. Leaving the coast at Ancona to cross the Apennines early in September, he bypassed the road to Rome, although a bold effort might have taken the city at this time. Agents had brought word that Hawkwood's White Company, promised for Urban's defense, had been held back by Florence for her own protection. Instead, against the advice of Amadeo of Savoy, Anjou took the lower road for Naples, and as the army passed through defiles and across gorges, between peaks "that touched the sky," calamity overtook them. Highland brigands, pulled by strings from Naples, attacked the baggage train and the rear guard escorting the treasure, with the

---

* In 1388 Giovanni de Mussi of Piacenza stated that a household of nine with two horses required a minimum income of 300 florins a year. In 1415 a wealthy Italian citizen spent 574 florins on his marriage celebration. A well-paid artisan at about this time earned approximately eighteen florins a year.

result that Anjou arrived at Caserta, within a day's march of Naples, very much poorer than when he set out. Reconnoitering terrain in advance was not part of medieval warfare because it was not part of tournaments. The clash was everything.

By this time it was November. On entering Neapolitan territory, Anjou had stopped for a week at Aquila to partake in welcoming ceremonies offered by partisans of his cause. The delays in his progress allowed time for Hawkwood, released by Florence, to come to his opponent's aid. Now in need of a quick decision, Anjou sent the traditional challenge to Durazzo demanding a time and place of battle. Charles III proved elusive. Fortified in Castel Nuovo, he counted on outlasting Anjou and exhausting his resources until he could be easily beaten and any territory he had meanwhile taken, regained. Professing himself overjoyed to accept Anjou's challenges, Charles kept him on the move, forcing him into the expense and fatigue of marches toward a combat that vanished at every approach.

In deepening anxiety by Christmastime, Anjou made a will and Amadeo, giving up hope of victory, proposed a negotiated peace. In return for Anjou relinquishing his claim to Naples, Charles of Durazzo was to relinquish his claim to Provence and give Anjou safe passage to the coast for return to France. Charles III rejected the terms. An arranged battle of ten champions on either side was then agreed upon and, as usual when the stakes were important, did not take place.

In February of 1383 an epidemic spread among the army in the mountains above Naples, carrying off large numbers, among them Amadeo of Savoy, at the age of 49. On March 1, a dreary year away from the snows of Savoy, the splendid green career came to an end. Hurriedly summoned, Anjou wept helpless tears at the deathbed.

Foiled and hungry, the Angevin forces retreated to the heel of Italy. All that remained of the kingly treasure was used to buy provisions. Anjou's gold and silver plate brought little money and even his nuptial crown, which he had brought to serve at his coronation, had to be sold. The resplendent hauberk embroidered in gold, worn over his armor, went too, and he wore in its place a simple cloth with fleur-de-lys painted in yellow. In place of the delicate meats and pastries he was accustomed to, he ate rabbit stew and barley bread. As the months went by, starving pack animals could not move and war-horses, "instead of pawing the ground and whinnying with pride, languished with lowered heads like common beasts."

Ever since he had left Paris, Anjou had been bombarding the Council by letter and messenger to fulfill its promise to finance a supplementary campaign against Naples under the command of Enguerrand de Coucy. While still in Avignon, he had urged his agent in Paris, Pierre Gérard, to make every effort to engage Coucy. No money was to be paid to him until he had committed himself in writing to join Anjou, but Gérard was instructed "always to proceed with this seigneur as graciously as possible." Pope Clement urgently supported Anjou's pleas to the crown, reporting "superb" offers from various parts of Italy and every promise of success, and expressing his deep chagrin at the refusal of the French Council to aid an enterprise on which the health of the Church depended. Nevertheless, Anjou was left dangling through the year of Roosebeke. Not until after the suppression of Paris, when the Treasury had been replenished by fines, was the crown ready to fulfill its promise. By this time Amadeo was dead and the "army of Xerxes" huddled in misery at Bari.

Coucy was ready and eager to go to Anjou's aid. He was in constant consultation in Paris with Anjou's chancellor, Bishop Jean le Fèvre, and repeatedly asked to know if Le Fèvre had obtained a positive reply from the King. At last, in April 1383, the Council agreed to give Anjou 190,000 francs, of which 80,000 represented aids levied on his own possessions. Just at that moment, England in a last infirmity of war hunger, launched yet another invasion. All energies were turned to meet it, and all men-at-arms, by order of the Duke of Burgundy, were prohibited from leaving the kingdom. Coucy's expedition was frustrated. An army was indeed organized, not for Italy but once again for Flanders where the English had seized Dunkirk.

Led by Henry Despenser, Bishop of Norwich, the English raid was the fruition of Urban's effort for a "crusade" against schismatic France. It began in scandal and was to end in fiasco. The moral harm done to papal obedience in England by the methods of financing the "crusade" outweighed anything the papacy could have gained, even with success. Friars as papal agents were endowed with "wonderful indulgences" and extra powers to sell or, worse, to refuse absolution "unless the people gave according to their ability and estate." Even the sacrament was at times withheld from parishioners who refused an offering to the crusade. Gold, silver, jewels, and money were collected, especially, according to Knighton, "from ladies and other women. . . . Thus the secret treasure of the realm, which was in the hands of women, was drawn out." Protest was re-invigorated and evoked one of Wyclif's last tracts, "Against Clerical Wars." Lollard preachers denounced "these worldly prelates . . . chief captains and arrayers of

Satan's battles to exile good life and charity." Because of the false nature of the absolutions, they said, "No tongue may tell how many souls go to hell by these cursed captains and Anti-Christs' jurisdictions and censures."

Norwich was a prelate not merely martial but actively bellicose. Though a bishop, he was described by Walsingham as "young, unbridled and insolent . . . endowed neither with learning nor discretion, experienced neither in preserving nor bestowing friendship." By the time he had gathered sufficient funds and a force of about 5,000, his intended allies in Ghent were sadly subdued. He succeeded, however, after landing at Calais, in quickly taking Gravelines, Dunkirk, and Bourbourg on the Flemish coast. After laying siege to Ypres without success, he turned his attentions to Picardy, then defended by Coucy as Captain-General. Norwich withdrew without a fight when half his force under the veteran Sir Hugh Calveley refused to follow him farther. A greatly superior French army having now taken the field, Norwich hurriedly shut himself up in Bourbourg while Calveley made for Calais. "By my faith," said that veteran captain in disgust, "we have made a most shameful campaign; none so poor or so disgraceful ever issued out of England." Such was the result, he said, of believing "this Bishop of Norwich who wished to fly before he had wings."

A huge French army settled down in August to the siege of Bourbourg, entertaining each other and visiting foreign knights in jousts and festivities of competitive splendor and valorous exploits designed "to raise the fame of their antique nobility." In these activities Coucy made an impressive showing, especially for his equestrian style. Mounted on a beautiful horse and leading several others caparisoned in all the heraldic arms belonging to his house, "he rode from side to side in the most graceful manner to the delight of all who saw him, and all praised and honored him for his great air and fine presence." Four months passed pleasurably before Bourbourg in very different mood from the fight against the commoners of the year before. The French exhibited no ardor for assault and, at the approach of winter, allowed the affair to be brought to an end through some tricky mediation by the Duke of Brittany. Norwich was bought off and went home to deficit and disgrace. England's military repute, already declining for a decade, sank further, supplying moralists with a text against the injustices and oppressions of men of the sword. "God's hand is against them," said Thomas Brinton, Bishop of Rochester, "because their hand is against God."

Although the belligerents could not know it, the Norwich invasion was destined to be the last of the century, though not of the war. Combat faded without bringing settlement between England and France any closer. Parleys began as usual after the siege of Bourbourg, but could agree on nothing better than a nine months' truce signed in January 1384. Coucy was not this time one of the negotiators because he was engaged in a private war on behalf of his future relative, the Duc de Bar, his daughter's prospective father-in-law, who very promptly paid him 2,000 francs to cover his expenses. Marie's marriage to Henri de Bar was afterward celebrated in November.

All this time the Duchesse d'Anjou and her husband's chancellor, Jean le Fèvre, were imploring the Council to deliver the promised aid. Anjou's situation now was needier than ever because he had been robbed by one of his own nobles of 80,000 to 100,000 francs collected for him by his wife (or, according to other versions, borrowed from the Visconti). The robber, who ten years later was to commit another crime of historic consequence, was Pierre de Craon, a knight of noble birth and large estates who had accompanied the Duke to Italy. Sent by Anjou to fetch the money, Craon returned via Venice where he dissipated most of it in extravagant parties, gambling, and debauchery, supposedly from a desire to display himself in a style suitable to the sovereign he represented. He kept what was left and did not rejoin the Duke.

Such casual criminality against his lord seems close to incredible unless someone interested in Anjou's failure and powerful enough to protect Craon from prosecution had put him up to it. That person could only have been the Duke of Burgundy, but that he would go so far as to ruin his brother seems far-fetched. When Craon returned to France, however, he did escape punishment through the protection of Burgundy to whose wife he was related.

The honor of France, in the eyes of the King and Council, could not allow Anjou to languish in failure nor give that much comfort to Pope Urban. In the spring of 1384, after truce was concluded with England, and after Burgundy, on the death of his father-in-law, entered into possession of Flanders, Coucy's campaign of rescue was launched at last. It was already late to save Anjou, but Coucy was not a captain to fly before he had wings. In the duel of arms and wits he was about to wage in the heart of Italy, he showed himself adroit, responsible, and gifted with that magic faculty of emerging invincible from surrounding disaster.

In May before leaving, he founded, as he had before the Swiss campaign, a perpetual daily mass for himself and his successors, this time at the Abbey of St. Médard near Soissons, assuring him double coverage. Toward the cost of his expedition, the crown supplied 78,000 francs, of which 8,000 were to be repaid by the Pope. Another 4,000 was given to Coucy in compensation for the non-payment of aids promised him in the preceding year. He assembled an army estimated at 1,500 lances, amounting with foot soldiers and archers to a total of about 9,000 men. Miles de Dormans, the former Chancellor, who had been eager to go for the past year, joined with 200 lances. The bulk of the force was evidently made up by mercenaries, partly recruited in Avignon, where Coucy went first for consultations with Clement.

In July he crossed the Alps by way of Mont Cenis bearing powers to conclude the marriage by proxy of Anjou's son and Bernabò's daughter. A message from Bernabò invited him to enter Milan with 200 of his highest-ranking companions, which Coucy, whether from pomp or caution, enlarged to 600. Welcomed "with much joy" by Bernabò outside the gates, they entered the city together, "but such was the great number of men that they broke the bridge." This seems to have been Coucy's only *faux-pas* and did not detract from opulent ceremonies and a daily parade of gifts during a visit that lasted two weeks.

Two weeks was not too long to chart a course through the labyrinthine rivalries of Italy. The interrelationships of Venice, Genoa, Milan, Piedmont, Florence, and assorted despots and communes of northern Italy were constantly shifting. As soon as one power joined another against a third for that season's advantage, all alliances and feuds changed partners as if in a *trecento* square dance. Venice feuded with Genoa, Milan played off one against the other and feuded with Florence and the several principalities of Piedmont, Florence feuded with its neighbors, Siena, Pisa, and Lucca, and formed various leagues against Milan; papal politics kept the whole mass quivering.

Coucy's first hazard lay underfoot in the mutual jealousy between Bernabò and his melancholy nephew Gian Galeazzo, who now ruled in Pavia since the death of his father in 1378. Subtle, secretive, and deceptively mild, Gian Galeazzo cultivated a public repute for timidity and a hidden will as strong and unprincipled as Bernabò's. In later years when he was better known, Francesco Carrara of Padua said of him, "I know Gian Galeazzo. Neither honor nor pity nor sworn faith ever yet inclined him to do a disinterested deed. If he ever seeks what is good, it is because his interest requires it, for he is without moral sense. Goodness, like hate or anger, is for him a matter of calculation." As an opponent, Carrara's opinion was naturally inimical but not necessarily invalid; the character it ascribed to Gian Galeazzo anticipated by more than a century Machiavelli's *Prince*.

Gian Galeazzo resented and feared Bernabò's intrusion on his own prior relationship with the French royal family. "Bernabò is making fresh alliances with France," warned his mother. "If he becomes related, he will seize upon your sovereignty." With his one remaining child against Bernabò's well-filled stable, Gian Galeazzo could not match his uncle in alliances. If he could not match him, he could remove him, a cold alternative that from this moment—as was later recognized—began to take shape in his mind.

Meanwhile, he quietly paid his share of the subsidy for Anjou and prepared to welcome Coucy to Pavia. It was ten years since their encounter at Montichiari which had so confirmed Gian Galeazzo's distaste for battle that he had never again taken the field. But Coucy did not appear in Pavia to renew the acquaintance, probably because Bernabò did not wish his nephew and the French envoy to meet.

Agitation in northern Italy was intense at news of Coucy's advent. Siena sent envoys secretly to Milan to bargain for support against Florence. Florence sent envoys to divert him from Tuscany by gracious words and protestations of friendship. Florentine diplomacy was conducted by the permanent chancellor, Coluccio Salutati, a cultivated scholar who could frame his foreign correspondence in elegant Latin rhetoric that reflected credit on the republic. The continuity of his office, which was equivalent to that of a chief administrator, gave him great influence, and the fact that his appointment was regularly renewed over a period of thirty years is evidence—given the turbulence of Florentine politics—of a man of remarkable political ability, not to say equanimity. His heart was in literature and the new humanism, but in the conduct of affairs he was efficient, diligent, learned, and genial, admired for his integrity and style. According to Gian Galeazzo, a state paper by Salutati carried in the political scales the weight of a thousand horsemen. This was Coucy's opponent.

In response to the Florentine greetings, Coucy was surpassingly gracious. "We met," states the report probably written by Salutati, "with joyful embraces and greetings and he spoke reassuringly and peacefully to us. He called us not friends and brothers but his very fathers and masters. . . . Not only did he promise to abstain from hostility toward us, but he pledged to support us with his army in our own affairs." Coucy had clearly learned the Italian manner. He assured the Florentines their fears were fanciful and promised to confine his passage to a strictly limited route. They accepted his assurances, perhaps less because they trusted them than because, with Hawkwood absent in Naples, they did not have an armed force capable of barring his way. Neutral but suspicious, they raised a company of 4,000 peasants and commoners to guard the route.

Starting in August, Coucy crossed the Apennines and entered the land of the "Tuscan miracle" on the west. Cypress stood out against the rich blue sky, vineyards and silver olive trees clung to the slopes. Between hills topped by castle or village, slow white oxen moved through a landscape hand-tended for 2,000 years. The French army penetrated harshly in a progress that was not the peaceful one Coucy had promised. To their *stupor et dolor* (shock and grief), as the Florentines afterward complained bitterly to the King of France, they learned "he was not the same toward us in his heart as he outwardly feigned." Partly as a form of intimidation to remind Florence to stay neutral, partly to pay and provision his mercenaries, Coucy exacted tribute from towns, looted villages, even seized castles. Florence sent more envoys crying, "Peace! Peace!" and offering rich gifts and further assurance of neutrality if he would bypass Florentine territory. Coucy continued to answer soothingly, but force once employed quickly became rapine, difficult to restrain.

"They not only stole geese and hens, robbed the dovecotes and made off with sheep, rams, and cattle," according to the Florentine complaint, "they actually stormed our unarmed walls and undefended homes as if they were at war with us. They took people captive and tortured them and forced them to pay ransom. They killed men and women in cruel ways and set fire to their empty houses."

As Coucy advanced, Florence learned with dismay that he was in communication with the exiled lords of Arezzo, an ancient and important hill town forty miles to the southeast which the Florentines had long coveted and were preparing to annex. Its history dated back to the Etruscans, its famous red glazed pottery to the Romans; from its cluster of towers with belvederes and balconies, St. Francis in Giotto's painting exorcised flying demons. In the strife of Guelfs and Ghibellines, its ruling family, the Tarlati, lords of Pietramala, had been overthrown in 1380, and the winning side, too weak to maintain control, had called in the help of Charles of Durazzo. He or his agents treated Arezzo as a conquered city subject to the usual sack and fines of inhabitants, who in consequence looked more favorably on Florence. After complex bargaining, the Florentines had all but concluded an arrangement to buy the city from Durazzo when Coucy's intervention threatened to wreck all their hopes. They learned that the exiled lords of Pietramala had offered to assist him in capturing the city and that he had concluded a treaty with them to that effect. Coucy's object was to gain a foothold for the Angevin cause and a position from which he could exert pressure on Florence for supplies. If he drew against himself Hawkwood's company from Naples, the forces opposing Anjou would thereby be weakened.

Between Coucy and Florence a duel now began. Approaching his goal, Coucy made heavier demands and gave fewer reassurances. In reply to a renewed Florentine protest against pillaging by his soldiers, he blamed it on the resistance of the inhabitants, and with cool arrogance demanded a tribute of 25,000 florins from Florence and 20,000 from Siena. The Signoria met in anxiety; some argued for paying, some for refusing, some for a token payment to maintain the façade of friendship and prevent assault by Coucy's men-at-arms. While sending forward envoys with various proposals, Florence warned Jacopo Carraciolo, the governor of Arezzo who was now in their pay, to fortify his walls, prepare to provision Florentine reinforcements when they should appear, and expect attack on September 18. With generous sums contributed by the bourgeois magnates, they began assembling an armed force.

For a week, while waiting the outcome of his demands, Coucy remained in the vicinity without advancing. Siena paid him 7,000 florins; Florence, without making refusal explicit, paid nothing. As if satisfied, Coucy resumed his march, but, instead of making for Arezzo, took the road southward toward Cortona. This diversion proved to be a ruse to relax the vigilance of Carraciolo. On the night of September 28–29, Coucy turned back toward Arezzo and, on reaching the city, divided his force in two groups. He sent one to assault the walls with great clamor and shouts, while he led the stronger section with his best knights silently around to the San Clemente gate on the other side. Crashing down the doors, the French poured through, crying, "Long live King Louis and the Sire de Coucy! Death to Guelfs and the Duke of Durazzo!" As Carraciolo's men-at-arms rushed to meet them, battle cries and clang of blows filled the city, combat surged through every street and around the old Roman amphitheater until the defenders gave way before superior numbers and retreated to the citadel. The lords of Pietramala regained their homes in triumph, and while Arezzo again suffered rape and pillage, Coucy claimed the city in the name of King Louis of Naples, Sicily, and Jerusalem.

At that moment Louis of Anjou had been dead for nine days. For a year and a half he had rusted in the heel of Italy, with no kingship but the title, while his army wasted and dwindled and some who could afford it took ship for home. With control of Bari and other coast towns on the Adriatic, he could be provisioned by sea and may not have been as entirely destitute as pictured by the monastic chroniclers who liked to enlarge on the theme of vainglory's fall. But he was immobilized for lack of funds. His impoverished knights rode on donkeys or marched on foot "to hasten the day of combat" but could find nothing more than occasional skirmishes. In September 1384, Anjou caught a severe chill after overexerting himself against looters in his army. Fever developed, and recognizing death's presence, the Duke, like his brother Charles V, completed his will on his last day. The dying seemed always to know when their hour was at hand, doubtless because cures were not expected and the onset of certain symptoms was recognized as fatal. How it happened that they were so often in condition at the end to dictate last wills or codicils is harder to explain, unless it was because dying was an organized ritual with many attendants to assist the process.

With passion for conquest undiminished, Anjou called in his will on Pope Clement to ensure that his son, Louis II, should succeed to the Kingdom of Naples, and on Charles VI to "brandish the sword of his incomparable power" to avenge Queen Joanna. He appointed Coucy as his viceroy to carry on the campaign, with a provision that he could not be removed except by order of the Duchesse d'Anjou confirmed by the King, Burgundy, and Berry. He died on September 20 in the castle of Bari in a room overlooking the sea. While his body in a lead coffin was shipped back to France for burial, and his forces disintegrated, Charles of Durazzo held funeral services suitable to his late rival's rank, and clothed his court in mourning.

Anjou's death was not yet known on the Arno when Florence was stunned to learn of Coucy's capture of Arezzo. The Balia or Council of Ten, appointed in times of crisis, hastily assembled. Letters and ambassadors were dispatched to Genoa, Bologna, Padua, Perugia, Verona, Naples, even to Milan, urging all to join Florence in a league against the invader whose presence was said to endanger all Italy. Hawkwood's company was summoned from Naples and Pope Urban was asked to levy a special tithe on the clergy for funds to drive the "schismatics" out of Italy and thwart the triumph of the Anti-Pope. In the midst of the furor, news arrived by way of Venice that the French claimant to Naples was dead. Florence rejoiced and redoubled her preparations to surround Coucy in Arezzo.

Unaware both of the storm rising around him and of Anjou's death, Coucy took pleasure in informing the Signoria of his capture of Arezzo, not doubting, he wrote smoothly, that they would be delighted by an event so happy for the partisans of King Louis. With even greater pleasure, the Signoria wrote back to the "illustrious lord and dearest friend" to inform him with "a great sting of grief" that Anjou had died and that several of his chief companions had already appeared in Venice on their way home. Coucy naturally did not believe it, suspecting a Florentine trick intended to discourage him.

To impress the inhabitants, he established himself in splendid style and set himself to win adherents for the Angevin claimant by keeping open table and receiving with largesse all comers who declared themselves partisans of his cause. But while besieging the citadel, he shortly became aware that he was being enveloped if not actually besieged himself by a Florentine force on the north and his former companion-in-arms, Sir John Hawkwood, on the south. At this juncture the purpose of his campaign collapsed when evidence reached him confirming the fact of Anjou's death.

Coucy discovered himself isolated in the center of Italy with no expectation of relief and no point in holding out. Rather, his problem was getting out. To have clung to Arezzo for the sake of pursuing the Angevin cause in obedience to Anjou's will would have been correct but doomed. Messages from a remainder of Anjou's followers urged him to enter the kingdom of Naples and be its Governor, but Coucy was not the knightly type of heroic fool either to march unthinking toward disaster or to accept it with brainless valor when it came. He meant to use his hold of Arezzo to extract himself without loss of prestige to the Angevin cause—and recover the cost of the campaign as well.

Siena, which had refused to join the Florentine league, was his lever. He offered to sell Arezzo to Siena for 20,000 florins, knowing that rivalry would force Florence to offer a better price including a safe-conduct through Tuscany. Florence had not recruited any very firm support for her league, owing to the fears of other states that she would use it for her own aggrandizement. Bernabò, in the interests of his French alliance, had advised regaining Arezzo by money rather than force and warned Florence that the King of France and his uncles might take harsh reprisals against Florentine merchants and bankers if Coucy were attacked.

Florence, too, knew when to put discretion before valor. Through Coucy, her prospect of acquiring Arezzo was now suddenly restored. Overtures were made for the surrender of Carraciolo, the city's governor, including an offer to pay the back wages of his men-at-arms. Given the prospect of pay which they had thought lost, Carraciolo's men let it be known to their chief that they were ready to abandon a useless resistance. Accordingly, he agreed to surrender on condition that Florence recompense him for damages suffered in defending the city. No combat without money was standard for the age of chivalry.

Because Florence had prepared to use armed force against Coucy, contrary to her promise of neutrality, she was concerned about possible reprisals by France. To forestall these, the Signoria addressed to Charles VI a voluminous recital of Coucy's wrongdoings: the pillaging and injuries, the demands for tribute, the dealing with rebels (the Pietramala) in Florentine territory. In sorrow, the letter told how, after feigning peaceful intentions, Coucy had acted in hostility like an enemy, how "we, even though unaccustomed to deceitful words, saw through his plans" and were saddened that "such a noble and high-minded man, especially of Gallic blood, whose proper and natural virtue is magnanimity, could allow himself to invent lies and set traps"; how, in the belief that he could not truly represent the King of France by such conduct, "we prepared an army to repel force by force"; how, finally, "we write this with grief and bitterness so that you may know that our actions are justified."

Having put that on the record, the republic reached amicable arrangements with Coucy in two skillfully drafted separate treaties of November 5. In the first, Enguerrand de Coucy, desirous of recognizing and recompensing the affection, devotion, and respect always shown by the Republic of Florence to the royal house of France, ceded Arezzo, its walls, fortresses, houses, furnishings, inhabitants, rights, and privileges to Florence in perpetuity. No mention of a consideration was made, in order that the treaty might appear purely as an act of policy by Coucy in the Angevin interest against Durazzo. He made it a condition that the Pietramala were to be restored to their properties, that Florence was to remain neutral with regard to Naples, that French envoys and messengers to Naples would be afforded free passage with the right to buy provisions, and that he and his men should enjoy the same conditions on returning to France.

The sum agreed on in the second treaty was twice what he had asked from Siena. Considering the great cost to the Sire de Coucy of taking the city of Arezzo, and considering that he had traversed Florentine territory "without causing damage" (Florence was flexible in these matters) and intended to depart in the same manner, the republic agreed to pay him 40,000 gold florins, of which three fourths were to be paid at once before cession of the city, and the remaining 10,000 either at Bologna, Pisa, or Florence according to his wish, within two weeks after his evacuation of Arezzo. In generous disposal of the citizens' property, the French were permitted to take away with them whatever they could carry on the day of departure.

For preserving appearances while gaining desired ends, the settlement was a diplomatic masterpiece. The losers were Durazzo, who was forced to accept an accomplished fact; the Pietramala, who, having expected to regain power, were enraged; and the people of Arezzo, whom nobody recompensed. In revenge, on the day of departure the Pietramala ambushed a French foraging party and lured others "into their homes by offers of food and afterward killed them." Coucy at once demanded punitive action by Florence to prove that such hostilities "are gravely displeasing to you and the friendship between us stands firm." Florence offered fulsome regrets and, in lieu of action, an artistic denunciation of the "detestable" Pietramala. Their family name, Tarlati, it was said, derived from a word meaning "rotten wood that has been gnawed by insect borers," while the name Pietramala, deriving from *pietra* meaning stone, suited them equally "for they are hard and unyielding in their crimes." With these colorful if not helpful remarks the duel between Florence and Coucy came to an end.

Mutual obligations were carried out. Florence paid 30,000 florins on November 15 and 17, Carraciolo surrendered on the 18th, Coucy evacuated Arezzo on the 20th. Avoiding the hostile populace he would have encountered by returning the way he had come, he crossed the mountains and returned along the eastern slope to Bologna, posting rear-guard units on the way to present the appearance of a victor's return. At Bologna on Christmas Day he received the final payment in full. He re-entered Avignon in January 1385, adding a passage over the Alps in midwinter to a remarkably scatheless record.

Coucy's gift, unusual for his time, was recognition of realities, as seen in the contrast between his conduct of an expeditionary force and Anjou's. The quest for the crown of Naples—however harshly judged by critics after the fact—was not necessarily destined for catastrophe. Anjou had as good a chance as and a better claim than his opponent. What defeated him was a late start, poor generalship, and a waste of time and resources on the ceremonial display of kingship before the thing itself was in hand. If he had led a rapid and spartan advance with all energies and resources applied to the objective, the outcome could well have been different. But the "if" asks for a modern attitude in a medieval age.

The social damage was not in the failure but in the undertaking, which was expensive. The cost of war was the poison running through the 14th century. The funds contributed by the crown and by Anjou himself, not to mention the sum stolen by Pierre de Craon, were squeezed from the people of France for a cause which could in no way, present or future, benefit them. This did not escape notice, nor soothe the popular mood. On hearing of Anjou's death, a tailor of Orléans named Guillaume le Jupponnier, when "overcome with wine," burst into a tirade in which can be heard the rarely recorded voice of his class. "What did he go there for, this Duke of Anjou, down there where he went? He has pillaged and robbed and carried off money to Italy in order to conquer another land. He is dead and damned, and the King St. Louis too, like the others. Filth, filth of a King and a King! We have no King but God. Do you think they got honestly what they have? They tax me and re-tax me and it hurts them that they can't have everything we own. Why should they take from me what I earn with my needle? I would rather the King and all kings were dead than that my son should be hurt in his little finger."

The record of the tailor's case states that his words expressed "what others dared not say." After arrest and imprisonment, he was pardoned by the Governor of Orléans.

Anjou's widow, born Marie of Brittany, a daughter of the saintly if ruthless Charles of Blois and his unyielding wife, pursued the crown of Naples on behalf of her son Louis II with the same strenuous pertinacity as her parents had pursued the dukedom of Brittany, and with no better results. In a life-long contest against Charles of Durazzo and his son, Louis II was no more successful than his father had been. While Naples passed to the rule of Aragon and then to the Spanish Bourbons, the Angevins persevered in their claim for two centuries with all the undismayed persistence of royalty in pursuit of a crown denied.

The other French aim in Italy—imposing Clement by force—though never attempted by Anjou, was not abandoned. Rather it became an increasing obsession. In the meantime, madness shadowed Pope Urban as he quarreled fatally with Charles of Durazzo and was driven from Naples. Employing mercenaries, he rampaged through Italy in ceaseless disputes, besieged and besieging, captive and rescued, sputtering anathemas and excommunications, dragging behind him the six captive cardinals whom he accused of conspiracy to put him under restraint. When the horse of one of them went lame, Urban had the unfortunate prelate put to death and his corpse left unburied by the roadside. Afterward he executed four of the remaining five. He did not grace the Church of Rome.

Pierre de Craon returned to France after Anjou's death, disposing of obvious riches. While many of his recent companions, remnants of Anjou's army, begged their way on foot out of Italy, he appeared at court with a magnificent retinue, exciting indignation. "Ha! False traitor," cried the Duc de Berry on seeing him enter the Council, "wicked and disloyal, you deserve death! It is you who caused my brother's death. Seize him, and let justice be done!" No one dared carry out the command in fear of Craon's Burgundy connection. Craon continued to ornament the court of Charles VI and to escape for a long time a relentless lawsuit by the Duchesse d'Anjou and her son, although ultimately he was ordered to pay back 100,000 francs.

Ironically, after escaping harm in Italy, Coucy suffered a fall from his horse in Avignon with serious injury to his leg. Possibly a compound fracture, it was severe enough to keep him confined to bed for nearly four months. As Anjou's viceroy, he took responsibility for the ragged veterans returning from Bari, distributing funds and mediating disputes. On the arrival of Anjou's widow to establish her son's claims in Provence, he visited her several times (presumably in a litter), advised her in the matter of Pierre de Craon, and "comforted her as best he could." During these visits he may well have met and talked with the author of one of the great commentaries of the 14th century.

Honoré Bonet, Benedictine Prior of Salon in Provence, was attached in some capacity to the Anjou household and living in Avignon during the years 1382–86 while writing his observations on the kind of experience in which Coucy was an actor. *The Tree of Battles* was an examination of the laws and customs of war and, inevitably, of its moral and social effects. His purpose in writing the book, Bonet stated, was to find an answer to the "great commotions and very fierce misdeeds" of his own time. His conclusion was blunt. Stated in the form of a question—"Whether this world can by nature be without conflict and at peace?"—his answer was, "No, it can by no means be so."

"I make a Tree of Mourning at the beginning of my book," he wrote, on which could be seen three things: the "tribulation such as never was before" of the schism; the "great dissension" among Christian princes and kings; and the "great grief and discord" among communities. Bonet examined many practical and moral questions—whether, if a man is captured while under safe-conduct, the guarantor is bound to ransom him at his own cost; whether a man should prefer death to flight from battle; what were a knight's rights to wages, including sick pay and pay while on leave; what were the rules of spoil. Through every discussion his governing idea was that war should not harm those who do not make war, while every example of his own time showed that it did. He is "heart-stricken to see and hear of the misery inflicted on poor laborers . . . through whom, under God, the Pope and all the kings and lords in the world have their meat and all their drink and clothing." In answer to the question whether it is permissible to take prisoner the "merchants, tillers of the soil, and shep-

herds" of the enemy, his answer was no: "All husbandmen and plow-
men with their oxen when they are carrying on their business" and any
ass, mule, or horse harnessed to a plow should have immunity "by
reason of the work they do." The reason was fundamental: security of
the laborer and his beasts benefits all because they work for all.

Bonet reflected the growing dismay at the "great grief and discord"
caused by daily violation of this principle. Monks like himself and poets
like Deschamps deplored openly the conduct of war not because they
were necessarily more sensitive than other men but because they were
articulate and accustomed to commit ideas to writing. With no illusions about chivalry, Bonet wrote that some knights were made bold
by desire for glory, others by fear, others by "greed to gain riches and
for no other reason." When *The Tree of Battles*, dedicated to Charles
VI, appeared in 1387, he did not suffer for its truths. On the contrary,
he was invited to court and appointed to pensions and positions. Like
other prophets, his fate was to be honored—and ignored.

Chapter 20

A Second Norman Conquest

While Coucy was still in Avignon, his diplomatic talents were assigned the delicate task of informing Pope Clement of the proposed marital alliance of the King of France to a house on the other side of the schism. The prospective bride was Elizabeth of Bavaria—or Isabeau, as she became known by the French equivalent of her name—a member of the Wittelsbach dynasty and a granddaughter to Bernabò Visconti. Bavaria, like all the German states, had remained in obedience to Urban, to the bitter disappointment of Charles V. A German marriage was nevertheless important to give weight against England, especially since Richard II was negotiating to marry Anne of Bohemia, daughter of the late Emperor.

Bavaria was the most powerful and flourishing of the German states, and the Wittelsbachs the wealthiest of the three families—the others being the Hapsburgs and the Luxemburgs—which at different times occupied the imperial throne. A Wittelsbach alliance was so desirable that Bernabò Visconti married no fewer than four of his children to scions of that house. Taddea, the second of these, bringing a dowry of 100,000 gold ducats, married Duke Stephen III of Bavaria, who, though he ruled jointly with two brothers, possessed every quality of the autocrat to excess. Reckless, prodigal, ostentatious, amorous, restless without a tournament or a war, he was well suited to a Visconti daughter, and when she died after twelve years of marriage, her sister Maddalena, with another dowry of 100,000 ducats, took her place. Isabeau, product of the first union, was in 1385 a pretty, plump fifteen-year-old German maiden destined for a lurid career.

Her marriage to Charles VI was first broached when her uncle, Duke Frederick, came to share in the pleasures of French chivalry at the siege of Bourbourg. He learned that a condition of betrothal to the

King of France was that the prospective bride be examined in the nude by ladies of the court to determine if she were properly formed for bearing children. Conveyed to his excitable brother, the proposal was indignantly rejected. What if she should be sent back? Duke Stephen demanded, and instantly tossed aside the offered crown. The alliance, however, was tactfully pursued by his uncle, Albert of Bavaria, ruler of Hainault-Holland, and by the Duke of Burgundy on the occasion of the famed double wedding of their sons and daughters. Stephen's consent was obtained by arranging that Isabeau should be sent to France on pretext of a pilgrimage, although Stephen warned his brother, who was to escort her, that if he brought her back, "You will have no more bitter enemy than I."

Rumors of the planned marriage, on reaching Milan, provoked the most sensational coup of the age—the ousting of Bernabò by his supposedly quiet and retiring nephew Gian Galeazzo. Bernabò's marriage policy had for some time been cutting into Gian Galeazzo's sovereignty, owing to Bernabò's habit of giving away, as dowries, Visconti territories or their revenues to which the nephew had equal title—and without consulting him. The prospect of Bernabò's granddaughter on the throne of France, and a renewed prospect of Bernabò's daughter Lucia on the throne of Naples, threatened to cut into Gian Galeazzo's French support. Lucia reappeared when the Duchesse d'Anjou, who had never ceased nagging her French relatives to try once more for Naples, succeeded in obtaining a tentative promise "in favor" of the attempt, and accordingly sent for Lucia to complete the proxy marriage to her son. This combination of circumstances propelled Gian Galeazzo to action.

In May 1385 he sent a message to his uncle saying that he was about to make a pilgrimage to the Madonna del Monte near Lago Maggiore and would be glad to meet with him outside Milan. His proposal seemed natural enough because Gian Galeazzo, though "subtle in intellect and wise in the ways of the world," was very devout, carrying a rosary and accompanied by monks wherever he went, and greatly concerned with penance and pilgrimage. He also relied on astrologers to select propitious moments for his decisions, and once refused to discuss a diplomatic matter at a particular time because, as he wrote his correspondent, "I observe astrology in all my affairs." These tastes and his apparent fear of his uncle, shown by doubling his guard and having all his food tasted, caused Bernabò to regard him with contempt. When a courtier, suspicious of Gian Galeazzo's message, warned of a possible plot, Bernabò scoffed. "You have little sense. I tell you I know my nephew." At age 76, after a lifetime of bullying, he was both overconfident and careless. Gian Galeazzo's plan depended on just that.

With two of his sons, but otherwise unprotected, Bernabò rode to the rendezvous outside the gates. Gian Galeazzo, accompanied by a large bodyguard, dismounted, embraced his uncle and, while holding him tightly, called out an order in German, upon which one of his generals, the *condottiero* Jacopo del Verme, cut Bernabò's sword belt while another, crying "You are a prisoner!", seized his baton of office and took him in custody. Immediately Gian Galeazzo's forces galloped through Milan and occupied its strong points. Because of his reasonable government of Pavia, the populace was ready to welcome him as a deliverer, and greeted him with cries of *"Viva il Conte!"* followed by their first thought on removal of the tyrant, "Down with taxes!" To smooth the transition, Gian Galeazzo allowed the mob to sack Bernabò's palace and burn the tax registers. He reduced taxes as one of his first measures and made up the difference from Bernabò's hoard of gold. Legitimacy or its appearance was supplied by summoning a Grand Council to endow him with formal dominion and by sending a legal transcript of Bernabò's crimes to all states and rulers.

The Milanese state was now controlled by a single ruler who was to loom ever larger as time went on. Bernabò's sons were neutralized, in the case of one by life imprisonment, in the case of the second by his own worthlessness, and by a lifetime pension for the third and youngest. The towns of Lombardy submitted uneventfully, and the tyrant himself was locked up in the fortress of Trezzo, where in December of the same year he died, supposedly poisoned by order of the usurper. Bernabò was buried in Milan with honors although without the baton of office, and his equestrian statue, already made at his design, was erected as he had planned.

The fall of the modern Tarquin amazed the world, with echoes reaching into the *Canterbury Tales*, where it is related in the "Monk's Tale" how "Thy brother's son . . . within his prison made thee to dye." Not the least of the consequences was to implant in the shallow if implacable heart of Isabeau of Bavaria a relentless desire for revenge upon Gian Galeazzo who had deposed, if not murdered the grandfather she had doubtless never known. Since the usurper was to emerge as one of the major figures of Europe and she as Queen of France, the results were grave and far-reaching.

At seventeen, Charles VI was an ardent, inconstant youth who rode nine courses in the lists at the tournaments in honor of the Burgundy double wedding. His martial appetite had been encouraged by his uncles for the sake of war in their own interests. Physically, "nature seemed to have been prodigal in her gifts" to him. Above average height, robust in figure, wearing his blond hair to his shoulder, he was frank, energetic, gracious, carelessly and excessively generous, giving to anyone and everyone regardless of what was in his Treasury, lacking in steadiness or seriousness. During a hunt when he was thirteen, a deer was reportedly taken wearing a golden collar inscribed in "ancient characters": *Caesar hoc mihi donavit.* Told that the deer must have been in the forest since the days of Julius Caesar "or some other emperor," the boy King was so enchanted that he ordered all the royal plate and other furnishings to be engraved with a deer wearing a collar in the form of a crown. No less easily inflamed in amours, he was the victim, according to the Monk of St. Denis, of "carnal appetites," and was equally quickly disenchanted. Instability trembled beneath outward health. His mother, Queen Jeanne, had suffered a phase of insanity in 1373, his heritage was a web of intermarriage, all his sisters but one had died before maturity.

The charm of Isabeau and the delights of marriage were suitably dwelt upon by his various aunts and uncles at the resplendent double wedding of Burgundy's son and daughter at Cambrai in April 1385. As a prince of great pretensions, Philip intended the ceremony to outshine any that had gone before. He borrowed the crown jewels from Charles VI, transported extra tapestries and special jousting horses from Paris, ordered special liveries made for the occasion of red and green velvet (the two most expensive colors), furnished all the ladies with gowns of cloth of gold, and supplied a thousand jousting lances for the tournament. Papal dispensations of consanguinity were obtained in duplicate, one from each Pope because the marriages spanned the schism. Gifts were distributed throughout festivities that lasted five days, and their cost was twice that of the clothes. The total cost was 112,000 livres, equal to one quarter the revenues of the Flemish-Burgundian state in a time of deep social anger and want.

Isabeau reached France in July after being tutored for four weeks, at the court of her Wittelsbach relatives in Hainault, in French dress, etiquette, and flirtation. The meeting with Charles took place at Amiens, where the French court had moved owing to renewed war in Flanders. The King, in a fever of excitement, arrived on July 13, the same day that Coucy arrived from Avignon "in great haste with news of the Pope," although what news is not recorded. Sleepless and agitated, Charles kept asking, "When will I see her?" and when he did, fell instantly enamored, gazing at the German girl with admiration and ardor. Asked if she was to become Queen of France, he replied forcefully, "By my faith, yes!"

Isabeau understood nothing of what was being said because her lessons had apparently left her innocent of the French language except for a few words spoken in a thick German accent. Her manner, however, was alluring, and Charles's impatience was such that the wedding followed hastily on July 17 to the accompaniment of numerous jokes about the hot young couple. "And if," concluded Froissart, "they passed that night together in great delight, one can well believe it." No such eager marriage was ever to sink to a sadder end, in madness, debauchery, and hate.

After Venus, Mars. Even before the truce with England was due to expire in October, the Scots had sent envoys to ask for a French force to join them "and make so great a hole in England that it should never be recovered." The pride of France welcomed the chance to show themselves not only strong enough to repel attack but ready to take the offensive. The English should be shown that they could not always be the aggressor but must "get accustomed themselves to being attacked"—in their own land, as Coucy had suggested to Charles V. Philip the Bold, who effectively controlled the government, arranged for Admiral de Vienne, "a knight of proven valor and a passion for glory," to take an expeditionary force to Scotland and prepare the way for a larger force to follow, which would be led by Clisson, Sancerre, and Coucy. Then, together with the Scots, they would "boldly penetrate" over the border.

Commanding eighty knights and a total force of 1,500 fully paid for six months in advance, Vienne crossed in the early summer of 1385, bringing a "free gift" of 50,000 gold francs to the King of Scotland and fifty suits of armor, including lances and shields, to his nobles. The Scottish envoys had indeed asked the French to bring equipment to arm a thousand Scots, which should have been a warning, but the realities of Scotland proved an unpleasant surprise. Castles were bare and gloomy with primitive conditions and few comforts in a miserable climate. The damp stone huts of clan chieftains were worse, lacking windows or chimneys, filled with peat smoke and the smell of manure. Their inhabitants engaged in prolonged vendettas of organized cattle-raiding, wife-stealing, betrayal, and murder. They had no iron to shoe their horses nor leather for saddles and bridles, which previously had been imported ready-made from Flanders.

Accustomed to "tapestried halls, goodly castles, and soft beds," the

French asked themselves, "Why have we come hither? We never knew what poverty meant until now." Their hosts were no better pleased with the visitors. They resented the luxury-loving French knights and welcomed them coldly. Instead of marching toward pitched battle with banners flying, they withdrew their forces when they learned that a large English army was advancing.

Diverted by a new outbreak in Flanders, the French army of reinforcement did not come. During enforced idleness, Admiral de Vienne's frustrated martial ardor turned to love; he engaged in a guilty amour with a cousin of the Scottish King which enraged his hosts "so that the Admiral was in danger of death." Whether the final quarrel was over this issue or because the Scots insisted that the French should pay the cost of their visit, the Admiral in any case undertook to bear the cost personally, hurriedly hired a number of ships, and departed.

Meanwhile, the party of Ghent, led by Artevelde's successor Francis Ackerman, had seized Damme, the port of Bruges at the mouth of the Scheldt where the French reinforcements for Scotland were to have been launched. The attack was prompted by the English, who were suffering the usual terrors spread by rumors of a French invasion. A French army, bringing the King fresh from his marriage bed, marched north to besiege Damme and, though suffering much from the heat, from English archers, and from an outbreak of plague, recaptured it after a siege of six weeks.

Punishment was savage, chiefly by the Burgundians, who burned and destroyed up to the gates of Ghent. Many prisoners, taken for ransom, were put to death to serve as an example. One of them at the block warned his executioners that "the King can kill men of strong heart, but though he exterminates all Flemings their dry bones will rise up to fight him again." The point was borne in upon the Duke of Burgundy that alienation of his own subjects was not in his best interests. A peace settlement without further penalties or fines was concluded in December at Tournai and efforts made afterward to restore Flanders' damaged commerce. But the harm done by decades of strife could not be undone; the great age of Flemish prosperity had passed.

Possibly stimulated by all the weddings, Coucy's remarriage at the age of 46 to a girl some thirty years his junior took place in February 1386. The bride was Isabelle, daughter of the Duc de Lorraine, "a very beautiful demoiselle of the noble and great generation of the house of Blois." She had been considered as a bride for the King during the interval when Stephen of Bavaria was recalcitrant, and was described as "of the King's age or very close," which would have made her sixteen to eighteen. Charles had been "near agreed" to the match until the Bavarian proposal was revived.

Little is known of the second Isabelle de Coucy except that after the marriage Enguerrand undertook a vast renovation of the castle from which it is possible (though not obligatory) to deduce that he did it to please a young and beautiful bride.

Following the marriage, a new northwest wing almost as grandiose in scale as the renowned *donjon* was added to the castle, along with many domestic improvements.* The new wing housed a grand banquet hall measuring 50 by 200 feet, called the Salle des Preux or Hall of the Nine Worthies, the heroes of history most admired in the Middle Ages. They were three ancients—Hector of Troy, Alexander the Great, and Julius Caesar; three Biblical Jews—Joshua, King David, and Judas Maccabeus; three Christians—King Arthur, Charlemagne, and the crusader Godfrey of Bouillon. An adjoining hall 30 by 60 feet, was dedicated to the feminine worthies, Hippolyta, Semiramis, Penthisilea, and other legendary queens. Each hall had an immense mantled chimney at either end, a high vaulted ceiling, and wide arched windows which let in broad bands of sunlight, unlike the narrow slits in the older walls. A raised tribune from which great personages and their ladies, separated from the crowd, could view the dances and entertainments was built into the Salle des Preux. Behind it stood the row of Nine Worthies in bas-relief, "carved by a hand so fine," wrote an admirer, "that if my eyes had not been witness I would never have believed that leaves and fruits and grapes and other delicate things could have been so perfectly fashioned in hard stone."

Among other additions were a fireplace and chimney for the lady's boudoir, now tucked into an angle between the new wing and the old; an indoor tennis court with carved wooden ceiling; a new stable in the lower court; parapets extended the length of the terraces; a double-arched space beneath the terrace to keep wood for fuel; a kennel with latrines "to make room for Bonniface and Guedon to lie"; a water tank six feet by eight and sixteen feet deep to supply water by four large stone conduits to the kitchens. New wooden ceilings were installed in the *donjon*, roofs throughout the castle were re-covered, gargoyles and gutters cleaned, and the windows of the upper chamber "which the Dame de Coucy's monkey had damaged" repaired.

---

* By a fluke of survival, the domestic accounts of Coucy-le-Château for the year 1386–87 remained in existence long enough for a local antiquarian, Lucien Broche, to publish a report of them in 1905–09. The originals disappeared during the First World War, in which Picardy suffered great destruction.

Craftsmen of every specialty were hired—a carriage-maker to cut down the carriage brought from Lorraine by the new Dame de Coucy, which was too wide for the gates and had to be reduced by a foot; wood-carvers to panel the ceilings of the Eagle Chamber and the oratory and dressing room of the Sire de Coucy, and to make two extension leaves for the banquet table for the new hall; iron-workers to replace old keys, locks, bolts, and hinges, in particular to make a new lock for the casket in the oratory of the Seigneur; plumbers to weld the kitchen sinks and drainage pipes; painters from Paris to decorate the walls and "to redress the white-and-red hoods of the Coucy livery with new quilting."

Much of the non-rented land, it appears from the accounts, was in vineyards, requiring considerable expense in planting, cultivating, and harvesting, and producing considerable income for the Seigneur. Other expenses went for the wages of bailiffs and tax-collectors, offerings to the chaplains of two chapels, charges for curing fish, replenishing live-stock, cutting wood, mowing and haying the fields, providing the clothes and equipment of the Seigneur and his retinue. Coucy's journeys to Soissons and other places show him generally accompanied by about eighty mounted knights, squires, and servants, and an astronomer, Maître Guillaume de Verdun, to carry out "certain necessities for him."

The second marriage like the first was not very prolific, which may reflect something about Enguerrand's marital relations or merely his prolonged absences. No son to carry on the dynasty and maintain the great barony was born, and only one daughter. Named Isabelle for her mother, she ultimately married the second son of the Duke of Burgundy. At an unknown date, probably some years later, the much desired son was finally born to Enguerrand—out of wedlock. Named Perceval and known as the Bastard of Coucy, he married in 1419 which suggests that he was the product of a late liaison. The identity of his mother is a blank. She may have been a rival of Coucy's wife or a substitute during his later tenure in the south as Lieutenant-General of Guienne. Evidently she was of some importance in Coucy's life, or he felt pride in a son, or both, because he acknowledged paternity and endowed Perceval with the seigneurie of Aubermont, a fief of the lordship of La Fère. The Bastard could thereafter call himself Sieur de Coucy and Seigneur d'Aubermont.

In the year of marriages, 1385–86, Coucy attended the wedding at Dijon of his Hapsburg relative and recent enemy, Duke Albert III, to a daughter of Philip the Bold. This was the year of the historic victory at Sempach when Swiss pikemen defeated the Hapsburgs, and it may be that Coucy's presence at Dijon for the wedding was connected with the Hapsburgs' desire for his support. In any event, his quarrel with his mother's family was apparently made up. "They ended always by accommodating," in the words of the discoverer of the document.

The Scottish fiasco failed to discourage French designs for the offensive. On the contrary, the design was now enlarged to a full-scale invasion of England, a true penetration, perhaps a second Norman Conquest. There was a strong body of sentiment which held that only a military victory by the French could finish off the war and assure the supremacy of the French Pope. Besides, England was known to be in great discord, and the nobility no longer united in support of the King but deeply disaffected. The Duke of Burgundy was initially the sponsor of the invasion plan, but when the decision was taken in April 1386, the Royal Council voted for it unanimously. Many were the same men who had served Charles V, but his controlling sense of the art of the possible was gone. Out of the "heap of ruins" after Poitiers, Charles had learned the discipline of adjusting ambitions to possibilities; his son's reign was to be spent unlearning it as fast as possible. A *folie de grandeur*, or just such "fantasies of omnipotence" as define megalomania, overtook the French as a distraught century was drawing to its close.

"You are the greatest King living with the greatest number of subjects," Burgundy told his nephew, "and it has occurred to me many times why we do not make this passage to England to crush the great pride of these English . . . and make this great enterprise one of eternal memory." When shortly after Easter the Duke of Lancaster left England with a large force in 200 ships to conquer the throne of Castile, the French opportunity was at hand. Information about each other's movements was known through French and English fishermen, who, ignoring hostilities, came to each other's aid at sea and exchanged catches, keeping trans-Channel communication open.

The French invasion fleet was planned to be the greatest "since God created the world." The original army that Clisson and Coucy were to have led to Scotland was to be the invasion force, swollen to awesome proportions. Chroniclers write in terms of 40,000 knights and squires, 50,000 horses, 60,000 foot soldiers, figures which were meant to be more impressive than precise. Preparations for Scotland had been well under way before the Flemish interruption and were now renewed in a colossal burst of activity. Money, as always, came first. A sales tax of 5 percent plus 25 percent on beverages had already been levied throughout the kingdom for the Scottish campaign, bringing in 202,000 livres. It was now renewed, as it was to be repeatedly, never bringing in enough.

Ships were hired or purchased from every part of Europe from Prussia to Castile, while French shipyards worked day and night. The 600 ships assembled in the previous year were more than doubled and the sight they made in the mouth of the Scheldt was "the greatest of its kind ever seen." Buonaccorso Pitti, the ubiquitous Florentine, saw 1,200 ships of which 600 were combat vessels mounted with the "castle" for archers. The French nobles, counting on recouping expenses from booty and ransoms in England, spared nothing in competitive splendor of gilded prows and silvered masts and sails striped with cloth of gold and silk. Admiral de Vienne commissioned a Flemish artist, Pierre de Lis, to paint his flagship red, adorned with his arms. Philip of Burgundy's black ship was decorated with the coats of arms of all his possessions, and flew silken banners bearing his bold device "*Il me tarde*," meaning approximately "I don't wait," repeated in gold on the mainsail. Coucy's ship, "one of the most sumptuous of the fleet . . . very large and richly decorated," met an unfortunate fate in the Seine, where it was moored. It was seized with two other ships in a daring raid up the river by a Portuguese admiral acting as an ally of the Duke of Lancaster.

Coucy was not immune to the hubris of the hour. His seal, attached to a receipt of October 1386 for payments connected with the invasion fleet, bears his arms combined with the royal leopard of England. Evidently he felt endowed with some permanent claim, perhaps in relation to his daughter Philippa, first cousin of the King of England. Coucy's personal contingent in the invasion army numbered 5 knights, 64 squires, and 30 archers.

The wide bays and estuaries of the Scheldt provided a huge, sheltered gathering place for the armada, with communication by land and sea and by inland canals to Bruges. Day after day the parade of supplies came in—2,000 barrels to hold biscuit, timber to make carts, portable handmills to grind wheat, cannonballs of iron and stone from Reims, ropes, candles, lanterns, mattresses and straw pallets, urinals, shaving basins, laundry tubs, gangplanks for horses, shovels, pickaxes, and hammers. Clerks wrote a ceaseless stream of orders, purchasing agents scoured Normandy and Picardy, Holland and Zeeland, and as far as Germany and Spain for provisions—for wheat to make 2,000 tons of biscuit, for salt pork and bacon, smoked mackerel, salmon, eels, and dried herring, dried peas and beans, onions, salt, 1,000 barrels (or four million liters) of French wine, and 857 barrels of wine from Greece, Portugal, Lepanto, and Rumania. The Duke of Burgundy ordered 101 beef cattle, 447 sheep, 224 hams, 500 fat hens, capons, and geese, containers of ginger, pepper, saffron, cinnamon, and cloves, 900 pounds of almonds, 200 of sugar, 400 of rice, 300 of barley, 94 casks of olive oil, 400 cheeses from Brie and 144 from Chauny.

Swords, lances, halberds, suits of armor, helmets "visored in the new fashion," shields, banners, pennants, 200,000 arrows, 1,000 pounds of gunpowder, 138 stone cannonballs, 500 ramming prows for the ships, catapults, and flame-throwers were collected. Armorers hammered and polished, embroiderers worked on banners, bakers made ship's biscuit, supplies were counted on delivery, packed, stored, and loaded into the holds. The roadsteads filled with cargo vessels, carracks, barges, galleys, and galleons.

Of all the preparations, the most stupendous was the portable wooden town to protect and house the invaders upon landing. A huge camp enclosing a place for each captain and his company, it was virtually an artificial Calais to be towed across the Channel. Its dimensions epitomized the fantasy of omnipotence. It was to have a circumference of nine miles and an area of 1,000 acres surrounded by a wooden wall 20 feet high reinforced by towers at intervals of 12 and 22 yards. Houses, barracks, stables, and markets where the companies would come for their provisions were to be laid out along prearranged streets and squares. William the Conqueror had brought a dismountable wooden fort to England in aid of his landing 300 years before, and similar devices had been used many times since, but nothing so daring in concept and size as this had ever before been attempted. Pre-fabricated in Normandy by the work of 5,000 wood-cutters and carpenters, supervised by a team of architects, it was to be packed and shipped in numbered sections, so designed that assembly at the beachhead could allegedly be accomplished in an unbelievable three hours. For belligerent purposes, the 14th century, like the 20th, commanded a technology more sophisticated than the mental and moral capacity that guided its use.

At the Scheldt the port overflowed with nobles, functionaries, craftsmen, and servants of every degree, all of whom had to be housed and paid. The missing brilliance of the Count of Savoy was made up by his son Amadeus VII, called the Red Count, who entertained everyone, whether humble, middle, or great, and turned away no one from his table without a meal. Eustache Deschamps, too, was on hand as laureate for the occasion, writing confidently,

Yours will be the land of England;
Where once there was a Norman Conquest,
Valiant heart will make war once more.

All the notable lords of France were present except the Duc de Berry, whose delayed arrival caused misgiving.

Impatience for embarkation was rising. The nobles stayed at Bruges "to be more at their ease," and every few days rode over to Sluys, where the King stayed, to learn if the day of departure had been decided. The answer was always tomorrow or next week or when the fog lifts or when the Duc de Berry comes. The mass of men crowded into the area was growing restless and disorderly. Many, including the poorer knights and squires, could not be paid, and the cost of living was going up as the local people raised prices. Knights complained that four francs could barely buy what formerly was worth one. The Flemings were sullen and quarrelsome, "for the common people bore a grudge in their minds for the battle of Roosebeke." They said to each other, "Why the Devil does not the King of France pass over into England? Are we not in poverty enough?"—although they admitted that "the Frenchmen make us no poorer."

All excuses for postponement now came to one—waiting for the Duc de Berry. His non-arrival was a sign that the invading spirit was not in fact unanimous, that doubts and conflicting interests were struggling behind the scenes, that a peace party represented by Berry was opposing itself to the war party.

Berry was too absorbed in acquisition and art to be interested in war. He lived for possessions, not glory. He owned two residences in Paris, the Hôtel de Nesle and another near the Temple, and built or acquired a total of seventeen castles in his duchies of Berry and Auvergne. He filled them with clocks, coins, enamels, mosaics, marquetry, illuminated books, musical instruments, tapestries, statues, triptychs painted in bright scenes on dazzling gold ground bordered with gems, gold vessels and spoons, jeweled crosses and reliquaries, relics, and curios. He owned one of Charlemagne's teeth, a piece of Elijah's mantle, Christ's cup from the Last Supper, drops of the Virgin's milk, enough of her hairs and teeth to distribute as gifts, soil from various Biblical sites, a narwhal's teeth, porcupine's quills, the molar tooth of a giant, and enough gold-fringed vestments to robe all the canons of three cathedrals at one time. Agents kept him apprised of curiosities, and when one reported a "giant's bones" dug up near Lyon in 1378, he at once authorized purchase. He kept live swans and bears representing his chosen device, a menagerie with apes and dromedaries, and rare fruit trees in his garden.

He ate strawberries with crystal picks mounted in silver and gold, and read by candlelight from six carved ivory candle-holders.

Like most affluent lords, he had a good library of classics and contemporary works; he commissioned translations from the Latin, bought romances from booksellers in Paris, and bound his books in precious bindings, some in red velvet with gold clasps. He commissioned from renowned illuminators at least twenty Books of Hours, among them two exquisite masterpieces, the *Grandes Heures* and *Très Riches Heures*. His pleasure was to see illustrated his favorite scenes and portraits, including his own. Delicate multiple-towered cities and castles, rural occupations, knights and ladies in garden, hunt, and banquet hall, clad in garments of surpassing elegance, ornamented the prayerbooks. The Duke himself usually appears robed in the pure sky blue, whose pigment was so precious that two pots of it were listed in an inventory of Berry's "treasures."

Berry introduced the newly invented pedal organ into his churches and bought a new jacket for four livres so that his cornettist who played so beautifully might perform a solo before Charles V. He had gold and pearls ground together for a laxative, and during enforced idleness when he was bled to relieve the effects of gluttony and an apoplectic tendency, he played at dice, his favorite pastime. In one game with knightly companions, he wagered his coral prayer beads for forty francs. Accompanied by his swans, bears, and tapestries, he moved continually from one of his castles to another, carrying half-finished works of art by artists at one place to be completed by those at another, taking part in local processions and pilgrimages, visiting monasteries, enjoying wine harvests in autumn, and sending home to the Duchess on one occasion in June new peas, cherries, and 78 ripe pears. He collected dogs, always searching for more, no matter how many he had, and when he heard of an unusual variety of greyhound in Scotland, obtained a safe-conduct from Richard II to allow four couriers on horseback to make the round trip to bring him back a pair.

The funds to gratify his tastes were wrung from the people of Auvergne, and of Languedoc when he was its governor, by the heaviest taxation in France of his time, sowing the hatred and misery that resulted in the insurrection of Montpellier and his own recall. Punishment of the Tuchin rising in 1383, when he was again governor in place of Anjou, was his most lucrative opportunity. Instead of death sentences on the leaders, he sold pardons and imposed on the communes an enormous fine of 800,000 gold francs, four times as much as the whole of Languedoc had been able to collect for the ransom of Jean II.

It was to be paid for by an unprecedented tax of 24 francs per hearth. Unchastened and unchanged, Berry was to go on spending for thirty more years until he had ruined his lands to pay his expenses and died insolvent in 1416 at the age of 76.

At the time when he was waited for at the Scheldt, he was 46, vain, pleasure-loving, obstinate, a prey to parasites, mediocre in mind and spirit, redeemed from vulgarity only by his love and fostering of beauty. Perhaps that lifelong passion was a reaction to his own ugly, coarse-grained features, which he perversely emphasized; the pug-nosed face appears on plates, seals, cameos, tapestries, altar panels, stained-glass windows, Books of Hours. According to a popular verse, the Duke wished to surround himself "only with snub-noses at his court."

Berry did not appear at the Scheldt until October 14. By that time the days were growing shorter and colder, the Channel rougher. Meantime in mid-September, disaster smote the portable town. Loaded aboard 72 ships, it was on the way from Rouen to the Scheldt when the convoy was attacked by an English squadron out of Calais and three of the French ships were captured, along with the master carpenter in charge of construction. Too big to enter Calais, two of the ships were towed to England and their sections of the town exhibited in London to the awe and rejoicing of the English. For the French the loss was a portent.

The Monk of St. Denis, never at a loss for omens, reported clouds of crows carrying lighted coals which they deposited on thatched barns, as well as one of the terrible storms which appear regularly at all dark moments of his chronicle and, in this case, tore up the tallest trees by their roots and destroyed a church by a thunderbolt. On the day after Berry finally arrived, the elements, "seemingly angered by the delay," flung the sea into an uproar and raised waves "like mountains" that shattered the ships and were followed by such rains as seemed that God was sending a new Flood. Many supplies, not yet loaded, were ruined.

Three weeks of indecision passed without action. In November the captains of 150 of the invasion ships submitted a list of reasons why embarkation was by now impossible: "Truthfully, the sea is cursed: item, the nights are too long; item, too dark [and through a long string of "items"], too cold, too rainy, too *fresques*. Item, we need a full moon; item, we need wind. Item, the lands of England are perilous, the ports are perilous; we have too many old ships, too many small ships, we fear the small ships may be swamped by the great ships. . . ." The unrelieved negatives hint at justification for a decision already taken.

The whole immense enterprise with all its investment in ships, arms, men, money, and provisions was called off, at least for the winter. The grand army disintegrated and departed, perishable supplies were sold to the Flemings below cost, the remainder of the portable town was given by the King to the Duke of Burgundy, who used it for construction in his own domain. Across the Channel, the English celebrated.

That Berry had "no wish to go to England" himself and did not wish the expedition to go was recognized at the time. Sentiment for a negotiated peace was growing on both sides, though always opposed by a war party in each country. Especially the mercantile estate wanted to end this "useless war," and many who recognized that it was getting nowhere argued for peace as a step toward ending the schism and uniting two great Christian kings against the Turks. Whether or not Berry thought in these terms, he was certainly concerned about the money absorbed by war, and he had been in communication with the Duke of Lancaster, who would have liked his country to be at peace with France in order to free him to pursue his ambitions in Castile. Under pretext of a peace parley, Berry and Lancaster had had a meeting earlier in the year from which both had emerged looking pleased, and a year later Berry, as a widower, negotiated to marry Lancaster's daughter, although that came to nothing.

Philip the Bold, even at the risk of leaving the kingdom in control of his brother, could have sailed without him if his will had matched the bold motto flying from his masts. But he feared the risk of a rising in Flanders if he left. The banners proclaiming "I don't wait" were hauled down and he waited after all. At the same time the Royal Council too developed doubts of military success. Long before the portents of barn-igniting crows and tree-uprooting storms, a report from Avignon mentioned "the great debate as to whether the King will invade or not."

The true determinant was probably reluctance at the water's edge. Crossing the Channel was an uncertain thing at best, and worse against "the terrible west wind" of the late season. Above all loomed a hostile beachhead on the other side. Facing that hazard, potential invaders, after making preparations as grandiose as those of 1386, have backed away—Napoleon for one, Hitler for another. Throughout the war in the 14th century the English had allied beachheads in Flanders, Normandy, or Brittany at their disposal, or their own ports at Calais and Bordeaux. Lacking that advantage, the French had never launched more than punitive raids with no attempt to hold land. In either direction no successful invasion of a hostile beachhead was ever carried out between 1066 and 1944.

If fear was a reason, it was not acknowledged. The invasion was considered only postponed until the following year, when a smaller version was to be launched under the command of the Constable and Coucy. In March 1387 Charles VI paid a ceremonial visit to Coucy-le-Château, partly to discuss plans, as indicated by a surviving document which refers to provisions for the "army" that the Sire de Coucy will take "for going to England." Doubtless also the King's visit was in furtherance of the crown's interest in Coucy's domain. This time no court poet documented the occasion, but a petty crime committed in the course of the visit elicited one of the royal letters of pardon which are windows on the life of the poor.

One Baudet Lefèvre, "a poor man with many children," took from the castle two tin serving platters used for service of the King's dinner, hid them under his tunic, and went to a hostel in the town, where he was seen by a sergeant of "our dear and beloved cousin, the Sire de Coucy," who asked him, "What are you doing here?" Baudet replied, "I am warming myself." As he was speaking, the sergeant saw the platters and arrested him. He was taken to prison in the castle, where he was also found to have taken a silver-gilt platter embossed with the royal mark. "In the prison he was like to have died, but that our pardon and grace was humbly begged, and since the said Baudet has always been a man of good life and honest speech with no other misdeeds on his record, we are pleased to grant him this grace and mercy," and to quit, remit, and pardon the supplicant, now and in the future, by "our special grace and royal authority" of all offense, fines, civil and criminal punishment which he may have sustained, and restore him and his good wife to their goods, and to let this be known to all officers of justice of the region and their lieutenants or successors now or in the future.

That all this was required in the King's name for the theft of three platters—and the word *theft* is not used in the document—suggests, beyond mere prolixity, the care taken to exhibit the King as protector of the poor.

In May, two months after the King's visit, Coucy attended a meeting of the Royal Council with Admiral de Vienne, Guy de la Tremoille representing Burgundy, Jean le Mercier, the King's minister, and others to confer on the renewed invasion of England. According to the Monk of St. Denis, the "shameful" departure of the King and nobles from the Scheldt had caused a painful impression upon all Frenchmen, with the result that it was felt necessary to erase the impression by striking a powerful blow at England, and to "commit there all the excesses of an enemy upon an enemy." Clearly the plan for conquest had receded to something more in the nature of a raid.

The expedition was to be split into two parts: one, commanded by the Constable, to leave from Brittany, and the other, commanded by the Admiral, Coucy, and Count Waleran de St. Pol, to leave from Harfleur in Normandy. Their objective was Dover. They were to take 6,000 men-at-arms, 2,000 crossbowmen, 6,000 "other men of war," enough food for three months including hay and oats for the horses, and armor in good condition. Intentions were certainly genuine, for in June a vessel of the Sire de Coucy was loaded at Soissons on the Aisne with foodstuffs, plate, cooking equipment, linens, arms, and tents to be delivered at Rouen. Coucy, Vienne, and the others were at Harfleur at this time. Coastal raids from Calais led by the fiery Sir Harry Percy, called "Hotspur," failed to halt preparations because Percy attacked northward in the wrong direction. The day for departure was fixed, all provisions loaded, every man given his wages for fifteen days, and "the journey so far forward that it was thought it could not be broken."

Contriving as best they could to interfere, the English found their cat's-paw this time in the chronic conspirator Jean de Montfort, Duke of Brittany. To determine where Montfort stood at any given time, as he tried to hold his balance between England and France, would have required the arts of a sorcerer. As parties of opposing policy developed within each country, his problem became more complicated and his deals ever more entangled. It is no wonder that, according to repute, he was a sovereign given easily to tears.

One constant in his sentiments was hatred of his fellow Breton and subject Olivier de Clisson, Constable of France. The feeling, which was mutual, did not preclude Montfort's making a treaty with Clisson in 1381 by which, "in consideration of the perfect love and affinity we have for our dear and well-beloved cousin and vassal, Messire Olivier, Seigneur de Clisson, Constable of France . . . we promise to be a good, true, and beneficient lord to the said seigneur . . . and to guard well his honor and the state of his person." Olivier promised reciprocal loyalties as vassal. Montfort's love and affinity turned to seething rage when Clisson arranged a marriage between his daughter and Jean de Penthièvre, son of Montfort's late rival Charles of Blois, and now heir to the duchy, since Montfort at that time had no sons.

Through various pressures and offers, England was working on Montfort to take action to frustrate the French invasion. At the same time he was involved with Burgundy and Berry. As a cousin of the Duchess of Burgundy, he was linked to her husband in that intense partisanship which automatically accompanied kinship through marriage in the Middle Ages. In May 1387 he had concluded a private treaty with the Duc de Berry. A common interest shared with both brothers was hostility to the Constable.

As Coucy had foreseen, the Constableship bred enemies, among whom the King's uncles came naturally to the fore. Any occupant of the office was a figure whose power could threaten theirs, and Clisson's personality stimulated the antagonism, the more so because of his wealth. He was making 24,000 francs a year from the Constableship, acquiring fiefs, building a palace in Paris, and lending money to everyone: to the King, the Duchesse d'Anjou, Berry, Bureau de la Rivière, and 7,500 florins in 1384 to the Pope. When debtors were late in repaying, as they usually were, he could afford to extend the loans and take a profit in larger securities and interest.

In June 1387 the one-eyed warrior was seized by Montfort in a coup as sensational as, and very similar to, the attack on Bernabò, though lacking its perfection. Montfort convoked a Parliament at Vannes which all Breton nobles were obliged to attend. During the proceedings he treated Clisson with the utmost amiability and afterward entertained him at dinner and invited him with his entourage to visit his new castle of Hermine near Vannes. Affably, Montfort conducted his guests on a tour of the building, visited the cellars to taste the wine, and on arriving at the entrance to the *donjon*, said, "Messire Olivier, I know no man this side of the sea who knows more about fortification than do you; wherefore I pray you mount up the stairs and give me your opinion of the construction of the tower, and if there are faults, I will have them corrected according to your advice."

"Willingly, Monseigneur," replied Clisson, "I will follow you."

"Nay, sir, go your way alone," the Duke answered, saying that while the Constable made his inspection he would converse with the Sire de Laval, Clisson's brother-in-law. Although Clisson had no reason to trust his host, he relied on security as a guest. He mounted the stairs, and as he entered the hall at the first level, a waiting body of men-at-arms seized and imprisoned him, loading him with three heavy chains, while throughout the castle other men closed doors and gates with violent banging.

At the sound, Laval's "blood trembled" and he stared at the Duke, who "became as green as a leaf." "For God's sake, Monseigneur,"

Laval cried, "what are you doing? Do not harm my brother-in-law, the Constable!"

"Mount your horse and go from hence," Montfort answered him. "I know what I have to do." Laval refused to leave without the Constable. At that moment another of Clisson's party, Jean de Beaumanoir, hurried up in anxiety. Montfort, who hated him too, pulled his dagger and, rushing upon him as if possessed, cried, "Beaumanoir, do you wish to be like your master?" Beaumanoir said that would honor him. "Do you wish, do you wish to be like him?" the Duke cried in a fury, and when Beaumanoir said yes, Montfort screamed, "Well then, I will put out your eye!" With shaking hand, he held the dagger before the man's eyes, but could not plunge it in. "Go, go!" he cried hoarsely. "You shall have no better nor worse than him," and ordered his men to drag Beaumanoir off to a prison chamber and load him, too, with chains.

Throughout the night Laval remained at the Duke's side, staying him by pleas and persuasions from ordering Clisson to be put to death. Three times Montfort gave the order to cut off his head or tie him in a sack for drowning, and twice the guards unloaded Clisson's chains preparatory to carrying out the order. Each time Laval, on his knees, managed at the last moment to dissuade the tortured Duke, reminding him how he and Clisson had been brought up together as boys, how Clisson had fought in his cause at Auray, how, if he killed him now, after inviting him to dinner and to his castle as a guest, "no prince shall be so dishonored as you . . . reproached and hated by all the world." If instead he held Clisson to ransom, he could gain great sums and towns and castles, for which Laval promised himself as guarantor.

To this suggestion Montfort at last responded. He wanted no pledge nor guarantor, but 100,000 francs in cash and the handing over to his deputies of two towns and three castles, including Josselin, Clisson's home, before the Constable would be released. Clisson had no choice but to sign the terms and remain incarcerated while Beaumanoir was sent to collect the money. "And if I should tell that such things happened and not tell openly the whole matter," wrote Froissart, "it would be a chronicle but no history."

As alarm at the Constable's disappearance spread rapidly, it was widely believed that he had been put to death, and instantly assumed by all that the voyage to England was "lost and broken." At Harfleur, Coucy, Vienne, and St. Pol had no thought of going ahead with the expedition without Clisson, even after it was known that he was alive. The Duke's terrible deed absorbed all minds, and the insult to the King represented by the seizure of his Constable took precedence over an act of war against England. The expedition with all its ships, provisions, and men-at-arms was abandoned as before, so easily as to raise a question whether the interruption may not have been welcomed. If the coup was designed to frustrate the invasion, it was a total success, but not for Montfort, who lacked the granite will of Gian Galeazzo.

Like the schism in the Church, like the brigandage of knights, like the worldliness of friars, Montfort's act was destructive of basic assumptions. It caused consternation. Knights and squires in anxious discussion said to each other, "Thereby no man should trust in any prince, since the Duke had deceived these noblemen." What would the French King say? Surely there never was such a shameful case in Brittany or anywhere else. If a poor knight had done such a deed, he would be dishonored forever. "In whom should a man trust but in his lord? And that lord should maintain him and do him justice."

On his release, Clisson, with only two pages, galloped straight for Paris in such a fury to obtain satisfaction that he is said to have covered 150 miles a day and to have reached the capital in 48 hours. The King, feeling his honor bound up with his Constable's, was eager for reprisal, but his uncles, who still governed for him, were markedly less so. They seemed indifferent to Clisson's losses, told him he should have known better than to accept Montfort's invitation, especially on the eve of embarking against England, and dampened any suggestion of martial action against the Duke. On this issue the division in the government opened between the uncles on the one hand, and the Constable—supported by Coucy, Vienne, Rivière, Mercier, and the King's younger brother Louis—on the other. Coucy insisted that the King must take cognizance and require Montfort to make restitution. The uncles, already jealous of Clisson's influence over the King and his close relations with Coucy and Rivière, wanted no major effort that would enhance his prestige. In the midst of the struggle, another crisis erupted.

A brash young exhibitionist, the Duke of Guelders, delivered by herald an astonishing and insolent challenge to Charles VI, announcing himself an ally of Richard II and therefore an enemy prepared to defy "you who call yourself King of France." His letter was addressed simply to Charles de Valois. This swaggering gesture by a petty German prince, ruler of a narrow territory between the Meuse and the Rhine, dumbfounded the court, although it had an explanation. The Duke of Guelders had recently accepted payment for declaring himself a vassal of the King of England and his challenge to the French King was a piece of troublemaking doubtless inspired by the English.

Charles was enchanted by the chivalric opportunity. He showered the herald with gifts and looked forward to spreading the glory of his name in personal war and "seeing new and far countries." Faced with two challenges at once, by Brittany on the west and Guelders on the east, the Council debated lengthily what to do. Some thought Guelders' gesture should be treated as pure "fanfaronade" and ignored, but again Coucy made an issue of the dignity not so much of the crown but of the nobles. He argued strenuously in the Council that if the King suffered such insults to pass unrequited, foreign countries would hold the nobles of France very cheap since they were the King's advisers and sworn to uphold his honor. He may have felt, too, that France had to do something after twice abandoning the attack on England. The fact that he clearly felt the issue personally impressed his listeners, and they agreed that he "understood the Germans better than anyone else because of his disputes with the Dukes of Austria."

This time Coucy found himself an ally of Philip the Bold, who strongly favored a campaign against Guelders in his own interests. Between Flanders and Guelders lay the Duchy of Brabant, in whose affairs Philip, with an eye to expansion, was deeply involved. Encouraging the King's enthusiasm, he committed France to war on Guelders, but the Council insisted on settling with Brittany first, for they said if the King and his nobles went off to fight Guelders, Montfort might open the way to the English.

Rivière and Admiral de Vienne, sent to treat with Montfort, met a sullen refusal to yield. The Duke would say only that he repented of nothing he had done to the Constable save for one thing: that he had let him escape alive. Nor would he excuse his seizure of a guest, "for a man ought to take his enemy wheresoever he can." Several months followed of pulling and tugging by all parties while Coucy at each delay kept up pressure in the Council. The issue hung fire as the year ended, taking with it a once supreme troublemaker, the withered viper Charles of Navarre.

After a last attempted poisoning—this time of Burgundy and Berry—Navarre died in horrid circumstances. Sick and prematurely old at 56, he was tormented by chills and shivering and at doctor's orders was wrapped at night in cloths soaked in brandy to warm his body and cause sweat. To keep them in place, the wrappings were sewn on each time like a shroud, and caught fire one night from the valet's candle as he leaned over to cut a thread. To the King's shrieks of pain, the brandy-soaked cloth flamed around his body; he lived for two weeks with doctors unable to relieve his agony before he expired.

In the new year the Council decided to send Coucy himself, as Montfort's former brother-in-law, in another effort to bring him to terms. No one, it was felt, would be more agreeable to the Duke nor "of greater weight"; with him would go Rivière and Vienne, making a mission of "three very intelligent lords." Informed of their coming, Montfort understood from Coucy's presence how heavily the matter weighed. He greeted him affectionately, offered to take him hunting and hawking, escorted him to his chamber, "sporting and talking of many idle matters as lords do when they have not been together for a long time." When it came to the issue, even Coucy's famed persuasiveness and "fine, gentle words" could not at first move him. He stood at a window looking out for a long time in silence, then turned and said, "How may any love be nourished when there is nothing but hate?" and repeated that he repented only of letting Clisson live.

It took two visits and Coucy's most reasoned and eloquent arguments and tactful hints of the weakness of Montfort's position—for in fact he had little support among his own subjects—to accomplish his object. After first persuading Montfort to give up Clisson's castles, he was sent back to get full restitution of the money and, most difficult of all, to push, wheedle, and drag the Duke to judgment in Paris. Desperately wanting to avoid Clisson, Montfort advanced a thousand excuses, but with added pressure from Burgundy, now anxious for a settlement, he was overborne. Against his alleged fear of assassination, Coucy persuaded him to go as far as Blois, where the King's uncles would meet him. With a safe-conduct from the King, reinforced by his own escort of 1,200 men, Montfort ventured up the Loire in a flotilla of six ships and, in June 1388, ultimately arrived at the gates of the Louvre in Paris. Restitution of Clisson's property and a formal pardon by the King were sealed by the usual formula of reconciliation in which the Duke and the Constable swore to be "good and loyal" sovereign and vassal respectively and, glaring at each other, drank from the same cup in token of "love and peace."

From the King, in token of royal appreciation, Coucy received a French Bible, and from history, through Froissart, a more memorable tribute. "And I knew four lords who were the best entertainers of others of all that I knew: they were the Duke of Brabant, the Count of Foix, the Count of Savoy, and especially the Lord of Coucy; for he was the most gracious and persuasive lord in all Christendom . . . the most well-versed in all customs. That was the repute he bore among all lords and ladies in France, England, Germany, and Lombardy and in all places where he was known, for in his time he had traveled much and seen much of the world, and also he was naturally inclined to be polite."

With these talents Coucy had brought to heel the most troublesome vassal since Charles of Navarre.

Chapter 21
The Fiction Cracks

The double collapse of the French invasion of England and, on the English side, the successive fiascos of the Buckingham and Norwich raids revealed the hollowness of knightly pretensions. Adding to the indignity, Austrian knights were slaughtered in 1385 by Swiss commoners at Sempach in a battle that reversed the verdict of Roosebeke.

The Austrians, expecting to duplicate the French massacre of "miscreants" of the non-warrior class, had dismounted to fight on foot as the French had in Flanders. But the Swiss had been trained in flexibility and rapid movement, just the opposite of the impacted line that had caused the Flemings' defeat. When the tide turned against the Austrians, their mounted reserves fled from the field without engaging, as Orléans' battalion had fled at Poitiers. Out of 900 in the Austrian vanguard, almost 700 corpses, including Duke Leopold's, lay on the field at the end.

What knights lacked in the fading 14th century was innovation. Holding to traditional forms, they gave little thought or professional study to tactics. When everyone of noble estate was a fighter by function, professionalism was not greater but less.

Chivalry was not aware of its decadence, or if it was, clung ever more passionately to outward forms and brilliant rites to convince itself that the fiction was still the reality. Outside observers, however, had grown increasingly critical as the fiction grew increasingly implausible. It was now fifty years since the start of the war with England, and fifty years of damaging war could not fail to diminish the prestige of a warrior class that could neither win nor make peace but only pile further injury and misery upon the people.

Deschamps openly mocked the adventure in Scotland in a long ballad with the refrain, "You are not now on the Grand Pont in Paris."

You who are arrayed like bridegrooms,
You who talk so well when you are in France
Of the great deeds you will do,
You go to conquer what you have lost:
What is it? Renown that for so long
Honored your country.
If you seek to recover it in battle,
Display your hearts, not your fancy clothes. . . .
You are not now on the Grand Pont in Paris.

Mézières, too, writing his *Songe du Vieil Pélérin* in 1388, did not restrain his scorn as Honoré Bonet had not restrained his reproaches. Because the knights had won a victory "by the hand of God at Roosebeke against a crowd of fullers and weavers, they take on vainglory and think themselves the peers of their ancestors, King Arthur, Charlemagne, and Godefrey of Bouillon. Of all the rules of war written by Assyrians, Jews, Romans, Greeks, and all Christians, this French chivalry does not keep one tenth, yet thinks there is no chivalry in the world of valor equal to theirs."

The nobles' fashionable clothes and habits of luxury, their private bedrooms where they shut themselves up till noon, their soft beds and perfumed baths and comforts on campaign were cited as evidence that knighthood had gone soft. The ancient Romans, as Jean Gerson, Chancellor of the University, remarked sarcastically some years later, "did not drag after them three or four pack horses and wagons laden with robes, jewels, carpets, boots and hose and double tents. They did not carry with them iron or brass stoves to make little pies."

More than soft beds and foppery, the moral failure of chivalry spread dismay. Instead of troubadours glorifying the ideal knight and ideal love in romantic epics, moralists now deplored in satire and allegory and didactic treatise what the knight had become—predator and aggressor rather than champion of justice. *Chansons de gestes* were no longer composed in the second half of the century, although, since the lusty *fabliaux* disappeared at the same time, the cause cannot be said to have been failure of the ideal so much as some mysterious failing of the literary spirit. The vices and follies and strange disorders of the time demanded moralizing, yet, ironically, it is Froissart's celebration of chivalry in its own image that endures.

In Italy, the complaint had a different source: knighthood was detached from nobility. "A few years ago," lamented Franco Sacchetti at the end of the century, "bakers, wool-carders, usurers, money-changers, and blackguards became knights. Why does an official need knighthood when he goes to preside over some provincial town? . . .

How art thou sunken, unhappy dignity! Of all the long list of knightly duties, what single one do these knights of ours discharge? I wish to speak of these things that the reader might see that knighthood is dead."

If Sacchetti's tone was morose, it was widely shared. With the courts of France and England ruled by minors and prey to factions, with the new Emperor Wenceslas proving a drunkard and a brute, with the Church split between two popes, each as remote from holiness as it was possible to be, no brilliance of the ruling class could cover its tarnish. Coucy was right in his perception of diminishing prestige, even if his suggested remedy was only to make matters worse.

The Guelders campaign of September–October 1388 proved that snafu was a military condition long before the word was coined. The expedition was mobilized on a scale out of all proportion to its petty issue or possible gain. Because of his relationships in Bar and Lorraine, which lay on the way, and his knowledge of the terrrain, Coucy was designated to recruit the lords of the area and plan the campaign. The preferable route lay through Brabant, but the towns and nobles of that duchy warned that they would never allow passage of a French army because it would cause more damage to their lands "than if the enemy were in the country."

A decision was perforce taken to march straight through the dark, forbidding forest of the Ardennes, where, Froissart remarks with awed inaccuracy, "no traveler had ever before passed." This necessitated sending surveyors to find a way through, followed by a force of 2,500 men to cut a road, an engineering task hardly less challenging than the portable town. The cost was paid for by a triple tax on salt and sales, for a purpose difficult to represent as defense of the realm. Perhaps for that reason, Coucy had been required to recruit in his own name as if for another expedition against the Hapsburgs, rather than in the name of the King.

Led by Coucy, a vanguard of 1,000 lances began the march, followed by the King and main body with "12,000" baggage carts, not counting pack animals. While en route, Coucy was suddenly detached for a mission to Avignon of unrecorded purpose but probably concerned with the plan that continued to obsess the French of conquering Rome for Clement. He returned—"to the great joy of the whole army"—within about a month, which, considering a journey of almost 500 miles each way, was energetic traveling.

Little combat and no glory were found at Guelders. The campaign bogged down in negotiations. Tents were wet after a summer of heavy rains, provisions rotted in the humidity, food was scarce despite a rich country. The return after honor had been satisfied by a negotiated apology from the Duke of Guelders, was wretched under more heavy rains. Roads were mud, horses stumbled over slippery logs and rocks, men were drowned in fording flooded rivers, and wagons of booty floated away. Knights, squires, and grand seigneurs came home without pride or profit, many of them sick or exhausted and blaming the Duke of Burgundy whose ambitions in Brabant they correctly held responsible. Coucy seems to have incurred no blame as he had incurred none in the insurrection of Paris. Since the start of the reign, the government of the uncles had dragged the country into ruinous expense for a series of grandiose projects ending in futility. At Guelders their credit ran out.

Awareness of bad government speaks through the omens and incidents inserted in the record by a censorious chronicler like the Monk of St. Denis. While the army for Guelders was being assembled, he reports, a hermit journeyed all the way from Provence to tell the King and his uncles that he had been instructed by an angel to warn them to treat their subjects more gently and lessen the burden of taxes and subsidies. The nobles at court scorned the hermit for his poverty and were deaf to his counsel, and though the young King treated him kindly and was disposed to listen, the uncles sent him away and levied the triple tax.

Deschamps' satire grew more caustic after the Guelders campaign, in which he had personally participated and fallen ill like others of an "intestinal flux." The military do not find their best friend in a war correspondent suffering from dysentery. Through many ballads, Deschamps' theme is unfavorable comparison with knights of the past. They had gained hardiness through long apprenticeship and training, ridden long journeys, practiced wrestling and throwing the stone, scaling forts, and combat with shield and sword. Now the younger men scorn training and call those who wish to instruct them cowards. They spend their youth eating and drinking, spending and borrowing, "polishing themselves white as ivory . . . each one a paladin." They sleep late between white sheets, call for wine on waking, eat partridges and fat capons, comb their hair to perfection, know nothing about the management of estates, and care for nothing but making money. They are arrogant, irreligious, weakened by gluttony and debauchery, and unfit for the profession of arms, "the heaviest in the world."

Denouncing them on the one hand for softness and indolence, Deschamps castigates them on the other for recklessness, improvidence, and bad judgment. In his *Lay de Vaillance*, they keep no order, no night watch or scouts or advance guard, give no protection to foragers, allow carts and provisions to be captured. "When bread lacked for a day or it rained in the morning, they cried, 'The army will starve!' " and "when they let provisions spoil on the ground, they wanted to turn back." They start out in winter, attack recklessly and in the wrong season, never ask the advice of the older men until after danger threatens, complain loudly when in trouble, and open themselves to defeat. "Because of mad recklessness, such armies are to be despised."

Deschamps is a scold but not an advocate of fundamental change or infusion of new blood into the nobility. He is bourgeois in sympathy, deplores injustice to the peasant, and writes ballads in praise of rural Robin and Margot for their love of France, but he denounces peasants who attempt to become squires and remove themselves from labor on the land. "Such rogues should be brought to justice and made to keep their class."

All of society is found corrupt in Mézières' *Dream of the Old Pilgrim*. Like Langland's *Vision of Piers Plowman*, it is an allegorical guidebook to the troubles of the age and, in addition, a plea for "reformation of all the world, all Christianity and especially the Kingdom of France." The pilgrim Ardent Desire and his sister Good Hope journey through the world to test the fitness of mankind for the return of the Queen of Truth and her attendants Peace, Mercy, and Justice, long absent from the earth. Mézières' message was urgent, his sense of wrongdoing profound, his prognosis somber.

As if in response, Charles VI at age twenty dismissed his uncles and assumed full sovereignty himself immediately upon returning from Guelders in 1388. The Cardinal of Laon, ranking prelate, proposed the motion at a meeting of the Council. A few days later he fell ill and died, "delivered from the fury and hate of the uncles of the King," and widely believed to have been poisoned by them.

Clisson later boasted to an English envoy that it was he who had made Charles VI "king and lord of his realm and put the government out of the hands of his uncles." Apart from Clisson's personal enmity, Coucy and others in the Council at the time were anxious to lift from the crown and themselves the further burden of the Dukes' unpopularity. The person most closely concerned, however, was the King's younger, cleverer, more dynamic brother and, for the time being, heir apparent, Louis, Duc de Touraine, soon to be known by his more familiar title, Duc d'Orléans.

Beginning in 1389, Louis of Orléans replaced the Duke of Burgundy in the Royal Council and for the rest of his brief, eventful life, already nearly half over, was to play a major role in French affairs, with a particular link to Coucy. A handsome pleasure-seeker and "devoted servant of Venus" who enjoyed the company of "dancers, flatterers, and people of loose life," he was also devoutly religious and used to retreat for two or three days at a time to the Celestine monastery, whose quarters in Paris (on the present Quai des Célestins) had been established by his father in 1363. A penitential order favored too by Philippe de Mézières, who had been the royal princes' tutor, the Celestins observed extreme rules of abstinence designed to promote concentration on eternity and disappearance of the body. Louis was much influenced by Mézières, whom he named his executor. He had evidently learned more from him than had his brother, for he was said to be the only member of the royal family who could understand diplomatic Latin. Something of a scholar for one of his station, he was also a compulsive gambler at chess and tennis as well as dice and cards. He played with his butler, his cup-bearer, and his carver, and at tennis with fellow nobles lost sums up to 2,000 gold francs.

Louis was as rapacious and ambitious for power as the uncles whom he ousted to make way for his ambition. The feud he thereby started was to end nineteen years later in his murder by his cousin Jean, son and successor of the Duke of Burgundy, tear France and Burgundy apart, and re-open the way to the English. Toward the end of his life he adopted a device of strange significance, the *camal*, a clerical hood or knight's mantle, which was said at the time to represent *Ca-mal* or *Combien de mal*, meaning how much evil is done in these days. Born to the century's last generation, Louis, for all his indulgences in pleasure, saw his world somberly. A verse of the time describes him as

> Sorrowing, even sad, yet beautiful;
> He seemed too melancholy for one
> Whose heart was hard as steel.

Coucy, though clearly associated with the ousting of the Dukes, nevertheless entertained Philip the Bold and his son the Count of Nevers immediately afterward. The Duke's accounts show that he and his son dined and slept at the castle on December 8 "at the expense of Monseigneur de Coucy," and that during the visit he presented a diamond ring to the Dame de Coucy and a brooch of sapphires and pearls to her baby daughter. Coucy was always worth cultivating.

The reorganized Council made a serious effort to end the Dukes' personal autocracy and restore the administrative system of Charles V. The Marmosets—Rivière, Mercier, and others—regained authority, bureaucracy was purged of the uncles' men, five commissioners of reform were appointed to seek out the worst abuses, remove corrupt officials, and replace them by "good men." As a step toward reconciliation with the bourgeois of Paris, the office of Provost of Paris and some, though not all, former municipal offices and privileges were restored. Measures were taken, or at least formulated, to improve sewage collection and restrict professional beggars, whose crutches and eye-patches and gruesome sores and stumps were stripped off each night in the district known by virtue of the transformations that took place there, as the Cour des Miracles.

The central problem of financing government was recognized in a series of ordinances dealing with financial and judicial reforms. Cancellation of the University's tax-exemption was one measure attempted by Rivière and Mercier with no good result, for it earned them the powerful enmity of the University to add to that of the Dukes.

At the same time in England, a more lethal drama of King against uncles and other opponents was taking place. The central figure was Philippa de Coucy's husband, Robert de Vere, ninth Earl of Oxford, King Richard's closest adviser and friend. Brought to court as a boy by virtue of his marriage to Philippa, Oxford gained a dominant influence over Richard, who was five years his junior and fatherless. He "managed the King as he pleased," and "if he had said black was white, Richard would not have contradicted him. . . . By him everything was done and without him nothing done."

The King at 21, slender, yellow-haired, pale-faced, with a skin that flushed easily, was "abrupt and stammering in his speech," over-splendid in dress, averse to war, ill-tempered with his domestics, arrogant and capricious. His Plantagenet pride, combined with Oxford's influence, shaped an erratic and willful sovereign who levied extortionate taxes to pay for his luxuries. Before his downfall, which finished off the Plantagenets, he invented the handkerchief, recorded in his household rolls as "little pieces [of cloth] made for giving to the lord King for carrying in his hand to wipe and clean his nose."

Government by favorite leans toward the arbitrary exercise of power, which in any case was Richard's natural tendency. He had made Oxford a Knight of the Garter and, at 21, a member of the Privy Council, and showered on him a stream of endowments—lands, castles, wardships, lordships, revenues—and a hereditary sheriffdom belonging to Buckingham's wife's family. This was unwise, but if autocrats always acted wisely they would not furnish history with moral lessons. The ruthless Buckingham, now Duke of Gloucester, did not need extra provocation to hate his nephew, whom he despised for his reluctance to pursue the war. Attracting the enemies of Oxford, Gloucester became the focus of the oppositionist party bent on curbing the power of the King's favorite.

The struggle reached a peak when Richard, on the occasion of a rebellion in Ireland, created for Oxford the unprecedented title of Marquis of Dublin and subsequently Duke of Ireland with precedence over all the earls. He was given regal powers to crush the rebellion, but instead of going to Ireland, which would at least have given the nobles the satisfaction of removing him from the scene, Oxford was smitten by love for a Bohemian lady-in-waiting of Richard's Queen. Such was his passion that he determined to divorce Philippa in order to marry the Bohemian lady, thus infuriating Philippa's royal uncles, the Dukes of Lancaster, Gloucester, and York. Despite the insult to the royal family, Richard was too hypnotized by Oxford to do other than "improperly and sinfully consent" to, and even assist in, his own cousin's repudiation. Oxford submitted to Rome an appeal for divorce based on "false testimony," Richard entreated Pope Urban for favorable consideration, and the Pope felt no compunction in complying since Philippa was of Clementist lineage.

Oxford's treatment of his wife was said by Froissart to be "the principal thing that took away his honor." Even his mother joined in the general condemnation and showed it by taking Philippa to live with her. Probably it was the fact of Philippa's royal blood and Oxford's personal unpopularity rather than moral indignation that excited all the disapproval. Although marriage was a sacrament, divorce was frequent and, given the right strings to pull, easily obtained. In *Piers Plowman* all lawyers are said to "make and unmake matrimony for money," and preachers complained that a man might get rid of his wife by giving the judge a fur cloak. In theory, divorce did not exist, yet marriage litigation filled the courts of the Middle Ages. Regardless of theory, divorce was a fact of life, a permanent element in the great disharmony between medieval theory and practice.

A formal appeal against Oxford and four other councillors of the King's party was presented in November 1387 by a group of lords known by virtue of their action as the Lords Appellant. When they appointed a Commission of Government headed by Gloucester with powers as Regent, Richard and Oxford gathered an army to assert the King's sovereignty by force of arms. The conflict came to a head in the so-called Battle of Radcot Bridge: facing superior forces, Oxford escaped by leaping into the river on horseback, after discarding part of his armor, and galloping away on the far side into the dusk. He took ship for Flanders, where he had taken the precaution to deposit large sums with Lombard bankers at Bruges.

A month later, in February 1388, the lords in a session known as the Merciless Parliament brought charges of treason against Oxford and the Chancellor, Michael de la Pole, Earl of Suffolk, who had also escaped. They were charged with conspiring to control the King, exclude his proper councillors, murder the Duke of Gloucester, impoverish the crown by grants to themselves and their relatives, override Parliament, and return Calais to the French King in exchange for aid against their domestic opponents. The Parliament sentenced Oxford and Suffolk in absentia to be hanged as traitors. Three others who had not escaped—the Chief Justice, the Mayor of London, and Richard's former tutor, Sir Simon Burley—were executed. Richard remained, humiliated and robbed of the friend he was never to see again. To abase a King and leave him on the throne has its dangers. Richard was to have his revenge.

Against Coucy's fierce opposition, Oxford was invited to France in 1388 on the grounds that it would be advantageous to obtain information from him about the quarrels in England. It may be, too, that Oxford had indeed made overtures about Calais. Although Coucy "hated him with all his heart," he was forced to acquiesce. Oxford came, was received at court and well entertained, but Coucy did not rest until, with the support of Clisson, Rivière, and Mercier, he prevailed upon the King to expel the dishonorer of his daughter from France. A residence was found for Oxford in Brabant, where, in 1392, he was killed in a boar hunt at the age of thirty. King Richard had his body brought back for reburial in England, and in an ornate if lonely ceremony, gazed mournfully upon the embalmed face and placed a ring on the dead finger of the great troublemaker. Meanwhile, the divorce having been annulled, Philippa remained the legal Countess of Oxford.

A royal grant made to Coucy at this time testified to the scars left by plague and war over the last decades. In November 1388 he was appointed Grand Bouteiller (Grand Butler) of France, the equivalent of chief seneschal or domestic steward to the crown. At the same time he was granted the privilege of holding two annual fairs of three days each, with the sale of all merchandise exempted from taxes. The language of the grant states that the town of Coucy had three times suffered "the fires of mischief, which occurred in the said town because of lack of laborers who died during the great mortality. And also owing to preceding wars, the inhabitants and community of the said town, castle and lands of Coucy were so impoverished, diminished and reduced in people, houses, manors, rents, revenues and all other goods and chattels, that the said town was in danger of becoming deserted and uninhabitable, and the vines, fields and other husbandries going to waste."

The intent of the grant, which followed a survey of the barony at the time of the King's visit to Coucy the year before, was clearly designed, in the royal interest as much as in Coucy's, to restore the health of a crucial domain. The barony is described by the grant as the "key and frontier" of the kingdom with borders reaching to Flanders and the Empire, and the castle as "one of the most notable and beautiful of the realm." By the "deserting and uninhabiting of the said town and castle, if that should happen, many great perils, damages and irreparable inconveniences could issue." The fact that the grant followed immediately upon the transfer of power to the group dominated by the Marmosets, Clisson, and Coucy himself, was certainly no coincidence.

From this time on, Coucy served as first Lay President of the Chambre des Comptes, a post associated with the office of Bouteiller, which originally had charge of the royal revenues and accounts. While he does not seem to have collected wages for the office, he continued to receive an annual pension from the crown. His domain, greatly enlarged by his many acquisitions, and now comprising 150 towns and villages, was apparently extensive enough to surmount the declining fortunes of lesser landowners.

Picardy, his native region, so often in the path of invasion, was "beaten and chastised," wrote Mézières, himself a Picard, "and today no longer flourishes." From places reduced to misery, the last peasants fled to other regions so that "at present," according to a complaint of 1388, "laborers cannot be found to work or cultivate the land." The marks of a century of woe—lowered population, dwindling commerce, deserted villages, ruined abbeys—were everywhere in France, and cause enough for the climate of pessimism. Certain communes in Normandy were reduced to two or three hearths; in the diocese of Bayeux several towns had been abandoned since 1370, likewise several parishes of Brittany. The commerce of Châlons on the Marne was reduced from 30,000 pieces of cloth a year to 800. In the region of Paris, according to an ordinance of 1388, "many notable and ancient highways, bridges, lanes, and roads" had been left to decay—gutted by streams, overgrown by hedges, brambles, and trees, and some, having become impassable, abandoned altogether. The same examples could be multiplied for the south.

The schism had caused physical as well as spiritual damage, as when a Benedictine abbey, already twice burned by the companies, was cut off from the revenue of its estates in Flanders and spent so much money on lawyers in various disputes that the Pope was obliged to reduce its tax from 200 livres to 40 for a period of 25 years. Other abbeys, robbed by the companies or depopulated by the plague, fell into indiscipline and disorder, and in some cases into disuse, their lands reverting to waste. Decreased revenue and rising costs impoverished many landowners, causing them to exact new fees and invent new kinds of taxes to impose on their tenants. When this hastened flight from the land, the nobles tried to prevent it by confiscating goods and by other penalties that increased the peasants' hostility.

Gathered together, the facts of decay convey too solid an impression. In real life every age is a checkerboard of light and dark. At the turn of the century the renowned Spanish knight Don Pero Niño, on a visit to France, left a picture of noble life as enchanted and bucolic in reality as it was often represented to be in tapestries and Books of Hours. The castle of Serifontaine, which he visited, was situated on the banks of a river in Normandy and furnished as richly "as if it had been in the city of Paris." Around it were orchards and gracious gardens, and a walled fishpond from which each day, by opening the conduits, enough fish could be taken to serve 300 people. The elderly and ailing but complaisant host, Reynaud de Trie, Vienne's successor as Admiral of France, possessed forty or fifty hounds, twenty horses of all kinds for his personal use, forests full of game great and small, falcons for hunting by the river, and for a wife, "the most beautiful lady then in France." She appears to have been remarkably privileged.

This lady "had her own noble dwelling apart from that of the Admiral," though connected by a drawbridge, and was attended by ten noble and richly dressed damsels who had no duties but to entertain themselves and their lady, for she had many serving maids as well. In the morning she and her damsels went to a grove, each with her Book of Hours and rosary, and said their prayers seated apart from each other and not conversing until they had finished. Returning to the castle, picking violets and other flowers as they went, they heard low mass in the chapel, after which they ate roasted larks and chicken from a silver plate accompanied by wine. Then, on finely saddled horses, together with knights and squires they rode in the country, where they made chaplets of flowers and sang "lays, virelays, roundelays, complaints, ballads and songs of all kinds which the French compose," harmonizing in voices "diverse and well-attuned."

At the elaborate main meal of the day in the castle hall, each gentleman sat beside a lady, and "any man who with due measure and courtesy could speak of arms and love was sure . . . that he would be heard and answered as his desire would have it." Minstrels played during the meal and for dancing by the knights and ladies afterward, which lasted for an hour and ended with a kiss. Spices and wine were served followed by a siesta, after which the company rose for heron-hunting with falcons by the river. There "you would have seen great sport, dogs swimming, drums beating, lures waving, and ladies and gentlemen enjoying delight beyond description." Dismounting in a meadow, they were served cold partridges and fruits and, while they ate and drank, made chaplets of greenery and returned to the castle singing.

At nightfall they had supper, played bowls or danced by torchlight "far into the night," or sometimes the Dame, perhaps bored by the cycle of pleasure, "went to seek distraction afoot in the country." After more fruits and wine, the company went to bed. In the decline of Rome, too, there must have been pockets of wealth and delight and serene days where trouble never penetrated.

Paris was another matter. Deschamps describes a raucous evening's entertainment, at an unspecified date, which began with dinner at Berry's residence, the Hôtel de Nesle, and moved on to a dice game in a tavern. The guests were Coucy and the three Dukes—Berry, Burgundy, and Bourbon—as well as "several good Lombards," and knights and squires, whose drinking and gaming in low-class surroundings inspired the poet to a lengthy if torpid tract against gambling.

Unhappily, Coucy figures also in a more spirited lament on the subject of baldness, in which Deschamps pleads for the return of head-coverings at court to spare the feelings of the bald, among whom he names himself and twelve great lords, including the Sire de Coucy. That baldness should be the only specific detail of his physical appearance to reach posterity is a sad trick of history, even if he was in good company. The Count de St. Pol, the Sire de Hangest, Guillaume de Bordes, bearer of the Oriflamme at Bourbourg, and other great knights and distinguished servitors of the late King were among the "skin-heads." Less fortunate were the *cheveux reboursés*—that is, those with little hair who carried combs and mirrors to keep their few strands combed over the bald spot. What is puzzling is that uncovered heads, a sign of shame, could have at any time become a fad—unless they were adopted as a kind of anti-chic by the dandies of the time in their craving, complained of by the preacher John Bromyard, "to devise some new piece of foppery to make men gaze at them in wonderment anew."

Deschamps was concerned with men as they are, not as they should be. Pimps, sorcerers, monks, scolds, lawyers, tax-collectors, prostitutes, prelates, rascals, female procurers, and a variety of repugnant hags populate his verses. As he grew older, his vision grew sourer, perhaps owing to the number of his ailments, including toothache, "the cruellest of sufferings." For a regimen of good health he advised drinking light red wine mixed with running water, abstaining from spiced drinks, cabbage, strong meats, fruits, chestnuts, butter and cream, and sauces of onion and garlic, dressing warmly in winter and lightly in summer, taking exercise, and never sleeping on the stomach.

Though he never lost his indignation at social injustice, Deschamps looked with a satiric eye on the human species, which though endowed with reason, prefers folly. The sins of the age he most condemned were impiety causing disobedience to God, pride that generates all other vices, sodomy the "unnatural" sin, sorcery, and love of money. In the new reign, though he held a post as *maître d'hôtel* to Louis d'Orléans, he felt himself displaced at court by frivolous and over-dressed young men of doubtful courage, equivocal habits, and uncertain faith. His complaint of court life was the same as is made of government at the top in any age: it was composed of hypocrisy, flattery, lying, paying and betraying; it was where calumny and cupidity reigned, common sense lacked, truth dared not appear, and where to survive one had to be deaf, blind, and dumb.

After fifty years, the purpose of the war had faded and men could hardly remember its cause. Although the Duke of Gloucester and the "boars" of England were as bellicose as ever, they could not raise the funds for another expedition. In France, the aborted invasion of England had drained desire for aggression. Anti-war sentiment was growing, even if, in the case of Mézières, it was in the interest of turning hostility against the infidel. "All Christendom has been disturbed for fifty years by your ambition to gain a little ground. The rights and wrongs of the matter have long been obscured and all Christians must now be held responsible for the shedding of so much Christian blood." To bring Christians together for a crusade was not seen by a man like Mézières as war but as the use of the sword for the glory of God.

After six months' parley, a three years' truce, but still no definitive settlement, was concluded in June 1389, with intricate provisions for negotiating each transfer of territory or sovereignty in case of dispute. With communication restored, Coucy was now able to send a messenger to Philippa in England "from his great desire to know certainly of her welfare." He was appointed Captain of Guienne to supervise the truce in the south and to guard and defend the country from Dordogne to the sea, including Auvergne and Limousin.

The news of peace was received by the common people, in at least one case, with skepticism and a curious revival of the prophecy once attributed to Coucy about the King and his spade. The citizens of Bois-Gribaut in the Limousin fell to discussing the news of the truce brought by a bourgeois of their village on his return from Paris. Some were unimpressed, saying they would soon be assembling against England again. A poor witless shepherd named Marcial le Vérit, who was said to have been held in prison by the English in great misery, expressed a more subversive opinion for which he was later arrested: "Don't you believe it. You will never see peace. As for me, I don't believe it, because the King has destroyed and pillaged Flanders as he did Paris. And what's more, the Seigneur de Coucy brought him a spade and told him that when he had destroyed his country, he would have to use that." The saying had evidently struck a responsive chord.

Coucy appeared as a symbol of another kind in a challenge addressed to him before the truce was signed by Thomas Mowbray, Earl of Nottingham and future Duke of Norfolk, one of the Lords Appellant whom Richard was courting and had appointed Earl Marshal of England for life. To this young man of 23, Coucy represented the epitome of chivalry; to encounter him in combat was to learn prowess and gain honor. When piety and virtue, the supposed springs of knightly conduct, were conspicuous by their absence, the cloak of honor and valor was all the more anxiously sought. Human beings of any age need to approve of themselves; the bad times in history come when they cannot.

As "a man of approved honor, valor, chivalry and great renown, as is known in many honorable places," Coucy was challenged by Nottingham to name a day and place for a joust of three points of the lance, three of the sword, three of the dagger, and three blows of the ax on foot. He was to send, sealed with his seal, "a good and loyal safe-conduct" from his King, and if Calais were chosen as the site, Nottingham would in turn supply a safe-conduct from his King. He suggested that the combat take place in front of "as many persons as you and I shall be prepared to supply with safe-conduct and lodging." No record exists of a reply or of any such joust taking place. Coucy was either uninterested or unwilling to engage while the truce was still pending.

Foiled of glory, Nottingham took up the famous challenge of St. Ingelbert in the following year when the dashing Boucicaut and two companions, angered by English boasting after the truce, offered to hold the lists against all comers in any form of combat for thirty days. Prudent counsel advised against re-opening a quarrel so soon after the truce for the whims of "wild young knights," and friends advised the three that it would be beyond their powers. Boucicaut was not one to be moved by prudence. At sixteen he had fought his first battle at Roosebeke where a huge Fleming, mocking his youth and small size, told him to go back to his mother's arms. Drawing his dagger, Boucicaut had plunged it into the man's side with the words, "Do the children of your country play games like these?" He and his companions maintained the lists of St. Ingelbert with great courage and he went on to become Marshal of France and share in Coucy's last adventure.

Nottingham's craving for combat was to have a darker conclusion. Ten years later it led him as Duke of Norfolk to the historic duel with Bolingbroke which was to precipitate the downfall of Richard II. Banished together with his opponent at the time of the duel, Nottingham was to die in exile within a year.

Moving from place to place, visiting, investigating, asking questions, Jean Froissart came to Paris in the month when the truce was signed to visit "the *gentil* Sire de Coucy . . . one of my seigneurs and patrons." In the twenty years since the death of his first patron, Queen Philippa of England, Froissart had enjoyed some support from the Emperor Wenceslas and had obtained a clerical living through the patronage of Guy de Châtillon, Count of Blois, with no duties but to continue his history. When Guy de Blois went bankrupt, Coucy had proposed Froissart for a canonry of Lille which had so far not materialized. Meantime,

> The good seigneur de Couci
> Often stuffed my fist
> With [a bag of] red-sealed florins.*

While the recipient of patronage is likely in turn to be generous with compliments, Froissart's for Coucy seem more than merely conventional; they add up to a distinct individual. "*Gentil*" was a word routinely applied to any important and well-considered noble, meaning no more than that he or she was nobly born; Coucy, in addition, is "subtle," "prudent," and especially "*imaginatif*" or "*fort-imaginatif*," meaning intelligent, thoughtful, or far-seeing, and the all-inclusive

---

* The original—"*M'a souvent le poing fouci/De beaux florins a rouge escaille*" —is obscure, but may refer to the fact that coins of good value, not worn or clipped, were often put in a bag tied at the top and sealed with colored wax, in this case a "red seal."

"*sage*" or "*très-sage*," which could mean wise, sensible, wary, rational, discreet, judicious, cool, sober, staid, well-behaved, steady, virtuous, or presumably any or all of these. He is also described as "*cointe*," meaning elegant in manner and dress, gracious, courteous, valiant—a compendium of the attributes of chivalry.

Book One of Froissart's *Chronicles*, in which chivalry immediately recognized a celebrator, had appeared in 1370, at once creating a wide demand. The oldest extant manuscript copy of Book One, now in the Royal Library of Belgium, bears the Coucy coat-of-arms.

Multiple copying of manuscripts was no longer the monopoly of lonely monks in their cells but the occupation of professional scribes who had their own guilds. Licensed in Paris by the University, supposedly to ensure accurate texts, the scribes were the agony of living authors, who complained bitterly of the copyists' delays and errors. The "trouble and discouragement" a writer suffers, wailed Petrarch, was indescribable. Such was the "ignorance, laziness, and arrogance of these fellows" that when a writer has given them his work, he never knows what changes he will find in it when he gets it back.

The rise of a bourgeois audience in the 14th century and the increased manufacture of paper created a reading public wider than the nobles who had known literature from recitation or reading aloud in their castle halls. The mercantile class, familiar by reason of its occupation with reading and writing, was ready to read books of all sorts: verse, history, romance, travel, bawdy tales, allegories, and religious works. Possession of books had become the mark of a cultivated man. Since the magnates and newly rich imitated the manners, ideals, and dress of the nobility, the chronicles of chivalry had a great vogue.

What books Enguerrand VII may have owned in addition to Froissart's *Chronicles* are not known except for those listed in the royal archives as gifts to him from the King. In addition to the French Bible from Genesis to Psalms, which he was given for his services in subduing the Duke of Brittany, he received in 1390 the romance of *King Peppin and His Wife Bertha Bigfoot* and the rhymed *Gestes de Charlemagne*, "well-inscribed on three columns to the page in a very large volume," which had belonged to the Queen and which "the King took from her and gave to Monsieur de Coucy."

Froissart arrived in Paris from the south, where he had visited another patron, the Count of Foix, and had been received by the Pope in Avignon. He had also attended the wedding of the Duc de Berry to a twelve-year-old bride, the occasion of much ribald comment. Eager for first-hand reports of these affairs, Coucy invited Froissart to accompany him on a journey to his fief at Mortagne. Riding together, they exchanged news, Coucy telling the chronicler what he knew of the truce parleys, and Froissart full of tales about his effulgent host at Foix. It appeared that the Count of Foix, who had the wardship of Berry's bride, had taken cool advantage of the Duke's ardor; he had strung out the marriage negotiations until Berry, in his impatience, agreed to pay 30,000 francs to cover the maiden's expenses while she had been Foix's ward.

In the course of persistent questioning, Froissart had drawn from the Count of Foix a contemporary view of the 14th century, seen from a position of privilege. The history of his own lifetime, Gaston Phoebus said, would be more sought after than any other because "in these fifty years there have been more feats of arms and more marvels in the world than in 300 years before." To him the ferment of the times was exciting; he had no misgivings. In the midst of events there is no perspective.

No misgivings about knighthood played a part in a frenzied celebration of that dignity on the occasion of the knighting of twelve-year-old Louis II of Anjou and his younger brother aged ten. In the ceremony's four days of all-too secular festivities staged in the royal Abbey of St. Denis, 14th century France relived the decadence of Rome, and indeed the knighting of little boys was not so far removed from the emperor who made a Consul of his horse. The surpassing pomp of the occasion and the selection of St. Denis as the site were intended to promote enthusiasm for the Angevin recovery of the Kingdom of Naples. Radical alterations were made in the abbey's precincts to accommodate tournaments, dances, and banquets. Religious services gave way to the hammering of carpenters and the coming and going of laborers and their materials. At the ceremony, after ritual baths and prayers, the two princelings, robed in floor-length furred mantles of double red silk, were escorted to the altar by squires holding naked swords by their points with golden spurs hanging from the hilts. In his enthusiasm for chivalric forms, Charles VI resurrected antique rituals which had fallen into disuse in his father's time and were already so faded that spectators "thought it all strange and extraordinary" and inquired what the rites signified.

The same nostalgia was enacted in the next day's tournament, when knights in polished armor were conducted to the lists by noble ladies "to imitate the gallantry of ancient worthies." Each of the ladies in turn drew from her bosom a ribbon of colored silk to bestow graciously upon her knight. After each day's jousts and tourneys, the celebrants "turned night into day" with dances, masquerades, feasting, drunkenness, and, according to the indignant Monk of St. Denis, "libertinage and adultery." Knighthood, represented by the two half-forgotten little principals, was not noticeably enhanced.

Government expenditure continued to mount through the year 1389 to an excess as extravagant as the uncles', although its purpose was civil rather than military. Its climax was the ceremonial entry into Paris of Isabeau of Bavaria, for her coronation as Queen, an event of spectacular splendor and unparalleled marvels of public entertainment. Though its cost contradicted the good intentions of the new government, the performance was in itself a form of government in the same sense as a Roman circus. What is government but an arrangement by which the many accept the authority of the few? Circuses and ceremonies are meant to encourage the acceptance; they either succeed or, by costing too much, accomplish the opposite.

Some of the Queen's thunder was stolen by Valentina Visconti, the new wife of Louis d'Orléans, who arrived just in time for the occasion. Since her marriage by proxy to Louis in 1387, the two intervening years had been required by her father, Gian Galeazzo, to amass her unprecedented dowry of half a million gold francs, plus Asti and other territories of Piedmont. Valentina was his only remaining child, to whom he was so attached that he left Pavia rather than be present at her departure, "and this was because he could not take leave of her without bursting into tears." As the daughter of his dead wife, Isabelle of France—and thus Louis of Orléans' first cousin—Valentina had grown up in a household which her father had made "a harbor for the famous, for men skilled in all learning and art whom he held in high honor." She spoke Latin, French, and German fluently, and brought her own books and harp with her to France. Thirteen hundred knights escorted her across the Alps, her trousseau may be extrapolated from a robe embroidered with 2,500 pearls and sprinkled with diamonds, her future household with Louis was carpeted in Aragon leather and hung with vermilion velvet embroidered with roses and crossbows. The household accounts show silk sheets costing 400 francs as New Year's gifts, but all the luxuries could not keep melancholy from pervading the marriage.

On the great day of the Queen's entry, the procession advanced along the Rue St. Denis, the main boulevard leading to the Châtelet and to the Grand Pont over the Seine. It was a ladies' day, with the duchesses and great ladies riding in richly ornamented litters escorted on either side by noble lords. Coucy escorted his daughter Marie and her mother-in-law, the Duchess of Bar, while his wife rode in another litter. The robes and jewels of the ladies were masterpieces of the embroiderers' and goldsmiths' arts, for the King wanted every previous ceremonial to be outdone. He had ordered the archives of St. Denis consulted for details of the coronations of ancient queens. The Duke of Burgundy, always a gorgeous dresser, needed no help; he wore a doublet of velvet embroidered with forty sheep and forty swans, each with a pearl bell around its neck.

Twelve hundred bourgeois led by the Provost lined the avenue, in gowns of green on one side of the street and gowns of crimson on the other. Such crowds of people had gathered to watch "as seemed that all the world had been there." Houses and windows the length of the Rue St. Denis were hung with silks and tapestries, and the street itself covered with fine fabrics "in such plenty as if they cost nothing."

Entering Paris through the Porte St. Denis, the procession passed under a heavenly sky of cloth stretched over the gate, filled with stars, beneath which children dressed as angels sang sweetly. Next on the way was a fountain spouting red and white wines, served by melodiously singing maidens with golden cups; then a stage erected in front of the Church of Ste. Trinité, on which was performed the *Pas Saladin*, a drama of the Third Crusade; then another firmament full of stars "with the figure of God seated in majesty"; then "a gate of Paradise" from which descended two angels with a crown of gold and jewels which they placed on the head of the Queen with appropriate song; then a curtained enclosure in front of St. Jacques within which men played organ music. At the Châtelet a marvelous mock castle and field of trees had been erected as the scene of a play dramatizing the "Bed of Justice." Its theme was the favorite popular belief that the King was invested with royalty in order to maintain justice in favor of the small against the great. Amid a flurry of birds and beasts, twelve maidens with naked swords defended the White Hart from the Lion and the Eagle.

So many wonders were to be seen and admired that it was evening before the procession crossed the bridge leading to Notre Dame and the climactic display. High on a tightrope slanting down from the tower of Notre Dame to the roof of the tallest house on the Pont St. Michel, an acrobat was poised with two lighted candles in his hands. "Singing, he went upon the cord all along the great street so that all who saw him had marvel how it might be." With his candles still burning, he was seen all over Paris and for two miles outside. The return of the procession from the cathedral at night was lighted by 500 torches.

The coronation and other festivities were thick with cloth of gold, ermine, velvets, silks, crowns, jewels, and all the gorgeous glitter that might dazzle the onlookers. A grand banquet was held in the same hall in which Charles V had entertained the Emperor, followed by a similar pageant (using what may have been the same props) showing the Fall of Troy with castles and ships moving about on wheels. At the high table with the King and Queen were seated only prelates and eight ladies, including the Dame de Coucy and the Duchess of Bar. The King wore his golden crown and a surcoat of scarlet furred with ermine which, considering that it was August, gave point to Deschamps' advice about light clothing in summer. Such was the crowding and heat of the hall that the Queen, who was seven months pregnant when she went through these five days of continuous ceremony in mid-August, nearly fainted and the Dame de Coucy did faint, and one table of ladies was overthrown by the press of people. Windows were broken open to let in the air, but the Queen and many ladies retired to their chambers.

The hot weather affected the tournaments too; so much dust was raised by the horses' feet that the knights complained, but the Sire de Coucy as usual "shone brilliantly." The King ordered 200 barrels of water to lay the dust, "yet next day they had dust enough and too much."

Forty of the leading bourgeois of Paris presented the King and Queen with gifts of jewels and vessels of gold in the hope of remittance of taxes. Carried by two men dressed as ancient sages, the gifts were enclosed in a litter covered by a fine silk gauze through which the sparkle of jewels and gleam of gold could be seen. This imaginative presentation was less persuasive than it deserved to be. Two months later, when the King left for a tour of the south to display his new-found sovereignty to the people and seek to relieve their oppressions, taxes were raised in Paris as soon as he left to pay for the cost of the Queen's entry and for the new journey, which in turn proved so sumptuous that it resulted not in lowered but in increased taxes. In a manipulation of the currency to aid the cost, the circulation of small silver coins of four pence and twelve pence, which were the common cash of the people, was forbidden in Paris, depriving the poor for two weeks of the means to purchase food in the market place. Who can say whether two weeks of hunger and anger weighed heavier in the balance than the miraculous vision of the acrobat on his tightrope and the fountains of running wine?

Chapter 22

The Siege of Barbary

oucy reached the age of fifty in 1390. He was now the leading noble, apart from the King's brother and maternal uncle, in the royal entourage, relied on equally for political mission and military command. He held official positions as Captain-General of Auvergne and Guienne and member of the Royal Council, but his adventures in his fiftieth year carried him far beyond these assignments.

When in September 1389 Charles VI set out with his brother Louis and his uncle Bourbon to confer with the Pope in Avignon and exhibit kingship in Languedoc, Coucy commanded the royal escort. The purpose of the journey was, first, to work out with Pope Clement a means of regaining sole control of the papacy, and, second, to mend the crown's fences in Languedoc, alienated by the oppressions of the Duc de Berry. Delegates from the south had told the King on their knees and in tears of the "crushing tyranny" and "intolerable exactions" of Berry's officers. Unless the King acted, they said, the 40,000 people of Languedoc who had already fled to Aragon would be followed by many more.

Now that there was truce with England, Charles was advised by Rivière and Mercier to make the journey in order to learn how his subjects were governed and make himself more beloved by them, for the sake of funds "of which he had great need." At 22, the age at which his father had been a mature ruler, Charles VI was a shallow youth, spending what he did not have in a cascade of largesse. Efforts of Treasury officials to stem the flow by writing alongside the names of recipients, "He has had too much" or "He should repay," were in vain.

Burgundy and Berry were greatly vexed to be informed by the King that they were not to accompany him on the journey but must remain on their own estates. Knowing that the order originated with

Rivière and Mercier, and that the King was going to "hold inquisitions" on those who had governed Languedoc, they consulted together and agreed that they must "dissemble this affront," but that the time would come "when those who have advised it shall repent of it." As long as they remained united, they told each other, others "cannot do us any injury for we are the greatest personages in France." "Such," writes Froissart in unblushing reconstruction, "was the language of these two dukes."

From Lyon, the King and his party continued the journey to Avignon by boat down the Rhône, a more comfortable form of travel than horseback. On such trips the royal suite would fill several boats including one with a room containing two fireplaces for the King, and others with kitchens and offices and a supply of plate and jewels to pawn for cash if necessary on the voyage. Charles's passage down the rushing Rhône must have included many stops to make himself known to towns en route, for the trip took nine days. Organized welcome was not very different then than now. As many as a thousand children dressed in the royal colors were stationed on wooden platforms to wave little flags "and make heard, as the King rode by, loud acclamations in his honor."

On October 30, clad in scarlet and ermine, Charles made his entry into the papal palace, where he was met by Clement and 26 cardinals, and attended a splendid banquet with all his party. He presented the Pope with a blue velvet cope embroidered in pearls in a design of angels, fleur-de-lys, and stars. Empty purse or not, "he wished to be spoken of even in foreign countries for the magnificence he displayed."

With no footing except in French support, Clement's papacy would have vanished like smoke, and the ruinous schism brought to an end, if the French had made that their object. But they did not. To admit error and cut losses is rare among individuals, unknown among states. States function only in terms of what those in control perceive as power or personal ambition, and both of these wear blinkers. To impose Clement on Italy by power politics or force of arms had never been feasible. It was Urban of Rome, crazy or not, and afterward his successor who had popular support as the true Pope. Ignoring the obvious, and the disparity between goal and means, the French pursued their aim with the blind persistence that amounts to frivolity.

In conferences with Clement, Charles VI and his counselors proposed to open his way to Rome and assist him to gain control of Italy by establishing Louis of Orléans in a revival of the cloudy Kingdom of Adria in the north, and Louis II of Anjou in the equally unattained Kingdom of Naples and Sicily in the south. To this end, Louis II,

brought to Avignon by his tireless mother, was given a grand coronation as King of Naples and Sicily (including Jerusalem). Coucy, again
chosen for grace and splendor on these occasions, performed the ceremony of serving the boy King on horseback, along with the Count of
Geneva, brother of Pope Clement.

Hardly were these arrangements completed when news was received that the Roman Pope, Urban the terrible, had been dead for
three weeks and his seat filled in haste and secrecy by the election of a
Neapolitan cardinal, Piero Tomacelli, as Boniface IX. Rome no more
than Avignon was prepared to give up its claim in favor of a negotiated
solution. Given no chance to take advantage of Urban's death, the
French and Clement now agreed to pursue the problem of removing
Boniface. Charles VI promised that on his return to France he would
"give attention to no other thing until he had restored the Church to
unity."

Lighter-hearted activities engaged the King while these matters
were being resolved. He and his brother Louis and young Amadeus of
Savoy, son of the late Green Count, "being young and giddy," spent
every night in song and dance with the ladies of Avignon, who warmly
praised the King for the many fine presents he lavished on them. The
Pope's brother acted as master of the revels. The most memorable of
the entertainments was a literary competition on an issue of courtly
love: whether fidelity or inconstancy brings the greater satisfaction.
Embodied in a group of poems called the *Cent Ballades,* the symposium
originated among four ardent young knights, including Boucicaut and
Comte d'Eu, a cousin of the King, who had been thrown together
while on a recent venture in the Holy Land. While temporarily imprisoned in Damascus, the four had passed the time by a debate in
verse, and on returning via Venice in time to join the gathering at
Avignon, had invited responses from noble friends and princes.

Louis d'Orléans contributed a ballad, as did Guy de Tremoille,
Jean De Bucy, a follower of Coucy's, and another Bastard of Coucy
named Aubert. He was Enguerrand's former squire and first cousin, a
son of his father's brother, subsequently legitimized by Charles VI
after Enguerrand's death. Nothing is known of him except that
Deschamps describes him as one of his "persecutors" among a group
overfond of wine. Although Enguerrand's friends and adherents
entered the competition, he himself did not, which is perhaps a minor
clue to personality.

Before the advent of the printing press, literature was enjoyed like
chamber music in groups. The audience for the *Cent Ballades* heard
the case for fidelity made in the name of an elderly knight representing

Hutin de Vermeilles, a real individual known for loyalty in love and respect for women. Hutin's argument is the traditional one that faithful love surpasses mere "delectation of the body" because it improves the lover, generates courtesy to all women for love of one, and enhances the warrior's prowess in his desire to rejoice the heart of his beloved. Love makes him more valiant in siege, raids, ambush, in vanguard or defense, pilgrimage to Jerusalem or crusade against the Turks. The case for Falsity, in turn, was made in the name of a woman called La Guignarde, who stresses the joys of promiscuity and the dangers of a serious liaison. "All lovers" are then called upon to judge the dispute.

Although a majority of the noble versifiers declare for Hutin and Loyalty, some are ambiguous. The Duc de Berry, who had just married his twelve-year-old bride, felicitates himself on having "escaped love" and recommends talking Fidelity and practicing Falsity. The same tone is taken by the Bastard of Coucy, who breathes passionate devotion and eternal love in each of his stanzas, and ends each with the refrain,

> *Aussi dist on, mais il n'en sera riens.*
> (So they say, but it comes to nothing.)

His is the most cynical of the ballads. Of the others, some are candid, some satirical, some ambivalent, a few serious but none expresses anything deeply felt, as they would have had the subject been knighthood. Courtly love was an accustomed game, not a motivating ideal to which men desperately clung and for which, like the knights who held the lists of St. Ingelbert, they staked their lives.

Moving on to Languedoc, Charles VI and his court made ceremonial progress through Nîmes, Montpellier, Narbonne to Toulouse, feted so grandly through richly decorated streets "that it was a marvel to see." Processions of all groups and classes, each in appropriate robes, welcomed him, and tables were set out at which the people could eat and drink. The King's larder was supplied by his subjects: at one town he was presented with a troop of sheep and twelve fat oxen as well as twelve hunting horses hung with silver bells. Meanwhile, his ministers inquired into conditions, ordered reforms, and lifted the heaviest taxes.

Royal intervention staged its greatest gesture at Béziers in the punishment of Berry's chief officer, the hated Bétizac. Secret inquiries of the King's ministers had disclosed many "atrocious acts and such great extortions as made the whole country cry out against him." Upon arrest and interrogation, Bétizac insisted that all the moneys, amounting to three million francs, had been duly paid over to the Duc de Berry and accounted for. His papers when seized appeared to confirm him. His conduct did not appear to warrant the death penalty, for, as certain of the investigators said, "How can he help it if the sums have been extravagantly spent . . . for this Duc de Berry is the most covetous man alive." Others disagreed, saying Bétizac had so impoverished the people "that the blood of these poor creatures cries out against him." He should have remonstrated with the Duke or, failing to restrain him, have informed the King and Council.

News of Bétizac's arrest brought a flood of public complaints showing how much he was hated by the people, and, at the same time, haughty letters from Berry acknowledging that all Bétizac had done had been done at his orders. Although the King wanted the Governor put to death, the Council was embarrassed to find judicial grounds for doing so, since his superior, Berry, had been appointed by the crown.

The problem was solved by finesse. Bétizac was privately informed that he would surely be sentenced to die and that his only hope was to declare himself a heretic. If he did, he would be handed over to the Church and sent for judgment to Avignon, where no one would dare condemn him because of the Pope's dependence on Berry, the most powerful and zealous of his supporters. Believing what he was told, "because those in peril of their lives are much confused in mind," Bétizac did as advised. He affirmed his guilt in errors of faith before the Bishop of Béziers, who, according to Church practice with confessed heretics, promptly handed him back to the civil arm for execution. Dragged to the stake in the public square, fastened by collar and chain and piled with faggots, Bétizac was burned and his bones hanged, to the joy of the populace. Berry was deprived of the lieutenancy of Languedoc and replaced by a team of royal reformers. The people of the province acclaimed the young King for his justice and voted him an aid of 300,000 francs.

Ambassadors from Genoa met the King at Toulouse, bringing a proposal for a "grand and noble enterprise" against the Berber Kingdom of Tunis. They wanted French chivalry to lead a campaign to suppress the Barbary pirates who, with the unofficial support of their sultan, harassed Genoese commerce, raided and plundered Sicily and the Mediterranean islands, and sold captured Christians in their slave markets. Assuming that France, since the truce with England, was free of inquietude, the Genoese felt that her knights, "having nothing to do, would be glad to join in the warfare." The proposed objective was Mahdia,* the pirates' main base and the best port on the Tunisian coast. With this great stronghold in Christian hands, the ambassadors told King Charles, the power of the Berber kings would be broken, and they could be destroyed or converted. Genoa offered to supply the necessary fleet, provisions, archers, and foot soldiers in return for the French combat arm—knights and squires only, no servants—led by a prince of the royal family to ensure a genuine commitment.

Given the infidel as enemy, the proposal was dressed in all the aura of a crusade, and doused in flattery. For her historic exploits against the infidels, said the ambassadors, the name of France was feared as far as India, enough in itself to halt Turks and Saracens.† The infidels, they warned, dominate Asia and Africa; they have entered Europe, they threaten Constantinople, frighten Hungary, occupy Granada. But supported by Genoa, a French campaign would be short, and the glory long. "A fine thing for your sovereignty," they told Charles, "for you are the greatest King among Christians and have so much renown."

The project was the scheme of that "very subtle man," Antoniotto Adorno, Doge of Genoa, whose oppressions had raised an opposition party among his subjects. He hoped to blunt its threat by aiding the business enterprise of the republic, and gain at the same time a powerful ally in case of need. While French knights were excited by the prospect, ministers were cautious. Short of a permanent peace with England, they disapproved of sending French strength out of the country; and the question of leadership was bound to arouse jealousies. Pending further consultation, the Genoese had to go home without a firm answer.

While at Toulouse, Coucy joined the royal party in a hunt which almost resulted in the sorely needed portrait that would have left his face to history. The hunters lost their way in a forest as night fell. Riding deeper and deeper into the dark maze, they could find no way out until the King vowed that if he escaped this peril he would donate the price of his horse to the chapel of Notre Dame de Bonne Espérance in the cloister of Carmes in Toulouse. In response, light broke through the sky, a path was seen, and next day the King duly fulfilled his vow, later commemorated by a fresco in the cloister containing the only known contemporary representation of Enguerrand de Coucy. Unfor-

---

* Called "Africa" or "*Auffrique*" by the Europeans of the time, and sometimes confused by them with Carthage, the ancient Tunis.

† Saracen was a term used indiscriminately for all Moslems, whether Berbers, Arabs, Moors, or Turks.

tunately, it shows no face. In the copies that survived the demolition of the cloister in 1808, he is seen among seven nobles in the train of the King, each identified by his coat of arms. They are Louis d'Orléans, the Duc de Bourbon, Henri de Navarre, Olivier de Clisson, Philippe d'Eu, Henri de Bar, and, lastly, Coucy, the only one with his face turned away from the viewer as if deliberately mocking posterity.

Shortly afterward he may have gone to Spain to arrange with the King and Queen of Aragon for the marriage of their daughter, Yolande, aged eight, to Louis II of Anjou. Froissart's account of this mission, which was designed to gain an ally in the Angevin quest of the crown of Naples, is a hopeless tangle of what could and could not have occurred. He states that Coucy escorted Anjou to an actual marriage, which in fact did not take place until 1400, and he sets the scene amid many other discrepancies of time and place. Nevertheless, a marriage contract was indeed concluded in 1390, and Coucy would have been the natural choice to negotiate it. The Duchesse d'Anjou had consistently sought his influence in her cause ever since her husband's death; moreover, Coucy was related by marriage and well known to the Queen of Aragon, who was the former Yolande de Bar, his son-in-law's sister. He had also served as proxy in young Louis' previous marriage to Bernabò Visconti's daughter, which had been neatly annulled when Bernabò fell from power.

In Froissart's version, the Duchesse d'Anjou entreated Coucy to escort her son to Spain and he "cheerfully agreed" to undertake the journey. Twelve-year-old Louis took leave of the Pope and his mother in tears, for "their hearts were wrung at the separation and it was uncertain when they should meet again." Coucy and his charge rode by land to Barcelona (250 miles or more from Avignon or 200 from Toulouse) and on their arrival the Queen of Aragon was "particularly pleased to see the Sire de Coucy" and thanked young Louis of Anjou for bringing him, saying that "everything would be the better for it." All this is natural enough although it probably did not happen; the fog of elapsed time has closed down over the facts.

If indeed he went to Spain, Coucy would have seen a country on the edge of turmoil. The peninsula below the Pyrenees was now experiencing the tail of the storm of insurrections that had swept through Europe a decade before. The long civil wars between Pedro the Cruel and his half-brother Enrique had trailed the ineluctable wake of pillage, oppression, and taxes. Social antagonism found vent against the Jews, who so regularly in history become a microcosm of the world's larger ills. In Spain their role had been more prominent and prosperous than elsewhere. Pedro the Cruel had employed them extensively as advisors and agents, besides keeping a Jewish mistress, and his preference was made a theme of Enrique's accusations until Enrique emerged the victor. Then he too used the Jews' financial services.

Popular hatred was inflamed by agitators who raised fears of the Jews' increasing influence and demanded cancellation of debts owed to Christ-killers. Given a religious motive, economic fear can rise to fury. A fanatic Archdeacon, Ferran Martínez, preached a version of Hitler's final solution. In 1391 murder, seizure of property, and forcible conversion of the Jews began, and this taste of violence soon turned into general insurrection against the clergy and propertied class, culminating in four days of terror in Barcelona. Protection of the Jews was denounced by the populace as treason to Christendom. Gradually, the rulers regained the upper hand, but aggression against the Jews had been too overt and physically damaging to be repaired. They were rendered vulnerable, and Spain susceptible, to the final expulsion one hundred years later.

Coucy is recorded again in Toulouse on January 5, 1390, and on January 28 appeared in Avignon, where he testified at hearings in behalf of the canonization of a French saint. The candidate was the nobly born Pierre de Luxemburg, a youth of great sanctity and great family, recently deceased at seventeen, whose nomination was intended to enhance the status of the French Pope. Clement's legitimacy could hardly be questioned if God had provided a saint within his sphere. Pierre's name had been put forward under the highest auspices, first by the Duchesse d'Anjou in 1388, then by the new Chancellor of the University of Paris, Pierre d'Ailly, in the name of the King.

A son of the chaste and pious Count Guy de St. Pol, who had died of the plague as a hostage in England, and of Jeanne de Luxemburg of the same family as the late Emperor Charles IV, Pierre had been orphaned at three and rather precociously renounced the flesh in an oath of perpetual chastity at six. He was said to have imposed the same vow on a twelve-year-old sister and to have reproached his brother for laughing, on the ground that the Gospels recorded that Jesus had wept but not laughed. At eight he was an overgrown, hollow-chested ascetic, who was sent to study in Paris, where he practiced fasting and self-flagellation and demanded to enter the austere and currently fashionable Célestin Order. Opposed in this wish by his guardians, he regularly visited the Order to share its bread and water and sleep on the bare ground fully clothed without removing belt or shoes in order to be ready for prayers at midnight without losing time.

His remarkable piety combined with high birth won him appointment as a canon at nine, as archdeacon some years later, as Bishop of Metz at fifteen and Cardinal at sixteen. The red robe did not discourage his austerities or lonely orisons. His life was "nothing but humility" and "always he fled from the vanities and superfluities of the world." He spent the greater part of the day and night in solitary prayer or in writing down his sins in a notebook by candlelight and confessing them twice a day to his chaplain. His urgency, like Catherine of Siena's loquacity, was sometimes too much for the chaplain, who occasionally feigned sleep when he heard Pierre knocking on his door in the middle of the night.

The boy Cardinal developed a faculty for miraculous cures: he was credited with saving the Duchesse de Bourbon from labor pains lasting two weeks, healing wounds suffered in a tournament by Guy de Tremoille, resurrecting a steward of the Duc de Bourbon who had been felled by a thunderbolt, and outside this rather limited circle, restoring to health a poor workman who had been tortured by brigands. When he died of consumption and self-imposed rigors in 1387, he was buried by his wish in the paupers' cemetery at Avignon, where his grave became an object of pilgrimage by the poor and sick, causing a "great marvel" at the visitations made there daily. Kings and nobles, including the Sire de Coucy, sent rich gifts and lamps of silver, and Froissart, who never missed the newsworthy, came to observe the crowds at the grave.

To ensure a foolproof case for canonization, the hearings on Pierre's qualifications lasted six months and took evidence from 72 witnesses on 285 different articles. As Witness Eight in the first week, Coucy testified from personal knowledge, telling how, when Pierre went to take possession of the Bishopric of Metz, he had required the men-at-arms of his brother, Count Waleran de Pol, to evict the Urbanist clerics who held the episcopal property. When Waleran demanded to be reimbursed from the revenues of the bishopric, Pierre had said he would rather die than bind the lands of the Church, whereupon such discord arose between the brothers that Coucy himself had to take custody of the Church property until a settlement could be reached. He added that he had known Pierre from childhood and marveled at his piety, nor had he ever seen at Avignon a youth of such virtue.

All the roll of witnesses was not enough. Whether Clement's own unholiness quailed before a question of sainthood or he hesitated for some other reason, he let the process lapse, and his own reputation as Anti-Pope kept it from being revived for 140 years. Pierre de Luxemburg was ultimately beatified but not canonized in 1527.

In company with the King and court, Coucy returned to Paris via Dijon, where the Duke of Burgundy was prepared to "dissemble"—as he did everything—in a very grand manner, with a view to restoring himself to favor. An entire book has been written about the festivities, liveries, banquets, tournaments, gifts, and costs of this occasion, but amidst the accumulating troubles of the 14th century these extravaganzas recur so regularly that astonishment fades.

Incidental to displaying political status, such festivities must have supplied economic stimulus. For the King's visit to Burgundy, tailors, embroiderers, goldsmiths, armorers, and all trades and crafts received orders for goods and services. The Duke alone ordered 320 new lances to present to competitors. All the towns of Burgundy which the King would visit en route received funds for cleaning and decorating and even repaving streets and squares. Dijon itself, with its forest of spires and bell towers and chimneys fitted with iron grills to keep storks from nesting, its narrow twisting streets and taverns of ill repute, had to begin by clearing away animal ordure. Dogs, cats, pigs, and sheep wandered freely through its dark wooden arcades, the pigs especially contributing to the filth and smells. Voracious feeders, quarrelsome and "unsociable," they were the subject of constant complaints for biting and, in one case, eating a child, for which the guilty animal was executed by hanging. Regulations prohibiting the keeping of pigs in the city and the disposal of their ordure in the river had little effect.

Because there was no hall large enough to accommodate all the guests, a gigantic tent requiring 30,100 ells of cloth was ordered to cover the palace courtyard. Thriftily, after the event, the cloth was cut up and sold in lots. The amount of fabric consumed for blue satin draperies to be hung in all the ducal rooms, for 300 gowns of silk and damask for attending ladies, and as many doublets of parti-colored velvet and satin for the knights, must have emptied Flanders. How many needlewomen were employed to embroider the draperies with the Duke's "*Il me tarde*" entwined with his wife's initials against a background of azure doves perched in a forest of orange and lemon trees? How many carpenters and laborers found work razing walls, cutting down trees, flattening the ground, and constructing covered grandstands for three days of tournaments in February weather? When the host alone had thirty war-horses on hand for the events, the total number would have required an army of grooms and stable hands. Jongleurs, actors of miracle plays, acrobats, and animal trainers flocked to the town to entertain the people while the nobles jousted.

Coucy, even at fifty, was a—or possibly *the*—prize-winner of the tournament, receiving a pearl-and-sapphire clasp from the Duchess in reward. In the farewell exchange of gifts (and careful account was kept of the price tag of each), Burgundy upstaged the King by giving him a more expensive present than the King gave to the Duchess. The ceremonies concluded with singing and dancing by the ladies and damsels, "for love of the King, the Duc de Touraine [Orléans], the Duc de Bourbon and the Sire de Coucy."

Soon after Charles's return to Paris, his promise to think of nothing but reuniting the Church was put aside in favor of Genoa's alluring enterprise against the Kingdom of Barbary. Here was a ready-made adventure with no need of the serious political maneuvering required in the papal cause. Crusade, even if it had little to do with the cross, gave prestige to the participants, not to mention the *privilogium crucis* allowing a moratorium on their debts and immunity from lawsuit. While "the fire of valor enflamed all hearts," certain cautions were observed: the Council limited the number of knights who could leave the country to 1,500, and none could go without the King's leave. All who joined were to equip themselves at their own expense and recruit no followers from outside their own domains.

Louis d'Orléans, bent on replacing his uncle of Burgundy as the dominant figure of the realm, wanted the command and showered gifts on influential nobles in the hope of acquiring it. His uncle exerted enough influence to keep it from him, on the grounds of Louis' youth and inexperience, thus adding more fuel to their rivalry. Burgundy had too many interests at stake at home to want to leave the country; Berry was out of favor and not a warrior. The Duc de Bourbon, eager to find glory in the footsteps of St. Louis, who had died on the shores of Tunis in his last crusade, was accordingly chosen, with Coucy as second in command.

In the gesture of a great prince, Coucy established a church and monastery before his departure. Since the religious life was acknowledged as superior to the secular, the founding of a religious institution was a way of partaking in the extra merit of the Church. Besides, as the Duke of Burgundy said when he founded a Carthusian monastery at Champmol in 1385, "For the soul's salvation nothing suffices like the prayers of pious monks."

Coucy chose the Célestin Order, whose extremities of renunciation had made it so paradoxically the favorite of a nobility steeped in world-liness. Was the preference indeed paradox, or was it spiritual discomfort and a need for penitence in a life so far removed from the principles it professed? The duality of life under the Christian faith showed itself in Louis d'Orléans' hastening from riches and pleasures and political intrigue to stony vigils in the Célestin cloister. Sharing the monks' austerities relieved the pricking of self-disgust. Even the Count of Foix, a hard-headed materialist well acquainted with wrath, vainglory, and other sins, composed his own "Book of Prayers" in which he acknowledged the great suffering that results from coming to believe that "God no longer exists and that good and evil fortunes come from the nature of things, without God being there. After that comes death, the death of body and soul."

Whatever solace the Christian faith could give was balanced by the anxiety it generated. In this anxiety, Chaucer toward the end of his life, in his envoy to the Parson's Tale, was moved to "revoke" his life's work—*The Canterbury Tales, Troilus and Criseyde, The Book of the Duchess,* and all the poems that were not pious—and to beg Christ to forgive him for writing these "worldly vanities . . . so that I may be one of those at the day of doom that shall be saved." Christianity held a tragic power indeed if the need for salvation could lead a man to recant his own creation.

The 13th century founder of the Célestin Order had as a youth chosen a hermit's life in a cave in order to devote himself to God while achieving the most complete renunciation of self and nature compatible with life. He had spent sixteen hours a day in prayer, wearing a hair shirt and fasting on water and cabbage leaves through six "Lents" of forty days each during the year. Attracting disciples and fame, he succumbed to election as Pope Célestin V; then, in bitter repentance, and in an act unique for the papacy, resigned, to return to self-affliction and the search for God. The order named for him, growing in favor with popes and kings, was exempted from tithes and authorized to grant 200 years of indulgences to truly penitential persons who visited its convents on holy days.

There is no evidence that Coucy made a habit of visits to the Order and none at all to suggest that he was a man troubled in spirit. In all likelihood, his choice did not reflect any burden of anxiety so much as the fact that the greater austerities practiced by the Célestin monks gave greater assurance of salvation to their patrons.

His charter, dated April 26, 1390, opens with the characteristic self-assurance of the Coucys: "Considering that the pilgrimage and the temporal and worldly goods of this transitory life are ordered among those who can, and know how, best to use and edify them, and to store up treasure for God who has loaned us these goods," and for the purpose of perpetual prayers for himself, his present wife, his ancestors and successors and all knights and ladies of his Order of the Crown, he ordains and establishes a monastery for twelve monks of the Célestin Order on his property at Villeneuve on the banks of the Aisne outside Soissons.

He endowed the monastery with 400 livres of annual income secured to the said Order by a copious variety of legal safeguards. And if at any time the income falls short of 400 livres, he specifies how the sum shall be made up so that the monks shall "peaceably possess the said revenues without any constraint of mortgage by us or our successors." In any future disputes, the monks shall have "the counsel, comfort and aid of us and our officers of justice, our councillors and servants as if it were our own quarrel." The Célestins evidently had a sharp lawyer working on the deed or else Coucy himself was taking great pains in the perpetual attempt of donors to outflank the future.

The foundation remained very much on his mind in coming years. When the buildings were still unfinished after a certain time, he added another 200 livres of annual income to bring them to completion. Later still he made over to the Célestins a fine large mansion in Soissons belonging to the *confrérie* of Archers in order that the monks might have a place of shelter in time of war and be enabled to continue the monastic life, which, judging from another gift, had increased in comfort. Informed that the monks had not enough wine—which their predecessors had done without—Enguerrand arranged for them to buy a vineyard large enough to provide a sufficient annual supply. Owing to a failure to sign the charter for this gift before his death, the vineyard was to become one of the monastery's several claims in an acrimonious suit against his heirs.

The noblest of the kingdom assembled for the enterprise against Barbary, joined by knights from Hainault and Flanders as well as an English party from Calais headed by the Duke of Lancaster's bastard son, John Beaufort, Earl of Somerset, progenitor of the Tudor line. Clisson the Constable stayed behind to guard the country and leave his opponent Burgundy no free hand. Otherwise the group included, besides Bourbon and Coucy, all the great names: Admiral de Vienne; Comte d'Eu, whose prominence was owed to family rank; Jean d'Harcourt VII; Philippe de Bar, brother of Coucy's son-in-law; Geoffrey Boucicaut, brother of the more famous Jean; Yvain, bastard son of the

Count of Foix; and a notable Gascon called the Soudic de la Trau, "one of the valiant knights of the world."

The King financed Bourbon to the extent of 12,000 francs and distributed more than 20,000 among the other lords. Bourbon borrowed another 20,000 from Louis d'Orléans, secured against the revenues of his estates. Coucy, who had just been paid 6,000 francs by the crown to cover his expenses in Avignon and Languedoc, and had borrowed 10,000 more from Louis d'Orléans, was "better supported than any" except Bourbon. He and Comte d'Eu brought, evidently between them, a following of 200 knights. Pope Clement gave a plenary indulgence, which was generous considering that his own purpose had been deflected, and perhaps overgenerous since it was supposed to apply only to a crusade for the recovery of Jerusalem. Indeed, except for Jerusalem, according to the honest Bonet, war "should not be made against unbelievers," because God had made the world for all and "we cannot and ought not to constrain or force unbelievers to receive Holy Baptism or the Holy Faith."

The French party met their Genoese transports at Marseille, from where they sailed to Genoa to take on provisions, archers and foot soldiers, and the foreign knights. The knights and squires numbered between 1,400 and 1,500 and the total force probably about 5,000, not counting perhaps 1,000 sailors to man some forty galleys and twenty cargo ships. Bourbon, Coucy, Comte d'Eu and the valiant Soudic went ashore to be entertained by the Doge of Genoa, who presented them with gifts of spices, syrups, prunes of Damascus, and "other liqueurs good for sickness." These did not make up for a shortfall in provisions. Bourbon had to supply an added 200 casks of wine, 200 flitch of bacon, and 2,000 chickens for the sick and wounded. Shortage of space required that many horses be left behind, which, to spare their upkeep, had to be sold at less than half their value. At the final moment, embarrassment arose as to which clergy should bless the fleet since Genoa and France acknowledged different papacies. For the convenience of war, allies might bridge the schism. In the end, two priests officiated, representing both popes.

These difficulties overcome, the imposing armada that prepared to sail on July 1, 1390, was a thrilling spectacle and for long afterward a favorite subject of the illuminators. Needless to name the verbal illuminator who wrote, "What a beautiful thing it is to see this fleet with the emblazoned banners of different lords glittering in the sun and fluttering in the wind, and to hear, when the musicians blow their clarions and trumpets, the sound of those voices carried and echoed over the sea."

Ill fortune was encountered almost at once when a furious storm off Elba dispersed the fleet and caused a delay of nine days before all were collected again at the rendezvous at Malta. In the last week of July the fleet sailed up to Mahdia, located on the downward curve of the north African coast 100 miles south and east of Tunis. The walled town stood at the center and highest point of a narrow mile-long peninsula, its well-fortified harbor defended by a chain and towers equipped with stone-hurling machines.

The invaders decided to send ashore a landing party under Coucy, to act as advance guard and distract the enemy while the main party landed next day. With the young and excitable Comte d'Eu as associate leader, Coucy's party of 600 to 800 men-at-arms supported by Genoese archers set forth in beach landing craft powered by oars. As the rowers thrust their vessels over the calm sea, the waters, partaking of the pathetic fallacy long before its time, "seemed to delight in bearing these Christians to the shores of the infidels." Landing craft usually carried up to twenty horses, whose riders mounted while on board and, with helmet down and lance in hand, landed through wide doors at the stern, charged the enemy, and if pursued, rode back aboard their vessel, which was then rowed out to sea again.

Coucy was the first ashore and drew up his party in battle formation to meet attack. None came. Warned of the coming invasion and believing his force inferior in arms to the Christians, the Berber Sultan Abou-'l-Abbas had decided to allow a landing without risking a fight. Thereafter, avoiding general battle, he would let the invaders wear themselves out against stone walls under the August sun while keeping them constantly harassed by glancing attacks until exhaustion, heat, failing supplies, and inability to bring up reinforcements defeated their efforts. It was the same strategy that Charles V had devised against the English, and that many times since then had served the defense well.

Confident of victory over the despised infidels, the crusaders established their camp of bright-colored tents before the city, with Bourbon's pavilion flying the fleur-de-lys at the center and the Genoese crossbowmen on the wings. They could blockade Mahdia by sea and by land across the waist of the peninsula, but the city had stored up some provisions and had access to fresh water through underground canals. Shaped like a triangle, it harbored a large population and a garrison of 6,000, supposedly in underground living quarters. Knowing that if Mahdia fell, the Christians could march unobstructed to the conquest of Tunisia, the Sultan had strengthened Mahdia's defenses at all points and called upon the aid of neighboring kings to assemble a field army in the hinterland.

For three days no move interrupted the invaders' siege preparations until on the third evening the Berbers suddenly poured with fierce yells from the fortress. Thanks to an alert system of guards around the Christian camp, they were thrown back, leaving 300 dead. The city resumed its silent resistance while the Christians, to prevent the horsemen from again dashing in, erected a four-foot-high barrier of stakes held together by rope, with crossed oars and lances serving as cover for archers, and guards posted every 120 feet.

From a distance the sound of drums and clarions signaled the approach of the Saracens' relief army, reported to number 40,000. Camping behind the city, they ventured no major offensive but kept up a series of stinging raids on swift horses, descending on the Christians when the sun was hottest, forcing them into combat in their heavy armor. The Europeans were "almost burned up" inside their steel while the Berbers wore cuirasses of quilted cloth or leather. If pursued, they dispersed rapidly, only to regroup and pursue the enemy, who, burdened by armor, lost many dead. Almost every day and sometimes at night for the next six to seven weeks, the skirmishes continued.

Genoese ships supplied the Christian camp by sea with provisions from Sicily and Calabria, but deliveries were irregular, leaving privation during the gaps. The heavy wine imported by the Genoese caused lethargy. Heat and thirst, wounds and fevers, and illness from bad water—the same conditions, except for plague, suffered by the crusade of St. Louis—preyed upon the besiegers. Swarms of insects as well as the impregnability of the town depressed their spirits. They tried to ration provisions and to encourage one another. "The Sire de Coucy in particular," according to loyal Froissart, "looked after the welfare of the poorer knights and squires whereas the Duc de Bourbon was indifferent, and sat cross-legged in front of his pavilion requiring everyone to address him through a third person with many reverences, not caring whether the lesser knights were embarrassed. The Sire de Coucy, by contrast, put them at ease. He was kind to all and behaved more graciously than the Duc de Bourbon who never conversed with the foreign knights and squires in the agreeable manner of the Sire de Coucy."

Having brought no battering rams to break down walls, the besiegers began construction of a huge assault tower on wheels. It was three stories high, to overtop Mahdia's walls, and forty feet square with enclosed sides. Meanwhile, the defenders, suffering from the blockade, sent envoys to parley. Conducted before Bourbon and Coucy, who listened attentively to the speech as translated by a Genoese, the envoys asked why the French and English knights had come to make war on those who had not harmed them. They said they had troubled only the Genoese, which was natural among neighbors, for it had been customary "to seize mutually all we can from each other."

The answer required care to be sure of making a good case for a just war. Bourbon and Coucy consulted with twelve of the leading lords and, evidently on the assumption that infidels were ignorant, replied that they came to make war on the Saracens because they were unbelievers "with no creed of their own," which made them enemies, and also to retaliate upon their forefathers "for having crucified and put to death the son of God called Jesus Christ."

"At this answer the Saracens did nothing but laugh, saying it was the Jews who had crucified Jesus Christ and not they." The parley evidently ended there.

Subsequently, a Berber and a Christian, meeting outside the walls, entered a dispute—probably not spontaneous, because the Berbers were looking for a way to take prisoners—on the relative merit of their religions. The Berber offered a challenge to decide the issue by the combat of ten champions from each side. Instantly responding, ten crusaders, including Guy and Guillaume de Tremoille, Geoffrey Boucicaut, and two English knights, presented themselves, while the camp buzzed in excited anticipation of the event. Only Coucy disapproved.

"Hold your tongues, you who never consider consequences," he said. "I see no advantage in this combat." Suppose the Saracens were to send not knights but mere varlets, what honor or advantage would be gained in defeating them? Suppose the challenge were a ruse to seize Christian knights as prisoners, of which they had so far taken none? Such a fight could not take Mahdia, whatever its outcome. Moreover, a trial at arms, especially with an unfamiliar enemy, should never be accepted without great deliberation nor without authority of the Senior Council and full knowledge of the challengers' identity by name and surname, rank and arms. Coucy rebuked the champions for indiscipline and for failure of the subordination to high command which ought to prevail in an army. In that concept he was ahead of his countrymen.

Although his advice won many adherents, others supported Comte d'Eu and Philippe de Bar, who insisted that the challenge, having been accepted, could not be disavowed and that combat must ensue. Led by Geoffrey Boucicaut, who in his "overflowing pride" offered to fight with twenty against forty, the champions duly rode forth in their armor to the appointed time and place. A throng of their comrades accompanied them, increasing in numbers by the moment until virtually all the able-bodied were present, leaving the camp guarded only by the sick under the command of Coucy. Seeing such numbers, the Berber champions preferred not to appear.

Intending to prevent the clash, doubtless on Coucy's advice, the Duc de Bourbon hurries up on his mule, to find himself surrounded by several thousand excited warriors. Fearing that he will not be obeyed if he orders retreat, he decides to let the occasion govern. Beginning with an attack on the enemy camp, battle is joined and fiercely waged. The Christians harm but cannot destroy the greatly superior Saracen army, and, suffocating in their armor, themselves suffer many losses. They are bathed in sweat, gasping for breath through open mouths and dilated nostrils, devoured by thirst. The wounded breathe their last in the arms of their comrades; the exhausted sink to the ground to lie motionless. By twilight even D'Eu counsels retreat on the ground that if the Saracens charge the camp, "there is no one there but the Sire de Coucy with a few men and many sick; they could all be lost," and the camp overrun.

Accounts differ widely as to casualties: two knights and four squires, according to Bourbon's biographer; no less than sixty, many of whom he names, according to Froissart. Whatever the number, they were lost in a pointless battle.

Frustration compounded the physical miseries of a siege that had lasted two months without result. Talk of raising the siege was heard. Grumblers said that skirmishing could never take the town. For every one of the enemy slain, ten could take his place because the Saracens were in their own country. Winter was coming with long and cold nights, and suspicion rose that the Genoese, "who are rude people and traitors," might desert, sailing away by night in their ships. Impatient at the long lapse in trade, the Genoese were indeed growing restless. They said they had expected the French to take Mahdia within two weeks but, as matters were going, they would never conquer the town, much less Tunisia, this year or next. Amid these doubts and discontents, a War Council was convened which agreed on a final major effort to take Mahdia by assault.

The day was carnage. Resistance of the Saracen field army, led by the Sultan's sons, was intense. Mahdia's garrison, fighting "in the certitude of a glorious reward in the other world," poured from the walls a shower of arrows, stones, and burning oil which succeeded in destroying the crusaders' great assault tower. Men-at-arms on ladders climbed to the very brink of the walls to be toppled back. Despite the strongest assaults, which almost carried one of the city's three gates, Mahdia could not be taken. The Berber field army was repelled, but, as so often in France, the walled city withstood its enemies.

Afterward, both sides were ready to end hostilities. The beleaguered Berbers, suffering invasion and blockade, had no advantage in prolonging war on their own soil. With their lighter arms and tactics, they could not hope for decisive victory in the field. The Genoese instigators of the enterprise were more than ready for withdrawal. While they negotiated terms with the Berbers, the invaders struck camp. Bright banners came down, tents were rolled up, withdrawal to the ships was completed nine weeks after the landing. "As you were the first to land, good cousin," said Bourbon to Coucy, "I wish to be the last to embark"—a less exigent choice.

The treaty concluded by the Genoese secured terms which the French were able to declare honorable, allowing them to depart without shame, if without victory. Indeed, at the last War Council held to discuss the terms, they convinced themselves they had done well. To maintain a siege for two months against three Saracen kings and a strong city, said the Soudic de la Trau, was a thing "as honorable as if I had been in three battles." Other speakers gladly took his cue, and all, including Coucy, agreed to accept the terms.

One more enterprise, the fourth since the Scottish fiasco, had ended in vain, not for lack of will or courage or fighting capacity, but from the headlong undertaking of a militarily impractical task. The strength of walls against men, the problems of siege to the besieger, the risks of overseas supply were as well known to knights as the inside of their helmets. They could have known the conditions of North Africa from the rout of St. Louis' two crusades, regardless of the time elapsed; 120 years ago was but yesterday insofar as change was expected. Military carelessness had some excuse, however. In a period of poor communication, advance intelligence was usually lacking. Mahdia's fortified strength could well have been unsuspected. Ignorance of the foe was a condition of the time; contempt for this foe, a condition of its mentality.

Froissart claimed that knights said to him afterward, "If the Sire de Coucy had been in command, the result would have been different." This is unlikely. Although lack of command structure played a part in the outcome, what principally vitiated the siege of Barbary was lack of a vital interest. When that was present, when the stakes were serious, as in the recovery of France under Charles V, a strategy compatible with its object was imposed, recklessness and improvidence disallowed. For the French, the Tunisian campaign was merely chivalric adventure with a religious overlay. What moved knights to war was desire to do deeds of valor augmented by zeal for the faith, not the gaining of a political end by force of arms. They were concerned with the action, not the goal—which was why the given goal was so rarely attained.

In France, where no word had been received of the expedition's fate, processions and prayers were held to implore God's mercy on the crusaders who fought in His name. Charles VI visited Coucy-le-Château in September, perhaps to comfort the young Dame de Coucy in her anxiety, or to inspect again a property coveted by the crown and which might soon be lordless. Rejoicing was loud when news came of the crusaders' return to Genoa in mid-October. More of the sick died there and others recovered slowly from their hardships. After a winter's crossing of the Alps, it was another six weeks before Bourbon and Coucy reached Paris, followed from time to time by their companions.

Interval and distance muted the truth. Despite a return without booty, ransom, or prisoners, they were greeted as if victorious (as were their opponents in Moslem halls). As far as France knew to the contrary, an impression of triumph over the infidel could prevail. There were no foreign correspondents in Tunisia to report, and no newspapers in France to publish, the frustrations of the campaign. Losses in killed and missing amounting to 274 knights and squires, or just short of 20 percent, left no negative impression; they were customary. In the end, France was admired for the undertaking, not least by Genoa, because the appearance of the French as her fighting allies sufficiently alarmed the Berbers to cause them for the present to reduce their piracy.

Eager to hear all that had happened, King Charles questioned Bourbon and Coucy and the rest. Not the least discouraged by their accounts, he declared that as soon as peace could be made with England and within the Church, he would gladly go with a royal army to those parts "to exalt the Christian faith and confound the infidels." Among the participants, memories of pain and futility faded, and when within a few years a new crusade was preached against the Turks, their attitude toward the foe was unchanged and their enthusiasm undeterred.

Chapter 23

In a Dark Wood

Undiscouraged by the equivocal result in Barbary, the French King and Council moved without pause to a more formidable venture: ending the schism by force of arms. The plan for a march on Rome to oust Pope Boniface and install Pope Clement was called the *Voie de Fait*, or Way of the Deed—that is, of force—as opposed to the Way of Cession, or voluntary mutual abdication of the popes, as advocated by the University. To march through Italy and take Rome by force was no less an undertaking than the invasion of England—so recently proved beyond French powers—but the policy-makers showed no hesitation. The Council took the decision at the end of November within a few days of Coucy's and Bourbon's return from Tunisia.

The plan was presented to the King as a prelude to crusade. He could not in good conscience, his ministers told him, take the cross against the Turks until the Church was reunited. "We can envision nothing finer nor more reasonable for you than to go to Rome with the power of men-at-arms and destroy this anti-pope Boniface. . . . Nothing could better occupy you. We may hope that this anti-pope and his cardinals, when they realize that you are coming against them with a strong army, will surrender to your mercy." After that grand consummation, the glowing prospect of continuing even to Jerusalem would be at hand.

When could he start? asked the King, immediately afire. He had been brought up under the ardent influence of Mézières, who had filled the court with his propaganda of crusade as France's destiny and the saving of society. Charles's advisers told him the campaign could begin at once, and plans were immediately set in motion. All the royal house were to be included; even the Duke of Brittany was invited because "they did not think it prudent to leave him behind." He predicted unpleasantly that the enterprise would "end in words."

A huge force of 12,000 lances was agreed upon, with departure set four months hence in March 1391 from a rendezvous at Lyon. The King and his brother were to lead 4,000 lances; Burgundy, Berry, and the Constable each 2,000; Bourbon and Coucy each 1,000; all to receive three months' pay in advance. The taxes required to raise such an army and maintain it in the field seem to have been lightly considered; financing the venture was as unrealistic as the Way of Force itself. When the Council met to authorize the rates, the usual omen in the form of a fearful storm made them hesitate. Was it God's signal against imposing new burdens on an already overburdened people?

The voice of the University spoke against the *Voie de Fait* more explicitly than lightning and thunder. In a stupendous twelve-hour sermon preached before the King and court on January 6, 1391, Jean Gerson, a young scholar already famed as a preacher, expressed the opposition. Twenty-seven years old and two years short of his doctorate in theology, Gerson was a protégé of the Chancellor Pierre d'Ailly, whom he was soon to succeed at the age of 31. As the struggle over the schism intensified, he was to become the foremost advocate of the supremacy of a Church Council over the Pope, and the most memorable French theologian of his age.

Gerson was a man proof against classification or generalization. A mystic in faith, he was rational in practice. As a lover of the golden mean, he distrusted the devotional excesses of other mystics and visionaries. As a churchman, he was both conformist and non-conformist. Humane in ideas, he harshly opposed the early French humanists in the great debate over the *Roman de la Rose*. Despite his dislike of visionaries, especially female, he was to be, in the last year of his life, one of only two theologians willing to guarantee the authenticity of the voices of Joan of Arc. This was not because he was what moderns would call a liberal, but because he understood the intensity of her religious faith. He was a compendium and a reflector of the ideas and intellectual influences of his age.

In earlier times he would have been a monk, but in the last hundred years the university had taken over from the monastery the main work of transmitting the knowledge of the past and pursuing it in the present. Entering the University of Paris at fourteen, Gerson had found theology and philosophy petrified in the arid syllogisms of the scholastics. In the great age of Aquinas, scholasticism had undertaken to answer all questions of faith by reason and logic, but reason had proved incapable of explaining God and the universe, and the effort faded, leaving only a hard shell of argument by logic, practiced, as Petrarch said in disgust, by "hoary-headed children." When they begin to "spew forth syllogisms," he advised taking flight. Gerson, like others of his troubled time, craved something more meaningful for the soul and found the alternative in mystic faith and direct communion with God.

He believed that society could be regenerated only through a renewal and deepening of faith in which "vain curiosity" had no place. Knowledge of God, he wrote, "is better acquired by penitent feeling than by intellectual investigation." He took the same view of the supernatural, affirming the existence of demons and reproving those who scoffed for lack of faith and the "infection of reason." Yet Gerson could not keep reason from breaking in. He scorned magic and astrologers' superstitions, and recommended careful examination of visions before giving them credence.

He disapproved of the Bible in the vernacular, yet, as a poet, teacher, and orator, he wrote many of his sermons and treatises in French so as to convey his meaning to simple minds and youthful understanding. Medieval educators in general spent much time composing sermons for children. Gerson in particular was concerned with their development, and uncommon in seeing them as persons distinct from adults. In a curriculum for Church schools, he urged the necessity of keeping a vigil lamp lit in the youngest children's dormitory to serve as a symbol of faith and to give light when "natural necessity" required their rising during the night. Reformation of the Church, he warned, must begin with the right teaching of children, and reform of the colleges begin with reform of elementary schools.

He advised confessors to arouse a sense of guilt in children with regard to their sexual habits so that they might recognize the need for penitence. Masturbation, even without ejaculation, was a sin that "takes away a child's virginity even more than if at the same age he had gone with a woman." The absence of a sense of guilt about it in children was a situation that must be changed. They must not hear coarse conversation or be allowed to kiss and fondle each other nor sleep in the same bed with the opposite sex, nor with adults even of the same sex. Gerson had six sisters, all of whom chose to remain unmarried in holy virginity. Some powerful family influence was surely at work here from which this strong personality emerged.

Sex was one factor in Gerson's violent rejection of Jean de Meung's *Roman de la Rose*. Meung's celebration of carnal love, his satire of Chastity, his enthronement of Reason, his free-thinking skepticism, his anti-clerical bias were all anathema to Gerson. When Christine de Pisan voiced her attack on Jean de Meung in 1399 in her *Epistle to the God of Love*, Gerson supported it in a sermon with all the passion of the book-burner. He denounced the *Roman de la Rose* as pernicious and immoral: it degraded women and made vice attractive. If he had the only copy in existence, he said, and it were worth 1,000 livres, he would not hesitate to consign it to the flames. "Into the fire, good people, into the fire!"

Admirers of Meung sprang to his defense in open letters to Christine and Gerson. The defenders, Jean de Montreuil, Gontier and Pierre Col, were clerics and scholars in the secretarial service of the crown. Together with like-minded academics, they were among those who had chosen another path than Gerson in reaction to the dusty answers of the scholastics. With their faith in human reason and recognition of natural instincts they were acknowledging the lay spirit. In that sense they were humanists, although not concerned with the classical researches of the humanist movement in Florence. What they admired in Meung was his free-ranging thought and bold attack on standard formulas. Among certain learned and enlightened men, Jean de Montreuil asserted, appreciation of the *Roman de la Rose* was such that they would rather do without their shirts than this book. "The more I study the gravity of the mysteries and the mystery of the gravity of this profound and famous work, the more I am astonished at your disapproval."

While fervent, this was not very specific. Pierre Col was more courageous, defending the sensuality that so offended Gerson. He asserted that the Song of Solomon celebrated love for the daughter of Pharaoh, not for the Church; that the female vulva represented by the Rose was held to be sacred, according to the Gospel of St. Luke; and that Gerson himself would one day fall in love, as had happened to other theologians.

The debate expanded. Christine replied with *Le Dit de la Rose* and Gerson with a magisterial essay, *Tractatus Contra Romantium de Rosa* in which allegorical figures carry their complaints against Jean de Meung before the "sacred court of Christianity" and he is appropriately condemned. Although Gerson had the last word in the controversy, he could not destroy the attraction of the book. It continued to be widely read into the 16th century, surviving even a pious attempt to "moralize" its images, in which the Rose was transformed into an allegory for Jesus.

While Gerson remained within the establishment, the search for faith was drawing others outside in movements away from institutional religion. People were seeking in lay communion a substitute for rituals grown routine and corrupt. Faith was all the more needed when the way seemed lost in a dark wood of alarms and confusions.

The damage done by the schism had deepened. Both the popes were absorbed in extravagant display for the sake of prestige and the search for more and more money to support it. Pope Boniface in Rome took cuts from usury and sold benefices to the point of scandal, sometimes re-selling the same office to a higher bidder and dating the second appointment previous to the first. He sold the right to hold as many as ten or twelve benefices at a time. Clement VII extracted "voluntary" loans and subsidies and piled up ecclesiastical taxes until his bishops in 1392 refused to pay, and pinned their protest to the doors of the papal palace in Avignon. As a dependent of France, he made over tithes on the French clergy to the crown, and in the many disputes arising from this, he took the crown's part against the clergy. No measures filled his need; he had to borrow from usurers and pawn the sacred treasures. At his death, it was said, the papal tiara itself was on pawn.

Within the Empire the effect of the schism was not greatly divisive because conditions were already so chaotic that they could not have been made much worse. Charles IV had taken the precaution before he died of having his eldest son, Wenceslas, crowned King of Bohemia and nominated Emperor ahead of time, but concord and unity did not come with the title. This was not surprising since Charles had apportioned rule of the imperial territories among Wenceslas' two brothers, an uncle and a cousin. Their interests were often at odds, the rival houses of Wittelsbach and Hapsburg were hostile, the twenty-odd principalities were insubordinate, the towns, fighting to maintain their privileges, formed leagues against the nobles. Revenues adequate for the exercise of central government could not be collected out of conditions of anarchy, and the authority of the Emperor was too superficial to control the situation.

Wenceslas IV was eighteen when he acceded to the throne in 1378 shortly after accompanying his father on the memorable visit to Paris. Although trained in government by his father, well educated and literate in Latin, French, German, and Czech, he lacked the character to dominate his circumstances. Despite his initial efforts to work out a balance of forces, the incessant warring of groups and classes, of towns versus princes, lesser nobles against the greater, Germans against Czechs, leagues against leagues, created a network of dissension that defied sovereignty—and destroyed the sovereign.

A tragic, ruined figure, Wenceslas emerges from the chronicles a kind of Caliban, half clownish, half vicious, a composite of half-truths and legends reflecting the animosities of his various sets of enemies.

Because his reign was the source of the Hussite revolt against the Church and of the rising Czech nationalism hostile to the Germans, Wenceslas suffered posthumously from both clerical and German chroniclers. The unfair advantage of the written word triumphs in the end. But even if exaggerated, the stories about Wenceslas are too much of a kind not to represent some body of truth.

Said by his partisans to be good-looking and well-mannered, he appears more generally as a "wild boar" who went on rampages at night with bad companions, burst into burghers' houses to rape their wives, shut up his own wife in a whorehouse, roasted a cook who served him a burned meal. According to these versions, he was sired by a cobbler, was born ugly and deformed (causing the death of his mother in giving him birth), soiled the baptismal water at his christening, and stained the altar by sweating profusely at his coronation at the age of two—all omens, although probably *ex post facto,* of an unholy reign. He was happy only when hunting, spending months at a time in the woods and at hunting lodges to the neglect of government, preferring the company of grooms and hunting companions whom he ennobled, to the anger of the barons. His early efforts to uphold justice and achieve order left him frustrated, he only made enemies by favoring one faction over another, his errors of judgment compounded a sense of inadequacy, he became incapable of pursuing a policy with any consistency, fled from his problems, and found refuge from incapacity in hunting and heavy drinking.

While it was common in Germany for a man in any rank of society to drink himself under the table, Wenceslas became a confirmed alcoholic. He grew increasingly irritable and black-tempered and indolent as a sovereign, stayed in Prague to the neglect of the rest of the Empire, and succumbed to fits of savagery in which he was thought sometimes to have "lost command of his reason." As if reflecting his master, one of the hounds that followed him everywhere was said to have attacked and killed his first wife, Joanna of Bavaria—although according to other sources she died of the plague and left a sorrowing husband too distressed—or possibly too drunk—to attend the funeral. Evidently not as repellent as he was later made out to be, he married a second Bavarian princess, reputedly very beautiful, who was said to have held him in great affection. Not so the Church, whose priests he pilloried, together with their concubines. His reign saw the notorious pogrom of 1389 when a priest leading a procession through the Jewish quarter of Prague on Easter Sunday was stoned by a Jewish child, causing the townspeople to turn out for the slaughter of 3,000 of the Jewish community. When the survivors sought justice from the

King, Wenceslas declared that the Jews deserved their punishment, and fined the survivors, not the perpetrators.

His most famous conflict came with the Church and ended in the canonizing of his victim. Its cause lay in the usual struggle of temporal versus ecclesiastical authority. Enmity reached a peak in 1393 when the Archbishop of Prague ordered his Vicar-General, John of Pomuk, to confirm the election of an abbot chosen by the monks over the candidate preferred by the King. Wenceslas in a fury threw the Archbishop, the Vicar-General, and two other prelates into prison; then, after releasing the Archbishop, tortured the others to extract a confession of the hierarchy's hostile designs. Maddened by their silence, the King himself reportedly seized a torch to apply to the victims' feet. Frightened by what he had done, he then offered to spare their lives in return for their promise on oath not to tell of their torture. When John of Pomuk proved too broken and suffering to sign the oath, Wenceslas, in a compulsion to destroy the evidence, had him bound hand and foot and thrown from a bridge into the Moldau to drown. John of Pomuk was subsequently canonized as a martyr and made the patron saint of all bridges.

The King's troubles mounted through the 1390s. He was drunk a great part of the time but not so incapacitated as to fail to aggrandize his Bohemian possessions at the expense of the great nobles. In consequence, he succeeded in uniting them in antagonism for long enough to enable them finally to depose him as Emperor in 1400, although he remained King of Bohemia.

Wenceslas' difficulties were not merely personal or temperamental. They were an epitome of his century. He too was lost in the dark wood of his time. Like Jean II of France, he was born to a task of government too heavy for him in an age when too much was going wrong. Like government, the Church in his country was failing in its task and giving rise to the strongest movement for reform in Europe. Taking its doctrine from Wyclif and named for Jan Hus, who was to be burned as a heretic in 1415, the Hussite rising opened the way to the Reformation a hundred years later. It also finished off Wenceslas by inducing an apoplectic fit of which he died in 1419.

In France the feverish atmosphere showed itself in 1389 when an impassioned controversy over the immaculate conception of the Virgin caused Dominican monks to be accused, like the Jews in the plague, of poisoning the rivers if not the wells. It happened that a Dominican, Jean de Montson, had propagated the view that the Virgin was conceived in original sin. He was condemned by the University of Paris, which upheld the opposite, Franciscan, view of her immaculate conception. When Montson appealed to Pope Clement, d'Ailly and Gerson went to Avignon to demand official approval of their opinion. Clement was in a dilemma. Montson's view was that of previous orthodoxy approved by Thomas Aquinas. If Clement denounced it, his own orthodoxy would be challenged by his rival in Rome. If he upheld it, he would be contradicting the University and arousing popular wrath in France. In the heat of this situation, angry threats pursued the Dominicans. Afraid for his life, Montson went over to Rome, leaving Clement free to declare for Immaculate Conception.

While devotion to the Virgin could still arouse such feeling, disbelief and irreverence were common at the end of the century, if the complaints of clerics and preachers reflect the true case. Scolding the laity was the cleric's normal occupation, but now the volume was rising. Many folk "believe in naught higher than the roof of their house," lamented the future saint Bernardino of Siena. His fellow monk Walsingham reported that certain barons of England believe "that there is no God, and deny the sacrament of the altar and resurrection after death, and consider that as is the death of a beast of burden, so is the end of man himself." Alongside evidence of failing faith may be put the unfailing succession of wills and bequests to shrines, chapels, convents, hermits, and sums for prayers and for pilgrimages by proxy. Few who professed disbelief during life took chances when they neared the end.

The too frequent use of excommunication for failure to take communion or keep feast days, so deplored by Gerson and other reformers, was a measure of the falling off of religious observance. Churches were empty and mass meagerly attended, wrote Nicolas de Clamanges in his great tract *De Ruina et Reparatione Ecclesiae* (The Ruin and Reform of the Church). The young, according to him, rarely went to church except on feast days and then only to see the painted faces and décolleté gowns of the ladies and the spectacle of their headdresses, "immense towers with horns hung with pearls." People kept vigils in church not with prayer but with lascivious songs and dances, while the priests shot dice as they watched. Gerson deplored the same laxity: men left church in the midst of services to have a drink and "when they hear the bell announcing consecration, they rush back into the church like bulls." Card-playing, swearing, and blasphemy, he wrote, occurred during the most sacred festivals, and obscene pictures were hawked in church, corrupting the young. Pilgrimages were the occasion for debauchery, adultery, and profane pleasures.

Irreverence in many cases was the by-product of a religion so much a part of daily life that it was treated with over-familiarity, but the chorus of reproof at the end of the century indicated a growing element of disgust. "Men slept in indifference and closed their eyes to the scandal," mourned the Monk of St. Denis. "It was a waste of time to talk of ways to reform the Church."

Indifference, however, like a vacuum in nature, is not a natural condition of human affairs. A new devotional movement arose at this time in the small trading towns of northern Holland, between desolate marshland and moor near the mouth of the Rhine—as if only in a remote corner of strife-torn Europe could fresh piety find a place to sprout. Because the members lived communally, they came to be known by their neighbors as the Brethren of the Common Life, although they referred to themselves simply as "the devout." Their purpose was to find direct union with God, and through preaching and good works create a devout lay society. They were not extremists like the earlier Brethren of the Free Spirit but simply, as they said, "religious men trying to live in the world"—meaning the lay world as distinct from the cloistered.

Gerard Groote, founder of the movement, was the son of a prosperous cloth merchant of Deventer in Holland. Born in the same year as Coucy, he spent a dissolute youth while studying law and theology at the University of Paris, where he dabbled in magic and medicine and made love to women "in every green woods and upon every mountain." Finding the scholars' disputations "useless and full of discord," he left the University to join the secular clergy, and after a career as a worldly pastor in Utrecht and Cologne, experienced a conversion. Giving away his property in Deventer to charity, he went forth to preach a gospel of dedication to God springing from an "inner kernel of devotion," rather than from baptism and the sacraments.

His zeal, gift of rhetoric, and an impressive personality attracted listeners in crowds that often overflowed the churches. People came to listen from miles away. Wearing an old gray cloak and patched garments, and trundling with him a barrel of books from which to confute critics after a sermon, Groote urged love of neighbors as well as of God, elimination of vice, and obedience to Christ's commandments. Lamenting the corruption and predicting the impending collapse of the Church, he preached to the clergy in Latin and to the laity in the vernacular. A disciple took down his words and another went ahead to post announcement of a coming sermon on the church doors of the next town. Enthusiasts met in groups to adopt his principles and gradually joined to practice them, living together in houses segregated by sex.

Association was voluntary, without the binding vow essential in the regular Orders, committing members to life apart from the world. Under the rules of Groote's *Devotia Moderna*, members were to live in poverty and chastity but, instead of begging like the friars, were to earn their living by teaching children and by two occupations not controlled by the guilds, copying manuscripts and cooking. Work, Groote believed, "was wonderfully necessary to mankind in restoring the mind to purity," although not so commerce: "Labor is holy, but business is dangerous." By the time he died of an illness in 1384, his followers' houses in Holland and the Rhineland numbered well over a hundred, with those for women being three times as many as those for men.

The communities' emphasis on individual devotion and their very existence without a vow or an official rule were in themselves a criticism of the authorized Orders. Voluntary self-directed religion was more dangerous to the Church than any number of infidels. Before he died, Groote was prohibited from preaching by the Bishop of Utrecht. When other churchmen afterward attempted to suppress the movement, his followers made vigorous and successful defense of their principles. At the Council of Constance in 1415, Gerson, though he disliked their doctrines, defended them against charges of heresy. Their communities survived because a climate of sympathy existed in their favor, and not only among the laity. Two years after Groote's death, the Brethren established their first formal monastery in association with the Augustinian Order, though still without vows. Although the movement remained small and limited, it was soon to produce in *The Imitation of Christ* by Thomas a Kempis, the most widely read religious book in Catholicism after the Bible.

In 1380, in the small town of Kempen, south of Deventer, a peasant's son was born to an evidently literate mother who kept a dame's school for the younger children of the town. At twelve, Thomas of Kempen—or a Kempis, as he came to be called—entered a school of the Common Life at Deventer, lived and studied with its disciples, and then joined an associated Augustinian monastery, where he remained for the rest of his 91 years. Loving books and quiet corners, he compiled the sayings and sermons of Groote and his disciples into a prolonged rhapsody on the theme that the world is delusion and the Kingdom of God is within; that the inner spiritual life is preparation for life everlasting. What he was saying over and over, through endless variations and admonitions, was that the life of the senses is without value, that the riches, pleasures, and powers of the world—the things most men want and rarely obtain—are no good to them anyway, but are only an obstacle on the way to eternal life; that the way to salvation lies in the abnegation of earthly desires and in the continual struggle against sin in order to make room for love of God; that man is born "with an inclination to evil," which he must conquer to be saved; that good lies in doing, not knowing—"I would rather feel compunction than know how to define it"; that only the humble in spirit are at peace—"it is much safer to be in subjection than in authority"; that to desire anything is to be "straightway disquieted"; that man is but a pilgrim in life, the world is an exile, home is with God.

Nothing of this was new or remarkable. *The Imitation of Christ* was what it said it was, an imitation of Christ's message, a consolation for the humble who are mankind's majority, a reassurance of the promise that their reward is to come hereafter. For a long time after Thomas' book appeared, so little was known about its author that Jean Gerson was supposed by some to be the Bacon behind this obscure northern Shakespeare.

In 1391 Gerson's plea against the Way of Force held the attention of the court from prime to vespers. Remembering how prison had closed over his predecessors, he pursued his argument at some risk, but as a native of Burgundy he had acquired the Duke as a patron, which may have made the sermon possible. He urged the crown to abandon the *Voie de Fait* with its "doubtful battle and spilling of blood," recommending rather a resort to augmented prayer and penitential processions. In a discreet rebuke, he deplored the gagging of the University on the subject of a Church Council, "for I have no doubt that if you had been better informed on what your very humble and devout daughter, the University of Paris, wished to say to you on this matter, you would very willingly have heard it, and great good would have come of it."

Boldly he suggested that the welfare of the papacy was subordinate to that of the Christian community as a whole, and that it would be "intolerable" if the Holy See, instituted for the good of the Church, became the instrument of its grave damage. He called on the memory of St. Louis, Charlemagne, Roland and Oliver, and the Maccabees to inspire Charles VI to remove the stain of the schism, a task Gerson did not hesitate to declare more important than a crusade against Islam. "What is greater than the union of Christendom? Who can better achieve that union than the most Christian King?"

Interference more material than Gerson's blocked the *Voie de Fait* for the time being. France could not go to war in Italy without the alliance or, at very least, the benevolent neutrality of Florence and

Milan, a prospect distinctly impeded by the fact of their being at war with each other. Each had rival advocates in France. Milan was represented by Valentina Visconti, wife of Louis d'Orléans. Louis dreamed of acquiring the promised Kingdom of Adria, still waiting to be carved out of the Papal States in return for French support. The dream depended on access to the wealth of Milan and on the collaboration of Louis' father-in-law in the *Voie de Fait*. Gian Galeazzo's interests were double-edged. He favored a Kingdom of Adria in friendly—that is, in French—hands, while at the same time he was wary of allowing France to become a power in Italy. He wanted a French alliance against Florence but he did not want to opt openly for Clement or commit himself to the *Voie de Fait*. While steering through these shoals, he had to frustrate the Florentine league against him, and confound the schemes of Bernabò's various sons and relations who were bent on his destruction.

News was spreading in Naples that the King of France and the Anti-Pope Clement were coming to Rome with a great army to reunite the Church. Clement himself was so sure of the program that he had ordered portable altars, riding saddles, pack saddles, blankets, and all equipment for a major move. Pope Boniface in great alarm begged the English to divert the French. This was accomplished not by a threat of war but by an offer of peace. English ambassadors came to France in February 1391 bringing an offer to negotiate a definitive treaty. Coucy and Rivière were delegated to confer with the English, to dine them and "keep them company." As evidence of serious purpose, the ambassadors said that King Richard's uncles, Lancaster and the bellicose Gloucester, would represent England at the parley. France could not refuse the momentous opportunity even if it meant postponing the *Voie de Fait*—which, of course, was the English purpose. The parley was set for the end of June and the march on Rome held in abeyance.

When June came, the English, having accomplished their original purpose, hung back from the edge of peace. At their request, the parley was postponed for another nine months until the following March. The truth was that England's counsels were sharply divided. King Richard and his two elder uncles, Lancaster and York, favored peace, while the relentless Thomas of Gloucester adamantly opposed it. In the generation since his father had fought France with no particular animus, the sense of underlying chivalric comradeship had shriveled. Gloucester, the youngest son, was fixed in his conviction that the French were perfidious and tricky and, by shifty legalities and ambiguous language, had cozened the English out of the gains confirmed in the Treaty of Brétigny. He refused to make peace until they rendered back "all such cities, towns, lands, and seigneuries" which they had falsely taken, not to mention 1,400,000 francs still owing on King Jean's ransom.

The real reason for his attitude lay deeper. Essentially, Gloucester and the barons of his party were opposed to peace because they felt war to be their occupation. Behind them were the poorer knights and squires and archers of England, who, unconcerned with rights or wrongs, were "inclined to war such as had been their livelihood."

At this moment, England's old ally, the Duke of Brittany, addicted as ever to feuding, suddenly re-opened his quarrel with France. Discarding a vassal's loyalty, he became more and more contentious and presumptuous, minting money bearing his own image, and assuming other rights of independent sovereignty. The French were anxious to bring him to submission before the date of the parley with the English, knowing that otherwise their uncovered flank would put them at a disadvantage. Coucy, one of the few persons acceptable to the irascible Duke, arranged for him to meet with the King and Council at Tours. Montfort came up the Loire attended by a suite of 1,500 knights and squires, in a convoy of five ships armed with cannon. For three months, from October to December 1391, the effort dragged on. Half slippery, half intransigent, Montfort could not be brought to terms. As a last resort, the King's daughter Jeanne, barely a year old, was offered in marriage to Montfort's son as the only means of attaching Brittany. The same solution had notably failed in the recent past to attach Charles of Navarre. With no great grace, after concluding the arrangement, Montfort went home "conserving all his hate."

While at Tours, Coucy was caught up in an affair that was to have bitter if posthumous irony for himself. It happened that the only son and heir of Count Guy de Blois died, leaving an enormous estate devoid of dynastic heirs. The limitless acquisitiveness of Louis d'Orléans focused at once on the property, which lay between his own domains of Touraine and Orléans. He and the King and Coucy rode over together from nearby Tours to visit the bereaved, and also bankrupt, father. Count Guy was the former fellow hostage in England who, to buy his liberty, had transferred his property of Soissons through King Edward to Coucy. Wild spending had since dissipated his great wealth; overeating and drinking had left him and his wife "overgrown with fatness" so that the Count could no longer mount his horse and had to be carried to the hunt in a litter. Given to fits of rage, he had once, in what appears to have been a 14th century habit, killed a knight with his dagger. Now he was old, sick, and childless, surrounded by swarms of quarreling would-be heirs.

32. *Papal palace at Avignon as it would have appeared in the 14th century. Engraving by Israel Sylvestre, c. 1650.*

33. 14TH CENTURY COINS

Pavillon d'or *of Philip VI*

Rome, coin of
Pope John XXII

Ange d'or *of Philip VI*

Florin, c. 1300, both faces

Franc of Jean II, both faces

Mouton d'or *of Jean II*

English noble, reign of Edward III

Écu d'or *of Charles VI*

34. *A Sienese army of 1363 depicted in the area where Coucy's campaign took place twenty years later. Fresco by Lippo Vanni, 1373, in the Sala del Mappamondo, Palazzo Pubblico, Siena.*

THE SWISS CAMPAIGN

*35, 36. The Gügler enter
Switzerland under the flags
of Coucy and England
(right) and the fight at
Fraubrunnen (below) showing
the flag of Bern (the Bear).
Both from the* Berner
Chronik, *c. 1400.*

37. *Sir John Hawkwood.*
Fresco by Paolo Uccello in
the Cathedral of Florence.

38. *Pierre de Luxemburg,*
with a cardinal's hat
on the altar drapery.
Portrait, c. 1400.

39. *Burning of the Jews.*
From Gilles li Muisis,
Antiquitates Flandriae,
14th century.

40. *A Jew wearing the circular*
badge. Detail from a 14th century
fresco of St. Helena's
discovery of the True Cross,
in the Cathedral of Tarragona.

41. *Christine de Pisan composing her works. From the manuscript of her* Oeuvres, *vol.* Poésies, *c. 1405.*

2, 43. *Jean de Berry (above), statue in the Cathedral of Bourges, and Philip of Burgundy (right), statue by Claus Sluter in the Champmol, Dijon.*

44. *Charles V receiving the translation of Aristotle's* Ethics *from Nicolas Oresme. From* Les éthiques d'Aristote, *1372 version.*

45. *Pope Urban VI. From a relief on the back of his sarcophagus in the Vatican Grotto, Rome, dated 1389.*

46. *Clement VII. Fragment of effigy at Avignon.*

47. *The siege of Mahdia. From Froissart's* Chronicles, *Louis de Bruges copy, c. 1460.*

48. Louis d'Orléans.
Portrait, c. 1420.

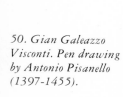

49. The Visconti
device: a viper
swallowing a man.

50. Gian Galeazzo
Visconti. Pen drawing
by Antonio Pisanello
(1397-1455).

51. *Froissart offering his* Chronicles *to Charles VI. From Froissart's* Chronicles, *c. 1450.*

52. *Gerson preaching at the Church of St. Bernard in Paris. From* Sermons sur la Passion, *illustrated by Baudoin de Lannoy, c. 1480.*

53,54. Bureau de la Rivière (left) and Cardinal Jean de La Grange. Both statues from La Grange buttress, Cathedral of Amiens.

55. Effigy of Guillaume de Harsigny at Laon.

56. DANSE MACABRE
Fresco in the Abbey of Chaise-Dieu at Riom, 15th century.

Death with Pope, Emperor, Cardinal, King, Patriarch, Knight, Bishop, Seigneur.

Death with Priest, Poet, Abbess, Merchant, Noblewoman, Sergeant, Lay Brother.

Death with Youth, Doctor of the Sorbonne, Troubadour, Benedictine, Serf, Franciscan, Child, Mother.

57. *Lamentation of the Virgin with St. John. From the* Rohan Hours, *c. 1420.*

58. *Massacre of the prisoners at Nicopolis. From Froissart's* Chronicles, *Louis de Bruges copy, c. 1460.*

59. *Posthumous portrait of Coucy commissioned by the Celestin monastery of Villeneuve-les-Soissons two hundred years after his death.*

60. *Ruins of the* donjon *of Coucy, after the German dynamiting of 1917.*

61. *Aerial view of Coucy-le- Château today.*

Coucy had much influence with Count Guy, besides holding a lien on his property deriving from money still owed on the Soissons transaction. As *"un grand traitteur"* (an accomplished negotiator), he was chosen by both parties to evaluate the estate and arrange its sale to Louis d'Orléans. Sale of dynastic property for cash was considered something of a disgrace. If Coucy was reluctant to act in such a matter—and there is no evidence that he was—he was handsomely, almost too handsomely, compensated by Louis for his services. When he succeeded in reducing Blois' asking price of 200,000 francs for his lands in Hainault by 50,000, or 25 percent, Louis paid him back the difference. At the same time, Louis acquitted Coucy of the debt of 10,000 florins loaned to him for the Tunisian campaign, "in consideration to our said cousin of the many and great services he has rendered to us." For the entire Blois estate Louis paid 400,000 francs from his wife's dowry, becoming thereby a territorial proprietor on a level with his uncles.

Froissart, who had been in the service of Guy de Blois before the days of the empty purse, delivered himself of the stern and rather surprising judgment that "The Sire de Coucy was greatly to blame in this matter." Perhaps he meant that Coucy should not have made money out of a transaction which Froissart considered ignoble. The worshiper of a caste often upholds higher ideals for it than its members. In the ultimate irony, Coucy's own domain after his death was to follow Blois' into Orléans' hands.

Rarely if ever at home, Coucy resumed his duties as Lieutenant-General in Auvergne and Guienne in January 1392, and came north again in March to accompany the King to the great parley at Amiens. In happy omen just before the parley, a son was born to Charles and Isabeau, their fifth child, of whom the two eldest were already dead. Paris celebrated in great emotion as bells pealed and bonfires flamed in the public squares. People filled the churches to thank God for a Dauphin and afterward sang and danced in the streets, where tables loaded with wine and food were set out for them by noble ladies and wealthy bourgeois. The object of their joy was to die at the age of nine, as were four more sons before one of the puny progeny survived to become the feckless Dauphin eventually crowned as Charles VII by Joan of Arc.

Extraordinary measures were taken to ensure that no quarrels arose between French and English retinues to disrupt the parley. The Council ordered French subjects on pain of death to abstain from all insults and provocative remarks or challenges to, or even talk of, combat. No one was to go out at night without a torch; any page or varlet who provoked a quarrel in a tavern was to earn the death penalty. Four companies of 1,000 guards each were to keep watch day and night to prevent assemblies with potential for trouble. If the fire bell rang, they were not to move from their posts but leave it to the regular fire companies to answer the alarm. The English were to be received with "greatest honors," treated with utmost courtesy, and entertained free of cost. Innkeepers were not to demand money from them but submit their accounts to the royal exchequer for payment.

These precautions expressed the French desire less for peace per se than for a settlement that would open the way to the *Voie de Fait* and to crusade. On the English side, the Dukes of Lancaster and York showed a similar sentiment, but the absence of Gloucester left an ominous hole. In recognition of Coucy's influence, the English Dukes had brought his daughter Philippa with them, no doubt hoping thereby to win his support for their terms. Philippa had expressed an ardent desire to see the father she barely knew, and Coucy had much joy in the meeting. His daughter "travelled in good state, but like a widow who had enjoyed little pleasure in her marriage."

In the presence of Charles seated on his throne, the parley opened at Eastertime in the utmost ceremony and grandeur, as if to support the great burden of its outcome. Lancaster knelt three times on his approach to the throne in the ritual of homage and was welcomed by the King with affectionate words, and by Burgundy and Berry with the kiss of peace. The splendor of the Duke of Burgundy was never more marvelous. He wore black velvet embroidered on the left sleeve with a branch of 22 roses composed of sapphires and rubies surrounded with pearls. On another day he wore a crimson velvet robe embroidered on each side with a bear in silver whose collar, muzzle, and leash sparkled with jewels. The great French lords, including Coucy, each gave a banquet for the English on successive nights at which knightly courtesies were exchanged and old acquaintances renewed.

Not all the precautions, free meals, and luxurious surroundings were enough to gain a peace. The parley lasted two weeks, but both parties knew it was useless. The English demand for more than a million francs in arrears on Jean's ransom was met by the French claim for an indemnity of three million for war damages on their soil. They went so far as to scale down their demand for the return of Calais to a demand that the city and walls be razed to make the place unusable. The English refused, considering that as long as they held Calais, "they wore the key to France on their belt." The sovereignty of Aquitaine was disputed as ever. Even when the French finally offered to pay the arrears on Jean's ransom and guarantee peaceable possession if not sovereignty of Aquitaine, in return for the razing of Calais, the English held back. They were not sure they wanted peace. When Charles urged the cause of the crusade, they said, as so often before, that they had no powers to conclude definitive terms, but would report back to their King. One more of the countless peace parleys came to nothing. Once more the truce was extended for yet another year. How hard it was to end a war.

Whether from disappointment or natural causes, King Charles fell ill in the midst of the parley, suffering from high fever and transports of delirium. Removed from Amiens to the quiet surroundings of the episcopal palace at Beauvais, where he was carefully nursed, he soon recovered, and by June had resumed hunting and his other pleasures. No ill omens were attached to the sudden strange illness, although they might well have been.

Chapter 24

Danse Macabre

istory never more cruelly demonstrated the vulnerability of a nation to the person of its chief of state than in the affliction of France beginning in 1392.

The circumstances that brought on the crisis arose from a struggle for power centering on the figure of Clisson, the Constable. As the main prop of the ministerial party, he was the object of the uncles' political enmity as well as of the Duke of Brittany's undying hatred. For as long as he retained the controlling military post with access to its immense financial advantages, and remained in partnership with the Marmosets and the King's brother, the uncles saw themselves kept at a distance from power. The Duke of Brittany feared him as a rival in Breton affairs and hated him the more fiercely because he had failed to kill him when he had had the chance. In their common desire to destroy Clisson, the interests of Brittany and the King's uncles met, and they maintained clandestine contact with each other.

Serving as a link between them was a Burgundian protégé, related to both the Duchess of Burgundy and the Duke of Brittany, the same sinister Pierre de Craon who had embezzled the Duc d'Anjou's funds in the Naples campaign. Since then he had flouted a court order to reimburse Anjou's widow, and had assassinated a knight of Laon but used his influence to secure a pardon. These derelictions had not prevented his finding favor in the royal circle of pleasure seekers. He evidently possessed the charm of wickedness. However, he angered Louis d'Orléans by informing his wife—apparently from an irresistible impulse to mischief—of an extra-marital passion which Louis had confided to him. Louis had even taken Craon to visit the beautiful, if too virtuous, lady who had resisted an offer of 1,000 gold crowns for her favors. On discovering Craon's betrayal, Louis in a rage took the tale to the King, who compliantly banished the troublemaker. Craon claimed he was removed because he had tried to make Louis give up engaging in occult practices and consorting with sorcerers.

Burning with resentment, he took refuge with the Duke of Brittany, who was his cousin. In Craon the Duke found the agent for another attempt to ruin Clisson. Because Clisson was married to a niece of the Duchess d'Anjou, he automatically shared that family's mortal enmity for Craon. On this basis Craon already suspected, and the Duke of Brittany easily persuaded him, that Clisson's hand was behind his banishment—which may have been true. Clisson is said to have discovered secret correspondence between Craon and the Dukes. In any event, Craon now "breathed only for vengeance."

On the night of June 13, 1392, having returned secretly to Paris, Craon waited in ambush at a street crossing where Clisson would pass on the way to his *hôtel*. With Craon in the darkness was a party of forty armored followers, enough to ensure overwhelming odds against an opponent in civilian circumstances. When a man really intended the death of a fellow noble, chivalry's codes were surprisingly non-inhibiting. Rather than challenge his enemy to open combat, Craon preferred to strike in the dark. Judging by his record, he was a man without moral sense, but he was not alone. Montfort too had violated honor, loyalty, and every other principle of chivalry when he had kidnapped Clisson. Clisson himself was no Roland. In the lifetime of these men, under the disruptive effects of plague, brigandage, and schism, normal codes of conduct disintegrated.

Escorted by eight attendants with torches but unarmed for combat, Clisson was returning on horseback from a party given by the King at St. Pol. He was discussing with his squires a dinner he was to give next day for Coucy, Orléans, and Vienne when suddenly the torchlight fell upon a dark mass of mounted men and on the faint gleam of helmet and cuirass. The assailants charged, extinguishing Clisson's torches and crying, "*A mort! A mort!*" Craon's men did not know whom they were attacking because the identity of the victim had been kept secret. They were appalled to hear their chief shout in his excitement, as with brandished sword he urged them forward, "Clisson, you must die!"

Clisson cried out to his unknown assailant, "Who are you?"

"I am Pierre de Craon, your enemy!" replied the leader openly, for he anticipated a corpse and an overturn of government in consequence. His men, stunned to discover themselves engaged in murdering the Constable of France, were hesitant in pressing the attack, "for treason is never bold." Armed only with a dagger, Clisson desperately defended himself until, struck by many blows, he was unhorsed. He fell into the doorway of a baker's shop, forcing open the door by the weight of his fall, just as the baker, hearing the racket, appeared in time to pull him into the house. Believing they had killed him, Craon and his party hastened away. The survivors among Clisson's squires found him in the shop, slashed by sword cuts, bathed in blood, and apparently lifeless. By the time the King, aroused from bed and informed of the awful news, reached the baker's shop, Clisson had recovered consciousness.

"How goes it with you, Constable?" pleaded Charles, stricken at the sight.

"Feebly, Sire."

"Who has done this to you?" When Clisson named his assassin, Charles swore that "no deed shall ever be so expiated as this. nor so heavily punished." He called for surgeons, who, on examining the Constable's hardened body, survivor of a hundred combats, promised his recovery. Carried to his residence, Clisson was "much cheered" by a visit from Coucy, who as his brother-in-arms was the first to be informed after the King.

Orders for the capture of Craon failed because the gates of Paris, still stripped of their bars since the insurrection, could not be closed. Learning that, unbelievably, Clisson lived, Craon escaped from the city, galloped as far as Chartres and thence to Brittany. "It is diabolic," he told the Duke in explaining his failure. "I believe all the devils of Hell, to whom the Constable belongs, guarded and delivered him out of my hands, for he suffered more than sixty blows by swords or knives and I truly believed him dead."

King Charles, feeling himself attacked in the person of the state's chief defender, pursued the assassin with insatiable fury. Two of Craon's squires and a page were beheaded on capture, as was the steward of his Paris residence for failing to report his return to the capital. A canon of Chartres who had given him shelter was deprived of his benefices and condemned to perpetual abstinence in prison on bread and water. Craon's properties and revenues were confiscated to the benefit of the Royal Treasury; his residences and castles were ordered razed. The King's excited state of mind communicated itself, as royal rage will, to his deputies. Admiral de Vienne, charged with making an inventory of Craon's fortune, reportedly evicted his wife and daughter without possessions or money, in nothing but the clothes they wore—after raping the daughter, according to one report—and helped himself to the rich furnishings and valuables of their residence. Perhaps he felt that Craon's treason justified this indecency, though his conduct was widely condemned by fellow nobles. Strange excesses flowed from the attempted murder of the Constable, as if Craon's act had released a contagion of evil.

Events moved from murder to war when the Duke of Brittany, on being ordered to surrender the culprit, denied all knowledge of him and refused to concern himself in any way. Thus defied, the King called for war on the Duke. Barely recovered from his illness at Amiens, Charles appeared often distraught and disconnected in speech. His physicians advised against a campaign, but, encouraged by his brother, he insisted. Burgundy and Berry, who depended on the Duke of Brittany as their ally in the political struggle, bent every endeavor to prevent it. The heat of family partisanship was added to the conflict by the Duchess of Burgundy, who was Montfort's niece and therefore took his side and hated Clisson with venomous intensity. Burgundian influence was certainly behind the asylum given to Craon. Berry, for his part, was said to have had prior knowledge of Craon's assault.

When it was learned that Clisson's will, dictated after the attack, left a fortune of 1,700,000 francs, not counting lands, the uncles' jealous rage at finding themselves outdone in the rewards of avarice knew no bounds. Such a fortune—greater than the King's, they let it be known—could have come from no honest source. The public was ready enough to believe it, for Rivière and Mercier, too, had amassed fortunes from government service and were generally disliked as both arrogant and venal. All these strifes and rancors festered behind the unstable King as he clamored for war.

The Council approved the campaign; the uncles, left out of the decision but bound to join the King, were augmented in their hatred of the ministers. "They dreamed of nothing but how to destroy them." The King, accompanied by Bourbon and Coucy, left Paris on July 1, moving westward by slow stages as knights and their retinues came up to join the march. Charles's ill health required protracted stops, and further delay was caused by waiting for the uncles. Hoping to forestall the war, they dallied and procrastinated, putting Charles in a frenzy of impatience. Scarcely eating or drinking, he was in Council every day, harping on the insult to him through his Constable, upset at any contradictions, refusing absolutely to be swerved from punishing the Duke of Brittany. Discord, arriving with Burgundy and Berry, spread to the army, where knights disputed the rights and wrongs of the enterprise. In reply to a second demand for Craon's surrender, Montfort again denied knowing anything about him. Charles, although declared "feverish and unfit to ride" by his physicians, would wait no longer.

In the heat of mid-August the march began from Le Mans on the borders of Brittany. On a sandy road under blazing sun, the King, wearing a black velvet jacket and a hat of scarlet velvet ornamented with pearls, rode apart from the others to avoid the dust. Two pages rode behind, one carrying his helmet, the other his lance. Ahead rode the two uncles in one group, and Louis d'Orléans with Coucy and Bourbon in another. As the party passed through the forest of Mans, a rough barefoot man in a ragged smock suddenly stepped from behind a tree and seized the King's bridle, crying in a voice of doom, "Ride no further, noble King! Turn back! You are betrayed!" Charles shrank in alarm. Escorts beat the man's hand from the bridle but because he appeared no more than a poor madman did not arrest him, not even when he followed the company for half an hour crying betrayal in the King's ears.

Emerging from the forest, the riders came out on an open plain at high noon. Men and horses suffered under the sun's rays. One of the pages, dozing in the saddle, let fall the King's lance, which struck the steel helmet carried by his companion with a loud clang. The King shuddered, then, suddenly drawing his sword, spurred his horse to a charge with the cry, "Forward against the traitors! They wish to deliver me to the enemy!" Wheeling and charging, he struck at anyone within reach.

"My God," cried Burgundy, "the King is out of his mind! Hold him, someone!" No one dared try. Warding off the blows but unable to strike back against the King's person, they milled around in horror while Charles rushed wildly against this one and that until he was exhausted, panting, and drenched in sweat. Then his chamberlain, Guillaume de Martel, whom he much loved, clasped him from behind while others took his sword and, lifting him from his horse, laid him gently on the ground. He lay motionless and speechless, staring with open eyes, recognizing no one. One or more knights (the number differs in different versions) whom he had killed in his frenzy lay near him in the dust.

Bold as always, Philip of Burgundy seized authority. "We must return to Mans," he decided. "This finishes the march on Brittany." Laid in a passing oxcart, the King of France was carried back while an appalled company, some already thinking furiously of the future, rode alongside. With scarcely a sign of life but his heartbeat, Charles remained in a coma for four days during which he was thought to be on his deathbed. His physicians could offer no hope, and other doctors who were called—Burgundy's, Orléans', Bourbon's—agreed after consultation that their science was powerless.

As the awful report of the King's madness spread, rumors of sorcery and poison were on every tongue, and popular emotion so aroused that the sick chamber had to be kept open to the public. All the tears and grief attending a royal demise filled the room and "all good Frenchmen wept as for an only son, for the health of France was tied to that of her King." Sobbing clergy conducted prayers, bishops led barefoot processions carrying life-size wax figures of the King to the churches, the people heaped their offerings on relics known for healing powers, and prostrated themselves before Christ and the saints to beseech a cure.

Few believed the affliction had natural causes. Some saw it as Divine anger at the King's failure to take up arms to end the schism; others, as God's warning against that very intention; still others, as Divine punishment for heavy taxes. Most believed the cause was sorcery, the more so because a great drought that summer dried up the ponds and rivers so that cattle died of thirst, waterborne transport ceased, and merchants claimed the worst losses in twenty years.

In a morbid time, belief in conspiracy rose to the surface. Whispers circulated against the Dukes. Why had the "phantom of the forest" not been arrested and interrogated? Had he been planted by the Duke of Brittany or by the uncles to cause the King to turn back? Had the King's excess of anger caused by the Dukes' delay brought on his madness? To allay public suspicions, Burgundy held a formal inquiry at which the King's doctors testified to Charles's previous illnesses.

Coucy too had summoned his personal physician, the most venerable and learned in France. He was Guillaume de Harsigny, a native of Laon aged 92, the same age as the century. After earning his degree at the University of Paris, he had traveled widely to enlarge his knowledge, studied under Arab professors at Cairo and Italians at Salerno, and eventually returned loaded with renown to his native Picardy. Nothing in human ills was unknown to him. Under his care—or by natural process coinciding with it—the King's fever subsided and intervals of reason returned in which the poor young man, not yet 25, recognized with horror what had befallen him. Within a month Charles's physical recovery had progressed well enough for Harsigny to take him to the castle of Creil high above the river Oise, where he could enjoy "the best air in the region of Paris." The court overflowed with joy and with praise for the skills of Coucy's physician.

The first four days, when Charles had been expected to die, gave the uncles their opportunity against the Marmosets. "Now is the hour," said Berry, "when I shall pay them back in kind." On the very day of the King's attack, someone with quick perception of Fortune's Wheel warned the Marmosets to be gone. On the next day while still at Le Mans, Berry and Burgundy, claiming authority as the King's eldest relatives, although in fact Louis was closer to the crown, dismissed the entire Council, disbanded the army, and seized the reins of government. Returning to Paris within two weeks, they convened a subservient Council which duly gave the government to Philip the Bold on the ground that Louis d'Orléans was too young, and deposed the Marmosets by judicial process. Rivière and Mercier, who had been unready to abandon power in time, were arrested and imprisoned, and their lands, houses, furnishings, and fortune confiscated. A more prescient colleague, Jean de Montagu, reputed to be a natural son of Charles V, took himself and his fortune to Avignon the moment he heard of the King's attack.

The ease of the overturn is almost baffling. Only the eclipse of the King and Clisson's wounds made it possible. Without royal authority to support them, Rivière and Mercier had no independent status; no regent had been named for the six-month-old Dauphin; Louis lacked the assurance and decisiveness to act, although he might have taken control if Coucy and Bourbon and the rest of the Council had been prepared to force the issue against the Dukes. Clearly, they were not. They could not be sure of military support because the leading nobles lacked cohesion. In the uncertainty of the King's condition, no one knew which way power would jump. Above all, the Constable was *hors de combat.*

With sure instinct Coucy seems to have made his choice quickly, for on August 25 he accepted a mission along with Burgundy's chamberlain, Guy de Tremoille, to inform the Duke of Brittany that the war against him was called off. In the fate of Rivière and Mercier he played a darker role. Although he had served closely with Rivière in many joint missions over the past fifteen years, Coucy was one of a group sent to seize his former partner in his castle, to which he had fled before the order for his arrest. Rivière was said to have opened his own door to his captors. Ten years later, after her husband and Coucy were both dead, Rivière's widow claimed that Coucy had taken coffers containing silver and gold plate and tapestries from the castle, although no such charge was ever made during the lifetime of the principals.

In the case of Mercier, however, Coucy benefited openly. By way of putting him under obligation, the Dukes gave him Mercier's principal castle of Nouvion-le-Comte in the diocese of Laon with all its rents and revenues. A ruler's bestowal upon one noble of the confiscated property of another was a routine means of attaching support. Whether or not Coucy had compunctions about accepting, to have refused would have marked him as an overt opponent of the Dukes.

In prison, Rivière and Mercier daily expected torture and execution, the normal fate of those who lost power. Rivière remained stoic, but Mercier was reputed to have cried so many tears that he almost lost his eyesight. Every day people came to the Place de Grève expecting to watch the dispatch of the prisoners. "Prudent, cold and far-seeing," Burgundy did not exact the final penalty. He preferred to be circumspect while there was still a chance of the King recovering sovereignty. Charles, as he improved, pressed for the release of his former councillors, and public opinion, in love and pity for the King, swung in their favor. Now it was remembered that Rivière had always been "gentle, courteous, debonair and patient with poor people." After eighteen months in prison both were finally released and banished from court, although their property was restored, presumably including Coucy's temporary acquisition.

The dismissal of Clisson was to be Burgundy's triumph. Forcing the issue, Clisson came to see him to inquire as Constable about measures for government of the realm. Philip looked at him malevolently. "Clisson, Clisson," he said between his teeth, "you need not busy yourself with that; the kingdom will be governed without your office." Then, unable to conceal the real source of his anger, he demanded "where the Devil" Clisson had amassed so great a fortune, more than his and Berry's put together. "Get out of my sight," he exploded, "for were it not for my honor I would put out your other eye!" Clisson rode home reflectively. That night, under cover of darkness, he left his *hôtel* with two attendants by the back gate and rode to his castle of Montlhéry, just south of Paris, where he could defend himself.

Raging at his escape, Burgundy again chose Coucy as agent against his own brother-in-arms. Along with Guy de Tremoille, he was named to command a force of 300 lances including many former comrades of the Constable, who were ordered to march by five different roads and not to return without Clisson dead or alive. This does not seem to have been one of Burgundy's more intelligent moves. Naturally warned by his friends in the party, Clisson escaped to his fortress of Josselin in Brittany, where on his own ground he could withstand attack. But his flight enabled Burgundy to use him as a scapegoat. He was tried in absentia, convicted as a "false and wicked traitor," deposed as Constable, banished, and fined 100,000 marks. Louis d'Orléans refused to ratify the proceedings, but throughout the overturn he never dared openly challenge his uncles.

Once again the Constable's sword was offered to Coucy, whom Burgundy was clearly anxious to have in his camp. If the post had not appealed to him in the last days of Charles V, it had even less attraction now, nor did he wish to become the beneficiary of his friend's fall. He "refused positively" to accept it, "even if it meant that he should be forced to leave France." The implied risk did not materialize. Finding

Coucy adamant, the uncles gave the post to the young Comte d'Eu, reportedly so that he might become wealthy enough to marry Berry's daughter.

Under the care of Coucy's physician, the King seemed restored to sanity by the end of September. Escorted by Coucy, he made a pilgrimage of thanks to Notre Dame de Liesse, a little church near Laon commemorating the miracle of three crusaders from Picardy who, while captives of the Saracens, had converted the daughter of the Sultan to Christianity and given her a statue of the Virgin, upon which they were promptly transported by air, along with the princess, to their native land. Charles returned via Coucy-le-Château, where in company with the Duke of Burgundy he dined on October 4, and still escorted by Coucy worshiped at St. Denis on his way back to Paris. Under the new regime, Coucy remained a leading member of the Council, dividing his time between attendance at its sessions and his functions as Lieutenant-General of Auvergne.

To the distress of the court, the wise and ancient Harsigny, refusing all pleas and offers of riches to remain, insisted on returning to the quiet of his home at Laon. He was awarded 2,000 gold crowns and the privilege of using four horses from the royal stables free of charge whenever he might wish to revisit the court. He never did. Several months later he died, leaving a historic effigy.

Harsigny's tomb was the first of its kind in the cult of death that was a legacy of the 14th century. His marble image does not show him in the pride of life at 33, as was customary in the hope of resurrection, when the chosen were expected to rise at the same age as Jesus Christ. Rather, following his specific instructions, the effigy is the visible image of the corpse inside the coffin. The recumbent body is shown exactly as it was in death, naked, in the extreme thinness of very old age with wrinkled skin stretched over the bones, hands crossed over the genitals, no drapery or covering of any kind, a stark confession of the nothingness of mortal life.

Before leaving his royal patient, Harsigny had advised against burdening him with the responsibilities of state. "I give him back to you in good health," he had said, "but be careful not to worry or irritate him. His mind is not yet strong; little by little it will improve. Burden him with work as little as you can; pleasure and forgetfulness will be better for him than anything else." This advice perfectly suited the Dukes. Sovereign in name only, Charles returned to Paris to dally with the ladies in the gardens of St. Pol and enjoy the amusements and festivities organized every night by his wife and brother. In relief from madness, frivolity abounded and the uncles did not interfere, "for so long as the

Queen and the Duc d'Orléans danced, they were not dangerous nor even annoying."

Court purveyors and moneylenders throve, mystery plays and magicians filled every hour, sorcerers and impostors found unlimited credulity, fashions went to extremes especially in hairdressing. Young men curled their locks and trimmed their beards in two points, while the elaborate braided shells worn by the ladies over their ears grew so fantastic and enormous that they had to turn sideways when passing through a doorway. Queen Isabeau and her sister-in-law Valentina vied with each other in novelties and opulence; dresses were loaded with jewels, fringes, and fantastical emblems. In the taverns people murmured against the extravagance and license. They loved the crowned youth, who for his affability and openhandedness and easy conversation with all ranks, was called Charles le Bien-aimé (the Well-beloved), but they deplored the "foreigners" from Bavaria and Italy and blamed the uncles for allowing dissipations unbecoming to the King of France.

Thrust to the head of the court as young boys not yet in their teens, Charles and Louis had none of their father's care for the dignity of the crown; they had neither discipline nor sense of decorum. Deprived of major responsibility, they made up for it in play, and adults' play requires constant new excesses to be entertaining.

On the night when these culminated in horror, Coucy was not present because he was in Savoy, using his negotiating talents to settle a tremendous family quarrel which had split the ruling house and all related noble families and created a crisis of hostility that threatened to block passage for the march on Rome. The issue, involving ducal families, dower rights, and of course property, derived from the fact that the Red Count, Amadeus VII, who had recently died at the age of 31, had left the guardianship of his son to his mother, a sister of the Duc de Bourbon, instead of to his wife, a daughter of the Duc de Berry. It was to take three months before Coucy and Guy de Tremoille succeeded in negotiating a treaty that brought the overblown fracas to an end and left the rival Countesses in "peaceable accord with their subjects."

On the Tuesday before Candlemas Day (January 28, 1393), four days after Coucy had left Paris, the Queen gave a masquerade to celebrate the wedding of a favorite lady-in-waiting who, twice widowed, was now being married for the third time. A woman's re-marriage, according to certain traditions, was considered an occasion for mockery and often celebrated by a charivari for the newlyweds with all sorts of license, disguises, disorders, and loud blaring of discordant music and clanging of cymbals outside the bridal chamber. Although this was a usage "contrary to all decency," says the censorious Monk of St. Denis, King Charles had let himself be persuaded by dissolute friends to join in such a charade.

Six young men including the King and Yvain, bastard son of the Count of Foix, disguised themselves as "wood savages," in costumes of linen cloth sewn onto their bodies and soaked in resinous wax or pitch to hold a covering of frazzled hemp, "so that they appeared shaggy and hairy from head to foot." Face masks entirely concealed their identity. Aware of the risk they ran in torch-filled halls, they forbade anyone carrying a torch to enter during the dance. Plainly, an element of Russian roulette was involved, the tempting of death that has repeatedly been the excitement of highborn and decadent youth. Certain ways of behavior vary little across the centuries. Plainly, too, there was an element of cruelty in involving as one of the actors a man thinly separated from madness.

The deviser of the affair, "cruelest and most insolent of men," was one Huguet de Guisay, favored in the royal circle for his outrageous schemes. He was a man of "wicked life" who "corrupted and schooled youth in debaucheries," and held commoners and the poor in hatred and contempt. He called them dogs, and with blows of sword and whip took pleasure in forcing them to imitate barking. If a servant displeased him, he would force the man to lie on the ground and, standing on his back, would kick him with spurs, crying, "Bark, dog!" in response to his cries of pain.

In their Dance of the Savages, the masqueraders capered before the revelers, imitating the howls of wolves and making obscene gestures while the guests tried to discover their identity. Charles was teasing and gesticulating before the fifteen-year-old Duchesse de Berry when Louis d'Orléans and Philippe de Bar, arriving from dissipations elsewhere, entered the hall accompanied by torches despite the ban. Whether to discover who the dancers were, or deliberately courting danger—accounts of the episode differ—Louis held up a torch over the capering monsters. A spark fell, a flame flickered up a leg, first one dancer was afire, then another. The Queen, who alone knew that Charles was among the group, shrieked and fainted. The Duchesse de Berry, who had recognized the King, threw her skirt over him to protect him from the sparks, thus saving his life. The room filled with the guests' sobs and cries of horror and the tortured screams of the burning men. Guests who tried to stifle the flames and tear the costumes from the writhing victims were badly burned. Except for the King, only the Sire de Nantouillet, who flung himself into a large wine-cooler filled with water, escaped. The Count de Joigny was burned to death on the spot, Yvain de Foix and Aimery Poitiers died after two days of painful suffering. Huguet de Guisay lived for three days in agony, cursing and insulting his fellow dancers, the dead and the living, until his last hour. When his coffin was carried through the streets, the common people greeted it with cries of "Bark, dog!"

This ghastly affair, coming so soon after the King's madness, was like an exclamation point to the malign succession of events that had tormented the century. Charles's narrow escape threw Paris into a "great commotion," and anger swept the citizens at the appalling frivolity which had so casually endangered the life and honor of the King. Had he died, they said, the people would have massacred the uncles and all the court; "not one of them would have escaped death, nor any knight found in Paris." Alarmed at these dangerous sentiments with their echo of the Maillotins' rebellion barely ten years past, the uncles prevailed on the King to ride in solemn procession to Notre Dame to appease the people. Behind Charles on horseback, his uncles and brother followed barefoot as penitents. As the involuntary agent of the tragedy, Louis was widely reproached for his dissolute habits. In expiation he built a chapel for the Célestins with marvelous stained glass and rich altar furnishings and an endowment for perpetual prayers. He paid for it with revenues given him by the King from Craon's confiscated property, leaving it a question as to whose soul was absolved.

The fatal masquerade came to be called the *Bal des Ardents*—Dance of the Burning Ones—but it could as well have been called the *Danse Macabre*, after a new kind of processional play on the theme of death that had lately come into vogue. Of uncertain origin and meaning, the name Macabre first appeared in writing in a poem of 1376 by Anjou's chancellor, Jean le Fèvre, containing the line, "*Je fis de Macabré le danse* (I do the Danse Macabre). It may have derived from an older *Danse Machabreus*, meaning "of the Maccabees," or from similarity to the Hebrew word for grave-diggers and the fact that Jews worked as grave-diggers in medieval France. The dance itself probably developed under the influence of recurring plague, as a street performance to illustrate sermons on the submission of all alike to Death the Leveler. In murals illustrating the dance at the Church of the Innocents in Paris, fifteen pairs of figures, clerical and lay, from pope and emperor down the scale to monk and peasant, friar and child, make up the procession.

"Advance, see yourselves in us," they say in the accompanying verses, "dead, naked, rotten and stinking. So will you be. . . . To live without thinking of this risks damnation. . . . Power, honor, riches are naught; at the hour of death only good works count. . . . Everyone should think at least once a day of his loathsome end," to remind him to do good deeds and go to mass if he wishes to be redeemed and escape "the dreadful pain of hell without end which is unspeakable."

Each figure speaks his piece: the constable knows that Death carries off the bravest, even Charlemagne; the knight, once loved by the ladies, knows that he will make them dance no more; the plump abbot, that "the fattest rots first"; the astrologer, that his knowledge cannot save him; the peasant who has lived all his days in care and toil and often wished for death, now when the hour has come would much rather be digging in the vineyards "even in rain and wind." The point is made over and over, that here is you and you and you. The cadaverous figure who leads the procession is not Death but the Dead One. "It is yourself," says the inscription under the murals of the dance at La Chaise-Dieu in Auvergne.

The cult of death was to reach its height in the 15th century, but its source was in the 14th. When death was to be met any day around any corner, it might have been expected to become banal; instead it exerted a ghoulish fascination. Emphasis was on worms and putrefaction and gruesome physical details. Where formerly the dominant idea of death was the spiritual journey of the soul, now the rotting of the body seemed more significant. Effigies of earlier centuries were serene, with hands joined in prayer and eyes open, anticipating eternal life. Now, following Harsigny's example, great prelates often had themselves shown as cadavers in realistic detail. To accomplish this, death masks and molds of bodily parts were made of wax, incidentally promoting portraiture and a new recognition of individual traits. The message of the effigies was that of the Danse Macabre. Over the scrawny, undraped corpse of Cardinal Jean de La Grange, who was to die in Avignon in 1402, the inscription asks observers, "So, miserable one, what cause for pride?"

The cult of the lugubrious in coming decades made the cemetery of the Innocents at Paris, with the Danse Macabre painted on its walls, the most desirable burial place and popular meeting place in Paris. Charnel houses built into the 48 arches of the cloister were donated by rich bourgeois and nobles—among them Boucicaut and Berry—to hold their remains. Because twenty parishes had the right of burial at the Innocents, the old dead had to be continually disinterred and their tombstones sold to make room for the new. Skulls and bones piled up under the cloister arches were an attraction for the curious, and bleak proof of ultimate leveling. Shops of all kinds found room in and around the cloister; prostitutes solicited there, alchemists found a market place, gallants made it a rendezvous, dogs wandered in and out. Parisians came to tour the charnel houses, watch burials and disinterments, gaze at the murals, and read the verses. They listened to daylong sermons and shuddered as the Dead One blowing his horn entered from the Rue St. Denis leading his procession of awful dancers.

Art followed the lugubrious. The crown of thorns, rarely pictured before, became a realistic instrument of pain drawing blood in the paintings of the second half of the century. The Virgin acquired seven sorrows, ranging from the flight into Egypt to the Pietà—the limp dead body of her son lying across her knees. Claus Sluter, sculptor to the Duke of Burgundy, made the first known Pietà in France in 1390 for the convent of Champmol at Dijon. At the same time, the playful smiling faces of the so-called Beautiful Madonnas with their gentle draperies and happy infants appear amid the gloom. Secular painting is gay and exquisite; Death never disturbs those lyrical picnics beneath enchanted towers.

The Black Death returned for the fourth time in 1388–90. Earlier recurrences had affected chiefly children who had not acquired immunity, but in the fourth round a new adult generation fell under the swift contagion. By this time Europe's population was reduced to between 40 and 50 percent of what it had been when the century opened, and it was to fall even lower by mid-15th century. People of the time rarely mention this startling diminution of their world, although it was certainly visible to them in reduced trade, in narrowed areas of cultivation, in abbeys and churches abandoned or unable to maintain services for lack of revenue, in urban districts destroyed in war and left unrepaired after sixty years.

On the other hand, it may be that when people were fewer they ate better, and proportionately more money circulated. Contradictory conditions are always present. Evidence of growing business exists alongside that of lowered trade. An Italian merchant who died in 1410 left 100,000 documents of correspondence with agents in Italy, France, Spain, England, and Tunisia. The merchant class had more money at its command than before, and its expenditures encouraged arts, comforts, and technological advance. The 14th century was not arid. The tapestry workshops of Arras, Brussels, and the famous Nicolas Bataille of Paris produced wonders which robbed stained glass of its primacy in decorative art. Mariners' maps reached new efficiency, allowing sea monsters to disappear from the lower corner in favor of accurate coastlines and navigational aids. Bourgeois money created a new audience for writers and poets and encouraged literature through the buying of books. Several thousand scribes were employed turning out copies to meet the demand of the 25 booksellers and *stationarii* of Paris. The flamboyant in architecture, with its lavish multitude of attenuated pinnacles, canopied niches, and lacy buttresses, expressed not only a technical exuberance but a denial, even a defiance, of decline. How to reconcile with pessimism the Milan Cathedral, that fantastic mountain of filigree in stone begun in the last quarter of the century?

Psychological effects are clearer than the physical. Never was so much written about the *miseria* of human life, and the sense of dwindling numbers, even if unmentioned, promoted pessimism about human fate. "What schal befalle hiereafter, God wot," wrote John Gower in England in 1393,

> —for now upon this tyde
> men se the world on every syde
> In sondry wyse so dyversed
> That it welnyh stant all reversed.

For men of affairs no less than poets, the insecurity of the time allowed little confidence in the future. The letters of Francesco Datini, merchant of Prato, show him living in daily dread of war, pestilence, famine, and insurrection, believing neither in the stability of government nor in the honesty of colleagues. "The earth and the sea are full of robbers," he wrote to one of his partners, "and the great part of mankind is evilly disposed."

Gerson believed he lived in the senility of the world when society, like some delirious old man, suffered from fantasies and illusions. He, like others, felt the time was at hand for the coming of Anti-Christ and the end of the world—to be followed by a better one. In popular expectation, Apocalypse would bring the return of a great emperor—a second Charlemagne, a third Frederick, an imperial messiah—who, coupled with an angelic pope, would reform the Church, renew society, and save Christendom. Churchmen and moralists in apocalyptic mood stressed more than ever the vanity of worldly things—though without visibly diminishing anyone's desire for, and pride in, possessions.

A pessimistic view of man's fate was the duty of the clergy in order to prove the need of salvation. It was by no means new to the 14th century. If Cardinal d'Ailly thought the time of Anti-Christ was at hand, so had Thomas Aquinas a hundred years before. If the corruption of the Church dismayed the devout, it had done so no less in the year 1040 when a monk of Cluny wrote, "For whensoever religion hath failed among the pontiffs . . . what can we think but that the whole human race, root and branch, is sliding willingly down again into the gulf of primaeval chaos?" If in a waning period Mézières' favorite dictum was "The things of this fleeting world go ever from bad to worse," he was matched by Roger Bacon, who had asserted in 1271, at the height of a dynamic period, "More sins reign in these days than in any past age . . . justice perisheth, all peace is broken."

The sentiments were not new, but in the 14th century they were more pervasive and more disparaging of the human kind. "Time past had virtue and righteousness, but today reigns only vice," is Deschamps' lament. How may safe-conducts be trusted? asks Christine de Pisan, discussing the failures of chivalry, "seeing the little truth and fidelity that this day runneth through all the world." Elsewhere she writes, "All good customs fail and virtues are held at discount. Learning which once governed is now of no account." Her complaint had some justification, for even the University had taken to selling degrees in theology to candidates unwilling to undertake its long and difficult studies or fearful of failing the examination. License to grant the degree was extended to other universities, even to towns which had no university, giving rise to the sarcastic saying, "Why not [a degree] from a pigsty?" Denouncing the age for decadence was in fashion, but the decadence was felt as real, and the sense of a moral decline from some better day in the past was insistent. The poets wrote for the very circles they denounced and they must have touched some responsive chord. Deschamps—who never left off scolding—was made chamberlain to Louis d'Orléans in 1382.

All ranks of life shared in the blame. Deeply shaken by the Peasants' Revolt, Gower wrote a jeremiad on the corruptions of the age called *Vox Clamantis*, in which he unfolds a "manifold pestilence of vices" among poor as well as rich. The unknown author of another indictment entitled it "Vices of the Different Orders of Society," and found all equally at fault: the Church is sunk in schism and simony, clergy and monks are in darkness, kings, nobles, and knights given over to indulgence and rapine, merchants to usury and fraud; law is a creature of bribery; the commons are plunged in ignorance and oppressed by robbers and murderers.

Mankind was at one of history's ebbs. At mid-century the Black Death had raised the question of God's hostility to man, and events since then had offered little reassurance. To contemporaries the *miseria* of the time reflected sin, and, indeed, sin in the form of greed and inhumanity abounded. On the downward slope of the Middle Ages man had lost confidence in his capacity to construct a good society.

The yearning for peace and for an end to the schism was widely voiced. A notary of Cahors said at this time that in all 36 years of his life he had never known his diocese without war. Thoughtful observers, conscious of social damage, called for peace as the only hope of reform, of re-uniting the Church, and of resisting the Turks, who had reached the Danube. In his *Dream of the Old Pilgrim*, written in 1389 to persuade Charles VI and Richard II to make peace, Mézières draws a pathetic and dramatic picture of an old woman in torn clothes, with disheveled gray hair, leaning on a cane and carrying a little book gnawed by rats. She was called Devotion, but is now called Despair because dwellers of her kingdom are in slavery to Mohammed, Christian trade is endangered, the eastern ramparts of Christendom menaced by enemies of the Faith.

"*Veniat Pax!*," the cry of Gerson's famous sermon of fifteen years later, was already sounding in people's minds. Few could tell what the war was fought for. In England, Gower thought it no longer a just war but one prolonged by "greedy lords" for gain. Let it be over, he cried, "so that the world may stand appeased." French peasants may be heard, if Deschamps is a good reporter, discussing the war as they reap. "It has gone on long enough," says Robin, "I know no one who does not fear it. Surely the whole thing is not worth a scallion."

"Nevertheless," replies hunchback Henry, sadly wise,

> "Each will have to take up his shield,
> For we'll have no peace till they give back Calais."

That is the refrain of each stanza and that was the sticking point. Anxious as they might be for an end to the state of war, the rulers of France were not prepared to conclude a permanent peace that left the open gate of Calais in English hands.

For the Duke of Burgundy, peace was a pressing necessity in order to restore the commerce between Flanders and England. It could only have been with his approval that a holy man called Robert the Hermit appeared at court, sponsored by the King's chamberlain, Guillaume Martel, to bring word that peace was Heaven's command. When returning from Palestine, the Hermit said, a voice had spoken to him out of a terrible storm at sea, telling him that he would survive the peril and that on reaching land he must go to the King and tell him to make peace with England, and warn that all who opposed it would pay dearly. Peace had its opponents as well as advocates.

The most important advocate—and most significant change in the situation—was the King of England. As autocratic as his father, but no soldier, Richard II wanted to end the war in order to reduce the power of the barons and promote a more absolute monarchy. His wish coincided with that of the Duke of Lancaster, who, having established his daughters as Queens of Castile and Portugal, wanted peace with France to protect their interests. "Let my brother Gloucester go make war on Sultan Bajazet, who is menacing Christendom on the frontiers of Hungary," he said; that was the proper sphere for those anxious to fight.

Through the joint efforts of Lancaster and Burgundy, parley was resumed in May 1393 at Leulinghen, a war-torn village on the banks of the Somme near Abbeville. For lack of housing, the delegates—Burgundy and Berry for France, Lancaster, Gloucester, and the Archbishop of York for England—and their retinues lived in tents, among which Philip of Burgundy's was naturally the focus of all eyes. It was made of painted canvas in the form of a castle with turrets and crenellated walls and a portcullis guarding the entrance beween two towers of wood. The main hall inside gave onto many separate apartments divided by little streets.

King Charles was theoretically if not actively present, housed in a nearby Benedictine abbey with a fine enclosed garden on the banks of the beautiful river. With his mind fixed on the adventure of crusade, the King of France, like the King of England, was ready to close a struggle begun before either of them had been born. Meetings of the parley were held in a chapel with a thatched roof and walls hung with tapestries depicting ancient battles to conceal the ruined murals behind. When Lancaster remarked that the delegates should not be looking at scenes of war when treating of peace, the tapestries were hurriedly removed and replaced by scenes of the last days of Christ. As senior uncles, Berry and Lancaster sat on elevated chairs with Burgundy and Gloucester next to them, and counts, prelates, knights, learned lawyers, and clerks ranged along the walls. Among the delegates moved a royal visitor, Leon V de Lusignan, called King of Armenia although in fact all that remained of his realm was Cyprus. Having lost that too to the Turks, he was a fervent voice importuning both the French Dukes and the English for a crusade.

The schism became an issue when Pope Clement sent the noble

Spanish Cardinal Pedro de Luna, well supplied with gold and magnificent gifts, to urge the legitimacy of the Avignonese papacy on the English. Angrily Lancaster said to him, "It is you, Cardinals of Avignon, who gave [the schism] birth, you who sustain it, you who augment it every day. Woe to you!" Burgundy did not argue the issue. He offered to ignore the schism in order to move the parley toward a treaty, leaving it to the University to work out the means of re-uniting the Church.

When it came to the French demand for the razing of Calais and the English demand for fulfillment of all the terms of the Treaty of Brétigny, the parties were as far apart as ever. Calais was "the last town we would ever give up," the English said, while the French insisted that territories which had resolutely refused to give their allegiance to England could not be forcibly transferred. At this impasse each side discreetly dropped pursuit of its major demand and moved to take up smaller issues one by one.

Dour and suspicious, Gloucester resisted every proposal. He complained that the French used ambiguous language, filled with "subtle cloaked words of double understanding" which they turned and twisted to their advantage—such words as Englishmen did not use, "for their speech and intent is plain." Already the stereotype of the crafty Frenchman and bluff Englishman was operating. At Gloucester's insistence, the English required that all proposals be reduced to writing so that they could carefully examine any wording which they found obscure or susceptible of two constructions. Then they would send their clerks to learn how the French understood it, and afterward require it to be either amended or removed, thereby lengthening procedures tediously.

Here was a real cause of difficulty in peace-making. Although English lords were French-speaking, the language was acquired, not native, and they did not feel secure in it. So great a noble as the first Duke of Lancaster, who wrote the *Livre des sainctes médecines*, says of his work, "If the French is not good I should be excused, because I am English and not well versed in French." Gloucester made the language problem an excuse for dragging his heels and delaying agreement, but mistrust of the French was real. Ever since Charles V's manipulation of the clauses of the Treaty of Brétigny, the English had approached—and balked at—settlements in fear of being gulled.

To influence Gloucester by his divine mission and eloquence, Robert the Hermit was summoned to the conference by Burgundy. In passionate words the holy man begged the Duke, "For the love of

God, do not longer oppose the peace." While the war of English and French tore Christianity apart, Bajazet and his Turks advanced. The duty of Christians, he pleaded, was to unite against the infidel.

"Ha, Robert," replied Gloucester, "I wish not to prevent a peace, but you Frenchmen use so many colored words beyond our understanding that, when you will, you make them signify war or peace as you shall choose . . . dissembling always until you have gained your end." Nevertheless, Gloucester had to subdue his intransigence in deference to the wishes of the royal nephew he despised. Short of an agreement on Calais, permanent peace was still elusive, but some progress was made in that the truce was extended for four years, during which various disputed territories were to revert to either side, clearing the way for final settlement.

In June, while the last clauses were being argued, madness again engulfed the King of France. Like the illness at Amiens foreshadowing his first attack, the second seizure coincided with a peace parley. Perhaps impatience at the long-drawn-out proceedings was a disturbing factor. This time the insanity returned more seriously than before and lasted for a longer period of eight months. For the rest of his life, which was not to end until 1422, thirty years after the first attack, Charles was intermittently mad, with remissions just often enough to preclude any stable government and to exacerbate the power struggle around a half-empty throne. In these thirty years the vicious contest between the factions of Orléans and Burgundy and the successors of each was to bring back the English and reduce France to a state as shattered and helpless as in the aftermath of Poitiers.

In the fit of 1393 the King's spirit "was covered by such heavy shadows" that he could not remember who or what he was. He did not know he was King, that he was married, that he had children, or that his name was Charles. He displayed two pronounced aversions: for the fleur-de-lys entwined with his own name or initials in the royal coat-of-arms, which he tried to deface in rage wherever he saw it, and for his wife, from whom he fled in terror. If she approached him, he would cry, "Who is that woman the sight of whom torments me? Find out what she wants and free me from her demands if you can, that she may follow me no more." When he saw the arms of Bavaria, he danced in front of them, making rude gestures. He failed to recognize his children although he knew his brother, uncles, councillors, and servants, and remembered the names of those long dead. Only his brother's neglected wife, sad Valentina, for whom he asked constantly, calling her his "dear sister," could soothe him. This preference naturally gave rise to rumors, fostered by the Burgundian faction, that Valentina had bewitched him by subtle poison. Given credence by the record of Visconti crimes and the Italian reputation for poisoning, the whisperers charged that Valentina was ambitious for greater place, having been told by her notorious father to make herself Queen of France.

Madness was familiar in the Middle Ages in all its varieties. William of Hainault-Bavaria, a nephew of Queen Philippa of England, "tall, young, strong, dark and lively," had been a raving maniac confined in a castle for thirty years, most of the time with both hands and feet tied. Sufferers from lesser derangement were generally not confined but moved among their neighbors like the deformed, the spastic, the scrofulous, and other misfits, and joined in the pilgrimages to Rocamadour in search of a cure. Madness as often as not was seen as curable and understood as a natural phenomenon caused by mental or emotional stress. Rest and sleep were prescribed, as well as bleeding, baths, ointments, potions made from metal, and happiness. Equally, it was seen as an affliction by God or the Devil to be treated by exorcism or by shaving a cross in the hair of the victim's head or tying him to the rood screen in church so that his condition might be improved by hearing mass.

No physician or treatment helped Charles VI in his later seizures. An unkempt, evil-eyed charlatan and pseudo-mystic named Arnaut Guilhem was allowed to treat Charles on his claim of possessing a book given by God to Adam by means of which man could overcome all affliction resulting from original sin. A prototype Rasputin who had gained the confidence of the Queen and courtiers, he insisted that the King's malady was caused by sorcery, but, failing himself to summon superior forces, was eventually ousted. Other quacks and remedies of all kinds were tried to no avail. Even doctors of the University called for discovery and punishment of the "sorcerers." On one occasion two Augustinian friars, after gaining no results from magic incantations and a liquid made from powdered pearls, proposed to cut incisions in the King's head. When this was disallowed, the friars accused the King's barber and the Duc d'Orléans' concierge of sorcery and, when they were acquitted, rashly transferred the accusation against Orléans himself. In consequence, the friars were brought to trial and torture, confessed themselves liars, sorcerers, and idolators in league with the Devil, and, on being divested of clerical status, were handed over to the secular arm and executed.

The obsession with sorcery in Charles's case reflected a rising belief in the occult and demonic. Times of anxiety nourish belief in conspiracies of evil, which in the 14th century were seen as the work of persons or groups with access to diabolical aid. Hence the rising specter of the witch. By the 1390s witchcraft had been officially recognized by the Inquisition as equivalent to heresy. The Church was on the defensive, torn apart by the schism, challenged in authority and doctrine by aggressive movements of dissent, beset by cries for reform. Like the ordinary man, it felt surrounded by malevolent forces, of which sorcerers and witches were seen as the agents carrying out the will of the Evil One. It was during this time, in 1398, that theologians of the University of Paris held the solemn conclave which declared the black arts to be infecting society with renewed vigor.

The poor mad King was a victim of these beliefs. "In the name of Jesus Christ," he cried, weeping in his agony, "if there is any one of you who is an accomplice in this evil I suffer, I beg him to torture me no longer but let me die!" After this piteous outburst, the government, in the hope of appeasing the anger of Heaven, passed an ordinance providing severe penalties for blasphemers and permitting confessors to attend prisoners condemned to die. Further, the Porte de l'Enfer (Gate of Hell) was renamed the Porte St. Michel.

In later years the King's seizures came and went unpredictably. In one year, 1399, he suffered six attacks, each more serious than the last until he was cowering in a corner believing himself made of glass or roaming the corridors howling like a wolf. In his intervals of sanity Charles wished to resume the function of kingship, though it had to be in mainly ceremonial capacity. At these times he is said to have resumed marital relations with Isabeau, who gave birth to four more children between 1395 and 1401—in itself no proof of paternity.

Frivolous and sensuous, still an alien with a thick German accent, humiliated by her husband's mad aversion, Isabeau abandoned Charles to his valets and to a girl she supplied to fill her place, a horse-dealer's daughter named Odette de Champdivers, who resembled her and was called by the public "the little Queen." The Queen herself turned to frantic pleasures and to adultery combined with political intrigue and a passionate pursuit of money. Insecure in France, she devoted herself to amassing a personal fortune and promoting the enrichment and interests of her Bavarian family. She extracted from Charles, lucid or not, assignments in her own and her children's names of land, revenues, residences, and separate household accounts. She acquired coffers of treasure and jewels which she stored in a variety of vaults. Her sway at court grew ever more extravagant and hectic, the ladies' dresses more low-necked, the amours more scandalous, the festivities more extreme. The Queen established a Court of Love at which both sexes took the parts of advocates and judges and discussed, according to a scornful contemporary, "in this ridiculous tribunal the most ridiculous questions."

Court life can produce ennui and disgust even in a Queen. In nostalgia for the bucolic, 400 years before Marie Antoinette, Isabeau built a *Hôtel des Bergères* (House of the Shepherds) at her property of St. Ouen, complete with gardens and fields, barn, stable, sheepfold, and dovecote, where she played at farming and took care of chickens and livestock. The King, as time went on, was rumored to be neglected to the point of penury, living unclean and even hungry in apartments where the paper windowpanes were torn and pigeons entered to leave their droppings. During one return of sanity he arrested the Queen's chamberlain and current paramour, had him imprisoned in chains, questioned under torture, and afterward secretly drowned in the Seine.

In the political struggle Isabeau attached herself where power lay. When Louis d'Orléans was named Regent, she joined him against Burgundy and was generally supposed to have become his mistress. When he was assassinated by Burgundy's son and successor, John the Fearless, she changed sides and moved into the camp and bed of Louis' murderer. In the vacuum created by a living but helpless King, France floundered, and the Queen, lacking any capacity to cope, became the tool of the ruthless forces—Burgundy and England—which moved into the vacuum. Hard-pressed in Paris, separated geographically and politically from the Dauphin, unable to mobilize support, she finally agreed to the infamous treaty which named the King of England heir to the throne of France in place of her own son. In the end, obese and depraved, she outlived her husband by fifteen years and was eventually to find an all too imaginative biographer in the Marquis de Sade.

Looking back from a perspective of some 200 years, the Duc de Sully, Henri IV's chief minister, characterized the reign of Charles VI as "pregnant with sinister events . . . the grave of good laws and good morals in France."

Chapter 25

Lost Opportunity

While the peace parley was meeting at Leulinghen in May-June 1393, Coucy was conferring with Pope Clement in Avignon, where he had gone after settling the Savoyard quarrel. His mission was the start of a major thrust over the next two years to install Clement in Rome and the French in the Papal States, transformed into a Kingdom of Adria. Both efforts turned upon the cooperation of Gian Galeazzo Visconti, whose concern in the venture was not so much the fate of the papacy as the expansion of Milan. Although personally religious, he seems to have had no strong feelings about one Pope or another, nor about the schism except to use it in his own interests. His object was to break the power of Florence and Bologna by drawing France into Italy in alliance with Milan.

Introspective, intelligent, rich, and melancholy, Gian Galeazzo was the master of *realpolitik* in Italy. His grasp had reached across the north, absorbing Verona, Padua, Mantua, and Ferrara, and probed down into Tuscany and the Papal States. He may have been aiming at a Kingdom of Lombardy, perhaps even of a united Italy, or he may have been playing the game for power's sake. In the politics of the schism, he ran a tortuous course between his Milanese subjects, who were loyal to the Roman Pope, and partnership with France, which meant opting for Clement. How he intended to sail through these straits was not clear. It was he, however, who had revived the idea that France should resume pursuit of the Kingdom of Adria, with his son-in-law Louis of Orléans as beneficiary. This scheme—which was now the object of Coucy's mission—had been argued with fervor and finesse by Visconti's seventy-year-old ambassador in Paris, Niccolo Spinelli, one of the ablest diplomats of the day. The Papal States, Spinelli argued, had earned nothing but hatred for the Holy See. In the thousand years since they had been given to the papacy, the most violent wars had been waged on their account, "yet the priests neither possess them in peace nor ever will be able to possess them." It would be better that they should renounce temporal lordship entirely "as a burden not only for themselves but for all Christians, especially Italians."

The French needed no persuasion to assume the burden, but they wanted the kingdom officially bestowed on Louis as a papal fief before they attempted its physical conquest. The Pope, however, wanted to have the Papal States in hand before he gave them away. Coucy, as the supreme persuader and the Frenchman best acquainted with the labyrinth of Italian politics, was charged with the task of convincing Clement to make the commitment in advance of conquest. He was accompanied on the mission by the Bishop of Noyon, a fellow member of the Royal Council known for his oratorical talents, and by the King's secretary, Jean de Sains, to keep the record. In "eloquent discourse," Coucy and the Bishop told the Pope that, failing a miracle, only the intervention of France could end the schism; alone Clement could do nothing. By enfeoffing Louis with the Kingdom of Adria, the Pope would regain a firm annual income from the patrimony, which had never been under papal control since the removal to Avignon. The King of France, the envoys said, recommended his brother as the person best fitted to undertake the conquest because "he is young and can work hard" and will have the aid of the Lord of Milan.

Clement balked on the grounds that he did not want to be known as the "liquidator of the papal heritage." That had not bothered him ten years before when he had given the Bull of Enfeoffment to the Duc d'Anjou, but he was no longer so sure of French capacity. Three French cardinals were called in for advice, including Jean de La Grange, Cardinal of Amiens, he who had once frightened Charles VI by his supposed intercourse with a familiar demon. He wanted some hard answers: how much money, how many men would France commit to the campaign, and how long would they be maintained in Italy? He wanted a promise of 2,000 men-at-arms led by substantial captains and nobles and supported by 600,000 francs a year for three years. The embarrassed envoys could not reply; their instructions of no less than seventeen "items" had contained nothing about military specifics. Cardinal de La Grange suggested smoothly that the Duc d'Orléans might begin his campaign and be enfeoffed with what he conquered as he progressed. Although they stayed for six weeks, Coucy and the Bishop could obtain no more than Clement's promise to send his own envoys to Paris for further discussion.

In France, the failure to conclude peace and the renewal of the King's madness—intensifying the struggle between Burgundy and Orléans—weakened the impetus for the Way of Force. The French were not prepared to move into Italy until they had settled with England. Indeed, when the English got wind of French plans, they conveyed a warning that they would break the truce if France took up arms against the Roman Pope. Mistrusting Gloucester's war party, the French sent heralds through the realm to order strengthening of defenses and repair of crumbling walls. In a renewed effort to train archers, an ordinance was issued prohibiting games. Tennis, which the common people were adopting in imitation of the nobles, and *soules*, a form of field hockey popular with the bourgeois and seldom played without broken bones, as well as dice and cards, were banned in the hope of encouraging practice in archery and the crossbow. This was the same effort Charles V had made in 1368 and it shows that the rulers were acutely conscious of the failure of French archery.

Skills were not lacking; the trouble was that French tactics did not allow archery an essential place. Combined action of archers and knights was not adopted; crossbow companies were hired and barely used. The reason was clearly a mixture of contempt for the commoner and fear for chivalry's primacy in battle. By 1393 the added fear of insurrection caused the new ordinance to have a short life. After a period during which practice with the bow and crossbow became very popular, the nobles insisted that the ban on games be revoked, fearing that the common people would gain too effective a weapon against the noble estate. They were caught in that common irony of human endeavor when one self-interest cancels out another.

Conflicting pressures were rising around the *Voie de Fait*. The Florentines sent an imposing mission of sixteen envoys to Paris to plead against a French alliance with Gian Galeazzo. They found an ally in the Duke of Burgundy, who, because of his Flemish subjects, had never been a strong partisan of Clement and was certainly not prepared to help him to Rome if it meant advancing Louis to be King of Adria as well as Regent. The Duke in turn found an ally—although he despised her—in Queen Isabeau, who would have supped with the Devil to harm Gian Galeazzo.

Publicly, the strongest influence against the *Voie de Fait* was that of the University, stronghold of the intellectual clerical establishment. Clerics of the University had never been happy with the Babylon of Avignon. Its consequences in simony and corruption and increasing materialism, in loss of prestige, in rise of protest and movements of dissent among Lollards and mystics, in nationalism stimulated by the French attempt to dominate the papacy and sharpened by rival states taking opposite sides in the schism, had brought the Church to low esteem. Historically, the breaking-up of the old unity of the Faith and the rise of nationalism were advanced, but not caused, by the schism. On the river of history, universality lay behind and break-up ahead, but men see what is immediately at hand and what they saw at the close of the 14th century was the schism's damage to society and a desperate need to re-unite the Church.

The faculty of theology was now openly advocating the Way of Cession despite the edict banning discussion of the subject. Gerson, in oral defense of his thesis on "Spiritual Jurisdiction" for a degree in theology in 1392, provided the doctrinal basis for mutual abdication of the popes. "If it is not profitable for the common good that authority should be retained, it ought to be relinquished," he argued, and boldly asserted that to retain authority in such case was mortal sin. Further, anyone who did not actively aid in ending the schism was morally guilty of prolonging it. This was a pointed reference to clerics willing enough to live with two papacies because of the increased number of benefices the situation provided. Gerson's public statement in Paris was a signal of the growing pressure, emphasized by Chancellor d'Ailly's presence in the chair. It attested also to Burgundy's protection, without which Gerson could never have dared to be so forthright.

In opposition, the drive for Italy was suddenly galvanized by a new offer made to Louis d'Orléans. He was asked to accept the sovereignty of Genoa, where domestic strife had reached that baleful point at which the foreigner is invited in. Whether the scheme was inspired by Gian Galeazzo, who wanted Genoa as a port for Milan, is unknown, but he clearly favored it in the belief that under his son-in-law's sovereignty, Genoa would be at his disposal. For Louis it was an extraordinary stroke of fortune, a foothold in the sun more achievable than his cousin Anjou's still unrealized claim to Naples, and a major step on the way to Adria.

His first act was to send Coucy again to Avignon accompanied by his personal representative, Jean de Trie, in addition to the Bishop of Noyon and the King's secretary as before. They were to ask again for the enfeoffment of Adria while postponing its conquest and the march on Rome for three or four years. The delay was intended to give Louis time to succeed in Genoa. Again the cardinals bargained closely— for money, for troops, for signed commitments by Charles and his brother, and other conditions which virtually precluded the Way of Force. But Clement at long last may have recognized that he was only precluding what had never been feasible. After many delays and excuses, which kept Coucy and his colleagues in Avignon for three months, they succeeded in obtaining the document of enfeoffment, to be confirmed as a Bull only when the King of France and his brother had approved the conditions. The envoys left Avignon on September 3, 1394. Two weeks later their entire effort was revealed as vain when they heard the stunning news that Clement was dead.

The schism which had raised Clement to the papacy was his executioner, by the hand of the University of Paris. Since January, when King Charles had recovered his reason, the University had been pressing hard for an audience to present its views. So far, the Duc de Berry, as Clement's warmest partisan, had blocked any such hearing, answering the University's appeals with violent reproaches and threats to "put to death and throw into the river the principal promoters of this affair." These vigorous sentiments were induced by "rich presents" received from Clement, who, having learned of the University's intentions, sent Cardinal de Luna to Paris to exert the financial persuasion that Berry best understood. At some point Burgundy must have offered his brother cogent argument to the contrary, for, in a surprising reversal, Berry suddenly replied to petitioners, "If you find a remedy acceptable to the Council, we will adopt it that very hour."

Cession, as enunciated by Gerson, was already the University's remedy. To give it as much public weight as possible, the faculty organized a popular referendum, with a ballot box placed in the cloister of St. Mathurin in which people were to drop their votes for a solution. From 10,000 votes counted by 54 masters of the different faculties, three solutions emerged, not including the Way of Force. Referendums do not commonly endorse an unwanted result. The Three Ways now proposed were, first, mutual abdication; second, if both popes continued obdurate, arbitration by a selected group; third, a General Council of the Church. The last was considered least desirable because a General Council was believed certain to divide into existing factions from which the schism would emerge as alive as ever.

Destined to dominate the opening decades of the next century, recourse to a Council was already a lengthening shadow. Both popes naturally detested it because it detracted from their authority. The theory of conciliar supremacy held that supreme authority in the Church lay in the General Council, from which the Pope derived his powers. "Some perverse men," raged Clement's rival, Boniface IX, "trusting in the arm of the flesh against the Lord, call for a Council. O damned and damnable impiety!"

Nevertheless, as hope of joint abdication faded, theologians on both sides increasingly discussed a Council and debated its problems. Who would convoke it? What was its legitimacy if convoked by temporal rulers? Did it have authority over the person of a Pope? If summoned by one pontificate in the present impasse, would its decisions be accepted by the other? How might both popes and both hierarchies ever be persuaded to act in concert? On June 30, 1394, a French royal audience heard the forbidden subject relentlessly exposed.

Arranged by Philip of Burgundy to present the University's findings from the referendum, the audience was held in great solemnity. The King was on his throne, with the royal Dukes and principal prelates, nobles, and ministers in attendance. The argument for cession in the form of a 23-page letter to the King was read by the Rector of the University, Nicolas de Clamanges, a friend of Gerson and d'Ailly. One of the humanists within the University, he was considered the finest Latin stylist in France and an orator unmatched for his "Ciceronian eloquence."

Clerical polemic in the Middle Ages was not cool. In a tirade of invective hurled at both popes, Clamanges piled up passion and hyperbole in his depiction of the suffering of the Church and the urgent and immediate need for a cure. Whichever of the two popes refused to accept one of the Three Ways, he proclaimed, should be treated as a "hardened schismatic and consequently a heretic"; a ravisher, not a pastor, of his flock; a "devouring wolf," not a shepherd, who should be driven from the fold of Christendom. If in their overconfidence the popes postponed any longer the offered remedy, they "will repent too late of having neglected reform . . . the harm will be incurable. . . . The world, for so long unhappy, is now on a dangerous slope toward evil."

"Do you think," he cried, in the eternal voice of protest, "that people will suffer forever your bad government? Who do you think can endure, among so many other abuses, your mercenary appointments, your multiple sale of benefices, your elevation of men without honesty or virtue to the most eminent positions?" Every day prelates are appointed who "know nothing of saintliness, nothing of honesty." Exposed to their extortions, "the priesthood has become a misery reduced to profaning its calling . . . by selling relics and crosses and chalices and putting at auction the mystic rites of the sacrament." Some churches hold no services at all. If the early Church fathers returned to earth, "they would find no vestige of their piety, no remnant of their devotion, no shadow of the Church they knew."

He spoke of Christianity as a laughingstock among the infidels, who hope that "our Church thus divided against herself will destroy herself by her own hands." He pointed to the rise of heretics, whose poison "like gangrene makes progress every day." He predicted that worse would come as internal strife within the Catholic Faith promoted dissension and disrespect. He raised all the arguments against a General Council and deflated each, quoting the Old Testament—Psalms, the Prophets, and the Book of Job—to establish its authority. "Has there ever been, will there ever be," he thundered, "a more urgent necessity for a Council than at this moment when the whole Church is convulsed in its discipline, its morals, its laws, its institutions, its traditions and oldest practices, spiritual as well as temporal—at this moment when it is menaced by frightful and irreparable ruin?"

Turning to the King, he did not hesitate to refer to Charles's personal tragedy, saying that if God had answered prayers to restore the King, it must be that he might awake to the interests of his people and of Holy Church, to eradicate "this horrible schism" and the *miseria* in its train. In the name of the University, he exhorted Charles to take the lead at once in working for a remedy if he did not wish to lose his title as Most Christian King.

Ignorant of Latin, the language of the oration, Charles listened graciously without understanding a word. Afterward a translation was ordered for the Royal Council, whose lay members, too, evidently knew no Latin. Clamanges' impassioned plea was ignored. Governments do not like to face radical remedies; it is easier to let politics predominate, and the politics that the court was currently engaged in was the effort, promoted by Louis and resisted by Burgundy, to establish Louis in Italy. The University was ordered by the King—or in his name—to abstain from further agitation. Its reply was to suspend courses in what amounted to a strike by the faculty, a method used successfully against a tax levy in 1392 although at the cost of many foreign students leaving Paris.

The University also circulated Clamanges' letter throughout Europe, not least to the See of Avignon, where it was presented to the Pope in a full assembly of cardinals. After reading a few lines, Clement's eyes filled with anger and he exclaimed, "This letter defames the Holy See! It is wicked, it is venomous!" Denouncing it as a calumny that "does not deserve to be read in public or private," he left the room in a rage and would neither listen nor speak to anyone. The cardinals read the letter through and, after conferring among themselves, concluded that postponement was indeed dangerous and that the Pope would have to accept the University's program. Summoned by Clement when he learned of their conference, they advised him that if he had the good of the Church at heart he must choose one of the Three Ways. Such was his indignation at this "traitorous cowardice" that within three days, on September 16, he died of a heart attack or apoplectic stroke, or, according to his contemporaries, of "profound chagrin." So ended Robert of Geneva, to be ultimately recorded as Anti-Pope by the Church.

The news of his death reached Paris six days later on September 22. Here at last was the moment to re-unite the Church painlessly, without use of force or a General Council—if the election of a successor to Clement could be prevented. "Never again will there be such an opportunity," wrote the University to the cardinals; "it is as though the Holy Ghost stood at the door and knocked." The Royal Council immediately dispatched a message in the name of the King to the Avignon cardinals, exhorting them "in the interests of all Christianity" to postpone their conclave until they received a "special and solemn" letter from the King of France which would follow.

Led by Marshal Boucicaut, the royal messengers galloped for Avignon, covering the 400 miles in the record time of four days. When they arrived, the conclave was already in session. The cardinals were anxious for union, but not at their own expense. They had been persuaded by the suave Spaniard, Cardinal de Luna, a former professor of canon law, that their position depended on their right of election, which must not be abridged. Divining the contents of the King's letter, they decided not to open it until the election was accomplished. But lest they be charged with sustaining the schism, they agreed to sign a written oath binding whichever of them was elected to resign if a majority of the cardinals called on him to do so. The oath bound them to work diligently for union of the Church "without fraud, deceit or machination whatsoever," and sincerely to examine without excuse or delay all possible ways to that goal "even to the point of ceding the papacy, if necessary." Eighteen of 21 cardinals signed, among them the most fervent exponent of union, Cardinal Pedro de Luna of Aragon.

In the conclave, when the name of one cardinal was proposed for election, he confessed in an agony of honesty, "I am weak and perhaps would not abdicate. Do not expose me to temptation!"

"I on the other hand," spoke up Cardinal de Luna, "would abdicate as easily as I take off my hat." All eyes turned to look at the colleague, now in his sixties, who had been a cardinal ever since the stormy election in Rome that had precipitated the schism. A learned and clever man of noble birth, subtle in diplomacy, austere in private life, an expert manipulator, he was a rigid opponent of Council though an ardent advocate of union. He was elected as Clement's successor on September 28, taking the name of Benedict XIII.

The second French embassy heard the news on their way to Avignon. On their arrival, the new Pope assured them of his intent to pursue every means of ending the schism and repeated his statement that he would abdicate if so advised as easily as taking off his hat, which he lifted from his head in illustration. His assurances in reply to the King mounted like a ladder to Heaven. He had accepted election only to end the "damnable schism," and would rather spend the rest of his life in "desert or cloister" than prolong it; if the King sent well-informed persons with definite proposals, he would accept them without hesitation and "execute them without fail"; he was "disposed, determined and resolved" to work for union and would accept the counsel of the King and his uncles "so that they rather than another prince may acquire the eternal glory that shall be the reward of so meritorious an effort."

De Luna may have been sincere but once he was on the papal throne, the duty to abdicate was fast replaced by the sense of right that supreme office breeds. The schism, like the war, was a trap not easy to get out of.

All this time Coucy had been in north Italy conducting, on behalf of Louis d'Orléans, a financial, political, and military campaign for the sovereignty of Genoa. The offer had come out of the city's chronic anarchy: the Grimaldi, Doria, Spinola, and other noble families, having been exiled and lacking cohesion, wanted a sovereign to restore them and deliver the city from bourgeois rule. Power swung from one bourgeois group to another, each of which installed a Doge until he was overthrown and exiled by opponents. No fewer than five Doges held office in 1393, giving way in 1394 to the return of Adorno, the Doge of the Tunisian campaign. Doges, parties, and exiled nobles exerted their various weights in the fluctuating balance of power between Florence and Milan.

As Lieutenant and Procurator General "in trans-alpine parts" for the Duc d'Orléans, Coucy established himself at Asti, which belonged to Louis as part of Valentina's dowry. He commanded some 400 lances and 230 archers recruited from among the best in France, and engaged an almost equal number of Gascon and Italian mercenaries. But without greatly superior numbers he could not expect to subdue Genoese territories by military conquest alone, if the local rulers were disposed to defend them. As in Normandy many years before, his strategy was to take castles and towns by negotiation backed by a show of force and assault only when required.

The nobles who had made the original proposal came to offer him their castles, but, being "prudent and subtle" and having experience of

Lombards and Genoese, Coucy did not trust too much in their promises and took care not to put himself in their power, even to the point of holding conferences in open fields rather than inside castle premises. Collaboration with the Genoese in Tunisia must have left an unpleasant impression.

Guided by Gian Galeazzo, who arranged contacts and lent money and soldiers, Coucy pushed his way through the Italian maze, recruiting and paying mercenary companies, negotiating the terms and price for submission of castles and territories, treating with Pisa and Lucca for their non-interference, sending out envoys to other parts of Italy to gather adhesions for the future Kingdom of Adria. The paper work was substantial, and through its survival in the archives a 14th century politico-military campaign can be seen at work. Recruiting was piecemeal: Guedon de Foissac comes with 2 knights, 19 squires, and 10 archers, Aimé de Miribel with 26 men-at-arms, Hennequin Wautre with 16 archers. Six Italian companies range in size from 10 to 350 "cavaliers." Bonnerel de Grimaut (probably Grimaldi) receives 100 gold florins for "showing the ways and means" by which the enterprise of Savona can be accomplished. Jerome de Balart, doctor of laws, and Luquin Mourre, squire, receive 100 gold florins for advice in the same project.

The territory of Savona, which had revolted against the Doge, is the crux of the advance, requiring delicate negotiations. When Gascon mercenaries are about to subject one of its vassal towns to "fire and blood" in revenge for the killing of three of their horses, they have to be hastily bought off at a cost of 96 écus, not too much to avoid hostilities which would make the cost of conquest greater. The approaches to Savona are opened by deals with surrounding lords for permission to pass through the valleys they command. Finally, Savona with its towns and castles is secured by "secret treaties" and payment of 6,990 gold florins.

Each castle whose allegiance is obtained is required to fly the Orléans flag and each lord is reimbursed by monthly installments on an agreed sum "until such time as the Duc d'Orléans is made master of Genoa." Forty members of the Spinola family receive collectively 1,400 florins a month for their allegiance and agreement to billet Coucy's forces in their towns and fortresses. Records of each transaction in the precise and architectural handwriting of the time make it plain that when knighthood was in flower, one of its primary interests was money.

The notaries who drew up these agreements and the ambassadors who confirmed them had to be paid, as well as couriers to and from Paris. Wages to men-at-arms and retainers to captains of companies were recorded, likewise twenty florins to Antonio de Cove, cannoneer, to fetch a *grosse bombarde* from a certain lord for the siege of a castle; eighteen florins to an envoy sent by Coucy to Pavia to borrow 400 florins from Gian Galeazzo; a silver goblet and ewer to Gian Galeazzo's secretary.

Not surprisingly, Coucy was constantly running out of ready cash, but the banking and credit network of the time kept him in operation. It enabled him to borrow 12,000 florins from one Boroumeus de Boroumeis, merchant of Milan, to be repaid by Orléans to the brothers Jacques and Franchequin Jouen, merchant-grocers of Paris. At another time Coucy pawned jewels and plate to pay his men-at-arms until 40,000 livres were brought by Orléans' chamberlain from Paris.

In November, after receiving plenipotentiary powers from the King of France and the Duc d'Orléans, Coucy concluded a treaty with Savona covering a mass of rights, guarantees, and obligations almost as complex as the Treaty of Brétigny. With this in hand, he moved to Pavia to arrange the definitive terms of Gian Galeazzo's share in the present venture and in the future *Voie de Fait*.

Twenty-one years had passed since Coucy and Gian Galeazzo had fought on opposite sides in the Battle of Montichiari. Did they reminisce over old times and remind each other how each had barely escaped with his life? Or were their relations purely formal? Did they compare notes on their respective monastic foundations, Coucy's for the Célestins at Soissons, Gian Galeazzo's for the Carthusians at Pavia, and did the Italian Prince say, as he had elsewhere, that he intended to build one "which will have no like in the world"? He did not live to see his boast fulfilled in the famous Certosa of Pavia.

He would doubtless have conducted Coucy through his archive of state papers and certainly through his library, whose collection had been started for his father by Petrarch. It contained the poet's copy of Vergil as well as his own and Boccaccio's works and Dante's *Commedia*. Steadily expanded by Gian Galeazzo's purchases to more than 900 volumes, it rivaled the library of Charles V at the Louvre and was open to bibliophiles and scholars whom the lord of Pavia liked to attract to his court. Its glories were the illuminated manuscripts he commissioned. Regardless of text, which might be Pliny or Horace, they illustrated the contemporary world in plants and animals, medical procedures, wedding processions, ships, castles, battles, banquets, and, not least, in the supreme Visconti *Hours*, in three portraits of Gian

Galeazzo himself. The artist, Giovanni dei Grassi, surrounded by his pots of pigment and precious gold leaf, was at work on the *Hours* in the year of Coucy's visit.

Undoubtedly Coucy would have seen the rising construction of the Milan Cathedral, of which his host had laid the foundations in 1386 in pious gratitude for his successful ouster of the impious Bernabò. While Gian Galeazzo gave a monthly subsidy of 500 florins, the building was a product of the popular will, pursued with an impulse so vigorous that the pillars of the nave were already completed. Participation and funds came from all classes. The Guild of Armorers came in a body to begin the work of carrying away rubble in baskets. Not to be outdone, the Drapers followed, then the College of Notaries, government officials, nobles, and others in a steady stream of voluntary labor. Districts of the city vied with each other in contributions. When the Porta Orientale gave an ass worth fifty lire and a day's work on the excavations, the Porta Vercellina gave a calf worth 150 lire. In the record of donations the whole of society appears: consecutive entries list three lire, four soldi from "Raffalda, prostitute," and 160 lire from the secretary of Valentina dei Visconti, Duchesa d'Orléans.

Coucy concluded two treaties with the lord of Milan, one providing for a joint force to take Genoa, the other concerning the *Voie de Fait*. In the second treaty Visconti undertook to provide a certain number of lances if the King of France came to Italy in person, and a more limited number if the leader were Orléans or—which was hardly likely—the Duke of Burgundy.

The reason for the reference to Burgundy remains hidden in the enigmatic statecraft of Gian Galeazzo. He was a ruler who always played both sides in pursuit of his goal and was prepared to abandon one for the other when necessary. In his need of an ally against Florence and Bologna, he could see that France, with an unstable King and a struggle between uncle and nephew for control of policy, was a shifting proposition, and the *Voie de Fait*, since the death of Clement, a fading prospect. While negotiating with Coucy, he was already mending relations with his technical overlord, the Emperor Wenceslas, who, like himself, needed support against domestic enemies. To confirm his imperial title, Wenceslas would have to undertake that hazard of emperors, the journey to Rome for formal coronation by the Pope. Visconti wealth would make it possible. In exchange for 100,000 florins in 1395, Wenceslas sold Gian Galeazzo the title of hereditary Duke of Milan with sovereignty over 25 cities. As the first such title in Italy, it marked the line where the age of city-states passed into the age of despots. It did not help Wenceslas, who was charged by his opponents with illegally alienating imperial territory and was ultimately deposed before ever becoming secure enough to make the journey to Italy.

While Coucy pushed forward the campaign against Genoa, another deal was arranged behind his back. A coalition of Florence, Burgundy, and Queen Isabeau induced Doge Adorno, as a means of keeping himself in office, to offer the sovereignty of Genoa to Charles VI, effectively thwarting Orléans and Visconti. On the edge of renewed madness in 1395, Charles could be manipulated. In the "grievous March" of that year, on being informed that the King had bought out Louis' interests in Genoa for 300,000 francs, Coucy discovered himself acting for a different principal. On the crown's instructions, he now negotiated a truce with the Doge Adorno, who promptly broke it by laying siege to regain Savona. In the course of the defense Coucy was immobilized for four days in July by a "wounded leg," which may have been a fresh injury or an effect of the old injury suffered ten years before. He can be glimpsed only intermittently in the documents, like a patch of sky through moving clouds.

By August the siege of Savona was raised, the sovereignty of Genoa confirmed in the King of France, and Coucy's campaign brought to an end. He is last seen with a suite of 120 horsemen leaving Asti on October 13 and reaching Turin the same evening on his way to yet another crossing of the Alps. On his return to France, Louis welcomed him with a gift—or a payment—of 10,000 francs "to help him over all he had suffered in Italy." In fact Coucy had gained for the crown of France, if not for the Duc d'Orléans, the long-sought foothold in Italy. French rule of Genoa was formally established in the following year. Overthrown by a popular uprising in 1409, it left a claim which Charles's and Louis' descendants, Charles VIII, Louis XII, and Francis I, were still pursuing into the 16th century.

While Coucy was engaged against Genoa, court and University coalesced in a concerted effort to unseat Benedict XIII. Although they knew him well, the French were offended by the election of a Spaniard, and he, though nobly born, did not have the kinship with Valois, Bourbons, and Counts of Savoy which had made Clement, from the French point of view, "one of us." An end to the schism became the more imperative as the tocsin for crusade rang more insistently. Hungarian ambassadors were on their way to France; the Patriarchs of Jerusalem and Alexandria had already arrived with a tale of woe.

Just as the humble Archbishop of Bari turned into a bully overnight as Urban VI, so the subtle and diplomatic Pedro de Luna turned righteous and inflexible as Benedict XIII. A heart-rending plea by the University not to put off "for a day, an hour, an instant" his intention to abdicate left Benedict unmoved, although the rhetoric of which Clamanges was again the author would have penetrated a conscience of granite. By resigning he would gain, wrote the University, "eternal honor, imperishable renown, a chorus of universal praise and immortal glory." If he postponed by one day, a second would follow, then a third. His spirit will weaken, flatterers and place-seekers will come with sweet words and gifts; under the mask of friendship, "they will poison your mind with fear of evil consequences and cool your zeal for this noble and difficult enterprise." The sweetness of honors and power will take hold. "If you are ready today, why wait until tomorrow? If you are not ready today, you will be less so tomorrow." The peace and health of the Church are in his hands. Should his rival refuse to abdicate when Benedict does, he will have condemned himself as "the most perverse schismatic," and proved to all Catholics the necessity of ousting him.

Unilateral abdication did not appeal to Benedict, nor was he persuaded that its moral effect could dislodge his rival. When Chancellor d'Ailly and his ardent and vocal colleague Gilles Deschamps came to Avignon as the King's ambassadors to add pressure, they found that the former De Luna's easy promise of taking off his hat had given way to a Spanish stubbornness bred "in the country of good mules."

Pressure was augmented in Paris. In February 1395 a conference of 109 prelates and learned clerics was convened in the King's name to decide on how to end the schism. After two weeks' deliberation, attended by archbishops, bishops, abbés, and doctors of theology, it voted 87 to 22 for the Way to Cession and renunciation of the Way of Force. Not entirely a matter of conviction, the vote reflected the ascendancy of the Duke of Burgundy. Prelates and theologians dependent for place on the patronage of one or another of the royal Dukes watched carefully the trend of events. Accordingly, as Burgundy or Orléans rose in power—usually Burgundy when the King was mad and Orléans when he was sane—their attitudes shifted, preventing a coherent policy.

The majority of the conference now renounced the *Voie de Fait*. It was declared "too perilous" and likely to involve the King of France in wars against all those obedient to the "Intruder" in Rome. Even if Boniface were defeated, said the prelates, the nations of England, Italy, Germany, and Hungary would still not accept Benedict XIII and "the schism would be stronger than it is now." The only hope was for Benedict to put his abdication in the hands of the King of France, who would then call upon his fellow sovereigns of the other obedience to obtain that of Boniface likewise. Despite the obvious flaws in this procedure, a decision for cession was clearly what the crown wanted. Without a French Pope as its beneficiary, the Way of Force had lost its attraction.

Adria and conquest of the Papal States vanished with the *Voie de Fait,* and with it any prospect for Benedict of ousting his rival by force of French arms. To convince him of this, the crown dispatched the most imposing embassy ever sent to Avignon, consisting of all three royal Dukes—Burgundy, Berry, and Orléans—supported by ten delegates of the University. Though softened by splendid gifts of Burgundian wines and Flemish tapestries, the message was a conscious assertion of royal will over the Church. It met an opponent unsurpassed in the techniques of evasion.

The issue was debated in polished discourse at a series of audiences, each opening on an appropriate text, with the usual "flowers of rhetoric" and many canonical and historical citations by each side. As a former professor at Montpellier, Benedict was not to be put down by the academics from Paris. While continually reasserting his willingness to work until death for union, he refused to be cornered into abdicating without a bilateral guarantee. Since here was the glaring weakness of the French case, he may have suspected that the French wanted him out mainly in order to install a French Pope in his place—and he may have been right. He twisted and evaded as the hunters pursued. When they demanded to see the text of the oath signed by the cardinals in conclave, he first refused, then offered to tell the substance in secret, then, when further pressed, to read it aloud without handing it over. When that too was rejected, he claimed a kind of executive privilege on the ground that resolutions of the conclave could not be communicated to anyone.

Forced to yield, he proposes a joint conference of both popes and both sets of cardinals. The visitors say this is impossible because of the Intruder's obstinacy, and that Benedict's voluntary cession is what is wanted. He asks for the proposal in writing. Gilles Deschamps replies that that is not necessary since it consists of but one word of two syllables: "cession." The Pope asks for time to reflect. During the pause, Burgundy invites the cardinals to give him their opinion "in good conscience as private persons, not as members of the Sacred College." They favor cession nineteen to one, the lone opponent being the Cardinal of Pampeluna, another Spaniard. When the cardinals put their opinion in writing, Benedict forbids them to sign the document. At an audience from which he excludes the University delegates he informs the Dukes that if they will support him, he will abandon to them the conquest and possession of the Papal States. They are deaf to the proposal.

The discussions have now lasted for two months, with the visitors coming across the river every day from Villeneuve, where they are staying. They discover one morning that during the night someone has burned the famous bridge by setting fire to boats moored to the piles. At once fearing "treason" and attack, they seize arms, but on second thought suspect the Pope. If the Spaniard is laughing on the other bank, it is privately. Swearing he has had nothing to do with the fire, he sends workmen to repair the bridge and arrange a temporary pontoon of boats tied together, hardly suitable for proud Dukes to ride across in dignity. The only alternative is crossing by boat, which is slow and insecure against the rushing waters. Disgusted, the visitors after consultation with the cardinals decide on one last appeal, which Benedict, still affirming his devotion to union, rejects. Defeated, the French depart after three months of empty effort. The schism remains unresolved.

With no assurance that his abdication would end the schism, Benedict cannot bear all the blame. Astonishingly, he won a champion in Nicolas de Clamanges, who had so furiously prophesied doom if the popes postponed abdication by a single day. In a decision which caused a storm at the University he now accepted office as Benedict's secretary, and was later to write of him that "though gravely accused, he was great and laudable and I believe him to have been a saintly man nor do I know anyone more praiseworthy." Did Nicolas act from conviction or was he bought? Since his motives are lost to us, let us believe them sincere.

Outraged by the outcome of its efforts, all the more because Benedict's original words had nourished high hopes, the University proposed two radical measures: it advised the King to withhold from Benedict the ecclesiastical revenues of France, a step amounting to a break with Avignon; and it advised the cardinals that if Benedict continued to refuse cession, he should be deposed by a General Council. The crown was not yet prepared to withhold obedience, though it was to come to that stage three years later. Fourteen years were to pass before Europe could achieve the momentary unity for a General Council, which even then did not succeed.

The University kept up its campaign. Letters went to rulers and other universities urging them to insist on cession by both popes. Doctors of Theology journeyed forth on horseback to preach in towns and provinces against the evils of the schism. In the course of denouncing the corruptions of the Church, they spread—with results they may not have intended—the demand for reform. The French crown sent envoys to the King of England and princes of Germany urging the way of mutual cession, and received everyone's earnest concurrence with as yet little practical result. Benedict XIII resisted every pressure. For nearly thirty years to come, despite French withdrawal of obedience, siege of Avignon, desertion by his cardinals, deposition by two Councils, and the rivalry of three other popes, he would not step down. Retreating to a Spanish fortress, he died in 1422 at the age of 94 still maintaining his claim.

Unexpectedly, the war, if not the schism, gave promise of ending at last. In March 1395, Richard II proposed a marriage between himself and Isabelle, daughter of the King of France. He was 29 years old, she six. As a way of by-passing the unyielding disputes to gain peace by other means, it was a bold move, even if peace was not its only motive.

Richard II had no use for what he termed this "intolerable war," nor did he share the animosity for France it had bred in most Englishmen. On the contrary, he admired France, desired to meet her King, and wanted peace in order to strengthen himself against his domestic opponents. He had ruled constitutionally for seven years since his rough treatment by the Lords Appellant, but his autocratic nature, intensified by that humiliation, craved absolute monarchy and the subjection of his enemies. Kingship, which can corrupt or improve, seems to have had a generally one-sided effect in the 14th century: only Charles V gained wisdom from responsibility. Richard was moody, profligate, despotic, emotional, and temperamentally if not physically aggressive. When his wife, Anne of Bohemia, sister of Wenceslas, died in 1394, he indulged the passion of his grief by ordering the royal manor of Sheen to be destroyed because she had died there. At her funeral, believing himself insulted by the behavior of the Earl of Arundel, one of the Lords Appellant, the King seized a staff and struck him to the ground.

Anne had been a sweet-natured woman of his own age who inspired, unlike her unhappy brother, only the most benign comments in the chronicles. Her death may have loosened some restraining influence, besides leaving Richard without a direct heir. To ensure his line, a second marriage was advisable, but the choice of a six-year-old child who was expressly spared consummation of the marriage until she was twelve suggests that an heir was not Richard's primary object. He wanted reconciliation with France in order to close off opportunities to the "boars" of England and, quite specifically, to gain French support, if need be, against them. His envoys were instructed to obtain assurance from the French King and from his uncles and brother "to aid and sustain Richard with all their power against any of his subjects."

That was hardly a normal request by one King of another, especially one so lately and still technically his enemy. Richard was only two years away from his grasp at absolute monarchy, the murder of Gloucester, the execution of Arundel, the banishment of Norfolk and Henry of Lancaster, and the series of compulsive provocations which in two more years were to lose him his crown and finally his life. Modern historians have suggested that in his last years he was overtaken by mental disease, but that is only a modern view of the malfunction common to 14th century rulers: inability to inhibit impulse.

Richard was King in a time of increasing tensions, suppressed but not eased since the Peasants' Revolt. Lawless bands of marauding knights and archers still spread disorder, heavy taxes were a constant complaint, Lollardy, despite the efforts to stamp it out, flickered everywhere. Its social no less than religious threat united crown and Church against it: the days of John of Gaunt's alliance with Wyclif were gone, although Lollards appeared in high places. During the Parliament of 1394–95 the movement suddenly surfaced with an inflammatory public statement of twelve "conclusions and truths for the reformation of Holy Church in England."

Supported by several members of the House of Commons, including the ever troublesome Sir Richard Stury and another knight who were both members of the Privy Council, a petition for the twelve reforms, written in English, was presented as a bill to Parliament. Simultaneously it was pinned in public view on the doors of St. Paul's and Westminster Abbey. The Twelve Conclusions were a mirror of the late medieval Church as seen by the dissatisfied; by those who wanted to believe and have faith but felt blocked by encrusted materialism and idolatry. They were the conclusions Wyclif had reached one by one, beginning with the two most threatening to Church and priesthood: temporal disendowment and denial of the "supposed miracle" of transubstantiation. Other rituals denounced in the list were vows of chastity, which in priests encouraged vice, and in women, who were "by nature frail and imperfect," led to many horrible sins; consecration or exorcism of physical objects, which was nothing but "jugglery," akin to necromancy; and pilgrimages to deaf images of wood and stone, which were a form of idolatry. The Tenth Conclusion was new—a virtual denial of the right to kill. It asserted that manslaughter in battle or by court of justice for any temporal cause was expressly contrary to the New Testament.

So alarmed were the bishops by the Twelve Conclusions that they summoned Richard home from Ireland, where he then was, to decree new measures of suppression. The King himself, in fury at the heresy, threatened to kill Sir Richard Stury "by the foulest death that may be" if he ever broke the oath to recant that was forced upon him. The Twelve Conclusions, however, were beyond the sovereign's power to kill. Lollardy had already found a response in Queen Anne's Bohemian retinue and through them formed a connection between the ideas of Wyclif and Jan Hus.

Richard's proposal of marriage, broached before the French Dukes went to Avignon, was not unanimously welcomed. Philippe de Mézières was its ardent advocate in the interests of crusade, as was the Duke of Burgundy in the interests of commerce. But the hostility of half a century was not easily dissipated. Berry and Orléans were both opposed, and when the proposal was debated in the French Council, several members objected on the ground that a marriage without a peace was unnatural. Coucy, if he had not been absent in Italy, might have shared that attitude. An incident of the same year shows him leaning over backward—perhaps because of his special connections— to maintain the formal relationship between enemies, even during a period of truce. Asked by Froissart, who was preparing to visit England, for letters of introduction to Richard and his uncles, Coucy refused "because he was a Frenchman" to write to the King, although he gave Froissart a letter to his daughter Philippa. If a letter to the King of England was impolitic, marriage to the King of England must indeed have appeared radical.

In the Council, Arnaud de Corbie, the Chancellor, advised acceptance on the ground that the marriage bond would strengthen the English King against the war party in his own country. The interests of peace prevailed. In July, 1,200 French gentlemen escorted a formal English embassy led by Earl Marshal Nottingham to the Council table in Paris. Agreement was reached on a dowry for Isabelle of 800,000 francs but no lands, and on a truce of 28 years. For the first time, a truce was long enough to represent a genuine forswearing of belligerent will—at least on the part of the negotiators. That was the difficulty.

If the French on whose soil the war was fought had, on the whole, had enough, too many English, personified in the Duke of Gloucester, had not. They were galled by a sense of having been bilked out of the gains confirmed in the Treaty of Brétigny. They ached to get satisfaction and saw the marriage putting it off forever. Footloose knights and yeomen were still attracted by the warring way of life and its loot on the continent. The commons, suffering from disrupted commerce and oppressive taxes, may have wanted peace, but they did not like the French marriage. They feared Richard would give away too much to the French; there were mutterings about Calais, and disappointment if not suspicion at the choice of a child queen and continued uncertainty about an heir.

Because of Gloucester's influence and popularity with the Londoners, Richard did not dare to conclude the alliance without his concurrence and that of his party. More than a year elapsed in the effort to obtain it. The French sent Robert the Hermit to add the weight of Heaven's command for peace, and to impress upon the English the Turkish menace which the Hermit knew from his travels in Syria. A visionary, even if he traveled with seven horses at the expense of the French King, was not the best choice to influence Gloucester. When, at the climax of his peroration, the Hermit warned, "Surely, whoever is or will be against the peace shall pay dearly for it be he alive or dead," Gloucester pulled him up with a sharp, "How do you know that?" Robert could only answer by "divine inspiration," which left the Duke unimpressed. He remained "hard-hearted against the peace," and by his words "condemned and despised greatly the Frenchmen."

Richard worriedly told Count Waleran de St. Pol, who had accompanied the Hermit, that Gloucester was trying to influence the people against a peace, perhaps even to "raise the people against me, which is a great peril." St. Pol, the hard-headed brother of saintly Pierre de Luxemburg, advised the King to win his uncle with fair words and great gifts until the marriage and peace were concluded. Then he could "take other counsel," because then he would be strong enough to "oppress all rebels, for the French King if need be shall aid you; of this you may be sure." The lubricator of politics was the same then as before and since. Richard promised Gloucester £100,000 and an earldom for his son worth £2,000 a year (which he later failed to make good) and, by various persuasions and pressures brought to bear by the Duke of Lancaster, secured a sullen acquiescence.

A proxy marriage and ratification of the truce were celebrated in Paris in March 1396, with Nottingham acting as proxy for the King. Nottingham now had occasion to meet the object of his esteem in entertainment if not in combat, for Coucy was one of those who acted as host to the English ambassadors during their three-week stay in the capital. After endorsement of the marriage contract by the barons of

England, Richard himself went to Calais in August, where in conferences with the Duke of Burgundy he went far to show himself a friend of France. He agreed to support the Way of Cession and persuade the Pope of Rome to resign, and, more realistically, he agreed to yield English footholds in Brittany. He went home again to make known the articles of peace to his countrymen, for he said he "could not firmly conclude a peace without the general consent of the people of England."

He returned in October for the climactic meeting with the King of France, held with all appropriate magnificence in a field of bright pavilions on the borders of Calais. Between two lines of 400 French knights and 400 English knights "with their swords in their hands," the two Kings advanced toward each other, each escorted by the uncles of the other. As they met and embraced, all 800 knights knelt, many weeping with emotion. Meetings, banquets, and merriment followed. The seven-year-old bride, swamped in scarlet velvet and emeralds, was handed over and formally married to Richard in November at Calais by the Archbishop of Canterbury. Enguerrand de Coucy was not present at the ceremonies nor to meet his daughter Philippa, who was in the English party, for he had already departed with the chief knights and nobles of the realm on the last crusade of any consequence in the Middle Ages.

The Kings were at peace, but all the old issues—disputed frontiers and territories, homages and reparations, Guienne and Calais—remained unresolved, and Gloucester's rancor abided. The French found that all the honors and entertainments and gifts of gold and silver they heaped on him in an effort to soften his antagonism went for nothing. He took the gifts and remained cold, hard, and covert in his answers. "We waste our effort on this Duke of Gloucester," Burgundy said to his council, "for as long as he lives there shall surely be no peace between France and England. He will always find new inventions and accidents to engender hatred and the strife between the realms." It did not take Gloucester, who would be dead within a year, to find these. Burgundy himself, through the fratricidal strife with Orléans carried on by his son, was as responsible as any. And the unending war had cut a gulf too deep to be easily pasted over. In England, Richard and Lancaster were the only genuine supporters of a pro-French policy, and both were dead three years after the French marriage. Animosity toward France endured. Not quite twenty years after the reconciliation, Henry V was to call to his followers, "Once more unto the breach!"

Chapter 26

Nicopolis

For fifty years Europeans had heard, more or less inattentively, the distant crash of the Turks' penetration in the East and the cries of distress marking their relentless advance. The Ottoman Turks were the last and destined to be the most enduring wave of warrior nomads who during the 11th to 13th centuries had swept out of the Asian steppes to overwhelm Asia Minor, as the Goths and Huns before them had overwhelmed Rome. Originally, the Ottomans had settled on the shores of the Black Sea in Anatolia as vassals of the preceding Seljuk Turks and guardians of the Seljuk frontier. When the Seljuk empire crumbled under the Mongol invasions of Genghis Khan and his successors, the trained, hard-fighting bands of the border chief Osman (whence the name Ottoman) declared their independence of Seljuk rule in 1300, and rose on the ruins of their predecessors. In 25 years, with all the brutal energy of a people on the way up, they conquered key cities and large tracts of Anatolia and mastered the shores of the thin blue straits separating Asia from Europe.

Across the straits on the European side stood Constantinople, capital of what was left of the Byzantine Empire. This eastern relic of the ancient Roman Empire was now finally disintegrating 800 years after Rome had succumbed to the earlier barbarians. Pushed back into Europe, it was a shrunken remnant of former greatness, its naval and commercial supremacy lost to Genoese and Venetians, its structure weakened by the same processes at work in the West—feudal service inadequately replaced by a money economy, Black Death, economic disruptions, religious dissent, workers' uprisings, warring peoples. Serbs and Bulgars, developing their own kingdoms, assaulted it on the west and a variety of small powers harassed it in the Aegean. Its provinces were disorganized, its military force dependent on mercenaries, its sovereignty torn apart by ferocious feuds around the throne. These feuds provided the opening through which the Ottoman Turks entered Europe.

The feuds began with the pretensions of John Cantacuzene, who as chief minister bore the title the "Great Domestic" and served as regent for John V Paleologus, child heir to the throne. In 1341 Cantacuzene declared himself joint—in reality, rival—Emperor as John VI. Through ensuing years of civil war he maintained his hold by purchasing the services of the hardy, disciplined Ottoman forces. When, at Cantacuzene's invitation, Sultan Orchan crossed the Hellespont in 1345, it was, in Gibbon's knell, "the last and fatal stroke" in the long fall of the ancient Roman Empire.

Murad I, Orchan's successor, gained a foothold on the European side with the capture in 1353 of Gallipoli, key to the Hellespont. Exactly 100 years later the Turks were to take Constantinople itself, but Cantacuzene, like other great actors in history, had no vision of the consequences inherent in his acts. Rather, to cement the collaboration with his new allies, he gave his daughter in marriage to Orchan in a Moslem ceremony, bridging the abyss between Christian and infidel without scruple—and without affecting his faith. Some years later, when forced to abdicate, the once "Great Domestic" became a monk and retired to write in cloistered calm a history of the times he had done so much to embroil.

Incurable discord at Constantinople gave the Turks the means to exploit their gateway at Gallipoli. Upon Cantacuzene's abdication, his former ward, John Paleologus, regained the throne (which accounts for the alarming succession of John VI by John V) only to plunge into a vicious family struggle in which sons and grandson, uncle and nephew over the next 35 years deposed, imprisoned, tortured, and replaced one another in various combinations with Murad I.

While assisting the Paleologi toward their mutual destruction, the Turks, like a hand opening out from the wrist at Gallipoli, expanded through the Byzantine and Bulgarian dominions. In 1365 Murad advanced his capital to Adrianople (Edirne) 120 miles inside Europe. In 1371 he defeated a league of Serbs and Bulgars on the river Maritza in Bulgaria. John V henceforth held part of his empire, and the Bulgar boyars their territories, as vassals of the Sultan. In 1389 a new league of Serbs, Rumanians, and their northern neighbors, the Moldavians, attempted to stem the Turks but were defeated by Murad in the decisive Battle of Kossovo, the grave of Serbian independence. The Serbian Czar and the elite of his nobles were killed and his son forced to accept vassalship to the Sultan. Murad himself was killed after the battle by a dying Serb who, feigning to have a secret to tell the Sultan, stabbed him in the belly when Murad leaned over to listen to him. However, the Sultan left his successor, Bajazet, the strongest power in the region. In the 35 years since their crossing of the Bosporus, the Turks had overrun the eastern Balkans up to the Danube and now stood at the borders of Hungary.

The division of their foes was the major factor in the Turkish advance. A legacy of bitter mistrust had separated Constantinople from the West ever since the Latin crusaders had penetrated the Eastern dominions. The old schism in Christianity between the Roman Catholic and Greek Orthodox churches left an implacable dispute over minor matters of ritual—the less fundamental they were, the greater the rancor—and made adversaries of the Balkan peoples. Bulgaria and Wallachia (the contemporary name for Rumania) and most of Serbia belonged to the Greek Church, as opposed to Hungary, which belonged to the Latin and was resented for its efforts to impose Roman Catholic clergy and gain political dominion over its neighbors. Mircea, *voyevod* or ruler of Wallachia, fought against the Turks at Kossovo, but, because of old animosities, was not anxious to make common cause with Hungary against the common enemy. The same was true of the Serbs, who in any case were precluded from doing so once they accepted the Sultan as overlord. This had been Murad's policy: to neutralize the Balkan rulers by leaving them in place under the obligation of homage. Because their kingdoms lacked unity, being no more than loose federations of semi-autonomous rulers, each could be picked off individually. One by one, Bulgarian, Bosnian, Serbian, and Wallachian rulers paid homage in order to avoid continuous Turkish raids. In areas of direct conquest, Murad divided the territory as fiefs among his followers, rooting them in Europe. Half the Turkish army at Kossovo already held land on the far side of the Bosporus.

Bajazet lost none of the impetus of his forebears. Chosen Sultan on the battlefield of Kossovo, he began by strangling his brother with a bowstring, a customary Turkish precaution, and proceeded at once to the business of shaking the Byzantine throne by assisting John VII to overthrow his grandfather. When John was in turn overthrown by his uncle, Manuel II, Bajazet besieged and blockaded Constantinople for seven years. In the meantime, he expanded his hold in Bulgaria, invaded Macedonia and Attica, and ravaged Bosnia and Croatia—taking more prisoners, it was said, than he left inhabitants. He was bold, enterprising, always on horseback, "equally avid for the blood of his enemies as he was prodigal with that of his soldiers." His vanguard of *ghazis*, instruments of Allah, fought with the extra zeal of holy war against the Christian infidels. A *ghazi*, according to Turkish definition, was "the sword of God who purifies the earth from the filth of polytheism," by which was meant the Christian Trinity.

In 1393, after occupying Tirnovo, capital of the eastern Bulgarian kingdom, Bajazet captured Nicopolis, the strongest Bulgarian fortress on the Danube. Situated on a height above the town of Nicopolis on the river's edge, it commanded what was then a ford of the Danube protected by a Wallachian fortress on the opposite bank. Two tributary rivers entered the Danube at the base of the castle which thus controlled communications through the interior as well as down the Danube. At this strategic site the European-Ottoman clash was to come.

When the Bulgarian Czar, Ivan Shishman, refused, though a vassal, to support the Turks' further advance with troops and provisions, Bajazet imprisoned him in Nicopolis. Growing impatient with the vassalage system, the Sultan subsequently had his prisoner strangled, reduced his kingdom to the status of a Turkish *sandjak* or province, and moved on against Vidin, capital of the western Bulgarian kingdom. When Sigismund, King of Hungary, sent envoys to demand by what right the Sultan abrogated Bulgarian sovereignty, Bajazet answered without words by simply pointing to the weapons and war trophies that hung upon his walls. Behind him he constructed a huge tower to fortify Gallipoli and a permanent port for his galleys. He raised imposing mosques at Adrianople and built caravansaries along the path of his advance. While his armed horsemen thrust forward in Europe, he continued to campaign and extend his hold in Anatolia. For the "fiery energy of his soul" and the speed of his marches, he earned the surname Ilderim, meaning Thunderbolt.

Following the capture of Nicopolis, King Sigismund's appeals to the West for help grew more pressing. His country was now the last organized state in Eastern Europe resisting the Turks and it still remembered the terror of the Mongol ravages that had swept and receded over the Danube plain in the last century. Though Hungary was "Queen of the surrounding countries," the resistance she could offer to the new invaders was hampered by incessant quarrels with Poland and Lithuania on the north, by the hostility of her neighbors to the south, and by divisions within its own ruling class and among its commoners. The country was a patchwork made up of a foreign sovereign, Hungarian nobles, native peasants living by an agriculture untouched by the West, and a merchant class of German immigrants who had developed the towns and remained alien in habit as they did in Bohemia and Poland.

Through a century of rule by the Angevin dynasty, the Hungarian crown was closely connected with the French court and continued to be so under the Luxemburg dynasty, which began with Sigismund. He became King in 1387 by virtue of marriage to the daughter of the last Angevin King, Louis the Great, who died without a male heir. Son of the late Emperor Charles IV and younger half-brother of Wenceslas, Sigismund was a less serious statesman than his father, more able and sensible than his distracted brother. Like Wenceslas, he was well educated and fluent in four languages. Tall, strong, and uncommonly handsome, with light-brown hair worn long and curled, he was intelligent and well-meaning as a ruler but pleasure-loving, extravagant, and licentious, with a record of scandalous love affairs. History knows him largely as Emperor in later life, but at this time he was only 28 and barely keeping his balance in precarious circumstances.

Succeeding as an outsider to the Hungarian crown at nineteen, he had faced comparison with a dynamic and powerful predecessor, the enmity of rebellious nobles, a domineering mother-in-law, and a rival to the throne in the person of that throne-surfeited Angevin heir, Charles of Durazzo. Through hectic years of cabals and assassinations, Charles of Durazzo and Queen-Mother Elizabeth of Hungary managed to destroy each other, and the rebellious nobles were more or less contained, despite such intensity of feeling as caused one of them to shout at Sigismund, "I will never bow to you, you Bohemian pig!" Preoccupied by these various challenges in his first eight years as ruler, Sigismund was not able to mobilize effective resistance to the Turks, who took advantage of the situation to ravage his borders.

Personally brave though tactless, hot-tempered and cruel when angered, Sigismund had survived. Like each of the Luxemburgs, he had distinctive characteristics. On being shown a relic said to be a bone of St. Elizabeth, he turned it over and remarked that it could just as well be that of a dead cobbler. Attending the Parlement at Paris to observe the courts of justice in operation, he heard a verdict given against a plebeian plaintiff named Seignet on the ground that he was no knight while the defendant was. To the astonishment of his retinue and assembled lawyers, judges, and onlookers, Sigismund rose, announced in a loud voice his right to make knights, summoned Seignet to him, bade him kneel, and dubbed him knight on the spot. Removing one of his gold spurs and his belt from which hung a dagger to represent a sword, he had one of his men put these insignia on the dumbfounded new knight, and "thus the King advanced the cause of the said Seignet."

While not oblivious to the Turkish advance, the West, having no great attachment to Constantinople, paid little serious attention to the danger until it reached Hungary. Every Pope in the last forty years had, it is true, called for crusade against the approaching infidel, some with real fervor, but the fervor was more for invigoration of the Faith than from a realistic appreciation of the danger. Such enterprises as were launched against the Turks were narrow in scope and motivated by special interests. The interest of the popes was to re-absorb the Eastern Church within the Latin fold; the interest of the Venetians and Genoese was to preserve their trading posts in the Black Sea and eastern Mediterranean; the interest of the Lusignans of Cyprus was to preserve their kingdom against the Turkish tide. The nearest thing to a united effort was the Latin League organized by Pope Clement VI in 1344, even before the Turks entered Europe. With the combined forces of the papacy, Venice, Cyprus, and the Hospitalers of Rhodes, Clement had hoped, by initial success against the Turks, to induce Constantinople to enter into alliance with the Latin League and reunite with the Roman Church. Victorious at the outset, the Latin fleet took Smyrna and destroyed 100 Turkish vessels, but the crusaders' land forces, paralyzed by disease, dissension, and irresolute leadership, made no headway and the campaign petered out in negotiated terms.

One further effort was made in the 1360s under the prodding of Pierre de Lusignan of Cyprus, whose interest was most immediate. After vainly touring the courts of Europe for three years trying to raise the forces for a crusade, he was able to mount an expedition from Cyprus in 1365 which triumphantly took the rich city of Alexandria in Egypt as a first step on the way to Jerusalem. Wishing to make sure of their immense booty, his followers insisted on sailing away with their gains, leaving Lusignan without enough forces to exploit his victory, or even hold it. Alexandria had to be given up.

At the same time, Amadeus of Savoy, whose aunt, Anne of Savoy, was Dowager Empress in Constantinople, led a remarkable campaign intending to join up with Lusignan. He succeeded in regaining Gallipoli, but this too was transitory. The Free Companies under Du Guesclin, who were supposed to march overland against the Turks from the West at the same time, never came. Amadeus, like Lusignan, lacked the forces to go farther, and within a few years Murad recovered Gallipoli.

In 1369 Constantinople itself called for help. In a desperate effort to excite the aid of the West, Emperor John V journeyed to Rome to abjure the schism between the Greek and Latin churches and offer himself as the first convert. He succeeded mainly in exciting the fury of his own clergy and laity, who repudiated his arrangements. Europe, preoccupied with the renewal of the Anglo-French war, was not interested.

The one person on record who consistently tried to energize a response proportionate to the challenge was Philippe de Mézières, although in his case, too, the enemy was irrelevant: crusade for its own sake was his great objective. For him it was a moral imperative, a philosopher's stone that would cure society's suffering and turn its evils to gold: quarrels and hostilities would cease, tyrants fall or reform, Christianity would convert Turks, Tatars, Jews, and Saracens and bring about the peace and unity of the world. But though he was an *exalté*, Mézières knew the Levant and the Turks at first hand, with the result that he understood the gravity of the problem and took it seriously.

As a young cleric drawn by ardor for the Holy Land, he had joined the crusade of the Latin League to Smyrna; later, as chancellor to Pierre de Lusignan of Cyprus, he lived close to the Turkish problem for many years and, on returning to the French court after Lusignan's death, made it his purpose in life to regain the East for Christianity. He recognized that this meant not reckless adventure, but organized serious warfare to meet an organized, disciplined foe whom he knew from Smyrna to be well trained, courageous, and ruthless. He conceived of the force needed as a national army to include bourgeois and common people serving as men-at-arms, and knights as leaders, motivated by virtue and zeal rather than greed. Like the Templars and Hospitalers of old, they would be dedicated to obedience, justice, and military discipline, and in the course of their great enterprise would revive the true ideals of knighthood. He founded, for this purpose, an Order of the Passion of Jesus Christ. As indicated by the name, his interest was moral, not military.

Mézières' insistent propaganda—which included the marvelous stage spectacle of the First Crusade performed for the Emperor's visit to Paris—undoubtedly had its effect on Charles VI and doubtless on others. In 1389 a firsthand report on the Turks was brought back by Boucicaut on his return from the Holy Land, where he had gone to ransom Comte d'Eu on the journey that produced the *Cent Ballades*. His recitals of all he had seen in the East, of his visit to Sigismund in Hungary, and his reception at Gallipoli by Sultan Murad, who had treated him nobly and given him magnificent gifts and a safe-conduct, heightened the young King's desire for the "glorious adventure." In the 1390s news from the East grew more urgent. When the peace parley of 1393 failed to conclude a treaty with England, Charles nevertheless urged Lancaster to consider a joint expedition against the Turks "to defend the faith and come to the aid of Hungary and the Emperor of Constantinople." But while peace with England hung fire, nothing could be done, and not until the Duke of Burgundy interested himself did anything happen.

Burgundy was still the principal mover of events. Before retrieving national power through the King's madness, he had been looking for a crusade to go on, with options divided between Prussia—which would serve no purpose except to keep warriors busy—and Hungary. In 1391 he sent Guy de Tremoille to Venice and Hungary to investigate the situation and, persuaded of sufficient grandeur in the cause to suit his requirements, planned a crusade, originally to be led by himself, Louis d'Orléans, and the Duke of Lancaster. In the end, none of the three went. Whether defense against the Turks was seen as a vital European interest is doubtful. Burgundy's personal interest in sponsoring the crusade was to magnify himself and his house, and since he was the prince of self-magnification, the result was that opulent display became the dominant theme; plans, logistics, intelligence about the enemy came second, if at all.

The first problem, as always, was finance. In 1394 Burgundy demanded an aid of 200,000 livres from Flanders, impoverished though it was by the years of civil war. Strenuous bargaining by the Flemish reduced the sum to 130,000, enough to initiate preparations of unsurpassed luxury in garments if not weapons. In January 1395 the Duke sent a second Tremoille brother, Guillaume, to inform Sigismund that an official request to the King of France for help would be favorably received.

Four imposing Hungarian knights and a bishop reached Paris in August. They told the court that Sultan Bajazet was assembling an army of 40,000 in order to subject Hungary to the fate of Bulgaria, Wallachia, and Serbia, and that unless the French sent help, the King of Hungary would soon be reduced to the last distress. They told how the cruel Turks held Christians in dungeons, carried off children to be converted to Islam, despoiled maidens, spared no one and nothing from sacrilege. Their King had given battle several times with unhappy result against this fearful and powerful enemy. However painful was such an admission, "the fate of Christians obliges us to say it." King Sigismund implored help "in the name of kinship and the love of God."

The English marriage having been arranged, King Charles was able to reply that, "as chief of the Christian Kings," it devolved upon him to prevent Christianity from being trampled underfoot by the Sultan and to punish his effrontery. Enthusiasm was general. Comte d'Eu, now Constable of France, and Boucicaut, now Marshal, proclaimed it the duty of every man of valor to undertake battle against the "miscreants," the word generally used for Moslems as for peasants and laborers, indicating contempt. Loaded with gifts and assurances of help, the Hungarian envoys returned, spreading word of the French crusade on their way through Germany and Austria and arranging provisions for its passage.

On his return from Italy, two months after the Hungarians' visit, Coucy found the court in great excitement over the crusade, and lost no time in taking the cross. After the habit of his kind, he never stayed home if he could help it. Burgundy, Orléans, and Lancaster had all withdrawn from the enterprise, owing to the negotiations with England which required their presence—or from reluctance to leave the vicinity of the throne. But the house of Burgundy remained in control in the person of the Duke's eldest son, Jean de Nevers, aged 24 and not yet a knight, whom his father proposed to put in nominal command. The predestined Cain (in Michelet's phrase) to his cousin Louis d'Orléans' Abel, the Count of Nevers showed few signs as yet of the decisive character that was to appear after his father's death. As Duke, he would be known as Jean Sans Peur (John the Fearless), meaning, it would seem, that he did not fear to do evil. Married at fourteen in the famous double wedding, he was already the father of two. Undersized, with a large head, hard features, graceless manners, and inelegant dress, he was the opposite in everything except ambition of his superb and charming cousin Louis. "Nature," wrote Michelet, "seemed to have fashioned him on purpose to hate the Duc d'Orléans."

While Nevers' royal blood and position gave éclat to the cause, his father recognized the need of more responsible leadership, which he evidently did not expect from either Constable d'Eu or Marshal Boucicaut, who were both under 35. He turned to Coucy as elder statesman and the most experienced warrior—since Clisson's disgrace—in the realm.

Since he had first marched at fifteen against the English, and at eighteen hunted down the Jacquerie, the range of Coucy's experience had extended over an extraordinary variety of combat, diplomacy, government, and social and political relationships. As son-in-law of Edward III, holding double allegiance to two kings at war, his position had been unique. He had seen war as captain or one of the top command in eleven campaigns—in Piedmont, Lombardy, Switzerland, Normandy, Languedoc, Tuscany, northern France, Flanders, Guelders, Tunisia, Genoa; he had commanded mercenaries, and fought as ally or antagonist of the Count of Savoy, Gregory XI, Hawkwood, the Visconti, the Hapsburgs, the Swiss, Navarrese, Gascons, English, Berbers, the Republic of Florence, and nobles of Genoa. As diplomat he had negotiated with Pope Clement VII, the Duke of Brittany, the Count of Flanders, the Queen of Aragon, with the English at peace parleys, and the rebels of Paris. He had had one temperamental and extravagant wife eight years his senior, and a second approximately thirty years his junior. He had served as adviser and agent of the two royal Dukes, Anjou and Orléans, as Lieutenant-General of Picardy and later of Guienne, as member of the Royal Council, as Grand Bouteiller of France, and had twice been the preferred choice for Constable. He had known and dealt with every kind of character from the ultra-wicked Charles of Navarre to the ultra-saintly Pierre de Luxemburg.

Not surprisingly, the Duke and Duchess of Burgundy sent for him and said, "Sir, we know well that above all other knights of France you are the most used and expert in all things, wherefore dearly we require that you would be companion to our son on this voyage and his chief counselor."

"Monseigneur and you, Madame," Coucy replied, "I will go, firstly for devotion to defend the faith of Jesus Christ; secondly, in that you do me so much honor as to give me charge of Monseigneur Jean your son. I shall acquit myself of the charge in all things to the best of my power." But, he added, he would prefer to be excused of the charge and let it be conferred rather on Comte d'Eu and Comte Jacques de la Marche, both related by blood to Nevers. (As a D'Artois, D'Eu shared the blood of the Valois, which was the chief reason he was Constable, while De la Marche, youngest of the crusaders, "without beard or moustache," was a Bourbon.)

"Sire de Coucy," answered the Duke, "you have seen much more than these two and know better the ordaining of an army in strange countries than either our cousin D'Eu or De la Marche, therefore we charge you and pray you to execute our request." Coucy bowed, saying, "Your prayer is my command," and agreed to accept if he had the aid of Guy and Guillaume de Tremoille and Admiral de Vienne. Clearly he, too, with unhappy percipience, had no great confidence in the younger men.

Because the problem of command was to be crucial in the outcome of the crusade, Burgundy's effort to name a "chief counselor" is significant, whether or not Froissart's report of the interview is verbatim. Writing history in terms of direct speech was a license medieval chroniclers allowed themselves. So did Thucydides. If we accept Pericles' speech to the Athenians, we need not balk at Burgundy's to Coucy. It has been questioned on the ground that Coucy's name does not appear as "chief counselor"—or at all—in the final list of Nevers' primary counselors, which consisted of the two Tremoilles and Odard de Chasseron, all of the Burgundian court, together with Philippe de Bar and Admiral de Vienne. Coucy, D'Eu, Boucicaut, De la Marche, and Henri de Bar made up a separate list whom Nevers could consult "when it seemed good to him." As an arrangement for the governance of a military campaign, this had flaws. It may reflect some sparring between Nevers and his father; more fundamentally, it reflects the absence of a *concept* of unity of command.

Emptied of occupation by the peace with England, knights took the cross with alacrity "to escape idleness and employ themselves in chivalry." Some 2,000 knights and squires are said to have joined, supported by 6,000 archers and foot soldiers drawn from the best available volunteers and mercenary companies. Just as he had set a record for opulence at the double wedding, Burgundy now determined that the equipment for his son's debut in war should be the most resplendent ever. Nevers' personal company of 200 were supplied with new livery of a "gay green," with 24 wagonloads of green satin tents and pavilions, with four huge banners painted with the crusade's emblem—a figure of the Virgin surrounded by the lilies of France and the arms of Burgundy and Nevers. Pennons for lances and tents, tabards for the trumpets, velvet saddle blankets and heraldic costume for twelve trumpeters were all embroidered with the same emblems in gold and silver, many encrusted with jewels and ivory. Kitchen equipment was made especially for the campaign as well as pewter tableware of forty dozen bowls and thirty dozen plates. Four months' wages in advance had to be paid before departure. The cost of all this outran the money raised from Flanders. New taxes were levied on all Burgundy's domains, including the traditional aid for knighting of the eldest son and for overseas voyage. Payment in lieu of participation in the crusade was exacted even from old men, women, and children. For further needs en route, the Duke negotiated loans from municipalities, tax farmers, Lombards, and other bankers.

Competitive splendor governed the preparations. Coucy's costs were covered in part by Louis d'Orléans, who paid him the remaining 6,000 livres due for the Genoa campaign in a flat sum, plus 2,000 to his son-in-law Henri de Bar and the expenses for seventeen knights and squires of Louis' household who were to follow Coucy's banner.

First among the foreign allies were the Knights Hospitalers of Rhodes, who, since the decline of Constantinople and Cyprus, held the dominant Christian position in the Levant; secondly, the Venetians, who supplied a fleet; and on land, German princes of the Rhineland, Bavaria, Saxony, and other parts of the Empire who had been recruited by the Hungarians and joined the French corps en route. Adventurers from Navarre and Spain, Bohemia and Poland, where French heralds had proclaimed the crusade, joined individually. The Italian states were too engaged in their usual intramural hostilities to send contingents, and the supposed English presence of which so much has been made is imaginary. No record exists of the financing necessary to send an English force abroad, nor of the necessary royal permission to leave the country. Neither Henry of Bolingbroke nor other "son of the Duke of Lancaster" could have led an English contingent, since they and most of the leading English nobles were present at Richard's marriage five months after the crusade's departure. Sporadic mention of English participants can be explained by the presence of Hospitalers of the English "tongue" who joined their brothers of Rhodes. The question that remains is not whether the English were present but why they were absent. It may be that as the contention between King Richard and Gloucester grew more vehement, each wanted his partisans near at hand; or it may be that the animosity left by the long war had cut deeply into the old brotherhood of chivalry, leaving the English with no taste for a crusade under French leadership.

Enthusiasm was not universal. Nevers' father-in-law, Albert, Duke of Bavaria and Count of Hainault, was not impressed by the need to expel the Turks or defend the Faith. When his son, William of Ostrevant, with a following of many young knights and squires, expressed a strong desire to go, Duke Albert curtly told him his motive was "Vainglory" and asked what reason he had "to seek arms upon a people and a country that never did us any damage." He said William would be better employed to use his forces for the recovery of family property unlawfully held by the neighboring lords of Frisia. Allowed a martial enterprise, William was happy to obey. The eastern frontier of Europe was far away and, given the communications of the time, the Turks seemed to most Europeans hardly more than a name.

The papal schism did not incommode the venture. Boniface, the Roman Pope, to whom Hungary, Venice, and the Germans were obedient, had been actively preaching the crusade since 1394. He wanted the prestige, as his late rival Clement had wanted the prestige of sponsoring a saint. Pope Benedict of Avignon sponsored the French. At Burgundy's request, he gave the customary plenary absolution to crusaders and special permission to take shelter with "schismatics" (the Greek Christians) and infidels.

The departure from Dijon on April 30, 1396, was a superb spectacle which could not fail to lift the hearts of observers. At the fulfillment of his dream, Mézières, however, could not rejoice. The humility of pilgrims, he wrote, did not grace the great procession: "they go like kings, preceded by minstrels and heralds in purple and rich garments, making great feasts of outrageous foods," and spending in one month more than they ought to in three. It would be the same as previous expeditions, ruined by extravagance and indiscipline, motivated by chivalry's love "for one of the great ladies of the world—Vainglory."

The crusaders' route took them via Strasbourg across Bavaria to the upper Danube and from there, using the river as transport, to rendezvous with the King of Hungary at Buda (Budapest). The joint armies would proceed from there against the Turks. Objectives, if vague, were not modest. After expelling the Turks from the Balkans, the crusaders planned to come to the aid of Constantinople, cross the Hellespont, march through Turkey and Syria to liberate Palestine and the Holy Sepulcher, and return after these triumphs by sea. Arrangements had been made for the Venetian fleet and galleys of the Emperor Manuel to blockade the Turks in the Sea of Marmora and for the Venetians to sail up the Danube from the Black Sea to meet the crusaders in Wallachia in July. As grandiose as the projected invasion of England and march on Rome, the program was unaffected by past frustrations. Nor had the siege of Mahdia, involving many of the same leaders, altered their contempt for the infidel as foe. The ranks of chivalry still believed that nothing could withstand their valor.

Rules of discipline were decreed by a War Council of March 28, which provided that a noble causing disruption was to lose horse and harness, a varlet drawing a knife in a quarrel to lose his hand, anyone committing robbery to lose an ear. The larger question of obedience to command—which military ordinances since the time of Jean II had tried and failed to solve—was left untouched. The Council of March 28 added a final provision that was to be determining at Nicopolis: "Item, that [in battle] the Count and his company claim the *avant garde*." Chivalry's sense of itself required valor to be proved in the front line. Victory required more.

Coucy did not travel with the main body because he was detached on a mission to the lord of Milan. Angry at the removal of Genoa from his sphere of influence, Gian Galeazzo was maneuvering to prevent its transfer of sovereignty to the King of France. Coucy was sent to warn him that his interference would be regarded as a hostile act. More than Genoa was behind the quarrel. Gian Galeazzo had turned against France, bitterly if not openly, because his beloved daughter Valentina was being subjected to a campaign of slander charging her with bewitching or poisoning the King. The vicious rumors were the work of Queen Isabeau, who wanted Valentina out of the way, perhaps from jealousy of her influence with the King, or to facilitate her own affair with Orléans, or as part of Isabeau's perpetual machinations with Florence against Milan, or something of each. Whispered in the taverns and markets, among a public ready to believe ill of the Italian foreigner, the rumors grew so rampant that mobs shouting threats gathered before Valentina's residence. Louis d'Orléans made no effort to defend his wife, but rather complied with Isabeau's objective by removing Valentina from Paris on the excuse of her safety. She was left to live in exile thereafter at her country residence at Asnières on the Seine, where, twelve years later, she died.

Valentina's removal occurred in April, the month of the crusade's departure, and was not taken lightly by her adoring father. He threatened to send knights to defend his daughter's honor, but his contemporaries believed he did more than that. For revenge upon France, he was said to have notified Bajazet of the crusaders' plan of campaign and to have kept him closely informed of its progress. The charge against Gian Galeazzo was probably a product of French animosity and the search for someone to blame after the appalling dénouement, but it could also have been true. A Visconti did not shrink from revenge, especially not the man who had so coolly dispatched his uncle to prison and death.

It is not impossible that Coucy may have inadvertently revealed the crusaders' plan of campaign to his host in Pavia. Gian Galeazzo was a strange, cheerless, secretive prince who would have concealed his paternal feelings. With regard to Genoa, however, Coucy's intervention was successful; sovereignty was duly transferred to the King of France in the following November. Coucy, accompanied by Henri de Bar and their followers, left Milan in May for Venice, where he requisitioned a ship from the Venetian Senate on May 17 to take him across the Adriatic. He embarked on May 30 for Senj (Segna), a small port on the Croatian coast. Evidence is lacking of his route thereafter, but the choice of Senj would indicate that he and his party traveled to Buda by the most direct way, a journey of some 300 miles through wild, rugged, and dangerous country.

He reached the rendezvous before Nevers, who was in no hurry. Stopping along the upper Danube for receptions and festivities offered by German princes, Nevers and his gorgeous companions in green and gold did not reach even Vienna until June 24, a month behind the vanguard under D'Eu and Boucicaut. A fleet of seventy vessels with cargo of wine, flour, hay, and other provisions was dispatched from Vienna down the Danube while Nevers enjoyed further festivities offered by his sister's husband, Leopold IV, Duke of Austria. After borrowing from his brother-in-law the huge sum of 100,000 ducats, which took time to arrange, Nevers finally arrived in Buda at some time in July.

Sigismund welcomed his allies with joy not unmixed with apprehension. Although the Hungarian nobles had taken the cross with enthusiasm, their loyalty to him was not perfect, and he foresaw difficulties in the problem of a combined march and a coordinated strategy with the visitors. The French were not disposed to take advice, and the habits of pillage and brigandage, grown routine in the last fifty years of warfare, had already been exhibited on their march through Germany.

Strategy also had to be coordinated with the ardent crusader Philibert de Naillac, Grand Master of the Hospitalers, and with representatives of the Venetian fleet. The 44 ships of Venice, carrying the Hospitalers from Rhodes, sailed through the Aegean into the Sea of Marmora, and some of them continued into the Black Sea and up the Danube, without meeting hostile action. Inferior at sea, the Turks did not challenge them, nor did they in turn blockade the Turks in Asia, which suggests that Bajazet and a large part of his forces were already on the European side.

Conflict immediately marked the War Council at Buda. Sigismund advised waiting for the Turks to take the offensive and then giving battle when they reached his borders where he exercised control, thus avoiding the difficulties of a long march and the uncertainties to be encountered in the doubtful territory of the schismatics. He had led a campaign against the Turks in Wallachia in the previous year, as a result of which Bajazet had sent heralds to declare war and to announce his intention to be in Hungary before the end of May. The Sultan had boasted that after chasing Sigismund out of Hungary he would continue on to Italy, where he would plant his banners on the hills of Rome and feed his horse oats on the altar of St. Peter's.

Now, by the end of July, he had not appeared. Reconnaissance parties sent out by Sigismund as far as the Hellespont showed no signs of the "Great Turk," causing the French to declare him a coward who did not dare face them. Sigismund assured them the Sultan would come and it were better to let him extend himself in a long march rather than undertake it themselves. But with his reputation as something of a lightweight, Sigismund had neither the authority, the force of character, nor the prestige to make his advice prevail. The French insisted they would chase the Turks out of Europe wherever they were found, and boasted that "if the sky were to fall they would uphold it on the points of their lances."

Chosen as spokesman for the allies (tending to confirm his position as "chief counselor"), Coucy rejected a defensive strategy. "Though the Sultan's boasts be lies," he said, "that should not keep us from doing deeds of arms and pursuing our enemies, for that is the purpose for which we came." He said the crusaders were determined to seek out the enemy. His words were upheld by all the French and foreign allies present at the Council, although they aroused a fatal jealousy in Comte d'Eu, who felt that as Constable he should have taken precedence as spokesman.

Sigismund was forced to acquiesce; he could hardly, at this point, hang back. The march went forward, down the left bank of the Danube. Part of the Hungarian army veered out to the north to gather in the reluctant vassal forces of Wallachia and Transylvania. The main body of the allies followed the wide, flat, dreary river, where the only life was the flickering of water birds in the brown water and an occasional fisherman's boat poking out from the reed-grown banks. The remainder of the Hungarians under King Sigismund brought up the rear. French indiscipline and debaucheries reportedly increased the farther they went. Suppers were served of the finest wines and richest foods, transported by boat. Knights and squires indulged themselves with prostitutes they had brought along, and their example encouraged the men in outrages upon the women of the countries through which they passed. The arrogance and frivolity of the French irritated their allies, causing continual conflicts. Pillage and maltreatment of the inhabitants grew unrestrained as they entered the schismatic lands, further alienating peoples already hostile to Hungary. Appalled by such conduct under the banner of the Virgin and in the cause of the cross, accompanying clerics pleaded for discipline and threatened the anger of God in vain. "They might as well," wrote the Monk of St. Denis, "have talked to a deaf ass."

The tale of French "wrongs, robberies, lubricities, and dishonest things," told from hearsay, is long and explicit and has grown over the centuries. The Monk of St. Denis, basing his account of the crusade on what was told him by a survivor, vibrates with moral disapproval. He treats the French crusaders throughout with utmost scorn and reproach, denouncing them for immorality and blasphemy, for games of dice, "the father of cheating and lies," and warning repeatedly of a dire outcome to punish their wickedness. Taking their cue from him, later historians waxed purple on the subject of a perpetual bacchanalia, of young knights spending whole days with their fallen women in shameful pleasures, of soldiers drowned in wine. To know the truth is beyond our reach, for it must be remembered that even the contemporary accounts were written *ex post facto* when the natural reaction was to blame the tragedy of the crusade on the moral failure of the crusaders. Had they been victorious, would they have been charged with so many rich and lurid villainies?

At Orsova, where the Danube narrows through a defile called the Iron Gates, the expedition crossed over to the right bank. The crossing on pontoons and in boats took eight days, though not because the army numbered anything like the 100,000 sometimes suggested. For such a number to cross would have taken a month. Chroniclers habitually matched numbers to the awesomeness of the event. Like the Black Death, the Battle of Nicopolis was to shed so dark a shadow that some reports of the number of combatants range up to 400,000, with the chroniclers of each side giving the enemy twice as many as their own. The nearest to a firsthand figure is that given by the German Schiltberger, a participant, not a chronicler. The servant—or "runner," as he calls himself—of a Bavarian noble, he was a boy of sixteen when captured by the Turks at Nicopolis, and wrote, or more likely dictated, his simple unadorned narrative from memory when he finally made his way home after thirty years in bondage to the Turks. He places the total Christian forces at 16,000. German historians of the 19th century arrived by various intricate processes at a figure of about 7,500 to 9,000 for the Christians and somewhere from 12,000 to 20,000 for the Turks. They note in passing the impossibility of feeding off the country men and horses in the scores, much less hundreds, of thousands. (Five hundred years later, on the same battleground in the Russo-Turkish war of 1877, as pointed out by a recent student of the problem, the opposing forces numbered 8,000 Turks against some 10,000 Russians.)

Vidin, the western Bulgarian capital held under Turkish suzerainty, was the crusaders' first conquest. Its native prince, having no great motive to fight for an alien conqueror against an overwhelming force of invaders, promptly surrendered, foiling the French of combat. Although the only bloodshed was the slaughter of Turkish officers of the garrison, the field of Vidin nevertheless served for the knighting of Nevers and 300 companions. They felt confirmed in confidence as they moved on; Turkish garrison forces were enough to hold the Bulgarians in vassalage but not enough to challenge the great Christian army.

The next objective, 75 miles farther on, was Rachowa (Oryekova), a strong fortress protected by a moat and a double ring of walls. Determined on deeds of arms, the French hastened by a night march to reach it ahead of their allies and arrived at dawn just as the Turkish defenders came out to destroy the bridge over the moat. In a fierce fight, 500 men-at-arms including Coucy, D'Eu, Boucicaut, De la Marche, and Philippe de Bar gained the bridge but against vigorous resistance could make no further headway until Sigismund sent up reinforcements. Rather than allow others to share the honor of the fight, Boucicaut would have rejected the aid, but in spite of him the forces combined and reached the walls as night fell. Next morning, before combat could be renewed, the Bulgarian inhabitants arranged to surrender the town to Sigismund on condition that their goods and lives would be spared. Violating the surrender, the French put the town to pillage and massacre, claiming later that the place was taken by assault because their men-at-arms had already scaled the walls. A thousand prisoners, both Turkish and Bulgarian, were seized for ransom and the town left in flames. The Hungarians took the action as an insult to their King; the French charged the Hungarians with trying to rob them of their glory; Sigismund's apprehensions were confirmed.

Leaving a garrison to hold Rachowa, the divided army moved on to Nicopolis, storming and seizing one or two forts and settlements on the way, but by-passing one citadel from which emissaries escaped to carry news of the Christian army to the Sultan.

Where was Bajazet? The question has been endlessly debated. Was he still in Asia or already on the march? He was to reach Nicopolis with a massive force within three weeks of the taking of Rachowa, too short a time, even given his reputation for speed, to have assembled and ferried an army across the straits. The allied fleet, which might have prevented his passage, engaged in no naval action. The likelihood is that Bajazet was already on the European side at the siege of Constantinople, where he learned of the crusaders' plan of campaign—if he was not already informed by Gian Galeazzo—through intercepting correspondence between Sigismund and the Emperor Manuel. Breaking off the siege, he marched with the forces he had, gathering others at garrisons en route.

As the key to control of the lower Danube and communications with the interior, Nicopolis was essential to the crusaders, who quite rightly made it their strategic objective. They came within sight of the fortress high on its limestone cliff on September 12. A road ran along the narrow space between the river's edge and the base of the cliff. On the inland side a ravine split the cliff into two heights dominating the lower town and descending steeply to the plain. Like the castle of Coucy, it was a site formed by nature for command. The so-called fortress was actually two walled and fortified enclosures or towns, the larger one on the bluff and the smaller below, each containing military, civil, and religious buildings and in the larger one a bazaar or street of shops. The French had no difficulty recognizing an objective as formidable as Mahdia, even without the knowledge that it was well supplied with arms and provisions and commanded by a resolute Turkish governor, Dogan Bey. Convinced that the Sultan must come to the defense of so important a stronghold, the Governor was prepared to fight for time, and resist, if necessary, to the end.

The French had brought no catapults or other siege weapons, as they had brought none against Barbary. Funds had been invested in silks and velvet and gold embroidery, cargo space packed with wines and festive provisions. Why drag heavy machinery a thousand miles across Europe for use against a contemptible enemy? Something fundamental in the culture determined these choices.

Boucicaut made light of the lack of siege weapons. No matter, said he, ladders were easily made and, when used by men of courage, were worth more than any catapults. Knighthood's zealot, Boucicaut at age twelve had served as the Duc de Bourbon's page in the Normandy campaign, at sixteen was knighted at Roosebeke, at 24 held the lists at St. Ingelbert for thirty days, the most admired exploit of his generation. Two years later, in 1391, he was created Marshal. Unable to endure repose, he had gone twice to fight with the Teutonic Knights in Prussia and, afterward, to the East to ransom D'Eu in Cairo and visit Jerusalem. In honor of an episode in Tunisia when the Saracens were supposedly stopped from attack by the descent from Heaven of two beauteous women in white bearing a banner with a scarlet cross, he created an Order of the White Lady with the stated purpose of providing defenders of the gentle sex whenever needed. He was the epitome, not the norm, of chivalry, and could well have expressed (although the words are those of Jean de Beuil, a knight of the next century) what it was that inspired his kind in an age of personal combat:

How seductive is war! When you know your quarrel to be just and your blood ready for combat, tears come to your eyes. The heart feels a sweet loyalty and pity to see one's friend expose his body in order to do and accomplish the command of his Creator. Alongside him, one prepares to live or die. From that comes a delectable sense which no one who has not experienced it will ever know how to explain. Do you think that a man who has experienced that can fear death? Never, for he is so comforted, so enraptured that he knows not where he is and truly fears nothing.

Neither impetuous assault nor mines deep enough to hold three men upright could force entry into Nicopolis. The lack of siege engines and the steep slopes made it impossible to take the place by storm, necessitating a siege by blockade. The crusaders invested Nicopolis on all sides, strictly guarded all exits, and, with the addition of the allied blockade in the river, settled down to let the garrison and inhabitants starve. Two weeks passed in slackening discipline, in feasting, games, debaucheries, and the voicing of contempt for the non-appearing enemy. Allies were invited to splendid dinners in tents ornamented with pictures; nobles exchanged visits, appearing every day in new clothes with long sleeves and the inevitable pointed shoes. Despite hospitality, sarcasm and jokes about the courage of their allies deepened ill-feeling in the army. In drunkenness and carelessness, no sentinels were posted. Natives of the region, alienated by pillage, brought in no information. Foragers, however, moving farther out each day, reported rumors of the Turks' approach.

In truth, the Sultan with cavalry and infantry had by now passed through Adrianople and was advancing at forced pace over the Shipka pass to Tirnovo. A reconnaissance party of 500 Hungarian horsemen, sent forward by Sigismund, penetrated to the vicinity of Tirnovo, seventy miles to the south, and brought back word that the "Great Turk" was coming indeed. The same word passing to the beleaguered and desperate inhabitants of Nicopolis set off shouts of celebration and the noise of trumpets and drums, which Boucicaut claimed was a ruse. Convinced that the Turks would never dare attack, he threatened to cut off the ears of anyone reporting rumors of their approach, as demoralizing to the camp.

Coucy was less inclined to sit in ignorance for pride's sake, and felt the need of action to arouse the camp. "Let us find out what sort of men our enemies are," he said. According to a veteran's account told to the chronicler Jehan de Wavrin fifty years later, Coucy was consistently gracious to the local allies and "willingly kept by him the good companions of Wallachia who were well acquainted with Turkish customs and stratagems." Always a practical warrior, he was one of the few to concern himself with the nature and whereabouts of the enemy. With Renaud de Roye and Jean de Saimpy, Burgundy's chamberlain, and a company of 500 lances and 500 mounted archers, he rode south. Learning that a large Turkish body was approaching through a pass, he detached a party of 200 horsemen to engage the enemy and by a feigned retreat to draw them into pursuit, enabling the rest of the troop, concealed in ambush, to take them in the rear. This was a regular tactic for use when the terrain favored it, and it worked on this occasion with complete success. As the Turks rushed past, the crusaders issued from their concealment among the trees crying, "Our Lady be with the Sire de Coucy!" and closed in upon them from behind while the French vanguard, turning back from its feigned flight, attacked from the front. Thrown into confusion, the Turks could not rally and suffered great slaughter. Giving no quarter, Coucy's troop killed as many as they could and left the field, "happy that they could escape thence and return as they came."

Coucy's victory shook the camp from its frivolities, but with two unfortunate effects: it increased French confidence and it aggravated the Constable's jealousy, "for he saw how the Sire de Coucy had the admiration of all the company and also of the foreigners." Fomenting discord, he accused Coucy of imperiling the army out of bravado and depriving Nevers of leadership and glory.

Sigismund convened a council of war. He proposed that the Wallachian foot soldiers should be sent forward to meet the enemy's vanguard, which was customarily a rabble of rough conscripts whom the Turks sent ahead of their main force for purposes of pillage. In battle they were exposed to the brunt of opponents' attack in order to tire them. They were not worthy, Sigismund said, of the combat of knights. When the shock of contact had been absorbed by the common soldiers, French chivalry, forming the crusaders' front line, could enter battle in full and fresh strength. The Hungarians and allies would follow to support their attack and keep the *sipahis*, or Turkish cavalry, from dashing in upon their flanks. The honor and glory of battle, Sigismund is supposed to have concluded, did not lie in the first blows but in the last—in those blows that finished the combat and decided the victory.

D'Eu furiously objected. French knights had not come so far, he said, to be preceded into battle by a miserable peasant militia more accustomed to flee than to fight. The knight's custom was not to follow, but to lead and to encourage others by his example. "To take up the rear is to dishonor us and expose us to the contempt of all." Moreover, as Constable, he claimed the front place; anyone ahead of him would do him a mortal insult—an obvious reference to Coucy. Boucicaut supported him warmly; Nevers, in the belief that Turkish sabers and scimitars could not resist the lances and swords of France, was easily persuaded along with the younger hotheads of his suite. Sigismund departed to make his own battle plan.

Apparently within hours—the accounts are confused—he sent back a message that Bajazet was now within six hours' march of Nicopolis. The crusaders, said to be carousing at dinner and befuddled with wine, rose in disorder, some scorning the report, some in panic, some hastily arming. All the flaws and dissensions of the campaign came to a head in an atrocious act. Supposedly for lack of guards to spare, the prisoners of Rachowa were massacred, perhaps with less compunction because they were schismatics and infidels. No chronicler mentions who gave the order, although the Monk of St. Denis and others recognized it as an act of "barbarism."

At daybreak, as ranks were forming under the banners of the leaders, Sigismund, in a last effort, sent his Grand Marshal to report that only the Turkish vanguard had been sighted and to plead against a hasty offensive without knowledge of how near or how numerous was the Sultan's main force. Scouts had been sent out and would return within two hours with the information necessary for a plan of battle. The crusaders could rest assured, said the Marshal, that if they waited they were in no danger of being surrounded. "Sirs, do as I advise, for these are the orders of the King of Hungary and his council."

Nevers, hastily summoning his own council, asked for the opinion of Coucy and Vienne, who advised obeying the King of Hungary's desire, which seemed to them wise. "He has the right to tell us what he wants us to do," Coucy said. D'Eu burst out, "Yes, yes, the King of Hungary wishes to have the flower and honor of battle." That was his reason and no other. "We are the vanguard. He granted it to us and now wants to take it back. Those who want to may believe him. I do not." Seizing his banner, he cried, "Forward, in the name of God and St. George, you shall see me today a valorous knight!"

This speech by the brainless Constable, a third choice for that office, was declared a "presumption" by Coucy. He asked for the comment of Vienne, who, as eldest knight, carried the sovereign banner of the crusade. "When truth and reason cannot be heard," replied the Admiral, "then must presumption rule." If the Constable wished to fight, he said, the army must follow, but it would be stronger if it advanced in unity with the Hungarian and allied forces. D'Eu obstinately refused to wait. The dispute grew angry, with the hotheads charging that their elders were moved not so much by prudence as by fear. The familiar slights of each other's courage were flung. If Coucy and Vienne submitted, it was because prudence cannot make a strong case against the mystique of valor.

D'Eu gave the signal to advance, with himself in command of the van. Nevers and Coucy commanded the main body. With their backs to the fortress and the town, the French knights on their war-horses, so brilliantly armored "that every man seemed a king," rode forward with their mounted archers toward the enemy coming down from the hills ahead. The date was September 25. The Hospitalers, Germans, and other allies remained with the King of Hungary, who no longer controlled events.

The impact of the French assault easily smashed the untrained conscripts in the Turkish front lines. With the hot taste of success, even against opponents so unequal, the knights plunged ahead against the lines of trained infantry. They came under volleys of lethal arrows and up against rows of sharpened stakes which the Turks had planted with the points at the height of a horse's belly. How the French broke through is unclear. Out of the welter of different versions, a coherent account of the movements and fortunes of the battlefield is not to be had; there is only a tossing kaleidoscope. There are references to horses impaled, riders dismounting, stakes pulled up, presumably by the French auxiliaries. The knights fought on with sword and battle-ax, and, by their ardor and heavy weight of their horses and weapons, appear to have dominated and routed the Turkish infantry, who circled back to take refuge behind their cavalry. Coucy and Vienne urged a pause at this stage to rest and restore order in the ranks and give the Hungarians time to come up, but the younger men, "boiling with ardor" and believing they had glimpsed victory, insisted on pursuit. Having no idea of the enemy's numerical strength, they thought that what they had encountered so far was his whole force.

Accounts tell of a scramble uphill, of the *sipahis* on the wings sweeping down for envelopment, of the Hungarians and foreign contingents caught in confused combat on the plain, of a stampede of riderless horses—evidently from the line of stakes, where, in the havoc, the pages could not hold them. At sight of the stampede, the Wallachians and Transylvanians instantly concluded that the day was lost and deserted. Sigismund and the Grand Master of Rhodes and the Germans rallied their forces against the Turkish envelopment and were fighting with "unspeakable massacre" on both sides when a critical reinforcement of 1,500 Serbian horsemen gave the advantage to the enemy. As a vassal of the Sultan, the Serbian Despot, Stephen Lazarevich, might have chosen passive neutrality like the Bulgarians on whose soil the struggle was being fought, but he hated the Hungarians more than the Turks, and chose active fidelity to his Moslem overlord. His intervention was decisive. Sigismund's forces were overwhelmed. Dragged from the field by their friends, the King and the Grand Master escaped to a fisherman's boat on the Danube and, under a rain of arrows from their pursuers, succeeded in boarding a vessel of the allied fleet.

The French crusaders, of whom more than half were unhorsed, struggled in heavy armor to the plateau, where they expected to find the debris of the Turkish army. Instead, they found themselves face to face with a fresh corps of *sipahis* held in reserve by the Sultan. "The lion in them turned to timid hare," writes the Monk of St. Denis unkindly. With harsh clamor of trumpets and kettle drums and the war cry "Allah is Great!" the Turks closed in upon them. The French recognized the end. Some fled back down the slope; the rest fought with the energy of despair, "no frothing boar nor enraged wolf more fiercely." D'Eu's sword arm slashed right and left as bravely as he had boasted it would. Boucicaut, filled with warrior's pride mixed with shame for his errors that had brought his companions to this fatality, fought with an unlimited audacity that carved a circle of death around him. Philippe de Bar and Odard de Chasseron were killed. The banner of Notre Dame clutched in the hand of Admiral de Vienne wavered and fell. Bleeding from many wounds, he raised it again and, while trying to rally the faint-hearted from flight, with banner in one hand and sword in the other, was struck down and slain. Coucy's outstanding figure was seen "unshaken by the heavy leather clubs of the Saracens that beat upon his head" and their weapons that battered his armor. "For he was tall and heavy and of great strength and delivered such blows upon them as cut them all to pieces."

The Turks closed round Nevers. His bodyguard, prostrating themselves in attitudes of submission, appealed wordlessly for his life. Holy war or not, the infidel was as interested in rich ransoms as anyone else, and spared the Count. Upon his surrender, the remaining French yielded. The Battle of Nicopolis was lost, the debacle complete. Thousands of prisoners were taken, all the crusaders' equipment, provisions, banners, and golden clothes fell to the victors. "Since the Battle of Roncesvalles when [all] twelve peers of France were slain, Christendom received not so great a damage."

Though Froissart could not have known it, his epitaph for the crusade was historically just. The valor of the French had been extraordinary and the damage they inflicted on the enemy sufficient to show that if they had fought united with their allies, the result—and the history of Europe—might have been different. As it was, the Turks' victory, by turning back the Western challenge and retaining Nicopolis, lodged them firmly in Europe, ensured the fall of Constantinople, and sealed their hold on Bulgaria for the next 500 years. "We lost the day by the pride and vanity of these French," Sigismund said to the Grand Master; "if they had believed my advice, we had enough men to fight our enemies."

The defeat was followed by a frightful sequel. As Bajazet toured the battlefield, hoping to find the corpse of the King of Hungary—and finding that of Vienne with the banner still held by his dead hand—he was "torn by grief" at the sight of his losses, which outnumbered the Christian. He swore he would not leave their blood unavenged, and the discovery of the massacre of the prisoners of Rachowa augmented his rage. He ordered all prisoners to be brought before him next morning. Jacques de Helly, a French knight who had seen service with Murad I, was recognized by Turkish officials and called upon to designate the leading nobles for ransom. Coucy, Bar, D'Eu, Guy de Tremoille, Jacques de la Marche, and a number of others in addition to the Count of Nevers were thus spared, as well as all those judged to be under twenty for forced service with the Turks.

The rest, an uncertain figure of several thousand, were marched naked before the Sultan, bound together in groups of three or four, with hands tied and ropes around their necks. Bajazet looked at them briefly, then signed to the executioners to set to work. They decapitated the captives group by group, in some cases cut their throats or severed their limbs until corpses and killers alike were awash in blood. Nevers, Coucy, and the rest were forced to stand by the Sultan and watch the heads of their companions fall under the scimitars and the blood spurt from their headless trunks. Boucicaut, dazed and wounded, was recognized in the line. Nevers fell on his knees before the Sultan and, by a pantomime of hands pressed together with fingers entwined, indicating that they were like brothers, capable of equal ransom, succeeded in having Boucicaut spared. The killing continued from early morning to late afternoon until Bajazet, himself sickened at the sight or, as some say, persuaded by his ministers that too much rage in Christendom would be raised against him, called off the executioners. Estimates of the number killed range—aside from the wilder figures—from 300 to 3,000.

The dead on the battlefield were many more, nor did all the fugitives reach safety. Some escaped the Turks only to drown in the Danube when the ships which they boarded in fleeing hordes became overloaded and sank. Afterward those on board knocked off others trying to get on. A Polish knight swam across in armor, but most who tried this feat went under. Fearful of treachery on Wallachian shores, Sigismund sailed to the Black Sea and Constantinople and eventually made his way home by sea. Those of his allies who succeeded in crossing the Danube and attempted to return by land found the country stripped by the Wallachians. They wandered in the woods, reduced to rags and misery, covering themselves with hay and straw. Robbed, ragged, and starving, many perished on their way; a few reached their homes, among them Count Rupert of Bavaria in beggar's clothes, who died of his sufferings a few days later.

Luxury and immorality, pride and dissension, superior Turkish training, discipline, and tactics all contributed to the fatal outcome. Nevertheless, what basically defeated the crusaders was the chivalric insistence on personal prowess—which raises the question: Why do men fight? Wars may be fought for the glorification of man's feelings about himself, or for a specific goal in power, territory, or political balance. Medieval war was not always impractical. Charles V cared nothing for glorification if he could only get the English out of France. In the campaigns of Normandy, Arezzo, and Genoa, Coucy used every other means first—money, diplomacy, and political bargains—and arms only last, to achieve a specific objective. For all his chivalric renown, of the kind that attracted Nottingham's challenge, he belonged rather to the school of Charles V than to that of Boucicaut, although he seems to have had a foot in each.

Within a few years of the deaths of Charles V and Du Guesclin in 1380, their pragmatism had been unlearned. It had been successful but aberrant. The chivalric idea reasserted itself and determined the choices made in the course of the Nicopolis campaign. Why, in a society dominated by the cult of the warrior, was extravagant display more important than the equipment of victory? Why was absolutely nothing learned from an experience as recent as Mahdia? All the grandiose projects of the last decade—invasion of England, Guelders, Tunisia, the *Voie de Fait*—were either castles in the air or exercises in futility. Why, after a less than glorious fifty years since Crécy, was the attitude of the French crusaders so steeped in arrogance and overconfidence? Why were they unable to take into account the fact of opponents who did not fight for the same values and who obeyed different rules? It can only be answered that a dominant idea is slow to change and that, regardless of everything, the French still believed themselves supreme in war.

The crusaders of 1396 started out with a strategic purpose in the expulsion of the Turks from Europe, but their minds were on something else. The young men of Boucicaut's generation, born since the Black Death and Poitiers and the nadir of French fortunes, harked back to pursuit of those strange bewitchments, honor and glory. They thought only of being in the vanguard, to the exclusion of reconnaissance, tactical plan, and common sense, and for that their heads were to roll in blood-soaked sand at the Sultan's feet.

Chapter 27

Hung Be the Heavens with Black

Dead, deserted, or captive, the great Christian army was no more. The way to Hungary was open, but the Turks had sustained losses too great to allow them to proceed. In that sense the crusaders had not fought in vain. An attack of gout suffered by Bajazet, which supposedly prevented him from advancing, evoked from Gibbon the proposition that "An acrimonious humor falling on a single fibre of one man may prevent or suspend the misery of nations." In reality, not gout but the limits of military capacity were the deciding factor. The Sultan turned back to Asia, after first sending Jacques de Helly, on his oath to return, to carry word of the Turkish victory and demand for ransoms to the King of France and Duke of Burgundy.

The ordeal of the prisoners, many of them wounded, on the 350-mile march to Gallipoli was cruel. Stripped of clothing down to their shirts, in most cases without shoes, with hands tied, beaten and brutalized by their escorts, they followed on foot at their captors' heels over the mountain range and down onto the plain. To nobles equestrian almost from birth, the indignity of the barefoot trek was as great as the physical suffering. At Adrianople the Sultan paused for two weeks. The next stage took the march across the great, empty, treeless plain stretching, as if without horizon, toward the Hellespont. Not a bush nor shelter nor person was to be seen. The sun blazed down by day; when it set, the winds were chill and the October nights cold. In alien hands, uncared for and barely fed, crushed by defeat and fearful of the Sultan's intentions, the prisoners were in circumstances more dire than they had ever known.

Coucy, eldest of the captives, never before a prisoner nor a loser—in which he was virtually unique for his time—survived only by a miracle, not a metaphoric miracle but one of faith. Clad only in a "little jacket," with bare legs and the final indignity of no head covering, he was on the point of collapse from cold and exhaustion. Believing himself about to die, he prayed for aid to Notre Dame of Chartres. Though the cathedral was not of his province, the Virgin of Chartres was highly renowned as having been seen in person and known to have performed miracles.

"Suddenly, where there had been no one seen along the road stretching far over flat country, a Bulgarian appeared who was not of a people favorable to us." The mysterious stranger carried a gown and hat and heavy cloak which he gave to the Sire de Coucy, who put them on and was so restored in spirit by this sign of heavenly favor that he found new vigor to continue the march.

In gratitude, Coucy was to leave 600 gold florins in his last will to Chartres Cathedral, which was duly paid after his death by Geoffrey Maupoivre, a physician who accompanied the crusade, shared the captivity, witnessed the miracle, and served as Coucy's executor. He recorded the circumstances for the chapter of Chartres in order that they might know the origin of the unexpected gift.

At Gallipoli the nobles among the captives were kept in the upper rooms of the tower, while the 300 common prisoners—the boy Schiltberger among them—who were the Sultan's share of the booty were held below. The worst of the harsh conditions was deprivation of wine, the Europeans' daily drink throughout their lives. When the ship bearing Sigismund from Constantinople passed through the Hellespont less than half a mile from shore, the Turks, unable to challenge it at sea, lined up their prisoners at the water's edge and called mockingly to the King to come out of his boat and deliver his comrades. Sigismund had in fact made overtures from Constantinople to ransom his allies, though they had cost him the war, but his means were depleted and the Sultan knew there was more money to be had from France.

Clinging to Europe's farthest edge, the prisoners could see the fatal shores of Troy across the straits where the most famous, most foolish, most grievous war of myth or history, the archetype of human bellicosity, had been played out. Nothing mean nor great, sorrowful, heroic nor absurd had been missing from that ten years' catalogue of woe. Agamemnon had sacrificed a daughter for a wind to fill his sails, Cassandra had warned her city and was not believed, Helen regretted in bitterness her fatal elopement, Achilles, to vent rage for the death of his friend, seven times dragged dead Hector through the dust at his chariot wheels. When the combatants offered each other peace, the gods whispered lies and played tricks until they quarreled and fought again. Troy fell and flames consumed it, and from that prodigious ruin Agamemnon went home to be betrayed and murdered. Since then, through some 2,500 years, how much had changed? The romance of Troy was a favorite of the Middle Ages; Hector was one of the Nine Worthies carved on Coucy's castle walls. Did he, the Odysseus of this new war, think of that ancient siege and hollow triumph as he gazed across the straits?

After two months at Gallipoli, the prisoners were transferred to Brusa, the Ottoman capital in Asia. Forty miles inland and enclosed by a crescent of mountains, Brusa foreclosed any idea of rescue and removed them even farther from contact with home. Everything depended on ransom. The wait until word could reach and return from France was long and the Sultan's temper uncertain in the interval. The prisoners feared he might order their deaths at any moment, as easily as they had sent to death the prisoners of Rachowa.

Unbelievable rumors trickled into Paris in the first week of December. That the infidel could have crushed the elite of France and Burgundy seemed unimaginable; nevertheless, anxiety mounted. In the absence of official news, the rumor-mongers were imprisoned in the Châtelet and, if convicted of lying, were to be condemned to death by drowning. The King, the Duke of Burgundy, Louis d'Orléans, and the Duc de Bar each sent separate envoys speeding to Venice and Hungary to learn news of the crusaders, to find them, deliver letters, and bring back replies. On December 16 trading ships brought news into Venice of the disaster at Nicopolis and of Sigismund's escape, but by Christmas Paris was still without official word.

On Christmas Day, Jacques de Helly "all booted and spurred" entered the Palace of St. Pol, where the court was assembled for the solemn rites of the day, and, kneeling before the King, confirmed the terrible truth of the defeat. He told of the campaign, the climactic battle, the "glorious deaths," and Bajazet's hideous revenge. The court listened in consternation. The King and Dukes questioned Helly intently. The letters he brought from Nevers and the other seigneurs were the first news of who was alive and, by omission, who was missing or dead. Weeping relatives crowded around to learn the fate of son or husband or friend. Helly assured his audience that the Sultan would accept ransom, for he "loved gold and riches." If Froissart may be believed (which he need not always be), the seigneurs present expressed themselves "fortunate to be in a world where there could have been such a battle and to have knowledge of so powerful a heathen

King as Amurath-Bequin" (one of the various versions of the name of this distant potentate), who, with all his lineage, "would derive honor from the great adventure." What signifies is not whether these sentiments were actually expressed, but that they were considered by Froissart the appropriate sentiments for the occasion. At the close of the audience, the rumor-mongers of the Châtelet were released.

The nobility felt "bitter despair," according to the Monk of St. Denis, and "affliction reigned in all hearts." Black garments appeared everywhere, and Deschamps wrote of "funerals from morn to eve." Prayers and tears filled the churches, with sorrow the more intense because the dead had received no Christian burial and the lives of the survivors were feared for. Mourning and lament spread through Burgundy, where so many families suffered a loss. On January 9, a day of solemn services for the dead in the capital and the provinces, "it was piteous to hear the tolling of the bells in all the churches of Paris." Hardly had the English marriage been celebrated and the burden of the old war lifted at last when rejoicing was stifled, as if God did not wish to allow mankind cause for joy.

The ladies of France sorrowed grievously for their husbands and lovers, "especially," says Froissart, always concerned for his patron, "the Dame de Coucy, who wept piteously night and day and could take no comfort." Probably at the suggestion of her brothers, the Duc de Lorraine and Ferry de Lorraine, who came to console and advise her, she wrote on December 31 to the Doge of Venice begging him to aid in arranging the ransom of her husband. Two envoys—Robert d'Esne, a knight of Cambresis with five attendants, and Jacques de Willay, *châtelain* of St. Gobain, one of the Coucy properties—were dispatched separately, expressly to arrange the deliverance of Coucy and Henri de Bar. They were sent and their expenses paid by Louis d'Orléans, rather than by the Dame de Coucy. With communications no faster than a man could travel, there could be no word for many months.

The problem of arranging ransom was riddled with anxiety because of the unfamiliarity of dealing with a sovereign outside Christendom, of whom only the worst might be expected. On the advice of Jacques de Helly, who reported the Sultan's exorbitant passion for the accoutrements of the hunt, a convoy of magnificent gifts, especially selected to appeal to him, was assembled to accompany the Duke's ambassadors. Twelve white gerfalcons, of a rare and costly species of which Gian Galeazzo reportedly sent two to the Sultan every year, were escorted each by its own falconer, together with falconers' gauntlets embroidered with pearls and precious stones. Ten handsome horses and ten hounds, caparisoned in the arms of Burgundy and conducted by grooms in the Duke's white-and-scarlet livery, were to make the journey to Turkey, along with saddles of rich work inscribed in "Saracen letters and flowers of overseas," saddle draperies with buckles in the form of golden roses, fine scarlet cloth of Reims believed unknown in the Orient, and, as a subtle compliment to Bajazet, tapestries of Arras depicting the history of Alexander the Great, from whom he claimed to be directly descended. All this was dispatched with the King's chamberlain, an experienced diplomat, and three noble ambassadors, officials of Burgundy, who departed on January 20, 1397, to negotiate the ransom. In haste to keep his oath to the Sultan, Jacques de Helly had already hurried on ahead with letters for the prisoners.

Reconciliation with Gian Galeazzo because of his known influence at the Ottoman court had suddenly become all-important. The ambassadors were directed to travel via Milan and convey to Gian Galeazzo, whose first wife had been a princess of France, the King's belated grant of the right to add the fleur-de-lys to the Visconti escutcheon, and to make every effort to obtain his help. Meanwhile, the first relay of envoys, sent in early December, had reached Venice, where they learned of the defeat and were endeavoring to make their way to the prisoners. Venice, whose interest in maintaining her trade in the Levant made her the link with the Moslem world—and something less than a wholehearted combatant in the crusade—served throughout as the center for news, travel arrangements, cash, and credit.

In Burgundy and Flanders the Duke's tax-collectors swarmed again. Hardly recovered from financing the crusade, his subjects were now required to salvage the survivors. The traditional aid for the lord's ransom was demanded from every town and county, plus a contribution from the clergy. The Duke met with bargaining and resistance and had to accept less than he asked for. The sums were not cash but payments to be drawn from revenues extending over months and years. Some were still being levied and disputed three years later. The cry, "Money! Money!", wrote Deschamps, resounded through his lifetime. Now and again, he says, the commoners, driven to distraction, rise and kill the tax-collectors, then, astonished by their success, collapse again, to be hounded once more by nobles with swords and lawyers with documents, crying in threatening voices, "Sà, de l'argent! Sà, de l'argent!"

In Brusa, Coucy had not fared well. Some accounts say that he fell into a deep chagrin and melancholy which nothing could lighten, that he insisted he would never see France again, that after so many adventures this was destined to be his last. His appraisal was realistic enough, more likely grounded in physical illness from wounds or disease in harsh conditions than in "mourning for the victory of Anti-Christ over the Christians," as suggested by L'Alouëte, first historian of the Coucy dynasty. At 56, he was not old, even though it is generally considered that old age came early in the Middle Ages. In fact, while a large proportion of the population died early, those who lived into their fifties and sixties were not venerable in body and mind nor considered so. Life-expectancy charts may reflect statistics, but not the way people see themselves. According to an anonymous poem of the mid-14th century, life's span was 72 years, consisting of twelve ages corresponding to the months of the year. At 18, the youth begins to tremble like March with the approach of spring; at 24, he becomes amorous as the blossoming of April, and nobility and virtue enter his soul along with love; at 36, he is at the summer solstice, his blood as hot as the sun of June; at 42, he has acquired experience; at 48, he should think of harvesting; at 54, he is in the September of life when goods should be stored up; age 60, the October of life, is the onset of old age; 66 is dark November when all green withers and dies and a man should think on death, for his heirs are waiting for him to go if he is poor and waiting more eagerly if he is rich; 72 is December, when life is as mournful as winter and there is nothing left to do but die.

Coucy had led an extraordinarily active life, never at rest, never pausing after one task before undertaking the next. He showed no signs of age or slackening when he undertook the crusade nor when he led the brilliant foray against the Turks on the day before the battle—the only successful French action of the campaign. Then came the disaster in a battle launched against his advice, defeat in an enterprise of which he had been given the guidance, the ghastly spectacle of his comrades and dependents slaughtered before his eyes, the shame and hardships of an ignoble captivity, the remoteness from home, uncertainty of rescue, and fear of a captor not bound by the rules. As one whose life, though anything but soft, had been singularly fortunate, Coucy was not conditioned for so much misfortune. Perhaps he recognized in the Battle of Nicopolis a profound failure of knighthood, and sensed in its outcome a time to die.

On February 16, 1397, preparatory to death, he drew up at Brusa his last will, or, more precisely, a lengthy codicil to a previous will. By this time he may have been removed from prison to better quarters under provisional liberty guaranteed by the rich and noble Francesco Gattilusio, Genoese Lord of Mitylene (Lesbos)—Coucy's "relative," according to Froissart. One of the independent lords of the Aegean islands called the Archipelago, Gattilusio was a man of influence at the

Ottoman court who, even without kinship, might well have given surety for a great French baron well known in Genoa. The Christian powers of the Archipelago under the shadow of the advancing Turks were acutely affected by the defeat at Nicopolis. The blow to the prestige, not to mention to the arms, of Christianity undermined their position, and the spectacle of prominent Christian nobles imprisoned and perhaps dying in infidel hands was a disturbing one for them. It was in their interest to secure a release, and reports of the prisoners' misery excited their pity. One merchant of the Archipelago, Nicholas of Aenos, sent a gift of fish, bread, sugar, and linens from his wife in addition to a loan of money. One can only hope that, by courtesy of Gattilusio, Coucy in his last days was not lodged on bare stone.

"Sound of mind but infirm of body, and considering that nothing is more certain than death and nothing uncertain but its hour," Coucy drew up his lengthy codicil in Latin, probably by the hand of Geoffrey Maupoivre, who was a Master of Arts as well as of Medicine. In the care and precision and nature of these instructions and their reflection of what was on a man's mind in his last hours, there is no better mirror of the Middle Ages.

"First and above all," he directs burial in France according to the terms of his previous will (which had specified burial of his body at Nogent and of his heart at his foundation of Ste. Trinité in Soissons). At the very end of the codicil, as if reminded of possible difficulties in embalming and transporting the body to France, he charges his executors with the return of his bones and heart, without fail. At a time when official belief insisted that the body was carrion and the after-life of the soul all that mattered, the extreme concern shown for every detail of disposal of the physical remains was remarkable.

Next in importance was Ste. Trinité, his heaviest investment in salvation. He orders for the monastery "a notable silver cross weighing forty Paris marks [about 23 pounds], a silver censer, two cruets for water and wine for use in the Divine service, a silver ewer for washing the hands of the priest, a fine and notable silver-gilt chalice of fitting weight and workmanship for such a monastery, four pairs of ornaments for the priest, deacon, and sub-deacon, of which three shall be for ordinary use and the fourth for the solemnities of important holy days."

In the further interest of his soul, bequests follow to no fewer than 21 separate churches and chapels, including Notre Dame de Chartres, "who, as we firmly believe, made for us a visible miracle." The other bequests range from 100 florins for the chapel of Pierre de Luxemburg at Avignon to 1,000 florins for Notre Dame de Liesse, where Coucy had escorted Charles VI after his first attack of madness, plus 100 florins each to five separate chantries in Soissons for prayers for his soul, and 6,000 to his executors for further prayers at their discretion. The sum of 1,000 florins was to be distributed among the poor of Paris, the same to the poor of his own domain, and 800 bequeathed to the Hôtel Dieu in Paris.

Unlike many nobles concerned with deathbed restitutions, Coucy evidently had no one he had wronged on his mind, but only some debts to be fulfilled. His only possessions at hand—a gown and a tapestry— are to be sold to pay his servants and to pay Abraham, "apothecary and merchant of Brusa," for medicines. Debts incurred on the voyage are to be paid by means of jewels he has deposited in Venice. The King of France is asked to hold his lands in France to ensure that revenues will be collected and used for all legacies he has directed. Geoffrey Maupoivre and Jacques d'Amance, Marshal of Lorraine (the duchy of his wife's family), are named executors, supplemented by Comte d'Eu, Boucicaut, and Guy de Tremoille for aid and counsel. These three together with Guillaume de Tremoille, Jacques de la Marche, and six other French knights witnessed and signed the document.

Two days later, on February 18, 1397, Enguerrand VII, Sire de Coucy and Count of Soissons, died in Brusa.

A whole man in a fractured time, he was the least compromised of his class and kind by brutality, venality, and reckless indulgence. His fellows have been well described by Clisson's biographer as "in turn refined and barbaric, generous and bloody, knavish and chivalrous, above mankind in their courage and love of glory, beneath mankind in their hates, their furious follies, their duplicity and savage cruelty." Coucy was distinct from most in being apparently immune from those furious follies. He saw his role steadily, accepted every responsibility but the constableship, remained sagacious in judgment, cool and capable in performance. In that steadiness, sagacity, and competence, and in commanding the respect and trust of all associates, he had many of the qualities of George Washington, short of leadership, which needs a cause to call it forth. If there have been mute inglorious Miltons in rural villages, presumably there have been unrealized Washingtons born in unpropitious times. The 14th century produced bourgeois leaders like the two Van Arteveldes, Etienne Marcel, Cola di Rienzi, but few from the noble class, partly because leadership was presupposed in the king, who, until the time of Charles V, personally led the nobles into battle. When Jean II was in captivity, the northern French nobles asked Charles of Navarre, because he was a king, to lead them against the Jacques. The nobility, however, had coherence only when it was threatened as a class. Otherwise, baronial interests were too sectional and habits of independence too strong to allow for a leader, even when the war against the English gradually built up a cause.

Coucy's English marriage set him apart during twelve crucial years. After his repudiation of England, following the death of his father-in-law, he began to emerge as a leading figure in the Normandy campaign and could have succeeded Du Guesclin as Constable if he had wanted to, but no concept of national leadership attached to that post, no body of public opinion or cohort of colleagues was asking to be led. The moment of what-might-have-been passed with the death of Charles V, and under the self-serving rule of the uncles, national purpose was frittered away. Enguerrand did not innovate nor rise above his time; he went with it, served it better than most, and died of its values. It was reduced by his going. "This Enguerrand VII," wrote the biographer of Boucicaut, "was esteemed the seigneur of most merit of his time."

Coucy's death was not known in Paris for two months. Robert d'Esne and, after him, Jacques de Willay learned of it in Venice on their way east. Still unaware on March 31, Louis d'Orléans in great solicitude sent a clerk of Coucy's estate to Turkey with clothing, having learned of the prisoners' impoverished condition. In April, Willay brought back the embalmed heart and body (or bones; whether the actual body was buried in France has been disputed). Only then was the Dame de Coucy notified that her husband was dead. According to the biographer of Boucicaut who tends normally to rhapsodize, she so bewailed her loss "that it seemed that heart and life would leave her, and never more did she wish to marry again, nor allow mourning to depart from her heart." A funeral of impressive grandeur was conducted by the Bishops of Noyon and Laon, the body (or other remains) being buried in an imposing tomb at Nogent, and the heart at Ste. Trinité, marked by a plaque showing an engraved heart superimposed over the Coucy arms. Deschamps wrote a dirge as if for a national event, lamenting "the end and death of Enguerrand the baron . . . mourned by every noble heart."

> O St. Lambert, Coucy, La Fère,
> Marle, Oisy and St. Gobain,
> Weep for your lord, the good seigneur
> Who served so well his sovereign
> With prowess great in many lands . . .
> Who for the faith in Turkey died.
> Let us pray God to pardon him.

In his day bright and beautiful,
Wise, strong, and of great largesse,
A true knight of labor hard
And no repose; in his great house,
He welcomed knights from morn to eve
Who came to join his company.
Preux and bold in Lombardy was he,
He took Arezzo, city of renown,
Made tremble Pavia and Milan.
Let us pray God to pardon him.

Many a heart is sad for him
That none is left to bear his arms. . . .

The stanzas continue, but, given an erratic meter combined with a rigid chain of only three rhymes winding through 55 lines, the charm of this and other 14th century French poetry is limited, and English, in any case, can do it no justice.

Ransom for the remaining prisoners was finally arranged in June 1397 after prolonged negotiations by the Duke's ambassadors at the Sultan's court. The sum was fixed at 200,000 ducats or gold florins, approximately equal in value to French francs. Burgundy's extravagant gifts misfired, it was said, convincing Bajazet that princes who could command such rare and precious things could pay very highly indeed. All the resources of the banking network were mobilized, chiefly under the direction of Burgundy's chief purveyor and banker, Dino Rapondi, a native of Tuscany with headquarters in Paris and Bruges. So widespread was his commerce that his name was said to be known wherever there were merchants. Through him, the King and his uncles acquired precious books, silks, furs, tapestries, fine linen shirts and handkerchiefs, amber and unicorn's horn and other curiosities. Rapondi advised raising the ransom money from the merchants of the Archipelago, who should be written to amiably and promised profit on the loans and credit they could arrange.

Meanwhile, Boucicaut and Guy de Tremoille, released on provisional liberty to seek funds in the Levant, had reached Rhodes, where Tremoille, evidently in weakened condition, fell ill and died at Eastertime. The Knights of Rhodes, anxious like the merchants about Christian prestige, pawned the plate of their Order to raise 30,000 ducats for a down payment on the ransom. The King of Cyprus added 15,000, and various merchants and wealthy citizens of the Archipelago made loans amounting to 30,000. Sigismund had grandly offered to subscribe half the ransom, but as he was perennially short of money, the best he could do was assign 7,000 ducats of revenues owed him by Venice. More than half the total was underwritten on behalf of Burgundy by Gattilusio, Seigneur of Mitylene.

On a down payment of 75,000, the prisoners were released on June 24 on their promise to remain in Venice until the entire sum was paid. One more of their number did not regain liberty. By a cruel justice, Comte d'Eu died on June 15, nine days before the release. Bajazet's farewell to the others was not courtly. Addressing Jean de Nevers, he said he disdained to ask him for an oath not to take up arms against him in the future. "Raise what power thou wilt and spare not, but come against me. Thou shalt find me ever ready to receive thee and thy company in the field in plain battle . . . for I am ready to do deeds of arms and ever ready to conquer further into Christendom." The Sultan then required the departing crusaders to witness the spectacle of his hunt conducted by 7,000 falconers and 6,000 huntsmen with hounds in satin blankets and leopards in diamond collars.

Weakened in health and even more in resources, the crusaders made no haste to regain France, or even Venice. To travel in indigence was unthinkable for a Prince of Burgundy. He and his companions stopped off at Mitylene, Rhodes, and other islands to rest and recover and borrow money wherever they could. The lady of Mitylene gave them all new shirts, gowns, and apparel of fine damask, "every man according to his degree." The Knights of Rhodes entertained them for a month. In Venice, which they did not reach until October, the financial transactions involving all parties connected with the crusade were intricate and tremendous. Through loans and guarantees, enough was collected to make up the ransom but not enough to go home in style.

Repayment of debts amounting to 100,000 ducats which they had incurred for living and traveling expenses since their release, together with the cost of the journey home in appropriate splendor, required nearly again as much as the ransom. The Duke and Duchess of Burgundy did not wish their son to travel through Europe and make his appearance in France looking like a fugitive. The Duke scraped every resource, to the point of reducing the pay and pensions of Burgundian officials, to supply his son with a magnificent retinue and provide gifts for all concerned. Dino Rapondi came to Venice with an order on the Duke's treasury for 150,000 francs and spent the winter arranging transfers of funds, of which repayment to the merchants of the Archipelago came last. Three years later the Seigneur of Mitylene was still owed the entire sum he had loaned, and a three-cornered transaction among Burgundy, Sigismund, and the Republic of Venice was not settled for twenty-seven years. These difficulties did not inhibit the

Duke's style of living. In 1399 he bought from Dino Rapondi two illuminated books for 6,500 francs and, in the next year, two more for 9,000 and 7,500 apiece.

An outbreak of plague in Venice while the crusaders were there caused them to remove to Treviso on the mainland, but took nevertheless the life of one more—Henri de Bar. If the epidemic was the Black Death, it had come full circle in Coucy's family, taking first his mother and now his son-in-law. It was a sad death so close to home, and in leaving Marie, who was the primary heir, both fatherless and a widow, it was to have a sad effect on the Coucy domain, so long coveted by the royal house.

The crusaders, of whom only Nevers, Boucicaut, Guillaume de Tremoille, and Jacques de la Marche were left among the leaders, along with some seven or eight other lords and knights, re-entered France in February 1398. They were received at the gates of Dijon with acclamation and gifts of silver presented by the municipality. In memory of his own captivity, Nevers liberated from the city prison, "by his own hand," all whom he found there. Dijon held solemn services for the dead crusaders, but thereafter the welcome was all celebration and joy.

In Paris the King gave his cousin a well-considered gift of 20,000 livres. The towns of Burgundy and Flanders vied for the honor of receiving him. On orders of his father, he made a triumphal progress to exhibit himself to the people whose taxes had bought his return. Minstrels preceded him through the gates, fetes and parades greeted him, more gifts of silver and of wine and fish were presented. Considering all the bereaved families of Burgundy whose sons did not return, the receptions probably represented not so much popular enthusiasm as organized joy, in which the 14th century excelled. Celebration was required for the prestige of the Duke and his heir, and the towns were happy enough to cooperate in expectation of the favors that generally accompanied such joyous occasions. The magistrates of Tournai expected Nevers' ceremonial entry to be graced by a plenary pardon, in which they were disappointed.

In pomp and minstrelsy, the culminating fiasco of knighthood was interred. After Nicopolis, nothing went right for France for many long years. The presiding values of chivalry did not change, but the system was in its decadence. Froissart found this in England too, where a friend of former times said to him, "Where are the great enterprises and valiant men, the glorious battles and conquests? Where are the knights in England who could do such deeds now? . . . The times are changed for the worse. . . . Now felonies and hates are nourished here."

The celebrations for Nevers could not conceal the defeat, and the moralists found in it reinforcement for pessimism. Mézières immediately composed an *Epistre Lamentable et Consolatoire*, Deschamps a ballade "For the French Fallen at Nicopolis," Bonet an allegorical satire in the form of an "Apparition of Master Jean de Meung," who appears in a dream to reproach the author for not protesting the evils that are destroying France and Christendom. Deschamps states openly that Nicopolis was lost "through pride and folly," although he lays some blame upon the Hungarians "who fled." Mézières similarly has hard words for the "schismatics," who, "for the great hate they bear the Latins," preferred to be subjects of the Sultan rather than of the King of Hungary. But essentially he sees the defeat as the consequence of the crusaders' lack of the four moral virtues necessary to any army: order, discipline, obedience, and justice. In the absence of these, God departs from an army, which then becomes easily discomfited, and this accounts for all the discomfitures since Crécy and Poitiers. Mézières' call for a new crusade aroused no response. The *Epistre Lamentable* was his last work. Eight years later his scolding and his passion were finally stilled in death. Like any Isaiah, he grew tiresome, but his yearning for goodness in society spoke for all the silent people who yearned for it too but left no record.

Bonet, while including the usual censure of knights for their soft life and love of capons and ducks, white shirts and fine wines, comes to something more basic. The knights leave the peasants behind because they think them "worth nothing," he writes, although the poor can endure hardship and coarse food, and, if armed, would wage a good fight, like the Portuguese peasants who fought bravely and killed many knights at Aljubarrota. (The reference is to a battle of 1385 in the same year and with similar results as the Swiss Battle of Sempach.) While Bonet and others had often in the past condemned the warrior for robbery and cruelty toward peasants, they were now ready to condemn chivalry's fundamental assumption that military capacity resided in none but the mounted knight. The chronicler of the *Quatre Valois*, writing at about this time, pointed out that the common soldier had been decisive in certain combats "and for this, poor men should not be held without honor nor in vile esteem." He cited a battle of the King of Cyprus against the Saracens in 1367, in which the day was saved by action of the sailors who remained to guard the ships, and this was by the will of Christ, who did not wish Christian chivalry to perish at the hands of the infidels, and moreover "wished to give an example to nobles. . . . For our Lord Jesus Christ wants no grandiloquence or vanity. He wishes victory to be gained by the common people so that the great should not take vainglory."

Vainglory, however, no matter how much medieval Christianity insisted it was a sin, is a motor of mankind, no more eradicable than sex. As long as combat was desirable as the source of honor and glory, the knight had no wish to share it with the commoner, even for the sake of success.

The Turkish victory had no immediate effect in Europe because Bajazet had to turn east against the rise of a fierce enemy in Asia. The rapid conquests of Tamerlane at the head of a revived Mongol-Turkic horde were comparable, in Gibbon's large words, "to the primitive convulsions of nature which agitated and altered the surface of the globe." Overrunning Anatolia, leaving a trail of ruined cities and pyramids of skulls, Tamerlane met and defeated the Ottoman army at Angora (Ankara) in 1402 and captured the Sultan alive. Kept in a wagon fitted with iron bars, Bajazet was dragged along on the Mongol path of conquest until he died of misery and shame—as if history had deliberately arranged a symmetrical retribution.

Absorbed in its own factions and schisms, Europe failed to seize the occasion to break the Ottoman hold on the Balkans. Except for a brave but minor expedition led by Boucicaut—the last trickle of the crusades—Constantinople could obtain no more help from the West; Sigismund was embroiled with the Germans and Bohemia; France and England were each torn by domestic conflict. Bajazet's son held his own against Tamerlane, the Mongol eruption subsided, Bajazet's grandson advanced again in Europe, and in 1453 his great-grandson Mohammed II conquered Constantinople.

At Coucy, rival ambitions swirled around the great barony with its castles of grandeur, its 150 towns and villages, its famous forests, its "many fine ponds, many good vassals, . . . much great nobility and inestimable revenues." Marie de Bar, Coucy's eldest daughter, and the Dame de Coucy, his widow, entered into a prolonged contest over the inheritance, Marie claiming the whole and the Dame de Coucy claiming half. Neither ceding, they lived in hostility, each in a separate castle of the domain with her captains and entourage of relatives, each pursuing lawsuits. At the same time the Célestins of Ste. Trinité brought a lawsuit against the widow, claiming that she had failed to carry out Coucy's last bequests to their monastery.

Meanwhile, Queen Isabeau, still concerned primarily with her parental family, was trying to promote a marriage between her father, Stephen of Bavaria, then in Paris as ambassador of the Empire, and the Dame de Coucy. This raised the prospect of the strategic domain passing into foreign hands, for it was feared that Marie might be pressured into allowing the house of Bavaria to take possession by purchase or otherwise. To frustrate this design, Louis d'Orléans pressured Marie (by "threats and menaces," according to one source) into selling the barony to him, disregarding the widow's claims on the ground that the barony was indivisible. Whether his motive was primarily the interests of France or his personal aggrandizement vis-à-vis the Duke of Burgundy is an open question. In any event, he acquired one of the greatest properties of northern France, which gave him a wedge between his uncle's two territories of Burgundy and Flanders. To confirm the patriotic motive, Marie was persuaded to state in the deed of sale, concluded November 15, 1400, that she "cannot put or transfer [the property] more securely for the good of the Kingdom of France than in the person of Monseigneur the Duc d'Orléans."

The purchase price was 400,000 livres, of which Louis paid only 60,000 down. Marie retained the usufruct of the domain and the use of the castles of La Fère and Du Châtelet for her residence, but legal disputes continued after the sale. By some means or other she was compelled to acquit Louis of 200,000 livres, or half the price, while the balance of 140,000 on the other half remained unpaid. No less than eleven lawsuits were brought by Marie against Orléans in an attempt to recover, before she died suddenly after a wedding feast in 1405, not without "a suspicion of poison." Her son Robert de Bar continued the litigation, both as plaintiff against Orléans and as defendant against the Dame de Coucy, who had not, after all, married Stephen of Bavaria and was still maintaining her dower rights in the courts. In 1408, after the death of Louis d'Orléans, Parlement allowed the widow's claim, but this lapsed a few years later when her daughter Isabel, who had married the brother of Jean de Nevers, died without an heir. Meanwhile Charles d'Orléans, Louis' son, remained in possession, and when Charles's son became King as Louis XII, the barony of Coucy passed, where it had long been desired, to the crown.

The tormented century sank to a close in keeping with its character. In March 1398 the Emperor Wenceslas and the King of France met at Reims in a renewed effort to end the schism of which they represented opposite sides. Charles VI had been persuaded that he would never recover from his affliction until the Church was re-united. To unseat Benedict, the University of Paris had proposed that France withdraw obedience, but before adopting this radical measure, one more attempt to obtain mutual abdication by the popes was to be tried. The assent of the Empire to exert pressure on Boniface was required, and this was the purpose of the assembly at Reims. Owing to the disabilities of the two major sovereigns, one incapacitated by alcohol and the other by insanity, the result was not what it might have been. Renewed madness was already darkening Charles's mind when he arrived and in the brief intervals when he was lucid, Wenceslas was drunk. The Emperor entered the negotiations in a stupor which he maintained by steady consumption while vaguely agreeing to anything that was proposed. When reason entirely deserted Charles, the assembly dispersed.

Persuasions and threats of force were brought to bear on both popes, and resisted. France resorted to withdrawal of obedience and even to a siege of the papal palace with Pope Benedict inside, but neither of these measures succeeded in effectively deposing him, and the first caused so much trouble that it had to be rescinded. Richard II, intent on friendship with France, agreed to demand the abdication of Boniface, which only succeeded in violently antagonizing the English, already disaffected by the King's misgovernment. The citizens of London, partisans of Gloucester, would now call the King nothing but Richard of Bordeaux (his birthplace) and were greatly excited against him, saying, "His heart is so French that he cannot hide it, but a day will come to pay for all."

Then happened in England those "great and horrible" events, the like of which, Froissart felt, had not been seen in all the history he had recorded. Convinced of plots against him, Richard removed Gloucester to Calais, where he was strangled with a towel, executed Arundel, banished Warwick and the Percys, and so aroused the fears and hates of his subjects that in 1399 his cousin Henry of Bolingbroke was able to depose him without a sword being raised in the rightful King's defense. Compelled publicly to resign the crown, Richard was transferred from the Tower to a more secluded prison, where, within a year, he died of purposeful neglect, or worse. The prop of peaceful relations with France was removed. Bolingbroke (now Henry IV) talked boldly of abrogating the truce, but usurpation breeds rebellion and he was too occupied in maintaining his throne to look for trouble abroad.

With these events, Froissart lost heart. If the sale of Guy de Blois' property had damaged his ideals, the deposition of the King of England shocked him profoundly, not for any love of Richard II, but because the act was subversive of the whole order that sustained his world. The sixty-odd years of his—and Coucy's—lifetime, which had seemed to him a pageant of unending interest and excitement, were closing in shadow. He glimpsed hollowness and could not continue; his history breaks off as the century ends.

If the sixty years seemed full of brilliance and adventure to a few at the top, to most they were a succession of wayward dangers; of the three galloping evils, pillage, plague, and taxes; of fierce and tragic conflicts, bizarre fates, capricious money, sorcery, betrayals, insurrections, murder, madness, and the downfall of princes; of dwindling labor for the fields, of cleared land reverting to waste; and always the recurring black shadow of pestilence carrying its message of guilt and sin and the hostility of God.

Mankind was not improved by the message. Consciousness of wickedness made behavior worse. Violence threw off restraints. It was a time of default. Rules crumbled, institutions failed in their functions. Knighthood did not protect; the Church, more worldly than spiritual, did not guide the way to God; the towns, once agents of progress and the commonweal, were absorbed in mutual hostilities and divided by class war; the population, depleted by the Black Death, did not recover. The war of England and France and the brigandage it spawned revealed the emptiness of chivalry's military pretensions and the falsity of its moral ones. The schism shook the foundations of the central institution, spreading a deep and pervasive uneasiness. People felt subject to events beyond their control, swept, like flotsam at sea, hither and yon in a universe without reason or purpose. They lived through a period which suffered and struggled without visible advance. They longed for a remedy, for a revival of faith, for stability and order that never came.

The times were not static. Loss of confidence in the guarantors of order opened the way to demands for change, and *miseria* gave force to the impulse. The oppressed were no longer enduring but rebelling, although, like the bourgeois who tried to compel reform, they were inadequate, unready, and unequipped for the task. Marcel could not impose good government, neither could the Good Parliament. The Jacques could not overthrow the nobles, the *popolo minuto* of Florence could not advance their status, the English peasants were betrayed by their King; every working-class insurrection was crushed.

Yet change, as always, was taking place. Wyclif and the protestant movement were the natural consequence of default by the Church. Monarchy, centralized government, the national state gained in strength, whether for good or bad. Seaborne enterprise, liberated by the compass, was reaching toward the voyages of discovery that were to burst the confines of Europe and find the New World. Literature from Dante to Chaucer was expressing itself in national languages, ready for the great leap forward in print. In the year that Enguerrand de Coucy died, Johan Gutenberg was born, although that in itself marked no turn of the tide. The ills and disorders of the 14th century could not be without consequence. Times were to grow worse over the next fifty-odd years until at some imperceptible moment, by some mysterious chemistry, energies were refreshed, ideas broke out of the mold of the Middle Ages into new realms, and humanity found itself re-directed.

Epilogue

In the next fifty years, the forces set in motion during the 14th century played themselves out, some of them in exaggerated form like human failings in old age. After a heavy recurrence in the last year of the old century, the Black Death disappeared, but war and brigandage were renewed, the cult of death grew more extreme, the struggle to end the schism and reform the abuses of the Church more desperate. Depopulation reached its lowest point in a society already weakened both physically and morally.

In France, Jean de Nevers, who had succeeded his father as Duke of Burgundy in 1404, turned assassin, precipitating a train of evils. In 1407 he employed a gang of toughs to murder his rival Louis d'Orléans in the streets of Paris. As Louis was returning to his hotel after dark, he was set upon by hired killers who cut off his left hand holding the reins, dragged him from his mule, hacked him to death with swords, axes, and wooden clubs, and left his body in the gutter while his mounted escort, which never seems to have been much use on these occasions, fled.

Protected from penalty by his ducal power, John the Fearless publicly defended his act, through a spokesman, as justifiable tyrannicide, charging Louis with vice, corruption, sorcery, and a long list of public and private villainies. Since Louis was associated in the public mind with the extravagance and license of the court and with its endless demand for money, John of Burgundy was able to make himself appear the people's champion by opposing the government's latest tax levy. In the void left by a mad King, the Duke filled the people's craving for a royal friend and protector.

Mortal hatreds and implacable conflict between Burgundians and Orléanists consumed France for the next thirty years. Regional and political groups formed around the antagonists, brigand companies employed by both sides re-emerged, leaving their smoking tracks of pillage and massacre. Each side raised the Oriflamme against the other, won and lost control of the helpless King and the capital, multiplied taxes. Administrative structures fell into disorder, finance and justice were abused, offices bought and sold, Parlement became a market place of corruption. The realm, declared an Orléanist manifesto, was sunk in crime and sin with God blasphemed everywhere, "even by churchmen and children."

The middle class rose in the same effort to oust corrupt officials and establish measures of good government as Etienne Marcel had led more than fifty years before—and with no more success. Impatient for immediate results, a turbulent collection of the butchers, skinners, and tanners of Paris, called Cabochiens after their leader Caboche, broke into fierce revolt, reproducing the revolt of the Maillotins with increased brutality. Inevitably the bourgeois reacted against them and opened the gates to the Orléanist party which suppressed the revolt, restored venal officials, canceled the reforms and persecuted the reformers. John of Burgundy, who had judiciously removed himself during the violence, was declared a rebel and, following the old pattern of Charles of Navarre, entered into alliance with the English.

Henry IV of England, after continuous struggle against Welsh revolt, baronial antagonists, and a son impatient for the crown, died in 1413, to be succeeded by the said son who at 25 was prepared, with all the sanctimonious energy of a reformed rake, to enter upon a reign of stern virtue and heroic conquest. Relying on the anarchy in France and his arrangements with the Duke of Burgundy, and hoping by military successes to unite the English behind the house of Lancaster, Henry V took up the old war and the threadbare claim to the French crown which had not gained in validity by passing to him through a usurper. On the pretext of various French perfidies, he invaded France in 1415 in Mars's favorite month of August, announcing that he had come "into his own land, his own country, and his own kingdom." After the siege and capture of Harfleur in Normandy, he marched north for Calais to return home for the winter. About thirty miles short of his goal, not far from the battlefield of Crécy, he met the French army at Agincourt.

The Battle of Agincourt has inspired books and studies and aficionados, but it was not decisive in the sense of Crécy, which, by leading to the capture of Calais, transformed Edward III's semi-serious adventure into a hundred years' war, nor in the sense of Poitiers, which determined the loss of confidence in the noble as knight. Agincourt merely confirmed both these results, especially the second, for not even

Nicopolis was so painful a demonstration that valor in combat is not the equivalent of competence in war. The battle was lost by the incompetence of French chivalry, and won more by the action of the English common soldiers than of the mounted knights.

Although Burgundy and his vassals held aloof, the French army that assembled to confront the invaders outnumbered them by three or four to one, and was as overconfident as ever. The Constable, Charles d'Albret, rejected an offer of 6,000 crossbowmen from the citizen militia of Paris. No change in tactics had been introduced, and the only technological development (except for cannon, which played no role in open battle) was heavier plate armor. Intended to give added protection against arrows, it had the effect of increasing fatigue and reducing mobility and play of the sword arm. The terrible worm in his iron cocoon was less terrible than before, and the cocoon itself sometimes lethal; knights occasionally died of heart failure inside it. Pages had to support their lords on the field lest, should they fall, they be unable to rise again.

The armies met in a confined space between two clumps of woods. Rain fell throughout the night while they waited to do battle and while the French pages and grooms, walking the horses up and down, churned the ground into a soft mud exactly suited for the slipping and stumbling of steel-clad knights. The French had not attempted to select a battleground where their superiority in numbers could be effectively deployed, with the result that they were drawn up for battle in three rows, one behind the other, with little room for action on the flanks, and forced to follow each other into the valley of mud. With no commander-in-chief able to impose a tactical plan, the nobles vied for the glory of a place in the front line until it was as compacted as the Flemish line at Roosebeke. Archers and crossbowmen were placed behind, where their missiles could not dilute the glory of the clash and were in fact useless.

The English, though tired, hungry, and dispirited by their numerical inferiority, had two advantages: a King in personal command and a disproportion of about 1,000 knights and squires to 6,000 archers and a few thousand other foot. Their archers were deployed in solid wedges between the men-at-arms and in blocks on the wings. Wearing no armor, they were fully mobile, and in addition to their bows, they carried a variety of axes, hatchets, hammers, and, in some cases, large swords hanging from their belts.

Under these conditions the outcome was more one-sided than any since the start of the war. In their overcrowding, the dismounted knights of the French front line could barely wield their great weapons and, hampered by the mud, fell into helpless disarray, which, when merging with the advance of the second line and tangled by flight, panic, and riderless horses, quickly became chaos. Grasping the situation, the English archers threw down their bows and rushed in with their axes and other weapons to an orgy of slaughter. Many of the French, impeded by their heavy armor, could not defend themselves, accounting for the several thousands killed and taken prisoner in contrast to a total English loss of 500, including at least one victim of probable heart failure. This was Edward Duke of York, one of Edward III's grandsons, who was 45 and fat and found dead on the battlefield without a wound. On the French side, three dukes, five counts, ninety barons and many others were killed, among them two of Coucy's family—his grandson Robert de Bar, and his third son-in-law, Philip Count of Nevers who fought in spite of his elder brother, the Duke of Burgundy. The list of prisoners was headed by Charles d'Orléans, the new lord of Coucy, who was to remain a captive for 25 years. Chivalry's hero, Marshal Boucicaut, too, was captured. Bungled Agincourt was his last combat; he died in England six years later.

After two years' pause, Henry V returned for the systematic conquest of territory. Improved technology in the use of gunpowder and artillery now made the difference, costing walled cities their immunity. As the era of the sword was ending, that of firearms began, in time to allow no lapse in man's belligerent capacity. In three years, 1417–19, Henry took possession of all Normandy while the French twisted and grappled in internal feuds. Two successive Dauphins died within a year of each other, leaving Charles, a hapless fourteen-year-old whom his mother pronounced illegitimate, as heir to the throne. The Cabochiens rose again in a rampage of savagery and murder. John the Fearless took control of the King and capital, while the Dauphin escaped below the Loire. Through a France divided against itself, Henry V hammered his advance. In the course of the English siege of Rouen, the defenders, to save food, expelled 12,000 citizens whom the English refused to let through their lines and who remained between the two camps in winter, subsisting on grass and roots or dying of cold and starvation. When the fall of Rouen posed a direct threat to Paris, the French factions were frightened into an attempt to close ranks against the enemy.

In 1419, after much stalling by the Duke of Burgundy, a meeting was arranged between him and the Dauphin to take place on the bridge at Montereau, about 35 miles southeast of Paris. The parties advanced toward each other filled with suspicion, harsh words were spoken as if the gods of Troy were again whispering evil, hands flew to swords, and as the Dauphin backed away from the scene, his followers fell upon the Duke, plunged their weapons in his body, and "dashed him down stark dead to the ground." Louis d'Orléans was avenged, but at bitter cost.

Reconciliation was broken off. Swearing revenge in his turn, Philip of Burgundy, the new Duke, entered into full alliance with Henry V, even recognizing his shopworn claim to the crown of Philip's own ancestors. Together they drew up the Treaty of Troyes between the King of England and the still living wraith of the King of France. By its terms, signed in 1420, the witless King and his foreign-born Queen, who never felt French, disowned the "so-called Dauphin" and accepted Henry V as successor to the throne of France and husband of their daughter Catherine. During Charles VI's lifetime Henry was confirmed in possession of Normandy and his other territorial conquests and was to share the government of France with the Duke of Burgundy.

The integrity of France had reached its lowest point. If a king had been captured at Poitiers, kingship itself was surrendered at Troyes. France the supreme was reduced to an Anglo-Burgundian condominium. Henry V's quick five-year campaign alone had not accomplished this: it was the work of a hundred years of disintegrating forces combined with the rise of the Burgundian state and the accident of the King's long-lived madness. But at this stage in the development of nationalism it was not a conquest that could succeed, no matter how careful the methods of Henry V. If a sense of Frenchness was already too strong to accept the transfers of sovereignty in 1360, it was that much stronger two generations later, as the parties to the Treaty of Troyes were clearly aware. They included a clause forbidding anyone to voice disapproval of the treaty and making such disapproval an act of treason.

There was, however, an occupied France and a free France below the Loire. The wretched Dauphin, with what stamina he possessed, refused to accept the treaty and retreated with his Council to Bourges in Berry, where he maintained a feeble heartbeat of the crown. After making a royal entry into Paris, Henry V returned home, leaving his brother, the Duke of Bedford, as his regent in France. History, or whatever *deus ex machina* arranges the affairs of men, indulges an occasional taste for irony. Less than two years later Charles VI and Henry V died within a month of each other, the son-in-law first so that he never wore the French crown. The claim passed to his nine-month-old son, and with it, through Catherine of France, the Valois curse. Madness was to overcome Henry VI as a grown man; the Dauphin, subsequently Charles VII, being illegitimate, escaped.

Once again it was said, "The forests came back with the English," as war and pestilence emptied the land. In Picardy, the invaders' perennial pathway, villages were left in blackened ruin, fields were uncultivated, disused roads vanished under brambles and weeds, un-peopled lands lay solitary where no cockcrow was heard. In the out-skirts of Abbeville, a starving peasant woman was found who had salted down the bodies of two children she had killed. Destruction spread as the English pursued a serious effort to make good the con-quest of France. Only the alliance of Burgundy and the exhaustion of a marauded and trampled country enabled them to take hold. No armed force, wrote Charles d'Orléans' secretary, could take the castle of Coucy during the wars, but by "interior treason" it was delivered for a time to the enemy and its beautiful chapel windows were "in large part stripped by profane hands."

Peasants fled the countryside to take refuge in the towns, where they hoped to find security and where they imagined people led a better life. In urban alleys and hovels they found the unskilled laboring class no better off than themselves. Among the overcrowded and un-dernourished, epidemics took a greater toll, and a weakened population became more vulnerable to typhus and leprosy as well as plague. De-clining trade and manufacture created unemployment and fostered hostility to the refugees. Some returned to the land to try to rebuild their villages and re-cultivate overgrown fields, some to live in the woods by trapping and fishing.

Statues of St. Roch and other saints invoked against plague and various forms of sudden death multiplied in the churches; the fashion for naked, skeletal effigies spread. Now in the 15th century the cult of death flourished at its most morbid. Artists dwelt on physical rot in ghoulish detail: worms wriggled through every corpse, bloated toads sat on dead eyeballs. A mocking, beckoning, gleeful Death led the parade of the Danse Macabre around innumerable frescoed walls. A literature of dying expressed itself in popular treatises on *Ars Moriendi*, the Art of Dying, with scenes of the deathbed, doctors and notaries in attendance, hovering families, shrouds and coffins, grave-diggers whose spades uproot the bones of earlier dead, finally the naked corpse awaiting God's judgment while angels and vicious black devils dispute for his soul.

The staging of plays and mysteries went to extremes of the horrid, as if people needed ever more excess to experience a thrill of disgust.

The rape of virgins was enacted with startling realism; in realistic dummies the body of Christ was viciously cut and hacked by the soldiers, or a child was roasted and eaten by its mother. In a 15th century version of the favorite Nero-Agrippina scene, the mother pleads for mercy, but the Emperor, as he orders her belly sliced open, demands to see "the place where women receive the semen from which they conceive their children."

Associated with the cult of death was the expected end of the world. The pessimism of the 14th century grew in the 15th to the belief that man was becoming worse, an indication of the approaching end. As described in one French treatise, a sign of this decline was the congealing of charity in human hearts, indicating that the human soul was aging and that the flame of love which used to warm mankind was sinking low and would soon go out. Plague, violence, and natural catastrophes were further signals.

With the English occupying the capital, courage had sunk low. Frenchmen did not lack who were ready to accept union under one crown as the only solution to incessant war and economic ruin. In most, however, resistance to the English tyrants and "Goddams," as they were called, was axiomatic, but it was uncoordinated and leaderless. The Dauphin was weak and spiritless, captive of unscrupulous or passive ministers. Unheralded, the courage came from society's most unlikely source—a woman of the commoners' class.

The phenomenon of Jeanne d'Arc—the voices from God who told her she must expel the English and have the Dauphin crowned King, the quality that dominated those who would normally have despised her, the strength that raised the siege of Orléans and carried the Dauphin to Reims—belongs to no category. Perhaps it can only be explained as the answer called forth by an exigent historic need. The moment required her and she rose. Her strength came from the fact that in her were combined for the first time the old religious faith and the new force of patriotism. God spoke to her through the voices of St. Catherine, St. Michael, and St. Margaret, but what He commanded was not chastity nor humility nor the life of the spirit but political action to rescue her country from foreign tyrants.

The flight of her meteor lasted only three years. She appeared in 1428, inspired Dunois, bastard son of Louis d'Orléans, and others of the Dauphin's circle to attack at Orléans, delivered the city in May 1429, and, on the wave of that victory, led Charles to the sacred ceremony of coronation at Reims two months later. Captured by the Burgundians at Compiègne in May 1430, she was sold to the English, tried as a heretic by the Church in the service of the English, and burned at the stake at Rouen in May 1431. Her condemnation was essential to the English because she claimed to have been moved by God, and if the claim were not disallowed, God, the arbiter in the affairs of men, would have been shown to have set His face against the English dominion of France. All the intensity and relentlessness of the inquisitors was pitted against her to prove the invalidity of her voices. Before the trial, neither Charles VII, who owed her his crown, nor any of the French made any effort to ransom or save her, possibly from nobility's embarrassment at having been led to victory by a village girl.

Jeanne d'Arc's life and death did not instantly generate a national resistance; nevertheless, the English thereafter were fighting a losing cause, whether they knew it or not. The Burgundians knew it. The installation of Charles as anointed King of France, with a re-inspired army, changed the situation, the more so as the English were distracted by rising frictions under an infant King. Recognizing the implications, the Duke of Burgundy gradually went over to the French, came to terms with Charles VII, and sealed an alliance by the Peace of Arras in 1435. Within a year, by action of an energetic new Constable, Paris was regained for the King, a signal to the realm of re-unification to come. No one could have said that the spark lit by the Maid of Orléans had become a flame, for her significance is better known to history than it was to contemporaries, but renewed hope and energy was in the air. The war did not end, and in fact grew more brutal as the English, out of the obstinacy that overtakes conquerors when the conquered refuse to succumb, persisted in an effort which the Burgundian defection from their cause had made hopeless.

All this time the dominant intellectual effort of Europe was engaged in continuous, contentious, and intense activity to end the papal schism and bring about reform within the Church. Both aims depended on establishing the supremacy of a Council over the papacy. As long as both popes persistently refused to abdicate, an agreed-upon ending of the schism was impossible, leaving a Council the only alternative. It was equally apparent that no Pope and College of Cardinals would override vested interests to initiate reform from within; therefore, only by establishing the authority of a Council could an instrument of reform be obtained. Serious theologians struggled seriously with these problems in a genuine effort to effect change and find a way to limit and constitutionalize the powers of the papacy. The issues aroused the fiercest philosophical and religious, not to say material, controversies, which were debated through a succession of Councils over a period of forty years. Summoned not from the center of the Church but from the circumference, by universities, sovereigns, and states, the Councils met at Pisa, Constance, and Basle.

At Pisa in 1409 the reform issue, eloquently sponsored by d'Ailly and Gerson, was suppressed while all energies were engaged in deposing both the Avignon and Roman popes and electing a single successor. This individual promptly died, to be replaced by a martial Italian, Baldassare Cossa, more *condottiere* than cardinal, who took the name of John XXIII. Since his two rival predecessors still clung to their Sees, the schism was now triple. In France's difficulties, the initiative passed to Emperor Sigismund, who summoned the memorable Council that met at Constance on imperial territory from 1414 to 1418.

With historic consequence for the Church, Constance took upon itself a third issue, the suppression of heresy, meaning all the dissident strains which had risen out of the malaise of the last century. Vitality in religion had passed to the dissidents, mystics, and reformers, and, in a negative sense, to practices of sorcery and witchcraft, although the emphasis on sorcery reflected accusations by the authorities more than it did actual practice. Being threatened, the Church responded by virulent persecution. Denunciations, trials, and burnings increased, and in its tortures of supposed heretics the Inquisition was as savage and ingenious in cruelty as any infidel Turk or Chinese. Witch-hunting was to reach epidemic proportions in the second half of the century, marked by the famous treatise *Malleus Maleficarum* of 1487, an encyclopedia for the detection of demonology and its devotees.

Constance was concerned with the more fundamental heresy of Jan Hus, ideologically the successor of Wyclif. Summoned to explain and defend his doctrines at Constance, he was condemned and burned at the stake in 1415. He might well have claimed, anticipating Bishop Latimer, that the flames in which he died lit the candle that would not be put out.

The Council also managed after a series of dramatic struggles with John XXIII, to depose him on charges of piracy, murder, rape, sodomy, and incest (of which Gibbon remarks that the "most scandalous" charges were suppressed) and elect Cardinal Colonna of Rome as Martin V. The previous Roman Pope having been induced to resign, and the still obstinate Benedict of Avignon being effectively isolated, the schism was declared closed, although it was to revive briefly over the issue of reform. The greater struggle between Council and papacy for supremacy remained. Under Martin V, the Papal States and their revenues were recovered, and the material, if not spiritual, gain in strength enabled the papacy under Martin's successor, Eugenius IV, to renew the conciliar contest at the Council of Basle. Like some wrestle of giants, this Council lasted for eighteen years.

Doctrinal controversies raged, groups seceded, rump councils convened, a rival Pope—no less than the reigning Count of Savoy, who could pay his own way—was elected as Felix V. Reforms and restrictions on the papacy were voted by one side and rejected by the other, while states and sovereigns were again divided by power politics. In the end, the reformers were defeated, Felix V resigned, and the Council of Basle was dissolved in 1449. The papacy, firmly Italian once more, acknowledged conciliar supremacy on paper but regained its primacy in fact. Its triumph, celebrated at the Jubilee of 1450, proved a phantom. The papacy was never again to be what it had been before the schism and the Councils. It had lost prestige in the first of these crises, and influence and control over the national churches in the second. In an expression of "Gallican liberties," a French synod in 1438 adopted reforms independently and restricted papal taxation of the French clergy. Movements and ideas generated by the conciliar struggle were moving ineluctably toward the Protestant secession.

Change in another sphere was registered in the Hussite wars, a movement fired by Czech nationalism and religious zeal to avenge the death of Hus. Its members were largely bourgeois and peasants (with some ambivalent support from the Czech nobility) and in their struggle against the warrior class, it was the bourgeois, not their opponents, who developed a new military tactic. They adopted the device of a "moving fort," consisting of a square or circle of baggage wagons chained together for defense against the charge of mounted horsemen. Squads armed with pikes, hand-held guns, and flails protected each gap between the wagons, and as success in defense led to the offense, the squads charged through these gaps against the enemy. In 1420 they defeated the forces led by Sigismund in a "crusade" to reestablish orthodoxy and, gaining confidence from the fear they inspired, undertook raids into Hungary, Bavaria, and Prussia as far as the Baltic, raising the prospect of a dominion of heresy. They fired cannon from within the wagon square and were the first force to make handheld firearms a major weapon. By the end of ten years a third of the Hussite force possessed these weapons.

Being human, they were afflicted with ideological conflict between moderates and radicals which ultimately broke their movement from within. At the Council of Basle, however, they were strong enough to compel the Church for the first time to conclude a treaty of peace with heretics. Like the Swiss, also largely an army of the non-noble class, they had learned to fight effectively because they were not wedded to glory nor bound to the horse.

During the 1420s and '30s, Henry the Navigator, Prince of Portugal and grandson of John of Gaunt, launched annual voyages into the Atlantic, exploring and claiming the Azores, Madeiras, and Canaries, and venturing down the west coast of Africa until the great western bulge was rounded in 1433 and the coasts of gold and ivory reached for the opening of new trade. Even if Prince Henry's initial motive was for the greater glory of the Order of Christ, of which he was General, his work and its impulse were modern. He took his place on the bridge between medieval and modern, where the humanists and scientists were crowding.

Change was uneven and erratic. The population of Europe had sunk to its lowest point by about 1440 and was not to rise for another thirty years. Rouen, which had a population of 15,000 before the Black Death, numbered only 6,000 citizens in the mid-15th century. The Cathedral of Schleswig, which made a comparison of its revenues of 1457 with those of 1352, found that rents and measures of barley, rye, and wheat were each down to about one third of what they had been. In many places, elementary schools had disappeared, not to return until modern times. In 1439 the Bourgeois of Paris, who kept a journal in these years, reported grass growing in the streets of the capital, and wolves attacking people in the half-populated suburbs. In the same year the Archbishop of Bordeaux complained that, owing to the curse of the *écorcheurs*, students could no longer seek the pearl of knowledge at universities, for "many have been taken on the way, imprisoned, stript of their books and goods and sometimes, alas! slain." The cost of a hundred years of war in aids and subsidies, poll taxes and indirect taxes and devalued currency was incalculable. Yet the forced summoning of so many Estates and parliaments for grant of funds may have strengthened the functioning of representative bodies even while the financial burden caused misery and class antagonism.

Few in the first decade under Charles VII could see signs of progress ahead. Through continual wars, civil and foreign, wrote Thomas Basin, a Norman chronicler of the reign, through the "negligence and idleness" of the King's officials, the "greed and slackness" of men-at-arms and the lack of military discipline, devastation reigned from Rouen to Paris, from the Loire to the Seine, over the plains of Brie and Champagne, and from the Seine as far as Laon, Amiens, and Abbeville. "And it was feared that the marks of this devastation would long endure and remain visible unless Divine Providence kept better watch over the things of this world."

Slowly, improbably, the tasks of ruling made a King of Charles VII, and better fortune brought better men into his service. The great bourgeois financier Jacques Coeur supplied a footing of money and credit, and siege artillery perfected by skilled gunners outside the ranks of chivalry broke the English hold on castles and towns with an efficacy unknown in the 14th century. Town after town opened its gates to the King's forces, the more readily because Charles VII accomplished at last the fundamental military reform that had defeated his grandfather Charles V. In 1444-45 he succeeded in establishing a standing army, incorporating and at the same time eliminating the lawless companies, the greatest scourge of the time. Under the new law, twenty *compagnies d'ordonnance* of 100 lances each were established, with two archers, a squire, a page, and a *valet de guerre* for each lancer, making a total of 600 per company. Officered by the most reliable of the mercenary captains, who recruited their own men, the new companies were paid and provisioned by the crown by means of regular annual taxation, and were quartered at strategic points throughout France. By relentless effort, the remaining *écorcheurs* were disbanded. Among signs of change at mid-century, none was more important than this innovation of the standing army. What it signified was a principle of order where all before—plague, war, and schism—had been agents of disorder.

Recovery was aided by England's fading will for conquest. Henry VI, as an adult, wanted peace. A feeble, uncertain King, he was the pawn of quarreling cabals among the barons and prelates. His competent uncle, the Duke of Bedford, was dead, leaving no one of outstanding status able to lead or terminate the war. By 1450 the French had recovered all of Normandy; towns surrendered as soon as the artillery train appeared. Even English Aquitaine had dwindled to little more than the environs of Bordeaux.

In 1453 at Castillon, the only remaining English foothold outside Bordeaux, the last battle was fought. Traditional roles were reversed, with foolhardy valor on the English side and bourgeois competence on the French. Castillon having surrendered to the French, Lord John Talbot, Earl of Shrewsbury, set out from Bordeaux to recapture it. According to Basin, he was habitually given to "impetuous daring rather than deliberate assault," and insisted, against the advice of an experienced lieutenant, on a frontal attack at the head of his mounted men-at-arms. The French, under the guidance of "a certain Jean Bureau, citizen of Paris, a man of small stature but of purpose and daring, particularly skilled and experienced in the use of [artillery]," had defended their camp by a ditch, a wall of earth reinforced by tree trunks, and "machines of war"—culverins, serpentines, arbalests, and various launchers of projectiles. Talbot and his knights threw themselves against these defenses and were repulsed by stones, lead, and missiles of every description. Talbot was killed and his army routed. Bordeaux itself fell soon after. Nothing was left of England's continental empire except Calais and an empty claim to the French crown.

The longest war was over, though perhaps few were aware of it. After so many truces and renewals, who could have realized that the end had come? Without ceremony or cease-fire, treaty or settlement, the adventure and agony of five generations faded away. National identities were formed by its passage. The Hundred Years' War, like the crises of the Church in the same period, broke apart medieval unity. The brotherhood of chivalry was severed, just as the internationalism of the universities, under the combined effect of war and schism, could not survive. Between England and France the war left a legacy of mutual antagonism that was to last until necessity required alliance on the eve of 1914.

In the same year as Castillon, madness overtook Henry VI, precipitating the same contest for control of the English crown that had so damaged France. Unemployed soldiers and archers returning to England took service with the baronial factions, adding their violence and weapons to the civil Wars of the Roses that now took the place of the war in France. In the same fateful year of 1453 the formidable defenses of Constantinople fell before the siege guns of Mahomet II. The Turks brought a siege train of seventy pieces of artillery headed by a super-bombard hooped with iron, drawn by sixty oxen and capable of launching cannonballs weighing 800 pounds. The fall of Byzantium has supplied a conventional date for the close of the Middle Ages, but an event more pregnant with change took place at the same time.

In 1453–54 the first document printed from movable type was produced by Gutenberg at Mainz, followed in 1456 by the first printed book, the Vulgate Bible. "The Gothic sun," as Victor Hugo put it with fitting grandiloquence, "set behind the gigantic printing press of Mainz." The new means of disseminating knowledge and exchange of ideas spread with unmedieval rapidity. Printing presses appeared in Rome, Milan, Florence, and Naples within the next decade, and in

Paris, Lyon, Bruges, and Valencia in the 1470s. The first music was printed in 1473. William Caxton set up his printing press at Westminster in 1476 and published that still unsurpassed work of English prose, Malory's *Morte d'Arthur*, in 1484.

With the Tudors on the English throne, a formal settlement between England and France was eventually concluded by the Treaty of Etaples in 1492, a year more significant for other reasons. The energies of Europe that had once found vent in the crusades were now to find it in voyages, discoveries, and settlements in the New World.

The Coucy lineage, after the death of Enguerrand VII, hung by the single thread of Marie's son Robert de Bar. Philippa died without issue. Isabel, offspring of Coucy's second marriage, died in 1411, followed or predeceased within six months by her only child, an infant daughter. Perceval, the Bastard of Coucy, left a will in 1437 leaving his *seigneurie* to the husband of Robert de Bar's daughter, from which it may be presumed that the only son of Enguerrand VII died without issue. Yet the single thread was to lead to a King. Robert de Bar's daughter Jeanne married Louis de Luxemburg, Constable of France, and in her turn bore a daughter who married a Bourbon of the branch descended from St. Louis. The grandson of this marriage, Antoine de Bourbon, married Jeanne d'Albret, Queen of Navarre, and the son of their marriage, with his white plume of Navarre and his famous concession—"Paris is worth a mass"—reached the throne as Henri IV. Courageous, quick-witted, amorous, reasonable, he was the most popular of all French Kings and—perhaps owing to a few genes from Enguerrand VII—a rational man.

The great barony of Coucy, after being united with the royal domain under Louis XII, son of Charles d'Orléans, remained the property of the Orléans branch of the royal house. During the minority of Louis XIV—whose brother Philippe d'Orléans carried the title Sire de Coucy—the formidable castle, originally built to overawe kings, became a focus of the Fronde, the league of nobles opposed to Cardinal Mazarin, the Regent. To destroy a base of his enemies, Mazarin in 1652 blew up parts of the castle, rendering it uninhabitable, though his means were inadequate to bring down the titanic *donjon*. An earthquake in 1692 shattered more of the castle and left a jagged crack from top to bottom of the *donjon*, but it still stood, guardian over the empty halls below. One hundred years later the barony's last seigneur was the Duc d'Orléans, called Philippe Egalité, who, as a member of the National Convention, voted for the death of Louis XVI and was himself a victim of the guillotine a year later. His property, including Coucy, passed to the state.

Meanwhile Enguerrand's Célestin monastery at Villeneuve de Soissons had been vandalized by the Huguenots, restored and ruined again in the battles of the Fronde, and sold as a private *château* when the Célestin Order was suppressed in 1781. Sacked during the Revolution, it passed through several hands until purchased by Count Olivier de la Rochefoucauld in 1861. Coucy's grasp at perpetuity was no more successful than most.

Under Napoleon III, the Commission of Historical Monuments recommended restoration of the castle of Coucy and, short of that, urgent work to prevent deterioration of the keep from the ravages of decay. The choice for restoration lay between Coucy and Pierrefonds, a later and more luxurious castle built in the late 14th century by Louis d'Orléans. Because Coucy would have cost three times as much to restore and Pierrefonds was preferred by the Empress Eugénie as being nearer to Paris, the choice went to the latter. Sadly, the architect Viollet-le-Duc, restorer of the medieval, turned away from the major military structure of the Middle Ages. "Beside this giant, the greatest towers known are but spindles," he wrote. All he could do was encircle the giant by two belts of iron, repair the roof and major cracks, and install a custodian to prevent further thefts of the castle's fallen stones.

Silent, deserted, inhabited by owls, the great landmark still inspired awe. Tourists came to gaze, archeologists to study its structure, artists to draw its plans and monuments. Life went on in the village at its base and along the road winding down the hill and through the valley to Soissons. The *donjon* was impervious to time, to the disorders of man and the disorders of nature, but not to those of the 20th century.

In 1917 Picardy, invaded once more, had been occupied for three years by the German army. Prince Rupprecht of Bavaria, commander of the Sixth Army, urged General Ludendorff, Chief of General Staff, to ensure that the castle of Coucy be spared as a unique architectural treasure of no current military value. Neither side, he pointed out, had attempted to use it for military purposes, and its destruction "would only mean a blow to our own prestige quite uselessly." Ludendorff did not like appeals to culture. Coucy having been unwisely called to his attention, he decided to make it an example of superior values. Rammed with 28 tons of explosives at his orders, the colossus raised by Enguerrand III in the age of the greatest builders since Greece and Rome was dynamited to the ground.

The outer walls, foundations, underground chambers and tunnels, portions of inner walls and doorways survive over acres of tumbled stones. Above a cracked lintel the unarmored knight still engages a lion in combat. For 700 years the castle had witnessed cycles of human endeavor and failure, order and disorder, greatness and decline. Its ruins remain on the hilltop in Picardy, silent observers as history's wheel turns.

Bibliography

I. MATERIAL RELATING SPECIFICALLY TO COUCY

A. MANUSCRIPTS AND SEALS
B. PUBLISHED WORKS

II. GENERAL

A. PRIMARY SOURCES
B. SECONDARY WORKS

ABBREVIATIONS

AESC	*Annales: Economies, Sociétés, Civilisations*
BEC	Bibliothèque de l'Ecole de Chartes
BN	Bibliothèque nationale
Ec HR	*Economic History Review*
EHR	*English Historical Review*
REH	*Revue des études historiques*
RH	*Revue historique*
RQH	*Revue des questions historiques*
SHF	Société de l'histoire de France
TRHS	*Transactions of the Royal Historical Society*

I. ON COUCY

A. MANUSCRIPTS

Archives du département de l'Aisne

H 325, folio 239: *Cartulaire-chronique de l'Abbaye de Nogent-sous-Coucy.* (Modern copy in Bib. de la ville de Noyon, Coll. Peigne-Delacourt, ms. 21.)

H 721: *Fondation du couvent des Célestins à Villeneuve-les-Soissons.*

Bibliothèque nationale, Paris

Fonds français, nouv. acq., Coll. Bastard d'Estang, 3653-4-5, 3638-9.

Coll. Clairembault, vol. 35, nos. 74–114; vol. 39, no. 81, dossier Coucy.

Pièces originales, 875, dossier Coucy, nos. 1–37.

Mss. Coll. Picardie, vol. x, fo. 207 ff.

Ms. fr. 18616, folios 94–141. *Mémoires pour faire servir à l'histoire des seigneurs de Coucy.* (Not an original work, this is a 16th century compilation of material drawn from L'Alouëte, Duchesne, and other sources.)

Ms. Latin 5149, *Historia monasterii SS Trinitatis Caelestinorum.*

Ecole de chartes

Lacaille, Henri, *Enguerrand VII, Sire de Coucy.* (Unpublished doctoral dissertation of 1890. The author's list of *pièces justificatives*—his sources—is unfortunately missing from the ms.) Cited in Notes as Lacaille, *thèse.*

SEALS

Archives nationales—Bureaux des sceaux

Coll. Clairembault, nos. 2838, 2841–2, 8644–6.

Coll. de la Flandre, no. 308.

Bibliothèque nationale—Cabinet des Médailles

Coll. Bastard d'Estang, nos. 28–28bis.

B. PUBLISHED WORKS

† indicates a primary source for the life of Enguerrand VII
†† indicates publication of primary documents

†L'ALOUËTE, FRANÇOIS DE, *Traité des nobles avec une histoire généalogique de la très-illustre et très ancienne maison de Couci et de ses alliances.* Paris, 1577.

ANCIEN, BERNARD, "*Les Couleurs d'Enguerrand VII, Sire de Coucy et Comte de Soissons.*" *Mémoire de la fédération des sociétés d'histoire et d'archéologie de l'Aisne,* vol. IX, 1963.

L'Art de vérifier les dates des faits historiques, par un Religieux de la Congrégation de St.-Maur, vol. XII. Paris, 1818.

††BARDY, HENRI, *Enguerrand de Coucy et les Grands Bretons.* Paris, 1860.

BELLOY, M. DE, *Mémoires historiques: 1, Sur la maison de Coucy encore existante.* Paris, 1770.

Bouet, M. G., *"Excursions à Noyon, à Laon et à Soissons."* Bull. *monumental sur les monuments historiques de la France,* 4th series, vol. IV.

††Broche, Lucien, *"Notes sur d'anciens comptes de la châtellenie de Coucy."* Bull. *de la Société académique de Laon,* vol. XXXII, 1905–9.

Chaurand, Jacques, *Thomas de Marle, Sire de Coucy.* Vervins, 1963.

††Delaville le Roux, J., *"Le Legs d'Enguerrand VII, Sire de Coucy, à la Cathédrale de Chartres."* Mémoires de la Société archéologique d'Eure-et-Loire, vol. IX, 1889.

†Duchesne, André, *Histoire généalogique des maisons de Guînes, d'Ardres, de Gand et de Coucy.* Paris, 1631.

Dufour, Etienne, *Coucy-le-Château et ses environs.* Soissons, 1910.

Duplessis, Dom Michel Toussaints Chrétien, *Histoire de la ville et des seigneurs de Coucy.* Paris, 1728.

††Durrieu, Paul, *"La Prise d'Arezzo par Enguerrand VII, Sire de Coucy, en 1384."* BEC, vol. XLI, 1880.

Duval, M. R., *"Histoire de l'Abbaye bénédictine de St. Nicolas-aux-bois au diocèse de Laon."* Mémoires de la Soc. Acad. de St.-Quentin, 4th series, vol. XII, 1893–96.

††Lacaille, Henri, *"Enguerrand de Coucy au service de Grégoire XI, 1372–74."* Annuaire Bulletin de la SHF, vol. XXXII, 1895. (A collection from the Vatican Archives of the letters of Gregory XI concerning Coucy's command in the War of the Papal League, 1372–74.)

††——, *"La Vente de la baronnie de Coucy."* BEC, vol. LV, 1894.

Larousse, *Grand Dictionnaire universel,* 1869, article "Coucy-le-Château."

Lefèvre-Pontalis, Eugène, *Le Château de Coucy.* Paris, 1909.

Lelong, Dom Nicolas, *Histoire ecclésiastique et civile du diocèse de Laon.* Châlons, 1783.

Lépinois, E. de, *Histoire de la ville et des sires de Coucy.* Paris, 1859.

††Mangin, *"Enguerrand VII, Sire de Coucy: Pièces inédites concernant son départ pour la Hongrie et sa mort."* Bulletin de la Soc. Acad. de Laon, vol. XXIV, 1882.

Mazas, Alexandre, *Vie des grands capitaines français du moyen age,* vol. III. 3rd ed. Paris, 1845. (Lively and interesting but unreliable and in some cases imaginary.)

Melleville, Maximilien, *Histoire de la ville et des sires de Coucy-le-Château.* Laon, 1848.

Moreau, Jules, *Notices sur les sires de Coucy.* Chauny, 1871.

††Roussel, l'Abbé R., *Histoire de l'abbaye des Célestins de Villeneuve-les-Soissons.* Soissons, 1904.

Sars, Comte Maxime de, *La Laonnais féodale,* vol. IV. Paris, 1931.

Savage, Henry L., *"Enguerrand de Coucy VII and the Campaign of Nicopolis."* Speculum, October 1939.

Viollet-le-Duc, E., *Description du château de Coucy.* Paris, 1880. (Largely repeated from his *Dictionnaire.*)

Zurlauben, Baron von Thurn und, *"Abrégé de la vie d'Enguerrand VII du nom, Sire de Couci."* Histoire de l'Académie royale des inscriptions et belles lettres, vol. XXV. Paris, 1759.

II. GENERAL

A. PRIMARY SOURCES

ALLMAND, C. T., ed., *Society at War: The Experience of England and France During the Hundred Years War.* Edinburgh, 1973. (Excerpts from contemporary texts.)

Anonimalle Chronicle (St. Mary's York). Ed. V. H. Galbraith. Manchester, 1927.

BARNIE, JOHN, *War in Medieval English Society.* Cornell University Press, 1974. (Excerpts from contemporary texts.)

BEAUREPAIRE, CH. DE, "*Complainte sur la Bataille de Poitiers.*" BEC, vol. XII, 1851.

BELL, CLAIR HAYDEN, ed., *Peasant Life in Old German Epics.* Columbia University Press, 1968. (Contains two 13th century narrative poems, "*Meier Helbricht*" and "*Der Arme Heinrich*," which, though not strictly applicable to 14th century France, are revealing of medieval peasant life.)

BERRY, DUC DE, *The Très Riches Heures of Jean, Duke of Berry.* Eds. Jean Longman and Raymond Cazelles, with preface by Millard Meiss. New York, 1969.

BOCCACCIO, GIOVANNI, *The Decameron.* Trans. Frances Winwar. New York, 1930.

BONET, HONORÉ, *The Tree of Battles.* Trans. and ed. G. W. Coopland. Harvard University Press, 1949.

BOUCICAUT. See Godefroy and *Livre des faits.*

BRIANS, PAUL, ed., *Bawdy Tales from the Courts of Medieval France.* New York, 1972.

BRUCKER, GENE, ed., *The Society of Renaissance Florence.* New York, 1971. (Excerpts from contemporary documents.)

——, *Two Memoirs of Renaissance Florence.* New York, 1967. (Contains excerpts from the journal of Buonaccorso Pitti.)

CHANDOS HERALD, *Life of the Black Prince.* Trans. M. K. Pope and E. C. Lodge. Oxford, 1910.

CHAPLAIS, PIERRE, "Some Documents Regarding the Fulfillment and Interpretation of the Treaty of Brétigny, 1361–69." *Camden Miscellany*, vol. XIX (Camden Third Series, vol. LXXX). London, 1952.

CHAUCER, GEOFFREY, *The Canterbury Tales.* Ed. Walter Skeat. New York, 1929.

CHRISTINE DE PISAN, *The Book of Fayttes of Armes and of Chyvalrye.* Trans. William Caxton. Ed. A. T. P. Byles. Oxford University Press, 1932.

——, *Le Livre des Fais et Bonnes Meurs du Sage Roy Charles V.* Ed. S. Solente. 2 vols. Paris, 1936–40.

Chronicle of Jean de Venette. Trans. Jean Birdsall. Ed. Richard A. Newhall. Columbia University Press, 1953.

Chronicon Angliae. See Walsingham.

Chronique du Bon Duc Loys de Bourbon. Ed. A. M. Chazaud. Paris, 1876. (Cited in Notes as *Chron. Bourbon.*)

Chronique de Jean de Bel. Eds. Jules Viard and Eugene Deprez. 2 vols. *SHF*, Paris, 1904–5.

Chronique normande du XIVe siècle. Eds. A. and E. Molinier. Paris, 1882.

Chronique des quatre premiers Valois, 1327–1393. Ed. Siméon Luce. *SHF*, Paris, 1862. (Cited as *Chron. 4 Valois.*)

Chronique des règnes de Jean II et de Charles V. Ed. R. Delachenal. 4 vols. *SHF*, Paris, 1910–20. (Cited as *Chron. J. & C.*)

Chronique du Religieux de Saint-Denys: La Règne de Charles VI, de 1380 à 1422. Trans. and ed. M. L. Bellaguet. 6 vols. Paris, 1839. (Cited as *Chron. C6.*)

Chronographia Regum Francorum (formerly designated *Chronique de Berne*). Ed. H. Moranvillé. 3 vols. *SHF*, Paris, 1891–97.

CUVELIER, J., *Chronique de Bertrand du Guesclin.* Ed. E. Charrière. 2 vols. Paris, 1839.

DELISLE, LÉOPOLD, *Les Collections de Bastard d'Estang à la Bibliothèque nationale.* Nogent-le-Rotrin, 1886. (Summaries of the contents of contemporary documents. Very valuable.)

DELISLE, M. L., ed., "*Un Pamphlet politique au XIVe Siècle*" (the *Tragicum Argumentum*). *Bull. historique et philologique, 1886.* Paris, 1887.

DEMAY, GERMAIN, *Inventaire des sceaux de la collection Clairembault,* vol. II. Paris, 1886.

——, *Inventaire des sceaux de la Flandre,* vol I. Paris, 1883.

DESCHAMPS, EUSTACHE, *Oeuvres complètes.* Eds. Marquis de Queux de Saint-Hilaire and G. Raynaud. 11 vols. Paris, 1878–1901.

DÍAZ DE GÓMEZ, GUTIERRE, *El Victorial: The Unconquered Knight, A Chronicle of the Deeds of Don Pero Niño, Count of Buelna.* Trans. and ed. Joan Evans. London, 1928.

DOUET-D'ARCQ, LOUIS, ed., *Choix de Pièces inédites relatives au règne de Charles VI.* 2 vols. Paris, 1863.

DUCKETT, SIR GEORGE FLOYD, ed., *Original Documents Relating to Hostages for John, King of France, and the Treaty of Brétigny in 1360.* London, 1890.

EGBERT, VIRGINIA WYLIE, ed., *On the Bridges of Medieval Paris; A Record of Early Fourteenth Century Life.* Princeton, 1974. (Excellent reproduction of illustrations with commentary; a beautiful piece of bookmaking.)

FROISSART, JEAN, *Chronicles of England, France and Spain.* Trans. Thomas Johnes, 2nd ed. in 2 vols. London, 1806. (Best for the general reader. Modernized language and some cuts.)

——, *The Chronicle of Froissart.* Trans. Lord Berners, 1523–25. Ed. W. P. Ker. 6 vols. London, 1902. (Text of the original translation with a useful introduction by the editor but no notes.)

——, *Chroniques.* Ed. Siméon Luce et al. 14 vols. Paris, 1869–1966. (The notes are a scholarly work in themselves, but the edition is difficult to use because of confusing organization and pagination. Cited as Luce-F.)

——, *Oeuvres.* Ed. Baron Kervyn de Lettenhove. 25 vols. Brussels, 1870–75. (The most useful edition for index, biographies, and editorial material. Cited as KL.)

——, "*Le Trettie du Joli Buisson de Jonece.*" *Collection des chroniques nationales françaises,* vol. X. Ed. J. A. Buchon. Paris, 1829.

GERMAIN, A., *Projet de descente en Angleterre . . . pour la délivrance du Roi Jean: Extrait de documents originaux inédits.* Montpellier, 1858.

GILLES LI MUISIS (ABBÉ DE ST. MARTIN DE TOURNAI), *Chronique et annales.* Ed. H. Lemaitre. *SHF.* Paris, 1906.

GODEFROY, THEODORE, ed., *Histoire de Maréchal de Boucicaut.* Paris, 1620. (This was the first publication of the *Livre des faits . . . de Boucicaut,* from the ms. in the BN, of which only one copy exists.)

GODFREY LE BAKER, *Chronicon.* Ed. Edwin M. Thompson (with parts translated). Oxford, 1889.

Grandes Chroniques de France, vol. IX (to 1350). Ed. Jules Viard. Paris, 1937.
——, vol. VI (to 1380). Ed. Paulin Paris. Paris, 1838.

GRAY, SIR THOMAS, *Scalacronica.* Trans. Sir Herbert Maxwell. Glasgow, 1905–7.

GUIBERT, ABBOT OF NOGENT, *Memoirs.* Trans. John L. Benton. New York, 1970.

HELLMAN, ROBERT, and RICHARD O'GORMAN, eds., *Fabliaux: Ribald Tales from the Old French.* New York, 1965.

HERLIHY, DAVID, ed., *Medieval Culture and Society.* New York, 1968. (Anthology of contemporary texts.)

JEAN LE FÈVRE, EVÊQUE DE CHARTRES, *Journal de Jean le Fèvre,* vol. I. Ed. H. Moranvillé. Paris, 1887.

JEAN JUVENAL DES URSINS, ARCHEVÊQUE DE REIMS, *Histoire de Charles VI.* Ed. Th. Godefroy. Paris, 1614. Also in *Nouvelle Collection des mémoires relatifs à l'histoire de France,* vol. II. Eds. J. F. Michaud and J. J. F. Poujoulat. Paris, 1881.

JOHN OF READING, *Chronica.* Ed. James Tait. Manchester, 1914.

KOENIGSHOFEN, JACOB VON, *Elsassiche und Strassburgische chronicke* (c. 1400). Ed. J. Schilter. Strasburg, 1698.

LANGLAND, WILLIAM, *The Vision of Piers Plowman.* Ed. Henry W. Wells. New York, 1935.

LANGLOIS, CHARLES VICTOR, *La Connaissance de la nature et du monde au moyen age d'après quelques écrits français à l'usage des laics.* Paris, 1911. (Contains *Image du monde, Roman de Sidrach,* and other encyclopedists. This is vol. III of what was later published as *La Vie en France au moyen age,* 4 vols., Paris, 1924–28. A collection of medieval writings on many subjects, this work is indispensable for a knowledge of the medieval mind.)

LA TOUR LANDRY, GEOFFREY, *The Book of the Knight of La Tour Landry.* Trans. G. S. Taylor. London, 1930.

Livre des faits du Mareschal de Boucicaut, in *Nouvelle Collection des mémoires relatifs à l'histoire de France,* vol. II. Eds. J. F. Michaud and J. J. F. Poujoulat. Paris, 1881. See also Godefroy.

MACHAUT, GUILLAUME DE, *Les Oeuvres.* Ed. Prosper Tarbé. Reims, 1849.

MÉNAGIER DE PARIS, LE, *The Goodman of Paris.* Ed. and trans. Eileen Power. London, 1928.

MÉZIÈRES, PHILIPPE DE, *Le Songe du Vieil Pèlerin.* Ed. with synopsis and commentary by G. W. Coopland. 2 vols. Cambridge University Press, 1969.

MURATORI, L. A., ed., *Rerum Italicarum Scriptores.* Milan, 1723–51.

NOHL, JOHANNES, *The Black Death: A Chronicle of the Plague Compiled from Contemporary Sources.* Trans. C. H. Clarke. London, 1971.

ORLÉANS, H. D., ed., *Notes et documents relatifs à Jean, Roi de France et à sa captivité en Angleterre*, vol. II. London, 1855–56.

OWST, GERALD R., ed., *Literature and Pulpit in Medieval England*. Cambridge University Press, 1933. (Texts of sermons.)

Petrarch . . . A Selection from His Correspondence. Eds. James Harvey Robinson and H. W. Rolfe. New York, 1898.

Polychronicon Ranulphi Higden. Ed. Joseph R. Lumby. Vol. VIII. London, 1882.

PROST, B., ed., *Inventaires mobiliers et extraits des comptes des ducs de Bourgogne*, vol. II. Paris, 1908–13.

Putnam's Dark and Middle Ages Reader. Ed. Harry E. Wedeck. New York, 1965.

ROBINSON, JAMES HARVEY, ed., *Readings in European History*, vol. I. Boston, 1904.

The Rohan Master, eds. Millard Meiss and Marcel Thomas, New York, 1973.

ROSS, J. B., and M. M. MCLAUGHLIN, eds., *The Portable Medieval Reader*. New York, 1973.

RYMER, THOMAS, *Foedera Litterae et Acta Publica*, vol. III, part II, 1367–77. London, 1830.

SCHILLING, DIEBOLD, *Berner Chronik*. Eds. H. Blesch and P. Hilber. Vol. I. Bern, 1943. (Incorporates chronicle of Konrad Justinger.)

SCHILTBERGER, JOHANN, *The Bondage and Travels of Johann Schiltberger*. Trans. J. Burden Telfer. Notes by P. Bruun. Hakluyt Society, 1879.

SECOUSSE, D., ed., *Mémoires pour servir à l'histoire de Charles II, roi de Navarre et comte d'Evreux*. 2 vols. Paris, 1755–58.

SERVION, JEHAN, *Gestez et Croniques de la Mayson de Savoye*. Ed. F. E. Bollati. 2 vols. Turin, 1879.

Songe du Vergier, in Pierre Dupuy, ed., *Traitez des droits et libertez de l'église gallicane*, vol. II. Paris, 1731.

VILLANI, GIOVANNI, *Chronicle of Florence*. Trans. Rose Selfe. London, 1906.

WALSINGHAM, THOMAS, *Chronicon Angliae, 1328–1388*. Ed. Sir Edward Maunde Thompson. London, 1874.

WARD, CHARLES FREDERICK, ed., *The Epistles on the Romance of the Rose and Other Documents in the Debate*. Chicago, 1911.

The Visconti Hours, eds. Millard Meiss and Edith Kirsch, New York, 1972.

WAVRIN, JEHAN DE, *Anchiennes Cronicques d'Engleterre*. Ed. Dupont. Vol. II. Paris, 1859.

WRIGHT, THOMAS, ed., *Political Songs and Poems Relating to English History (1327–1483)*. 2 vols. London, 1859.

——, *A Volume of Vocabularies*. London, 1857.

B. SECONDARY WORKS

* indicates works of special value or unique material

ABRAHAMS, ISRAEL, *Jewish Life in the Middle Ages*. Philadelphia, 1958.

ANQUETIL, LOUIS PIERRE, *Histoire de France*, vol. II. 3rd ed. Paris, 1829.

*ANSELME, PÈRE, *Histoire généalogique et chronologique de la maison royale*, vol. VIII. Paris, 1733. (Contains most of the higher nobility including the Coucys.)

ARIÈS, PHILIPPE, *Centuries of Childhood.* Trans. New York, 1962.

ARMITAGE-SMITH, SYDNEY, *John of Gaunt.* London, 1904.

ARTZ, FREDERICK B., *The Mind of the Middle Ages, A.D. 200–1500.* New York, 1953.

ATIYA, AZIZ SURYAL, *The Crusade in the Later Middle Ages.* London, 1938.

——, *The Crusade of Nicopolis.* London, 1934.

AUTRAND, FRANÇOISE, "*Culture et mentalité: les librairies des gens du parlement au tempts de Charles VI.*" *AESC*, September-October 1973.

BALDWIN, FRANCES E., *Sumptuary Legislation and Personal Regulation in England.* Johns Hopkins University Press, 1926.

BAPST, GERMAIN, "*Les Spectacles et les réjouissances des fêtes publiques au moyen age.*" *Revue Bleue*, vol. XLVIII, 1891.

BARANTE, GUILLAUME-PROSPER, BARON DE, *Histoire des ducs de Bourgogne, 1364–1477.* Vol. II. Paris, 1839.

BARNES, JOSHUA, *The History of Edward III.* Cambridge, 1688.

BARON, HANS, "Franciscan Poverty and Civic Wealth as Factors in the Rise of Humanistic Thought." *Speculum*, January 1938.

BARON, SALO W., *A Social and Religious History of the Jews,* vols. IX–XI. Columbia University Press, 1965–67.

BATIFOL, LOUIS, "*Le Châtelet de Paris vers 1400.*" *BEC*, 1896.

BAUDRILLART, H., *Histoire du luxe.* Paris, 1881.

BEAN, J. M. W., "Plague, Population and Economic Decline in the Later Middle Ages." *EcHR*, April 1963.

BÉDIER, JOSEPH, and PAUL LAZARD, *Histoire de la littérature française,* vol. I. Paris, 1923.

BERESFORD, MAURICE, and JOHN B. HURST, *Deserted Medieval Villages.* London, 1971.

BISHOP, MORRIS, *Petrarch and His World.* Indiana University Press, 1963.

BLOCH, MARC, *French Rural History.* Trans. (*Les Caractères originaux de l'histoire rurale française.*) Berkeley, 1973.

——, *Feudal Society.* Trans. (*La société féodale.*) University of Chicago Press, 1971.

——, *Seigneurie française et manoir anglais.* Paris, 1960.

BLOOMFIELD, MORTON W., *Piers Plowman as a Fourteenth Century Apocalypse.* Rutgers University Press, 1961.

BOISSONADE, P., *Life and Works in Medieval Europe.* Trans. Eileen Power. New York, 1927.

BONNARD, CAMILLE, *Costumes historiques des XIIe, XIIIe, XIVe, et XVe siècles.* Paris, 1861.

BOUDET, MARCELLIN, *La Jacquerie des Tuchins, 1363–1384.* Paris, 1895.

BOUTRUCHE, ROBERT, *La crise d'une société.* Paris, 1947.

BOWSKY, WILLIAM, "The Impact of the Black Death upon Sienese Government and Society." *Speculum*, January 1964.

BOYER, MARJORIE, "A Day's Journey in Medieval France." *Speculum*, October 1951.

BRADDY, HALDEEN, "Froissart's Account of Chaucer's Embassy in 1377." *Review of English Studies*, January 1938.

——, "The Historical Background of the *Parlement of Foules*." *Review of English Studies*, April 1935.

BRADLEY, CAROLYN G., *Western World Costume*. New York, 1954.

BRIDBURY, A. R., "The Black Death." *EcHR*, November 1973.

BROWN, ELIZABETH A. R., "Taxation and Morality in the 13th and 14th Centuries." *French Historical Studies*, April 1973.

CALMETTE, JOSEPH, *Chute et relèvement de la France sous Charles VI et Charles VII*. Paris, 1945.

The Cambridge Medieval History, vol. VII. Cambridge University Press, 1968.

CAMPBELL, ANNA M., *The Black Death and Men of Learning*. Columbia University Press, 1931.

CARCO, FRANCIS, *La Danse des morts comme la décrite François Villon*. Geneva, 1944.

CARPENTIER, ELISABETH, "*Autour de la peste noire: famines et épidémies dans l'histoire du XIVe siècle*." *AESC*, November-December 1962.

——, *Une Ville devant la peste: Orvieto et la peste noire de 1348*. Paris, 1972.

CARTELLIERI, OTTO, *The Court of Burgundy*. New York, 1929.

CAZELLES, RAYMOND, "*Etienne Marcel au sein de la haute bourgeoisie d'affaires*." *Journal des Savants*, January-March 1965.

——, "*Les Mouvements révolutionnaires du milieu du XIVe siècle et le cycle de l'action publique*." *RH*, October-December 1962.

——, "*Le Parti navarrais jusqu'à la mort d'Etienne Marcel*." *Bull. philologique et historique*, vol. II, 1960.

——, "*La Peste de 1348-49 en Langue d'oil; épidémie prolitarienne et enfantine*." *Bull. philologique et historique*, 1962, pp. 293-305.

——, *La Société politique et la crise de la royauté sous Philippe de Valois*. Paris, 1958.

CHAMBERLIN, E. R., *The Count of Virtue: Giangaleazzo Visconti, Duke of Milan*. New York, 1965.

CHAMBERS, E. K., *The Medieval Stage*. London, 1903.

CHANEY, EDWARD F., *La Danse macabre*. Manchester University Press, 1945.

CHAZAN, ROBERT, *Medieval Jewry in Northern France*. Johns Hopkins University Press, 1973.

CHEYNEY, EDWARD P., *The Dawn of a New Era, 1250-1453*. New York, 1962. (A useful general history with excellent bibliographies.)

*CHOTZEN, TH. M., "Yvain de Galles in Alsace-Lorraine and in Switzerland." *Bull. of the Board of Celtic Studies*, 1928.

CHUBB, THOMAS CALDECOTT, *The Life of Giovanni Boccaccio*. New York, 1930.

CIPOLLA, CARLO M., *Money, Prices and Civilization in the Mediterranean World*. Princeton University Press, 1956.

CIRCOURT, ALBERT DE, "*Le Duc Louis d'Orléans: ses enterprises en Italie*." *RQH*, 1889, in two parts, vols. XLV and XLVI.

COGNASSO, FRANCESCO, *Il Conte Verde*. Turin, 1930.

COHEN, GUSTAVE, *Histoire de la mise en scène dans le théâtre religieux français du moyen age*. Paris, 1951.

——, *La Vie littéraire en France au moyen age*. Paris, 1949.

*COHN, NORMAN, *The Pursuit of the Millennium*. New Jersey, 1957. Reissue. Oxford University Press, 1970.

COLLAS, EMILE, *Valentine de Milan*. Paris, 1911.

COLLINS, ARTHUR, *Life of Edward Prince of Wales, Commonly Called the Black Prince*. London, 1740.

COLLIS, MAURICE, *The Hurling Time*. London, 1958. (A first-rate popular book on English affairs for the period 1337–81.)

CONNOLLY, JAMES L., *Jean Gerson, Reformer and Mystic*. Louvain, 1894.

CONTAMINE, PHILIPPE, *Guerre, état et société à la fin du moyen age*. Paris, 1972.

COOK, ALBERT S., "The Last Months of Chaucer's Earliest Patron" (Lionel, Duke of Clarence). *Trans. of the Connecticut Academy of Arts and Sciences*, vol. XXI, December 1916.

COPLESTON, F. C., *A History of Medieval Philosophy*. London, 1972.

CORDEY, JEAN, *Les Comtes de Savoie et le roi de France pendant la guerre de cent ans*. Paris, 1911.

COUDERC, CAMILLE, *Album de portraits d'après les collections du Département des Manuscripts*. Paris, 1910.

COULTON, G. G., *The Black Death*. London, 1929.

——, *Chaucer and His England*. New York, 1908.

——, *The Chronicler of European Chivalry*. London, 1930.

——, *Five Centuries of Religion*. Cambridge University Press, 1936.

*——, *Life in the Middle Ages*. Reissue (4 vols. in 2). Cambridge University Press, 1967.

*——, *Medieval Panorama*. Cambridge University Press, 1938. Reprint. New York, 1955.

*COVILLE, A., *Les Premiers Valois et la guerre de cent ans (1328–1422)* (vol. IV of Lavisse, *Histoire de France*). Paris, 1902.

*COX, EUGENE L., *The Green Count of Savoy*. Princeton University Press, 1967.

CRAWFURD, RAYMOND, *Plague and Pestilence in Literature and Art*. Oxford, 1914.

CREIGHTON, MANDELL, BISHOP OF LONDON, *A History of the Papacy*, vol. I. Boston, 1882.

CROCE, BENEDETTO, *History of the Kingdom of Naples*. Trans. University of Chicago Press, 1970.

CUTTINO, G. P., "Historical Revision: The Causes of the Hundred Years War." *Speculum*, July 1956.

CUTTS, REV. EDWARD L., *Scenes and Characters of the Middle Ages*. London, 1930.

DANDLIKER, KARL, *Geschichte der Schweiz*, vol. I. Zurich, 1900.

DARMESTETER, MARY (DUCHAUX), *Froissart*. Trans. E. F. Poynter. New York, 1895.

D'AVENEL, VICOMTE GEORGES, *L'Evolution des moyens de transport*. Paris, 1919.

*DAVID, HENRI, *Philippe le Hardi, Duc de Bourgogne et co-régent de France de 1392 à 1404: le train somptuaire d'un grand Valois*. Dijon, 1947.

DAVIS, WILLIAM STEARNS, *Life on a Medieval Barony*. New York, 1923.

DEAUX, GEORGE, *The Black Death, 1347*. London, 1969.

*DELACHENAL, ROLAND, *Histoire de Charles V*. 5 vols. Paris, 1909–31. (As a collection of information and reference guide to the sources, this is the single most essential work.)

*Delaville le Roux, J., *La France en Orient au XIV siècle: expéditions du Maréchal Boucicaut*, vol. I. Paris, 1886.

Delbouille, Maurice, *Le Roman du castelain de Couci et de la dame de Fayel*. Paris, 1936.

Delisle, Léopold, *Recherches sur la librairie de Charles V*. Paris, 1907. (Part II includes inventories of libraries of Charles VI and Duc de Berry.)

Denifle, Henri, *La Désolation des églises, monastères et hopitaux en France pendant la guerre de cent ans*, vol. I. Paris, 1899. (A detailed and documented history of the war in France up to the death of Charles V, this book is much more than its title suggests.)

Dierauer, Johannes, *Geschichte der Schweizerrischen Eidgenossenschaft*, vol. I. Gotha, 1887.

Dingwall, John Eric, *The Girdle of Chastity*. London, 1931. (On the chastity belt.)

Duby, Georges, *Rural Economy and Country Life in the Medieval West*. Trans. N.p., 1968.

Dumas, Georges, and Suzanne Martinet, *L'Histoire de l'Aisne vue à travers les archives*. Laon, 1971.

Dupont, Jacques, and Cesare Gnudi, *Gothic Painting*. Geneva, 1954.

Durrieu, Paul, "Manuscripts de luxe exécutés pour des princes et grands seigneurs françcis." *Le Manuscrit*, vol. II, 1894.

*——, "Le Royaume d'Adria." *RQH*, vol. XXVIII, 1880.

Emerton, Ephraim, *Humanism and Tyranny: Studies in the Italian Trecento*. Harvard University Press, 1925.

Enlart, Camille, *Manuel d'archéologie française; vol. III, Le Costume*. Paris, 1916.

Evans, Joan, *Art in Medieval France*. Oxford University Press, 1948.

——, *Life in Medieval France*. London, 1969.

Evans, Joan et al., eds., *The Flowering of the Middle Ages*. London, 1966.

Fawtier, R., "La Crise d'une société devant la guerre de cent ans." *RH*, January 1950.

——, *Ste. Catherine de Sienne*. Paris, 1922.

Flick, Alexander C., *The Decline of the Medieval Church*, vol. I. New York, 1930.

Focillon, Henri, *The Art of the West in the Middle Ages*, vol. II. New York, 1969.

Fossier, Robert, *La Terre et les hommes en Picardie jusqu'à la fin du XIIIe siècle*. 2 vols. Paris, 1968.

Fowler, Kenneth, *The Age of Plantagenet and Valois*. New York, 1967.

——, *The King's Lieutenant: Henry of Grosmont, First Duke of Lancaster, 1310–61*. London, 1969.

——, ed., *The Hundred Years War*. London, 1971.

Frank, Grace, *The Medieval French Drama*. Oxford, 1954.

Franklin, Alfred, *Dictionnaire historique des arts, métiers et professions*. Paris, 1905.

——, *Les Rues et les cris de Paris au XIIIe siècle*. Paris, 1874.

——, *La Vie privée d'autrefois*, vol. I, *L'Annonce et la réclame;* vol. VII, *Le Hygiène*. Paris, 1890.

"Froissart and His Patrons." *Times Literary Supplement*, 11 December 1937.

FUNK, ARTHUR L., "Robert le Coq and Etienne Marcel." *Speculum*, October 1944.

GABOTTO, FERDINANDO, *L'Eta del Conte Verde in Piemonte, 1350–83;* vol. XXXIII, *Miscellanea di Storia Italiana*. N.p., 1895.

GABRIEL, ASTRIK L., "The College System in the 14th Century Universities," in Utley, q.v.

GAGNIERE, SYLVAIN, *The Palace of the Popes at Avignon*. Trans. Caisse nationale des monuments historiques, 1965.

GAIRDNER, JAMES, *Lollardy and the Reformation in England*, vol I. London, 1908.

GASQUET, FRANCIS AIDAN, ABBOT, *The Black Death of 1348 and 1349*. 2nd ed. London, 1908.

GAUPP, FRITZ, "The Condottiere John Hawkwood." *History*, March 1939.

GAUTIER, LÉON, *La Chevalerie*. Paris, 1890. (New edition with index.)

GAYLEY, CHARLES M., *Plays of Our Forefathers*. New York, 1907.

GAZEAU, M. A., *Les Bouffons*. Paris, 1882. (On jesters.)

GIRVAN, RITCHIE, "The Medieval Poet and His Public." *English Studies Today*, 1952.

*GREEN, MARY ANNE EVERETT (MRS. J. R.), *Lives of the Princesses of England*, vol. III. London, 1851. (Based on extensive and scholarly research in the Wardrobe and Household rolls and other documents, this is essential for Isabella de Coucy.)

GREGOROVIUS, FERDINAND, *History of the City of Rome in the Middle Ages*, vol. VI. Trans. A. Hamilton. London, 1906.

GROSJEAN, GEORGES, *Le Sentiment national dans la guerre de cent ans*. Paris, 1927.

HALE, JOHN, ROGER HIGHFIELD, and BERYL SMALLEY, *Europe in the Late Middle Ages*. London, 1965.

HAMMER, J. VON, trans., *Histoire de l'empire ottoman*, vol. I. Paris, 1836.

HARDY, B. C., *Philippa of Hainault and Her Times*. London, 1910.

D'HAUCOURT, GENEVIÈVE, *La Vie au moyen age*. Paris, 1968.

HAY, DENYS, *Europe in the 14th and 15th Centuries*. London, 1966. (A useful general history.)

HAYWARD, FERNAND, *Histoire de la maison de Savoie, 1000–1554*. Paris, 1941.

HEARNSHAW, F. J. C., "Chivalry and Its Place in History," in Prestage, q.v.

HECKER, J. F. C., *The Epidemics of the Middle Ages*. Trans. London, 1844.

HEERS, JACQUES, *L'Occident aux XIVe et XVe siècles*. Paris, 1970.

HENNEMAN, JOHN B., "Militarism, Politics and Finance in Late Medieval France." Unpublished. 1976.

——, *Royal Taxation in Fourteenth Century France*. Princeton University Press, 1971.

——, "Soldiers, Society and State Finance in France, 1350–1450." Unpublished. 1974.

HERLIHY, DAVID, *Medieval and Renaissance Pistoia*. Yale University Press, 1967.

——, "Population, Plague and Social Change" in Molho, q.v.

HEWITT, H. J., *The Black Prince's Expedition of 1355–1357.* Manchester University Press, 1958.

*——, *The Organization of War Under Edward III, 1338–62.* Manchester University Press, 1966.

HILLAIRET, JACQUES, *Connaissance du vieux Paris.* 3 vols. Paris, 1951–54.

——, *Dictionnaire historique des rues de Paris,* 2nd ed. in 2 vols. Paris, 1964.

HILTON, R. H., "Peasant Movements in England Before 1381." *EHR,* 2nd series, vol. II, no. 2, 1949.

HONORÉ-DUVERGÉ, SUZANNE, "*Participation navarraise à la bataille de Cocherel.*" *Les Cahiers Vernonnais,* no. 4, 1964.

——, "*L'Origine du surnom de Charles le mauvais,*" in *Mélanges à Louis Halphen.* Paris, 1951.

The Horizon Book of the Middle Ages, Morris Bishop et al. London, 1968.

HUGHES, DOROTHY W., *Illustrations of Chaucer's England.* London, 1919.

HUGHES, PENNETHORNE, *Witchcraft.* London, 1952.

HUIZINGA, JOHAN, "The Political and Military Significance of Chivalric Ideas in the Late Middle Ages," in his *Men and Ideas.* Trans. New York, 1959.

*——, *The Waning of the Middle Ages.* London, 1968. (First published 1924.)

HUTCHISON, HAROLD F., *The Hollow Crown.* London, 1961. (Richard II.)

HUTTON, JAMES, *James and Philip van Artevelde.* London, 1882.

HYMA, ALBERT, *The Brethren of the Common Life.* Michigan, 1930.

IBN-KHALDOUN, *Histoire des Berbères,* vol. III. Trans. Paris, 1934.

JACKSON, W. T. H., *The Literature of the Middle Ages.* Columbia University Press, 1962.

JACOB, E. F., *Essays in Later Medieval History.* Manchester University Press, 1968.

JAMES, M. R., "Twelve Medieval Ghost Stories." *EHR,* July 1922.

JARRETT, BEDE, *The Emperor Charles IV.* New York, 1935.

——, *Social Theories of the Middle Ages, 1200–1500.* London, 1926.

*JARRY, EUGÈNE, "*Le Retour de la croisade de Barbarie (1390).*" *BEC,* vol. LIV, 1893.

——, *La Vie politique de Louis de France, Duc d'Orléans, 1372–1407.* Paris, 1889.

*——, "*La 'Voie de Fait' et l'Alliance Franco-Milanese, 1386–95.*" *BEC,* vol. LIII, 1892.

JOLY, M. A., "*De la Condition des Vilains au Moyen Age d'après les fabliaux.*" *Mémoires de l'Académie nationale des sciences, arts et belles-lettres de Caen,* 1882.

JONES, MICHAEL, *Ducal Brittany, 1364–99.* Oxford University Press, 1970.

JORGA, NICOLAS, *Philippe de Mézières, 1327–1405, et la croisade au XIVe siècle.* Paris, 1896.

JORGENSEN, JOHANNES, *Saint Catherine of Siena.* London, 1938.

JUSSERAND, J. J., *English Wayfaring Life in the Middle Ages.* London, 1950. (Contains far more information than the title indicates.)

KEEN, MAURICE, "Brotherhood in Arms." *History,* February 1962.

——, *A History of Medieval Europe.* New York, 1967.

——, *The Laws of War in the Late Middle Ages.* London, 1965.

——, "Robin Hood, a Peasant Hero." *History Today,* October 1958.

KILGOUR, RAYMOND L., *The Decline of Chivalry as Shown in the French Literature of the Late Middle Ages.* Harvard University Press, 1937.

KIRKLAND, DOROTHY, "The Growth of National Sentiment in France before the Fifteenth Century." *History*, June 1938.

KLEMM, FRIEDRICH, *A History of Western Technology.* New York, 1959.

KOUSEV, A., *"Contribution à l'histoire des forteresses médiévales sur le bas Danube." Bull. du Musée national à Varna*, vols. III and IV (XVIII–XIX), 1967–68.

KROLLMAN, CHRISTIAN, *The Teutonic Order in Prussia.* Trans. Preussenverlag, 1938.

LA CHESNAYE-DESBOIS ET BADIER, FRANÇOIS A. A. DE, *Dictionnaire de la noblesse*, vol. VI. Paris, 1865.

LACROIX, PAUL, *France in the Middle Ages: Customs, Classes, and Conditions.* Trans. New York, 1963.

LAGARDE, GEORGES DE, *La Naissance de l'esprit laïque au déclin du moyen age.* 6 vols. Paris, 1934–42.

LAGUILLE, LOUIS, *Histoire de la province d'Alsace.* Strasbourg, 1927.

LEA, HENRY CHARLES, *A History of the Inquisition of the Middle Ages.* Rev. ed. in 3 vols. London and New York, 1906.

*LEADER-TEMPLE, JOHN, and GIUSEPPE MARCOTTI, *Sir John Hawkwood: The Story of a Condottiere.* London, 1889.

LECARPENTIER, GEORGES, *"La Harelle, revolte rouennaise de 1382." Moyen Age*, 2nd series, vol. VII, 1903.

LEFEBVRE DES NOETTES, RICHARD, *L'Attelage: le cheval de selle à travers les ages.* 2 vols. Paris, 1931.

LEFF, GORDON, "Heresy and the Decline of the Medieval Church." *Past and Present*, November 1961.

——, "In Search of the Millennium." *Past and Present*, April 1958.

*LEFRANC, ABEL, *Olivier de Clisson, connétable de France.* Paris, 1898. (Excellent biography.)

LEGRAND, H., *Paris en 1380: plans de restitution.* Paris, 1868. (In same series as Le Roux de Lincy, q.v.)

LE GRAND D'AUSSY, PIERRE J. B., *Histoire de la vie privée des français.* 3 vols. Paris, 1815.

LEHOUX, FRANÇOISE, *Jean de France, Duc de Berri.* 4 vols. Paris, 1966.

LERNER, ROBERT E., *The Age of Adversity.* Cornell University Press, 1968.

LE ROUX DE LINCY, M., and L. M. TISSERAND, *Paris et ses historiens au XIVe et XVe siècles* (in series *Histoire générale de Paris*, ed. Baron Haussmann). Paris, 1867.

LESTOCQUOY, JEAN, *Histoire de la Picardie.* Paris, 1970.

*LEWIS, P. S., *Later Medieval France.* London, 1968.

LEYERLE, JOHN, ed., "Marriage in the Middle Ages." Symposium, *Viator*, vol. IV, 1973.

LINDNER, THEODOR, *Geschichte des deutschen Reiches unter König Wenzel.* 2 vols. Braunschweig, 1875.

LOCKE, A. AUDREY, *War and Misrule, 1307–99.* London, 1920.

LOOMIS, LAURA HIBBARD, "Secular Dramatics in the Royal Palace, Paris, 1378, 1379." *Speculum*, April 1958.

Lot, Ferdinand, *L'Art militaire et les armées au moyen age*, vol. I. Paris, 1946.

Lot, Ferdinand, and Robert Fawtier, *Histoires des institutions françaises au moyen age*, vol. II. Paris, 1958.

Luce, Siméon, *La France pendant la guerre de cent ans*. 2 vols. Paris, 1890–93.

——, *Histoire de Bertraud du Guesclin et son epoque*. Paris, 1876.

*——, *Histoire de la jacquerie*. Paris, 1895.

McFarlane, K. B., "England and the Hundred Years War: War, the Economy and Social Change." *Past and Present*, July 1962.

Macfarlane, Leslie, "An English Account of the Election of Urban VI, 1378." *Bull. of the Institute of Historical Research*, May 1953.

MacKinnon, James, *The History of Edward the Third*. London, 1900. Reprint. London, 1974.

McKisack, May, *The Fourteenth Century*. Oxford, 1959.

*McLaughlin, Mary Martin, "Survivors and Surrogates: Parents and Children from the Ninth to the Thirteenth Centuries," in *The History of Childhood*. Ed. Lloyd de Mause. New York, 1975. (An original and informative study full of evidence that does not support the generalizations of the editor.)

*Mâle, Emile, *L'Art religieux de la fin du moyen age en France*. 2nd ed. Paris, 1922.

Manley, John M., "Three Recent Chaucer Studies" and correspondence. *Rev. of English Studies*, July 1934 and April 1935.

Masson, A. L., *Jean Gerson*. Lyon, 1894.

Meiss, Millard, *French Painting in the Time of the Duke of Berry: Patronage of the Dukes*. 2 vols. London, 1967. *The Limbourgs*. 2 vols. New York, 1974.

——, *Painting in Florence and Siena After the Black Death*. Princeton, 1951.

——, "The Problem of Francesco Traini," *Art Bulletin*, vol. XV, 1933.

Mesquita, D. M. Bueno de, *Giangaleazzo Visconti, Duke of Milan*. Cambridge University Press, 1941.

Michelet, Jules, *Histoire de France*. Rev. ed. in 6 vols. Paris, 1861. (First published 1833–46.)

Milman, Henry Hart, *History of Latin Christianity*. London, 1867.

*Mirot, Léon, *Les Insurrections urbaines au debut de règne de Charles VI, 1380–83: leurs causes, leurs conséquences*. Paris, 1905. (Indispensable.)

——, "La Politique française en Italie sous le règne de Charles VI (1380–1422)." *REH*, October-December 1933.

——, "Sylvestre Budes et les Bretons en Italie." *BEC*, vol. LVII, 1897.

——, *Une Grande Famille parlementaire aux XIVe et XVe siècles: les d'Orgemonts*. Paris, 1913.

*——, "Une Tentative d'invasion au Angleterre pendant la guerre de cent ans (1385–86)." *REH*, July-September and October-December 1915.

Miskimin, Harry A., *Money, Prices, and Foreign Exchange in 14th Century France*. Yale University Press, 1963.

Moisant, J., *Le Prince noire en Aquitaine*. Paris, 1894.

Molho, Anthony, ed., *Social and Economic Foundations of the Italian Renaissance*. New York, 1969.

Mollat, Guillaume, *Les Papes d'Avignon, 1305–78*. 9th ed. Paris, 1950.

Mollat, Michel, *Genèse médiévale de la France moderne*. Paris, 1970. (With many uncommon and well-chosen illustrations.)

——, *La Vie et la pratique religieuse aux XIVe et XVe siècles . . . en France.* Paris, 1963.

*MOLLAT, MICHEL, and PHILIPPE WOLFF, *Ongles bleues, Jacques et Ciompi.* Paris, 1970.

MORANVILLÉ, HENRI, *Etude sur la vie de Jean le Mercier.* Paris, 1888.

——, ed., *Le Songe véritable: pamphlet politique d'un parisien du XVe siècle.* Paris, 1891. (For biographical notes on personages of the reign of Charles VI.)

MORRALL, JOHN B., *Gerson and the Great Schism.* Manchester University Press, 1960.

MUIR, DOROTHY, *A History of Milan under the Visconti.* London, 1924. (Confused and unreliable but worth reading.)

MULLER, JOHANN VON, *Der Geschichten Schweizerischen Eidgenossenschaft.* Leipzig, 1825.

MUNTZ, E., "*L'Argent et le luxe à le cour pontificale d'Avignon.*" RQH, 1899.

MUZZY, DAVID S., *The Spiritual Franciscans.* New York, 1907.

NOONAN, JOHN T., *Contraception: A History of Its Treatment by Catholic Theologians and Canonists.* Harvard University Press, 1965. (Covers a wider area of sexual theories than contraception alone.)

OAKESHOTT, R. EWART, *A Knight and His Horse.* London, 1962.

OMAN, SIR CHARLES, *A History of the Art of War in the Middle Ages,* vol. II. 2nd ed. London, 1924.

*ORIGO, IRIS, *The Merchant of Prato, 1335–1410.* New York, 1957. (No better book exists for the understanding of a real person of Coucy's period.)

ORNATO, EZIO, *Jean Muret et ses amis, Nicolas de Clamanges et Jean de Montreuil.* Geneva and Paris, 1969.

PAINTER, SIDNEY, *French Chivalry.* Johns Hopkins University Press, 1940.

PALMER, J. J. N., "The Anglo-French Peace Negotiations, 1390–96." *TRHS,* vol. XVI, 1966.

——, *England, France and Christendom, 1377–99.* London, 1972.

PANNIER, LÉOPOLD, "*Le Livre des cent ballades et la résponse du Bâtard de Coucy.*" *Romania,* vol. I, 1872.

PERNOUD, REGINA, *Histoire de la bourgeoisie en France.* Paris, 1960.

PERROY, EDOUARD, "The Anglo-French Negotiations at Bruges, 1374–77." *Camden Miscellany,* vol. XIX (Camden Third Series, vol. LXXX). London, 1952.

——, "*Economie contractié dans les crises du XIVe siècle.*" *AESC,* April-June 1949.

——, *The Hundred Years War.* Trans. New York, 1965.

*——, "Social Mobility Among the French Noblesse." *Past and Present,* April 1962.

——, "Wage Labour in France in the Later Middle Ages." *EHR,* December 1955.

*PETIT, ERNEST, *Entrée du rois Charles Six à Dijon, 1390.* Dijon, 1885.

——, *Itinéraires de Philippe le Hardi et de Jean Sans Peur.* Paris, 1888.

PIRENNE, HENRI, *Histoire de Belgique,* vol. II. Bruxelles, 1922.

——, *A History of Europe,* vol. II. New York, 1958.

POLLARD, A. F., *The Evolution of Parliament.* London, 1926.

POLLARD, ALFRED W., *English Miracle Plays, Moralities and Interludes.* Oxford, 1927.

POOLE, R., *Wycliffe and the Movements for Reform in the Fourteenth Century.* London, 1911.

POSTAN, M. M., "The Costs of the Hundred Years' War." *Past and Present,* April 1964.

——, "Some Social Consequences of the Hundred Years' War." *EHR,* vol. XII, 1942.

POWELL, J. ENOCH, and KEITH WALLIS, *The House of Lords in the Middle Ages.* London, 1968.

POWER, EILEEN, "The Position of Women," in *The Legacy of the Middle Ages.* Eds. G. G. Crump and E. F. Jacob. Oxford, 1926.

PRESTAGE, EDGAR, ed., *Chivalry: A Series to Illustrate Its Historical Significance and Civilizing Influence.* New York, 1928.

PUTNAM, GEORGE HAVEN, *Books and Their Makers During the Middle Ages,* vol. I. New York, 1896.

RAYNAUD, GASTON, *Les Cent Ballades: poème du XIVe siècle.* Paris, 1905.

RENOUARD, YVES, *The Avignon Papacy.* Trans. London, 1970.

——, "La Peste noire de 1348–50." *Rev. de Paris,* March 1950.

ROBBINS, HELEN, "A Comparison of the Effects of the Black Death on the Economic Organization of France and England." *Jour. of Political Economy,* August 1928.

ROBBINS, RUSSELL HOPE, *Encyclopaedia of Witchcraft and Demonology.* New York, 1959.

ROGOZINSKI, JAN, "Urban Violence in the Three Worlds of the Middle Ages: The French Perspective." Unpublished. December 1972.

RONCIÈRE, CHARLES DE LA, *Histoire de la marine française,* vol. II. Paris, 1899.

ROSENTHAL, JOEL T., *The Purchase of Paradise: Gift-giving and the Aristocracy, 1307–1485.* Toronto, 1972.

ROSETTI, R., "Notes on the Battle of Nicopolis." *Slavonic Review,* vol. XV, 1936–37.

RUNYAN, TIMOTHY J., "Ships and Mariners in Later Medieval England." Unpublished. 1976.

RUSSELL, JEFFRY B., *Witchcraft in the Middle Ages.* Ithaca, 1972.

RUSSELL, JOSIAH COX, *British Medieval Population.* Albuquerque, 1948.

——, "Effects of Pestilence and Plague, 1315–85." *Comparative Studies in Society and History,* July 1966.

——, "Medieval Population." *Social Forces,* May 1937.

——, "Populations in Europe, 500–1500," in *Fontana Economic History of Europe.* London, 1969.

SABINE, ERNEST L., "City Cleaning in Medieval London." *Speculum,* January 1937.

SADE, MARQUIS DE, *Histoire secrète d'Isabelle de Bavière, reine de France.* Ed. Gilbert Lely. Paris, 1953.

SALTMARSH, JOHN, "Plague and Economic Decline in England in the Later Middle Ages." *Cambridge Historical Jour.,* vol. VII, no. 1, 1941.

SAPORI, ARMANDO, *The Italian Merchant in the Middle Ages.* Trans. New York, 1970.

SCHEVILL, FERDINAND, *History of Florence.* New York, 1961.

——, *Siena: The Story of a Medieval Commune.* New York, 1909.

SCHNYDER, PIERRE, "*Le Flagellantisme à travers les siècles.*" *Archives de Psychologie,* January 1932.

SEARLE, ELEANOR, and ROBERT BURGHART, "The Defense of England and the Peasants' Revolt." *Viator,* vol. III, 1972.

SEDGWICK, HENRY DWIGHT, *Edward the Black Prince.* Indianapolis, 1932.

SEE, HENRI, *Les Classes rurales et le régime domaniel en France au moyen age.* Paris, 1901.

SEEBOHM, F., "The Black Death and Its Place in English History." *Fortnightly Rev.,* vol. II, 1865.

SHEARS, F. S., *Froissart.* London, 1930.

SHERBORNE, JAMES, "The Battle of La Rochelle." *Bull. of the Institute of Historical Research,* University of London, May 1969.

——, "Indentured Retinues and English Expeditions to France." *EHR,* October 1964.

SISMONDI, J. C. L. S., *Histoire des républiques italiennes du moyen age,* vols. IV and V. Paris, 1840.

SNELL, FREDERICK, *The Fourteenth Century.* Edinburgh, 1899.

SOUTHERN, RICHARD W., *Western Society and the Church in the Middle Ages.* London, 1970.

STANLEY, ARTHUR, "Sir John Hawkwood." *Blackwood's,* March 1929.

STEIN, HENRI, *Archers d'autrefois: archers d'aujourd'hui.* Paris, 1925.

STRAYER, JOSEPH R., "France: The Holy Land, the Chosen People, and the Most Christian King," in *Action and Conviction in Early Modern Europe.* Eds. T. K. Rabb and J. E. Siegel. Princeton University Press, 1969.

——, *On the Medieval Origins of the Modern State.* Princeton University Press, 1970.

SUPINO, I. B., *Il Camposanto di Pisa.* Firenze, 1893.

TERRIER DE LORAY, HENRI, MARQUIS DE, *Jean de Vienne, amiral de France.* Paris, 1877.

THIBAULT, MARCEL, *Isabeau de Bavière: la jeunesse, 1370–1405.* Paris, 1903.

THOMPSON, JAMES WESTFALL, "The Aftermath of the Black Death and the Aftermath of the Great War." *American Jour. of Sociology,* March 1920.

——, *Economic and Social History of Europe in the Later Middle Ages.* New York, 1931.

*THORNDIKE, LYNN, *A History of Magic and Experimental Sciences,* vols. III and IV. Columbia University Press, 1934.

THRUPP, SYLVIA, "Plague Effects in Medieval Europe," *Comparative Studies in Society and History,* July 1966.

TIPTON, CHARLES L. "The English at Nicopolis." *Speculum,* October 1962.

TOURNEUR-AUMONT, J. M., *La Bataille de Poitiers et la construction de la France.* Paris, 1940.

——, "*Originalité militaire de Du Guesclin.*" *Moyen Age,* March 1938.

TREASE, GEOFFREY, *The Condottiere.* New York, 1971.

TREVELYAN, GEORGE, *England in the Age of Wyclif.* London, 1899.

TURNER, RALPH E., "Economic Discontent in Medieval Western Europe," *Jour. of Economic History,* Supplement VIII, 1948.

ULLMAN, WALTER, *The Origins of the Great Schism*. London, 1948.

UTLEY, FRANCIS L., ed., *The Forward Movement of the 14th Century*. Ohio University Press, 1961.

VAISSÈTE, JEAN JOSEPH, and CLAUDE DE VIC, *Histoire générale de Languedoc*, vol. IV. Paris, 1730–45.

VALERI, NINO, *L'Italia nell' Età dei Principati* (vol. V of *Storia d'Italia*). Verona 1949.

*VALOIS, NOËL, *La France et le grand schisms d'occident*. 4 vols. Paris, 1896–1902.

VAUGHAN, RICHARD, *Philip the Bold*. London, 1962.

VERNOT D'AUBEUFF, ABBÉ AUBERT DE, *Histoire des Chevaliers Hospitaliers de St. Jean de Jérusalem*, vol. II. Amsterdam, 1781.

VIOLLET-LE-DUC, E., *Dictionnaire raisonné de l'architecture de France du XIe au XVIe siècle*. 10 vols. Paris, 1861–75.

——, *Military Architecture of the Middle Ages*. Trans. Oxford, 1860.

VUATRIN, GABRIEL, *Etude historique sur le connétable*. Paris, 1905.

WHITE, LYNN, "Medieval Astrologers and Late Medieval Technology." *Viator*, vol. VI, 1975.

——, *Medieval Technology and Social Change*. Oxford, 1962.

——, "Technology Assessment from the Stance of a Medieval Historian." *American Historical Rev.*, February 1974.

——, "Technology and Invention in the Middle Ages." *Speculum*, vol. XV, 1940.

WILKINS, ERNEST HATCH, *Petrarch's Eight Years in Milan*. Cambridge, 1958.

WORKMAN, HERBERT, *John Wyclif: A Study of the Medieval Church*. Oxford, 1926.

WRIGHT, EDITH, "Medieval Attitudes Toward Mental Illness." *Bull. of the History of Medicine*, vol. VII, no. 3, March 1939.

WRIGHT, THOMAS, *A History of Domestic Manners and Sentiment in England*. London, 1862.

WULF, MAURICE DE, *Philosophy and Civilization in the Middle Ages*. Princeton, 1922.

WYLIE, JAMES HAMILTON, *The Reign of Henry the Fifth*. 3 vols. Cambridge, 1919.

ZACOUR, NORMAN P., "Talleyrand: The Cardinal of Périgord 1301–1364." *Trans. of Am. Philosophical Soc.* New Series, vol. 50, part 7. Philadelphia, 1960.

*ZIEGLER, PHILIP, *The Black Death*. New York, 1969. (The best modern study.)

ZURLAUBEN, BARON VON THURN UND, "Histoire d'Arnaut de Cervole, dit l'Archiprêtre." *Histoire de l'Académie royale des inscriptions et belles-lettres*, vol. XXV. Paris, 1759.

Reference Notes

References are given for most quotations and for curious, debatable, or relatively obscure items for which an inquiring reader might want to know the source. I have not documented the better-known facts, events, and general conditions, which can be found in standard histories. With regard to quotations from the chronicles and other contemporary writers such as the Ménagier, La Tour Landry, Chaucer, Langland et al., I have given page references where it seemed important. Otherwise, when the source is named in the text and the work appears in the Bibliography, I have not thought it necessary to cite the page. This applies especially to Froissart, both for the sake of reducing bulk and because I read or consulted different editions (Berners, Johnes, Kervyn Lettenhove, Luce) at different times, resulting in too many variants.

ABBREVIATIONS

AN	Archives nationales
BN	Bibliothèque nationale
CMH	*Cambridge Medieval History*, vol. VII
DBF	*Dictionnaire de biographie française*, 1933– (in progress; at the time used by the author, this had reached the letter F)
DNB	*Dictionary of National Biography*
KL	Kervyn Lettenhove edition of Froissart
LUCE-F	Luce edition of Froissart
OCFL	*Oxford Companion to French Literature*

Foreword

p. xiii THOMPSON: *Aftermath*, 565.
  xiv SISMONDI: *Républiques*, chap. 38. The original is *"ne fut point heureuse pour l'humanité."* "A PERIOD OF ANGUISH": Heers, 111.
  PERROY: *Hundred Years*, x.
  xvi COMTE D'AUXERRE: Delachenal, I, 207, n. 3.
  ISABEAU OF BAVARIA, A BLONDE: Mazas, IV, 181. "DARK AND LIVELY": *CMH*, 375.
  xvii HUNGARIAN HISTORIAN: Otto Zarek, *A History of Hungary*, trans., London, 1939.

Chapter 1—"I Am the Sire de Coucy": The Dynasty

3 SOURCES FOR THE CASTLE AND *donjon:* Viollet-le-Duc, *Dict.*, II, 440–41; III, 113–14; V, 34, 74–75; 79; Larousse, *Grand Dictionnaire universel*, V, 1869; Dufour; Lefèvre-Pontalis. COMPARISON TO THE PYRAMIDS: q. Dufour, 21.

4 *"Coucy à la merveille!":* L'Art de vérifier. *"Roi ne suis":* Duchesne, 205. CASTLE BUILT IN SEVEN YEARS: Viollet-le-Duc, *Dict.*, V, 74.

5 "WORTHY OF NERO": Antoine d'Asti, secretary of Charles, Duc d'Orléans, inheritor of the Coucy domain. Description of the castle written 1410, q. Dufour, 58.

6 "ONE OF THE KEYS OF THE KINGDOM": so described in a suit over disputed property brought in 1407 by the Duc d'Orléans against Coucy's grandson, Robert de Bar, based on the claim that the barony must be held as a whole by its seigneur in order that he may "better resist those who come against the said kingdom," q. Jarry, *Orléans*, 240. (The date 1447 given by Jarry must be a typographical error.)

7 ff. HISTORY OF THE DYNASTY: Duchesne, 185–274; *L'Art de vérifier*, 219 ff.; Sars, passim; Duplessis.
  ENGUERRAND I AND SYBIL: Guibert of Nogent, 148–50.
  "RAGING WOLF": Suger in *Vie de Louis VI le Gros*, q. Ross & McLaughlin, 267–73.

8 ORIGIN OF THE COUCY ARMS: Ancien, based on Duchesne and L'Alouëte. Other versions in *Rev. Nobiliare*, 1865, vol. III, q. Lacaille *thèse;* also *Histoire de la ville de Marle*, q. Chaurand, 67–68. See also Dumas & Martinet, 17; Duckett, 19.
  THOMAS DE MARLE'S CAREER: Guibert of Nogent, 170, 184–85, 199, and dynastic sources.

9 CHARTER OF COUCY-LE-CHÂTEAU: Sars, 170; Larousse, *Gr. Encyc.*

10 ENGUERRAND III: Lelong, 281, 286–87.

11 HIS CONSTRUCTIONS AT COUCY: Viollet-le-Duc, *Dict.*, IV, 233–34.

p. 12 AMIENS, "HIGHER THAN ALL THE SAINTS": J. Brandicourt & J. Desobry, *The Cathedral of Amiens,* undated brochure issued by the Cathedral.

DUC DE BERRY AND CHAPEL WINDOWS: Dufour, 51.

COINED OWN MONEY: Sars, 194.

COUCY OWED 30 KNIGHTS: Lot & Fawtier, 517.

13 ENGUERRAND IV: for his trial, in addition to dynastic sources, see Margaret Wade Lafarge, *St. Louis,* Boston, 1968, 175–76.

VALUE OF 20 SOUS: Perroy, "Wage Labour," 45, n. 1; Jusserand, 46–47, 51.

15 "OF THE GOOD TOWNS": Georges Chastellain, q. Cartellieri, 76.

"EXPOSURE OF THEIR BODIES": q. Bloch, *Feudal,* 451.

AQUINAS, "COMMON GOOD": q. Jarret, *Social,* 18. "PRINCES ARE INSTITUTED": ibid.

"NOT ONE OF US": Girard de Roussilon, q. Oakeshott, 53.

16 GARIN LI LOHERAINS: q. Gautier (Eng. ed.), 281.

BERTRAND DE BORN: q. Bloch, *Feudal,* 293. DANTE PUT HIM IN HELL: *Inferno,* XXVIII.

17 "NOT PROPER FOR A NOBLE": Lewis, 175, 180. SONS OF NOBLES AS MERCHANTS: Cazelles, *Société politique,* 290.

"SHALL HAVE NO CAUSE": Bonet, 131.

18 KNIGHT WITH 32 COATS-OF-ARMS: He was Jacques de Lalaing; Cartellieri, 75.

DURATION OF NOBLE FAMILIES: Lewis, 176–77.

DISAPPEARANCE RATE OF 50 PERCENT: Perroy, "Social Mobility." CLUSEL AND GUICHARD VERT: ibid.

19 SUMPTUARY LAWS: Baldwin, passim.

IN FLORENCE: Origo, 290, 298, 300–301. IN FRANCE: Franklin, *Rues et cris,* 35–36.

20 KNIGHTON: q. Baldwin, 69.

21 GIRALDUS CAMBRENSIS: q. Shears in Prestage, 57. UNCOUTH GERMANS: Bonet, 204. "MOST CHIVALROUS SOJOURN": q. Michelet, III, 255. DON PERO NIÑO: q. Díaz de Gómez (Evans trans.), 133.

FRENCH LANGUAGE, MARCO POLO, ST. FRANCIS, VENETIAN SCHOLAR: Artz, 350; Cheyney, 248–49.

LONDON BRIDGE: Jusserand, 23–24. FRENCH DOLLS: Bradley, 136.

22 FRENCH IVORIES: E. Mâle, *Art et artistes du moyen age,* Paris, 1927, 313–14.

"YOU PARIS MASTERS": q. E. R. Chamberlin, *Life in Medieval France,* London, 1967, 118. "TWO LIGHTS OF THE WORLD": q. Coville, 394.

23 CEREMONY OF THE *rissoles:* Dufour, 62–64; Lelong, 181.

Chapter 2—Born to Woe: The Century

24 BALTIC SEA: J. C. Russell, *Fontana,* 24. CASPIAN SEA: Carpentier, "*Autour de la peste noire.*"

p. 24 PEOPLE EATING CHILDREN: Russell, op. cit.

26 BISHOP DENIED BURIAL: *CMH*, 280.

27 CHILDREN OF PRIESTS: Flick, 175–76. AND OTHER DISPENSATIONS: ibid., 121–22.
ALVAR PELAYO, "I FOUND BROKERS": q. ibid., 180.
UNFIT CLERGY, BOY OF SEVEN ET AL.: ibid., 174.
BISHOP OF DURHAM: Coulton, *Panorama*, 128.

28 HENRY OF HEREFORD: q. Cohn, 133–34.
JOHN XXII, GOLD CLOTH AND FURS: Origo, 8.
"RICH, INSOLENT AND RAPACIOUS": q. Hay, 277. CARDINAL'S TEN STABLES: *CMH*, 282.

29 PETRARCH ON "BABYLON OF THE WEST": Robinson, *Readings*, I, 502–3.
LATRINES OF THE PAPAL PALACE: Gagnière. AMBASSADOR FROM ARAGON: Origo, 7.
ST. BRIGITTA, "A FIELD FULL OF PRIDE": q. Hay, 277.

30 ARCHBISHOP OF CANTERBURY'S COMPLAINT: q. Cutts, 242–43.
MATTEO VILLANI: q. Emerton, 178.

31 14TH CENTURY POEM: T. Wright, *Political Songs*, I, 264–66.
"DID NOT BEHAVE AS FRIARS OUGHT": q. Jusserand, 170.
ST. FRANCIS AND BREVIARY: ibid., 166.
MONKS LENT MONEY AT INTEREST: Coulton, *Panorama*, 269.

32 "MUSTARD POTTIS": q. Jusserand, 171–72.
BOILING AN EGG: Ménagier de Paris, 295.
FEAST OF FOOLS: Chambers, 294, 315, 325–27; Gayley, 49–50.

33 "THE THORN FALLS OUT": *Chron. C6*, I, 317. WOMAN ACCUSED OF INCEST: Cohen, 327.

34 PETRARCH, "A HARD AND WEARY JOURNEY": *Correspondence*, 398.
"TURN THEE AGAIN": q. Herlihy, *Med. Culture*, 409.

35 GASCON SEIGNEUR: He was Amanieu d'Albret VI, q. Boutruche, 177.
JOINVILLE ON THE POOR: q. Shears in Prestage, 64.

37 ST. AUGUSTINE: q. Coulton, *Panorama*, 369. ST. JEROME: q. Pirenne, *Europe*, 229.

38 "DEVIL ON THE LID": q. Pirenne, loc. cit. DATINI'S MOTTO: Origo, xiv.
PHILIPPE DE BEAUMANOIR: q. Mollat & Wolff, 46.

40 *Confréries:* Mâle, 167 ff.; M. Mollat, *Vie*, 91–103.

41 JACQUES DE VITRY: q. Davis, 271, and Evans, *Med. France*, 34.

42 TEMPLARS ACCUSED OF BLACK ARTS: Jeffry Russell, 195–96, 198.

43 "AND HE WOULD HAVE CONFESSED": q. *CMH*, 318–19.

44 MOLAY'S CURSE: The eyewitness report by Godfrey of Paris is quoted in *Nouv. biog. générale*, ed. Hoefer, Paris, 1861. See also Marcel Lobet, *Histoire des Templiers*, Liège, 1944, 225; M. Reynouard, *Procès et condamnation des Templiers*, Paris, 1805, 113.

45 "BAD LAME QUEEN": Coville, 399. PHILIP VI and THE BEATIFIC VISION: Lea, III, 590, 593; *Cath. Encyc.*, II, 430; Coville, 14.

46 THREAT TO BURN THE POPE: reported by Giovanni Villani, q. J. B. Christophe, *Histoire de la Papauté*, Paris, 1853, II, 30.
PHILIP ARRANGES MARRIAGE OF ENGUERRAND VI: Duchesne, 262–63.

47 EMPEROR LUDWIG AND DAUGHTER: Jarrett, *Social*, 58.

Chapter 3—Youth and Chivalry

p. 49 ENGLISH PREACHER ON MOTHER AND CHILD: q. Owst, 34–35.

50 KNITTING ON FOUR NEEDLES: White, "Technology Assessment" with illus. *Ancren Riwle:* q. McLaughlin, 153, n. 90.

INFANT MORTALITY ESTIMATED: McLaughlin, 111.

PHILIP OF NOVARA: *"Des iiii tenz d'aage d'ome"* [The four ages of man] in Langlois, II, 210–11.

51 ADVICE ON ETIQUETTE: Ménagier, 10, 14–17, 20, 24, 47, 204, 209, 215, 219; T. Wright, *Manners,* 275; Christine de Pisan, *Livre des trois vertus,* q. Power, 318; Fra Benvenisco da Ripa, *Zinquanta cortesi da Tavola* [Fifty courtesies at the table], q. Aries, 381. On absence of advice on child-rearing, see Power, 420.

BARTHOLOMEW OF ENGLAND and ALDOBRANDINO OF SIENA: q. McLaughlin, 115, 137, 144, n. 31.

52 HALF THE POPULATION UNDER 21: J. C. Russell, *Fontana,* 31.

53 BOCCACCIO, "BIRDS, WILD BEASTS": *Questioni d'Amore,* chap. 5, q. *Putnam's Reader,* 188.

54 CHRONICLER'S COMPLAINT OF SHORT TUNICS: Jean de Venette, q. Luce, *Jacquerie,* 37.

MARCH, "IN WHICH THE WORLD BEGAN": Nun's Priest's Tale.

55 A SCHOLAR OF OXFORD: Thorndike, III, 143. MENTAL DEPRESSION AN ILLNESS: ibid., 251. TRIANGULATION BY A MONK: Davis, 338.

WINDMILLS MUST PAY TITHES: White, *Med. Tech.,* 89.

TRAVEL—DISTANCES AND CONDITIONS: Boyer; Jusserand, 123; Hay, 363; d'Haucourt, 17; Cipolla, 534; Boissonade, 287; T. Wright, *Manners.*

56 VENICE-TO-BRUGES POSTAL SERVICE: Origo, 99.

SIR HERVÉ DE LÉON: Coulton, *Panorama,* 325. PILGRIMS' "HERTES BEGIN TO FAYLE": ibid.

57 DESCHAMPS ON GERMAN INNS: q. Coopland in notes to Mézières, I, 36.

KNEW THE WORLD WAS ROUND: Bartholomew of England, *Image du Monde* and others in Langlois, *Connaissance.*

58 AS A FLY ON AN APPLE: *Image,* q. ibid., 78. DISTANCE FROM THE STARS: ibid., 79.

UNIVERSE IN GOD'S ARMS: Mâle, 298. MOON, ECLIPSE, RAIN, TIME BETWEEN THUNDER AND LIGHTNING: *Image du Monde,* 97–100.

VIEWS OF INDIA, PERSIA: ibid., 83–84.

GARDEN OF EDEN: Howard Patch, *The Other World,* Harvard University Press, 1950.

59 "THEY ARE AS GOD PLEASES": ibid., 93.

BOOK OF SIDRACH: Langlois, *Connaissance,* 224 ff.

60 DANTE, CHANTED BY BLACKSMITHS, AND PUBLIC LECTURES ON: Cheyney, 260.

61 ITALIAN BIOGRAPHICAL DICTIONARY: Bandini of Arezzo, *Fons memorabilium universi,* q. Thorndike, III, 562.

p. 61 CATHERINE'S HUSBAND: He is named Conrad de Hardeck in *L'Art de vérifier*, 237, and Conrad de Magdebourg by La Chesnaye-Desbois.

62 CATHERINE'S CARE FOR SON'S EDUCATION: BN, ms. fr. 18616.

64 JOHN OF SALISBURY: q. Coulton, *Panorama*, 242. JOHN THE BLIND DUG UP SYNAGOGUE: Jarrett, *Charles IV*, 104, n. 1. HIS DEATH: Froissart on Crécy.

65 COST OF HELMET AND WAR-HORSE: Contamine, 656.

66 ST. BERNARD ON TOURNAMENTS: Gautier, 272.

67 KEEP HIS TEETH AND NAILS CLEAN: Painter, 135.
Châtelain de Coucy: Delbouille, passim.
"MELANCHOLY, AMOROUS AND BARBARIC": Gaston Paris, q. in Larousse, *Gr. Encyc.*, XIII, 34.

68 EDWARD III AND COUNTESS OF SALISBURY: *Chron. Jean le Bel*, 30–34; *Chron. normande*, 54, 59–60; Luce-F, II, 346, and IV, xviii–ix.

69 IDENTITY OF JEAN LE BEL: Snell, 339; Coville, 413.
TEUTONIC KNIGHTS HUNTED PEASANTS FOR SPORT: Pirenne, *Europe*, II, 110.

Chapter 4—War

70 LONGBOW: Stein, 66; Lot & Fawtier, 528.
Ribauds (CANNON): Oman, 211–17; *Chron. Jean de Venette*, 157, n. 45.

71 "OH, THE COWARDLY ENGLISH": Walsingham, q. KL, III, notes, 491. FISH DRANK SO MUCH FRENCH BLOOD: *Melsa Chron.*, q. notes to *Chron. Jean de Venette*, 154, n. 27.

72 EDWARD III, "CHARM" AND "PETULANCE": *CMH*, 438.

73 AQUINAS ON "JUST WAR": q. Jarrett, *Social*, 193; Painter, 157. "RIGHT OF SPOIL": Keen, *Laws*, 65, 74–75, 140.
MICHELET ON BRITTANY: from the famous "Tableau de France" in the *Histoire*, II, 7–18.

74 CHARLES DE BLOIS—CHARACTER: Huizinga, *Waning*, 178. BAREFOOT IN THE SNOW: ibid.
HURLED 30 HEADS: Mackinnon, 219; see also Roujoux, *Hist. des rois et des ducs de Bretagne*, 1839, III, 127; A. Clauziou, *Hist. de Bretagne*, 1941, 97–98.

76 QUEEN JEANNE ON BRUGES: q. Mollat & Wolff, 25.
MATTHEW OF WESTMINSTER ON WOOL: q. Thompson, 61.
COURTRAI, LOSSES MADE UP BY ENNOBLEMENT: Bloch, *Feudal*, 324–25.

80 ARTEVELDE STRIKES FLEMISH KNIGHT: Pernoud, 214.
ARTEVELDE'S DEATH: Froissart.
"*Il piccolo re*": q. Tourneur, 467.

81 *Double et louche:* III, 250.

82 ADVICE OF PARLIAMENT IN 1344: Barnes, 303.
SHIPS FOR EXPEDITIONARY FORCE: Hewitt, *Organization*, 51, 76; Coopland, in notes to Mézières, I, 59.
RECRUITMENT AND PROPAGANDA: Oman, 126; Hewitt, op. cit., 30, 159.

84 MILITARY OBLIGATION OF TOWNS: Contamine, 33, 176. ROUEN, NARBONNE, NÎMES: Henneman, *Royal*, 116, 120, 122, 135, 147.

p. 84   KNIGHTS' RATES OF PAY: Contamine, 622–23, 626. THE *montre:* ibid., 537.
ARMOR AND HELMET: Oakeshott, 15, 43; Cutts, 344–45; Contamine, 656.

85   "TERRIBLE WORM": q. Lefranc, 137, from an unnamed contemporary poem, not further identified. MACE FAVORED BY MARTIAL CLERICS: Davis, 196.

86   FRENCH DISDAINED MISSILES: Evans, *Life*, 140. ARCHER AS "COWARD": q. Davis, 190.
CROSSBOW BANNED BY CHURCH: Painter, 21.

87   CRÉCY: The battle is described in all the chronicles. A useful summary is in Lot, 340–50.
ENGLISH ARCHERS PROTECTED BOWSTRINGS: *Chron. Jean de Venette*, 43. The subject of the wet and dry bowstrings and whether, when wet, they shrink or stretch has been a question of intense discussion among the Crécy buffs, and even of physical experiment by one historian who soaked bowstrings in water to determine the answer.

89   "15 DENIERS WORTH THREE": *Chron. 4 Valois*, 14.
ESTATES' DISPLEASURE VOICED: Perroy, *Hundred Years*, 121.

90   ISABELLE'S BETROTHAL TO LOUIS DE MALE: *Chron. Jean le Bel*, II, 135–39; *Chron. normande*, 84–86, 276, n. 7; Luce-F, IV, nn. 1–2, 34–37; *Grandes Chrons.*, ed. Viard, IX, 292; *Chron. Jean de Venette*, 47–48, 184–85, n. 27; *Chron. de Jean de Noyal*, ed. Molinier, *Bull. SHF*, 1883, 253. Song about Isabelle is in Jean de Venette, 48. Summary of the sources in Henry Lucas, *The Low Countries and the Hundred Years' War*, 1929, 559–65.

91   CALAIS REDUCED TO EATING EXCREMENT ("*Toutes ordures par droite famine*"): q. *CMH*, 349.
NUMBERS ENGAGED IN CRÉCY-CALAIS: Postan, *EHR*.

Chapter 5—"This Is the End of the World": The Black Death

The chief sources used for this chapter were Campbell; Carpentier; Crawfurd; Coulton, *Black Death;* Gasquet; Hecker; Ziegler; also Barnes; Bowsky; Bridbury; Cazelles, *Peste;* Deaux; Meiss, *Painting . . . After the Black Death;* Nohl; Renouard: Saltmarsh; Seebohm; Thompson; Thrupp. On the Jews: Abrahams; Salo Baron; Chazan, and *Encyclopedia Judaica*, Jerusalem and New York, 1970–71.

92   "DEATH IS SEEN SEATED": Simon de Covino, q. Campbell, 80.

93   "COULD INFECT THE WORLD": q. Gasquet, 41.
WELSH LAMENT: q. Ziegler, 190.

94   "DOGS DRAGGED THEM FORTH": Agnolo di Tura, q. Ziegler, 58.
"OR IF NO MAN IS PRESENT": Bishop of Bath and Wells, q. Ziegler, 125.

95   "NO BELLS TOLLED": Agnolo di Tura, q. Schevill, *Siena*, 211. The same observation was made by Gabriel de Muisis, notary of Piacenza, q. Crawfurd, 113.

p. 95   GIVRY PARISH REGISTER: Renouard, 111. THREE VILLAGES OF CAMBRIDGESHIRE: Saltmarsh.

PETRARCH'S BROTHER: Bishop, 273. BROTHER JOHN CLYN: q. Ziegler, 195.

96   APATHY; "AND IN THESE DAYS": q. Deaux, 143, citing only "an old northern chronicle."

AGNOLO DI TURA, "FATHER ABANDONED CHILD": q. Ziegler, 58.

"MAGISTRATES AND NOTARIES": q. Deaux, 49. ENGLISH PRIESTS TURNED AWAY: Ziegler, 261.

97   PARENTS DESERTING CHILDREN: Hecker, 30. GUY DE CHAULIAC, "A FATHER": q. Gasquet, 50–51.

NUNS OF THE HÔTEL DIEU: *Chron. Jean de Venette*, 49.

PICARDS AND SCOTS MOCK MORTALITY OF NEIGHBORS: Gasquet, 53, and Ziegler, 198.

CATHERINE DE COUCY: *L'Art de vérifier*, 237. AMIENS TANNERS: Gasquet, 57. "BY THE JOLLITY THAT IS IN US": *Grandes Chrons.*, VI, 486–87.

98   JOHN OF FORDUN: q. Ziegler, 199. SIMON DE COVINO ON THE POOR: Gasquet, 42. ON YOUTH: Cazelles, *Peste*.

KNIGHTON ON SHEEP: q. Ziegler, 175. WOLVES OF AUSTRIA AND DALMATIA: ibid., 84, 111. DOGS AND CATS: Muisis, q. Gasquet, 44, 61.

99   BAVARIAN CHRONICLER OF NEUBERG: q. Ziegler, 84. WALSINGHAM, "THE WORLD COULD NEVER": Denifle, 273.

"OH HAPPY POSTERITY": q. Ziegler, 45.

GIOVANNI VILLANI, "*e dure questo*": q. Snell, 334.

100   PHYSICIANS OF VENICE: Campbell, 98. SIMON DE COVINO: ibid., 31. GUY DE CHAULIAC, "I WAS IN FEAR": q. Thompson, *Ec. and Soc.*, 379.

THUCYDIDES: q. Crawfurd, 30–31.

101   CHINESE ORIGIN: Although the idea of Chinese origin is still being repeated (e.g., by William H. McNeill, *Plagues and People*, New York, 1976, 161–63), it is disputed by L. Carrington Goodrich of the Association for Asian Studies, Columbia Univ., in letters to the author of 18 and 26 October 1973. Citing contemporary Chinese and other sources, he also quotes Dr. George A. Perera of the College of Physicians and Surgeons, an authority on communicable diseases, who "agrees with me that the spaces between epidemics in China (1334), Semirechyé (1338–9) and the Mediterranean basin (1347–9) seem too long for the first to be responsible for the last."

REPORTS FROM THE EAST: Barnes, 432; Coulton, *Black Death*, 9–11.

102   ANONYMOUS FLEMISH CLERIC, "MOST TERRIBLE": His correspondence was edited in the form of a chronicle by De Smet, in *Recueil des chroniques de Flandres*, III, q. Ziegler, 22. GENTILE DA FOLIGNO, "COMMUNICATED BY AIR": Campbell, 38.

REPORT OF THE UNIVERSITY OF PARIS: Hecker, 51–53; Campbell, 15.

103   M. VILLANI, "EXTERMINATION OF MANKIND": q. Meiss, *Painting . . . After the Black Death*, 66. ROUEN PROHIBITS GAMBLING: Nohl, 74.

104   AT MESSINA, DEMONS LIKE DOGS: Coulton, *Black Death*, 22–27.

PEST MAIDEN: Ziegler, 85.

CANTACUZENE: Barnes, 435. PIERS PLOWMAN, "PURE SIN": B text, V, 13.

105   CLEMENT VI, "SENSUAL VICES": Gregorovius, VI, 334.

p. 106 DOCTORS' SKILLS: Thorndike, III, 249–51. CATARACTS: Gilles li Muisis, *Chron.*, q. in Intro. x. SKIN GRAFTS: M. Rowling, *Life in Medieval Times*, New York, 1973, 192. See also Arturo Castiglione, *A History of Medicine*, New York, 1946, 398–99.

107 SEWAGE DISPOSAL: Thrupp; Coulton, *Panorama*, 456; Sabine.

108 VISCONTI MEASURES: Hecker, 58. LEICESTERSHIRE AUTOCRAT RAZED NOSELEY: letter to author, 25 June 1974, from Lord Hazelrigg, direct descendant of the autocrat, and present proprietor of Noseley Hall.

LEGEND OF ST. ROCH; "IN THESE SAD TIMES": q. Mâle, 190. "GOD IS DEAF": Passus X, line 79.

109 "HOSTILITY OF GOD": q. Campbell, 132.

JEWS' INTENT TO "KILL AND DESTROY": *Chron. Jean le Bel*, I, 225, and Gilles li Muisis, 222.

WELL-POISONING: *Chron. Jean de Venette*, 50; S. W. Baron, XI, 160. "RIVERS AND FOUNTAINS": from *Jugement du Roi de Navarre*, 70.

112 RABBI MOSES OF COUCY: *Encyc. Jud.*, VI, 167; VII, 19.

JEWS' BADGE AND POINTED HAT: Abrahams, 287; Enlart, 435.

WILLIAM OF NEWBURGH: q. Coulton, *Panorama*, 359.

113 TRIALS IN SAVOY: Cox, 60–70; "Black Death" in *Encyc. Jud.*

CLEMENT'S BULL: Luce-F, IV, 101.

114 FLAGELLANTS: Cohn, 125–37; *CMH*, chap. 10; Lea, II, 882; Hecker, 34–39; Schnyder, 279–89.

115 MASSACRES AT WORMS, FRANKFURT, COLOGNE, MAINZ, ERFURT: Cohn, 138–39; Heinrich Graetz, *History of the Jews*, Philadelphia, 1894, IV, 109.

116 DUKE ALBERT II OF AUSTRIA: S. W. Baron, XI, 163.

"LIKE NIGHT PHANTOMS": q. Cohn, 139.

JEWS RETURN TO ERFURT: S. W. Baron, IX, 224.

117 DICE INTO PRAYER BEADS: Gasquet, 60.

PIERS PLOWMAN: Passus IX, ed. Wells, 110.

M. VILLANI, "BETTER MEN": q. Coulton, *Black Death*, 66–68.

118 ORVIETO: Carpentier, *Ville*, 190. PENALTY FOR INTERCOURSE BETWEEN CHRISTIAN AND JEW: ibid., 196.

EMPEROR CHARLES IV, "PRECIOUS KNOWLEDGE": Campbell, 150. CORPUS CHRISTI: ibid., 150.

119 PETRARCH ON BOLOGNA: ibid., 159–60.

DECLINE IN POPULATION: J. C. Russell, "Med. pop."; Carpentier, *AESC*; Bowsky; Heers, 101–5; Hay, 76.

120 EFFECTS ON LABOR: Perroy in *EHR*; Seebohm, 269, 273; Helen Robbins, 473–76; Heers, 108–11.

121 JUBILEE YEAR: Gregorovius, 323–25. "A PONTIFF SHOULD MAKE HIS SUBJECTS HAPPY": q. G. Mollat, *Papes*, 86.

TREASURY OF MERIT: Jusserand, 170.

122 A MILLION VISITORS: Meiss, 80.

BEQUESTS, ST. GERMAIN: Ziegler, 78. SIENA: Bowsky, 26. FLORENCE: Meiss, 78.

CARDINAL-LEGATE ATTACKED IN ROME: Gregorovius, 325.

"*Bene quidem*": Coulton, *Black Death*, 59.

p. 123   "WICKEDER THAN BEFORE": *Chron. Jean de Venette*, 51. CLEMENT, "WHAT CAN YOU PREACH": ibid., 55–56.

LOTHAR OF SAXONY: q. Campbell, 144.

124   TRAINI'S FRESCO: Meiss, "Traini"; Supino, 73–80.

Chapter 6—The Battle of Poitiers

127   EXECUTION OF COMTE D'EU: This affair, generating a mass of gossip and speculation, is treated at length by all the chroniclers—Jean le Bel, *Chron. J. & C.*, *4 Valois*, Gilles li Muisis, *Normande*, and Froissart, with extensive notes in Luce-F, IV, and KL Biog. Index, and discussion in Cazelles, *Société pol.*, 249–52.

"*Ung bien hastif homs*": *Chron. 4 Valois*, 16–17.

128   "A VERY CRUEL LADY": KL, IV, 202.

GIRARD D'ORLÉANS, COURT PAINTER: Dupont & Gnudi, 134.

ORDINANCE OF 1351: Lot; Tourneur, *Poitiers*.

129   GILLES LI MUISIS ON MONEY: q. Lewis, 58.

130   GARTER'S HISTORIAN: Elias Ashmole, *The History of the Most Noble Order of the Garter*, London, 1715.

ORDER OF THE STAR: Michelet, III, 294–95; Coville, 92; Contamine, 186–87; Huizinga, *Men and Ideas*, 204; Anquetil, 402. For the Battle of Mauron, in which the members were slaughtered, see *Chron. normande*, 106, and Luce-F, IV, notes.

131   COMBAT OF THIRTY: KL, V, 514.

133   MURDER OF CHARLES D'ESPAGNE: all the chronicles, especially *Chron. 4 Valois*, 25–28.

134   RIOT AT OXFORD: Trevelyan, *English Social History*, London, 1949, I, 49.

FRANCESCO ORDELAFFI: Emerton, 170.

ENGLAND, CORONERS' ROLLS: Coulton, *Panorama*, 371.

135   VILLAGE GAMES: Origo, 42. CITIZENS OF MONS: Huizinga, *Waning*, 22–23.

136   CHARLES OF NAVARRE, LETTERS TO POPE AND EDWARD III: Denifle, 99.

137   EDWARD III, "ON THE WORD OF A KING": "*In verbo regiae veritatis dicimus et contestamur fideliter coram Deo*," q. Denifle, 103–4, from text in Secousse and Rymer.

138   "HARRYING AND WASTING": letter to Bishop of Winchester, q. Sedgwick, 117.

139   HENRY OF LANCASTER: Fowler, *King's Lieutenant*, 106–10.

141   ENGUERRAND IN THE PICARDY CAMPAIGN: *Chron. 4 Valois*, 41. For this campaign see also *Chron. Jean de Venette* and Denifle.

142   JEAN'S SEIZURE OF CHARLES OF NAVARRE AND EXECUTION OF NORMAN NOBLES: all the chronicles and summary in Delachenal, I, 140–57.

143 ff. BATTLE OF POITIERS: On the English side the chief sources are *Anonimalle*, Chandos Herald, Godfrey le Baker; and on the French side, *Grandes Chrons.*, *Chron. 4 Valois*, *Chron. normande*, Froissart. Hewitt's

Black Prince is the most thorough recent account; Tourneur-Aumont devotes a whole book to it, infused with a special thesis; Delachenal, Denifle, Lot, and MacKinnon give full accounts.

p. 145 TALLEYRAND DE PÉRIGORD: Zacour, 8, 24.

152 SIRE DE FERTÉ-FRESNEL: Delachenal, I, 397.

RUINED KNIGHTS: for documents illustrating these cases, see Moisant, 59–61; Delachenal, I, 248, n.

"COMPLAINT OF THE BATTLE OF POITIERS": Beaurepaire.

Chapter 7—Decapitated France: The Bourgeois Rising and the Jacquerie

For the physical events of this chapter, from the meeting of the Estates to the death of Marcel, the chief primary source is *Chron. J. & C.*, vol. I, with additional material from *Chron. 4 Valois, Chron. normande*, Jean de Venette, Jean le Bel, and Froissart. These are supplemented by the notes of their respective editors and by the modern accounts of Delachenal, vol. I, and Coville.

156 ROBERT LE COQ'S LIBRARY: Autrand, 1220.

DAUPHIN'S BASTARD SONS: *Chron. normande*, 136; Delachenal, I, 110, n. 2.

GOSSIP ABOUT HIS PATERNITY: ibid., 68, 69, n. 2.

157 MARCEL'S UNCLE, FATHER- AND BROTHER-IN-LAW: Cazelles, *"Etienne Marcel,"* 415–17.

FINANCE OFFICERS "WHO TRAVEL IN POMP": Mézières, Coopland, I, 417–18. *Renart le Contrefait*: q. Evans, *Life*, 42.

158 TAX SURVEY OF 1292: Franklin, *Vie privée*, I, 12; Evans, ibid., 49–50.

159 ff. CONDITIONS OF PARIS: Franklin, *Rues, Dict., Vie privée*, VII, 12–13; Batifol; Hillairet; Legrand; Coulton, *Panorama*, 308; Coville, 427–28.

160 ENGLISH VISITOR ON BOOKSELLERS: q. Evans, ibid., 131.

162 GRAND ORDINANCE: Coville, 119–21.

163 FREE COMPANIES: Luce, *Jacquerie*, 9–28; Denifle, passim; Gray, *Scalacronica*, 130–31; Gregorovius, 317 ff.; Delachenal, II, 28. "WRITE SORROW ON THE BOSOM OF THE EARTH": Shakespeare, *Richard II*, act III, sc. 2.

164 FRA MONREALE: Gregorovius, 356–66; Hale, Highfield & Smalley, 102–3; Oman, 293.

165 *Società dell' acquisito*: Lot, 397, n. 1. CERVOLE RECEIVED BY THE POPE: Luce-F, V, 95; Gregorovius, 395.

KNOLLYS: *DNB*.

166 EUSTACHE D'AUBRECICOURT: Luce-F, V, 160; Delachenal, II, 40–42.

167 "TRAGIC ACCOUNT": M. L. Delisle, *Tragicum Argumentum*.

168 JEAN'S ENTRY INTO LONDON: John of Reading, 206; *Brute Chron.*, q. Green, 197.

HIS EXPENDITURES AS A CAPTIVE: Orléans, 29, 42–43; Delachenal, II, 78–79; Putnam, 312; Gazeau.

169 MICHELET'S COMMENT: III, 360.

p. 169 ENGUERRAND ACCOMPANIES CHARLES OF NAVARRE: *Chron. 4 Valois*, 64; see also Cazelles, *"Parti navarrais."*

171 ff. CONDITIONS OF THE PEASANT: H. See, 540–624; Bloch, *Rural*, 80–94; Perroy, "Wage Labour"; Mollat & Wolff, 19–20; Davis, 268–70; Fossier, 358–59; *Horizon*, 238; Helen Robbins; Turner, "Ec. Discontent"; Viollet-le-Duc, *Dict.*, VI, 292; Bell, *Old German Epics.*

173 COST OF PLOW: Fossier to aurhor.

"BATHING WAS COMMON": Gasquet, 64. DIET: Luce, *Guesclin*, 57; Thrupp, 483; Contamine, 654; *Horizon*, 238.

174 COMFORTABLE PEASANT OF NORMANDY: Duby, 518–19. DOWRIES: Mollat & Wolff, 17–20.

Merlin Merlot: Joly, 452–53. DEMONS REFUSE TO CARRY HIS SOUL: ibid., 458.

175 *Le Despit au Vilain:* ibid., 460–61.

176 JACQUERIE: For the outbreak and subsequent events, the major source is Luce, *Jacquerie*, invaluable for its documentation of royal pardons issued after the event, which, in the course of stating the circumstances in each case, gives a picture more true to life than the chronicles. In addition, *Chron. Jean le Bel*, II, 256; KL, VI, 44–58; *Chron J. & C.*, I, 177–78; *Chron. normande*, 127–28; *Chron. 4 Valois; Chron. Jean de Venette.*

179 ATTACK AT MEAUX: KL, VI, 477; *Chron. J. & C.*, 180–84.

180 NOBLES APPEAL TO CHARLES OF NAVARRE: Luce, *Jacquerie*, 147.

181 COUCY'S PRESENCE: *Chron. 4 Valois*, 74. According to the terms of the subsequent Treaty of Calais in 1360, the persons who followed Charles of Navarre "during the troubles" were to receive pardons from the King of France. Coucy's name does not appear either in the list of 300 persons who had been followers of Charles or in a second list of 300 who received pardons from King Jean: Secousse, II, 177–81, 181–85.

"THEY FLUNG THEMSELVES": *Chron. Jean de Venette.*

182 "20,000" KILLED: Secousse, Mem. 239.

184 COUCY GUARDS HIS TERRITORY: *Chron. Jean le Bel*, II, 277; KL, VI, 99.

"DID NOT LIKE THE SAID BISHOP": *Chron. Jean le Bel*, II, 260; Denifle, 224.

Chapter 8—Hostage in England

185 COUCY NAMED HOSTAGE IN TREATY OF LONDON: Delachenal, II, 408.

"THEY SAID THE TREATY WAS DISPLEASING": q. ibid., 87.

186 EDWARD'S EXPEDITIONARY FORCE: Knighton, q. Locke, 53; Hewitt, *Edw.*, 31, 51, 88; Fowler, *Lanc.*, 198–200.

"AS THE STARRES HAVE INFLUENCE TO PRODUCE": Sir Richard Baker, *Chron. of Kings of England*, q. Barnie, 104.

187 FRENCH RAID ON WINCHELSEA: Gray, *Scalacronica*, 152; Orléans, 50–51, Delachenal, II, 158.

188 ENGLAND IN A PANIC: from the Calendar of Close Rolls, q. Hewitt, *Edw.*, 19.

p. 189 BLACK MONDAY, "FOUL DARK DAY": *Chron. of London*, q. Thompson, 101; Knighton and *Eulogium*, q. Delachenal, II, 191.

DESIGNATION OF HOSTAGES: *Chron. 4 Valois*, 122; *Chron. normande*, 155, n.

190 TREATY OF BRÉTIGNY: the text occupies 33 pages in *Chron. J. & C.*, I, 267–300. See also Duckett, 7–8.

COUCY'S CONTRIBUTION TO RANSOM: Lépinois, 165.

191 VISCONTI MARRIAGE: Chamberlin, 31–35; Cook, 49 ff.

VILLANI QUOTED: ibid., 49, n. 55.

PHILIP THE BOLD EARNS HIS NAME: Froissart.

192 FROISSART SAILS WITH THE HOSTAGES: Shears, 12–13. WALTER SCOTT: *Old Mortality*, chap. 35.

CHAUCER WITH THE HOSTAGES, and HIS RANSOM: Coulton, *Chaucer*, 25–26.

193 "COUCY SHINED IN DANCING": KL, VI, 392.

GOD OF LOVE IN *Roman de la Rose:* lines 2149–53, 2166–72.

194 POSTHUMOUS PORTRAIT: now in the Museum of Soissons.

DUC D'ORLÉANS' 16 SERVANTS: Coulton, *Chaucer*, 33.

195 FROISSART ON THE GERMANS: Luce-F, V, 289.

KING EDWARD NOT FLUENT IN ENGLISH: Coulton, *Panorama*, 237. ENGLISH COMPLAINT OF 1340: q. Darmesteter, 13. JOHN OF TREVISA: q. Gasquet, 234; Campbell, 177.

"ARRAYED AS FOR WAR" and STATUTE OF 1362: Hewitt, *Edw.*, 175.

196 PLAGUE OF 1361: *Chron. 4 Valois*, 130–31; John of Reading, 150, 364; *Polychronicon*, 411; Saltmarsh; Carpentier, *Ville*; G. Mollat, *Papes*, 106; Coville, 160–61.

PROPHECY OF JEAN DE LA ROQUETAILLADE: *Chron. Jean de Venette*, 61–62; Cohn, 105–6.

197 LONDON, ONE-THIRD EMPTY, and SANITATION: *Sabine*.

198 BUXEAUL: Duby, 523.

DESOLATION OF CHURCHES: M. Mollat, *Vie*, 4, 9. UNIVERSITY OF MONTPELLIER: Campbell, 156–57.

PETRARCH'S ACCOUNT OF FRANCE: text from his *Epistolae de Rebus Familiaribus* in Cook, 23–24. MISSION FROM GALEAZZO AND ORATION AT COURT: Wilkins, 217–24.

199 DAUPHIN'S SORROWS and NAVARRE'S POISON PLOT: *Gr. Chrons.*, VI, 166, 222; Delachenal, II, 268–69.

CITIZENS OF LA ROCHELLE AND CAHORS: Froissart. ST. ROMAIN DE TARN: Hewitt, *Edw.*, 151.

RINGOIS OF ABBEVILLE: *Gr. Chrons.*, VI, 91; Delachenal, II, 178, n. 4.

200 TREATY OF THE "LILIES" AND COUCY: Letters of King Jean naming Coucy and other correspondence in this matter are collected in Rymer, 72, 694, 700, 702; see also Lehoux, I, 171.

201 FIGHT AT BRIGNAIS: Lot, 404–5; Cox, 164.

JEAN CONSIDERS MARRYING JOANNA OF NAPLES: Orléans, H.D., *Notes et documents*.

202 JEAN'S RETURN TO CAPTIVITY: KL, Ia, 119; Duckett, 9; Delachenal, II, 351.

203 JEAN'S DEATH AND FUNERAL: *Chron J. & C.*, I, 339–41; Michelet, III, 368.

Chapter 9—Enguerrand and Isabella

p. 204 ISABELLA: The facts of Isabella's life, household, possessions, and finances are in Green, 164–228, who collected them from extensive original research in the Wardrobe Accounts, Close Rolls, Pipe Rolls, and various contemporary English chronicles. On Isabella's character, see Hardy, 168, 182.

205 BÉRARD D'ALBRET: KL, Biog. Index, XX, 20.

207 "ONLY FOR LOVE": *Polychronicon*, 365.

JOAN OF KENT: KL, II, 243.

208 LADIES IN MALE ATTIRE AT TOURNAMENTS: Knighton, q. J. Cammidge, *The Black Prince*, 1943, 108.

PLUCKING EYEBROWS: La Tour Landry, 96.

DUENNA'S ADVICE IN *Roman de la Rose*: lines 13,879–14,444, trans. in Herlihy, *Med. Culture.*

209 AGNES AND MACHAUT: Machaut, xiv, xvii.

CHASTITY BELT: Dingwall, 4, 76, 160.

DESCHAMPS, *"Suis-je belle?"*: q. Cohen, *Vie*, 293–95.

210 JEAN DE CONDÉ'S TALE: Hellman & O'Gorman, 24–25. OTHER *fabliaux:* ibid., also Brians, *Bawdy Tales.*

211 VINCENT DE BEAUVAIS: q. Owst, 378.

212 PETRARCH RENOUNCES THE FLESH: *Correspondence*, 62, 92, 403. "WHERESOEVER BEAUTY SHOWS": Master Rypon, a 14th century preacher, q. Owst, 48.

213 QUESTIONS OF SEX AND SIN: Noonan, 249, 274, 279, 283, 293–94.

SODOMY "AGAINST NATURE" AND "WORST OF SINS": Aquinas, *Summa Theologica*, q. Noonan, 339–40.

214 ILLUMINATED MS. DEPICTING IRE AS A WOMAN: Mâle, 331–33. AQUINAS ON WOMAN'S PLACE: *Summa Theologica*, q. Jarrett, *Social*, 72, 74. BONET, "MAN IS NOBLER": 194.

215 DUNMOW FLITCH: For text of the oath, see *Reader's Encyclopedia*, ed. W. R. Benét, New York, 1948.

216 NUNS "LIKE DOGS CHAINED UP TOO MUCH": q. Jarrett, *Social*, 82.

WOMEN'S DEATH RATE: J. C. Russell, *Fontana*, 29.

JACOBA FELICIE: Power, 422. NOVELLA D'ANDREA: Will Durant, *Story of Civilization*, V, 4.

217 MARCIA ORDELAFFI: Emerton, 177–87.

CHRISTINE DE PISAN: Coville, 410–11. POEM ON WIDOWHOOD: ibid. (trans. BT).

OTHER WORKS AND POEMS: Huizinga, *Waning*, 111–12, 123, 286.

218 CONTROVERSY ON *Roman de la Rose:* Kilgour, 136; Masson, 174.

219 ON JOAN OF ARC: Jarrett, *Social*, 86.

220 MARRIAGE OF ENGUERRAND AND ISABELLA: documents in Rymer, 773, 778.

A LADY'S CARRIAGE: Avenel, 49–50; Jusserand, 48–49.

221 ENGUERRAND MADE EARL OF BEDFORD: Issue Rolls, 40 Edw. III, q. Green, 206; also Barnes, 667, 670.

COUCY ACQUIRES SOISSONS: KL, VII, 232–34.

Chapter 10—Sons of Iniquity

p. 222 ONE OF THE WORST OF THE CAPTAINS, he was Anichino Baumgarten: Cox, 138–40.

223 PHILIP OF BURGUNDY AND ARNAUT DE CERVOLE: Zurlauben, *Cervole*, 162. BERTUCAT D'ALBRET: KL, XI, 228. SEGUIN DE BADEFOL: ibid., XX, 232–36. AIMERIGOT MARCEL: ibid., XIV, 164.

224 INNOCENT VI, PASTORAL LETTER: M. Mollat, *Vie*, 5, 30. "IF GOD HIMSELF WERE A SOLDIER": q. Kilgour, 26. COMPANIES DEMAND PAPAL ABSOLUTION: Denifle, 185.

225 HAWKWOOD: Leader-Temple & Marcotti and Gaupp, passim. "NOTHING WAS MORE TERRIBLE": q. Leader-Temple & Marcotti, 27. "*Perfidi scelera-tissimi*": ibid., 14. "DID NOT ROAST AND MUTILATE": q. Stanley, 401. "AN ITALIANIZED ENGLISHMAN": q. Gaupp, 308.

226 CUVELIER ON DU GUESCLIN: 1, 5. In the opinion of Edouard Perroy (*Hundred Years*, 148), Du Guesclin "enjoyed a popularity out of all proportion to his talents and exploits. . . . [He was] a mediocre captain, incapable of winning a battle or being successful in a siege of any scope . . . swollen with self-importance." See also Michelet, IV, 4. BATTLE OF COCHEREL: Luce-F, VI, 131; Lot, 436.

227 DU GUESCLIN AND ASTROLOGERS: Lewis, 26; Thorndike, III, 586. CHARLES V AND SAME: Campbell, 128; Pernoud, 224. THOMAS OF PISANO: Thorndike, II, 801–2; III, 611, 615.

228 ENRIQUE ELDEST OF FATHER'S TEN BASTARDS: *Chron. Jean de Venette*. Notes, 304, n. 2.

228 "THE TYRANNY OF RHYME": Delachenal, III, 455.

229 DU GUESCLIN, CARDINAL, ET AL. AT VILLENEUVE: Cuvelier, verses 7530–7620, trans. in D. F. Jamison, *Life and Times of Bertrand du Guesclin*, 1864, 260–65.

231 BLACK PRINCE ENCOURAGED TROOPS "UNDERHAND": Froissart, Johnes ed., I, 383. "DID SO MUCH DAMAGE": ibid. "HE DID NOT VALUE A KNIGHT": Cuvelier, q. Sedgwick, 195–97.

Chapter 11—The Gilded Shroud

232 COUCY'S CHARTER OF LIBERTIES: text in Melleville, 103–6.

235 CHÂTEAU OF HESDIN, MECHANICAL JOKES: Vaughan, 205. SWAN FESTIVAL OF PICARDY: Le Grand d'Aussy, II, 23. FORKS, listed in an inventory of Charles V's household in 1379: Le Grand d'Aussy, III, 179.

236 TROUSSEAU OF BLANCHE DE BOURBON: Evans, *Flowering*, 174. "BUSYING THEMSELVES WITH OTHER THINGS": q. Coulton, *Life*, I, 204. COMMUNION WAFERS' MAGICAL POWERS: Lea, I, 50.

237 COMMUNION AND CONFESSION ONCE A YEAR: M. Mollat, *Vie*, 72. "THIS I

KNEW NOT": Jacques de Vitry, q. Coulton, *Life*, I, 57. RELIGIOUS OB-
SERVANCE IN NORTHERN FRANCE: M. Mollat, *Vie*, 72–73.

CHARLES V: Christine de Pisan, *Charles V*, passim; Coville, 183–85.

TAILLEVENT: Evans, *Flowering*, 172.

p. 238 47 JEWELED CROWNS: Vaughan.

CHARLES V'S ILLNESSES AND ABSCESS: KL, IX, 280–82; Delachenal, I, 14; II,
306–11. Froissart's account, according to Delachenal, V, 389, is a "tissue of
fables."

CHARLES V'S LIBRARY: Christine de Pisan, *Charles V*, II, 13; Coville, 189.

239 CLARENCE'S RETINUE: Cook (a study in detail of the entire affair). CLARENCE
IN PARIS: *Chron. J. & C.*, II, 41; Rymer, 845. VISITED BY COUCY: Green, 208.

240 AMADEUS' PURCHASES: Cordey, 184–85.

VISCONTI FAMILY: Chamberlin, 15–30, 67–70; also Cook, 16, 18; Muir, 70.

241 CASTLE OF PAVIA: Corio, *Storia di Milano*, q. Chamberlin, 119. "FINEST
DWELLING": J. A. Symonds, *Age of Despots*, q. Cook, 43. PETRARCH:
Correspondence, 323–25.

MILAN: Mesquita, 2–3; Chamberlin, 13–15; Molho, 30.

242 WEDDING: Cook; Chamberlin, 42–43. For presence of Froissart and
Chaucer, see Jarrett, *Charles IV*, 5, and Coulton, *Chaucer*, 48, 50.

243 KING EDWARD'S OFFER TO PLEDGE CALAIS: Vaughan, 5.

244 COUCY SELLS BURGUNDY PEARL NECKLACE: Luce, *Cent ans*, I, 96.

PHILIP OF BURGUNDY'S HABITS: Luce, *Cent ans*, II, 206; Petit, *Itinéraires*,
490–91; Vaughan, 6, 197.

COUCY "FINEST SHOWING": Luce-F, VII, 130.

245 PETRARCH TO BOCCACCIO: *Correspondence*, 213–14.

Chapter 12—Double Allegiance

246 CHARLES CONSULTS UNIVERSITIES: Chaplais, 55.

"SORE TROUBLED IN THEIR MYNDES": Froissart. BONET ON DOUBLE ALLE-
GIANCE: 167–68.

COUCY'S HAPSBURG INHERITANCE: Duplessis, 119–20; Zurlauben, *Enguerrand
VII*, 170–73, has collected the evidence; also Lacaille, *thèse*, 17–20.

247 COUCY'S SEAL OF 1369: AN, *Service des sceaux;* No. 308 in Demay,
Flandre, attached to a document of 14 November 1369 stamped *Sigillum
Engueranni filii ducisse Austrie domini de Couciaco et comitis Suession-
ensis et Bedfordis.* Bears the device *Semper.* A similar seal of 1376 (No.
8644 in Demay, *Clairembault*) bears the device *Sans plus* and shows a
shield quartered 1 and 4 *vairé* and 2 and 3 *fascé.* Anselme, 542, gives a
further description of Coucy's seals with the upright figure.

CONTRACT WITH MONTBÉLIARD, and MANIFESTO TO STRASBOURG AND COLMAR:
KL, VIII, cxxx, n. 3; Bardy, 13–14.

DOCUMENT DATED PRAGUE: mentioned by Galbraith in notes to *Anonimalle
Chron.*, 117. Copied for the author at the Public Record Office (Mem-
oranda Roll, 13 Richard II, Michaelmas Communia, Recorda, fourth

membrane after 19), the document is an "inspection" made in 1390 of earlier letters patent to Robersart, and repeats the full text of Coucy's letter given under his seal "at Prague in Bohemia on the 14th day of January of the year 1369 [1370]."

p. 248 ITALY INFESTED BY BRIGANDS: John Bromyard, q. Owst, 174; Origo, 153, 275–76.

249 BERNABÒ VERSUS THE PAPACY: Gregorovius, 408; Milman, VIII, 14–16.
PUBLIC ATTRIBUTED URBAN'S ELECTION TO GOD: Milman, VIII, 13.

250 URBAN'S RETURN: ibid., 20; Jarrett, *Charles IV*, 156. CONDITION OF ROME: Pirenne, *Europe*, 23–24; Flick, 213.

252 ENGUERRAND WITH COUNT OF SAVOY IN ITALY: Cox, 264–68; Cognasso, 197; Gabotto, 201–2.
PASSAGE OF THE ALPS: Cox, *The Eagles of Savoy*, Princeton, 1974, 339–43.

254 VILLANI ON HAWKWOOD'S COMPANY: This is Filippo Villani, q. Cook, 25.

255 ORDERS OF VISCONTI'S PARENTS: q. Chamberlin, 58.
PAPAL CORRESPONDENCE AND CONTRACTS WITH COUCY: Lacaille, *An. Bull. SHF*, 187–206, gives the full texts from the Vatican Archives.

257 ff. CAMPAIGN OF THE PAPAL LEAGUE and BATTLE OF MONTICHIARI: *Annales Mediolanensis* in Muratori's *RIS*, chaps. cxxxv–vi, 752–56 (trans. for the author by Phyllis G. Gordan); Corio, *Historia di Milano*, q. Mazas, 187–90; Servion, 198–205; Leader-Temple & Marcotti, 72–78; Lacaille, *thèse*, 26–31; Cox, 276–77; Chamberlin, 58–60; Cognasso, 208.

260 TITLE OF SIRE DE COUCY HELD HIGH: KL, Ib, 17, n. 5.

261 APPOINTED MARSHAL: Luce-F, VIII, cxxxii.
NEUTRALITY HELD HONORABLE: KL, VIII, 291–93. CHEVALIER DE CHIN: ibid., 21, 24.
BATTLE OF ENRIQUE AND PEDRO: Luce-F, VII, xxxii, n. 1.

262 BLACK PRINCE'S ILLNESS: That it was dropsy is stated by Denifle, 497, and Lefranc, 108. English biographers avoid naming this unheroic malady.

264 BATTLE OF LA ROCHELLE: In addition to Froissart and *Chron. 4 Valois*, Roncière, 15–16; Sherborne; Runyan.

266 CAPTAL DE BUCH HELD IN PRISON: *Chron. J. & C.*, III, 62–78; Keen, *Laws*, 90; Delachenal, III, 186–87.
COUCY INTERCEDES: KL, VIII, 401–2.

267 LANCASTER'S LONG MARCH: Walsingham, q. MacKinnon, 552; Lot, 367–68; Delachenal, III, 302.

Chapter 13—Coucy's War

269 BURGUNDY'S EXPENSES: Delachenal, IV, 568.

270 PROPOSAL TO COUCY TO LEAD COMPANIES: KL, VIII, 369, 372. RIVIÈRE, MERCIER: Lefranc, 217–18; Coville, 220.
COUCY LENT MONEY TO BERRY: Lehoux, I, 358, n. 3.
BRETON COMPANIES AND THE POPE: Mirot, *"Budes,"* 590; Denifle, 583.
OWEN OF WALES: Chotzen. COUCY'S CONTRACT WITH HIM: ibid., 236.

p. 271 CANNON AT SIEGE OF ST. SAUVEUR: *Chron. 4 Valois*, 253; Delachenal, IV, 527–28.

ALSATIAN CHRONICLE: Koenigshofen, 334–35.

272 COUCY'S CHANTRIES AT NOGENT: BN, *Fonds fr.*, *nouv. acq.* no. 3653, no. 293, and a later "vidimus" of this document, *nouv. acq. fr.* 20510, *pièce* 48.

CAPTAL'S MASSES: Lewis, 204.

PRINCESS OF WALES' THREE PRIESTS: Rosenthal, 15.

COUCY'S LETTERS TO IMPERIAL VICAR AND CITIES: Bardy, 17; Zurlauben, *Enguerrand VII*, 177.

273 RAVAGES IN ALSACE: Bardy, 23–25.

274 ff. INVASION OF THE AARGAU: Sources for the Swiss campaign are: Dierauer, 287–92; Dandliker, 547–52; Muller, 201–18 (translated for the author by Kathie Coblenz); also Bardy, 17–29; Chotzen, 234–38; Laguille, 309–10; Zurlauben, 177–80. Chotzen includes a list of the original Swiss chronicles.

MORGARTEN AND LAUPEN: Oman, 235–46.

276 FROISSART'S VERSION: KL, VIII, 376–78.

279 FRAUBRUNNEN, BALLADS ON THE BATTLE: R. Liliencron, ed., *Die Historischen Volkslieder des Deutschen vom 13 bis 16 Jahrhundert*, Leipzig, 1865, I, 88–90; Chotzen, 238.

FRAUBRUNNEN, INSCRIPTION ON STONE MONUMENT: copied by the author and translated by Prof. E. A. R. Brown.

280 HAPSBURG SETTLEMENT WITH COUCY: Delachenal, IV, 583, n. 5; Zurlauben, *Enguerrand VII*, 180 (who undertakes to dispose of the errors of all previous historians).

281 COUCY COMMISSIONED TO ACT AGAINST COMPANIES: Delachenal, IV, 584, n. 1; Lehoux, I, 380, n. 9.

EDWARD'S GRANTS TO ISABELLA: Green, 213–16. ALICE PERRERS: *Chron. Angl.*, Thompson, xlviii.

282 "LADY OF THE SUN": q. Green, 210, n. 2.

COUCY'S FRIENDS URGE HIM TO TURN FRENCH, and HIS MISSION TO ENGLAND: KL, VIII, 378–80. On double allegiance, see Keen, *Laws*, 89–91.

Chapter 14—England's Turmoil

The major contemporary narrative source for English affairs in this period is Thomas Walsingham's *Chronicon Angliae*, which unfortunately does not exist in English (although Thompson's notes are useful). Those like myself not fluent in Latin must depend on quotations and excerpts in English by other historians. The somewhat less lively *Anonimalle Chronicle* has been translated by V. H. Galbraith. Secondary sources on the condition of England used for this chapter are Jusserand, McKisack, Postan, Saltmarsh, Seebohm, and Trevelyan. Although the last, which was Trevelyan's first book, may lag behind modern scholarship, it is far ahead in general interest and a comprehensive view of the social milieu.

285 "NOT STRONGER IN MIND THAN A BOY OF EIGHT": *Chron. Angl.*, q. Collis, 186, n. 2.

p. 285 "WHEREBY THE JUSTICES BE AFRAID": a statute of 2 Rich. II, q. Jusserand, 76.

286 BISHOP OF ROCHESTER: q. ibid., 86.

COMMONS COMPLAIN OF LABORERS AND SERVANTS: Jusserand, 147–48, from Rymer, V, 668.

"GATHER TOGETHER IN GREAT ROUTS": q. Seebohm, 274.

287 FOUR VILLAGES OF GLOUCESTER: Beresford & Hurst, 8. FIVE CHURCHES OF NORFOLK: Saltmarsh, 24.

WYCLIF: Poole; Trevelyan, passim; Cheyney, 211–24.

288 PRIESTS LICENSED TO KEEP A CONCUBINE: MacKinnon, 563. CONFESSOR IN CASES OF ADULTERY: Lea, I, 31.

EUCHARIST WITHHELD: ibid., 28. MISBEHAVIOR OF CLERICS: Coulton, *Life*, I, 96, 99–100. WORLDLY CLERICS' CLOTHING: Jusserand, 55.

289 LOLLARDY AMONG THE NOBLES: Cheyney, 217.

290 *Horribles expenses:* q. McKisack, 386, n. 1.

PURVEYORS "SEIZE ON MEN": J. R. Green, *Short History of England*, I, 455–56.

GOOD PARLIAMENT: In addition to sources at head of chapter, MacKinnon; Harold I. Nelson, "Thomas Walsingham and the Crisis of 1376" (unpublished ms.); A. F. Pollard; Powell & Wallis; Stubbs' *Constitutional History*.

291 COUCY AS EARL OF BEDFORD: A search of the Close Rolls, Parl. Rolls, and Parl. Writs made for the author at the Public Record Office disclose no evidence that Coucy was summoned to or attended the Parliament of 1376, although he *was* summoned as Earl of Bedford to the Parliament of 43 Edw. III (1370) (*The Dignity of a Peer of the Realm; Reports from the Lords' Committees* . . . , London, 1829, IV, 645).

293 ISABELLA AND COUCY VISIT BLACK PRINCE: KL, VIII, 379.

294 HIS DEATHBED, WILL, AND MONUMENT: Chandos Herald, 170; *Chron. Angl.*, q. Trevelyan, 27; Collins, 300–301; *DNB.*

296 COUCY ADVISES INVASION: Froissart, q. Lépinois, 178.

297 KING EDWARD'S PHYSICIANS "DESPAIRED": *Anonimalle*, 95. COUCY'S MISSION TO FLANDERS: Lacaille, *thèse*, 40.

QUEEN'S ILLNESS: *Chron. 4 Valois*, 244; Delachenal, IV, 536. PAYMENTS TO COUCY: BN, *Pièces originales*, 875, dossier 19, 660 Coucy. MARIE DE COUCY: Lehoux, I, 392, 398, n. 7.

COUCY IN PARLEYS WITH THE ENGLISH: KL, VIII, 383–84; Barnes, 906–7.

298 CHAUCER'S PRESENCE: Braddy; Manley; also F. N. Robinson, Introduction to *Chaucer's Complete Works.*

SUBSTANCE OF THE PARLEYS: Delachenal, V, 4; Delisle, *Coll. BE*, No. 1425; Perroy, "Anglo-French."

301 EDWARD'S DEATH; JUBILEE YEAR PASSED UNNOTICED: J. J. Jusserand, *Piers Plowman*, London, 1894, 53.

ISABELLA'S MOVEMENTS: KL, XXI, 41; Green, 215–17, from Rymer, VII, 153.

302 ROBERSART: Collins, 237, 249.

Songe du Vergier: q. Delachenal, IV, 601–2

DIALOGUE WRITTEN BY D'AILLY: q. Kirkland, 18.

p. 302 COUCY'S LETTER OF RENUNCIATION: text in KL, XXI, 41–42, and in Rymer, VII, 172, from Patent Roll, 1 Richard II.

303 TRUSTEESHIP FOR ISABELLA: *DNB;* Green, 219, from Rymer, IV, 60; Hardy, 309.

304 ESTATES SETTLED ON PHILIPPA: Lacaille, *"Vente,"* 574, n. 1.
FRENCH RAIDS AND EFFECT ON ENGLAND: Searle & Burghart.

305 SIR JOHN ARUNDEL AND LANCASTER: *Chron. Angl.,* q. ibid., 382, and in Delachenal, V, 30.

Chapter 15—The Emperor in Paris

306 CHARLES IV, CHARACTER AND APPEARANCE: Matteo Villani, q. Cox, 189; Jarrett, *Charles IV,* 219–24.

308 WELCOMING PARTY AT CAMBRAI, and SUBSEQUENT ACCOUNT OF THE EMPEROR'S VISIT: *Chron. J. & C.,* II, 200–276; Christine de Pisan, *Charles V,* II, 90–132.

310 CHANCELLOR'S CHRONICLER: Pierre d'Orgement, the Chancellor, is believed to have supervised, or possibly himself written, the *Chron. J. & C.:* Delachenal, I, xviii.
BANQUET DISHES: from menus listed by the Ménagier, 226–36.

311 VISIT TO SAVOY, PLATTERS SERVED ON LANCES: Cox, 197.
BANQUET BY VIDAME DE CHARTRES: Le Grand d'Aussy, III, 343.
DRAMA AND STAGECRAFT: Mâle, 36–37; Artz, 356–60; Cohen, *Theatre,* 49, 93–94, 99, 162, 273; Gayley, 33–34, 75–80, 214, 263–64; Frank, 115–35; A. W. Pollard, xli.

313 LOLLARD PREACHER: q. A. W. Pollard, xxii.
SIEGE OF JERUSALEM STAGED: in addition to the primary accounts, Loomis.

315 BEAUTÉ-SUR-MARNE: Luce, *Cent ans,* II, 41–44.
GREAT THEOLOGIAN ON CONSENT OF THE GOVERNED: Jean Gerson, q. Lewis, 94.

316 BRETHREN OF THE FREE SPIRIT: *Chron. J. & C.,* II, 163–64; Cohn, chap. 8; Leff.

317 BÉGUINES A RETREAT FROM "MARITAL BONDS": Southern, 329. BIBLE IN FRENCH: Cohn, 161.
ANJOU, "THE WORLD BROUGHT TO NOTHING": q. Campbell, 151.

318 DEMONOLOGY AND SORCERY: Lea, III, 464; J. B. Russell, 208–14; P. Hughes, passim.

319 ORESME: Thorndike, III, 428–38, 466–68; q. Coopland in notes to Mézières, I, 25.

Chapter 16—The Papal Schism

Based on the Italian and French chroniclers, the two major modern authorities for the events of this chapter are Valois, vol. I, and Ullman, supplemented by Creighton, Flick, McFarlane, and of course Delachenal, especially for the role of Charles V. Sources other than these are cited below. All quotations from St. Catherine are from Jorgensen, unless otherwise cited.

p. 320 ABBOT OF MONTMAYEUR: Sismondi, IV, 412.

"FOR WITH NO OTHER QUARREL": The French governor quoted was Marshal Boucicaut. Godefroy, *Boucicaut*, 2–3.

321 "AS IF THESE TIMES": Neri di Donato, q. Jorgensen, 171.

ROBERT OF GENEVA: Valois, I, 109; conflicting versions of his appearance are from Muratori and the chronicler Dietrich of Niem, q. Ullman, 163.

322 BRETONS' SWORDS BLESSED BY THE CARDINAL: Mirot, *"Budes."*

MASSACRE OF CESENA: Leader-Temple & Marcotti, 119–22. *"Sangue et sangue!":* Lot, 417; Sismondi, IV, 422.

BERNABÒ'S DAUGHTER MARRIES HAWKWOOD: Leader-Temple & Marcotti, 126.

323 "MAN OF BLOOD" and "BUTCHER OF CESENA": Delachenal, V, 143. "PEOPLE NO LONGER BELIEVE": q. ibid., 121.

325 JOHANNES TAULER: Mâle, 89, 107. ST. BRIGITTA: ibid., 89–90.

326 CATHERINE'S LETTER TO HAWKWOOD: q. Leader-Temple & Marcotti, 82–83.

CATHERINE IN AVIGNON: Delachenal, IV, 598.

327 ON THE RETURN TO ROME: from the Cartier edition of her letters, q. ibid., 596, nn. 3, 4, 5.

ECCLESIASTICAL EXTORTIONS, IN GERMANY: *CMH*, 280. PRIESTS DESERTED: ibid. AS TAVERNERS AND HORSE-DEALERS: M. Mollat, *Vie*, 43.

BRIGITTA, "FEAR OF GOD": q. Jorgensen, 160.

CATHERINE ON REFORM: q. Ullman, 60–61.

328 CHARLES V, "ROME IS WHEREVER": q. Renouard, *Papacy*, 64.

GREGORY'S RETURN TO ROME: Froissart, Berners ed., II, 505; Jarrett, *Charles IV*, 209–11. HIS FATHER: Jorgensen, 237. ONE OF HIS BISHOPS: Renouard, *Papacy*, 66.

330 URBAN REGARDED AS MAD: Ullman, 53; Creighton, 83; *Cath. Encyc.*

332 MICHELET, "NO EPOCH MORE NATURALLY MAD": IV, 8.

"OH, UNHAPPY MEN": q. Ullman, 67–68.

333 JUAN I, "WHAT GOVERNMENT": q. Delachenal, V, 171.

335 EFFECTS OF THE SCHISM: *Chron. C6*, I, 85–87; Michelet, IV, 8; Huizinga, *Waning*, 21.

BONET ON THE SCHISM: 92–93.

336 MONK OF ST. DENIS, "LIKE A PROSTITUTE": *Chron. C6*, I, 91.

ANJOU AND CLEMENT AND KINGDOM OF ADRIA: Valois, I, 145, 167–68; Durrieu, *"Adria."*

337 UNIVERSITY RESISTS and ARREST OF ROUSSE: *Chron. C6*, I, 87.

338 WYCLIF ON INDIVIDUAL SALVATION: q. Trevelyan, 141.

339 NO ONE HAD ENTERED PARADISE: q. Huizinga, *Waning*, 29.

Chapter 17—Coucy's Rise

343 KING "SORROWED LONG": *Gr. Chrons.*, q. Delachenal, V, 20.

343 ff. CHARLES OF NAVARRE'S TREASON AND PLOTS: *Chron. J. & C.*, II, 286 ff., and documents in Secousse; Coville, 246–47; Delachenal, V, 180–218.

344 FOIX, "IMPETUOUS PASSIONS": q. Tarbé in notes to Machaut, XIX. AFFAIR OF GASTON: *Chron. C6*, I, 365; also Froissart; and Tarbé, op cit.

p. 345   NORMANDY CAMPAIGN: KL, IX, 56, 61–63, 77–78.

347   COUCY AND CLISSON: Lefranc, 189, 270. COMRADESHIP OF BROTHERHOOD-IN-ARMS: see Keen, *Laws*, 138.

CLISSON'S CAREER: Lefranc, 24–37, 58–68, 132–34.

348   "ALWAYS IN PERFECT HARMONY": ibid., 270. ASSASSINATION OF OWEN OF WALES: Froissart, Berners ed., III, 15.

349   POLICY ON BRITTANY and TRIAL OF MONTFORT: Moranvillé, *Mercier*, 76–81; Delachenal, V, 242–45.

COUCY AS A "PEER OF FRANCE": Froissart says specifically, in connection with Coucy's campaign in Italy in 1372–74, "*et li uns des xii pers*": KL, VII, 419. On the somewhat elastic nature of the twelve French peers, see Bloch, *Feudal*, 333–35; Lot & Fawtier, 297, n. 1.

350   KING'S VISIT TO COUCY: *Chron. J. & C.*, III, 215; Lacaille, *thèse*, 59; Moranvillé, *Mercier*, 70–72, 319.

DESCHAMPS: Coville, 401, 407–9; Gaston Raynaud, 27; intro. and notes to Queux edition of Deschamps' works, vol. XI. BALLADE ON COUCY: Deschamps, I, 269 (Trans. B.T.).

PURCHASE OF GREAT FIEFS: see Lewis, 191.

351   MARRIAGE NEGOTIATIONS: Lehoux, I, 439.

COUCY'S ORDER OF THE CROWN: Deschamps, Queux ed., II, 35 (on the twelve qualities of the crown), and IV, 115. Duplessis, 89; Zurlauben, *Enguerrand VII*, 183.

352   JOHN PHILPOT: *Chron. Angl.*, q. Barnie, 108–9; McKisack, 403.

353   REVOLT OF GHENT, "ON THE FOLLIES OF PRINCES": q. Hutton.

353 ff.   OPPRESSION AND UPRISING IN LANGUEDOC, and PUNISHMENT OF MONTPELLIER: *Chron. J. & C.*, II, 365–76; Delachenal, V, chap. 6.

354   "KILL ALL THE RICH!": q. Mollat & Wolff, 182.

"CUT OPEN BODIES": q. Delachenal, V, 303, n. 3.

356   ENGLISH TAX OF 1379: Trevelyan, 100–103. MISCALCULATION OF THE TAX BASE: it was derived from an estimate of the number of English parishes at 40,000–50,000 when in fact they numbered about 9,000, see Coulton, *Five Centuries*, III, 449.

ARUNDEL'S VOYAGE: *Chron. Angl.*, q. Collis, 225–27, and *DNB;* Froissart, Berners ed., III, 11; Roncière, 65–66. HIS 52 SUITS OF CLOTHES: Baldwin, 74.

COMMONS' PROTEST AND GOVERNMENT'S REPLY: Jusserand, 124–25, from Parl. Rolls, 2 Rich. II.

357   "ALL THE WITTE OF THIS WORLDE": B text, xiii, 173.

358   COUCY OFFERED CONSTABLESHIP: KL, IX, 237–38; Lefranc, 211–12.

SCOPE OF THE OFFICE: Vuatrin, 89–90; Lefranc, 230–31.

359   COUCY NAMED CAPT.-GEN. OF PICARDY and GIVEN MORTAIGNE: KL, IX, 243; Duchesne, 267; Duplessis, 91–92.

BUCKINGHAM EXPEDITION: KL, IX, 260–91; *Chron. C6*, I, 7. PREPARATIONS: Sherborne, EHR.

360   CLISSON ON THE ENGLISH: KL, VIII, 302.

"THEY CAN BETTER LIVE IN WAR": KL, XIV, 314.

361   DOCUMENTS ON COUCY'S MOVEMENTS: Luce-F, xcix, n. 8.

Immobilis quasi lapis: q. Coville, 264.

p. 362 ff. CHARLES V'S DEATHBED and THE PROBLEM OF TAXES: Coville in *CMH*, 265–66; Perroy, *Hundred Years*, 173–74; Delachenal, V, 408–10.

363 *Songe du Vergier:* q. Mirot, *Urbaines*, 6, n. 1.

TEXT OF KING'S ORDINANCE: ibid., 4.

364 PRECEDENTS: Brown, "Taxation and Morality."

"TO THEIR GREAT DISCOMFORT": *Anonimalle*, q. Collis, 230.

Chapter 18—The Worms of the Earth Against the Lions

On the conditions, taxation, and sentiments of the working class, the chief sources used for this chapter are Mollat & Wolff, *Ongles Bleues;* Turner, "Economic Discontent"; Perroy, "Wage Labour"; Pirenne, *Europe*, 103–12; Boissonade, 303–7; Thompson, *Econ. and Soc. Hist.;* Carpentier, *Ville*, 220–21.

For the Ciompi: Mollat & Wolff, 144–62; Turner; Schevill, *Florence*, 277–83; contemporary texts in Brucker, *Society*, 233–39.

For the insurrections in France and associated events, the chief primary sources are: *Chron. C6* by the Monk of St. Denis, vol. I (especially for Paris), and *Chron. 4 Valois* (especially for Rouen), plus Froissart in KL, IX. The most detailed secondary studies are Mirot's *Insurrections urbaines* and, for Rouen, Lecarpentier's *"Harelle."*

On the Peasants' Revolt in England, so much has been written that it is hardly necessary to cite references except, for convenience, McKisack, Trevelyan, Keen's "Robin Hood," and a good account in Collis. The chief primary sources are *Anonimalle*, Malverne's continuation of *Polychronicon*, and Froissart.

For Ghent, Hutton should be added to the sources mentioned above on the working class, and Froissart.

365 "LET HIM GO TO THE DEVIL!": q. Luce-F, *Notes*, X, xliii.

367 LAON REFUSED COUCY: Lacaille, *thèse*, 64–65.

ANJOU TOOK 32 BOOKS: Delisle, *Lib. Chas. V*, 136–37.

369 "WORMS OF THE EARTH": q. Jacob, 192, and Origo, 66.

371 CARDINAL DE LA GRANGE: *Chron. 4 Valois*, 283; Jean Juvenal des Ursins, q. Moranvillé, *Mercier*, 83–84, and Lefranc, 217.

372 COUCY PAYING SPIES: BN, Clairembault, vol. XXXV, No. 92.

374 "TOURNAMENTS OF THE RICH," "EVIL PRINCES," JOHN BROMYARD, FRANCISCAN FRIAR: q. Owst, 293, 299, 301, 310–11.

377 "VILLEINS YE ARE": q. McKisack, 418.

"DAYS OF WRATH AND ANGUISH": Walsingham, q. ibid., 414.

378 "TOKENS OF GRETE VENGAUNCE": T. Wright, *Political Songs*, I, 252. WALSINGHAM ON FRENCH RAIDS: q. Barnie, 103. FLORENTINE DIARIST: Paolo Sassetti, q. Brucker, *Society*, 42.

VILLANI, "IT SHOULD BE": q. Mollat & Wolff, 133–34.

381 BUONACCORSO PITTI: q. Mollat & Wolff, 172.

384 COUCY NEGOTIATES WITH THE REBELS: KL, IX, 447; Luce-F, X, xlv, n. 1; also *Chron. de Berne* reprinted in KL, notes, X, 456–57; Mirot, *Insurrections*, 152–55. COUCY'S *hôtel:* Roussel, 24, n. 1, and Hillairet, *Dict.*, entry

under "St. Jean-en-Grève."

p. 386 TUCHINS: *Chron. C6;* Boudet, passim; also Mollat & Wolff, 10–35, 184–85. RIOTERS OF BÉZIERS IN PLOT: Mollat & Wolff.

386 ff. FLANDERS CAMPAIGN and BATTLE OF ROOSEBEKE: *Chron. Bourbon* (the author, Chateaumorand, was a participant) in addition to *Chron. C6*, I, *Chron. 4 Valois*, and Froissart in KL, X; also Lot, 451–52, and Hutton. COUCY'S RETINUE IN ARMY FOR FLANDERS: BN, Clairembault 35, *pièce* 2628, nos. 99 and 100.

390 COUCY PROPOSED AS CONSTABLE FOR THE BATTLE: KL, X, 160–63.

392 COUCY IN THE BATTLE OF ROOSEBEKE: in addition to *Chron. Bourbon*, *Chron. de Berne* in KL, X, 477–79.

396 "THE SIRE DE COUCY HAD NOT FEARED": KL, notes, X, 501. DESCHAMPS, "THEREFORE THE INNOCENT": q. Coulton, *Life*, 111, 112.

Chapter 19—The Lure of Italy

The chief contemporary sources for Anjou's campaign for Naples are *Chron. C6*, vol. I, and the *Journal* of Jean le Fèvre. The fullest secondary account is in Valois, vol. II. Additional material from Valeri, 230–31, and on Amadeus of Savoy from Cox, 330–37.

Coucy's campaign in Italy is fully documented in Durrieu's "*Prise d'Arezzo*" (Bibliog. I, B) using the *Documenti degli Archivi Toscani . . . Comune di Firenze*, published 1866, and other Italian sources. Lacaille's *thèse* adds material on the proceedings of the Florentine Signoria taken from the Chronicle of Naddo da Montecatini, in *Delizie degli eruditi Toscani*, vol. XVIII, Firenze, 1784. The *Chron. de Berne*, reprinted in KL, XI, 442–43, and Jean le Fèvre are further sources. As part of Anjou's venture, Coucy's campaign is covered also in Valois, II.

398 BOCCACCIO ON NAPLES AND OTHER QUOTATIONS IN THIS PARAGRAPH: Croce, 52.

399 "GORGED WITH BOOTY": *Chron. C6*, I, 165.

400 GIOVANNI DI MUSSI (footnote): Herlihy, *Pistoia*, 3, 266.

402 EFFORTS TO ENGAGE COUCY: Jean le Fèvre, 47–48; Valois, II, 443–45. NORWICH CRUSADE, HIS CHARACTER: *DNB*. EXTORTIONS: Trevelyan, 268–69. SACRAMENTS WITHHELD: Barnie, 24.

403 CALVELEY, "BY MY FAITH": q. Barnie, 27. BOURBOURG, "THEIR ANTIQUE NOBILITY": *Chron. C6*, I, 281. COUCY'S IMPRESSIVE SHOWING: KL, X, 254; also Johnes ed. of 1805–6, VI, 313. BISHOP OF ROCHESTER: q. Barnie, 28.

404 NEGOTIATIONS WITH DUC DE BAR: Lacaille, *thèse*, 78. COUCY, MASSES AT ST. MÉDARD: BN, *Pièces originales* 875, dossier Coucy.

405 COUCY VISITS BERNABÒ: Mesquita, 28. GIAN GALEAZZO, CARRARA'S OPINION: q. Sismondi, V, 76.

406 HIS MOTHER'S WARNING: q. Chamberlin, 74. A STATE PAPER BY SALUTATI: q. Schevill, *Florence*, 320. "WE MET WITH JOYFUL EMBRACES": Full texts of the Florentine correspondence concerning Coucy's campaign are printed in Durrieu,

"*Arezzo.*" The report of the meeting with Coucy and the complaint of his march are from the Signoria's letter to the King of France of 20 October 1384, which is also given in full (in Latin) in KL, XI, 442–49.

p. 409 ANJOU'S WILL: Valois, II, 76–83. DURAZZO'S SERVICES: *Chron. C6*, 339, n. 3.

410 MESSAGES FROM ANJOU'S FOLLOWERS: Jean le Fèvre, 79.

411 CORRESPONDENCE ON THE PIETRAMALA: Coucy to Florence, 18 November 1384; Signoria to Coucy, 24 November 1384, in Durrieu, "*Arezzo,*" 189–90.

413 GUILLAUME LE JUPPONNIER: Douet-d'Arcq, I, 59.
"HA! FALSE TRAITOR": q. Collas, 144–45.

414 COUCY IN AVIGNON: KL, X, 323; Lehoux, II, 109, n. 1.
BONET: 63, 68, 81, 117–19, 153, 160, 188.

Chapter 20—A Second Norman Conquest

For events and quotations concerning the invasion of England, the Monk of St. Denis (*Chron. C6*, I) and Froissart (KL, XII) may be generally taken for granted as the original sources, supplemented by Mirot's "*Une tentative,*" Terrier de Loray's life of Vienne, and Roncière's history of the French navy.

416 ISABEAU OF BAVARIA, WITTELSBACHS AND VISCONTIS, STEPHEN OF BAVARIA, MARRIAGE NEGOTIATIONS ET SEQ.: Thibault, 12–42, in addition to the chroniclers.

417 GIAN GALEAZZO'S OUSTER OF BERNABÒ: Sismondi, V, 50; Mesquita, 15–36; Chamberlin, 74–82; Cook, 19. ACTIVITY OF THE DUCHESSE D'ANJOU: Jean le Fèvre, 97; Lehoux, II, 125 ff.

419 CHARLES VI and DEER WITH THE GOLDEN COLLAR: *Chron. C6*, I, 71.
BURGUNDY DOUBLE WEDDING: in addition to the chroniclers, Vaughan, 88; *CMH*, 374.
COUCY ARRIVES IN "GREAT HASTE": Anselme, 542.

420 ff. EXPEDITION TO SCOTLAND: *Chron. C6*, I, 351.

421 FRENCH BROUGHT 50 SUITS OF ARMOR: *Book of Pluscarden*, q. Locke, 84. See also P. Hume Brown, *History of Scotland*, Cambridge, 1929, I, 191–92. The statement in some of the earlier histories that Coucy was a member of this expedition was based on a misreading of a reference in one ms. of Froissart to a Seigneur de Courcy, corrected by Terrier de Loray, 204, n. 2. (The inconvenient Sire de Courcy causes a further error with regard to Coucy's second wife—see notes to chap. 25, p. 650.)
COUCY'S REMARRIAGE: KL, X, 347; Duchesne, 267–68; Zurlauben, *Enguerrand VII*, 182.
RENOVATION OF THE CASTLE: Broche 340 ff.; Dufour, 50–54; Evans, *Art*, 166.

423 PERCEVAL, BASTARD OF COUCY: AN, Demay, Coll. Clairembault, Nos. 2841–42; Duchesne, 273.
COUCY AT HAPSBURG-BURGUNDY WEDDING: Broche, 135. He is the archivist quoted.

p. 424 ROYAL COUNCIL VOTED UNANIMOUSLY: *Chron. C6*, I, 429–31.

"YOU ARE THE GREATEST KING LIVING": *Chron. Bourbon*, q. Mirot, 429, n. 3.

FISHERMEN: ibid., 441.

FRENCH INVASION FLEET: In addition to the sources listed above, material from the *Chronique de Tournai* and other primary sources is quoted by Palmer, *England, France*, 77–79.

425 BURGUNDY'S MOTTO: Terrier de Loray, 214.

COUCY'S SHIP: Roncière, 89.

COUCY'S SEAL: AN, Demay. Coll. Clairembault, I, 2838. HIS RETINUE: KL, XXI, 45.

426 WILLIAM THE CONQUEROR: Cutts, 391.

DESCHAMPS, NORMAN CONQUEST: q. Mirot, 455.

427 DUC DE BERRY: Luce, *Cents ans*, I, 212–27; Wylie, II, 405–32; Dupont & Gnudi, 150–51.

428 HOUNDS FROM SCOTLAND: Jusserand, 125, from Rymer for 3 April 1396.

FINED LANGUEDOC: Boudet, 64–65.

429 "SNUB-NOSES": q. Wylie, II, 399, n. 5.

FLEET CAPTAINS' LIST OF "ITEMS": text from *Chron. de Tournai*, q. Vaughan, 50.

430 THIS "USELESS WAR": Walsingham, q. Barnie, 129.

431 CHARLES VI VISITS COUCY: Broche, 341–43.

BAUDET LEFÈVRE: text of the pardon, which recounts the circumstances, in Mangin (Bibliog. I, A), 42, n. 1.

432 COUCY'S VESSEL LOADED AT SOISSONS: Broche, 342.

432 ff. MONTFORT-CLISSON AFFAIR: Froissart, Berners ed., IV, 440–59; Lefranc, 279, 304–24; Moranvillé, *Mercier*, 112–13.

435 COUCY'S INSISTENCE ON RESTITUTION: KL, XIII, 84.

GUELDERS AFFAIR: *Chron. C6*, I, 523–25. VASSAL FOR MONEY: Perroy, *Hundred Years*, 191; GUELDERS' LETTER TO CHARLES VI: text in Douet-d'Arcq, I, 78.

436 COUCY ARGUES IN COUNCIL: KL. XIII, 84.

DEATH OF CHARLES OF NAVARRE: *Chron. C6*, I, 473, and Froissart.

437 COUCY'S MISSION TO MONTFORT: KL, XIII, 136, 337 ff.

KING'S GIFT OF A BIBLE: Lacaille, *thèse*, 117, from Delisle. FROISSART'S TRIBUTE: Berners ed., V, 163.

Chapter 21—The Fiction Cracks

As before, events and quoted statements not otherwise identified may be presumed to come from *Chron. C6*, I, or Froissart.

438 DESCHAMPS, "NOT ON THE GRAND PONT": Queux ed., I, 156–57.

439 MÉZIÈRES QUOTED: Coopland ed., 524–25.

SOFT BEDS AND PERFUMED BATHS: preachers q. in Owst, 412. GERSON: q. Kilgour, 184.

SACCHETTI: q. Jacob Burckhardt, *Civilization of the Renaissance in Italy*, New York, 1960 (paperback ed.), 262.

441 DESCHAMPS ILL ON CAMPAIGN: Raynaud in Deschamps, Queux ed., XI, 296. An excellent analysis of Deschamps' life, work, and opinions may be

found in this long essay by Queux's editorial successor. Ballads discussed here are in II, 214–26, 226–35. See also Kilgour, 64.

p. 442 LOUIS D'ORLÉANS: *Chron. C6;* Jorga, 505; Collas, 143, 296.

443 CAMAL: Evans in notes to Díaz de Gómez, 153. VERSE: q. Mary Duchaux (Darmesteter), *A Short History of France,* 1918, 86.

BURGUNDY VISITS COUCY: Petit, *Itinéraires,* 203; Prost, 475.

444 RICHARD DESCRIBED: *Vita R. Ricardi II,* ed. Hearne, 1729, q. Locke, 110. HANDKERCHIEF: Hutchison, 239.

446 GRAND BOUTEILLER and PRIVILEGE OF TWO FAIRS: Duplessis, notes, 121; Duchesne, 268–69; Lacaille, *"Vente,"* 574–75; DBF, IX, 873. Text of the King's grant in Lépinois, 209–11. ON THE OFFICE OF GRAND BOUTEILLER: Lot & Fawtier, 54.

447 COMPLAINT OF 1388: q. Denifle, 594.

MARKS OF DECLINE: Denifle, 594; Jusserand, 43–44. The Benedictine abbey was St. Nicolas-aux-Bois, diocese of Laon: Denifle, 706.

448 DON PERO NIÑO AT SERIFONTAINE: Díaz de Gómez, 134–38. The host served as Admiral of France from 1397 to 1405, which places the date of the visit about 1405–6.

449 DESCHAMPS' BALLAD ON RAUCOUS EVENING: Queux ed., VII, 253. ON BALD-NESS: Ballade 867. Obscurities in the language of this ballade were elucidated by Prof. Howard Garey of Yale.

BROMYARD ON FOPPERY: q. Owst, 408.

450 DESCHAMPS' AILMENTS, SINS HE CONDEMNED, COMPLAINT OF COURT LIFE: Raynaud in Deschamps, Queux ed., XI, 296–97, 303–5.

COUCY SENDS MESSAGE TO PHILIPPA: Green, 227, from Rymer. NAMED CAPTAIN OF GUIENNE: KL, XIV, 25.

451 MARCIAL LE VÉRIT: from text of pardon in Douet-d'Arcq.

NOTTINGHAM'S CHALLENGE: text in KL, notes, XIV, 398–99.

452 BOUCICAUT AT ROOSEBEKE: KL, notes, X, 481.

COUCY PROPOSED FROISSART FOR CANONRY AT LILLE: Shears, 55–56.

VERSE ON COUCY AS PATRON: KL, Ia, 345. The meaning of *rouge escaille* was suggested in consultation by Profs. Howard Garey and Harry Miskimin of Yale.

453 COUCY OWNED OLDEST FROISSART MS.: KL, notes, Ib, 224. This copy passed from Coucy's great-granddaughter Jeanne de Bar to the royal library when Louis XI confiscated the books of her husband, Louis of Luxemburg. Listed as ms. II 88 in the Royal Library of Brussels (and as #6941 in the *Catalogue des Mss.* by Van den Gheyn), the copy has the Coucy coat-of-arms on fo. 16 r.

PETRARCH'S COMPLAINT: *Correspondence,* 28.

BOOKS GIVEN TO COUCY: Lacaille, *thèse,* 117, from Delisle, *Cat. de la librairie du Louvre,* III, nos. 19, 1160.

455 VALENTINA VISCONTI: Chamberlin, 89–91, 109–12; Collas, 48 ORLÉANS HOUSEHOLD: Lacroix, 74–75.

QUEEN'S ENTRY: Both Froissart and the Monk of St. Denis were eyewitnesses.

456 BURGUNDY'S CLOTHES: Vaughan, 43.

ON THE "BED OF JUSTICE": Bapst.

Chapter 22—The Siege of Barbary

p. 458 TREASURY OFFICIALS, "HE HAS HAD TOO MUCH": *Chron. C6*, I, 609.

459 CHARLES VI IN AVIGNON: Froissart; *Chron. C6*, I; Valois, II, 152–54.

460 *Cent Ballades:* Pannier, passim; Raynaud, xxxvi–xlix, li–v, lxiv–viii, 226–27.

BASTARD OF COUCY: La Chesnaye-Desbois.

461 KING'S TOUR OF LANGUEDOC and BÉTIZAC AFFAIR: *Chron. C6*, I; *Chron. Bourbon;* Froissart; Coville, 304–5.

462 GENOESE AMBASSADORS: *Chron. C6*, I, 653; Mirot, "*Politique*," 10.

463 FRESCO IN THE CLOISTER OF CARMES: Vaissète, IV, 396; Sabine Coron-Lesur, unpublished dissertation on the *Couvent des Grands Carmes de Toulouse*, 140–43, supplied through the kindness of Prof. Philippe Wolff of Toulouse. A copy of the fresco, generally known as "The Vow of Charles VI," exists as an engraving in the Musée Paul Dupuy in Toulouse, and is reproduced in Vaissète, IV, plate XX-C, in G. Lafaille, *Annales de la ville de Toulouse*, 1687, I, 143, and in a number of later volumes. Lacking differentiation of faces, it is of little interest.

464 ff. SPANISH MISSION: That Coucy could have gone to Spain in the course of the tour of Languedoc is unlikely but not impossible. The documents show him to have been with the King at Toulouse for the founding of the Ordre de l'Espérance on an unknown date in December, and again (or still) there on January 5 when his signature was added to the King's treaty with the Count of Foix (Vaissète, ed. of 1885, IX, 938–51, X, notes, 125–29; Lacaille, *thèse*, 127–28). He reappeared at Avignon on January 28 to testify in the *Processus* of Pierre de Luxemburg. This allows two intervals—one of unknown length in December and one of 23 days in January—when he might have gone to Barcelona and back, although the time element is very tight. No evidence exists to support Froissart's version of his role in the Anjou-Aragon marriage. According to R. Oliver Bertrand, *Bodas Reales entre Francia y la Corona de Aragon*, Barcelona, 1947, 203, a marriage contract *was* concluded and a dispensation from Clement VII obtained in 1390, but the contract itself was not found. Researches by Richard Famiglietti at the BN and AN and in the published French and Spanish sources, and a search of the documents in the Archivo de la Corona de Aragon at Barcelona (commissioned through the kindness of Prof. J. N. Hillgarth) found no evidence of a journey by Coucy in connection with the Anjou-Aragon marriage.

465 PIERRE DE LUXEMBURG: Baring-Gould, *Lives of the Saints*, VII, 85–88; Jorga, 460–62; Valois, II, 300, 362–66; Huizinga, *Waning*, 179–80. Testimony in the *Processus* for canonization occupies 133 double-column folio pages in *Acta Sanctorum*, Paris, 1863–1940, vol. XXVIII, in which Coucy's testimony appears on pp. 464–65, 468, 472, 476, 488.

467 THE ROYAL VISIT TO DIJON: Petit, *Entrée*, passim; KL, Ia, 556.

468 "FOR THE SOUL'S SALVATION": q. Cartellieri, 29.

COUCY'S FOUNDATION OF CÉLESTIN MONASTERY: Roussel, 19–24.

p. 469 FOIX'S "BOOK OF PRAYERS": Pierre Tucoo-Chala, *Gaston Febus*, Pau, 1976, 103.

COUCY'S CHARTER: BN, *Fonds Latins*, 5149, published in Roussel, 193–96, and (in part) in Duplessis, 158–59.

470 ff. THE ENTERPRISE AGAINST BARBARY: *Chron. Bourbon*, 218–57, is the chief primary source, taking precedence in this episode over Froissart (KL, XIV) and *Chron. C6*, I, 650–57 et seq. Secondary accounts: Delaville le Roux, 166–200; Mirot, "*Politique*"; Atiya, *Crusade in Later Middle Ages*.

471 BONET ON WAR AGAINST UNBELIEVERS: 126–27.

472 STRATEGY OF ABOU-'L-ABBAS: Ibn-Khaldoun, 118–19.

474 COUCY DISAPPROVES THE CHALLENGE: *Chron. Bourbon*, 233.

477 CHARLES VI VISITS COUCY: Jarry, "*Voie de Fait*," 224.

Chapter 23—In a Dark Wood

478 "WE CAN ENVISION NOTHING FINER": KL, XIV, 280–81. On the *Voie de Fait* in general, Froissart and *Chron. C6*, I, continue to be the narrative sources. Valois, II, and Mirot, "*Politique*," are modern accounts.

479 JEAN GERSON: Morrall, passim.

ON JOAN OF ARC: *CMH*, 810.

PETRARCH ON THE SCHOLASTICS: *Correspondence*, 222–23.

480 ff. GERSON'S OPINIONS: Copleston, 278; Thorndike, IV, 108, 114, 128. ON CURRICULUM FOR SCHOOLS: Gabriel. ON CHILDREN'S SEXUAL HABITS: Ariès, 106–7.

CONTROVERSY OVER *Roman de la Rose*: Bédier & Lazard, 98–99.

481 GERSON, "INTO THE FIRE"; KL, Ia, 221, n. 1.

JEAN DE MONTREUIL AND PIERRE COL: Huizinga, *Waning*, 113–15, 308–9.

482 BONIFACE, SALE OF BENEFICES: Creighton, 116–17. CLEMENT PAWNS TIARA: Coville, 314–15.

WENCESLAS IV: Lindner, II, 170–77; Kamil Krofta, "Bohemia in the 14th Century," chap. 6 in *CMH*; Jules Zeller, *Les Empereurs du XIVe siècle*, Paris, 1890, 450–52.

483 DRUNKENNESS IN GERMANY: Lindner, II, 174. POGROM OF PRAGUE: Baron, IX, 160 ff., 202, 318.

484 CONTROVERSY OVER THE IMMACULATE CONCEPTION: Michelet, ed. of 1840, IV, 57; Creighton, 112.

485 BERNARDINO OF SIENA: q. G. G. Coulton, *Inquisition and Liberty*, London, 1938, 45. WALSINGHAM ON UNBELIEF: q. Jusserand, 224.

CLAMANGES AND GERSON ON IRREVERENCE: q. M. Mollat, *Vie*, 65.

486 BRETHREN OF THE COMMON LIFE: Hyma, passim; Southern, 331–52.

487 GROOTE AND THOMAS A KEMPIS: ibid.

488 *Imitation of Christ* ASCRIBED TO GERSON: Coville, 416–17.

GERSON'S SERMON: Valois, II, 395.

489 CLEMENT PREPARES FOR ROME: Coville, 302.

THOMAS OF GLOUCESTER: KL, XIV, 314–15, 384; XV, 165, 240.

490 GUY DE BLOIS: KL, XIV, 370; Barante, II, 36–38.

p. 490 COUCY'S ROLE: Jarry, *Orléans*, 85; Lacaille, *thèse*, 138; KL, XVI, 71.

491 PRECAUTIONS TAKEN AT AMIENS: KL, XIV.

492 COUCY AND PHILIPPA: ibid., 378.

BURGUNDY'S CLOTHES: Barante, II, 39.

Chapter 24—Danse Macabre

494 ff. THE CRAON-CLISSON AFFAIR: *Chron. C6*, II, 3 ff., and KL, XIV, 316–20, are the basic narrative sources. They are combined in a lively account by Barante, II, 46–55. Modern accounts in Coville, 305; *CMH*, 372; Lefranc, 349–56. Admiral de Vienne's conduct: Lefranc, 356. On Craon personally, see *DBF* and Bio. Index in KL.

CRAON'S ASSASSINATION OF A KNIGHT OF LAON: KL, notes, XV, 362.

495 SECRET CORRESPONDENCE OF THE UNCLES WITH DUKE OF BRITTANY: Sismondi, *Histoire des Français*, Paris, 1828, II, 597.

497 ff. CAMPAIGN AGAINST BRITTANY and THE KING'S MADNESS AT LE MANS: *Chron. C6*, II, 19–25; KL, XV, 40–49; Barante, II, 59–81; Moranvillé, 89, 124–26, 149.

499 GUILLAUME DE HARSIGNY: Edouard Fleury, *Antiquités et monuments du département de l'Aisne*, Paris, 1882, 242–43. Also Mâle.

500 COUCY IN RIVIÈRE'S ARREST: KL, XV, 63–64, and notes, 365; Lefranc, 367.

RECEIVES MERCIER'S PROPERTY: KL, XV, 67; Moranvillé, 158, 161, 163.

501 BURGUNDY AND CLISSON: Lefranc, 365–67.

COUCY REFUSES CONSTABLESHIP: KL, XV, 97.

502 COUCY ESCORTS KING TO LIESSE: Lacaille, *thèse*, 142; *DBF*, IX, 873.

HARSIGNY'S EFFIGY: now in the museum at Laon. The inscription reads *"Deo et Nature reddo simplicia. Acta compositi sint Deo Grata."* Allowing for ambiguities of language, the translation could be: "I give back to God and nature my [bodily] elements. May the deeds of the whole [man] be pleasing to God."

503 LADIES HAD TO TURN SIDEWAYS TO PASS THROUGH DOORWAYS: described by Juvenal des Ursins, q. Collas, 75.

COUCY IN SAVOY: Duchesne, 269–70.

CUSTOMS AT SECOND MARRIAGES: M. Mollat, *Vie*, 57.

504 ff. DANCE OF THE SAVAGES: *Chron. C6*, II, 65–71; KL, XV, 77, 85–87, 89–90, 92; *Chron. Valois*, 328; Barante, II, 95–99. Huguet de Guisay's character is from *Chron. C6*.

505 LOUIS' CÉLESTIN CHAPEL: *Chron. C6*, II, 75; Jorga, 506.

505 ff. *Danse Macabre:* Carco; Chaney; Huizinga, *Waning*, 139–41. On origin of the phrase, in addition to the above, *OCFL*. CHURCH OF THE INNOCENTS MURALS: Chaney, from verses and woodcuts in Guyot Marchant's *Danse Macabre*, c. 1485. EFFIGY OF CARDINAL DE LA GRANGE: now in Musée Calvet, Avignon; illustrated in Joseph Girard, *Avignon: ses monuments*, Marseille, 1930. A thorough if pedestrian listing of such effigies with illustrations appears in Kathleen Cohen, *Metamorphosis of a Death Symbol: The Transi Tomb in the Late Middle Ages and Renaissance*, Berkeley, 1974.

506 CEMETERY OF THE INNOCENTS: Mâle, 360; Huizinga, *Waning*, 144; Carco, 29.

p. 507 SEVEN SORROWS OF THE VIRGIN: Mâle, 125. BEAUTIFUL MADONNAS: One of the most characteristic and charming is the statue of the Madonna of the Bird at the church of Notre Dame du Mathuret in Riom in Auvergne. POPULATION REDUCED BY 50 PERCENT: Russell, "Effects of Pestilence," 470; Carpentier, *AESC*, 1082–83.

508 ff. PESSIMISM: Gower, from *Confessio Amantis*. DATINI: q. Origo, 116. GERSON: q. Thorndike, *History*, IV, 115. MONK OF CLUNY: q. Coulton, *Life*, I, 2. MÉZIÈRES: q. Coopland ed., I, 255. ROGER BACON: q. Coulton, *Life*, II, 57. DESCHAMPS: q. KL, Ia. 440–41. CHRISTINE DE PISAN: q. ibid.; SAFE-CONDUCTS: from her *Book of Fayttes*, XIX. UNIVERSITY SELLING DEGREES: Coville, 395.

509 "VICES OF THE DIFFERENT ORDERS": q. T. Wright, *Political Songs*, I, lxxxiv–vi.

510 NOTARY OF CAHORS: Denifle, 827.

GOWER ON WAR: q. Barnie, 123, 131. "NO PEACE TILL THEY GIVE BACK CALAIS": q. Locke, 95.

511 PARLEY AT LEULINGHEN: *Chron. C6*, II, 77–83; Froissart (who was present), Berners ed., VI, 110–21.

512 THOMAS OF GLOUCESTER: ibid.

513 CHARLES VI'S PERIODS OF MADNESS: *Chron. C6*, II, 87–91, 405, 455; Barante, II, 110–11, 223–24; Collas, 260; Thibault, 222–24.

514 WILLIAM OF HAINAULT: Darmesteter, 38. ON MENTAL ILLNESS: E. Wright, 356.

515 ISABEAU'S CONDUCT: Collas, 297; Thibault, 265, 281, 290, 316. "THIS RIDICULOUS TRIBUNAL": Juvenal des Ursins, q. Mazas, IV, 181. Founded in 1400 with the intention of honoring women and cultivating poetry, the *Cour Amoureuse* included one member who was convicted of attempted rape in 1405, and another who kidnapped a *dame d'honneur* (whom he later married after repudiating his wife). Among other members of all classes were the vocal advocates of the *Roman de la Rose*, Jean de Montreuil, and Pierre and Gontier Col. (A. Piaget, "*Cour Amoureuse*," *Romania*, XX, 447.)

516 MARQUIS DE SADE: see Bibliography. Written in 1813, this was his last book, not published until 1953. Sade claimed to have found at Dijon the transcript of the trial of Louis de Bourdon, the Queen's lover, who revealed under torture her part in the crimes of the reign. Unhampered by the disappearance of the transcript in the destruction of the library by the "Huns of the French Revolution," the Marquis was able, 40 years after reading it, to write the biography ascribing to Isabeau responsibility for every "drop of blood spilled in this terrible reign." In his version, she prostituted herself to Craon to contrive the attack on Clisson, gave Charles the poisons that caused his madness, arranged for the appearance of the madman in the forest of Mans, planned the fatality of the Dance of the Savages, acted as accomplice in the murder of her former lover Louis d'Orléans, coupled in the slums with thieves and murderers, poisoned three of her own children, and delivered Joan of Arc to the Inquisition. Sade was a one-cause historian.

p. 516 DUC DE SULLY: q. François Guizot, *Hist. of France,* trans., New York, 1885, III, 9.

Chapter 25—Lost Opportunity

For the efforts to end the schism, the death of Clement, the election of Benedict, and his refusal to abdicate, the chief primary source is the Monk of St. Denis (*Chron. C6,* II, 131–317), who was obviously more interested in, and closer to the struggle than Froissart (KL, XIV–XV). Both are supplemented by Valois, II–III; Jarry, "*Voie de Fait,*" 523–41; Creighton. Where not otherwise stated, the above are the sources for the events in this chapter that relate to the schism.

517 SPINELLI'S ARGUMENT: q. Chamberlin, 153.

518 COUCY'S MISSION TO AVIGNON: KL, XIV, notes, 422–26; Durrieu, "*Adria,*" 13–64; Jarry, *Orléans,* 117; Mirot, "*Politique,*" 527; Lehoux, II, 296.

519 NOBLES FEARED COMMONERS' ARCHERY: *Chron. C6,* II, 131. Also Jean Juvenal des Ursins, q. Fowler, *Plantagenet and Valois,* 177.

520 GERSON'S ORAL DEFENSE: Morrall, 34–36.

COUCY AGAIN IN AVIGNON: same sources as above: KL, ibid.; Durrieu, 72–75; Jarry, *Orléans,* 121; Jarry, "*Voie de Fait,*" 517; Mirot, "*Politique,*" 530–31.

522 NICOLAS DE CLAMANGES: Ornato, 16; *DBF* and Michaud, *Biographie universelle.* Text of his address in *Chron. C6,* II, 135 ff.

523 TRANSLATED FOR THE COUNCIL: Jarry, "*Voie de Fait,*" 523.

524 "AS THOUGH THE HOLY GHOST": q. Creighton, 129.

400 MILES IN FOUR DAYS: Hay, 363.

525 ff. COUCY'S CAMPAIGN FOR GENOA: The major sources are Jarry's *Orléans,* 134–56, and Delisle's summaries of the documents in the Coll. Bastard d'Estang at the BN, *Fonds fr., nouv. acq.* 3638–9 and 3653–4–5. These contain some three dozen documents covering transactions by Coucy. Payments to him from the crown are in BN, *Pièces originales,* 875, dossier Coucy. Lacaille, *thèse,* 156–94, adds references from Italian sources. Froissart is the source for Coucy holding conferences with the Genoese outdoors (KL, XV, 221–22). Modern authorities: Jarry, "*Voie de Fait,*" 532–37; Mesquita, 157–58; Mirot, "*Politique,*" 533–35.

527 VISIT TO PAVIA: BN, Coll. Bastard d'Estang, 231, 234.

528 GIOVANNI DEI GRASSI: Meiss & Kirsch.

BUILDING OF THE CATHEDRAL: Chamberlin, 122–26, 173–75.

529 COUCY'S "WOUNDED LEG": Jarry, *Orléans,* 161.

532 CLAMANGES GOES OVER TO BENEDICT: Valois, III, 270, n. 4; Creighton, 433–34. Further on this episode: Ornato, 27, 33–41.

533 BENEDICT DIED AT 94: *CMH,* 301.

534 "TO AID AND SUSTAIN" RICHARD II: q. McKisack, 476, from Rymer, VII, 811.

LOLLARD TWELVE "CONCLUSIONS": Gairdner, I, 43–44.

535 THREATENED TO KILL SIR RICHARD STURY: Hutchison, 155.

COUCY REFUSED "BECAUSE HE WAS A FRENCHMAN": Froissart, Berners ed., VI, 130.

p. 536 GLOUCESTER, ROBERT THE HERMIT, WALERAN DE ST. POL: ibid., VI, 161–68, 211–12.

537 MARRIAGE OF ISABEL AND RICHARD: Froissart, Berners ed., 224–29. Froissart's statement that the only French lady to accompany Isabel to England was the Dame de Courcy (KL, XV, 306) became Coucy in Lord Berners' translation (VI, 229) and accounts for Mrs. Green's error (228) in identifying this lady, who was later to bring back the news of Richard's deposition, as Coucy's second wife.

Chapter 26—Nicopolis

Apart from Schiltberger's sparse account told 30 years after the event (see p. 554), the primary Western sources for the crusade to Nicopolis are the *Livre des faits du bon messire Jean le Maingre, dit Bouciquaut* (Godefroy ed., pp. 78–104), written at about the time of the subject's death in 1421 (by an "anonymous cleric" according to OCFL, although Kervyn Lettenhove—XX, 372—believed the author was Christine de Pisan); the Monk of St. Denis (*Chron. C6*, II, 485–519); and Froissart, KL, XV, 218–328, passim. These are the bases for the spirited accounts by Abbé Vertot in the 18th century and Barante in the early 19th. KL's notes add material from Dom Plancher's *Histoire Générale de Bourgogne*, Dijon, 1739–81. The most thorough modern account and a classic work is Delaville le Roux, *La France en Orient*, Book III, chaps. 1–5, whose wealth of notes fills in a mass of information. Where not otherwise cited, the events in this chapter are drawn from the above sources.

Atiya's *Nicopolis*, usually cited (by English-speaking historians) as the standard work, supposedly draws on an impressive bibliography of Turkish sources, but little evidence of this appears in the text. With minor exceptions, not all of them accurate, this book is not much more than a reworking of Delaville. Rosetti supplies a useful survey from all sources of estimated numbers engaged in the crusade. Savage points up the importance of Coucy's offensive. Tipton contributes an original and valuable investigation of the supposed English role.

540 HALF THE TURKISH ARMY HELD LAND IN EUROPE: Oman, 344.
A *ghazi*, "THE SWORD OF GOD": q. Anthony Luttrell, "The Crusade in the 14th century" in Hale, Highfield & Smalley, 139.

541 A FORD OF THE DANUBE AT NICOPOLIS: Kousev, 70. This does not seem to jibe with accounts of fugitives of the battle drowning in attempts to swim across.
BAJAZET ANSWERED WITHOUT WORDS: Hammer, 323.

542 SIGISMUND, "YOU BOHEMIAN PIG!": Otto Zarek, *The History of Hungary*, trans., London, 1939, 182.
BONE OF ST. ELIZABETH: q. Wylie, II, 432, n. 4.
AT PARLEMENT OF PARIS: Douet-d'Arcq, I, 382.

544 MÉZIÈRES' ORDER OF THE PASSION: Kilgour, 148–62.

546 JEAN DE NEVERS, APPEARANCE: Michelet, IV, 45; Calmette, 57–58.

548 EQUIPMENT: David, 37, from Plancher, *Bourgogne*, III, 149.

549 SUPPOSED ENGLISH PARTICIPATION: The evidence refuting it has been effec-

tively presented by Tipton, leading to his conclusion, "No Englishman whatsoever can be identified as positively among the crusading army," 533.

p. 550   "THEY GO LIKE KINGS": q. Jorga, 489.

551   SLANDER OF VALENTINA: chronicles, and Mesquita, 203; Chamberlin, 176.
GIAN GALEAZZO SUPPOSEDLY INFORMED BAJAZET: KL, XV, 253, 262, 329, 338.

554   ESTIMATE OF NUMBERS: Lot, 456; Rosetti, 633–35.

556   "HOW SEDUCTIVE IS WAR!": Jean de Beuil, *Le Jouvencel*, 2 vols. SHF, Paris, 1887, II, 20–21.

557   COUCY'S ATTACK: Wavrin, 149; KL, XV, 314; Savage, 437–40.

561   COUCY SEEN "UNSHAKEN": *Livre des faits*, Godefroy ed., 97.
SIGISMUND, "WE LOST THE DAY": Schiltberger, ed. notes, 109.

562   BAJAZET SWEARS REVENGE: Schiltberger, 4.

Chapter 27—Hung Be the Heavens with Black

Livre des faits . . . de Boucicaut (Godefroy ed., 104–14), Froissart, and *Chron. C6*, II, continue to be the main primary sources. It may be assumed that these and Delaville le Roux, chaps. 6–9, are the sources for material not otherwise cited.

564   MARCH OF THE PRISONERS: from the account of Geoffrey Maupoivre in Delaville, "*Le Legs d'Enguerrand VII*" (Bibliog. I, B).

565   COUCY'S MIRACLE: ibid.

566   "FORTUNATE TO BE IN A WORLD": KL, XV, 334.

567   DESCHAMPS ON FUNERALS: Queux ed., VIII, 85–86.
DAME DE COUCY WRITES TO DOGE: XV, 426. ORLÉANS' MESSENGERS: Mangin, 45–46, 52–54; BN, *Fonds fr., nouv. acq.* 3638–9, nos. 268–9, 308, 456.
GIFTS FOR BAJAZET: Barante, II, 201; Jarry, *Orléans*, 185–86.

568   DESCHAMPS, "MONEY!": q. Gustave Masson, *Story of Medieval France*, 1888.

569   L'ALOUËTE: 182.
ANONYMOUS POEM ON TWELVE AGES: q. Mâle, 303–4.

570   NICHOLAS OF AENOS: *Livre des faits*, q. Atiya, *Nicopolis*, 105.
COUCY'S WILL: published in *Testaments enregistrés au parlement de Paris sous le règne de Charles VI*, ed. A. Tuetey, in *Documents inédits, Mélanges historiques, nouv. série*, Paris, Imp. nat., 1858, III, 39–44.

571   COUCY'S DEATH: The assumption made by some historians that he died alone, the Sultan having moved on, taking the prisoners with him and leaving Coucy behind because he was too ill to travel, cannot be reconciled with the eight signatures to his will. The Sultan and French prisoners did indeed move on to Mikalidsch, two days' journey from Brusa, where Burgundy's envoy Guillaume de l'Aigle met them, supposedly in January. Either that date is an error or the prisoners must have returned to Brusa—perhaps because of Coucy's imminent death—in time to sign the will.

"REFINED AND BARBARIC": Lefranc, Intro., x.

p. 572 "SEIGNEUR OF MOST MERIT": *Livre des faits*, Godefroy, 2nd ed., The Hague, 1711, 81.

572 RETURN OF COUCY'S REMAINS: Duplessis, 103. DAME DE COUCY: Godefroy, 1620, 106. FUNERAL: KL, XV, 357, 437; XVI, 31. TOMB: destroyed (presumably) in the destruction of Nogent-sous-Coucy; the plaque from Ste. Trinité is now in the museum of Soissons. DESCHAMPS' DIRGE: Queux ed., Ballad 1366.

573 ff. RANSOM AND RETURN OF THE PRISONERS: In addition to the sources at the head of the chapter, Vaughan, 71–77. BURGUNDY'S GIFTS MISFIRED: Bavyn ms., *Mémoires du voiage fait en Hongrie par Jean dit Sans-Peur, Comte de Nevers*, q. Atiya, *Nicopolis*, 103. BURGUNDY'S BOOKS BOUGHT FROM DINO RAPONDI: Durrieu, *Mss. de luxe*, 163, and Putnam, 275.

575 TOURNAI EXPECTED A PARDON: Delaville, 320, n. 2.

576 *Epistre Lamentable*: Jorga, 500–503; also reprinted as anonymous in KL, XVI, 444–523. BONET'S SATIRE: q. Kilgour, 158–60, 172–73.
Quatre Valois: Chron. 4 Valois, 187, 192.

577 BAJAZET IN WAGON WITH BARS: On this famously disputed question, Gibbon (VI, 370–84) cites French, Italian, Turkish, and Greek sources to refute the claim of Persian historians that the story is a fable reflecting "vulgar credulity." Gibbon's editors (Milman, Guizot, Wenck, and Smith) accept the explanation of Von Hammer that the so-called iron cage was a mistranslation of the Turkish word *hafe* meaning a covered litter, in this case covered by a latticework made of iron. See also F. Schevill, *History of the Balkan Peninsula*, New York, 1922, 190.
COUCY'S "MANY FINE PONDS": as described in the suit brought by Robert de Bar, q. Lacaille, "*Vente*," 594. FAMILY LITIGATION: ibid.

578 PROPOSED MARRIAGE TO STEPHEN OF BAVARIA: originating in *Chron. C6*, II, 765, the erroneous statement that the marriage was concluded was repeated by Duchesne and Duplessis and others down the line until corrected by Thibault, 355. SALE OF THE PROPERTY TO ORLÉANS: Lacaille, "*Vente*," 574–87; Jarry, *Orléans*, 239–42, 311.

Epilogue

583 ORLÉANIST MANIFESTO, SUNK IN CRIME AND SIN: q. Enid McLeod, *Charles d'Orléans*, New York, 1970, 63.
AGINCOURT: Wylie, II, 108–230. An eyewitness account of the battle from the *Chronicle* of Jehan de Wavrin is quoted in Allmand, 107–11.

584 HEAVY ARMOR AND HEART FAILURE: Oman, 377.

587 "FORESTS CAME BACK WITH THE ENGLISH": q. Evans, *Life*, 141. DESOLATION OF PICARDY AND STARVING WOMAN OF ABBEVILLE: Lestocquoy, 47–48. COUCY DELIVERED TO THE ENEMY: Antoine d'Asti, q. Dufour, 51.
REALISTIC HORRORS ON STAGE: Cohen, 149, 267.

588 CONGEALING OF CHARITY: Mâle, 440.

591 HUSSITE "MOVING FORT": Oman.

592 POPULATION, ROUEN: Cheyney, 166. SCHLESWIG: Heers, 106.

p. 592   THOMAS BASIN: *Histoire de Charles VII*, ed. Charles Samaran, Paris, 1933, I, 87, q. Fowler, *Plantagenet and Valois*, 150–51.

593   CASTILLON: ibid., q. Allmand, 11–13.

594   TURKS' SIEGE TRAIN: Oman, 357–58.

VICTOR HUGO: q. Mâle, 295.

595   COUCY LINEAGE: La Chesnaye-Desbois; Anselme, V, 243, VII, 566; *L'Art de vérifier*, 243; Melleville, 20. PERCEVAL HAD NO HEIRS: Duplessis, 107.

FATE OF THE CASTLE AND MONASTERY: Duchesne, 672; *L'Art de vérifier*, 219; Dufour, 21, n. 1; Viollet-le-Duc, *Coucy*, 30–31; Roussel, 42.

596   RUPPRECHT OF BAVARIA: His intervention was related by him to Friedrich P. Reck-Malleczewen, *Diary of a Man in Despair*, trans., New York, 1970, 196. LUDENDORFF'S 28 TONS OF DYNAMITE: *Histoire de Coucy*, pamphlet of Ass'n . . . Coucy-le-Château, by R. Leray, J. Vian, and H. Crepin.

Index